UNIVERSITY OF NOTTINGHAM
WITHDRAWN
FROM THE LIBRARY
60 0368598 1
D1621305

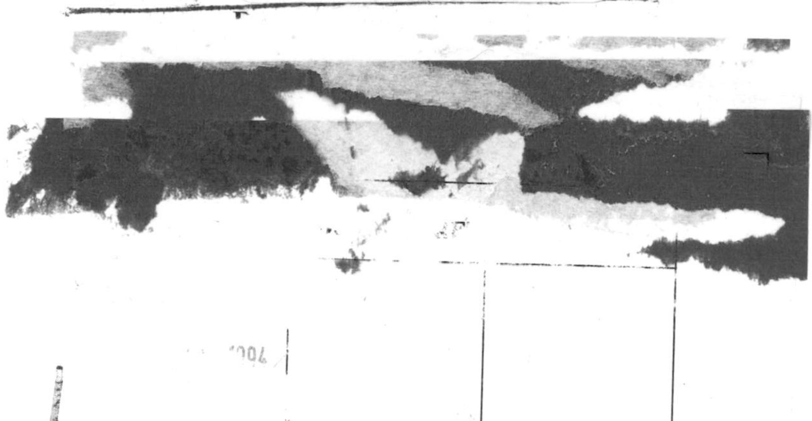

UNOTT

A GUIDE TO OLD ENGLISH

A GUIDE TO OLD ENGLISH

FIFTH EDITION

Bruce Mitchell
Fellow Emeritus of St Edmund Hall, Oxford
Fred C. Robinson
Douglas Tracy Smith Professor of English, Yale University

A Guide to Old English © Bruce Mitchell 1964, 1968
A Guide to Old English revised with Texts and Glossary
© Bruce Mitchell and Fred C. Robinson 1982
A Guide to Old English Revised with Prose and Verse Texts and Glossary © Bruce Mitchell and Fred C. Robinson 1986
A Guide to Old English Fifth edition © Bruce Mitchell and Fred C. Robinson 1992

First edition 1964
Second edition 1968
Reprinted 1971, 1975, 1978, 1981
Revised (3rd) edition with texts and glossary 1982
Reprinted with corrections 1983, 1984 (twice)
Revised (4th) edition with prose and verse texts and glossary 1986
Reprinted 1987, 1988 (with corrections and revisions), 1990, 1991
Fifth edition 1992

Blackwell Publishers
108 Cowley Road, Oxford OX4 1JF, UK

Three Cambridge Center
Cambridge, Massachusetts 02142
USA

All rights reserved. Except for the quotation of short passages for the purposes of criticism and review, no part of this publication may be reproduced, stored in a retrieval system, or transmitted, in any form or by any means, electronic, mechanical, photocopying, recording or otherwise, without the prior permission of the publisher.

Except in the United States of America, this book is sold subject to the condition that it shall not, by way of trade or otherwise, be lent, re-sold, hired out, or otherwise circulated without the publisher's prior consent in any form of binding or cover other than that in which it is published and without a similar condition including this condition being imposed on the subsequent purchaser.

British Library Cataloguing in Publication Data
A CIP catalogue record for this book is available from the British Library.

Library of Congress Cataloging in Publication Data
Mitchell, Bruce, 1920–
A guide to old English / Bruce Mitchell, Fred C. Robinson – 5th ed.
p. cm.
6003685281
Includes bibliographical references and indexes.
ISBN 0-631-16656-4 ISBN 0-631-16657-2 (pbk)
1. English language – Old English, ca. 450–1100 – Grammar.
2. English language – Old English, ca. 450–1100 – Texts. 3. Anglo-Saxons. I. Robinson, Fred C. II. Title.
PE131.M5 1992
429'.82421–dc20 90-24627
CIP

Typeset by Joshua Associates Limited, Oxford
Printed and bound in Great Britain by Billing & Sons Ltd, Worcester

In Memoriam

DONOVAN F. MITCHELL

AND

IRENE K. MITCHELL

'Everyman, I'll go with thee
  And be thy *Guide*.'
And if you don't learn Old English,
  Then Devil take your hide.

Foreword to the Fifth Edition

The *Guide* aims at making easier the initial steps in the learning of Old English. It is intended for beginners and will, it is hoped, prove especially useful to those wishing to acquire a reading knowledge of the language. But potential specialists in philology should find it a help in their preliminary studies of the essential grammar. The *Guide* can be used by students working with or without a teacher; for the latter, a section on 'How to Use this Guide' has been provided.

In general, the *Guide* devotes more space than is usual to the simple explanation of difficult points and to ways of reducing rote learning and of solving problems which arise for the reader of Old English texts. Part One is divided into seven chapters – Preliminary Remarks on the Language, a simple treatment of Orthography and Pronunciation, Inflexions, Word Formation, Syntax (where stress is laid on the important differences between Old and Modern English), a brief Introduction to Anglo-Saxon Studies in which language and literature, history, and archaeology, are discussed, and a highly selective Bibliography for the beginner. Part Two consists of Texts (with notes), and Glossary. Phonology is not treated in a separate section, but is integrated with the grammar, important sound-changes being treated briefly when they provide the accepted explanation of apparent irregularities in inflexion. Those seeking more information on sound-changes and their relation to accidence are recommended in the first place to the work by R. F. S. Hamer cited in §9 Note. But the *Guide* aims at being self-contained, as far as it goes. Chapter 6, An Introduction to Anglo-Saxon Studies, is, like the rest of the book, addressed to the beginner. Its aim is to give in short compass basic facts and background information which will illuminate the prose and verse texts and stimulate the student to pursue paths of interest. This accounts for the mention of some works which to the expert may seem 'popular' or 'out of date', e.g. Jessup's *Anglo-Saxon Jewellery* (§220), with its four colour plates and forty monochrome plates, and Fisher's *Introduction to Anglo-Saxon Architecture and Sculpture* (§220), with over one hundred monochrome plates. The books on metalwork by Wilson and by Hinton, on architecture by Taylor and Taylor, and on sculpture by Cramp and by Bailey – all cited in §258 – are more up to date and offer more detailed information. But in the interests of the beginner, we have retained the simpler books, just as we have provided a Glossary instead of referring him or her to one of the dictionaries.

The prose texts are arranged in order of increasing difficulty. The first three selections are normalized throughout, and palatal ċ and ġ are distinguished from velar *c* and *g*. The texts in the fourth selection are not normalized, but a few peculiarities have been removed to ease transition to the unnormalized texts in the remainder of the readings. The Glossary is extremely detailed, with heavy parsing of words recorded. Similarly, the notes are full, and cross-references to the grammatical explanations in the *Guide* are frequent. So full an apparatus may seem at times to encumber the student with more help than is necessary, but our intention is to make it possible for the student to begin reading Old English from the outset, without obliging the teacher to take up particular topics in the grammar in a particular sequence before assigning texts for translation. Although individual teachers and readers are thus freed to cover the fundamentals of the language in whatever sequence suits their taste, we do think that the order of topics laid out on pages 3 to 5 is recommended both by logic and by our own experience.

The prose and verse texts selected are on the whole those which have traditionally been offered to beginning students to read. We have resisted the temptation to substitute novel selections for the familiar ones: such passages as King Alfred's Preface, the story of Cædmon, the conversion of Edwin, and Cynewulf and Cyneheard, have been chosen by generations of teachers and scholars as the appropriate introductory texts precisely because these are the essential ones for the proper orientation of beginners towards both the literature and culture of Anglo-Saxon England. Replacement of any or all of these with different selections might give the veteran teacher a refreshing change from the canon, but it would also deprive beginning students of important reference points in their initial study of Old English literature.

The fifth edition rectifies some errors and omissions in text and bibliographies, and fills two gaps regretted by past users of the book. By including Ælfric's life of St. Edmund we provide a specimen of the important Old English genre of the saint's life and also introduce students to Ælfric's alliterative prose. By presenting in Appendix C a brief, general introduction to Old English metre with examples from the poems in the *Guide* we hope to enhance students' appreciation of the verse selections.

Bruce Mitchell's original obligations are recorded in the Forewords to the first and second editions. Thanks are now due to Sarah Ogilvie-Thomson of St. Edmund Hall, Oxford, Daniel Donoghue of Harvard University, and Traugott Lawler of Yale University. We should emphasize that in the poetic texts, as in the prose texts, we make no claim to originality in our emendations and interpretations. Rather we have tried to select what seemed to us the best scholarly view on each point, and usually this has been the view that enjoys a majority consensus among editors and scholars. We have made no effort to name the scholars who originated and have subscribed to the interpretations selected, for this, it seemed to us, would have cluttered the commentary without serving the student's needs. We make wholesale and grateful acknowledgement here to the Old English scholarly tradition on which we have drawn in preparing this book.

BRUCE MITCHELL

Gregory the Great, 1991 FRED C. ROBINSON

Contents

Abbreviations and Symbols

LANGUAGES AND DIALECTS

Gmc.	Germanic	nWS	non-West-Saxon
IE	Indo-European	OE	Old English
Lat.	Latin	OHG	Old High German
ME	Middle English	WS	West-Saxon
MnE	Modern English		

Before the name of a language or dialect

e = Early   l = Late   Pr = Primitive

GRAMMATICAL TERMS

acc.	accusative	nom.	nominative
adj.	adjective	pass.	passive
adv.	adverb	p.d.	see §100
conj.	conjunction	pers.	person
cons.	consonant	pl.	plural
dat.	dative	poss.	possessive
dem.	demonstrative	prep.	preposition
fem.	feminine	pres.	present
gen.	genitive	pret.	preterite
imp.	imperative	pret.-pres.	preterite-present
ind.	indicative	pron.	pronoun
inf.	infinitive	ptc.	participle
infl.	inflected	sg.	singular
inst.	instrumental	st.	strong
masc.	masculine	subj.	subjunctive
neut.	neuter	wk.	weak

's' may be added where appropriate to form a plural.

SYMBOLS

>	became
<	came from
*	This precedes a form which is not recorded. Usually it is a form which probably once existed and which scholars reconstruct to explain the stages in sound-changes; see §103.3.

Sometimes it is a form which certainly never existed but which is invented to show that one sound-change preceded another. An example is *ċierfan* in §100, note.

¯ over a letter denotes a long vowel or diphthong.

˘ over a letter denotes a short vowel or diphthong.

˘̄ means 'short and long', e.g. *ĕ̄* in §100.

– ˘ in §41 denote a long and short syllable respectively.

´ ` × denote respectively a syllable carrying full, secondary, or no, stress.

[ ] enclose phonetic symbols.

How to Use this Guide

This section is particularly addressed to those of you who are working without a teacher. We hope that when you have finished with this book you will not disagree too strongly – as far as elementary Old English grammar is concerned, at any rate – with the pithy observations made by Dr Johnson to Boswell in 1766:

> People have now-a-days, said he, got a strange opinion that everything should be taught by lectures. Now, I cannot see that lectures can do so much good as reading the books from which the lectures are taken. I know nothing that can be best taught by lectures, except where experiments are to be shown. You may teach chemistry by lectures. – You might teach making of shoes by lectures!

THE IMPORTANCE OF READING AND PARSING

The ability to recognize forms in the texts you are reading and an awareness of the basic structure of Old English are far more important than a parrot knowledge of the paradigms. Hence, from the beginning, you must get into the habit of analysing and thoroughly understanding each form you meet in your texts. Here you will find 'parsing' a great help. Since this word is taboo in many places, it had better be explained if it is to be used here.

All it means, of course, is recognizing what part of speech the word is – noun, pronoun, adjective, verb, and so on – and what particular form the word has in your sentence. If you are uncertain about the meaning of the parts of speech listed below or of other terms such as 'article', 'infinitive', or 'participle', you are advised to consult A. J. Thomson and A. V. Martinet *A Practical English Grammar* (3rd ed., Oxford, 1980, or 4th ed., Oxford, 1986) or David Crystal *A Dictionary of Linguistics and Phonetics* (2nd ed., Basil Blackwell, 1985).

The information needed when parsing Old English words is:

Noun: Meaning, gender, number, case, and the reason for the case, e.g. accusative because it is object, genitive denoting possession, or dative of the indirect object.

Pronoun: Same as for noun. Here you need to know the noun to which the pronoun refers. (If it is a relative pronoun, see §162.)

Adjective: Same as for noun. Sometimes, of course, an adjective is used with a noun, sometimes it is used alone, either as a complement or where a noun is more usual, e.g. 'The good often die before their time'.

Verb: If you have the infinitive, you merely need the meaning. Otherwise you need to work out the person, number, tense, and mood, and then deduce the infinitive. Unless you are familiar with the verb, you will have to do all this before you can find its meaning. For hints on how to do it, see §134.

Adverbs and interjections (a name given to words like 'Oh!', 'Alas!', and 'Lo!') will give little trouble. It is important to notice the case of a word governed by a preposition, for a difference in case sometimes indicates a difference in meaning; see §§213–214. Conjunctions are a greater source of difficulty. Lists of them are given in §§168, 171, and 184, and references to discussions on them are set out in 'Understanding the Syntax' below.

Note

The importance of gender varies. Sometimes it is obvious, sometimes it is of no real importance. But at times it provides a vital clue. Thus in *Hē ġehīerþ þās word and þā wyrcð*, *þās* and *þā* could be acc. sg. fem. or acc. pl. Only the fact that *word* is neuter will tell us that we must translate 'He hears these words and does them'.

LENGTH MARKS

Long vowels have been marked (¯) throughout,with the exception noted below. A knowledge of the length of vowels (or 'quantity', as it is called) is essential for proficiency in reading, for accuracy in translation (compare *god* 'god' with *gōd* 'good'), for the understanding of OE metre, and for the serious study of phonology. Hence, when you learn the inflexions, you will need to remember both the form of the word and the length of its vowels. Long vowels are marked in the Texts and you should take advantage of this by noting carefully those which occur in both familiar and unfamiliar words.

But since the length-marks are not shown in the Old English manuscripts, many editions of prose and verse texts do not show them. Examples are the standard editions of the Anglo-Saxon Chronicle and of the Homilies of Ælfric and Wulfstan, the texts published by Methuen (in their Old English Library) and by the Early English Text Society, and *The Anglo-Saxon Poetic Records* (published by Columbia University Press) which contain all the extant poetry. You will have to use one or more of these works fairly early in your career. In the hope that you will find the transition to such texts easier if you have already seen short passages in the form in which they appear in these works, we have not regularized the spelling (see §3) or marked vowel-length in the illustrative quotations in chapters 5 and 6. Most of the passages quoted are taken from texts which appear in Part Two. You can use these passages by writing them out, marking in the length-marks yourself, and then comparing them with the correct version. You can check individual words in the Glossary. But you will find it more interesting if you track down the context of the longer prose passages and those in verse with the help of the references in the Glossary. By so doing, you will improve your knowledge of vowel quantity and widen your acquaintance with OE literature.

LEARNING THE INFLEXIONS

Those who want to test their knowledge of the paradigms and to try their hand at translating into Old English (a very useful way of learning the language, especially important since no-one speaks it today) will find A. S. Cook *Exercises in Old English* (Ginn, 1895) a useful book. There are second-hand copies about. *An English—Anglo-Saxon Vocabulary*, compiled by W. W. Skeat and printed for private distribution only by the Cambridge University Press in 1879, was reprinted in 1976 by J. D. Pickles of Cambridge, England.

We suggest that those coming to this book without any knowledge of Old English learn the inflexions in the order set out below. But remember that texts must be read and an understanding of the syntax acquired at the same time. Hints on how to do this are given later in this section.

1 Read §§1–4.

2 Now work through §§5–9. Make sure that you can recognize the new letters *æ*, *þ*, and *ð*, and practise reading aloud the Practice Sentences (Text 1), following generally the natural stress of MnE.

3 Now read §§10–12.

4 The next step is to learn the paradigms in A below, in the order in which they are set out there.

5 (*a*) When you have learnt the pronouns, nouns, and adjectives, in A, you can see whether §§77–81 help or hinder you. Experience on this point differs.

(*b*) When you have learnt the verbs in A, you should read §§131–134.

6 You can now turn to the paradigms referred to in B below. B contains what may be called the 'derived paradigms', i.e. those which can be derived from the paradigms set out in A when certain sound-changes are understood. The sound-changes are presented in the hope that they will make your work easier, not as an end in themselves. Thus, if you meet a word *hwatum* in your reading, you will not be able to find out its meaning unless you know that it comes from an adjective *hwæt* 'active, bold'. You will know this only if you have read §70.

7 The paradigms in C are important ones of fairly frequent occurrence

which need not be learnt all at once. When you come across one of them in your reading, you can consult the relevant section. In this way, you will absorb them as need arises.

8 Because of the dialectal variations and inconsistencies in spelling noted in §§2–3, there are many ways of spelling even some of the most common words in the language; for examples, see the word *se* in the Glossary. If all the possible forms of this and other words were given in the paradigms in chapter 3, you would not see the wood for the trees. So those less common variants which occur in the texts will be found as cross-references in the Glossary.

A Key Paradigms

These paradigms must be known thoroughly. At this stage, concentrate on them alone; disregard anything else in these sections.

1 The pronouns set out in §§15–21. Note particularly §19. (The dual forms in §21 may be passed over at first.)
2 *Nama* (§22) and, after reading §§63–64, *tila* (§65).
3 Now read §§26–32.
4 *Stān* (§33), *scip/word* (§34), and *ġiefu/lār* (§§47–48).
5 The strong declension of the adjectives (§§66–67).
6 Now read §§14, 87–89, and 115.
7 *Fremman* (§§116–117) and *lufian* (§§124–125).
8 *Habban* (§126), *bēon* (§127), and *weorþan* (Appendix A.3 (*b*)).
9 The principal parts of the strong verbs (§§90–95).
10 The conjugation of strong verbs (§§110–113).

B Derived Paradigms

The paradigms in this group may be derived from those in A as follows:

1 From *nama*, those in §§23–25.
2 From *stān*, *scip*, or *ġiefu*, those in §§35–44, 48–51, and 52–60. See now §13.
3 From *tila* and *til*, those in §§68–73.
4 From *fremman*, those in §§116–123.
5 From *lufian*, those in §§124–125.
6 From §§90–95, those in §§96–109.
7 From §§110–113, those in §114.

Note
Some nouns which often go like *stān*, *scip*, or *ġiefu*, once belonged to other declensions. As a result, they sometimes have unusual forms which may cause you difficulty

in your reading. It might be just as well if you learnt to recognize these fairly early in your career. They include: *ċild* (§34), *hæleþ* and *mōnaþ* (§44), some nouns in *-e* (§§45–46), the feminine nouns discussed in §§49 and 51, the relationship nouns (§60), and the *u*-nouns (§§61–62).

C Other Paradigms

1 Other Strong Nouns (§§45–46 and 61–62).
2 Comparison of Adjectives (§§74–76).
3 Numerals (§§82–86).
4 Verbs
 (*a*) Class 3 weak verbs (§126).
 (*b*) *Dōn* and *gān* (§128).
 (*c*) *Willan* (§§129 and 211).
 (*d*) Preterite-present verbs (§§130 and 206–210).
5 Adverbs (§135).

LEARNING THE VOCABULARY

Many OE words are easily recognizable from their MnE counterparts, though sometimes the meaning may be different; see §4 and look up the word 'lewd' in the Oxford English Dictionary.

Other words differ in spelling and pronunciation as a result of changes in ME and MnE. The short vowels *e, i, o, u,* have remained relatively constant (see §7). But the long vowels and the diphthongs have sometimes changed considerably. Words with a long vowel in OE sometimes appear in MnE with the vowel doubled, e.g. *fēt* (masc. pl.) 'feet' and *dōm* (masc.) 'doom'. Sometimes, they have *-e* at the end, e.g. *līf* (neut.) 'life' and (with, in addition, one of the differences discussed below) *hām* (masc.) 'home' and *hūs* (neut.) 'house'.

Correspondences like the last two are more difficult to spot. Yet a knowledge of them is easily acquired and will save you much hard work. Thus, if you know that OE *ā* often appears in MnE as *oa*, you will not need to use the Glossary to discover that *bār* (masc.) means 'boar', *bāt* (fem. or masc.) 'boat', *brād* 'broad', and *hār* 'hoar(y)'. Words like *āc* (fem.) 'oak', *hlāf* (masc.) 'loaf', and *hlāfas* (masc. pl.) 'loaves', will not present much more difficulty.

The table which follows will help you to recognize more of these correspondences. But it is not complete and the correspondences do not always apply. Thus OE *hāt* is MnE 'hot' and you may find it interesting to look up in a glossary or dictionary the four OE words spelt *ār* and see what has happened to them.

OE spelling	*MnE spelling*	*Vowels*	*Consonants*
fæt (neut.)	vat	æ = a	f = v
rǣdan	read	ǣ = ea	
dǣd (fem.)	deed	ǣ = ee	
lang	long	an = on	
hālġ	holy	ā = o	
hām (masc.)	home	ā = o.e	
āc (fem.)	oak	ā = oa	c = k
hlāf (masc.)	loaf		hl = l
ecg (fem.)	edge		cg = dge
dēman	deem	ē = ee	
frēosan	freeze		s =z
ċild (neut.)	child		ċ =ch
miht (fem.)	might		h = gh
scip (neut.)	ship		sc = sh
līf (neut.)	life	ī = i.e	
ġiellan	yell	ie = e	ġ = y
ġiefan	give	ie = i	ġ = g
dōm (masc.)	doom	ō = oo	
mūs (fem.)	mouse	ū = ou.e	
nū	now	ū = ow	
synn (fem.)	sin	y = i	
mȳs (fem.)	mice	ȳ = i.e	

See §253 for a book which may help you to learn the vocabulary.

The principles on which words were formed in OE are set out in §§136–138. Once you understand these, you will be able to deduce the meaning of some new words by their similarity to words you already know; see §136. For correspondences in endings, see §138.

UNDERSTANDING THE SYNTAX

The fundamental differences between the syntax of Old English and that of Modern English are set out in §§139–153. These, and §§182–183, should be studied as soon as you can read simple sentences with some degree of fluency and before you pass on to the connected passages of Old English recommended below. Other sections which should be read fairly soon are §§154–155, 157–158, and 160 (noun clauses and their conjunctions), §162 (relative pronouns), §§166–167 and §§169–170 (conjunctions introducing adverb clauses), §189 note, and §§195–199 (the uses of the tenses and the syntax of the resolved verb forms).

The remaining parts of the syntax should be used for reference when the need arises; note especially the topics mentioned in §§141–142 and the lists of conjunctions in §§168, 171, and 184. When you begin to feel some confidence, you can try the exercise in §172.

If at first you find these sections too long and complicated, you are advised to use one of the books cited in §256.

TEXTS TO READ

Part Two of this book starts with a selection of prose texts for beginners, the texts being carefully coordinated with the explanations in the grammar sections. After you have worked your way through these, you will be ready for the poems, which are similarly annotated. This combination of texts should provide a foundation from which you can advance to *Beowulf* and to the prose and verse texts available in Methuen's Old English Library and the Manchester Series.

READING THE TEXTS

Before beginning to read the texts you should do two things: first, study carefully the introduction to the Glossary, and second, familiarize yourself with the function words and word-patterns listed in §§168 and 171. While reading the texts, you should make careful use not only of the Glossary, but also of the Index of Words.

WES ÞU HAL

It now remains for us to wish you success – and pleasure – in your studies. In 991, before the battle of Maldon, Byrhtnoth called across the cold waters of the river to his Danish foes:

> Nu eow is gerymed; gað ricene to us,
> guman to guþe; god ana wat
> hwa þære wælstowe wealdan mote.
> (*The Battle of Maldon*, ll. 93–95)

This can be paraphrased

> 'Now the way is clear for you; O warriors,
> hasten to the battle; God alone knows
> how things will turn out'.

It is our hope and wish that *your* efforts will prosper – *Wel þe þæs geweorces!*

Part One

I

Preliminary Remarks on the Language

§1 Professor Campbell defines Old English as 'the vernacular Germanic language of Great Britain as it is recorded in manuscripts and inscriptions dating from before about 1100'. It is one of the Germanic group of the Indo-European family of languages. Those who are unfamiliar with this concept should read about it in one of the histories of the English language cited in the Bibliography.

§2 There are four dialects distinguishable in the extant monuments – Northumbrian, Mercian, Kentish, West-Saxon. The differences are apparent in the spelling; otherwise, of course, we should not know about them. After 900 West-Saxon was increasingly used as a standard written language. It is for this reason that, initially at any rate, you learn West-Saxon. But even here the spelling conventions were never as rigidly observed as they are in Great Britain or America today, where compositors, typists, and writers, in different parts of the country use the same spelling, no matter how different their pronunciations may be.

§3 Most OE primers therefore attempt to make things easier for the beginner by 'normalizing', i.e. regularizing, the spelling by eliminating all forms not belonging to the West-Saxon dialect. But difficulty arises because two stages can be distinguished – early West-Saxon (eWS), which is the language of the time of King Alfred (*c.* 900), and late West-Saxon (lWS), which is seen in the works of Ælfric (*c.* 1000). Professor Davis, in revising Sweet's *Anglo-Saxon Primer*, followed Sweet and used eWS as his basis. Quirk and Wrenn's *Old English Grammar*, however, normalizes on the basis of Ælfric's lWS. For the beginner, the most important difference is that eWS *ie* and *īe* appear in lWS texts as *y* and *ȳ*; this accounts for such differences as Sweet *ieldra, hīeran*, but Q. & W. *yldra, hȳran*. Another is that *ea* and *ēa* may be spelt *e* and *ē* in lWS (and sometimes in eWS) texts, e.g. *seah* and *scēap*, but *seh* and *scēp*. Since the other differences will scarcely trouble you and since there are some disadvantages in the use of lWS, the paradigms are given here in their eWS forms and the sound laws are discussed with eWS as the basis. Any important variations likely to cause difficulty – apart from those mentioned here – will be noted. Full lists of all dialectal variants will be found in the appropriate section of Campbell's *Old English Grammar*.

In the sections on syntax, the spelling of a standard edition has generally been followed, though occasionally an unusual form has been silently regularized. This should ease the transition to non-normalized texts.

Similarly, in the prose texts provided for reading, we have moved from totally normalized to non-normalized texts. We have not normalized the poems.

§4 As has been explained in the Foreword, this book, after a brief discussion of orthography and pronunciation, deals with accidence, word formation, and syntax (including word-order), and attempts simple explanations of those sound-changes which will help you to learn the inflexions. Other sound-changes, the metre of poetry, and semantics, are not discussed. It is important, however, to remember that many common words have changed their meaning. *Sellan* means 'to give', not just 'to give in exchange for money, to sell'. *Eorl* cannot always be translated 'earl' and *dēor* and *fugol* mean, not 'deer' and 'fowl', but 'any (wild) animal' and 'any bird' respectively. It is also important to note that, while Old English literature was written and/or transmitted by Christians, the Christian poetry was largely written in an originally pagan vocabulary which embodied the values of the heroic code. However, it does not follow that the poetry is rich in pagan elements. You will find that words like *lof* in *The Seafarer* and *wyrd* in *The Wanderer* have acquired Christian connotations. On this point, see further §§218 and 236–246. The Bibliography contains references to useful introductory discussions on all the topics not discussed in this book.

2

Orthography and Pronunciation

I ORTHOGRAPHY

§5 As a glance at the facsimile of the OE manuscript on page 254 will show, the letters used by Anglo-Saxon scribes were sometimes very like and sometimes very unlike those used today, both in shape and function. Printers of Anglo-Saxon texts generally use the equivalent modern letter form. Hence the sounds [f] and [v] are both represented by *f*, and the sounds [s] and [z] by *s* because the distinctions were less significant in OE; on these and other differences in representing the consonants, see §9. On the value of *y*, which represents a vowel now lost, see §7.

The following symbols are not in use today: *æ* (ash), which represents the vowel in MnE 'hat', *þ* (thorn) and *ð* (eth or, as the Anglo-Saxons appear to have called it, *ðæt*), both of which represent MnE *th* as in 'cloth' and in 'clothe'. Capital *ð* is written *Ð*. To make the learning of paradigms as simple as possible, *þ* has been used throughout chapter 3.

The early texts of the Methuen Old English Library used the runic 'wynn' *ƿ* instead of *w* and the OE letter *ʒ* for *g*. In the latest volumes, these have been discarded.

As is customary, the punctuation in quotations and selections from OE is modern. But see the Note on the Punctuation of Old English Poetry which follows selection 18 in Part Two.

II STRESS

§6 The stress usually falls on the first syllable, as in MnE, e.g. mórgen 'morning'. The prefix *ġe-* is always unaccented; hence *ġebīdan* 'await'. Two main difficulties occur:

1 Prepositional prefixes, e.g. *for-*, *ofer-*, can be either accented (usually in nouns or adjectives, e.g. *fórwyrd* 'ruin') or unaccented (usually in verbs, e.g. *forwíernan* 'refúse').

2 Compound words in which both elements retain their full meaning, e.g. *sǣ-weall* 'sea-wall', have a secondary stress on the root syllable of the second element. There is some dispute about three-syllabled words with a long first syllable (see §26). Some say that *bindende* 'binding' and *timbrode*

'built' have a pattern like MnE 'árchàngelsͯ', not like 'hástiͯlyͯ'. But not everyone agrees.

III VOWELS

§7 Short vowels must be distinguished from long vowels, which are marked (¯) in this book (except as noted on pp. 2–3). Approximate pronunciations of OE vowels for those working without a teacher are given as far as possible in terms of Received Standard English.

a as the first vowel in 'aha'
ā as the second vowel in 'aha'
æ as in 'mat'
ǣ as in 'has'[1]
e as in 'bet'
ē approx. as in 'hate', but a pure vowel [cf. German *See*]
i as in 'tin'
ī as in 'seen'
o as in 'cough'
ō approx. as in 'so', but a pure vowel [cf. German *so*]
u as in 'pull' [NOT 'hut']
ū as in 'cool'
y as *i*, with lips in a whistling position [French *tu*]
ȳ as *ī*, with lips in a whistling position [French *ruse*]

Vowels in unstressed syllables should be pronounced clearly. Failure to distinguish gen. sg. *eorles* from nom. acc. pl. *eorlas* is characteristic of ME, not of OE.

IV DIPHTHONGS

§8 If you are not sure of the distinction between vowels and diphthongs, you should consult a simple manual of phonetics. It is important to realize that OE words such as *heall*, *hēold*, *hielt*, which contain diphthongs, are just as much monosyllables as MnE 'meat' and 'field' (in which two letters represent one vowel) or MnE 'fine' and 'base', which contain diphthongs. The OE diphthongs, with approximate pronunciations, are

ea = æ + a
ēa = ǣ + a
eo = e + o

[1] If you experiment, you will notice that the vowel in 'has' is longer than that in 'mat', though MnE [æ] is frequently described as a 'short vowel'.

ēo = ē + o
ie = i + e[1]
īe = ī + e

A short diphthong is equal in length to a short vowel, a long diphthong to a long vowel. But remember that, like the MnE word 'I', they are diphthongs, not two distinct vowels such as we get in the *ea* of 'Leander'.

V CONSONANTS

§9 All consonants must be pronounced, e.g. *c* in *cnapa*, *g* in *gnæt*, *h* in *hlāf*, *r* in *þǣr*, and *w* in *wrītan* and *trēow*.

Double consonants must be pronounced double or long. Thus, when you see *-dd-*, as in *biddan*, pronounce it as you do when you say 'red *D*', not as you do when you say 'ready'.

Most of the consonants are pronounced in the same way as in MnE. The main exceptions are set out below.

The letters *s*, *f*, *þ*, and *ð*, are pronounced voiced, i.e. like MnE *z*, *v*, and *th* in 'clothe', between vowels or other voiced sounds, e.g. *rīsan*, *hlāfas*, *paþas*, and *hēafdes*. In other positions, including the beginning and end of words, they are voiceless, i.e. like MnE *s*, *f*, and *th* in 'cloth', e.g. *sittan*, *hlāf*, *pæþ*, and *oft*. This accounts for the different sounds in MnE 'path' but 'paths', 'loaf' but 'loaves', and the like. Initial *ġe-* does not cause voicing; *findan* and its past ptc. *ġe-funden* both have the sound *f*.

The differences described in the preceding paragraph are due to the fact that the pairs *f* and *v*, *s* and *z*, and voiceless and voiced *þ* 'th', were merely variants ('allophones') in OE and not sounds of different significance ('phonemes'). This means that, whereas in MnE speech the distinctions between 'fat' and 'vat', 'sink' and 'zinc', and 'loath' and 'loathe', depend on whether we use a voiceless or voiced sound, both OE *fæt* 'fat' and OE *fæt* 'vat' could be pronounced with initial *f* or *v*, according to dialect.

At the beginning of a word ('initially') before a vowel, *h* is pronounced as in MnE 'hound'. Otherwise it is like German *ch* in *ich* [ç] or *ach* [x], according to the front or back quality of the neighbouring vowel. It can be pronounced like *ch* in Scots *loch*.

Before *a*, *o*, *u*, and *y*, *c* is pronounced *k* and *g* is pronounced as in MnE 'good'. Before *e* and *i*, *c* is usually pronounced like *ch* in MnE 'child' and *g* like *y* in MnE 'yet'. In Part One, the latter are printed *ċ* and *ġ* respectively, except in the examples quoted in chapters 5 and 6.

[1] The original pronunciation of *ie* and *īe* is not known with any certainty. It is simplest and most convenient for our purposes to assume that they represented diphthongs as explained above. But by King Alfred's time *ie* was pronounced as a simple vowel (monophthong), probably a vowel somewhere between *i* and *e*; *ie* is often replaced by *i* or *y*, and unstressed *i* is often replaced by *ie*, as in *hiene* for *hine*. Probably *īe* had a similar sound.

After or between back vowels, *g* is pronounced [ ], like the *g* sometimes heard in dialectal German *sagen*. Those without a teacher can pronounce it as *w* in words like *dragan* and *boga*.

The combinations *sc* and *cg* are usually pronounced like MnE *sh* and *dge* respectively. Thus *scip* 'ship' and *ecg* 'edge' are pronounced the same in both OE and MnE. But in *ascian* 'ask' (1/34, p. 164), *-sc-* is pronounced *-sk-*.

Note

A more detailed account of the pronunciation of Old English will be found in §§9–19 of *Old English Sound Changes for Beginners* by R. F. S. Hamer (Basil Blackwell, 1967).

3

Inflexions

INTRODUCTION

§10 Following (as most primers do) the conventional terminology, we distinguish in Old English the following parts of speech: nouns, adjectives, pronouns (including articles), verbs, adverbs, prepositions, conjunctions, and interjections.

§11 Like most inflected languages, OE distinguishes number, case, and gender, in nouns, pronouns, and adjectives. The numbers are singular and plural; a dual is found in the 1st and 2nd pers. pron. where, e.g. *wit* means 'we two', *ġit* 'you (ye) two'. The main cases are nominative, accusative, genitive, and dative, but in certain parts of the adjective and pronoun declensions an instrumental occurs; where it does not, the dative does its work. If you are unfamiliar with the concept of 'case', you are recommended to consult the sections listed under that word in the Index of Subjects.

§12 There are three genders – masculine, feminine, and neuter. Gender sometimes agrees with sex, e.g. *se mann* (masc.) 'the man', *sēo sweostor* (fem.) 'the sister', or with lack of it, e.g. *þæt scip* (neut.) 'the ship'. This is often called 'natural gender'. But grammatical gender is often opposed to sex, e.g. (with persons) *se wīfmann* (masc.) 'the woman', *þæt wīf* (neut.) 'the woman', and (with inanimate objects) *se stān* (masc.) 'the stone', *sēo ġiefu* (fem.) 'the gift'. These opposing tendencies, which contribute to the later disappearance of grammatical gender in English, sometimes produce 'lack of concord'; see §187.2. Compounds follow the gender of the second element; hence *þæt wīf* (neut.) + *se mann* (masc.) = *se wīfmann* (masc.).

§13 OE nouns are traditionally divided into two groups – weak and strong. Generally, the gender of nouns must be learnt. The form of the demonstrative is the main clue (see §§16–17). The following nom. sg. endings, however, are significant:

Weak Masc.:	*-a*
Strong Masc.:	*-dōm*, *-els*, agent nouns in *-end* and *-ere*, *-hād*, concrete nouns in *-ing* and *-ling*, *-scipe*
Strong Fem.:	*-nes(s)*, abstract nouns in *-ing/ung*, *-rǣden*, *-þo/þu*
Strong Neut.:	*-lāc*

Notoriously ambiguous is the ending *-e*; see §77. On these endings, see further §§136–138.

§14 Verbs. The differences between strong and weak verbs and the system of conjugating the OE verb are described in §§87–89. New developments, many of them important for MnE, are outlined in §§199–203.

I PRONOUNS

§15 You are now ready to learn your first paradigms. The demonstrative *se* serves as a definite article. Both *se* 'that' and *þes* 'this' can be used with nouns, e.g. *se mann* 'the man', or as pronouns, e.g. *hē sorgaþ ymb þā* 'he is concerned about those (them)'.

§16 *se* 'the, that'

	Singular			*Plural*
	Masc.	*Neut.*	*Fem.*	*All genders*
Nom.	se	þæt	sēo, sīo	þā
Acc.	þone	þæt	þā	þā
Gen.	þæs	þæs	þǣre	þāra, þǣra
Dat.	þǣm, þām	þǣm, þām	þǣre	þǣm, þām
Inst.	þȳ, þon	þȳ, þon		

§17 *þes* 'this'

	Singular			*Plural*
	Masc.	*Neut.*	*Fem.*	*All genders*
Nom.	þes	þis	þēos	þās
Acc.	þisne	þis	þās	þās
Gen.	þisses	þisses	þisse, þisre	þissa, þisra
Dat.	þissum	þissum	þisse	þissum
Inst.	þȳs	þȳs		

§18 3rd Pers. Pron.

	Singular			*Plural*
	Masc.	*Neut.*	*Fem.*	*All genders*
Nom.	hē 'he'	hit 'it'	hēo, hīo 'she'	hīe, hī 'they'
Acc.	hine	hit	hīe, hī	hīe, hī
Gen.	his	his	hire	hira, hiera, heora, hiora
Dat.	him	him	hire	him, heom

§19 The following similarities in these declensions may be noted:

1 neut. sg. gen. dat. inst. are the same as the corresponding masc. forms;
2 nom. and acc. neut. sg. are the same;
3 gen. and dat. fem. sg. are the same;
4 pl. is the same for all genders;
5 acc. fem. sg. is the same as nom. and acc. pl.
6 masc. and neut. dat. sg. is the same as dat. pl.

Note too the way in which the masc. and neut. sg., while agreeing with one another except in the nom. and acc., differ markedly in inflexion from the fem.

§20 *Hwā* is interrogative 'who?' or indefinite 'anyone, someone'. It is not a relative pronoun in OE; see §159.

	Masc. and Fem.	*Neut.*
Nom.	hwā	hwæt
Acc.	hwone	hwæt
Gen.	hwæs	hwæs
Dat.	hwǣm, hwām	hwǣm, hwām
Inst.	hwȳ	hwȳ, hwon

Compare *hwā/hwæt* and *se/þæt*. The main difference is that the masc. and fem. of *hwā* are the same. This is understandable if we think of what *hwā* means.

§21 1st and 2nd Pers. Prons.

	Singular	*Dual*	*Plural*
Nom.	iċ 'I'	wit 'we two'	wē 'we'
Acc.	mē, meċ	unc	ūs
Gen.	mīn	uncer	ūre
Dat.	mē	unc	ūs

	Singular	*Dual*	*Plural*
Nom.	þū 'thou'	ġit 'you two'	ġē 'ye, you'
Acc.	þē, þeċ	inc	ēow
Gen.	þīn	incer	ēower
Dat.	þē	inc	ēow

The easiest way to learn these is to compare them with their MnE equivalents (the main differences are in pronunciation) and with one another.

Note

Unlike the indeclinable gen. forms *his*, *hire*, *hira* (§18), the six gen. forms given here can also be declined strong like adjs. (§63) to agree with nouns, e.g. 3/70 *mīnne cræft.* We cannot tell whether *mīn* in 2/54 and 55 means 'my' (poss. adj.) or 'of me' (poss. pron.).

II NOUNS AND SOUND-CHANGES RELEVANT TO THEM

Weak Nouns

§22 The basic paradigm of the weak or *-an* nouns is *nama* 'name' (masc.):

	Singular	*Plural*
Nom.	nama	naman
Acc.	naman	naman
Gen.	naman	namena
Dat.	naman	namum

Notes

1 Any noun with the nom. sg. ending *-a* is weak masc.

2 All other cases have the ending *-an* except gen. pl. *-ena* and dat. pl. *-um*.

Once *nama* is known, the rest follows quite simply without learning further paradigms.

§23 The weak fem. noun *sunne* 'sun' is declined exactly as *nama* apart from the nom. sg.

§24 The weak neut. noun *ēage* 'eye' is declined exactly as *nama* except that, as in all neut. nouns, the nom. and acc. sg. are the same.

§25 Nouns with a nom. sg. ending in a long vowel or diphthong form their oblique cases (i.e. any case other than the nom.) by adding the consonant of the inflexional ending. So *ġefēa* (masc.) 'joy' has oblique cases *ġefēa/n* except for gen. pl. *ġefēa/na* and dat. pl. *ġefēa/m*.

Some Technical Terms

§26 You now need to know some phonological terms. 'Short vowel' as in MnE 'hit' and 'long vowel' as in the second syllable in MnE 'machine' will present no difficulty. The word *wer* 'man' has a short vowel and is a short syllable. The word *stān* 'stone' has a long vowel and is a long syllable. Such words as *cniht* 'young man' and *cræft* 'strength' have a short vowel. But, since the short vowel is followed by *two* consonants, the syllable is long; cf. the rules of Latin prosody. To summarize, we have

short-stemmed monosyllables[1]	*wer, bæc, feoh*
long-stemmed monosyllables	*stān, cniht, crēap*
short-stemmed dissyllables	*miċel, yfel*
long-stemmed dissyllables	*ēþel, engel*

Forms like *metodes* and *bysiġe* are called 'trisyllabic' and the *o* or *i* is sometimes called the 'medial vowel'.

§27 It is also important to distinguish open and closed syllables. An open syllable ends in a vowel, e.g. *hē* 'he'; a closed syllable ends in a consonant, e.g. *stān* 'stone'. This is clear enough. But difficulty arises with dissyllables. You must take on trust that the gen. sg. *stānes* is divided *stā/nes* (cf. MnE 'stone' but 'sto/ning'), while the infinitive *limpan* divides *lim/pan* (cf. MnE 'limb pad'). So we have

open syllables	*hē*	*stā/nes*
closed syllables	*stān*	*lim/pan*

§28 'Sometimes', it has been observed, 'things may be made darker by definition.' This must not deter us from attempting to define high and low

[1] The 'stem' of a word may be defined as that portion to which the inflexional ending is added, e.g. *scip* + *-es* = gen. sg. *scipes*. The stem of words ending in a vowel can usually be found by dropping the final vowel. So *ende* has stem *end-* + *-es* = gen. sg. *endes*.

vowels and back and front vowels. The adjectives 'high, low, back, front' all refer to the position in the mouth occupied by some part of the tongue. The tip of the tongue is not usually important; here it is assumed to be near or touching the lower front teeth. We are concerned with the movement of that part of the tongue which is highest when we pronounce a particular vowel.

§29 What follows is a conventionalized diagram showing the parts of the mouth in which the vowels are pronounced.

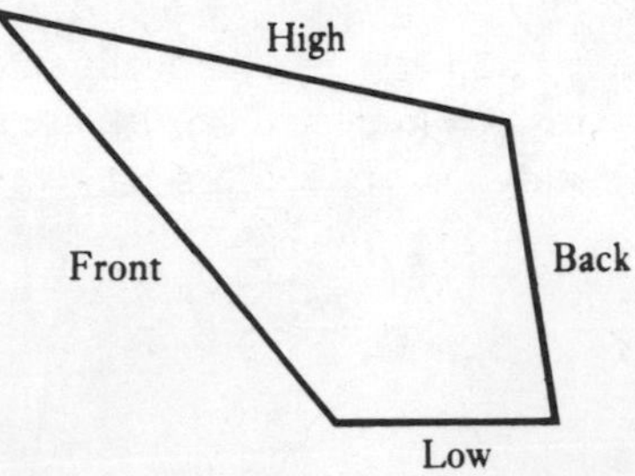

In the front vowels, the 'front' of the tongue is raised towards the hard palate. In the back vowels, the 'back' of the tongue is raised towards the soft palate. To understand this, you may well need the help of a tutor and of a book on the phonetics of your own 'accent' of English. But you can try the following experiment, observing with the aid of a mirror the movements of jaw, lips, and tongue:

1 Practise individually the sounds you have learnt for the OE vowels *i, e, æ, a, o, u*.

2 Sing them in a rough scale in the order given in 1, with the tip of the tongue near or touching the lower front teeth.

§30 Observe:

1 with *i, e, æ*,

(*a*) a gradual lowering of the jaw;
(*b*) a gradual lowering of the (front of the) tongue;
(*c*) the roughly natural position of the lips, i.e. neither unduly spread out nor rounded;
(*d*) a general feeling that the sounds are being made in the front of the mouth.

2 With the transition from *æ* to *a* a backward and slightly downward movement of the tongue.

3 with *a, o, u*,

(*a*) progressive raising of the jaw and of the (back of the) tongue;
(*b*) the way in which the lips become more rounded, i.e. form a progressively smaller circle;
(*c*) the general feeling of 'backness'.

§31 From this, it should be clear why *i*, *e*, *æ*, are called front vowels and *a*, *o*, *u*, back vowels. Another way of feeling the difference is to pronounce the diphthongs made up of *i* + *u*, *e* + *o*, and *æ* + *a*, for if you do this you will feel the backward movement of the tongue. (The two latter sounds will be close to the OE diphthongs *eo* and *ea* respectively.) But you will not feel a great downward movement; roughly speaking, *i* and *u* are pronounced with the highest part of the tongue about the same height in the mouth. Similarly with *e* and *o* and with *æ* and *a*. Now, if you draw the vowel diagram again and try to plot these vowels as you pronounce them, you will get something like this:

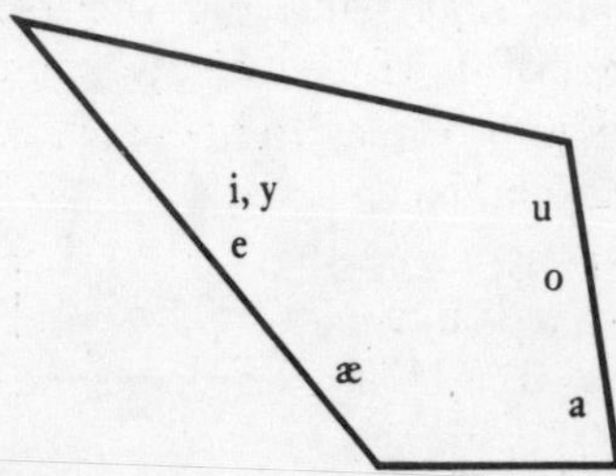

Since we can distinguish *i*, *u*, as high vowels and *æ*, *a*, as low vowels, we can now describe *i* as a high front vowel, *a* as a low back vowel, and so on.

§32 Of course, this is far from being a scientific description of the vowel sounds and you will need to consult a book on phonetics if you wish to learn more. Its incompleteness is illustrated by the fact that OE possesses another high front vowel *y* which (unlike the high front vowel *i*) has lip rounding. (If you try to pronounce the second vowel in 'machine' and to purse your lips at the same time, you will get a rather strained and tense *ȳ*.) But this outline will suffice for our present purposes.

Strong Nouns like *stān* (masc.) and *scip* (neut.)

§33 Here we can take the masc. and neut. nouns together and deal with the fem. separately; cf. §19. The basic paradigm is the masc. *stān*:

	Singular	*Plural*
Nom.	stān	stānas
Acc.	stān	stānas
Gen.	stānes	stāna
Dat.	stāne	stānum

Notes

1 nom. and acc. sg. the same;

2 nom. and acc. pl. the same – the characteristic strong masc. *-as* which gives the MnE 's' plural;

3 gen. pl. in *-a*;

4 dat. pl. in *-um*. This is spelt *-an* or *-on* in some late texts.

§34 In the neut. we find

	Singular	*Plural*	*Singular*	*Plural*
Nom.	scip	scipu	word	word
Acc.	scip	scipu	word	word
Gen.	scipes	scipa	wordes	worda
Dat.	scipe	scipum	worde	wordum

These differ from *stān* and from one another only in the nom. and acc. pl. where the short-stemmed *scip* has *scipu* while the long-stemmed *word* remains unchanged; for this absence of *-u*, cf. *ġiefu/lār* (§48) and *sunu/hand* (§61).

Ċild 'child' may follow *word* or may add *r* before the pl. endings – *ċildru, ċildra, ċildrum*; hence MnE 'children', with final *n* from the weak declension. *Ǣġ* 'egg' has nom. acc. pl. *ǣġru*.

§35 Many nouns are exactly like *stān* (e.g. *āþ* 'oath', *dōm* 'judgement', *wer* 'man'), like *scip* (e.g. *god* 'god', *hof* 'dwelling'), or like *word* (e.g. *hūs* 'house', *wīf* 'woman'). But some differ in that, while THEY HAVE PERFECTLY NORMAL ENDINGS like those of *stān*, *scip*, or *word*, THEY SHOW SOME ABNORMALITY IN THE STEM (see §26, note) as the result of certain 'sound-changes' or 'sound-laws'. These 'sound-laws' are not laws in the same sense as the law of gravity is one. People who jump off cliffs always have fallen and (as far as we know) will continue to fall, irrespective of what language they spoke or speak. But each language undergoes different changes at different periods. And the 'sound-laws' in which these changes are summed up are the result of observation by later scholars. Sometimes one of these 'laws' appears not to operate. This, however, is usually because something in a particular word or form prevented it. In such cases, another 'sound-law' was deduced to explain the exception. Thus the sound which was Gmc. *a* usually turns up in OE as *æ*. But in the nouns discussed in §36 we sometimes find *æ*, sometimes *a*. It was as a result of observing such differences that scholars first deduced the sound-changes. We can follow in their steps by examining the full paradigms of two nouns, noting the similarities and dissimilarities between them and regular nouns of the same declension, and so deducing the sound-changes necessary to explain the forms we have.

§36 These nouns are *dæġ* (masc.) 'day' and *fæt* (neut.) 'vessel':

	Singular	*Plural*	*Singular*	*Plural*
Nom.	dæġ	dagas	fæt	fatu
Acc.	dæġ	dagas	fæt	fatu
Gen.	dæġes	daga	fætes	fata
Dat.	dæġe	dagum	fæte	fatum

Observe:

1 that their endings are the same as in *stān* and *scip* respectively;
2 that they are short-stemmed monosyllables;

3 that the stem vowel of the nom. sg. is *æ*;
4 that both have *æ* throughout sg., *a* throughout pl.;
5 that where they have *a*, the ending is, or begins with, a back vowel;
6 that where they have *æ*, there is either no ending or an ending which is, or begins with, a front vowel.

Hence we can deduce that *æ* is found in a closed syllable (*dæġ*) or in an open syllable + a front vowel (*dæġes*), but appears as *a* in an open syllable + a back vowel (*dagas*). A simple rule is that these monosyllabic nouns have *æ* in the sg. stem, *a* in the pl. stem.

§37 Long-stemmed monosyllables ending in a vowel or diphthong + *h* take the endings of *stān* or *scip* but show absorption of *h* when it occurs between two vowels. Subsequently the unaccented vowel is also absorbed. Thus the gen. sg. of *scōh* (masc.) 'shoe' is **scōhes* > **scōes* > *scōs*. The paradigm is

Singular: *nom.* scōh, *acc.* scōh, *gen.* scōs, *dat.* scō
Plural: *nom.* scōs, *acc.* scōs, *gen.* scōna (§38), *dat.* scōm

§38 The same thing happens in short-stemmed monosyllables ending in a vowel or diphthong + *h*. But even without the *h* and the vowel, these words appear to have taken roughly the same time to pronounce. (A little experimenting will convince you that this is reasonable.) Hence the stressed vowel or diphthong is lengthened. So we get (these are the recorded forms)

eoh (masc.) 'horse', but gen. sg. *ēos*
feoh (neut.) 'money', but gen. sg. *fēos*, dat. sg. *fēo*

Theoretically, the gen. pl. of *feoh* should be **fēo* < **feoha*, but *fēona*, with the weak ending *-ena*, occurs – doubtless because *fēo* was ambiguous. So also *scōna* (§37).

§39 Loss of *h* with lengthening of the stem vowel or diphthong occurs between *r* or *l* and a vowel in monosyllabic nouns like *mearh* (masc.) 'horse' and *wealh* (masc.) 'foreigner'. The endings are those of *stān*.

	Singular	*Plural*	*Singular*	*Plural*
Nom.	mearh	mēaras	wealh	wēalas
Acc.	mearh	mēaras	wealh	wēalas
Gen.	mēares	mēara	wēales	wēala
Dat.	mēare	mēarum	wēale	wēalum

Note
Here the diphthong of the first syllable has been shown lengthened (as in *fēos*), so that the first syllable of *mēares* is the same length as *mearh*. But metrical and place-name evidence shows that forms with a short diphthong, e.g. *meares*, also occurred under the influence of the short sound in *mearh*; in these, the whole word is the metrical equivalent of *mearh*.

§40 The forms of *bearo*, *-u* (masc.) 'grove' and *searo*, *-u* (neut.) 'device' are

	Singular	*Plural*	*Singular*	*Plural*
Nom.	bearo	bearwas	searo	searo
Acc.	bearo	bearwas	searo	searo
Gen.	bearwes	bearwa	searwes	searwa
Dat.	bearwe	bearwum	searwe	searwum

Thus they add the endings of *stān* and *word* respectively to the stems which before vowels become *bearw-* and *searw-* respectively; cf. §71.

§41 We turn now to dissyllabic nouns which take the endings of *stān*, *scip*, or *word*.

Compounds like *ġewrit* 'writing' and *ġebed* 'prayer' (both neut.), where the stress falls on the second syllable, follow *scip*.

Dissyllabic nouns which are compounds of two nouns, or of an adjective or adverb and a noun, have the second element declined, but not the first, e.g. *hron-fisc* (masc.) 'whale', *hēah-clif* (neut.) 'high cliff', and *in-gang* (masc.) 'entrance'.

Other dissyllables with their stress on the first syllable may follow one of four patterns:

		Masc.	*Neut.*
(*a*)	⏑́ –	*cyning* 'king'	*fæ̅reld* (also masc.) 'journey'
(*b*)	–́ –	*Hengest* 'Hengest'	*īsern* 'iron'
(*c*)	–́ ⏑	*engel* 'angel'	*hēafod* 'head'
(*d*)	⏑́ ⏑	*metod* 'creator'	*werod* 'troop'

Types (*a*) and (*b*) are quite regular and follow *stān* or *word* without any variations of stem or ending.

§42 Type (*c*) – long-stemmed dissyllables – add the endings of *stān* or *scip*. But they lose the medial vowel when an ending is added:

	Singular	*Plural*	*Singular*	*Plural*
Nom.	engel	englas	hēafod	hēafdu
Acc.	engel	englas	hēafod	hēafdu
Gen.	engles	engla	hēafdes	hēafda
Dat.	engle	englum	hēafde	hēafdum

Note

This loss of the medial vowel occurs only when an inflexional ending beginning with a vowel is added or (to put it another way) when this medial vowel is in an open syllable. Thus *engel* and *hēafod* have dat. pl. *englum* (NOT **enge/lum* – medial *e* is in an open syllable) and *hēafdum* (NOT **hēafo/dum* – *o* is in an open syllable). Since all the endings of *stān* and *scip* begin with a vowel, the simple statement made above suffices here. But the qualification is important for adjectives; see §68.

§43 Nouns of type (*d*) – short-stemmed dissyllables – are

	Singular	*Plural*	*Singular*	*Plural*
Nom.	metod	metodas	werod	werod
Acc.	metod	metodas	werod	werod
Gen.	metodes	metoda	werodes	weroda
Dat.	metode	metodum	werode	werodum

The masc. nouns therefore follow *stān* exactly. The neut. nouns remain unchanged in the nom. and acc. pl.; in other words, they are like *word*, not *scip*.

§44 But, as Dr. Johnson wisely observed, 'it may be reasonably imagined that what is so much in the power of men as language will very often be capriciously conducted'. For analogy often interferes with the historically correct forms given in §§42–43. A child learning to speak English today hears those around him forming past tenses of verbs by adding the sound *t*, e.g. 'baked', or *d*, e.g. 'sighed'. So quite naturally he says 'I maked a mud-pie today' or 'I buyed a hat in the shop today'. Thus the process of analogy can produce forms not accepted by most speakers of English today. But since we now have pretty strict notions of 'correctness', we tend to say to children 'No dear, I made a mud-pie' or 'I bought a hat', thereby helping to preserve the now-accepted form.

But many such variant forms are recorded in Old English texts. Alongside the regular nom. and acc. pls. *hēafdu* and *werod*, we find *hēafod*, *hēafodu*, and *weredu*.

Similarly, the process of analogy and earlier differences in some of the words themselves cause type (*d*) nouns ending in *l*, *r*, *m*, or *n*, to appear sometimes with no medial vowel in oblique cases. Thus *fugol* (masc.) 'bird' appears, like *engel*, without the medial vowel, and *wæter* may have gen. sg. *wæteres* or *wætres*, and nom. and acc. pl. *wæter*, *wætru*, or *wæteru*.

Hæleþ (masc.) 'man' and *mōnaþ* (masc.) 'month' may have nom. and acc. pl. the same or may add *-as*.

Masculine and Neuter Nouns in *-e*

§45 Masc. nouns with nom. sg. in *-e* are always strong, for weak masc. nouns have nom. sg. in *-a*. Neut. nouns in *-e* can be strong or weak (see §24). Historically speaking, strong nouns in *-e* belong either to a sub-class of the *stān/scip* declension or to another declension. As a general rule, it is safe to say that they drop the *-e* of the nom. sg. and add the endings of *stān* or *scip* as appropriate. Examples are

1 masc.: *ende* 'end', *here* 'army', *wine* 'friend', *stede* 'place';
2 neut.: *wīte* 'punishment', *rīce* 'kingdom', *spere* 'spear'.

The long-stemmed neuters, being dissyllabic in nom. sg., remain dissyllabic in the nom. acc. pl. *wītu*, *rīcu*.

§46 Words like *wine* and *stede* may have nom. and acc. pl. *wine* and *stede*. A few masc. nouns have only the *-e* form in the nom. and acc. pl.; they include names of people, e.g. *Seaxe* 'Saxons' and *Dene* 'Danes', and the common nouns *ælde* 'men' and *lēode* 'people'.

Other forms you need to be able to recognize in your reading are

1 nom. acc. pl. *rīċiu* alongside *rīċu* 'kingdoms';

2 forms with -(*i*)*ġ*(*e*)-, e.g. nom. acc. pl. *her*(*i*)*ġ*(*e*)*as* alongside *heras* 'armies'.

Strong Feminine Nouns

§47 The basic paradigm is *ġiefu* 'gift':

	Singular	*Plural*
Nom.	ġiefu	ġiefa, -e
Acc.	ġiefe	ġiefa, -e
Gen.	ġiefe	ġiefa, -ena
Dat.	ġiefe	ġiefum

Note the following endings:

1 *-e* in acc. gen. and dat. sg.;
2 alternative nom. acc. pls. *-a*, *-e*;
3 weak *-ena* in gen. pl. alongside *-a*;
4 dat. pl. in *-um*.

§48 The long-stemmed monosyllable *lār* 'teaching' is identical except for nom. sg.; for absence of *-u* cf. *scipu/word* (§34) and *sunu/hand* (§61).

	Singular	*Plural*
Nom.	lār	lāra, -e
Acc.	lāre	lāra, -e
Gen.	lāre	lāra, -ena
Dat.	lāre	lārum

§49 Some fem. monosyllables with long front vowels, e.g. *cwēn* 'queen', originally had nom. and acc. sg. the same and *-e* in nom. acc.pl. Later most of them (by a perfectly natural confusion) sometimes followed *lār*. But it is important to note that *brȳd* 'bride', *cwēn* 'queen', *dǣd* 'deed', etc. may be acc. as well as nom. sg. in your texts, and that all the long-stemmed fem. monosyllables may have *-a* or *-e* in nom. acc. pl.

§50 Long-stemmed dissyllables, e.g. *sāwol* 'soul' and *ċeaster* 'city', take the endings of *lār*, but (like *engel* and *hēafod* in §42) lose the medial vowel in trisyllabic forms.

§51 Some abstract nouns ending in *-þu* and *-u*(*-o*) can remain unchanged in the oblique cases (i.e. any case other than the nom.), e.g. *iermþu* 'poverty' and *ieldu* 'age'.

i-Mutation

§52 A sound-change which affects certain nouns and verbs must now be explained. The vowel *i* and the related consonant written in phonetic script [j] and pronounced as the first consonant in MnE 'yes' are high front sounds. When in OE one of these followed a stressed syllable, the vowel of that stressed syllable was subject to what is called '*i*-mutation'.[1] In simple terms, the organs of speech and the mind of the speaker got ready for the high front sound too soon and in the process

the low front vowels were dragged up or 'raised'
and the back vowels were pulled forward or 'fronted'.

The *i* or [j] is usually lost but may appear in OE as *e* or *i*.

§53 This change can be explained (unscientifically) in terms of the diagram in §31 (p. 22) as follows:

1 The low front vowels *æ* and *e* move up one place.

2 The back vowels *a* and *o* are pushed straight forward to the corresponding front position.

3 *u* keeps its lip-rounding and goes forward to the rounded *y* described in §32.

The sections which follow give a Table of Correspondences in which the unmutated vowel (as it appears in OE) is shown on the left, and the OE mutated equivalent on the right.

Table of Correspondences

§54 Again in terms of the diagram on p. 22, the low front vowels are raised; only the short ones are affected.

æ̆	:	ĕ
ĕ	:	ĭ

Note
i is not affected because it cannot go any higher.

§55 The back vowels are fronted; both short and long are affected here.

	ā̆	:	ǣ̆
	ō̆	:	ē̆
	ū̆	:	ȳ̆[2]
But	ă + m, n	:	ĕ + m, n

§56 The diphthongs *ea* and *eo* (short and long) are affected.

ē̆a	:	ī̆e
ē̆o	:	ī̆e

[1] Unstressed vowels are sometimes affected. But this need not concern us here.
[2] Both *ō̆* and *ū̆* were fully rounded – *ō̆* to *œ̄̆* and *ū̆* to *ȳ̆*. But *œ̄̆* was usually unrounded to *ē̆*.

§57 Thirteen sounds are therefore affected – 2 front vowels, 7 back vowels (including *ă* in two ways), and 4 diphthongs. You should cull your own examples. A very good way to find some is to look at the strong verbs and to compare the stem vowel of the infinitive with the stem vowel of the 2nd and 3rd pers. sg. pres. ind.; see §112.1 and Appendix A. In most of them you will find the non-mutated vowel in the infinitive and its mutated equivalent in the 2nd and 3rd pers. sg. pres. ind. The *i* which caused *i*-mutation in these two forms has either disappeared or become *e*. For further effects of *i*-mutation, see Appendix B, pp. 159–60 below.

Nouns affected by *i*-Mutation

§58 Typical paradigms for those masc. and fem. nouns affected by *i*-mutation are *mann* (masc.) 'man' and *bōc* (fem.) 'book':

	Singular	*Plural*	*Singular*	*Plural*
Nom.	mann	menn	bōc	bēċ
Acc.	mann	menn	bōc	bēċ
Gen.	mannes	manna	bēċ, bōce	bōca
Dat.	menn	mannum	bēċ	bōcum

Notes

1 nom. and acc. sg. the same;

2 gen. sg. masc. like *stān*;

3 gen. and dat. pl. regular;

4 the mutated equivalent of the vowel of the nom. sg. appears in the dat. sg. and nom. and acc. pl. (with no inflexional ending);

5 the gen. sg. with the mutated vowel in the fem. nouns. This should not cause difficulty because the gen. and dat. sg. fem. are usually the same. *Bōce* arises by analogy with *lāre*.

Most of the masc. examples can be recognized by thinking of the MnE plural of the corresponding word, e.g. 'foot' (*fōt*), 'man' (*mann*), 'tooth' (*tōþ*). Most of the fem. nouns have become regular in MnE, e.g. 'book' (*bōc*), 'oak' (*āc*), 'goat' (*gāt*), but a few survive, e.g. 'goose' (*gōs*), 'louse' (*lūs*), 'mouse' (*mūs*).

§59 The nouns *frēond* 'friend' and *fēond* 'enemy', which are formed from pres. ptcs. of verbs, can follow *stān* or can have *īe* in dat. sg. and nom. and acc. pl.; cf. *mann*.

§60 Nouns ending in *-r* which denote relationship are: *fæder* 'father' and *brōþor* 'brother' (both masc.), *mōdor* 'mother', *dohtor* 'daughter', and *sweostor* 'sister' (all fem.). It is difficult to systematize these nouns, for many analogical variations exist, but the following observations may help:

1 All are regular in the gen. and dat. pl., ending in *-a* and *-um* respectively and losing the medial vowel if long-stemmed (§42).

2 All can have the nominative singular form in all remaining cases except for

(*a*) *fæder* which takes *-as* in nom. acc. pl.;

(*b*) *brōþor*, *mōdor*, *dohtor*, which may show *i*-mutation in dat. sg., viz. *brēþer*, *mēder*, *dehter*. These forms may also occur in gen. sg., by analogy with fem. nouns such as *lār* (§48), in which gen. and dat. sg. are the same.

u-Nouns

§61 A few masc. and fem. nouns belong to the *u*-declension. They may be short-stemmed dissyllables with final *-u*, e.g. *sunu* (masc.) 'son' and *duru* (fem.) 'door', or long-stemmed monosyllables, e.g. *feld* (masc.) 'field' and *hand* (fem.) 'hand'; for the absence of *-u* in the latter cf. *scipu/word* and *ġiefu/lār*. Typical paradigms are *sunu* (masc.) and *hand* (fem.):

	Singular	*Plural*	*Singular*	*Plural*
Nom.	sunu	suna	hand	handa
Acc.	sunu	suna	hand	handa
Gen.	suna	suna	handa	handa
Dat.	suna	sunum	handa	handum

Notes

1 Nom. and acc. sg. are the same.

2 All other cases end in *-a* except of course the dat. pl. *-um*.

Other nouns which belong here are *wudu* 'wood', *ford* 'ford', and *weald* 'forest' – all masc.

§62 Masc. nouns like *feld* and fem. nouns like *duru/hand* are all to some extent influenced by *stān* and *ġiefu/lār* respectively and so hover uneasily between two declensions; hence gen. sg. *feldes* and the like. But the most important point to note here is that the ending *-a* is sometimes a dat. sg. in the texts, e.g. *felda*, *forda*, *wealda*.

III ADJECTIVES

Introduction

§63 Most adjectives can be declined strong or weak. Important exceptions are *ōþer* and the poss. adjs. *mīn*, *þīn*, etc. (see §21), which are declined strong, and comparatives, which end in *-a* in nom. sg. masc., e.g. *blindra* 'blinder', and are declined weak.

On participles, see §111.

§64 Which form of the adjective is used depends, not on the type of noun with which it is used, but on how it is used. The strong form is used when the adj. stands alone, e.g. 'The man is old' *se mann is eald*, or just with a noun, e.g. 'old men' *ealde menn*. The weak form appears when the adj. follows a dem., e.g. 'that old man' *se ealda mann*, or a poss. adj., e.g. 'my old friend' *mīn ealda frēond*. You can remember that the strong forms stand alone, while the weak forms need the support of a dem. or poss. pron.

Weak Declension

§65 The paradigm is *tila* 'good':

	Singular			*Plural*
	Masc.	*Neut.*	*Fem.*	*All genders*
Nom.	tila	tile	tile	tilan
Acc.	tilan	tile	tilan	tilan
Gen.	tilan	tilan	tilan	tilra, -ena
Dat.	tilan	tilan	tilan	tilum

The long-stemmed *gōda* 'good' is declined exactly the same. Here the endings are identical with those of the weak noun of the same gender with one addition – the strong form of gen. pl. *tilra* is generally preferred to *-ena*, except in eWS. The dat. pl. *-um* is frequently replaced by *-an* in WS texts and in lWS *-an* is found in the gen. pl. too. Stem changes in the weak declension of the adjectives follow the rules set out in §§68–73.

Strong Declension

§66 The paradigm is *til* 'good', which has a separate inst. form in the masc. and neut. sg.:

	Singular		
	Masc.	*Neut.*	*Fem.*
Nom.	til	til	tilu
Acc.	til*ne*	til	tile
Gen.	tiles	tiles	til*re*
Dat.	til*um*	til*um*	til*re*
Inst.	tile	tile	

	Plural		
	Masc.	*Neut.*	*Fem.*
Nom.	tile	tilu	tile, -a
Acc.	tile	tilu	tile, -a
Gen.	til*ra*	til*ra*	til*ra*
Dat.	tilum	tilum	tilum

Notes

1 Nom. and acc. pl. masc. end in *-e*, e.g. *cwice eorlas* 'living noblemen'; the ending *-as* belongs to the nouns only. This *-e* is sometimes found in fem. and neut. pl.; see §81.

2 All the other endings are familiar. Those italicized have already been met in the pronouns (§§16–18). The remainder are endings found in *stān*, *scip*, and *ġiefu*, respectively.

§67 The long-stemmed monosyllable *gōd* 'good' varies only in the nom. sg. fem. *gōd* as against *tilu* (cf. *lār/ġiefu*) and in the nom. and acc. neut. pl. *gōd* as against *tilu* (cf. *word/scipu*).

Stem Changes in Adjectives

§68 Long-stemmed dissyllables such as *hāliġ* add the weak or strong endings given above as appropriate. The medial vowel is not lost before endings beginning with a consonant, i.e. in closed syllables – hence *hāliġ/ne, hāliġ/re, hāliġ/ra*.

When the ending begins with a vowel, the medial vowel sometimes disappears; cf. the nouns *engel* and *hēafod* (§42) and *sāwol* (§50). Thus *hāliġ* has gen. sg. masc. strong *hālġes*. But analogical variations are common, and we find *hāligan* alongside *hālgan, hāliġes* alongside *hālġes*, and so on.

In the nom. sg. fem. and nom./acc. pl. neut. *hāliġ* (cf. *lār/word*), *hāligu* (cf. *ġiefu/scipu*), and *hālgu* (with loss of vowel) are all found.

§69 Short-stemmed dissyllabic adjectives show forms with no medial vowel more frequently than the corresponding nouns (§§43–44). Thus *miċel* 'great' may have acc. sg. fem. *miċele* or *miċle*, while *moniġ* 'many' and *yfel* 'evil' have dat. pl. *monigum* or *mongum* and gen. sg. masc. *yfeles* or *yfles*, respectively.

§70 Short-stemmed monosyllabic adjectives with the stem-vowel *æ* follow *glæd* 'glad', here declined strong:

	Singular		
	Masc.	*Neut.*	*Fem.*
Nom.	glæd	glæd	gladu
Acc.	glædne	glæd	glade
Gen.	glades	glades	glædre
Dat.	gladum	gladum	glædre
Inst.	glade	glade	

	Plural		
	Masc.	*Neut.*	*Fem.*
Nom.	glade	gladu	glade
Acc.	glade	gladu	glade
Gen.	glædra	glædra	glædra
Dat.	gladum	gladum	gladum

Here *æ/a* fluctuation occurs. As in the nouns (§36), we find *æ* in a closed syllable, i.e. in the simple form *glæd* and when an ending beginning with a consonant is added, e.g. *glæd/ne*. In open syllables, however, the adjectives have *a* irrespective of whether a front or back vowel follows, e.g. *gla/des, gla/dum*. This is the result of analogy.

§71 Adjectives like *ġearo, -u* 'ready' take the endings of *gōd*. Hence in the strong declension, they remain unchanged in the nom. sg. all genders, acc. sg. neut., and nom. and acc. pl. Before consonants, the stem is *ġearo-* – hence *ġearone, ġearore, ġearora,* but before vowels it is *ġearw-* – hence *ġearwes, ġearwum*; cf. §40. Write out the paradigm. Then see A. Campbell *O.E. Grammar*, §649.

§72 Adjectives such as *hēah* 'high' and *fāh* 'hostile' usually lose their final *h* and contract where possible; cf. §§37 and 38. *Hēah* may have acc. sg. masc. strong *hēanne* or *hēane*.

§73 Adjectives in *-e*, e.g. *blīþe*, behave like the corresponding nouns (§45). Hence they drop the *-e* and add the endings of *til*.

Comparison of Adjectives

§74 Most adjectives add the endings *-ra, -ost* to the stem. Thus we find *lēof* 'dear', *lēofra* 'dearer', *lēofost* 'dearest'. Similarly *glæd* 'glad', *glædra* 'gladder', but *gladost* 'gladdest' (see §70). The comparative is declined weak, the superlative strong or weak (see §64).

§75 Some adjectives, however, add the endings *-ra, -est*, and show an *i*-mutated vowel in the stem, e.g.

eald 'old'	ieldra	ieldest
ġeong 'young'	ġingra	ġingest
lang 'long'	lengra	lengest
strang 'strong'	strengra	strengest
hēah 'high'	hīerra	hīehst

§76 Irregular are:

lȳtel 'little'	lǣssa	lǣst
miċel 'great'	māra	mǣst
yfel 'bad'	wiersa	wierst
gōd 'good'	betera, sēlra	betst, sēlest

These, of course, can be compared with their MnE equivalents.

IV OBSERVATIONS ON NOUN, ADJECTIVE, AND PRONOUN DECLENSIONS

§77 The weak declension of nouns and adjectives, with *-an* throughout except in a few easily remembered places (see §§22–25), presents little difficulty. The weak masc. noun can always be recognized by *-a* in nom. sg. However, *-e* of the weak fem. and neut. is also found in strong masc. and neut. nouns. But a noun with final *-e* in nom. sg. cannot be strong fem.

§78 Nouns with their nom. sg. ending in a consonant are strong, but can be any gender. See again §13.

§79 In the strong nouns and the strong declension of the adj., the characteristic endings should be noted. The gen. pl. of the noun is *-a*, of the adj. *-ra*. But the weak ending *-ena* is found in nouns like *feoh/fēona* and *ġiefu/ġiefa* or *ġiefena*, and in the adj. The endings *-ne* (acc. sg. masc.) and *-re* (gen. and dat. sg. fem.) are found in adjs. (strong forms) and prons.

§80 Certain similarities may be noted in the declension of strong nouns, the strong form of the adj., and the dem. and pers. prons. (less 1st and 2nd pers.; on these, see §21). These are

1 neut. sg. nom. and acc. are always the same;
2 nom. and acc. sg. of masc. NOUNS are always the same;
3 nom. and acc. pl. are always the same;
4 gen. and dat. fem. sg. are always the same (with the reservations made in §§58 and 60);
5 within the same declension
 (*a*) masc. and neut. gen. sg. are the same;
 (*b*) masc. and neut. dat. sg. are the same;
 (*c*) masc. and neut. inst. sg. are the same.

§81 A possible source of confusion is the fact that in prons. and adjs., the acc. fem. sg. is the same as nom. and acc. pl., e.g. *þā/þā, þās/þās, hīe/hīe, cwice/cwice*. This last form *cwice* is properly the masc. pl. But in later texts especially, the ending *-e* is often used for all genders in the strong form of the adj., rather than *-u* or *-a* (§66).

V NUMERALS

§82 The numerals from 1 to 10 are

	Cardinal	*Ordinal*
1	ān	forma
2	twēġen	ōþer
3	þrīe	þridda
4	fēower	fēorþa
5	fīf	fīfta
6	siex	siexta
7	seofon	seofoþa
8	eahta	eahtoþa
9	nigon	nigoþa
10	tīen	tēoþa

§83 When declined strong, *ān* means 'one'; when declined weak *āna*, it usually means 'alone'. Only the first three cardinal numbers are regularly declined.

Ordinals are declined weak, except *ōþer* which is always strong.

§84 *Twēġen* 'two' and *bēġen* 'both' are declined alike. In the nom. and acc. they have

Masc.	twēġen	*Neut.*	twā, tū	*Fem.*	twā
	bēġen		bā, bū		bā

The gen. and dat. are the same for all genders:

twēġra, twēġ(e)a;	bēġra, bēġ(e)a
twǣm;	bǣm

§85 In the nom. and acc. of *þrīe* 'three' we find

Masc.	þrīe	*Neut.*	þrēo	*Fem.*	þrēo

The gen. and dat. are *þrēora, þrim*.

§86 A knowledge of the remaining numerals is not essential at first. The meaning of many is obvious, e.g. *twēntiġ, þrītiġ, fēowertiġ, fīftiġ*, and those which occur in your texts will be glossed. Full lists will be found in any of the standard grammars. Roman numerals are often used.

VI STRONG VERBS AND SOUND-CHANGES RELEVANT TO THEM

Introduction

§87 Like MnE, OE has two types of verbs – weak and strong. The weak verb forms its preterite and past participle by adding a dental suffix, the strong verb by changing its stem vowel; cf. MnE 'laugh, laughed' and 'judge, judged' with MnE 'sing, sang, sung'. The strong verbs are nearly all survivals from OE; new verbs when made up or borrowed today join the weak conjugation. Thus the strong verb 'drive, drove, driven' survives from OE. When in the thirteenth century 'strive' was borrowed from the French, it followed the pattern of 'drive' because the two infinitives rhymed; hence we get MnE 'strive, strove, striven'. But we conjugate the comparatively new verb 'jive', not 'jive, jove, jiven', but 'jive, jived', i.e. as a weak verb.

§88 Such patterns as 'drive, drove, driven' and 'jive, jived' are called the 'principal parts' of the verbs. It is essential for you to know the principal parts of the Old English verbs. This is important because, if you do not know the patterns which the various verbs display in their principal parts, you will be unable to find out their meaning. You will be in the same position as a foreign student of English looking up 'drove (verb)' in his dictionary. For he can only find out what it means by knowing that it is the preterite of 'drive'.

§89 Both weak and strong verbs in OE distinguish

1 two tenses – present and preterite;

2 indicative, subjunctive, and imperative, moods, in addition to two infinitives – one without *to*, and one (the inflected infinitive) with *to* – and two participles, the present and the past (or second);

3 two numbers – singular and plural. The dual is found only in the 1st and 2nd person pronouns and is used with plural verb forms;

4 three persons, but only in the singular of the present and preterite indicative. All plurals and the singular of the subjunctives are the same throughout;

5 one voice only – the active. One true passive form survives from an earlier stage of the language, viz. *hātte* 'is called, was called'.

On the syntax of these forms and on the beginnings of new methods of expressing verbal relationships, see §§195 ff.

Principal Parts of the Strong Verbs

§90 These verbs show a change of vowel in the stressed syllable in the principal parts. This is known as 'gradation' and the vowels which change – e.g. *ī, ō, i* in 'drive, drove, driven' – are known as the 'gradation' series. The origin of these is to be found in the shifting stress of the original IE language (which later became fixed, usually on the first syllable, in OE). We can see how the pronunciation of a vowel can change according to the amount of stress the syllable carries if we compare the pronunciation of the following three versions of the same MnE sentence:

Cán he do it?
Can hé do it?
Can he dó it?

In the first, the vowel of 'can' has its full value; in the second, a reduced value; and in the third, it has almost disappeared and has what is sometimes called 'zero' value. Such variations in IE may well have been perpetuated when the stress became fixed.

§91 No MnE strong verb has more than three vowels in its gradation series; some, e.g. 'bind, bound, bound', have only two. But in OE, four parts of the verb may be distinguished by different vowels – the infinitive, two preterites, and the past participle, e.g. *crēopan* 'creep', *crēap, crupon, cropen*. But (for various reasons) the same vowel may occur more than once in the same verb. So we find, with three different vowels, *bindan* 'bind', *band, bundon, bunden*, and, with two only, *faran* 'go', *fōr, fōron, faren*.

§92 Many primers show five vowels for the strong verbs, viz. inf. (*crēopan*), 3rd sg. pres. ind. (*crīepþ*), pret. sg. or 1st pret. (*crēap*), pret. pl. or 2nd pret. (*crupon*), past ptc. (*cropen*). See §113. 1 & 2. The 3rd sg. pres. ind. is not part of the gradation series; its stem vowel is the *i*-mutated equivalent of the vowel of the inf. and can be deduced from that vowel; see §57. So, when learning a strong verb, you will need to remember four vowels – those of the inf., two preterites, and the past ptc. There are in OE seven different 'classes' of verbs, each with a different gradation series. Each type can be recognized by its 'uniform' or recognition symbol. This is the distinctive vowel-consonant combination apparent in the infinitive. So, in addition to the gradation series, you need to know the 'uniform' or recognition symbol which will enable you to tell the class to which a verb belongs.

§93 Verbs characteristic of these classes are

Class	*Inf.*	*1st Pret.*	*2nd Pret.*	*Past Ptc.*
I	scīnan 'shine'	scān	scinon	scinen
II	crēopan 'creep'	crēap	crupon	cropen
	brūcan 'enjoy'	brēac	brucon	brocen
III	breġdan 'pull'	bræġd	brugdon	brogden
IV	beran 'bear'	bær	bǣron	boren
V	tredan 'tread'	træd	trǣdon	treden
VI	faran 'go'	fōr	fōron	faren
VII	(*a*) healdan 'hold'	hēold	hēoldon	healden
	(*b*) hātan 'command'	hēt	hēton	hāten

Roman numerals are here used for the classes of strong verbs, arabic numerals for those of the weak verbs. Thus *scīnan* I 'shine' and *lufian* 2 'love' tell us both the type and class of verb. Class VII verbs are sometimes called 'reduplicating' (abbreviation 'rd.'). Note The past ptc. frequently has the prefix *ġe-* (§6).

§94 From a study of these and the lists of strong verbs set out in Appendix A, the following gradation series will emerge:

Class	*Recognition Symbol*	*Inf.*	*1st Pret.*	*2nd Pret.*	*Past Ptc.*
I	*ī* + one cons.	ī	ā	i	i
II	*ēo* + one cons.	ēo	ēa	u	o
	ū + one cons.	ū			
III	See §102				
IV	*e* + one cons.[1]	e	æ	ǣ	o
V	*e* + one cons.[2]	e	æ	ǣ	e
VI	*a* + one cons.[3]	a	ō	ō	a
VII	See §104				

§95 The gradation series of verbs in classes I and II are quite regular. Class III presents special difficulties because the stem vowels of most verbs are affected by one of several sound laws. For purposes of explanation, we

[1] Usually a liquid (*l*, *r*). But note *brecan* 'break'. On the verbs with nasals, see §103.2.
[2] Usually a stop (*p*, *t*, *c*, *d*, *g*) or spirant (*f*, *þ*, *s*).
[3] *Standan* 'stand', with *-n-* in inf. and past ptc., belongs here.

can take the verb *breġdan* 'pull' as the basic paradigm in terms of which all the other verbs can be explained. *Breġdan* shows the following pattern:

III	*e* + TWO cons.	e	æ	u	o

A few other verbs, e.g. *streġdan* 'strew', *berstan* 'burst', *þerscan* 'thresh',[1] show the same vowel pattern. But the remainder fall into four groups which are represented by the verbs *weorpan* 'throw'/*feohtan* 'fight', *helpan* 'help', *ġieldan* 'pay', and *drincan* 'drink'. To understand the variations in these verbs, we have to know something about certain sound-changes.

Breaking

§96 The first of these is the diphthongization of a front vowel when it is followed by a consonant or group of consonants produced in the back of the mouth. When moving from a front vowel to a back consonant, the organs of speech do NOT perform the equivalent of the quick march, in which one foot is lifted cleanly from the ground and put down again 30 inches or so further on. They glide more or less smoothly from one position to another, as your feet do when you are dancing a waltz. You can see the result of this process in an exaggerated form if you imagine that you have fallen overboard from a ship and are calling out 'Help'. If you call out loudly and long (you had better do this in a desert place!), you will find that the vowel of the word 'Help' is 'broken' as you glide from the front position of *e* to the back position of *lp*. If you spell it as you are pronouncing it, you will write something like 'Heulp'. Try the same experiment with words like 'bell', 'fell', 'tell'. You will probably find that a 'glide' develops between the short front vowel *e* and the following *l*. A similar process took place in OE. It is called 'breaking'.

§97 For our purposes, its most important effects are

1 before *h*, *h* + cons., *r* + cons.[2]

ǣ > ěa
ě > ěo

In terms of the diagram in §31, the organs of speech glide back to the back vowel nearest in height to the front vowel from which they started. (See §8, where we assume that the symbol *ea* is pronounced *æa*.)

2 before *l* (here made in the back of the throat) + cons.

ǣ > ěa

But ě is not usually affected before *l*. We can call this 'limited breaking'; it occurs before *l*, with which the word 'limited' begins!

[1] *Berstan* and *þerscan* were originally **brestan and *þrescan*, with two medial consonants. But the *r* 'changed places'. This change, known as 'metathesis', is not uncommon; cf. OE *brid* with MnE 'bird'.

[2] Here *r* was probably made with the tip of the tongue curved back.

Note
ĕ does break before *lh*. See §133.2 for an example.

3 before *h* and *h* + cons.

ī > īo > very often ēo

§98 We can now return to the verbs of class III where the basic gradation series is *e, æ, u, o* (§95). If we examine *weorpan* and *feohtan*, we find

weorpan	wearp	wurpon	worpen
feohtan	feaht	fuhton	fohten

Here the medial cons. groups *-rp-* and *-ht-* cause *e* and *æ* to break but do not affect the back vowels *u* and *o*. Hence we get as the gradation series, NOT *e, æ, u, o,* but *eo, ea, u, o*.

§99 In *helpan*, however, the medial group *-lp-* produces only limited breaking and so we get

helpan	healp	hulpon	holpen

where only the 1st pret. *ea* differs from the basic series of *breġdan*, the *e* of the infinitive remaining unchanged.

Influence of Initial *ġ, sc, ċ*

§100 The results of the next sound-change to affect the verbs of class III are seen most commonly in the WS dialect, with which we are mainly concerned. Here the initial palatal consonants *ġ, sc*, and *ċ*, caused the following front vowels *ĕ* and *ǣ̆* to become *ĭe* and *ĕa* respectively. The effect may be produced by an emphatic pronunciation of these consonants, which will produce a glide between the consonant and vowel. A modern parallel may be found in the prolonged 'Yes' in the sentence 'Well, yes, I suppose so' used when one gives hesitating assent or grudging permission; we might spell our pronunciation something like 'Yies'. This change is sometimes called 'palatal diphthongization' (p.d. for short). It is because of it that we find the inf. *ġieldan*. For further examples, see §103.1.

Note
The pret. *ġeald* could be the result of breaking or of p.d. But such forms as *ċeorfan*, which show *eo* < *e* as the result of breaking, suggest that breaking took place before p.d.; if it had not, we should have had **ċierfan* by p.d. P.d. can take place in such forms as *ġieldan* because *e* did not break before *-ld-* and hence remained until p.d. took place.

Influence of Nasals

§101 The last sound-change which affects verbs of class III is found in verbs in which the first of the two medial consonants is a nasal *m* or *n*. In these circumstances, *i* appears instead of *e*, *a* instead of *æ*, and *u* instead of *o*. So we get

drincan dranc druncon druncen

with *i, a* (sometimes *o*; see §103.2), *u, u* instead of *e, æ, u, o*.

Summary of the Strong Verbs of Class III

§102 The following table summarizes class III verbs. Each of series (*b*)–(*e*) is to be explained by the appropriate sound-change operating on series (*a*). See also §§116 and 133.5.

Sound-Change	*Symbol*	*Example*	*Gradation Series*			
(*a*) Basic Series	*e* + 2 cons.	*breġdan*	e	æ	u	o
(*b*) Breaking before *r* + cons.	*eo* + *r* + cons.	*weorpan*	eo	ea	u	o
h + cons.	*eo* + *h* + cons.	*feohtan*				
(*c*) Limited breaking before *l* + cons.	*e* + *l* + cons.	*helpan*	e	ea	u	o
(*d*) Palatal diphthongization	palatal + *ie* + 2 cons.	*ġieldan*	ie	ea	u	o
(*e*) Nasal	*i* + nasal + cons.	*drincan*	i	a	u	u

The Effects of Sound-Changes on other Strong Verbs

§103 Some of these sound-changes affect verbs of other classes.

1 P.d. is seen in:
Class IV *scieran* 'cut', which has *ie, ea, ēa, o* instead of *e, æ, ǣ, o*;
Class V *ġiefan* 'give' with *ie, ea ēa, ie*, instead of *e, æ, ǣ, e*,
and in the class VI infinitive *scieppan* 'create'.

2 Nasals influence class IV *niman* 'take' with *i, a/o, ā/ō* (fluctuation

between *a* and *o* is not uncommon before nasals) and *u* instead of *e, æ, ǣ, o*. On *niman* and *cuman* 'come' see also §109.

3 Breaking before *h* with subsequent loss of *h* between a diphthong and a vowel (see §§37–38) affects the infinitives of the contracted verbs of classes I, V, and VI. The stages can be set out thus:

I	*wrīhan	> *wrēohan	> wrēon 'cover'	
V	*sehan	> *seohan	> sēon 'see'	
VI	*slahan	> *slæhan[1]	> *sleahan	> slēan 'strike'

4 The infinitives of contracted verbs of class II are affected by loss of *h* only, e.g.

*tēohan > tēon 'draw'

5 The contracted verbs of class VII – *fōn* 'take' and *hōn* 'hang' – have a complicated phonology; detailed explanation would be out of place here. But see §108.

6 On the principal parts of contracted verbs, see §§107–108. On 3rd sg. pres. ind. of contracted verbs, see §114. On the 'weak presents' of classes V–VII, see §116.

Strong Verbs of Class VII

§104 Strong verbs of class VII show the following characteristics:

1 the same stem vowel in inf. and past ptc. (except *wēpan*);

2 the same stem vowel in 1st and 2nd pret. – either *ēo* or *ē*. On this basis the two sub-classes (*a*) and (*b*) are distinguished.

Important verbs here are: *cnāwan* 'know', *feallan* 'fall', *weaxan* 'grow' (all VII(*a*)), and *drǣdan* 'fear' and *lǣtan* 'let' (both VII(*b*)). It is worth noting that none of them can be mistaken for strong verbs of any other class, for the stem vowels of the inf. are different. But see further §§131–134.

Grimm's Law and Verner's Law

§105 Certain consonant changes which distinguish the Gmc. languages from the other IE languages were first formulated by the German philologist Grimm (of the Fairy Tales) and hence are known as Grimm's Law. But the fact that the expected consonant did not always appear in the Gmc. languages puzzled philologists until the Danish grammarian Karl Verner explained that the differences depended on the position of the stress in the original IE form of the word.

§106 Grimm's Law accounts (*inter alia*) for the variations between Latin (which in the examples cited keeps the IE consonant) and OE seen in such pairs as

[1] This variation must be taken on trust. (Those interested can compare §§35–36.)

Lat.	*piscis*	OE	*fisc*	(*p/f*)
Lat.	*frater*	OE	*brōþor*	(*t/þ*)
Lat.	*genus*	OE	*cynn*	(*g/c*)
Lat.	*dentem*	OE	*tōþ*	(*d/t*)

But, if *fisc* corresponds to *piscis* and *brōþor* to *frāter*, we should expect **fæþer* alongside *păter*. But we have *fæder*. Verner explained exceptions like this.

We can see the sort of thing which happened if we compare MnE 'éxcellent' and 'ábsolute' on the one hand with MnE 'exám.' and 'absólve' on the other. In the first pair, the stress falls on the first syllable and the consonants which follow are voiceless; we could spell the words 'eks-' and 'aps-'. In the second pair, the stress is on the second syllable, the consonants are voiced, and the words could be spelt 'egz-' and 'abz-'. Similar variations, said Verner, arose in Pr. Gmc. because of similar differences. Greek φϱάτηϱ = Latin *frāter* was stressed on the first syllable. Hence in its Pr. Gmc. equivalent the medial *t* developed regularly by Grimm's Law to voiceless *þ* (cf. MnE 'cloth') in Pr. OE.[1] But Greek πατήϱ = Latin *păter* was stressed on the second syllable. So in Pr. Gmc. the voiceless *þ* which arose from the *t* by Grimm's Law was voiced to the sound in MnE 'clothe'. This voiced sound subsequently became *d*.

§107 Many standard histories of the English language explain these two Laws in detail; for us their most important effect is seen in the OE strong verbs, where Verner's Law accounts for certain variations in the medial consonant. Thus in class I we find

snīþan snāþ snidon sniden

Here the *þ* of the inf. and 1st pret. is the consonant we should expect by Grimm's Law. The *d* of the 2nd pret. and past ptc. (which originally had the accent on the second syllable) is the Verner's Law form. Similarly we find

II	ċēosan	ċēas	curon	coren

and in contracted verbs (which originally had *h* in the inf.; see §§103.3 and 103.4)

I	wrēon	wrāh	wrigon	wrigen
V	sēon	seah	sāwon	sewen

In these strong verbs, the Verner's Law forms occur in the 2nd pret. and the past ptc., while the inf. and 1st pret. are regular. This is historically 'correct'; we see from the verbs marked † in Appendix A that by Verner's Law TH in the inf. and 1st pret. is LIKELY to be replaced by D in the 2nd pret. and past ptc., S by R, and (mostly in contracted verbs) H by G, W, or (in *hōn* and *fōn*: see below) by NG.[2]

[1] Its voicing (§9) comes later; see A. Campbell *Old English Grammar*, §444.

[2] Verner's Law forms are also seen in such related pairs as *ċēosan* 'choose'/*cyre* 'choice' and *rīsan* 'rise'/*rǣran* 'raise'. See §136.

§108 The word 'LIKELY' is emphasized because the Verner's Law forms sometimes occur where historically they should not. Thus the principal parts of the contracted verbs of class VII are

hōn	hēng	hēngon	hangen
fōn	fēng	fēngon	fangen

Here the Verner's Law *ng* is extended into the 1st pret.; the same may be true of the *g* in

VI	slēan	slōg	slōgon	slæġen[1]

Sometimes, on the other hand, the Verner's Law forms are completely eliminated, as in *mīþan* I 'conceal' and *rīsan* I 'rise'; this has happened to all Verner's Law forms in MnE except 'was/were'. This process of systematizing or regularizing by the elimination of odd forms is sometimes called 'levelling'. But, as we see from verbs like *scrīþan*, with past ptc. *scriden* or *scriþen*, its results are often capricious because it is not conducted consciously and logically.

§109 These and other levellings which occur in OE can be seen as the first signs of two great changes which overtook the strong verbs as English developed through the centuries. First, we today distinguish fewer classes of strong verbs. For example, the verbs of class V have gone over to class IV. Thus, while OE *specan, tredan, wefan*, have *e* in their past ptcs., MnE 'speak', 'tread', 'weave', have *o*; cf. *beran* IV. Second, while in OE the stem vowels of the 1st and 2nd prets. are different except in classes VI and VII, they are today the same (again except in 'was/were'). The beginnings of this process are seen in *cuman* IV 'come' and *etan* V 'eat', where the vowel of the 2nd pret. is found in the 1st pret. too. The marked confusion of forms in *niman* IV 'take' also results from this levelling. Perhaps you can work out for yourself why *findan* has a 1st pret. *funde*.

Conjugation of the Strong Verb

§110 Our wanderings through what have been called 'the dusty deserts of barren philology' lead us now to the conjugation of the strong verb, here exemplified by *singan* III. Points which must be carefully noted when conjugating these and all strong verbs are set out below; on the uses of the tenses and moods, see §§195–198 and 173–179.

§111 *Singan* 'sing' *sang sungon sungen* is conjugated

		Present Indicative	*Preterite Indicative*
Sg.	1	singe	sang
	2	singest	sunge
	3	singeþ	sang
Pl.		singaþ	sungon

[1] But *slōh* does occur, and ME forms suggest that the *g* in *slōg* may be merely a spelling variant of *h*.

	Present Subjunctive	*Preterite Subjunctive*
Sg.	singe	sunge
Pl.	singen	sungen

Before a 1st or 2nd pers. pron., the plural endings can be reduced to *-e*, e.g. *wē singaþ* but *singe wē*.

Imp. Sg.	sing	*Pl.*	singaþ
Inf.	singan	*Infl. Inf.*	tō singenne
Pres. Ptc.	singende	*Past Ptc.*	(ġe-)sungen

Participles may be declined like adjectives. Strong and weak forms occur, as appropriate.

§112 In the present tense, note:

1 The stem vowel of the inf. appears throughout except in 2nd and 3rd pers. sg. pres. ind., where its *i*-mutated equivalent is found if there is one. Hence *sing(e)st, sing(e)þ* but (< *bēodan*) *bīetst, bīett*.

2 The common WS reduction in these forms whereby the *e* of the endings *-est* and *-eþ* disappears. If this leaves a combination which is difficult to pronounce, it is simplified. So from *bīdan* 'wait for', we get _bīdeþ_ > *_bīdþ_ > *_bītþ_ > _bītt_. (Try this simple phonetic process for yourself.) Similarly, *bīteþ* from *bītan* 'bite' is also reduced to *bītt*. Hence theoretically *se mann bītt þæt wīf* could mean 'the man is waiting for the woman' or 'the man is biting the woman'.[1] But, in the absence of newspaper reporters in Anglo-Saxon times, this ambiguity does not cause practical difficulty. The most important consequences for you are that 2nd pers. sg. pres. ind. ending in *-tst* and 3rd pers. sg. pres. ind. ending in *-tt* may be from verbs with *-tan* (e.g. *bītan*), *-dan* (e.g. *bīdan*), or *-ddan* (e.g. *biddan*). Since *-sest* and *-seþ* both become *-st, ċīest* may be either 2nd or 3rd pers.[2]

3 The endings of the imp. – sg. NIL, pl. *-aþ*.

4 The imp. pl. is the same as the pres. ind. pl.

5 The subj. endings sg. *-e* and pl. *-en*, which also occur in the pret.

6 The pres. subj. sg. is the same as the 1st pers. sg. pres. ind.

§113 In the preterite tense, note:

1 The so-called pret. sg. occurs in TWO PLACES ONLY – 1st and 3rd sg. pret. ind. Hence it is better called the 1st pret.

2 The vowel of pret. pl. (better called the 2nd pret.) is found in all other places in the pret. Hence *þu sunge* may be either pret. ind. or pret. subj.

3 In actual practice, a similar ambiguity exists throughout the pret. pl. Many primers and grammars show *-on* as the ind. ending and *-en* as the subj. ending. But (generally speaking) this distinction does not hold in the manuscripts. This is because the process which led to the reduction of all

[1] *Bīdan* 'wait for' can take gen. or acc.

[2] See further, Appendix A.

the inflexional endings to *-e*, *-es*, *-en*, and so on, in ME had already begun in OE. MnE, with its fixed spelling system, still spells differently the second syllables of 'pukka', 'beggar', 'baker', 'actor', and (in some places) 'honour', all of which are pronounced the same by many speakers in Great Britain, and by some in other countries. But in OE the spelling system tended to be more phonetic and we often find scribes writing down in the manuscripts forms which represent the pronunciation they actually used and not the forms which are shown in the grammars. As a result, you may find in your reading pret. pl. forms ending, not only in *-on* and *-en*, but also in *-æn*, *-an*, and *-un*. Any of these may be ind. or subj. Hence the only places in the pret. of the strong verbs where ind. and subj. are clearly distinguished are the two places where the ind. has the 1st pret. form; see 1 above.

4 The variations in the medial cons. caused by Verner's Law; see §§107–108.

§114 Two groups of strong verbs present special difficulties in the present tense. The first – those in classes V and VI with weak presents – are discussed in §116. The others are the contracted verbs, exemplified here by *sēon* V 'see'. Only the present tense is given, for in the pret. it follows the rules given above.

	Present Indicative		*Present Subjunctive*
Sg. 1	sēo		sēo
2	si(e)hst		sēo
3	si(e)hþ		sēo
Pl.	sēoþ		sēon
Imp. Sg.	seoh	*Pl.*	sēoþ
Inf.	sēon	*Infl. Inf.*	tō sēonne
Pres. Ptc.	sēonde		

Note

We have already seen in §103.3 that *sēon* is a form produced by breaking and loss of *h*. The whole of the pres. tense except 2nd and 3rd sg. pres. ind. (forms which always require special attention in both strong and weak verbs) is affected by these two sound-changes, e.g.

1st sg. pres. ind. *iċ sehe > *iċ seohe > *iċ sēoe > iċ sēo

and so on for the other forms. But the 2nd and 3rd sg. pres. ind. are different. The vowel changes are the result of *i*-mutation; see §112.1. But *h* occurs in these forms because the *e* of the ending disappeared (see §112.2) before the *h* could be lost between vowels. Because the *h* did not disappear, the vowels remained short; cf. the imp. sg. *seoh*.

You may care to note that the pres. subj. sg. is the same as the 1st pers. sg. pres. ind. (*sēo*) and that the subj. pl. and the inf. are the same (*sēon*). This is true of all contracted verbs.

VII WEAK VERBS AND SOUND-CHANGES RELEVANT TO THEM

Introduction

§115 There are three classes of weak verbs in OE. As in MnE, these verbs form their pret. and their past ptc. by the addition of a dental suffix. Normally the stem vowel is the same throughout; for exceptions, see §§122–123 and 126. As will become apparent, the inflexional endings of the strong and weak verbs have much in common.

Class 1

§116 Class 1 of the weak verbs is divided into two sub-classes:
(*a*) exemplified by *fremman* 'do' and *nerian* 'save';
(*b*) exemplified by *hīeran* 'hear'.

	(*a*)	(*a*)	(*b*)
Present Indicative			
Sg. 1	fremme	nerie	hīere
2	fremest	nerest	hīerst
3	fremeþ	nereþ	hīerþ
Pl.	fremmaþ	neriaþ	hīeraþ
Imperative			
Sg.	freme	nere	hīer
Pl.	fremmaþ	neriaþ	hīeraþ
Present Subjunctive			
Sg.	fremme	nerie	hīere
Pl.	fremmen	nerien	hīeren
Preterite Indicative			
Sg. 1	fremede	nerede	hīerde
2	fremedest	neredest	hīerdest
3	fremede	nerede	hīerde
Pl.	fremedon	neredon	hīerdon
Preterite Subjunctive			
Sg.	fremede	nerede	hīerde
Pl.	fremeden	nereden	hīerden
Inf.	fremman	nerian	hīeran
Infl. Inf.	tō fremmenne	tō nerienne	tō hīerenne
Pres. Ptc.	fremmende	neriende	hīerende
Past Ptc.	(ġe-)fremed	(ġe-)nered	(ġe-)hīered

Participles may be declined like adjectives.

Like *fremman* are most verbs with short vowel + a double consonant, e.g. *cnyssan* 'knock'. The strong verbs of classes V and VI such as *biddan* 'pray' and *hebban* 'lift' are like *fremman* THROUGHOUT THE PRESENT.[1]

Like *nerian* are nearly all verbs ending in *-rian* (for exceptions, see §132.1). The class VI strong verb *swerian* is like *nerian* THROUGHOUT THE PRESENT.

Like *hīeran* are verbs with a long vowel + a single consonant, e.g. *dēman* 'judge', and verbs with a short vowel + two consonants not the same, e.g. *sendan* 'send'. A few verbs of the same pattern as *fremman*, but with a different history, also belong here; they include *fyllan* 'fill'. The strong verb *wēpan* (class VII(*a*)) is like *hīeran* THROUGHOUT THE PRESENT. Its past ptc. is *wōpen*.

As is shown in §117, all the verbs of this class have an *i*-mutated vowel throughout the stem except those discussed in §§122–123.

§117 A glance at the conjugation of these three verbs will show that *fremman* sometimes loses an *m*, *nerian* its *i*, and that (compared with *fremman* and *nerian*) *hīeran* sometimes loses an *e* in the inflexional endings. These 'losses' (an unhistorical name, as we shall see below) occur in the following places:

1 2nd and 3rd sg. pres. ind.;

2 imp. sg.;

3 throughout the pret. The pret. stems of these three verbs are respectively *fremed-* (with one *m*), *nered-* (with no *i*), and *hīerd-* (with no *e*);

4 in the past ptc., except that *hīeran* usually has *hīered*.

Note

These variations can be explained briefly as follows. The infinitive of *fremman* was once **framjan*.[2] The *j* – a high front sound – operated like *i* and caused *i*-mutation of *a*, which before *m* became *e*. But *j* had another property denied to *i*; in short-stemmed words it caused lengthening or doubling of any cons. (except *r*) which preceded it, and then disappeared. So **framjan* > *fremman*. In **nærjan* the *j* merely caused *i*-mutation and remained as *i*; hence *nerian*.

But in the places where *fremman* 'loses' an *m*, the inflexional ending originally began with *i*. So e.g., the 3rd sg. pres. ind. of **framjan* was **framjiþ*. Here the *j* was absorbed into the *i* before it could cause doubling; so we get **framiþ*. The *i* caused *i*-mutation and then became *e*, giving *fremeþ*. Similarly **nærjiþ* > **næriþ* > *nereþ*. Similarly, absence of *j* in the pret. gave *fremede* and *nerede*. In *hīeran* and the other verbs of sub-class (*b*), the details and the results are different, and can be taken on trust for the time being.

[1] The only verbs with double medial cons. which are strong throughout belong to class III (e.g. *swimman*, *winnan*) and to class VII (e.g. *bannan*, *feallan*). Verbs whose infinitives rhyme with any of these four are always strong. See further §133.5.

[2] *j* here and elsewhere is the sound written [j] in phonetic script and pronounced something like MnE *y* in 'year'. It is a high front sound which can be made by saying *i* and then closing the gap between the tongue and the hard palate.

§118 Once these variations are understood, we can observe certain similarities in the inflexional endings of the weak verbs of class 1 and those of the strong verbs. These are

1 The pres. ind. endings of the weak verbs are the same as the endings of the strong verbs. The *-est* and *-eþ* of the 2nd and 3rd sg. pres. ind. are subject to the same reductions as occurred in these forms in the strong verbs (§112.2). However, the weak verbs generally show more unreduced forms than the strong verbs.

2 The pres. and pret. subj. endings are the same in both weak and strong verbs.

3 The pres. subj. sg. is the same as the 1st pers. sg. pres. ind.

4 The endings of the pret. pl. ind. are the same.

5 The endings of the imp. pl., the pres. ptc., and the infs. respectively are the same.

6 The imp. pl. is the same as the pres. ind. pl.

§119 Important differences are seen in

1 the imp. sgs. *freme* and *nere*, where the strong verbs have no final *-e*; cf. *hīer* (see §117.2);

2 the pret. ind. sg., where the endings are *-e*, *-est*, *-e*.

§120 As in the strong verbs, the pret. pl. endings *-on* and *-en* are ambiguous; see §113.3. In lWS the 2nd sg. ending *-est* is often extended to the subj. Hence the pret. ind. and subj. can no longer be distinguished in the weak verbs.

§121 Certain simplifications occur in the pret. and the past ptc.:

1 If in forming the pret. a double consonant followed another consonant, it was simplified. Hence *sendan* has pret. *sende*, not **sendde*.

2 A ptc. such as *sended* may be simplified to *send*.

3 After voiceless sounds (e.g. *p*, *s*, *t*) the dental suffix becomes *t*, e.g. *mētan* 'meet' has *mētte*; cf. MnE 'judged' with 'crept'.

4 **-cd-* appears as *-ht-*. Hence *tǣċan* 'teach' has pret. *tǣhte*, past ptc. (*ġe-*)*tǣht*.

§122 In MnE we have some weak verbs which change their stem vowel in the pret. and the past ptc. as well as adding the dental suffix. They include 'sell/sold', 'tell/told', 'seek/sought', 'buy/bought', 'bring/brought', and 'think/thought', which were weak verbs of class 1 in OE and had the same irregularity even then. There were more of them in OE, for some have disappeared, e.g. *reċċan* 'tell', and some have become regular weak verbs, e.g. *streċċan* 'stretch'.[1] It is simplest just to learn these in the first instance. The most important ones are

[1] As you will see from §121.4, the verb *tǣċan* 'teach' usually has the same vowel throughout in WS, but *tāhte, tāht*, do occur.

Inf.	*Pret. Sg.*	*Past Ptc.*
sēċan 'seek'	sōhte	sōht
sellan 'give'	sealde	seald
cwellan 'kill'	cwealde	cweald
þenċan 'think'	þōhte	þōht
brenġan 'bring'	brōhte	brōht
þynċan 'seem'	þūhte	þūht
bycgan 'buy'	bohte	boht
wyrċan 'work'	worhte	worht

§123 The irregularity of these verbs is due to the fact that there was no *i* in the pret. or the past ptc. to cause *i*-mutation. Hence, while their present tenses have an *i*-mutated vowel like all the other verbs of this class, the vowel of the pret. and past ptc. is unmutated. This can be seen clearly by comparing *sēċan* (< **sōkjan*) with *sōhte/sōht*. However, the parallels in most verbs are obscured by other sound-changes which affected the vowel of the pret. and past ptc. They are

1 Breaking, e.g. *cwellan/cwealde*. Here the *æ* which once occurred throughout has been *i*-mutated to *e* in the pres. and broken to *ea* by the *ld* in the pret.

2 Loss of *n* before *h* with lengthening of the preceding vowel so that the word takes the same time to pronounce. This accounts for *þenċan/þōhte*, *þynċan/þūhte*, and *brenġan/brōhte*. Note that the strong inf. *bringan* usually replaces *brenġan*.

3 A change by which Gmc. *u* under certain conditions became OE *o*. This accounts for the variations in *bycgan/bohte* and *wyrċan/worhte*, where an original *u* has been *i*-mutated to *y* in the pres. and has changed to *o* in the pret.

4 On the derivation of weak verbs of class 1, see Appendix B.

Class 2

§124 The weak verbs of class 2 present few problems. The traditional paradigm is *lufian* 'love'. The long-stemmed *lōcian* 'look' has exactly the same endings.

	Present Indicative	*Preterite Indicative*
Sg. 1	lufie	lufode
2	lufast	lufodest
3	lufaþ	lufode
Pl.	lufiaþ	lufodon
	Present Subjunctive	*Preterite Subjunctive*
Sg.	lufie	lufode
Pl.	lufien	lufoden

Imp. Sg.	lufa	*Pl.*	lufiaþ
Inf.	lufian	*Infl. Inf.*	tō lufienne
Pres. Ptc.	lufiende	*Past Ptc.*	(ġe-)lufod

All weak verbs of class 2 have an infinitive ending in *-ian*. However, most verbs ending in *-rian* belong, not to class 2, but to class 1(*a*) following *nerian*. But *andswarian* 'answer', *gadrian* 'gather', *timbrian* 'build', and one or two other verbs in *-rian*, usually follow *lufian*.

§125 Points to note in the conjugation of *lufian* are

1 The *i* disappears in the 2nd and 3rd sg. pres. ind., the imp. sg., all forms of the pret., and the past ptc. These are exactly the same places where *fremman* 'loses' its *m*, *nerian* its *i*, and *hīeran* its *e*.

2 The *-a* in 2nd and 3rd sg. pres. ind. *lufast, lufaþ*, and in imp. sg. *lufa*. So far the verb ending *-aþ* has always signified imp. or pres. ind. pl. In these verbs, *-aþ* is sg., *-iaþ* pl. Beware of this when reading your texts.

3 The *-od* in the pret. stem *lufod-* and in the past ptc. *lufod* where *fremman* has *-ed*.

Apart from these differences, the weak verbs of classes 1 and 2 are conjugated the same.

Class 3

§126 Class 3 contains four weak verbs – *habban* 'have', *libban* 'live', *secgan* 'say', and *hycgan* 'think'. These are conjugated:

Present Indicative					
Sg.	1	hæbbe	libbe	secge	hycge
	2	hæfst	leofast	sæġst	hyġst
		hafast	lifast	seġ(e)st	hogast
	3	hæfþ	leofaþ	sæġþ	hyġþ
		hafaþ	lifaþ	seġ(e)þ	hogaþ
Pl.		habbaþ	libbaþ, leofaþ	secgaþ	hycgaþ
Present Subjunctive					
Sg.		hæbbe	libbe	secge	hycge
Pl.		hæbben	libben	secgen	hycgen
Imperative					
Sg.		hafa	leofa	saga, seġe	hoga, hyġe
Pl.		habbaþ	libbaþ, leofaþ	secgaþ	hycgaþ
Preterite Indicative					
Sg.		hæfde	lifde, leofode	sæġde, sǣde	hog(o)de
Pl.		hæfdon	lifdon, leofodon	sæġdon, sǣdon	hog(o)don
Preterite Subjunctive					
Sg.		hæfde	lifde, leofode	sæġde, sǣde	hog(o)de
Pl.		hæfden	lifden, leofoden	sæġden, sǣden	hog(o)den

VIII ANOMALOUS VERBS

Bēon

§127 *Bēon, wesan* 'be' has forms from different stems.

Indicative	*Pres.*	*Pres.*	*Pret.*
Sg. 1	eom	bēo	wæs
2	eart	bist	wǣre
3	is	biþ	wæs
Pl.	sind(on), sint	bēoþ	wǣron
Subjunctive			
Sg.	sīe	bēo	wǣre
Pl.	sīen	bēon	wǣren
Imperative			
Sg.	wes	bēo	
Pl.	wesaþ	bēoþ	

On the distinction in meaning between *eom* and *bēo*, see §196.

Dōn and gān

§128 *Dōn* 'do' and *gān* 'go' have

Present Indicative		
Sg. 1	dō	gā
2	dēst	gǣst
3	dēþ	gǣþ
Pl.	dōþ	gāþ
Imp. Sg.	dō	gā
Pret. Ind. Sg.	dyde	ēode
Past Ptc.	ġedōn	ġegān

Note

i-mutation in 2nd and 3rd pers. sg. pres. ind.

The remaining forms can be constructed with the help of §118.

Willan

§129 *Willan* 'wish, will' has

	Present Indicative	*Present Subjunctive*
Sg. 1	wille	wille
2	wilt	wille
3	wile	wille
Pl.	willaþ	willen
Pret.	wolde	

Preterite-Present Verbs

§130 Some very common verbs have a strong past tense with a present meaning (cf. Lat. *novi* 'I know') and a new weak past tense. Thus *wāt* 'I know, he knows' *witon* 'they know' belongs to class I; cf. *scān, scinon*. Its new past tense is sg. *wiste* pl. *wiston*. Such verbs are called preterite-present verbs. The most important ones are

Meaning	*Inf.*	*Pres. Ind. Sg.* 1, 3	2	*Pres. Ind. Pl.*	*Pret. Sg.*
'possess'	āgan	āh	āhst, āht	āgon	āhte
'grant'	unnan	ann	—	unnon	ūþe
'can, know how to'	cunnan	cann	canst	cunnon	cūþe
'avail, be of use'	*dugan	dēah	—	dugon	dohte
'dare'	*durran	dearr	dearst	durron	dorste
'remember'	gemunan	ġeman	ġemanst	ġemunon	ġemunde
'be able'	magan	mæġ	meaht	magon	mihte, meahte
'be allowed to, may'	*mōtan	mōt	mōst	mōton	mōste
'be obliged to'	*sculan	sceal	scealt	sculon	sceolde
'need'	þurfan	þearf	þearft	þurfon	þorfte
'know'	witan	wāt	wāst	witon	wiste, wisse

IX IS A VERB STRONG OR WEAK? TO WHICH CLASS DOES IT BELONG?

§131 If we assume that you can recognize on sight the strong contracted verbs, the four weak verbs of class 3 (§126), and the verbs discussed in §§127–130, the system set out below will enable you to answer the questions at the head of this section.

Verbs in *-ian*

§132 1 Verbs in *-rian* are class 1 weak.
Exceptions:

(*a*) *swerian* 'swear' (class VI strong with a weak present);

(*b*) *andswarian* 'answer' and a few other verbs which can follow *lufian* 'love'; see §124.

2 All other verbs in *-ian* are class 2 weak.

Verbs in *-an*

§133 These are either strong or class 1 weak. You will find that the recognition symbols for the strong verbs set out in §94 are almost always reliable. Thus if a verb ending in *-an* has *ī* + one cons. in the infinitive, it is probably class I strong. If it has *ū* + one cons., it is probably class II strong. And so on. Exceptions include

1 The strong verbs of classes V, VI, and VII (*wēpan* 'weep'), with weak presents. These too should be recognized on sight.

2 *Fēolan* 'press on' looks like class II strong, but belongs to class III, as the 1st pret. *fealh* shows. (**Felhan* > **feolhan* by breaking (§97.2) > *fēolan* by loss of *h* + lengthening; see §38.)

3 A verb with *ǣ* + one cons. may be either strong or weak; *lǣtan* 'let' is class VII strong, *lǣdan* 'lead' is class 1 weak.

4 For weak verbs with *ī* and *ēo*, see Appendix A.1 and 2.

5 Verbs with a short vowel + a double cons. are mostly weak class 1, e.g. *fremman*. The recognition symbols of the strong verbs of class III will enable us to distinguish *swimman* 'swim' and *winnan* 'fight' as class III strong; note *i* before the nasals compared witth the *e* of *fremman. Bannan* 'summon', *spannan* 'span', *feallan* 'fall', and *weallan* 'boil', are class VII strong. On *bringan*, see §123.2. On *hringan* and *ġeþingan*, see Appendix A.3.

§134 When you are reading Old English, your problem will often be to find the infinitive from which a certain verb form is derived. Let us take *bītt*, *stæl*, and *budon*, as examples.

For *bītt*, we note *-ī-* and *-tt*. Together these suggest the syncopated 3rd sg. pres. ind. of a verb of class I. The ending *-tt* we know to be a reduction of *-teþ* or *-deþ*. This gives us two possibilities – *bītan* 'bite' or *bīdan* 'await'. The context should determine which we have. In a text which does not mark long vowels, *bitt* could also be from *biddan* V 'ask'.

For *stæl* we note *-æ-*. This suggests the 1st pret. of class IV or V. Hence the inf. is *stelan* 'steal'. The medial *l* decides for class IV.

Budon is perhaps more difficult. Is it strong or (since it ends in *-don*) weak? If it is strong, the medial *u* and the single cons. suggest class II. Therefore the inf. could be *bēodan* or **būdan*. The glossary decides for *bēodan* 'command'. If it were a weak pret., the inf. would be *buan*. This would not fit *būan* 'dwell' with pret. pl. *būdon* unless the text did not mark long vowels. If this were the case, the context would again decide.

The verbs discussed in §122 present a problem, but you will soon become familiar with their preterites.

X ADVERBS

Formation

§135 Characteristic endings of adverbs are *-e* (e.g. *hraþe* 'quickly'), *-līce* (e.g. *hrædlīce* 'quickly'), and *-unga* (e.g. *eallunga* 'entirely'). The ending *-an* usually means 'from', e.g. *norþ* 'north, northwards' but *norþan* 'from the north'.

The gen. and dat. can be used adverbially; see §§190 and 191.

The negative adverb is *ne*. For its use, see §184.4.

Comparison

Adverbs are normally compared by adding *-or*, *-ost*, e.g. *oft* 'often' *oftor oftost*, and (dropping the *-e* of the positive) *swīþe* 'greatly' *swīþor swīþost*.

Some have an *i*-mutated vowel in the comparative and superlative, e.g. *lange* 'long' *leng lengest* and *feorr* 'far' *fierr fierrest*.

A knowledge of the equivalent OE adjectives and MnE adverbs will enable you to recognize in reading the irregular comparatives and superlatives of the adverbs *wel* 'well', *yfle* 'evilly', *mičle* 'much', and *lȳt* 'little'.

4

Word Formation

INTRODUCTION

§136 Old English acquired new words in three ways – by borrowing from other languages (see §234), by making compounds of two words already existing in the language, e.g. *sǣ-weall* 'sea-wall', and by adding affixes to existing words to change their function or meaning, e.g. *blōd* (neut.) 'blood' but *blōd-iġ* 'bloody, blood-stained', and *bēodan* 'command' but *for-bēodan* 'forbid'. A knowledge of these last two methods and of the formative elements used will help you to deduce the meaning of many words which may at first sight seem unfamiliar.

It is also important to realize that parts of speech were not interchangeable in OE as they often are in MnE. Thus the OE noun *drinc* has a corresponding verb *drincan* whereas today 'drink' is both a noun and a verb. Similarly the OE adjective *open* and the verb *openian* are both represented by MnE 'open'. Such correspondences are fairly obvious. But others are more difficult to spot because they are obscured by sound-changes. You may be able to deduce for yourself the change which causes the variations in the following pairs: *scrūd* (neut.) 'clothing' *scrȳdan* 'clothe'; *dōm* (masc.) 'judgement' *dēma* (masc.) 'a judge'; *hāl* 'whole, in good health' *hǣlan* 'heal, make whole'. If you cannot, see §§52–57 and Appendix B. Other groups of related words have different vowels from the same gradation series (see §90), e.g. *beran* 'carry', *bǣr* (fem.) 'bier', and the ending *-bora* (masc.) 'bearer, carrier', which often occurs in compounds such as *sweord-bora* 'sword-bearer'. Both these sound-changes and Verner's Law (§§105–108) obscure the relationship between *ċēosan* 'choose' and *cyre* (masc.) 'choice', where *y* is an *i*-mutation of *u*.

Notes

1 On the gender and declension of nouns formed by compounding or by the addition of suffixes or endings, see §§12, 13, and 41.

2 The work by Madden and Magoun mentioned in §253 adopts a 'packaging principle' by which parent words, their immediate derivatives, and those related by *i*-mutation and gradation, are grouped together. This makes for ease of learning, and is one of the reasons why the book is so useful.

I COMPOUNDING

§137 The process of forming new words or compounds by joining together two separate words which already exist was common in OE. Some of the possible arrangements are exemplified below.

Nouns can be formed by combining

1 Noun and noun, e.g. *hell-waran* (masc. pl.) 'inhabitants of hell', *niht-waco* (fem.) 'night-watch', *scip-rāp* (masc.) 'ship-rope', *storm-sǣ* (masc. or fem.) 'stormy sea';

2 Adjective and noun, e.g. *eall-wealda* (masc.) 'ruler of all', *hēah-clif* (neut.) 'high cliff', *hēah-ġerēfa* (masc.) 'high reeve, chief officer', *wīd-sǣ* (masc. or fem.) '(open) sea';

3 Adverb and noun, e.g. *ǣr-dæġ* (masc.) 'early day, first dawn', *eft-sīþ* (masc.) 'return', *inn-faru* (fem.) 'expedition', *inn-gang* (masc.) 'entrance'.

Adjectives are found consisting of

1 Noun and adjective, e.g. *ælmes-ġeorn* 'alms-eager, generous, charitable', *ār-weorþ* 'honour-worthy, venerable', *dōm-ġeorn* 'eager for glory', *mere-wēriġ* 'sea-weary';

2 Adjective and adjective, e.g. *hēah-þungen* 'of high rank', *hrēow-ċeariġ* 'sad' (lit. 'sad-anxious'), *wīd-cūþ* 'widely known', *wīs-hycgende* 'wise-thinking';

3 Adverb and adjective, e.g. *ǣr-gōd* 'very good', *forþ-ġeorn* 'forth-eager, eager to advance', *wel-þungen* 'well-thriven, excellent', *wel-willende* 'well-wishing, benevolent';

4 Adjective and noun, e.g. *blanden-feax* 'having mixed hair, gray-haired', *blīþe-mōd* 'of kindly mind, friendly', *hrēowiġ-mōd* 'gloomy-minded, sad', *salu-pād* 'dark-coated'.

In all these words the first element is uninflected; cf. *folc-lagu* (fem.) 'law of the people, public law' with *Godes* (gen.) *lagu* 'God's law' and *wīn-druncen* 'wine-drunk' with *bēore* (dat.) *druncen* 'drunk with beer'. But compounds do occur with an inflected first element, e.g. *Engla-lond* 'land of the Angles, England' (but cf. *Frēs-lond* 'Frisian land, Frisia') and *eġes-full* 'full of terror, terrible, wonderful' (but cf. *synn-full* 'sinful').

Note

Compounds of three elements are sometimes found, e.g. *wulf-hēafod-trēo* (neut.) 'wolf-head-tree, gallows, cross'.

Today, when we are faced with a new object or idea, we often express it by a compound made up of foreign or of native elements, e.g. 'tele-gram' and 'astro-naut', but 'one-up-man-ship' and 'fall-out'. But OE often 'translated' foreign words. Sometimes the elements of a foreign word were represented by OE equivalents, e.g. *god-spel* (neut.) 'good news', based on *evangelium*, for 'gospel',[1] *þrī-nes* (fem.) representing *Trini-tas* 'The Trinity', and Ælfric's grammatical terms *fore-set-nes* (fem.) for Lat. *prae-positio* 'preposition' and *betwux-āleġed-nes* (fem.) 'between-laid-ness' for Lat. *inter-jectio* 'interjection'. Sometimes the word was analysed into its concepts and these were rendered into English, e.g. two words for 'Pharisees' – *sundor-halgan* (masc. pl.) 'apart-holies' and *ǣ-lārēowas* (masc. pl.) 'law-teachers'. That these processes are now less natural for speakers of English can be seen in two ways. First, many native compounds such as *tungol-cræft* (masc.) 'star-craft' for 'astronomy' and *lār-hūs* (neut.) 'lore-house' for 'school' have disappeared from the language. Secondly, proposed replacements like the sixteenth-century 'hundreder' for 'centurion' or the nineteenth-century 'folk-wain' for 'bus' seem to us ridiculous, whereas to Germans *Fernsprecher* 'far-speaker' for our Greek-derived 'telephone' is not unnatural, though they do, of course, use *Telephon*.

To help provide the many synonyms beginning with different letters which were essential for the *scop* (poet) working in the alliterative measure, the Anglo-Saxon poets made great use of compounds. Of special interest is the kenning, a sort of condensed metaphor in which (a) is compared to (b) without (a) or the point of the comparison being made explicit; thus one might say of the camel 'The desert-ship lurched on'. So the sea is *hwæl-weġ* (masc.) 'whale-way', a ship *ӯþ-hengest* (masc.) 'wave-horse', and a minstrel *hleahtor-smiþ* (masc.) 'laughter-smith'.

We find too that many set phrases inherited from the days when the poetry was composed orally survive in the lettered poetry. These 'oral-formulae' are set metrical combinations which could be varied according to the needs of alliteration. Thus the phrase 'on, over, across the sea' can be expressed by one of the prepositions *on, ofer, ġeond*, followed by the appropriate case of one of the following words: *bæþ-weġ* 'bath-way', *flōd-weġ* 'flood-way', *flot-weġ* 'sea-way', *hwæl-weġ* 'whale-way' (all masc.), *hran-rād* 'whale-road', *swan-rād* 'swan-road', and *seġl-rād* 'sail-road' (all fem.). References to further discussions on these points will be found in §§265–266.

II THE ADDITION OF AFFIXES

§138 These can be divided into prefixes – elements placed at the beginning of words to qualify their meaning – and suffixes. The effect of many which survive today is obvious; we may cite the prefix *mis-* as in *mis-dǣd* (fem.) 'misdeed', prepositions or adverbs used as prefixes, e.g. *ofer-mæġen* (neut.) 'superior force' and *ūt-gān* 'go out', adjectives ending in *-full, -iṡc*,

[1] You should look up the noun 'gospel' in O.E.D. to find out why *godspel* has *ŏ* when the OE equivalent of 'good' is *gōd*.

and *-lēas*, e.g. *synn-full* 'sinful', *ċild-isċ* 'childish', and *feoh-lēas* 'moneyless, destitute', and nouns ending in *-dōm, -ere, -scipe* (all masc.) and *-nes, -nis, -nys* (fem.), e.g. *wīs-dōm* 'wisdom', *fisc-ere* 'fisherman', *frēond-scipe* 'friendship', and *beorht-nes* 'brightness'. Others which occur frequently but are not so easily recognizable are set out below.

Prefixes

ā- 1 Sometimes it means 'away', as in *ā-fȳsan* 'drive forth'.

2 But sometimes it seems to have no effect on the meaning, e.g. *ā-galan* 'sing'.

ǣġ- It generalizes prons. and advs., e.g. *ǣġ-hwā* 'everyone' and *ǣġ-hwǣr* 'everywhere'.

be- 1 In some words *be-* is the same as the prep. 'about', e.g. *be-gān* 'surround' and *be-rīdan* 'ride round, surround'.

2 Sometimes it is a deprivative, e.g. *be-dǣlan* 'deprive' and *be-hēafdian* 'behead'.

3 It can make an intransitive verb transitive, e.g. *be-þenċan* 'think about' and *be-wēpan* 'bewail'.

for- It is an intensifier, e.g. *for-bærnan* 'burn up, consume', *for-lorenness* (fem.) 'perdition', and *for-heard* 'very hard'.

ġe- 1 In some nouns it has the sense of 'together', e.g. *ġe-fēra* (masc.) 'companion' and *ġe-brōþru* (masc. pl.) 'brothers'.

2 In verbs, it sometimes has a perfective sense, e.g. *ġe-āscian* 'find out' and *ġe-winnan* 'get by fighting, win'; hence its frequent use in past ptcs.

on-, *an-* 1 In verbs like *on-bindan* 'unbind' and *on-lūcan* 'unlock', it has a negative sense.

2 Sometimes it means 'against', as in *on-rǣs* (masc.) 'attack'.

or- 1 This is a deprivative in *or-mōd* 'without courage, despairing' and *or-sorg* 'without care, careless'.

2 It can also mean 'early, original, primaeval' (cf. *or* (neut.) 'beginning, origin'), e.g. *or-eald* 'of great age', *or-ieldu* (fem.) 'extreme old age', and *or-þanc* (masc.) 'inborn thought, ingenuity, skill'.

tō- 1 Sometimes it is the same as the prep. *tō*, e.g. *tō-cyme* (masc.) 'arrival' and *tō-weard* (prep.) 'towards'.

2 But with verbs it frequently means separation, e.g. *tō-drīfan* (trans.) 'drive apart, disperse, scatter' and *tō-faran* (intrans.) 'go apart, disperse'.

un- 1 This is sometimes a negative prefix, e.g. *un-friþ* (masc.) 'un-peace, war' and *un-hold* 'unfriendly'.

2 Sometimes it is pejorative, as in *un-ġiefu* (fem.) 'evil gift' and *un-weder* (neut.) 'bad weather'.

wan- This is a deprivative or negative prefix, e.g. *wan-hāl* 'not hale, ill' and *wan-hoga* (masc.) 'thoughtless man'.

wiþ- Its primary sense in compounds is 'against', e.g. *wiþ-cēosan* 'reject', *wiþ-cweþan* 'reply, contradict', *wiþ-drīfan* 'repel', and *wiþ-feohtend* (masc.) 'enemy, opponent, rebel'.

ymb- This means 'around', e.g. *ymb-gang* (masc.) 'circuit, circumference' and *ymb-lǣdan* 'lead round'.

Suffixes

Nouns

-aþ, -oþ This forms masc. nouns, e.g. *herg-aþ* 'plundering' and *fisc-oþ* 'fishing'.

-end This equals '-er', as in *Hǣl-end* (masc.) 'Healer, Saviour' and *wīġ-end* (masc.) 'fighter, warrior'. It derives from the pres. ptc. ending *-ende*.

-hād This introduces masc. nouns and equals MnE '-hood', as in *ċild-hād* 'childhood' and *woruld-hād* 'secular life'.

-ing 1 In masc. nouns it means 'son of', e.g. *Ælfred Æþelwulf-ing* 'Alfred son of Æthelwulf', or 'associated with', e.g. *earm-ing* 'wretch' and *hōr-ing* 'adulterer, fornicator'.

2 In fem. nouns, it equals *-ung*; see below.

-mǣl 1 The noun *mǣl* (neut.) 'measure, fixed time' appears in compound nouns, e.g. *fōt-mǣl* (neut.) 'foot's length, foot' and (with the dat. pl. used adverbially; see §191.3) *floc-mǣlum* 'in (armed) bands' and *ġēar-mǣlum* 'year by year'.

2 In the sense 'mark, sign', it appears in compound nouns, e.g. *fȳr-mǣl* (neut.) 'fire-mark', and also in compound adjectives; see below.

-rǣden This forms fem. abstract nouns, e.g. *hierd-rǣden* 'guardianship, care, guard'.

-þ(o), -þ(u) This is used to form fem. abstract nouns, e.g. *fǣh-þ(o)* 'hostility' and *ierm-þ(u)* 'misery, poverty'. Note that *ġeogoþ* 'youth' is fem.

-ung, -ing This is found in fem. abstract nouns formed from verbs, e.g. *bod-ung* 'preaching' and *rǣd-ing* 'reading'.

Adjectives

-en 1 This is the ending of past ptcs. of strong verbs.

2 It is also found in adjectives with an *i*-mutated vowel in the stem, e.g. *ǣttr-en* 'poisonous' and *gyld-en* 'golden'.

-iġ This equals MnE '-y', as in *cræft-iġ* 'powerful, mighty' and *hāl-iġ* 'holy'.

-līċ This, originally the same word as *līċ* (neut.) 'body', equals MnE '-ly, -like', e.g. *heofon-līċ* 'heavenly' and *ċild-līċ* 'child-like, childish'.

-mǣl This element, listed above under Nouns, also occurs in compound adjectives, e.g. *grǣg-mǣl* 'of a grey colour', *hring-mǣl* 'ring-marked, ornamented with a ring', and *wunden-mǣl* 'with curved markings'.

-sum This occurs in words like *wynn-sum* 'delightful, pleasant' (cf. 'winsome') and *hīer-sum* 'hear-some, obedient'.

Adverbs

See §135.

Verbs

-an The most common infinitive ending for strong and weak verbs. (For the *-an* in class 1 weak verbs, which was originally **-jan*, see Appendix B.)

-ian The infinitive ending for class 2 weak verbs. Verbs borrowed from Latin are usually conjugated according to this class, e.g. *declinian* 'decline' < *declināre* and *predician* 'preach' < *praedicāre*.

-rian See §132.1.

-sian This is the infinitive ending of a subclass of weak 2 verbs formed from adjectives and nouns, e.g. *clǣnsian* 'cleanse' and *rīcsian* 'be powerful, reign'.

-ettan This infinitive ending is used to form a subclass of weak 1 verbs from adjectives and nouns, e.g. *lāþ-ettan* 'hate, loathe', *līc-ettan* 'pretend', and *sār-ettan* 'lament'.

-lǣċan This infinitive ending is also used to form a subclass of weak 1 verbs from adjectives and nouns, e.g. *ġe-ān-lǣċan* 'unite' and *ġe-þwǣr-lǣċan* 'consent'.

5

Syntax

INTRODUCTION

§139 Syntax has been described as the study of 'the traffic rules of language'. If this is so, you are offered here only a simplified Anglo-Saxon highway code, designed to deal with constructions likely to worry the beginner. OE syntax is recognizably English; in some passages the word-order at least is almost without exception that of MnE. At other times, we seem to be wrestling with a foreign language. Some of the difficulties arise from idiosyncrasies due to the Germanic ancestry of OE. Another reason, which obtains mostly in the early writings when OE prose was in a formative state, is that Alfred and his companions were struggling to develop the language as a vehicle for the expression of complicated narrative and abstract thought. They achieved no little success, but had their failures too. The breathless but vigorous account of the Battle of Ashdown (the annal for 871 in the Parker MS of the Anglo-Saxon Chronicle), which sweeps us along on a surging current of simple sentences joined by *ond*, is not untypical of the early efforts of prose writers who were not translating from Latin. There is only one complex sentence in the whole piece (the last but one). That the writer gets into trouble with it is symptomatic; cf. the account of the sea-battle of 897 in the same manuscript, where what has happened is not particularly clear on first reading. This inability to cope with complicated ideas is more apparent in the translated texts, where the influence of the Latin periodic structure often produces stilted prose, as in the story of Orpheus and Eurydice in King Alfred's translation of Boethius. Even Alfred's original prose is sometimes twisted in the same way, e.g. the sentences discussed in §172. Perhaps Latin, being the language of the Church, the language from which many works were translated, and the only model available, was accorded a status denied to it (or to any other original) today.

§140 Another source of difficulty becomes apparent from a study of the major differences between OE and MnE. It is sometimes said that OE is the period of full inflexions, ME the period of levelled inflexions (all with the vowel *e*, e.g. *-e*, *-es*, *-en*, as opposed to the endings of OE with their different vowels), and MnE the period of no inflexions. This statement points to the vital truth that MnE depends on word-order and prepositions to make distinctions which in an inflected language are made by the case endings. However, it needs qualification. That there are still a few inflexions in MnE is of little importance. But it might be less misleading to say that OE is a 'half-inflected' language. Firstly, it has only four cases and remnants of a fifth left of the eight cases postulated for the original IE language. Secondly, as has been pointed out in §189 note, there is often no distinction in form between nominative and accusative. Hence word-order is often the only thing which enables us to tell which is subject and which is object; consider *Enoch gestrynde Irad and Irad gestrynde Mauiahel* (and so on) 'E. begat I. and I begat M.' (cf. *Caesarem interfecit Brutus*) and *Hi hæfdon þa ofergan Eastengle and Eastsexe* 'They had then conquered the East Anglians and the East Saxons'. These and many similar examples support the view that the Anglo-Saxons already had the feeling that the subject came first. If we did not have evidence for this, we should have to hesitate instead of automatically following the modern rule and taking *Oswold and Ealdwold* as the subject in the following lines from *Maldon*, for the order object, subject, verb, is possible in OE (see §147):

Oswold and Ealdwold ealle hwile,
begen þa gebroþru, beornas trymedon

'O. and E., the two brothers, all the time encouraged the warriors'. (More is said in §147 on the triumph of the order 'subject verb'.) Thirdly, prepositions followed by an oblique case are often used to express relationships which could be expressed by case alone; cf. *ond þa geascode he þone cyning lytle werode . . . on Merantune* 'and then he discovered the king [to be] at Merton with a small band (inst. case alone)' with *eode he in mid ane his preosta* 'he went in with one of his priests (*mid* + inst. case)'. All these things suggest a language in a state of transition. The implications of this for the future development of English are mentioned briefly in §231; here we are concerned with it as another source of difficulty.

§141 Important differences between OE and MnE are found in the following:

the position of the negative (§§144.1 and 184.4);
the use of the infinitives (§205);
the uses of moods and tenses of the verb (§§195 ff.);
the resolved tenses[1] and the function of the participles therein (§§199 ff.);
the meaning of 'modal' auxiliaries (§§206 ff.);
agreement (§187);
the meaning and use of prepositions (§§213–214).

§142 Features found in OE, but not in MnE, include

strong and weak forms of the adjective (§§63 and 64);
some special uses of cases (§§188–192);

[1] This term is explained in §199.

some special uses of articles, pronouns, and numerals (§§193–194);

the use of a single verb form where MnE would use a resolved tense or mood (§195).

idiomatic absence of the subject (§193.7).

But the main difficulty of OE syntax lies, not in these differences, but in the word-order of the simple sentence or clause, and in the syntax of the subordinate clauses. These fundamental topics are accordingly treated first; if any of the points mentioned in this or the preceding section cause immediate difficulty, see the Contents and read the appropriate section. The order of clauses within the complex sentence is very similar to that of MnE, and will cause little difficulty.

I WORD-ORDER[1]

§143 If we take subject and verb as the fundamental elements of a sentence, we shall find that the following arrangements are common in OE prose:

S.V., where the verb immediately follows the subject;

S. . . . V., where other elements of the sentence come between subject and verb;

V.S., where the subject follows the verb.

The same orders are also found in the poetry. But, like their successors, the Anglo-Saxon poets used the language much more freely than the prose writers did. Hence the comments made below apply to the prose only. But the word-order in the poetry will not cause you much difficulty if you understand what follows.

§144 As in MnE, the order S.V. can occur in both principal and subordinate clauses, e.g. *he hæfde an swiðe ænlic wif* 'he had a most excellent wife' and *þe getimbrode his hus ofer sand* 'who built his house on sand'. Therefore it cannot tell us whether a clause is principal or subordinate, except in the circumstances discussed in §§150 ff. It is also found after *ond* 'and' and *ac* 'but', e.g. *ond his lic liþ æt Winburnan* 'and his body lies at W.'.

There are naturally variations of this order. Some are found in both OE and MnE. Thus an adverb precedes the verb in *Se Hælend ða het þa ðeningmen afyllan six stænene fatu mid hluttrum wætere* 'The Saviour then ordered the servants to fill six stone vessels with pure water'. The indirect object precedes the direct object in *Romane gesealdon Gaiuse Iuliuse seofon legan* 'The Romans gave Gaius Julius seven legions', but follows it in *ac he forgeaf eorðlice ðing mannum* 'but he gave earthly things to men'.

[1] In these sections, the following abbreviations are used: S. (subject), V. (verb), O. (object), Adv. (adverb or adv. phrase). A MnE sentence such as 'Do you sing?' is characterized by v. (auxiliary verb) S.V. Round brackets indicate that the feature in question is optional.

Arrangements not found in MnE are

1 The position of the negative *ne* 'not' immediately before the verb. This is the rule in all three OE word-orders; see §184.4.

2 The placing of a pronoun O., which would be unstressed, between S. and V. when a noun O., which would carry some stress, would follow V. Thus *we hie ondredon* 'we feared them' is an idiomatic variation of the order S.V. rather than an example of S. . . . V.

3 The possibility that an infinitive or a participle may have final position, e.g. *he ne meahte ongemong oðrum monnum bion* 'he could not be among other men' and *Eastengle hæfdon Ælfrede cyninge aþas geseald* 'The East Angles had given King Alfred oaths'. On the order S.V. in non-dependent questions, see §160.

§145 The order S. . . . V. is most common in subordinate clauses, e.g. *se micla here, þe we gefyrn ymbe spræcon* 'the great army which we spoke about before' and *gif hie ænigne feld secan wolden* 'if they wished to seek any open country', and after *ond* 'and' and *ac* 'but', e.g. *Ac ic þa sona eft me selfum andwyrde* 'But again I immediately answered myself'. But it also occurs in principal clauses, e.g. *Ða reðan Iudei wedende þone halgan stændon* 'The cruel Jews in their rage stoned the saint' and *Stephanus soðlice gebigedum cneowum Drihten bæd* . . . 'Stephen however on bended knees besought the Lord . . .'. Hence the order S. . . . V. does not certify that a clause is subordinate. With this order, the verb need not have final position, but may be followed by an adverbial extension, e.g. *ær he acenned wæs of Marian* . . . 'before He was born of Mary' and . . . *þæt hi wel wyrðe beoð þære deoflican ehtnysse* . . . 'that they will be very worthy of devilish persecution'. On this order in non-dependent questions, see §160.

§146 The order V.S. occurs in MnE in questions with the verbs 'to have' and 'to be', e.g. 'Have you the book?' and 'Are you there?', and in a few other set phrases or constructions, e.g. 'said he', 'Long live the King!', 'be he alive or be he dead', and 'Had I but plenty of money, I would be in Bermuda'. It must not be confused with the normal interrogative word-order of MnE, which is v.S.V., e.g. 'Have you found him?', 'Is he coming?', and 'Do you see him?' In OE the order V.S. is found in

1 Positive non-dependent questions either with or without interrogative words, e.g. *Hwær eart þu nu, gefera?* 'Where are you now, comrade?' and *Gehyrst þu, sælida?* 'Do you hear, sailor?'

2 Negative non-dependent questions, e.g. *ne seowe þu god sæd on þinum æcere?* 'Did you not sow good seed in your field?'

3 Positive statements, e.g. *Wæs he Osrices sunu* 'He was Osric's son' and *Hæfde se cyning his fierd on tu tonumen* 'The king had divided his army in two'.

4 Negative statements, e.g. *Ne com se here* 'The army did not come'.

5 In subordinate clauses of concession and condition, e.g. *swelte ic, libbe ic* 'live I, die I', i.e. 'whether I live or die'.

6 In principal clauses introduced by certain adverbs; cf. MnE 'Then came the dawn'. On the value of this word-order for distinguishing principal from subordinate clauses, see §§150 ff.

Notes

1 The orders described in 3 and 4 above are NOT necessarily emphatic.

2 In *Matthew* 20: 13, we read: *Eala þu freond, ne do ic þe nænne teonan: hu, ne come þu to me to wyrcenne wið anum peninge?* 'Friend, I do thee no wrong; lo, didst thou not come to me to work for one penny?' Here exactly the same word-order is used first in a statement (order 4 above) and then in a question (order 2 above).

§147 Other word-orders may, of course, occur. Some which are used for emphasis are also found in MnE, e.g. *Gesælige hi wurdon geborene* ... 'Blessed they were born', *Micelne geleafan he hæfde* ... 'Great faith he had', and (with a MnE preposition replacing the OE dative case) *þam acennedan Cyninge we bringað gold* ... 'To the newborn King we bring gold' and *Gode ælmihtigum sie ðonc* 'To God Almighty be thanks'. But the order O.V.S. found in *deman gedafenað setl* 'a seat is the proper place for a judge' would be impossible today because, in a MnE sentence of the pattern 'Man flees dog', what precedes the verb must be the subject. Consider what happens to the meaning of the spoken sentence if the word-order is altered. 'Dog flees man', 'Fleas dog man', and even 'Fleas man dog', all mean something different. The absence of endings and the interchangeability of MnE parts of speech have left word-order the only guide and the absolute master. The gradual triumph of this order S.V.O. is one of the most important syntactical developments in English. Its beginnings can be seen in OE. Thus in *Matthew* 7: 24 *ælc þæra þe þas min word gehyrð and þa wyrcð, bið gelic þæm wisan were, se his hus ofer stan getimbrode*, the two subordinate clauses have S. ... V. But in *Matthew* 7: 26 *And ælc þæra þe gehyrð þas min word, and þa ne wyrcð, se bið gelic þam dysigan men, þe getimbrode his hus ofer sandceosel*, they both have S.V. This suggests that any difference there may have been between these orders was disappearing. Again, the old preference for V.S. after an adverb (compare modern German) is at times conquered by the new preference for S.V., e.g. *Her cuomon twegen aldormenn* 'In this year two chiefs came' but *Her Hengest 7 Æsc fuhton wiþ Brettas*[1] 'In this year H. and A. fought against the Britons'. Of course, in OE, where the distinction between the nominative and accusative is not always preserved, freedom sometimes lead to ambiguity, e.g. *Đas seofon hi gecuron* ..., where only the context tells us that *hī* is the subject. In MnE 'these seven they chose' is unambiguous because of 'they' and because, while the order O.S.V. is possible, the order S.O.V. is not.

[1] 7 is a common MS abbreviation for *ond* which is often reproduced by editors.

II SENTENCE STRUCTURE

Three difficulties in sentence structure must now be discussed.

Recapitulation and Anticipation

§148 The first is this. In their attempts to explain complicated ideas, Anglo-Saxon writers often had recourse to a device similar to that used by some modern politician who has the desire but not the ability to be an orator, viz. the device of pausing in mid-sentence and starting afresh with a pronoun or some group of words which sums up what has gone before. A simple example will be found in Alfred's Preface to the translation of the *Cura Pastoralis*. Alfred, having written (or dictated) *Ure ieldran, ða ðe ðas stowa ær hioldon* 'Our ancestors who previously occupied these places' pauses as it were for thought and then goes on *hie lufodon wisdom* 'they loved wisdom', where *hīe* sums up what has gone before and enables him to control the sentence. Compare with this the orator's gesture-accompanied 'all these things' with which he attempts to regain control of a sentence which has run away from him. Other examples of recapitulatory pronouns will be found in *7 þæt unstille hweol ðe Ixion wæs to gebunden, Leuita cyning, for his scylde, ðæt oðstod for his hearpunga. 7 Tantalus se cyning ðe on ðisse worulde ungemetlice gifre wæs, 7 him ðær ðæt ilce yfel filgde ðære gifernesse, he gestilde* 'And the ever-moving wheel to which Ixion, King of the Lapithae, was bound for his sin, [that] stood still for his (Orpheus's) harping. And King Tantalus, who in this world was greedy beyond measure and whom that same sin of greed followed there, [he] had rest'. More complicated examples will be found in *hergode he his rice, þone ilcan ende þe Æþered his cumpæder healdan sceolde* 'He (Hæsten) ravaged his (Alfred's) kingdom, that same province which Æthered, his son's godfather, had the duty of holding', where *his rīċe* is qualified by the rest of the sentence, and in the second passage discussed in §172.

The common use of a pronoun to anticipate a noun clause may be compared with this. A simple example is

þa þæt Offan mæg ærest onfunde,
þæt se eorl nolde yrhðo geþolian

lit. 'Then the kinsman of Offa first learned that thing (the first *þæt*), that the leader would not tolerate slackness'. We have perhaps all had this experience at the hand of some leader, but MnE would dispense with the tautologic *þæt* in giving it expression. In *þæs ic gewilnige and gewysce mid mode, þæt ic ana ne belife æfter minum leofum þegnum* lit. 'That thing I desire and wish in my mind, that I should not remain alone after my beloved thanes', the pronoun *þæs* anticipates the following *þæt* clause. It is in the genitive after the verbs *ġewilnian* and *ġewyscan*. The pronoun *hit* is sometimes found similarly used, e.g.

þæt is micel wundor
þæt hit ece God æfre wolde
þeoden þolian, þæt wurde þegn swa monig
forlædd be þam lygenum. . . .

Here the first *þæt* is in apposition with the *þæt* clause in l.2 while *hit* anticipates the *þæt* clause in l.3: lit. 'That is a great wonder that eternal God the Lord would ever permit it, that so many a thane should be deceived by those lies'. Dependent questions may be similarly anticipated, e.g. *Men þa þæs wundrodon, hu þa weargas hangodon* lit. 'Men then wondered at that, how the criminals hung' (where *þæs* is genitive after *wundrodon*) and

Hycgað his ealle,
hu ge hi beswicen

lit. 'All [of you] take thought about it, how you may deceive them' (where *his* is genitive after *hycgað*).

Note
It is possible that in the sentence 'He said that he was ill', 'that' was originally a demonstrative – 'He said that: he was ill' – which gradually became a part of the noun clause. If so, the introduction of the second *þæt* or of *hit* illustrates clearly the difficulty our ancestors seem to have had in collecting and expressing complicated thoughts.

The Splitting of Heavy Groups

§149 The second thing which sometimes helps to make OE seem a foreign language is a tendency to split up heavy groups. Thus we say today 'The President and his wife are going to Washington'. But the more common OE arrangement was 'The President is going to Washington, and his wife'. Examples of this tendency are common. We find

1 A divided subject in *eower mod is awend, and eower andwlita* 'your mind and your countenance are changed'. Note here the word-order S.V. and the singular verb; cf. MnE 'Tom was there and Jack and Bill and all the boys'.
2 A divided object in *þa he þone cniht agef 7 þæt wif* 'when he returned the child and the woman'.
3 A divided genitive group in *Inwæres broþur 7 Healfdenes* 'the brother of I. and H.'.
4 Divided phrases in *þa þe in Norþhymbrum bugeað ond on East Englum* 'those who dwell in Northumbria and East Anglia'.
5 Separation of adjectives governing the same noun in *þæt hi næfre ær swa clæne gold, ne swa read ne gesawon* 'that they never before saw such pure, red gold'.

But such groups are not always divided, e.g. *Her Hengest 7 Horsa fuhton wiþ Wyrtgeorne þam cyninge* 'In this year, H. and H. fought against King W.'.

Correlation

§150 The third thing which makes us feel that OE is a foreign language is its marked fondness for correlation. This may have its origin in, and so be a more sophisticated manifestation of, the same feeling of insecurity in the face of the complicated sentence which produced the awkward repetitions already discussed. But it later becomes a very important stylistic device which such an outstanding writer as Ælfric exploited to the full. Consider the following sentence from his Homily on the Passion of St. Stephen: *þider ðe Stephanus forestop, mid Saules stanum oftorfod, þider folgode Paulus, gefultumod þurh Stephanes gebedu* 'Where Stephen went in front, stoned by the stones of Saul, there Paul followed, helped by the prayers of Stephen'. Note:

1 that both the principal and subordinate clause contain the same elements;

2 the word-order S.V. in the subordinate clause *þider ðe Stephanus forestop* and V.S. in the principal clause *þider folgode Paulus*. This is regular OE (see §151) but produces a chiasmus;

3 that the word-order 'prepositional phrase + participle' in the first clause is reversed in the second. Again, both are good OE, but the change produces another chiasmus;

4 the change from *Saules* to *Paulus* – a sermon in itself.

It is (we can say) certain beyond all doubt that Ælfric was influenced by Latin prose style; it is hard to see how it could have been otherwise. But it is equally important to realize that this powerful and moving sentence – parallel yet doubly chiastic and with the effective contrast between Saul and Paul – contains nothing which is not 'good Old English'. It follows therefore that we must avoid the tendency (often found in critics of Milton's *Paradise Lost*) to rush around slapping the label 'Latinism' on anything which deviates in the slightest from our preconceived notions of the norms of ordinary speech.

§151 Much of the difficulty with correlative pairs arises from the fact that (with a few exceptions such as *ġif*... *þonne* 'if ... then') the conjunction and the adverb have the same form, e.g. *þā* can mean both 'when' and 'then'. For the interrogatives (with the possible exception of *hwonne* 'when, until') were not used to introduce adjective or adverb clauses in OE; see §159 n. 2. Sometimes the indeclinable particle *þe* is added to the conjunction, e.g. in the passage discussed in §150 *þider ðe* means 'whither' and *þider* 'thither'. But this is by no means the rule. Sometimes the context helps, e.g. we can safely translate *þa se cyng þæt hierde, þa wende he hine west* as 'When the king heard that, then he turned (reflexive) west'. But the word-order is an even more useful and reliable guide, for it may be taken as a pretty safe rule for prose that, when one of two correlative *þā* clauses has the word-order V.S., it must be the principal clause and *þā* must mean 'then'. The temporal clause introduced by *þā* 'when' may have the order S. ... V., e.g. *þa he on lichoman wæs* 'when he was in the flesh', or S.V., e.g. *þa þunor ofslog XXIIII heora fodrera* 'when thunder killed twenty-four of their foragers'. The adverb *þā* may be repeated within the subordinate clause, e.g. *þa he þæt þa sumre tide dyde* 'when he did that on one particular occasion', where it need not of course be translated. Doubled *þā*, as in *ða þa seo boc com to us* 'when the book came to us' and *þa þa Dunstan geong man wæs* 'when Dunstan was a young man' usually introduces a subordinate clause, as the word-order in these examples testifies. Ælfric is very fond of this device.

§152 Other correlative pairs with which we can use word-order to determine which of the clauses is principal are

þonne . . . þonne 'when . . . then'
þǣr . . . þǣr 'where . . . there'
þider . . . þider 'whither . . . thither'

On the distinction between *þā* and *þonne*, see §168, s.v. *þonne*.

Note
Correlative pairs to which this rule does not regularly apply include: *ǣr . . . ǣr, nū . . . nū, siþþan . . . siþþan, swā . . . swā, þanon . . . þanon, þēah . . . þēah*; on these, see §168. *þēah . . . hwæþre* 'though . . . yet' and *ġif . . . þonne* 'if . . . then' present no problems. It should also be noted that the word-order S.V. often occurs after adverbs other than those discussed above; see §147 for an example after *Hēr*, and note *nu todæg hi underfengon Stephanum* 'now today they received Stephen' and *On deaðe he wæs gesett . . .* 'he was placed in death . . .'. S.V. seems to be more common in such sentences when the subject is an unstressed pronoun, as in the last two examples, but often occurs with a noun subject, as in the example in §147. Compare §144.2.

Exceptions to the rule do exist. But you should view with suspicion any you meet, for the punctuation of some modern editions is sometimes at fault. Remember, however, that the rule does not apply to the poetry and that correlation is not essential, e.g.

> þa he þa wið þone here þær wæst abisgod wæs, 7 þa hergas wæron þa gegaderode begen to Sceobyrig on Eastseaxum, 7 þær geweorc worhtun, foron begen ætgædere up be Temese

'When he was occupied against the army there in the west, and the [other] Danish armies were assembled at Shoebury in Essex, and had made a fortress there, they both went together up along the Thames'.

§153 The value of this rule can be demonstrated from the following complicated passage in the Old English version of Bede's account of the poet Cædmon (selection 9, paragraph 2):

> Ond he for þon oft in gebeorscipe, þonne þær wæs blisse intinga gedemed, þæt heo ealle sceolden þurh endebyrdnesse be hearpan singan, þonne he geseah þa hearpan him nealecan, þonne aras he for scome from

þæm symble ond ham eode to his huse. þa he þæt þa sumre tide dyde, þæt he forlet þæt hus þæs gebeorscipes ond ut wæs gongende to neata scipene, þara heord him wæs þære neahte beboden, þa he ða þær in gelimplicre tide his leomu on reste gesette ond onslepte, þa stod him sum mon æt þurh swefn ond hine halette ond grette ond hine be his noman nemnde.

We can begin by underlining the verbs in the second sentence: *dyde, forlēt . . . ond ūt wæs gongende, wæs . . . beboden, ġesette ond onslēpte, stōd . . . ond . . . hālette . . . ond grētte . . . ond nemnde*. Now the corresponding conjunctions for these five verbs or groups of verbs are *þā . . . þā, þæt, þāra, þā . . . ðā*, and *þā. þæt* introduces a noun clause (§155) and *þāra* an adjective clause (§162). From our word-order rule, we know that '*þā* subject *þā*' introduces a subordinate clause, '*þā* V.S.' a principal clause. Hence the last *þā* means 'then', the syntax of the sentence is clear, and we can translate fairly literally: 'When he did that on one particular occasion, namely left the feast-hall and went out to the stall of the cattle, the care of which had been entrusted to him for that night [and] when in due time he stretched his limbs on the bed there and fell asleep, then a certain man appeared to him in a dream and saluted him and greeted him and called upon him by name'.

Similarly, in the first sentence, we have three *þonne* clauses, viz. *þonne þǣr wæs . . . , þonne hē geseah . . . þonne ārās hē. . . .* The rule instantly tells us that the last is the principal clause 'then he arose . . .'.

III NOUN CLAUSES

Introduction

§154 This heading traditionally comprehends dependent statements, desires (commands, wishes, etc.), questions, and exclamations. The OE patterns conform very closely to those of MnE, apart from the use of *þæt* and *hit* to anticipate a noun clause (see §148).

Dependent Statements and Desires

§155 Dependent statements are introduced by *þæt*, e.g. *ða ðohte he ðæt he wolde gesecan helle godu* 'then he thought that he would seek the gods of hell', or *þætte* (= *þæt þe*), e.g. *ic wene ðætte noht monige begiondan Humbre næren* 'I believe that there were not many beyond the Humber'. *þæt*(*te*) is sometimes repeated, as in the second sentence discussed in §172, and is sometimes not expressed, e.g. *Swa ic wat he minne hige cuðe* 'So I know he perceived my intention'.

Dependent desires are also introduced by *þæt*, e.g. *bæd þæt hyra randas rihte heoldon* 'requested that they should hold their shields properly', or *þætte*.

þæt clauses are, however, more common in OE than their equivalent in MnE, for they are often found where we should use an accusative and infinitive (as in the last example, where we should say 'requested them to hold their shields properly') or some other construction.

§156 The verb of the *þæt* clause may be indicative or subjunctive. Two questions arise – first, 'What is the significance of the two moods?' and second 'When must the subjunctive be represented in translation?' The first is usually answered in some such way as this:

The *indicative* is used when the content of the noun clause is presented as a fact, as certain, as true, or as a result which has actually followed or will follow.

When the *subjunctive* occurs, some mental attitude towards the content of the noun clause is usually implied; one of the following ideas may be present – condition, desire, obligation, supposition, perplexity, doubt, uncertainty, or unreality.

There is some truth in this. Thus the subjunctive is the natural mood in dependent desires, e.g. *ic ðe bebiode ðæt ðu do* . . . 'I command that you do . . .'. But the indicative sometimes occurs after verbs of commanding, compelling, and the like, e.g. *he bebead Tituse his suna þæt he towearp þæt templ* and *and ðurh ðine halige miht tunglu genedest þæt hi ðe to herað*. Here the indicative emphasizes that the action desired actually took place; hence the translations might read 'Titus carried out his father's command and destroyed the temple' and 'through your holy power you compel the stars to worship you'. These and similar clauses could be called result clauses or noun clauses with the indicative showing that the event actually took place. But 'a rose by any other name . . .'.

Similarly, in dependent statements, the indicative shows that the speaker is certain of the factuality of what he says and is vouching for its truth, e.g. *ic wat þæt þu eart heard mann* 'I know that you are a hard man', . . . *ðe cyðan* . . . *ðæt me com swiðe oft on gemynd* . . . 'to make known to you that it has often come into my mind . . .', and *þonne wite he þæt God gesceop to mæran engle þone þe nu is deofol* 'let him know therefore that God created as a great angel the creature who is now the devil'. But the subjunctive appears when no certainty is implied about a happening in the future, e.g. *Hit wæs gewitegod þæt he on ðære byrig Bethleem acenned wurde* 'It was prophesied that He should be born in the city of Bethlehem', when the truth of another's statement is not vouched for, e.g. *Be þæm Theuhaleon wæs gecweden . . . þæt he wære moncynnes tydriend, swa swa Noe wæs* 'About that Deucalion it was said that he was the father of mankind, as Noah was', or when it is denied, e.g. *Nu cwædon gedwolmen þæt deofol gesceope sume gesceafta, ac hi leogað* 'Now heretics said that some creations were the work of the devil but they lie'. This distinction between the indicative and the subjunctive is seen clearly in *Ne sæde þæt halige godspel þæt se rica reafere wære, ac wæs uncystig and modegode on his welum* 'The holy gospel did not say that the rich man was a robber, but that he was mean and exulted in his wealth'.

However, the rule does not tell the whole truth. The indicative does not always state a fact, e.g. *And gif hit gelimpþ þæt he hit fint* 'And if it happens that he finds it', nor does the subjunctive always imply uncertainty, doubt, or the like, e.g. *Mine gebroðra, uton we geoffrian urum Drihtne gold, þæt we andettan þæt he soð Cyning sy, and æghwær rixige* 'My brothers, let us offer our Lord gold, that we may confess that He is [the] true King and rules everywhere'; they all believe this. Again, in *Se wisa Augustinus . . . smeade hwi se halga cyðere Stephanus cwæde þæt he gesawe mannes bearn standan æt Godes swyðran* 'The wise Augustine . . . enquired why the holy martyr Stephen said that he saw the Son of Man standing at God's right hand', the subjunctive *gesāwe* does not mean that Augustine is casting doubt on Stephen's statement; it is probably due in part to the 'attraction' of the subjunctive form *cwǣde* and in part to the influence of the verb *cweðan* itself. For, when introducing a dependent statement, *cweðan* prefers the subjunctive, *cȳðan* the indicative. This may reflect some original difference in meaning such as 'I (think and) give it as my opinion' as against a more objective 'I (know and) make it known'. Perhaps originally *cweðan* always had the subjunctive and *cȳðan* the indicative, and perhaps this situation would have continued if language were always a strictly logical activity in which verbs of thinking took the subjunctive and verbs of knowing the indicative. But it is not. We tend to say 'I think he may come' and 'I know he will come'. But 'I know he may be here in ten minutes, but I can't wait' and 'I think that he is without doubt the cleverest boy in the school' show that no hard and fast rules can be laid down. Each situation must be judged on its merits.

Hence we may say that, while the rule set out above often works, fluctuation between the subjunctive and the indicative in OE noun clauses is often of little significance. It is just as dangerous to place too much reliance on the presence of a subjunctive in OE as it would be to draw firm conclusions about a modern speaker's attitude from the fact that he started his sentence with 'I know that . . .' rather than 'I think that . . .'.

So the answer to our second question 'When must the subjunctive be represented in translation?' can only be something indefinite like 'When the situation demands it'. It is, for example, unnecessary to bring out the fact that a verb of denying or supposing is followed by a subjunctive referring to some past act, for the verb 'to deny' or 'to suppose' is in itself enough to give a modern reader the necessary information. The subjunctive which will be most frequently represented in MnE is that in which some doubt or uncertainty arises over an action which, at the time of speaking, is still in the future. Such a subjunctive, of course, occurs most commonly in dependent desires.

Dependent Questions

§157 Questions fall into two main divisions – those in which the questioner seeks new information, e.g. *Hwær eart þu?* 'Where are you?' and *Hwy stande ge ealne dæg idele?* 'Why do you stand all day idle?', and those in which he asks his hearer to choose between alternatives expressed or implied in the question, e.g. *'Wilt þu we gað and gadriað hie?' Đa cwæð he: 'Nese'* ' "Do you wish us to go and gather them?" And he answered "No".' [But he could have answered 'Yes'.] Rhetorical questions may, of course, be of either type.

§158 Those questions which seek new information present little difficulty. The dependent question will include the interrogative word of the non-dependent question. This may be a pronoun (e.g. *hwā* 'who' and *hwæt* 'what'), an adjective (e.g. *hwelċ* 'which, what sort of'), or an adverb (e.g. *hū* 'how' and *hwǣr* 'where'). Other common adverbs are *hwider* 'whither', *hwanon* 'whence', *hwonne* 'when' (see §159 n. 2), *hwȳ* and *hwæt* 'why', and combinations of a preposition + an oblique case of *hwæt*, e.g. *tō hwæs* 'whither', *for hwon* and *for hwȳ* 'why'. These questions may be anticipated by a demonstrative or personal pronoun; see §148.

Note
Some of these interrogative words can also be used indefinitely, e.g. *hwā* can mean 'someone, anyone' and *hwǣr* 'somewhere, anywhere'.

§159 In MnE many of these interrogative words can also be used as relative pronouns, e.g. 'The man who . . .', 'The place where . . .', and so on. This use seems to stem (in part at least) from OE sentences of the type 'I know you, what you are' and 'Consider the lilies of the field, how they flourish', in which the main verb has as objects both a noun (or pronoun) and a clause containing a dependent question. A convenient OE example is a possible reading of *The Wanderer* ll. 23b–27

ond ic hean þonan
wod wintercearig ofer waþema gebind,
sohte sele dreorig sinces bryttan,
hwær ic feor oþþe neah findan meahte
þone þe in meoduhealle mine wisse

'and I, miserable, with winter in my heart, made my way thence over the frozen expanse of the waves, sadly seeking the hall of a giver of treasure, [sadly seeking] far and near where I might find one who in the mead-hall might know of my origins'.

Here the two objects of *sōhte* are *sele* and the *hwær* clause.

Note 1
The first object of *sōhte* is *sinces bryttan* in our text (piece 16), where the attractive compound *seledrēoriġ* 'sad for a hall' is accepted. But the fact that this interpretation is possible emphasizes that the *hwǣr* clause is interrogative, not adjective. It could not qualify *bryttan*.

Similarly in

> Ne meahte hire Iudas . . .
> sweotole gecyþan be ðam sigebeame
> on hwylcne se hælend ahafen wære

hwylċne is strictly an interrogative introducing a noun clause, object of *gecȳþan*, and the literal sense is 'Nor could Judas . . . tell her beyond doubt about the victorious tree, [tell her] on which tree the Saviour was raised up'.[1] It is easy to see how such juxtaposition of noun and interrogative would lead to the use of the interrogative as a relative. But this stage has not been reached in OE.

Note 2
Hwonne 'when, until' is perhaps furthest advanced of all the OE interrogatives on the way to becoming a word which could introduce adverb and adjective clauses. Those who are interested may care to look at the ways in which *hwonne* is used in the following examples: *Andreas* l. 136 (noun clause); *Riddle* 31 l. 13 (adjective clause); *Genesis* l. 2603 (adverb clause of time 'when'); *Genesis* l. 1028 (adverb clause of time 'whenever'); and *Andreas* l. 400 (adverb clause of time 'until'). I have put in brackets the interpretation which seems to offer the most convenient translation. But careful consideration will show that an Anglo-Saxon might have regarded all these as noun clauses – if he ever thought about it.

§160 Non-dependent questions inviting a choice between alternatives can be asked in two ways in OE:

1 by the word-order V.S. (as in MnE) – for examples see §§146.1 and 146.2;

2 with *hwæþer* (*þe*) and the word-order S. . . . V., e.g. *Hwæþer þe þin eage manful is?* 'Is your eye evil?', or S.V., e.g. *Hwæðer ic mote lybban oðþæt ic hine geseo?* 'May I live until I see him?'

As in MnE, dependent questions of this type are normally introduced by an interrogative word – either *hwæþer* 'whether', e.g. *Lætaþ þæt we geseon hwæðer Elias cume* 'Let us see whether E. comes', or *ġif* 'if', e.g. *frægn gif him wære niht getæse* 'asked if the night had been pleasant to him'. An occasional example like 'He asked was anybody there' occurs (e.g. *Elene* ll. 157 ff.); in these the original word-order is retained but the tense has been changed.

In the examples cited above, the alternative 'or not' is implied. But it is occasionally expressed, e.g. *Anra gehwylc wat gif he beswuncgen wæs oððe na*

[1] The OE relative construction occurs in

> . . . ond geflitu ræran
> be ðam sigebeame on þam soðcyning
> ahangen wæs . . .

'to stir up controversy about the victorious tree on which the true King was crucified . . .'. Note the difference in mood – *wǣre* above but *wæs* here.

'Each man knows whether he was beaten, or not'. An unusual example of the type of question under discussion here occurs in *Genesis* ll. 531 ff., where the conjunctions are *þēah . . . þe* 'whether . . . or'.

The remarks made about mood in dependent statements also apply in general to dependent questions.

The Accusative and Infinitive

§161 This construction, well known in Latin, e.g. *Solon furere se simulavit* 'Solon pretended to be mad', and in MnE, e.g. 'I know him to be dead', is also an OE idiom. The subject accusative may be expressed, as in

> Het þa hyssa hwæne   hors forlætan,
> feor afysan,   and forð gangan

'He then ordered each of the warriors to release his horse [and] drive it away, and to go forth', but is often left unexpressed, as in *ond ðe cyðan hate* lit. 'I order [someone] to make known to you . . .', and *he het hi hon on heam gealgum* lit. 'he ordered [someone] to hang them on the high gallows' (where *hīe* is the object of *hōn*). In the last two examples, the subject accusative is not expressed, either because everybody knows or because nobody cares who is to perform the action. In these, it is very convenient to translate the infinitives *cȳðan* and *hōn* as if they were passive – 'I order you to be told' (or '. . . that you be told . . .') and 'he ordered them to be hanged'. Much time has been spent in idle controversy over the question whether these infinitives were actually passive; what is important is that, when the subject accusative of the accusative and infinitive is not expressed, the active infinitive can usually be *translated* as a passive.

IV ADJECTIVE CLAUSES

Definite Adjective Clauses

§162 Definite adjective clauses are those which refer to one particular antecedent, e.g. 'This is the man *who did it*' as opposed to indefinite clauses whose antecedent is unspecified, e.g. '*Whoever did it* will be caught'. As in Latin, the relative pronoun agrees with its antecedent (expressed or implied) in number and gender, but takes its case from the adjective clause. There are various ways of expressing it in OE.

1 The indeclinable particle *þe* is very common when the relative is the subject, e.g. *Ic geseah þa englas þe eower gymdon* 'I saw the angels who took care of you', *ælc þæra þe ðas min word gehyrð* 'each of those who hears these my words', and *swa swa hit gewunelic is þæm ðe on wuda gað oft* 'as is customary among those who frequently go in the wood'. It occurs fairly often when the

relative is the object, e.g. *her onginneð seo boc þe man Orosius nemneð* 'here begins the book which one calls Orosius'. It very occasionally functions as a relative in the genitive or dative. Examples are *of ðæm mere ðe Truso standeð in staðe* 'from the sea on whose shore Truso stands' and *oð ðone dæg þe hi hine forbærnað* 'until the day on which they burn him'.

2 In these last two examples, however, the case of the relative pronoun is not immediately clear because *þe* is indeclinable. So the appropriate case of the third person pronoun was sometimes added. Thus there is no ambiguity in *Eadig bið se wer, þe his tohopa bið to Drihtne* 'Blessed is the man whose hope is in the Lord' or in

þæt se mon ne wat
þe him on foldan fægrost limpeð

'That (object) the man for whom it goes very pleasantly on the earth does not know'.

Note
This combination sometimes occurs when the relative is nominative, e.g. *Paris Psalter* 67 l. 4 (*þe hē*) and, with first person pronouns, *Riddle* 12 l. 14 (*þe iċ*) and *Christ* l. 25 (*þe wē*). With the second person pronoun the regular combination is *þū þe* or *ġē þe*; see *The Review of English Studies* 15 (1964), 135–137.

3 The appropriate case of the demonstrative *se, sēo, þæt* is often used as a relative, e.g. *se hearpere, ðæs nama wæs Orfeus, hæfde an wif, seo wæs haten Eurydice* 'the harper, whose name was Orpheus, had a wife who was called Eurydice', *eall þæt ic geman* 'all that I remember', and *fif Moyses boca, ðam seo godcunde æ awriten is* 'five (of the) books of Moses in which the divine law is written'. Here there is no ambiguity about case and number, but we cannot always be sure whether the pronoun is demonstrative or relative.

4 But there is no ambiguity for us in sentences like . . . *and wæs se soþa Scyppend, seþe ana is God, forsewen* '. . . and the true Creator, who alone is God, was rejected', in which both antecedent and relative have the same case, for *þe* certifies that we have a relative pronoun and *se* tells us its case. This can be called the *seþe* relative. Again, there is no ambiguity for us in sentences like *þa com he on morgenne to þam tungerefan, se þe his ealdormon wæs* 'Then he came in the morning to the steward, who was his superior' and *þystre genip, þam þe se þeoden self sceop nihte naman* 'the cloud of darkness, for which the Lord Himself made the name "night" ', for the presence of the particle *þe* after *se* and *þām* makes it clear that we have to do with a relative pronoun, while *se* and *þām* tell us its case. This pattern, in which the *se* element has the case required by the adjective clause only, can be called the *'seþe* relative. In both these patterns, although the elements are written sometimes together, sometimes separately, by the scribes, the *se* element tells us the case of the relative pronoun.

Note
In the nominative, these combinations can mean 'he who' or 'the one who' or 'whoever'; cf. §164.

5 So far, then, we can say that the OE relatives are the indeclinable particle *þe*, to which the personal pronoun can be added to remove ambiguities of case, and the demonstrative pronoun *se, sēo, þæt* in the case required by the *adjective* clause, either alone or followed by the indeclinable particle *þe* to make clear that we have a relative and not a demonstrative pronoun.

§163 The comments which follow may be useful when you have mastered §162.

1 Another example of the *'seþe* type like those in §162.4 is

> Se wæs Hroþgare hæleþa leofost
> rice randwiga, þone ðe heo on ræste abreat

'That man was the most beloved of heroes to Hrothgar, a mighty shield-warrior whom she (the monster) killed in his resting-place'. But a word of warning is necessary here, because you are likely to meet sentences which seem to contain this combination, but do not. Thus in *gedo grenne finul XXX nihta on ænne croccan þone þe sie gepicod utan* 'put green fennel for thirty nights into a jar which is covered with pitch on the outside' and in

> syððan hie gefricgeað frean userne
> ealdorleasne, þone ðe ær geheold
> wið hettendum hord ond rice

'when they learn our lord to be dead, he who in the past guarded our treasure and kingdom against enemies', *þone þe* is not an accusative relative, for *þone* has the case of the *principal* clause agreeing with its antecedent. Formally, *þone* belongs to the principal clause and we can therefore say that the relative in these examples is *þe*. But they differ from the second and third sentences quoted in §162.1 (where the demonstrative is the only antecedent) in that there is already an antecedent and the demonstrative is therefore superfluous. In earlier times *þone* was no doubt stressed in such sentences – 'our lord . . . that one . . . he'. But there may be some truth in the view that in our sentences *þone* belonged rhythmically to the adjective clause and was felt as part of the relative; hence we can (if we wish) distinguish the relative in which the demonstrative has the case of the principal clause but is not the antecedent, as the *se'þe* relative. There is no real difficulty in the pattern seen in the *ðā ðe* clause in example B in §172, where the two clauses require different cases (acc./nom.) but where *ðā* can be either nominative or accusative. But you should be on the alert for examples of what is here called the *se'þe* type.

Notes

1 Examples in which real ambiguity occurs are rare. But there is one in *Beowulf* ll. 2291–93:

Swa mæg unfæge eaðe gedigan
wean and wræcsið se ðe Wealdendes
hyldo gehealdeþ.

If the relative pronoun is *se'þe, hyldo* (indeclinable feminine) is the subject of the adjective clause, *ðe* is accusative, and the translation would read 'So may an undoomed man whom the favour of the Almighty protects easily survive both woe and banishment'. If the relative pronoun is *seþe*, it is nominative, *hyldo* is accusative, and the translation would read 'So may an undoomed man who retains the favour of the Almighty . . .'.

2 Sometimes, when the relative pronoun is in a case other than the nominative, the personal pronoun follows a relative of the *se'þe* type. This enables us to tell immediately the case of the relative pronoun, e.g.

se biþ leofast londbuendum
se þe him God syleð gumena rice

'that one is most beloved by land-dwellers to whom God gives the kingdom of men' and *se, se þe him ær geþuhte þæt him nan sæ wiþhabban ne mehte þæt he hine mid scipum afyllan ne mehte, eft wæs biddende anes lytles troges æt anum earman men, þæt he mehte his feorh generian* 'he to whom it once had seemed that no sea was so great (lit. could stop him) that he could not fill it with ships, finally asked a wretched man for one little boat so that he could save his life'. See also *Dream of the Rood* ll. 85–6.

2 A not uncommon idiom is found in the sentence about Tantalus quoted in §148. The antecedent *Tantulus* is followed by two adjective clauses joined by *ond*. In the first, *ðe . . . gīfre wæs*, the relative pronoun is nominative. The second is *him . . . ðǣre gīfernesse*. Here the relative pronoun is [*þe*] *him* 'whom'. But it is idiomatic not to repeat the *þe*; *him* warns us of the change of case from nominative to dative.

Another idiom is found in

Nis nu cwicra nan
þe ic him modsefan minne durre
sweotule asecgan.

Here the antecedent is *nān cwicra*. The relative pronoun is *þe him. Iċ* is the subject of the adjective clause. So we have 'There is no one alive to whom I dare reveal my thoughts'. When the relative pronoun is *þe* + personal pronoun and another pronoun is the subject of the adjective clause, the latter comes between the two elements of the relative. So *þe iċ him*.

3 The indeclinable relative *þe* always precedes any preposition which governs it; see the sentence about Ixion quoted in §148.

4 The adjective clause need not immediately follow the antecedent.

5 *Þæt* often combines antecedent and relative pronoun. It must then be translated 'what', e.g. *he hæfde ðeah geforþod þæt he his frean gehet* 'he had, however, done what he promised his lord'. This survived into eMnE, e.g. in the Authorized Version *John* 13:27 'That thou doest, do quickly'. In

gode þancode
mihtigan drihtne, þæs se man gespræc,

þæs is genitive after *þancode* and we might expect *þe*: 'thanked God for that which the man spoke'. But this is probably an example of *þæt* 'what' – 'thanked God, the mighty Lord, for what the man spoke'.

6 In MnE the difficulty of combining an adjective clause and a verb of saying or thinking often produces a 'grammatical error', e.g. 'This is the man whom they thought would revolutionize the teaching of English' where we should have '. . . who, they thought, . . .'. The same problem arises in OE and often results in what seems to us a somewhat incoherent arrangement, e.g. *Đa eode he furður oð he gemette ða graman gydena ðe folcisce men hatað Parcas, ða hi secgað ðæt on nanum men nyton nane are, ac ælcum men wrecen be his gewyrhtum; þa hi secgað ðæt walden ælces mannes wyrde* 'Then he went on further until he met the terrible goddesses whom the people of that land call the Parcae, who (they say) show no mercy to any man, but punish each man according to his deserts; these (they say) control each man's fate'. A result acceptable in MnE can be obtained in these examples by omitting the *ðæt*. Sometimes, however, the subject is expressed twice, e.g. *in þære cirican seo cwen gewunade hire gebiddan, þe we ær cwædon þæt heo Cristen wære*. Here we need to omit *þæt hēo* to get the sense: 'in that church the queen who, we said formerly, was Christian, was wont to say her prayers'. But even this is clumsy and needs polishing.

7 Attempts have been made to lay down the rules which governed the use of the various relative pronouns in OE. They have not succeeded, largely because the vital clue of intonation is denied to us.

Indefinite Adjective Clauses

§164 The relative pronouns used in definite adjective clauses also appear in the indefinite ones, e.g.

þa wæs eaðfynde þe him elles hwær
gerumlicor ræste sohte

'Then it was easy to find whoever (= the man who) sought a bed for himself elsewhere, further away',

heold hyne syðþan
fyr ond fæstor se þæm feonde ætwand

'thereafter kept himself further away and in greater safety whoever escaped the enemy', *sægde se þe cuþe* . . . 'he who knew said . . .' (the *seþe* relative; see §162.4), and *Se þe gewemð Godes tempel, God hine fordeð* 'Whoever defiles God's temple, God will destroy him' (the *'seþe* relative; see again §162.4).

As has already been noted, the interrogatives *hwā* 'who', *hwǣr* 'where', and the like, are not used alone in OE as relatives; see §159. But they are used in the indefinite relatives *swā hwā swā* 'whoever', *swā hwæt swā* 'whatever', *swā hwǣr swā* 'wherever', and so on. One example will suffice – *swa hwa swa þe genyt þusend stapa, ga mid him oðre twa þusend* 'whoever compels thee [to go] one mile, go with him two'.

Mood

§165 The adjective clause usually has its verb in the indicative, even when it is in dependent speech. But the subjunctive may occur in the following situations:

1 When the principal clause contains an imperative or a subjunctive expressing a wish, e.g. *Matthew* 5: 42 *syle þam ðe þe bidde* Authorized Version 'Give to him that asketh thee'. However, the fact that the indicative is found in such circumstances, e.g. *Matthew* 19: 21 *becyp eall þæt þu ahst* Authorized Version 'sell that thou hast', shows that the mood varies with the speaker's attitude and not with any automatic 'law of symmetry'. In the first example, there is uncertainty because the asker is as yet unknown and indeed may not exist; we could translate 'Give to anyone who may ask'. In the second, the young man's possessions exist and are known to him. For, as the story tells us, 'he went away sorrowful, for he had great possessions'.

2 When the principal clause contains a negative, e.g. the second sentence discussed in §163.2. But this again is no automatic rule. The subjunctive is found only when the content of the adjective clause is put forward as unreal; in the example, there is no such person in existence nor probably could there be. But in *Beowulf* ll. 1465–7

Huru ne gemunde mago Ecglafes
eafoþes cræftig, þæt he ær gespræc
wine druncen

'However, the son of Ecglaf, powerful in his might, did not remember what he had said before, when drunk with wine', Unferth (*mago Ecglāfes*) actually had spoken the words, but he did not now remember them; the poet could have said that he had forgotten them. In this example, the *ne* negates merely the verb of the principal clause, not the whole idea which follows; hence the indicative in the adjective clause.

3 When the principal clause contains a rhetorical question, e.g.

Hwa is on eorðan nu unlærdra
þe ne wundrige wolcna færeldes . . . ?

'Who is there on earth among the unlearned who does not wonder at the motion of the clouds . . . ?' The answer demanded is, of course, 'No-one'. Such examples are exactly parallel to those discussed in 2 above, for the poet could easily have said 'There is no-one on earth . . .'.

4 When a limiting adjective clause[1] has as antecedent a genitive depending on a superlative, e.g.

> Niwe flodas Noe oferlað,
> . . .
> þone deopestan drencefloda
> þara ðe gewurde on woruldrice.

Here the poet is saying that Noah sailed over the deepest deluge that could ever be or have been. Similar examples occur in *Beowulf* ll. 2129 ff., *Genesis* ll. 626 ff., and *Daniel* ll. 691 ff. In these the subjunctive is used to imply that all the possible examples of floods, griefs, women, and cities, respectively are being considered – those which the writer knows about, those which have happened without his knowledge, and those which may yet happen. That the 'superlative + genitive' does not automatically cause the subjunctive is shown by examples like

> . . . ond hi þa gesette on þone selestan
> foldan sceata, þone fira bearn
> nemnað neorxnawong . . .

'and then he placed them in the best regions of the earth, which the sons of men call Paradise', where the non-limiting adjective clause has the indicative.

V ADVERB CLAUSES

Introduction

§166 The conventional classification will serve us here. It distinguishes eight types – place, time, purpose, result, cause, comparison, concession, condition. On the whole, you will find that these clauses are fundamentally very similar to their counterparts in MnE. The main differences to be noted are:

1 the conjunctions themselves;
2 the methods of correlation, linked with
3 the word-order within the clauses. On these two points, see §§150–153;
4 a more frequent use of the subjunctive mood. Sometimes it is used by rule and is of little significance for us, sometimes it makes an important distinction. On this, see §§173–180.

§§167–171 contain a discussion of the conjunctions and alphabetical lists

[1] In the sentence 'The soldiers who (that) were tired lay down' the adjective clause does not merely describe the soldiers; it limits the action of lying down to a particular group – those who were tired. Hence it is a 'limiting' clause. But in 'The soldiers, who were tired, lay down' the adjective clause merely tells us something more about all the soldiers. Hence it is 'non-limiting'.

of non-prepositional and prepositional formulae with their main uses. §§173–180 discuss each type of clause in turn, outlining briefly the conjunctions and moods used in them and any other points of special interest.

§167 If we adopt a purely formal classification, we can detect in MnE at least five types of conjunction. Consider the following series of clauses:

1 Christ died, *that* we may live.
2 Christ died, *so that* we may live.
3 *So* boldly did Christ speak, *that* all men listened.
4
5
6 Christ died, *to the end that* we may live.
7 *To this end* Christ died, *that* we may live.

In OE, we can find comparable examples to these and can fill in the missing items 4 and 5:

1 *... he biþ geseald hæþnum mannum þæt hie hine bysmrian* '... he will be given to heathen men that they may mock him'.

2 *Hæfde se cyning his fierd on tu tonumen, swa þæt hie wæron simle healfe æt ham, healfe ute* 'The king had divided his army into two, so that at any one time half were at home, half in the field'.

3 *He ... swa anræd þurhwunode þæt he nolde abugan to bismorfullum leahtrum* 'he ... remained so resolute that he was unwilling to turn aside to shameful sins'.

4 *... ond ðæs ðe ðu gearo forwite hwam ðu gemiltsige, ic eom Apollonius, se Tyrisca ealdormann* '... and, so that you may know who is receiving your mercy, I am Apollonius, Prince of Tyre'.

Note: This use of *ðæs ðe* is a rare one, but it is included to complete the series.

5 *Ic wat þæt nan nis þæs welig þæt he sumes eacan ne þyrfe* 'I know that there is no man so wealthy that he does not need more of something'.

6 *And ic hyne nyste, ac ic com and fullode on wætere, to þam þæt he wære geswutelod on Israhela folce* 'And I knew him not, but I came and baptized [him] in water, to the end that he might be manifested to the people of Israel'.

7 [the Heavenly King] *þe to ði com on middangeard þæt he of eallum ðeodum his gecorenan gegaderode* ... '[the Heavenly King] who to this end came into the world that he might gather his chosen from all nations'.

So we find

	MnE	*OE*
1	'that'	*þæt*
2	'so that'	*swā þæt*
3	'so ... that'	*swā ... þæt*

4		*þæs þe*
5		*þæs . . . þæt*
6	'to the end that'	*tō þām þæt*
7	'to this end . . . that'	*tō þī . . . þæt*

On the variations *þe/þæt* in 4 and 5 and *þām/þī* in 6 and 7, see §169.

We can therefore speak of prepositional conjunctions (6 and 7) and non-prepositional conjunctions (1–5). We can speak of simple conjunctions (1), grouped conjunctions (2, 4, and 6), and divided conjunctions (3, 5, and 7). MnE has no exact equivalent for types 4 and 5. Their real force cannot be brought out literally today because *þæs* is the genitive of *þæt* used adverbially and we no longer have a genitive of 'that' to use in this way. So we must translate them either 'so that' and 'so . . . that', which brings out the adverbial force only, or 'to the end that' and 'to the end . . . that', which brings out the adverbial force and at the same time demonstrates the important truth that a good many functions of the OE cases have been taken over by MnE prepositions. Other examples of this type in OE include:

(*a*) *þȳ . . . þȳ* (the instrumental of *þæt*) in comparisons, the ancestor of MnE '*the* more, *the* merrier' (lit. 'by that much . . . by that much');

(*b*) *þā hwīle þe* 'while'; where we have an accusative of duration of time turned into a conjunction by the addition of the indeclinable particle *þe*;

(*c*) *þȳ lǣs* (*þe*) MnE 'lest'. On the use of *þe* in (*b*) and (*c*), see §169.

For practical purposes, the best grouping is a twofold one – non-prepositional conjunctions, simple, grouped and divided (i.e. items 1–5), and prepositional conjunctions or formulae, grouped and divided (items 6–7). The following sections contain separate alphabetical lists of the most important OE conjunctions in these two groups, with any comments necessary on their use. Examples are often given from poems you are likely to read.

Non-Prepositional Conjunctions

§168 (Note: The list mentions any adverbial and prepositional uses of the conjunctions discussed and any pronominal forms with which they may be confused.)

ǣr

1 Prep. 'before'. As prep. it also introduces prep. conjs. of time; see §171.

2 Adv. 'formerly'. Often a sign of the pluperfect; see §197.4.

3 Temporal conj. 'before'. Often takes the subj. But this need not be brought out in translation.

būtan, būton

1 Prep. 'without'.

2 Conj. 'except that, but' + ind.

3 Conj. 'unless, if not' + subj.

ġif

1 Conj. 'if, whether' introducing dependent questions.

2 Conj. 'if' introducing conditional clauses.

hwonne

Conj. 'when'. Originally an interrogative introducing questions, it shades into a temporal conj. 'when, until'; see §159 n. 2.

nefne, nemne, nymþe

The Anglian equivalent of *būton*; you will meet it mostly in the poetry, e.g. *Beowulf* l. 1552.

nō ðȳ ǣr

Adv. 'none the sooner, yet . . . not, not yet'. Not a conj.

nū

1 Adv. 'now'.

2 Conj. 'now that, because', often combining the ideas of time and cause; it takes the ind. and is not used when a false reason is given. It usually refers to a state in the present, e.g. (with present tense) *Maldon* l. 222 and (with preterite tense to be translated as perfect) *Maldon* l. 250. In the latter example, the state in the present is the result of an action completed in the past.

oð

1 Prep. 'until, up to' of time or place. As a prep. it also introduces prep. conjs. of time; see §171.

2 Conj. 'until' marking temporal and/or local limit.

sam . . . sam

Conj. 'whether . . . or' in concessive clauses.

siþþan

1 Adv. 'after'.

2 Conj. meaning

(*a*) *ex quo* 'since'.

(*b*) *postquam* 'after'.

(*c*) sometimes 'when, as soon as'.

swā

1 Adv. 'so, thus'. It usually refers back, but may anticipate what is to come.

2 Conj. alone and in combination. The following main uses can be distinguished:

(*a*) In indefinite combinations

in adjective clauses; see §164.

in clauses of place, e.g. *swā hwǣr swā* 'wherever' and *swā wīde swā* 'as widely as'.

in clauses of time, e.g. *swā hraþe swā* 'as quickly as', *swā lange swā* 'as long as', *swā oft swā* 'as often as', and (*swā*) *sōna swā* 'as soon as'.

(*b*) With the superlative
e.g. *swa ðu oftost mæge* 'as often as you can' and *swa hie selest mihton* 'as well as they could, as best they could'.

(*c*) In clauses of comparison
swā 'as'.
swā swā 'as, just as'.
swā . . . swā 'so . . . as, as . . . so'.
swā . . . swā swā 'so . . . as'.

(*d*) Other uses
swā + subj. often means 'as if', e.g. *Wanderer* l. 96.
swā can sometimes be translated 'as far as', e.g. *Elene* l. 971, or 'wherever', e.g. *Andreas* l. 1582.
swā can sometimes be translated 'because'.
swā sometimes means 'so that'.
Frequently it is 'a rather characterless connective, shading into concession, result, or manner, as the case may be, and, with the negative, corresponding to Modern English "without", "not being" ' e.g. *Hi fuhton fif dagas, swa hyra nan ne feol* 'They fought for five days without any of them falling'.

For *swā . . . swā* 'either . . . or', see §184.3.
With a comparative, *swā . . . swā* means 'the . . . the', e.g. *swa norðor swa smælre* 'the further north, the narrower'.

Note
swā is sometimes translated as a relative pronoun. This is misleading; see *The Review of English Studies* 15 (1964), 140.

swā þæt
Conj. 'so that' introducing result clauses. No unambiguous examples of purpose clauses after *swā þæt* have been noted. But the distinction is often a very fine one, e.g. *swa þæt he mehte ægþerne geræcan*, which might mean either 'was able to reach' or 'might reach'; see §§120 and 207.

swā . . . þæt
Conj. 'so . . . that'. Like its MnE equivalent, it usually introduces result clauses.

swelċe, swilċe, swylċe
1 It can be a form of the pron. *swelċ* 'such, such a one, such as, which'.
2 Conj. 'such as', e.g. *Beowulf* l. 757, where it would be *swylċne* if it were the pronoun. In *Dream of the Rood* l. 92 *swylċe swā* may be translated 'just as'.
Frequently we can not tell whether we have 1 or 2, e.g. *Seafarer* l. 83. This does not matter.
3 Adv. 'likewise, also'.

4 Conj. 'as if' with subj. or without verb, e.g. *swelce him to gamenes* 'as if in fun for them'.

5 Conj. 'because'.

þā

1 Acc. sg. fem. and nom. acc. pl. of *se*.

2 Adv. 'then'.

3 Conj. 'when'. Used only with pret. ind. of a single completed act in the past. For further explanation, see under *þonne*.

4 *þā . . . furþum* = Lat. *cum . . . primum* 'as soon as', e.g. *Beowulf* l. 465.

5 In *Maldon* l. 5 (quoted in §148) *þā . . . ǣrest* may mean 'as soon as'.

þā hwīle þe

Conj. 'as long as, while' (lit. 'during that time in which', i.e. acc. of duration of time + particle *þe*). It is found only eight times in the poetry, where *þenden* (an older word) is preferred for stylistic reasons. *The Battle of Maldon* contains four of these eight examples.

þanon

1 Adv. 'thence'.

2 Conj. 'whence'.

þǣr

1 Adv. of place 'there'. Sometimes it can be translated 'then'.

2 With *wæs*, equals MnE 'there was . . .', e.g. *Beowulf* l. 2105.

3 Conj. 'where', alone, doubled *þǣr þǣr*, or correlative *þǣr . . . þǣr*. (Sometimes it can be translated 'when' or 'because'.)

4 Conj. 'whither, to the place where', e.g. *Dream of the Rood* l. 139.

5 Conj. 'wherever', e.g. *Beowulf* l. 1394.

6 Conj. 'if', especially with pret. subj. of type 3 conditions (§179), e.g. *Beowulf* l. 2730.

7 Introducing a wish with subj. 'if only', e.g. *Metres of Boethius* 8 l. 39.

þæs

Gen. sg. neut. of *þæt* used as an adv.

1 of time 'from that, after'.

2 of extent or comparison 'to that extent, so'; see under *þæs (þe)*, *þæs . . . þe*, *þæs . . . þæt*.

þæs (þe)

1 Gen. sg. masc. or neut. of the relative pronoun; see §162.

2 Conj. of time 'when, after, since', sometimes shading into 'because'.

3 Comparative conj. 'as'.

4 After verbs like *þancian*, see §163.5.

þæs . . . þæt

Conj. 'so . . . that' introducing consecutive clauses, e.g. *Beowulf* ll. 1366–7 and *Seafarer* ll. 39 ff. *þæs . . . þæt* is commoner in the poetry; prose writers prefer *swā . . . þæt*.

Notes

1 The subject for the *þæt* clause in *Beowulf* l. 1367 is absent. Some take *þæt* as rel. pron. 'who'; this would be an early example of the use of *þæt* without regard to gender. Such absence of a subject is, however, idiomatic; see §193.7 and *Christ* ll. 241 ff. where *þæs ... þæs* is followed by *þe* in what may be an adjective or a consecutive clause. *Metres of Boethius* 28 contains examples of *þæt* and *þe* in clauses which seem the same. It is dangerous to say dogmatically that the former are consecutive clauses with unexpressed subjects, the latter adjective clauses. But this may have been the original situation.

2 In *Seafarer* ll. 39 ff. *þæs ... þæs* ... is paralleled by *tō þæs* (3 times); see §171.

þæs ... þe

See *þæs ... þæt*.

þæt

1 Neut. dem. and rel. pron. 'that, which, what'; see §§162 and 163.5.

2 Conj. introducing noun clauses; see §155.

3 Conj. 'so that' introducing:

(*a*) clauses of purpose with subj.

(*b*) clauses of result with ind. After verbs of motion, it can be translated 'until'.

(*c*) with ambiguous verb forms, clauses which may be either purpose or result. Often the context makes clear which it is.

4 Conj. introducing some local and temporal clauses where its use is idiomatic, as in MnE, e.g. *Beowulf* l. 1362 and *Maldon* l. 105.

þe

1 In texts which do not mark long vowels, *þe* = *þē* can be a spelling for *þȳ*.

2 Indeclinable rel. pron.; see §162.

3 Subordinating particle turning an adv. into a conj.; see §169.

4 *þēah ... þe* in *Genesis* ll. 531–2 = 'whether ... or'.

5 Conj. of time 'when', e.g. *Beowulf* l. 1000. This is not a common use.

6 Sometimes a comparative conj. 'as'; *Maldon* l. 190 is a possible example.

þēah, þēh

1 Adv. 'yet, however'.

2 Alone, or with *þe*, concessive conj. 'although', nearly always with the subj.

3 On *Genesis* l. 531 see s.v. *þe* 4.

þenden

1 Adv. 'meanwhile'.

2 Temporal conj. 'as long as, while'. See *þā hwīle þe* above.

þider

1 Adv. of place 'thither'.
2 Conj. of place 'whither'.

þon mā þe

Conj. 'more than', a rare alternative to a comparative + *þonne* in negative sentences. Its literal meaning is *mā* 'more' *þon* (inst. of *þæt* expressing comparison) 'than this' *þe* 'namely' (see §169).

þonne

1 Adv. of time 'then', frequently correlative with *ġif*.
2 Conj. of time 'when':
(*a*) with preterite tense, frequentative 'whenever'.
The difference between *þā* and *þonne* in the past is made clear by a study of the second paragraph of Bede's account of the poet Cædmon, which is quoted in §153. *þā* is used only of a single completed act in the past; note *þa he þæt sumre tide dyde* 'when he did that on one particular occasion'. *þonne* is frequentative 'whenever'; note *oft . . . þonne* 'often . . . whenever'. Cf. Modern German *als* and *wenn.*
(*b*) in the present and future 'whenever' in both senses:
(i) of a single act to be performed at some unknown time, e.g. *Beowulf* l. 3106.
(ii) 'whenever' frequentative of repeated acts, e.g. *Riddle* 7 l. 1.
As in MnE, the distinction is not always clear; cf. 'I'll see him whenever he comes' with *Beowulf* l. 23.
3 Comparative conj. 'than':
(*a*) with full clause following, e.g. *Maldon* l. 195.
(*b*) with contracted clause following, e.g. *Beowulf* l. 469.
(*c*) sometimes = 'than that' when two clauses are compared, e.g. *Maldon* ll. 31–33.

þȳ

1 Inst. of *þæt* in the combination *þȳ . . . þȳ* (lit. 'by that much . . . by that much') MnE 'the . . . the', e.g. *Maldon* ll. 312–13.

2 Alone, or in the combination *þȳ þe*, 'because', e.g. *Genesis* l. 2626 and *Daniel* l. 85.

þȳ lǣs (þe)

Conj. 'lest' introducing negative clauses of purpose, almost always with the subj.

Prepositional Conjunctions

§169 Basically these consist of a preposition + an oblique case of *þæt* (+ *þæt* or *þe*).

Note

The case used depends on the preposition. Thus, since *for* governs the dat. or inst., we find in the manuscripts *for þæm, for þam, for þan, for þon, for þy, for þi* – all variant spellings of the dat. or inst. (*ð* may appear instead of *þ* in any of these spellings.) The formulae are sometimes written together, e.g. *forþon*. In the discussions which follow, one particular form of the prepositional formula (such as *for þæm*) includes all these variant spellings unless the contrary is specifically stated. *To* sometimes governs the gen. instead of the dat. or inst.; so we find *to þæs* in addition to *to þæm* etc.

These conjunctions probably grew out of an originally adverbial use of a prepositional phrase such as occurs in *ond for ðon ic ðe bebiode ðæt ðu* . . . 'and for that (= 'therefore') I command you that you . . .' and in *for þan wearð her on felda folc totwæmed* . . . 'because of that the army here in the field was divided . . .'. Such phrases were then used as conjunctions by the addition of *þe* or *þæt* to indicate the new function, e.g. . . . *ond he hi him eft ageaf, for þæm þe hiora wæs oþer his godsunu* . . . 'and he afterwards returned them to him, because one of them was his godson . . .'. Here *þe* warns us that the combination is a conjunction. We can call *þe* (if we wish) a subordinating particle. This is the general function of *þe* and its use as a relative pronoun is probably a special adaptation; see §162. We can perhaps get nearest to its original force by translating it as 'namely'. So, in the example above, we have 'and he afterwards returned them to him, for that [reason], namely, one of them was his godson'.

These formulae can be used in two ways. Thus *for þǣm* sometimes refers *back* to a reason already given as in the second example above – '[Some fled.] Therefore the army was divided'. Here it is equivalent to MnE 'therefore'. But sometimes it refers *forward* to a reason yet to be given, as in the third example above, where the *þe* warns us not to relax because something – the reason – is still to come, and so tells us that *for þǣm* means 'because' and not 'therefore'.

Sometimes *þæt* is used instead of *þe*, e.g. *forþan þæt he wolde Godes hyrde forlætan* 'because he wished to desert God's flock'. This use of *þæt* becomes more common as we move from OE to ME and still survives in Chaucer's metrically useful 'if that', 'when that', and the like.

So far we have distinguished *for þǣm* adverb 'therefore' from *for þǣm þe* conjunction 'because'. But this distinction was not long preserved by the Anglo-Saxons. They could distinguish adverb and conjunction by the context, word-order, and intonation, just as we can distinguish the use of 'who' in 'The man who did that is a fool' from its use in 'The soldiers, who were tired, lay down'. So they sometimes dispensed with the subordinating particle and used the formula as a conjunction without *þe* or *þæt*, e.g. *Wuton agifan ðæm esne his wif, forðæm he hi hæfð geearnad mid his hearpunga* 'let us give the man back his wife, because he has earned her with his harping'.

Like other adverbs and conjunctions such as *þā* (see §§150 ff.), prepositional conjunctions may be used correlatively. Examples are *forðæm we habbað nu ægðer forlæten ge ðone welan ge ðone wisdom forðæmðe we noldon to ðæm spore mid ure mode onlutan* 'and for that reason we have now lost both the wealth and the wisdom, because we would not bend to the track with our minds', and, without *þe* in the conjunction, *For þon nis me þæs þearf . . . to secgenne, for þon hit longsum is, ond eac monegum cuð* 'For this reason, there is no need for me . . . to speak of it, because it is long and also known to many'.

So now we have

for þǣm adv. 'therefore'
for þǣm þe conj. 'because'
for þǣm conj. 'because'

and the correlative combination *for þǣm . . . for þǣm* (*þe*), 'for this reason . . . because'.

One further variation needs to be recorded. We have already seen that conjunctions can be divided. An OE example of a divided prepositional conjunction is *þa comon for ðy on weg ðe ðara oðerra scipu asæton* lit. 'those (men) got for that away, namely, the ships of the others had gone aground' and so 'those escaped because the others' ships were aground'. The causal conjunction is *for ðȳ . . . ðe*, divided by *on weg*.

§170 Since all these arrangements are possible with the prepositional conjunctions, it follows that, when in your reading you meet *for þǣm* or some such combination, it may be

1 an adverb used alone;
2 a conjunction used alone;
3 an adverb used correlatively with a prepositional conjunction;
4 the first part of a divided prepositional conjunction. If it is this, you will need to find the following *þe* or *þæt*.

The combination *for þǣm þe* is almost always a conjunction. But sometimes MnE 'for' will be a better translation than 'because'.

§171 The remarks made in §170 about *for þǣm* and *for þǣm þe* apply to all the prepositional conjunctions set out in the list which follows. It contains all that you are likely to meet. You should note, however, that these combinations may occur 'in their own right' and may not be true prepositional conjunctions. Thus *mid þǣm þæt* does not mean 'while' or 'when' in *ealles swiþost mid þæm þæt manige þara selestena cynges þegna forðferdon*; we must translate 'most of all by the fact that (lit. 'with that, namely') many of the king's best thanes died'.

æfter + dat., inst.
Adv. and conj. 'after'.

Note
æfter is never used alone in OE as a conj. But it does occur as an adv.

ǣr + dat., inst.
Adv. and conj. 'before'.

Note
ǣr is used alone as a conj. and adv.; see §168.

betweox + dat., inst.
Conj.'while'.

for + dat., inst.
See §§169–170 above. *For* alone as a conj. is late.

mid + dat., inst.
Conj. 'while, when'.

oþ + acc.
Conj. 'up to, until, as far as' defining the temporal or local limit.
It appears as *oþþe, oþþæt*, and *oð ðone fyrst ðe* 'up to the time at which' (a good example of how *þe* can turn a phrase into a conj.).

Note
oþ can be used alone as a conj.; see §168.

tō + dat., inst.
Conj. 'to this end, that' introducing clauses of purpose with subj. and of result with ind.

tō + gen.
Conj. 'to the extent that, so that'.

wiþ + dat., inst.
Conj. lit. 'against this, that'. It can be translated 'so that', 'provided that', or 'on condition that'.

An Exercise in Analysis

§172 Now you are in a position to 'try your strength' by analysing and translating the following sentences *before* consulting the key given below:

A. Ond for ðon ic ðe bebiode ðæt ðu do swæ ic geliefe ðæt ðu wille, ðæt ðu ðe ðissa woruldðinga to ðæm geæmetige, swæ ðu oftost mæge, ðæt ðu ðone wisdom ðe ðe God sealde ðær ðær ðu hiene befæstan mæge, befæste.

B. Forðy me ðyncð betre, gif iow swæ ðyncð, ðæt we eac sume bec, ða ðe niedbeðearfosta sien eallum monnum to wiotonne, ðæt we ða on ðæt geðiode wenden ðe we ealle gecnawan mægen, ond gedon, swæ we swiðe eaðe magon mid Godes fultume, gif we ða stilnesse habbað, ðætte eall sio gioguð ðe nu is on Angelcynne friora monna, ðara ðe ða speda hæbben ðæt hie ðæm befeolan mægen, sien to liornunga oðfæste, ða hwile ðe hie to nanre oðerre note ne mægen, oð ðone first ðe hie wel cunnen Englisc gewrit arædan.

In A, we have

1 three noun clauses introduced by *ðæt* – one the object of *bebīode*, one the object of *ġelīefe*, and one which is perhaps most simply explained as being in explanatory apposition to the clause *ðæt ðū dō*.

2 an adjective clause introduced by *ðe*.

3 two prepositional formulae –
for ðon adverb used alone 'therefore' and
tō ðǣm . . . ðæt used as a divided prepositional conjunction.

4 two *swā* clauses, one of comparison (*swǣ iċ ġelīefe*) and the other of time (*swǣ ðū oftost mæġe*).

5 an adverb clause of place introduced by *ðǣr ðǣr*.

In B, we have

1 two noun clauses –
the *ðæt* clause subject of *ðyncð* 'seems', which begins after *ðyncð* and has *ðæt*, the subject, and the object, repeated after *wiotonne*. It has two verbs – *wenden* and *ġedōn*;
the *ðætte* clause object of *ġedōn*.

2 four adjective clauses –
the *ðā ðe* clause, where the relative pronoun does not clearly tell us its case (see §163.1);
two *ðe* clauses, excluding that mentioned in 7;
the *ðāra ðe* clause.

3 two conditional clauses introduced by *ġif*.

4 a *swā* clause of comparison.

5 a clause of purpose or result introduced by *ðæt* (following *hæbben*).

6 a clause of time introduced by *ðā hwīle ðe*. Here we must understand *oðfæste wesan*.

7 two prepositional formulae –
for ðȳ adverb 'therefore';
the temporal conjunction *oð ðone first ðe*, where *ðe* can be described as a relative pronoun 'until the time at which'.

These and similarly complicated sentences in Alfred's Preface to the *Cura Pastoralis* show the problems which faced the first men to write in English prose about difficult and complicated subjects. But they and later writers overcame them, often triumphantly.

Clauses of Place

§173 The main conjunctions are:

1 *þǣr* 'where', 'whither', *þider* 'whither', and *þanon* 'whence'. These may introduce definite and indefinite clauses.

2 *swā hwǣr swā* 'wherever' and *swā hwider swā* 'wherever, whithersoever'.

The prevailing mood is the indicative. In examples like *Beowulf* l. 1394 *ga þær he wille*, the subjunctive reflects the subjunctive in the principal clause, the indefiniteness of the adverb clause, and probably also the fact that the whole expression means 'no matter where he goes' and therefore has a concessive force. For other examples see *Genesis* ll. 2723–4 and a passage from Gregory's *Dialogues* where MS C reads *Far þu þider þe þu wille* and MS H *Far þu nu swa hwider swa þu wille* 'Go wherever you wish'.

Clauses of Time

§174 1 Conjunctions whose primary meaning is 'when' or 'while' are: *þā, þonne, mid þām (þe), þā hwīle (þe), þenden*, and *swā lange swā*.

2 Conjunctions whose primary meaning is 'after' are: *siððan* and *þæs þe*. *Æfter* is not used alone as a conjunction in OE.

3 'Before' is rendered by *ǣr* either alone or introducing a prepositional formula.

4 Conjunctions whose primary meaning is 'until' are: *oð, oð þe, oð þæt*, and *hwonne*; on the last, see §159 n. 2.

All these conjunctions usually take the indicative with the exception of *ǣr*, which prefers the subjunctive, and *hwonne*, which always seems to take the subjunctive (except in *Exodus* l. 251, which is therefore suspect).

Note

Doubtless the fact that both *ǣr* and *hwonne* clauses refer to a time AFTER the action of the verb of the main clause has something to do with the subjunctive, but the same is true of *oð þæt* which prefers the indicative. The interrogative origin of *hwonne* is also relevant. There are other factors too, but when they have all been investigated, we have to fall back on 'the attitude of the speaker' to explain some variations in mood.

The conjunctions which prefer the indicative may take the subjunctive if circumstances demand. Thus cf. *Beowulf* l. 1374 and l. 1485, in both of which *þonne*, while frequentative and/or indefinite and referring to the future, has the indicative after an indicative principal clause, with *Luke* 14: 13 *Ac þonne þu gebeorscype do, clypa þearfan* 'When you make a feast, call the poor', where the imperative *clypa* imparts to the sentence a further element of wishing and uncertainty which is reflected in the subjunctive *dō*. Again, while *þonne* frequentative in the past is followed by the preterite indicative, e.g. *Beowulf* ll. 1580 ff., it has the subjunctive when the time reference was to the future at the time of speaking. (We may call this the 'future-in-the-past'.) In these circumstances, the reference may be to a single act, e.g. *þa bæd he hine þæt he him þæs arwyrþan treos hwylcne hwego dæl brohte, þonne he eft ham come* 'he asked him to bring a little bit of that precious tree when he came home again' – *þonne*, the conjunction appropriate to a single act in the future, is retained for the future-in-the-past – or to a series of acts, e.g. *He þa ... geworhte anes fearres anlicnesse of are, to ðon, þonne hit hat wære, 7 mon þa earman men oninnan don wolde, hu se hlynn mæst wære þonne hie þæt susl þæron þrowiende wæron* 'He then made the likeness of a boar in brass with the object [of showing] how, when it was hot and the wretches had been put inside it, the noise would be greatest when they were undergoing the torture'.

Clauses of Purpose and Result

§175 Since a result is often a fulfilled purpose and a purpose a yet-to-be-completed result, these two have much in common. Both can be introduced by the following conjunctions: *þæt, þætte, swā þæt*, and *swā ... þæt*, though the last two are rare in purpose clauses. *þæs ... þæt* and *tō þæs ... þæt* occasionally introduce result clauses, more commonly in the poetry than in the prose. *þȳ lǣs* (*þe*) 'lest' is found only in negative clauses of purpose.

It is generally agreed that purpose clauses take the subjunctive, result clauses the indicative. This proposition cannot be proved, for it is only by classifying all clauses with the subjunctive as purpose and all clauses with the indicative as result that we can deduce the rule. This is clearly a circular argument. But it seems likely enough when we think of MnE usage.

Note
Much time has been spent on arguing whether a clause with the indicative can be purpose. This seems a pointless terminological controversy. A much-discussed example is *Elene* ll. 930 ff., where the indicative *wiðsæcest* is used of an event which has yet to take place. Some describe the *þæt* clause as purpose, some as result. The indicative clearly reflects the speaker's belief that a future event is sure to take place. In one sense it is therefore a probable result regarded by the speaker as certain. But it does not seem to have taken place. So in another sense it is an unfulfilled purpose which someone once thought certain to be fulfilled. Hence the indicative reflects the certainty of the speaker, when he spoke, that the event would take place. And that seems all that we can usefully say. Cf. *Husband's Message* ll. 26 ff.

The subjunctive occurs in result clauses under much the same conditions as in adjective clauses (see §165). They are:

1 When the principal clause contains an imperative or a subjunctive expressing a wish, e.g. *alswa litel þu gewurþe þet þu nawiht gewurþe* 'may you

become so small, that you become nothing'. Here the result is expressed as a tendency. A more difficult example is

> . . . ne huru on weg aber þone halgan gast,
> þæt he me færinga fremde wyrðe

'. . . nor take away thy Holy Spirit so that he quickly becomes a stranger to me'. Here the result has not actually taken place. It is a possible future result of an action not yet performed. It is not the purpose or wish of the speaker that the Holy Spirit should depart from him. His purpose would require a *þæt . . . ne* or *þȳ lǣs* 'lest' clause. It may be a purpose attributed by the speaker to God. But from the speaker's point of view it is a result he is anxious to avoid.

Sometimes it is impossible to decide whether a clause with a subjunctive after an imperative should be classified as purpose or result, e.g. *Andreas* ll. 1182–3 and *Andreas* ll. 1332–3

> Gað fromlice,
> ðæt ge guðfrecan gylp forbegan

'Go quickly to humble the warrior's pride'. But this is probably a distinction without a difference; cf. *Elene* ll. 930 ff. discussed above.

2 When the principal clause contains a negative which implies that the content of the result clause is doubtful or unreal, e.g. *Beowulf* ll. 1366–7, where the poet means that no human being could possibly know. This should be compared with *Beowulf* ll. 1520–1 and *Maldon* ll. 117–19, where we have examples of litotes in which the negatives refer only to the verbs immediately following them. Hence 'He did not withhold the blow' means 'He gave him a very severe blow'. Thus a result which has actually taken place will not be put into the subjunctive under the influence of a negative in the principal clause.

3 When the principal clause contains a rhetorical question, e.g. *Andreas* ll. 1372–3

> Hwylc is þæs mihtig ofer middangeard,
> þæt he þe alyse . . .

'Who is there on earth so powerful that he can free you?' or '. . . powerful enough to be able to free you?' This of course means 'There is no-one . . .'; cf. §165.3.

Causal Clauses

§176 The main causal conjunctions are the *for* formulae, *nū*, and *þæs* (*þe*). *þe*, *þȳ*, and *þȳ þe*, are sometimes found.

When the true cause is given, the causal clause has an indicative verb. The subjunctive is regularly used for a rejected reason, e.g. *Ne cwæþ he þæt na forþon þe him wære ænig gemynd þearfendra manna, ah he wæs gitsere* . . . 'He said that, not because he cared at all about needy men, but because he was a miser . . .'.

Clauses of Comparison

§177 1 Comparisons involving 'than' are expressed in OE by *þonne* or (occasionally and only after a negative principal clause) *þon mā þe*. There is a strong tendency for the *þonne* clause to have the subjunctive when the principal clause is positive, e.g. *Ic Ælfric munuc and mæssepreost, swa þeah waccre þonne swilcum hadum gebyrige, wearþ asend* . . . 'I Ælfric, monk and mass-priest, though weaker than is fitting for such orders, was sent . . .', and the indicative when the principal clause is negative, e.g. *Beowulf* ll. 247–9. However, exceptions are not uncommon.

2 Comparisons involving 'as' may be expressed by

(*a*) *swā* 'as' or *swā swā* 'just as';
(*b*) *swā . . . swā* 'so . . . as, as . . . so';
(*c*) *swā* + superlative;
(*d*) *swylċe* 'such as';
(*e*) *swylċe . . . swā* 'such . . . as';
(*f*) *þæs* (*þe*), e.g. *Beowulf* l. 1341 and (with a superlative) *Beowulf* l. 1350.

For further details, see the appropriate word in §168. The prevailing mood in these clauses is the indicative.

3 Comparisons involving 'the . . . the' are expressed by *þȳ . . . þȳ*, e.g. *Maldon* ll. 312–13. The verbs are in the indicative.

4 Comparisons involving hypothesis are expressed by *swā* or *swilċe* 'as if' followed by the subjunctive. When the time reference is to the past, the preterite subjunctive is found in the 'as if' clause, e.g. *Wanderer* l. 96 and *Finnsburh* l. 36. When it is to the present, we find the present subjunctive in the 'as if' clause, e.g. *Christ* ll. 179–81 and ll. 1376–7. The preterite subjunctive is not used of the present as it is in OE type 3 Conditions (see §179.4) or in MnE 'He runs as if he were tired'; the MnE equivalent of the OE idiom would be 'He runs as if he be tired'.

Clauses of Concession

§178 1 Simple concessive clauses are usually introduced by *þēah* (*þe*) 'though'. The prevailing mood is the subjunctive, whether the concession is one of fact or hypothesis.

Note

Sometimes we have *þēah . . . eall*, as in *Beowulf* l. 680 *þeah ic eal mæge*. Here *eall* is an adverb, perhaps with the sense 'easily'. But this probably represents a stage in the development of 'although'; see *OED* s.v. *all* C adv. II 10, and note that in such ME examples as *The Pardoner's Tale* lines 371, 449, and 451 (line references to Skeat's edition), *al* is still an adverb and the concession is expressed by the word-order V.S.

2 Disjunctive concessions are expressed by *sam* . . . *sam* 'whether . . . or'. In such clauses, the subjunctive is the rule, e.g. *sam hit sy sumor sam winter* 'whether it is summer or winter'.

3 As in MnE, an element of concession is often present in indefinite adjective clauses (e.g. *Beowulf* ll. 942 ff. and ll. 142–3) or in indefinite adverb clauses of place (e.g. *Genesis* ll. 2723 ff.) or time (e.g. *Genesis* ll. 1832 ff.). On the possibility that there was a special OE idiom expressing indefinite concession, see Klaeber's note on *Beowulf* l. 968.

4 Concession can sometimes be expressed by putting the verb first without any conjunction. The two most common types are *swelte ic, libbe ic* 'whether I live or die' and *hycge swa he wille* 'let him think as he will', 'no matter what he thinks'. The first type often occurs in the form *wylle ic, nylle ic* 'willy nilly'.

Clauses of Condition

§179 1 In earlier versions of this *Guide*, I classified conditional clauses according to a system traditionally used for Latin and Greek. I have abandoned this because it does not really fit OE. I now distinguish these three types:

(1) (a) conceded and (b) denied conditions, e.g. (a) 'If you think that [and you have said that you do], you are wrong', and (b) 'Seek if you dare [but you do not]'.

(2) open conditions, e.g. 'If you think that [and I do not know whether you do or not], you are wrong', 'If you thought that [and you might], you would be wrong', and 'Seek if you dare [and you may or may not]'.

(3) rejected or imaginary conditions, e.g. 'If you believed this [but you do not], you would be wrong', 'If you had believed this [but you did not], you would have been wrong', and 'If [= Imagine that] you saw a mouse ruling over men, you would think it strange'.

In OE, conditions of all three types may be introduced by *ġif* 'if'. *þǣr* 'if' sometimes introduces type 3 conditions.

2 Conditions of types 1 and 2 fall into two main groups – those in which both clauses have the indicative, e.g. *Maldon* ll. 34–5 and ll. 36–41, and those in which the verb of the principal clause is imperative or expresses a wish in the subjunctive. In these latter sentences, the 'if' clause usually has the subjunctive, e.g. *sec, gif þu dyrre* 'seek if you dare'. This point is well illustrated by the two almost parallel *ġif* clauses in *Beowulf* ll. 445–53.

3 It is not always immediately clear whether a condition belongs to type 1 or 2, e.g. *Fed ðonne min sceap gif ðu me lufige* (cf. *John* 21: 15–17) – here Peter

says that he does love Christ and ultimately proves that he does – and *sec, gif þu dyrre* (quoted above from *Beowulf* l. 1379) – here Beowulf does dare when the time comes.

4 Type 3 conditions regularly have the preterite subjunctive in both clauses, e.g. *ac hit wære to hrædlic, gif he ða on cild-cradole acweald wurde* . . . 'it would have been too early if He (Christ) had been killed in His cradle . . .' and perhaps (with *þǣr* and in dependent speech)

> and þæt wiste eac   weroda Drihten,
> þæt sceolde unc Adame   yfele gewurðan
> ymb þæt heofonrice,   þær ic ahte minra handa geweald

'and the Lord of Hosts also knew that things would turn out badly between Adam and me about that heavenly kingdom, if I had control of my hands'.

Note

The use of 'perhaps' here is important. In MnE we can distinguish unreality in the past, present, and future, by means of the verb alone, e.g.

> If he had been here, it wouldn't have happened.
> If he were here, it wouldn't be happening.
> If he were coming, it wouldn't happen.

But (as is pointed out in more detail in §§195–198) the OE verb was not as flexible an instrument as the MnE verb. Hence an Anglo-Saxon had to use the preterite subjunctive in all these examples. In other words, he could say that a thing was unreal or impossible, but he was unable to say when it could not happen unless he used an adverb or some other device.

Thus both the OE examples cited in this section have the preterite subjunctive. But the first refers to something which did not happen in the past, while the second might refer to something which is impossible at the time when Satan spoke – the implication being 'if only I had control of my hands now, but I haven't'. But it could also be translated 'God knew that trouble would arise between Adam and me if I were to have control of my hands'.

This raises a further difficulty and explains the 'perhaps'. Does this interpretation mean that there was a possibility that Satan might have control of his hands (type 2 condition) or that such a thing was impossible when God spoke? The issue here is complicated by questions of God's foreknowledge, though perhaps our own knowledge of the story enables us to dismiss the latter possibility. But enough has been said to make it clear that the Anglo-Saxon 'rule' that 'unreality is timeless' is not without its advantages.

A clearer example is *Beowulf* ll. 960–1, discussed in §198.

5 *Būtan* and *nymþe, nemne, nefne* both have two meanings – 'unless' and 'except that'. If they take the subjunctive, they usually mean 'unless', e.g. *Beowulf* l. 966 and l. 1056. If they take the indicative, they usually mean 'except that', e.g. *Beowulf* l. 1560 and l. 1353.

6 'On condition that' may be expressed by *ġif* or by the *wiþ* formula (see §171).

7 Conditions expressed by the word-order V.S. without a conjunction – e.g. 'Had I plenty of money, I would be lying in the sun in Bermuda' – occasionally occur in OE prose, e.g. *eaðe mihte þes cwyde beon læwedum mannum bediglod, nære seo gastlice getacning* 'this saying could easily be concealed from laymen were it not [for] its spiritual meaning'. The only certain example in the poetry is *Genesis* ll. 368–70; here it is arguable whether a line is missing or whether the poet deliberately left the *þonne* clause unfinished to obtain a dramatic effect.

8 On comparisons involving hypothesis, see §177.4.

Adverb Clauses Expressing Other Relationships

§180 The divisions outlined above are for convenience only and are far from being watertight, for one relationship often involves another. Thus, while clauses of time with *oþ* (*þæt*) often shade into result, and *þæt* after verbs of motion can often be translated 'until', other temporal clauses may contain elements of cause or of condition. Similarly, indefinite adjective clauses are often the equivalent of conditional clauses, e.g. *Beowulf* ll. 1387–8. See also §178.3.

Note
This latter relationship is very clearly seen in some ME sentences which contain an adjective clause which must be rendered by a conditional clause in MnE, e.g. Hall *Selections from Early Middle English*, p. 54 l. 11 and l. 21 (cf. p. 54 l. 16) and *Sir Gawain and the Green Knight* l. 1112.

Other Ways of Expressing Adverbial Relationships

§181 1 Parataxis; examples will be found in §§182–186.
2 Participles; see §204.
3 Infinitives; see §205.
4 Prepositional phrases, e.g. *mid* expressing condition *mid Godes fultume* 'with God's help, if God helps us'; *þurh* expressing cause *þurh þæs cyninges bebod* 'by command of the king'; and *þurh* expressing time *þurh swefn* 'in a dream, while he dreamt'.

VI PARATAXIS

Introduction

§182 The Anglo-Saxons were far from primitive. At the time of the Norman Conquest, England – although she no longer led Western Europe in monastic learning, as she had in the eighth century – was fruitful ground for new forms of devotion, was famous for her craftsmen, and had a well-developed economy and the most advanced administration north of the

Alps. It is of special interest here that her language was far more developed for the expression of both prose and poetry than any other contemporary European vernacular and that authors using it sometimes rose to very great heights. Look for example at the poem *The Dream of the Rood* and at the magnificent passage beginning *Ne forseah Crist his geongan cempan* in Ælfric's Homily on the Nativity of the Innocents.

Some of the reasons for the belief that Old English was a primitive language have been discussed in §§148–152. Another is the frequent use of parataxis. Some writers, steeped in the periodic structure of Latin and Greek, seem unable or unwilling to believe that parataxis can be anything but a clumsy tool used by people who did not know any better. Certainly, S. O. Andrew (in *Syntax and Style in Old English*) does well to draw our attention to inconsistencies in the editorial punctuation of Old English texts. But he allows himself to be swayed too much by his conviction that good writing must necessarily be periodic. Today, when the long and complicated sentence is losing favour in English, we will perhaps be more in sympathy with the constructions described in the following paragraphs, more able to appreciate the effect they produced, and less likely to believe that the juxtaposition of two simple sentences was necessarily less dramatic or effective than one complex sentence. During his journey to the Underworld in search of Eurydice, Orpheus met the Parcae. *Ða ongon he biddan heora miltse; ða ongunnon hi wepan mid him*, the story continues. Here the word-order supports the view that the two sentences are independent (see §151), and suggests that the writer is giving equal prominence to the two ideas. The effect he was after can perhaps be achieved by the translation 'Then he asked for their pity and they wept with him'. At the end of the same story, the final disappearance of Eurydice is related thus: *Ða he forð on ðæt leoht com, ða beseah he hine under bæc wið ðæs wifes; ða losade hio him sona* 'When he came into the light, he looked back towards his wife. Straightway she disappeared from his sight'. Here a powerful dramatic effect would be lost if we took only one of the clauses with *þā* + V.S. as principal.

§183 The term 'parataxis', with its adjective 'paratactic', has been abandoned by some writers because of its ambiguity. Here it is used in a purely formal sense to mean a construction in which sentences are not formally subordinated one to the other. 'Asyndetic' and 'syndetic' mean respectively without and with conjunctions such as *ond* and *ac*. The term 'co-ordinating' (often used for the MnE equivalents 'and', 'but', and so on) is avoided here because in OE *ond* and *ac* are frequently followed by the order S. . . . V. (see §145), which is basically a subordinate order. The opposite of 'parataxis' is 'hypotaxis', which implies the use of one or more of the conjunctions discussed in §§154–180. Examples follow.

Hypotaxis: When I came, I saw. When I saw, I conquered.
Asyndetic Parataxis: I came. I saw. I conquered.
Syndetic Parataxis: I came and I saw and I conquered.

List of Conjunctions and Adverbs Commonly Used

§184 On word-order after these words, see §§144 and 145.

1 Those meaning 'and', 'both . . . and', etc. (traditionally called 'cumulative'):

and, ond 'and' (see below);
ǣghwæþer (*ġe*) . . . *ġe* . . . (*ġe*) '(both) . . . and . . . (and)';
(*ǣġþer*) (*ġe*) . . . *ġe* . . . (*ġe*) '(both) . . . and . . . (and)';
ēac 'also, and'; *ġe* 'and'; *ġe* . . . *ġe, ǣġþer* . . . *and* 'both . . . and'.

The *ond* clause can of course imply more than mere continuity and is often the equivalent of an adverb clause. Thus *ofer Eastron gefor Æþered cyning; ond he ricsode V gear* could be translated 'During Easter Æthered died after ruling five years'. This of course often happens today, especially in conversation.

2 Those meaning 'but', 'however', etc. (traditionally called 'adversative'):

ac 'but, on the contrary'; *furþum* 'also, even';
hūru 'however, indeed', etc.;
hwæþere 'however, yet'; *swāþēah* 'however, yet';
þēah 'however, yet' (see also §178);
þēahhwæþere 'however, yet'.

3 Those meaning 'either . . . or' (traditionally called 'alternative'):

hwīlum . . . *hwīlum* 'at one time . . . at another time';
(*ǣġþer*) *oþþe* . . . *oþþe*; *swā* . . . *swā*; *þe* . . . *þe*.

4 Those involving a negative:

nā, ne, nō 'not';
(*nāhwæðer ne*) . . . *ne* . . . (*ne*) 'neither . . . nor . . . (nor)';
nalles, nealles 'not at all, not';
(*nāðor ne*) . . . *ne* . . . (*ne*) '(neither) . . . nor . . . (nor)';
nǣfre 'never'; *næs* 'not' (a short form of *nalles*).

An example of 'not only . . . but also' will be found in *na þæt an þæt he wolde mann beon for us, ðaða he God wæs, ac eac swylce he wolde beon þearfa for us, ðaða he rice wæs* 'not only was He willing to become man for us when He was God, but He was also willing to become poor for us when He was rich'.

The following points should be noted:

(*a*) The OE verb is normally negated by *ne* immediately preceding it. But if the negative is stressed, as in *Wanderer* l. 96 and *Seafarer* l. 66, *nā* (= *ne* + *ā*) or *nō* (= *ne* + *ō*) is used. In *Phoenix* l. 72 the MS *no* is unstressed and should probably be emended to *ne* as a scribal anticipation of *o*.

(*b*) The arrangement seen in *Ne com se here* — *Ne* + V.S. – is common in negative principal clauses; see §146.4.

(*c*) Contraction of the negative *ne* with a following word beginning with a vowel, *h*, or *w*, produces *nis* from *ne is*, *næfde* from *ne hæfde*, *noldon* from *ne woldon*, and so on.

(*d*) *Ne* not before a finite verb is a conjunction, e.g. *ne tunge ne handa* 'neither tongue nor hands', *ne leornian ne tæcan* 'neither to learn nor to teach'.

(*e*) *Nā* and *nō* are used to negate words other than finite verbs, e.g. *He wæs Godes bydel ond na God* 'He was God's messenger and not God'.

(*f*) One negative does not cancel out another, as it does in formal MnE. The OE use is similar to that seen in such non-standard sentences as 'I didn't do nothing to nobody'; cf. *on nanum men nyton nane are* '[they] show mercy to no-one'. This could be added to the list of things which make some people think of OE as a primitive language; see §182.

(*g*) On a 'semi-subordinating' use of *ne*, see §185.2.

5 Those meaning 'for' (traditionally called 'illative'). A useful article by T. B. Haber on MnE 'for' (*American Speech* 30 (1955), 151) states: 'The only practical conclusion is that the conjunction has two uses, subordinating and co-ordinating, and that punctuation is of no significance in identifying either.' In other words, MnE 'for' can sometimes be replaced by 'because'. In OE, the situation is even more complicated, for *forþon* can mean, not only 'for' and 'because', but also 'therefore'. No rule can be laid down for distinguishing these uses; see §§169–70.

Parataxis without Conjunctions

§185 Two main types of asyndetic parataxis may be distinguished.

1 Here the two sentences are of equal status, as in the well-known *Veni. Vidi. Vici*. Examples are especially common in the poetry, e.g. *Beowulf* ll. 1422–4 and *Maldon* ll. 301–6.

2 Examples of the second type occur in *Eadmund cyning awearp his wæpnu, wolde geæfenlæcan Cristes gebysnungum* and *þa comon þeofas eahta, woldon stelan þa maðmas*, where the clauses beginning with *wolde* and *woldon* respectively could be translated 'wishing to imitate Christ's example' and 'intending to steal the treasures'. Note

(*a*) These clauses do not themselves contain a grammatically-expressed subject.

(*b*) They are actually, though not formally, subordinate to the clause which precedes them; for this reason they are sometimes said to be in 'semi-subordination'.

(*c*) They explain the motive for the action of the principal clause and are the equivalent of an adverb clause of purpose or cause.

This idiom occurs with verbs other than *willan*, e.g. *he sæt on ðæm muntum, weop ond hearpode* which can conveniently be translated 'he sat on the mountains, weeping and harping'. Similar examples occur with an initial negative, e.g. *Beowulf* ll. 1441–2 'Beowulf arrayed himself in princely armour without (or 'not') worrying about his life'.

Some Special Idioms

§186 1 ... *wæs gehāten* '... was called' is frequently used independently of the rest of the sentence, e.g. *mid heora cyningum, Rædgota ond Eallerica wæron hatne* 'with their kings, [who/they] were called R. and E.' (note the change from the dative to the nominative case) and *þa wæs sum consul, þæt we heretoha hataþ, Boetius wæs gehaten* 'there was a certain consul – we use the word *heretoha* – [who/he] was called B.'. Cf., with the verb 'to be' only, ... *gefor Ælfred, wæs æt Baðum gerefa*, 'A., [who/he] was reeve at Bath, died'.

2 For '*swā* + negative + indicative', see §168 s.v. *swā* 2(*d*).

VII CONCORD

§187 The main rules of agreement in OE are set out below. They will present little difficulty to any reader with a knowledge of an inflected language.

1. Nouns, Pronouns and their Modifiers

(*a*) They agree in number, gender, and case, e.g. *se Ælmihtiga Hælend* 'the Almighty Saviour', *ðæs eadigan apostoles* 'of the blessed apostle', and *and þe cwicne gebindaþ* 'and will bind you alive'.

Note
The masc. ending *-e* in nom. acc. pl. of adjectives is often used for fem. and neut., especially in later texts.

(*b*) The participle in a participial phrase usually shows similar agreement, e.g. *Hinguar and Hubba, ge-anlæhte þurh deofol* 'H. and H., united by the devil'. But it need not, e.g. *Abraham geseah þær anne ramm betwux þam bremelum be þam hornum gehæft* 'A. saw there a ram caught among the brambles by his horns'.

(*c*) *Gehāten* 'called' with a noun usually has the nominative irrespective of the case of the word with which it is in apposition, e.g. *into anre byrig, Gaza gehaten* 'into a city called Gaza'; cf. *for ðy hit man hæt Wislemuða* 'therefore we call (lit. 'one calls') it W.' where the nominative *Wīslemūða* is the equivalent of the modern italics or inverted commas, and the second example in §186.1.

(*d*) After *wesan* and *weorþan* the participle often agrees with the subject, e.g. *hie wurdon ofslægene* 'they were slain' and *þe mid him ofslægene wæron* 'who were killed with them'. But it need not, e.g. *þa wurdon hiora wif swa sarige on hiora mode ond swa swiðlice gedrefed* . . . 'then their wives became so sorrowful and so greatly distressed in mind . . .'. See further §§201–203. So too with adjectives.

(*e*) After *habban*, the participle may agree with the object or may remain uninflected; see §200.

2. Pronouns and their Antecedents

(*a*) They agree in number and gender, e.g. *to þæm cyninge . . . he . . . his feores* 'to the king . . . he . . . for his life'; *anne flotan . . . se* 'a pirate . . . he (lit. 'that')'; and *se hearpere . . . ðæs nama* 'the harper, whose name'.

(*b*) The main exceptions arise from the conflict between natural and grammatical gender, e.g. *ðæs hearperes wif* (neut.) . . . *hire sawle* 'the harper's wife . . . her soul' and *an swiðe ænlic wif, sio wæs haten Eurydice* 'a most excellent wife, who was called E.'. Similarly, in a passage from the Preface to the *Cura Pastoralis* (selection 5, end of first paragraph) we find *ðone wīsdōm* followed first by the grammatically right masculine *hiene* and then by the neuter *hit* which seems appropriate to us. Thus there are already signs that the feeling for grammatical gender is weakening.

Note

Agreement in case between pronoun and antecedent is a matter of chance, not principle, despite Quirk and Wrenn *An Old English Grammar* §121(*c*). In the examples they cite, *rōde* and *hēo* do not agree in case and the relative *ðāra þe* would have to be replaced by the acc. pl. *þā* of the declined relative *se*, i.e. *ðāra* has the case of the principal clause; see §163.1.

(*c*) Special uses of *hit, þæt, hwæt*, and the like, in which these neuter pronouns are used without regard to the number and gender of the noun to which they refer, should be noted, e.g. *þæt wæron eall Finnas* 'they were all Lapps' and *Hwæt syndon ge . . . ?* 'Who are you . . . ?' See further §168 s.v. *þæs . . . þæt*, note 1.

3. Subject and Verb

(*a*) Subject and verb agree in number and person. Dual pronouns are followed by plural verbs.

(*b*) Collective nouns and indefinite pronouns cause much the same problems as they do today, e.g. *an mægð . . . hi magon cyle gewyrcan* 'a tribe . . . they can make cold' and *þonne rideð ælc, and hit motan habban* 'then each man rides, and [they] can have it'.

(*c*) With *ond þæs ymb XIIII niht gefeaht Æþered cyning ond Ælfred his broður*, where *gefeaht* is singular, cf. 'Here comes Tom, and Jack, and all the boys'.

(*d*) When the relative pronoun *þāra þe* means 'of those who', the verb of the adjective clause can be singular or plural.

VIII THE USES OF THE CASES

These will not present much difficulty to those familiar with an inflected language. On the cases used after prepositions, see §§213–214.

Nominative

§188 The case of the subject, of the complement, and of address, e.g. *Gehyrst þu sælida?* 'Do you hear, seaman?' See also §187.1(*c*).

Accusative

§189 1 The case of the direct object.

2 It also expresses duration of time, e.g. *ealne dæg* 'all day', and extent of space, e.g. *fleon fotes trym* 'to flee one foot's pace'.

Note
It is important to realize that already in OE the nominative and accusative are frequently the same. In the plural they are always the same except in the 1st and 2nd pers. pron. In the singular, many nouns have the same form in the nominative and accusative, and the distinction depends on the form of any demonstrative or possessive adjective, or on that of any adjective, which may qualify the noun. See further §140.

Genitive

§190 1 The case of possession, e.g. *Hæstenes wif* 'Hæsten's wife'.

2 The subjective genitive – *þæs cyninges bebod* 'the king's command', i.e. 'the king commanded' – differs in function from the objective genitive – *metodes ege* 'fear of the Lord', i.e. 'we fear the Lord'.

3 The genitive may describe or define, e.g. *swete hunig and wynsumes swæcces* 'honey sweet and of pleasant taste', *ðreora daga fæsten* 'a fast of three days', and *an lamb anes geares* 'a one-year-old lamb'.

4 The partitive genitive is common, e.g. *an hiora* 'one of them' and *þreora sum* 'one of three'. See also §194.

5 The genitive is used adverbially, e.g. *dæges ond nihtes* 'by day and night', *micles to beald* 'much too bold', *upweardes* 'upwards', *þæs* 'therefore, so, after that'.

6 The genitive occurs after some adjectives, e.g. *þæs gefeohtes georn* 'eager for the fight', and after some verbs, e.g. *fanda min* 'try me' and *hie þæs fægnodon* 'they rejoiced at that'. The glossary gives you this information when you need it.

Dative

§191 1 The case of the indirect object, e.g. *ond he hi him eft ageaf* 'and he afterwards gave them back to him'.

2 It may express possession, e.g. *him on heafod* 'on his head'.

3 It may express time, e.g. *hwilum* 'at times' and *ðære ylcan nihte* 'in the same night'. Other adverbial uses include *flocmælum* 'in (armed) bands' and *gearmælum* 'year by year'.

4 The dative absolute is used in imitation of the Latin ablative absolute, e.g. *gewunnenum sige* 'victory having been gained'.

5 The dative occurs after some adjectives, e.g. *ise gelicost* 'most like to ice', sometimes after comparatives, e.g. *sunnan beorhtra* 'brighter than the sun', and after some verbs, e.g. *þæt he him miltsian sceolde* 'that he should have mercy on him'. Here too the glossary will help you.

Instrumental

§192 Where there is no special instrumental form (and sometimes when there is), the dative serves.

1 The instrumental expresses means or manner, e.g. *þone ilcan we hataþ oþre naman æfensteorra* 'we call the same by another name – evening star', *fægere ende his lif betynde* 'closed his life with a fair end' (but cf. the dative in *geendode yflum deaþe* 'ended with an evil death'), and *hlutre mode* 'with a pure mind'.

2 It expresses accompaniment, e.g. *lytle werode* 'with a small band'.

3 It expresses time, e.g. *þy ilcan geare* 'in the same year'.

IX ARTICLES, PRONOUNS, AND NUMERALS

Articles and Pronouns

§193 1 There are no 'articles' as such in OE. The demonstrative *se* does duty for 'the' and 'that', the demonstrative *þes* means 'this', e.g. *Her on þysum geare for se micla here, þe we gefyrn ymbe spræcon* . . . 'In this year went the great army which we spoke about before . . .'. Sometimes, however, *se* can be translated 'this', e.g. *anne æþeling se wæs Cyneheard haten — 7 se Cyneheard wæs þæs Sigebryhtes broþur* 'a princeling who was called C. and this C. was the brother of the S. already mentioned'.

2 The demonstrative is frequently not used in OE where we would use it today, e.g. *wælstowe gewald* 'command of the battlefield', and, from the poetry (where its absence is even more common), *fram beaduwe* 'from the battle' and *Oddan bearn* 'the sons of Odda'. But the reverse is sometimes true, e.g. *sio lar* 'learning'.

3 In examples like *Æþered cyning* we have either absence of a demonstrative pronoun 'Æthered the King' or (more likely in view of *Iohannes se godspellere* 'John the Evangelist') a different arrangement of appositional elements 'King Æthered'. Hence *Æþelwulf aldormon* might be the equivalent of 'General Smith'.

4 The indefinite article is even rarer; thus we find *holtes on ende* 'at the edge of a wood', *to wæfersyne* 'as a spectacle', and *on beorg* 'onto a mountain'. *Ān* is sometimes used, e.g. *to anum treowe* 'to a tree' and *an wulf* 'a wolf'. But usually *ān* and *sum* mean something more, e.g. *an mægð* 'a certain tribe' and *sum mon* 'a certain man'. Sometimes these words have an even stronger sense, e.g. *þæt wæs an cyning* 'that was a peerless King', 'that wás a King', and *eower sum* 'a particular one among you', 'your leader'. In this sense, and as the numeral 'one', *ān* is strong. Meaning 'alone', it is usually weak, e.g. *he ana*, but may be strong, e.g. *ðone naman anne* 'the name alone'.

5 *Se* is also used as a relative pronoun; see §162.3. Sometimes, as in *Beowulf* l. 1296, it may be either demonstrative or relative. But the difficulty is of little practical consequence.

6 The third person pronoun is sometimes used ambiguously, so that we cannot readily tell to whom it is referring. A well-known series of examples is found in the story of Cynewulf and Cyneheard (selection 6, third paragraph). But this is rather the result of inexperience in handling the language than of defects in the language itself, for later in its development, OE managed to make the meaning clear with no more pronouns at its disposal. The same is, of course, true of MnE.

7 A pronoun subject is frequently not expressed. Often the subject not expressed is the same as that of the preceding clause. But the absence of a subject does not certify that it has not changed; see, e.g. *Maldon* ll. 17–21, where the subject changes twice in l. 20 without any pronoun. A pronoun object may be similarly unexpressed, e.g. the sentence quoted in §167.6. Sometimes, however, *sē* is used instead of *hē* to make clear that a subject has changed, e.g. *Maldon* ll. 150 and 227. This avoids the ambiguity which could arise from a repeated or an absent *hē*, e.g. *Maldon* l. 286 and *Beowulf* l. 57.

Numerals

§194 The cardinal numerals can be used

1 as adjectives agreeing with a noun, e.g. *þrim gearum ær he forþferde* 'three years before he died' and *mid XXXgum cyningum* 'with thirty kings';

2 as nouns followed by a partitive genitive, e.g. *to anre þara burga* 'to one of the cities' and *þritig cyninga* 'thirty kings'.

X VERBS

On the detailed uses of the indicative and subjunctive in subordinate clauses, see the discussions on the appropriate clause.

The Uses of the Present and Preterite Tenses

§195 As we have seen in §89, the OE verb distinguished only two tenses in conjugation – the present and the preterite. Hence, despite the fact that the beginnings of the MnE resolved tenses are found in OE (see below), the two simple tenses are often used to express complicated temporal relationships. This is one of the things which made Professor Tolkien once say in a lecture that most people read OE poetry much more quickly than did the Anglo-Saxon minstrel, reciting or reading aloud as he was to an audience which needed time to pick up the implications of what he was saying. And this would apply, not only to the subject-matter, especially to the hints and allusions which frequently had great significance, but also to the relationships between paratactic sentences such as those discussed in §§182–185 and to the actual relationship in time between two actions both of which were described by a simple tense of a verb. Thus it is important for us to understand what these simple tenses could imply.

§196 The present expresses, not only a continuing state as in *Wlitig is se wong* 'The plain is beautiful', and *ðeos woruld nealæcð þam ende* 'this world is drawing near to its end', but also the passing moment, the actual 'now' for which MnE often uses a continuous tense, e.g. *hwæt þis folc segeð* 'what this people are saying, say now'. It is also used for the future, e.g. *þas flotmenn cumaþ* 'these seamen will come', and (as in equivalent examples in MnE) for the future perfect, e.g. *seþe þæt gelæsteð, bið him lean gearo* 'a reward will be ready for him who does (shall have done) that', and (with a subjunctive *gefeohte* as explained in §179.2) *gif hwa gefeohte on cyninges huse, sie he scyldig ealles his ierfes* 'if anyone fight (shall have fought) in the king's house, let him forfeit all his property'.

In the principal clause in the last sentence, the subjunctive *sīe* expresses a command and could be translated 'he shall forfeit'. The present subjunctive can also express a wish, e.g. *abreoðe his angin* 'may his enterprise fail', or a prayer, e.g. *God þe sie milde* 'May God be merciful to you'.

The only verb which has a special future form is the verb 'to be', where *bið* and its forms are used for the future, e.g. *bið him lean gearo* above, and for the statement of an eternal truth (a use sometimes called 'gnomic'), e.g. *wyrd bið ful aræd* 'Fate is quite inexorable' and *þonne bið heofena rice gelic þæm tyn fæmnum* 'Then the Kingdom of Heaven is like unto (the) ten virgins'. But *is* may do the same job, e.g. *Heofena rice is gelic þæm hiredes ealdre* 'The Kingdom of Heaven is like unto a man that is an householder'.

The historic present rarely, if ever, occurs.

§197 The preterite indicative is used

1 of a single completed act in the past;

2 of an act continuing in the past. Both of these are exemplified in *soðlice þa ða men slepon, þa com his feonda sum* 'truly, while men were sleeping, one of his enemies came';

3 for the perfect, e.g. *ic mid ealre heortan þe gewilnode* 'I have wished for Thee with all my heart';

4 for the pluperfect, e.g. *sona swa hie comon* 'as soon as they had come' and (with a strengthening *ǣr*) *and his swura wæs gehalod þe ær wæs forslægen* 'and his neck, which had been cut through, was healed'. (Cf. the use of *ǣrur* in *Dream of the Rood* l. 108.) But see *Anglo-Saxon England* 4 (1975), 17–20.

§198 The preterite subjunctive may refer to the past, e.g. *ond ge wiðsocon þæt in Bethleme bearn cenned wære* 'and you denied that a child was born in Bethlehem', or to the future-in-the-past, e.g. the two sentences quoted at the end of §174.

It has already been pointed out in §179.4 that unreality is timeless in OE. An interestingly ambiguous example of this is seen in *Beowulf* ll. 960–1

Uþe ic swiþor
þæt ðu hine selfne geseon moste . . . !

Here Beowulf might be saying to Hrothgar either

'I could wish that you could see Grendel now'; in other words 'I wish that he hadn't got away'

or 'I could wish that you could have seen Grendel yesterday'; in other words 'I wish that you had been at the fight and had seen how badly wounded he was'

or 'I could wish that you could see Grendel tomorrow'; in other words 'I wish that we could find his body and so know that he is dead'.

But the context strongly suggests the second.

The Resolved Tenses
Introduction

§199 This term is used to mean tenses made up from a participle (present or past) or an infinitive together with the verb 'to be', the verb 'to have', or one of the 'modal' verbs (see §206), e.g. MnE 'He is coming', 'He is come', 'He has come', 'He will come'. The beginnings of these forms are seen in OE, with one important difference which throws light on their origin. A MnE example will explain this. In *Ephesians* 6: 14, the Revised Version reads 'Stand therefore, having girded your loins with truth'. If we parsed 'having girded', we would perhaps call it the perfect participle of the verb 'to gird', with 'your loins' its object; at any rate, we would say that it was part of the verb 'to gird'. But the Authorized Version reads 'Stand therefore having your loins girt about with truth'. Here 'your loins' is the object of the participle 'having' and 'girt about with truth' is a phrase describing 'your loins'; hence 'girt' is adjectival rather than verbal. That this was its original function in such phrases in OE becomes clear when we study the agreement of some of the examples cited below; to make this point, it will be convenient if we take first the ancestor of the MnE perfect tense with 'have'.

The Verb 'to have' as an Auxiliary

§200 Examples in which the participle is adjectival are *he us hafað þæs leohtes bescyrede* 'he has us deprived of that light' (where the present tense of *habban* is followed by *bescyrede* a past participle acc. pl. strong, agreeing with *ūs*) and *ac hi hæfdon þa heora stemn gesetenne and hiora mete genotudne* 'but then they had their term of service finished and their food used up' (where a past tense of *habban* is followed by two participles both of which are declined acc. sg. masc. strong, agreeing with *stemn* and *mete*, the objects of *hæfdon*). These are clearly the ancestors of the MnE perfect and pluperfect respectively.

But examples also occur in which there is no such declining of the past participle to agree with the object, e.g. *Eastengle hæfdon Ælfrede cyninge aþas geseald* 'The East Anglians had oaths given to King Alfred' and *Hæfde se cyning his fierd on tu tonumen* 'The king had his army divided in two'; cf. §187.1(*b*). This was, of course, a necessary stage in the development of the MnE perfect and pluperfect tenses. The modern arrangement in which the participle precedes the object instead of having final position is found in such examples as *Nu ðu hæfst ongiten ða wanclan truwa þæs blindan lustes* 'Now you have realized the fickle loyalty of blind pleasure'.

The Verb 'to be' as an Auxiliary of Tense

§201 1 It is found with the present participle as the ancestor of the MnE continuous tenses. But here too the participle was originally adjectival rather than verbal. It should also be noted that the OE combination is not the exact equivalent of the modern usage. Often it means the same as the corresponding simple tense, e.g. *þa wæs se cyning openlice andettende þam biscope* 'Then the king openly confessed to the bishop', though it may give greater vividness. (This construction is now agreed to be of native rather than of Latin origin.) But sometimes it implies that an action continued for some time, e.g. *ond hie þa . . . feohtende wæron* 'and then they kept on fighting' and *ða ða se apostol þas lare sprecende wæs* 'while the apostle was explaining this teaching'. In these examples, it comes close to the modern use.

2 The verb 'to be' is also found with the past participle forming the perfect and pluperfect of intransitive verbs, e.g. *Swæ clæne hio* [= *lar*] *wæs oðfeallenu on Angelcynne* 'So completely was learning fallen away in England' (where the participle is declined nom. sg. fem. strong, agreeing with the subject) and *hu sio lar Lædengeðiodes ær ðissum afeallen wæs* 'how the learning of Latin was fallen away before this' (where the participle is not declined). Here too the participle was originally adjectival rather than verbal.

The Passive

§202 Only one OE verb had a synthetic passive, viz. *hātte* 'is called', 'was called', e.g. *se munuc hatte Abbo* 'the monk was called A.'. Otherwise the idea was expressed by the impersonal *man* 'one' with the active voice, e.g. *Her mon mæg giet gesion hiora swæð* 'Here one can still see their track', or by the verbs 'to be' or 'to become' with the past participle, e.g. *to bysmore synd getawode þas earman landleoda* 'the miserable people of this land are (have been) shamefully ill-treated', *Æfter þæm þe Romeburg getimbred wæs* 'After Rome was (had been) built', and *æfter minum leofum þegnum þe on heora bedde wurdon mid bearnum and wifum færlice ofslægene* 'after my beloved thanes who became (have been) suddenly killed in their beds with their wives and children'. The inflexions in the first and third of these examples show that here too the participle is adjectival rather than verbal. But again the participle was not always declined, e.g. *hie beoð ahafen from eorðan* 'they are raised from the earth'. (Can we definitely say it is not declined in the example about Rome?)

§203 The difference between the forms with *wesan* and those with *weorðan* is not well-defined. The former sometimes seem to emphasize the state arising from the action, e.g. *he eall wæs beset mid heora scotungum* 'he was completely covered with their missiles' and (showing the continuing state by the use of *bið*) *ne bið ðær nænig ealo gebrowen* 'nor is any ale brewed there', and the latter the action itself, e.g. *þær wearþ se cyning Bagsecg ofslægen* 'there King B. was killed' (lit. 'became slain'). But this does not always hold; cf. e.g. *on þæm wæron eac þa men ofslægene* 'on it too the men were slain'. Such fluctuations are natural in a developing language. The fact that the *weorðan* form of the idiom disappeared suggests that the language found other ways of making the distinction when it was necessary, e.g. *þær se cyning ofslægen læg* 'where the king lay slain'; it was, claims J. M. Wattie, 'the only false start' in the development of the MnE verb.

Other Uses of the Present and Past Participles

§204 1 Present and past participles are found as nouns, e.g. *brimliþendra* 'of the seamen' and *He is se frumcenneda* 'He is the first-born', and as adjectives, e.g. *þinne ancennedan sunu* 'your only son'.

2 They also introduce phrases which may be the equivalent of adjective clauses, e.g. the sentences quoted in §187.1(*b*), or which may express various adverbial relationships, such as time, e.g. *þæt man his hlaford of lande lifigendne drife* 'that one should drive his lord from the land while he still lives', or cause, e.g. *me þearfendre* 'to me in my need'. (What sex is the last speaker?)

3 Together with a noun or a pronoun, a participle may be inflected in the dative case in imitation of a Latin ablative absolute; see §191.4.

4 Sometimes the exact grammatical status of such a phrase is not certain. Thus the first two words in *astrehtum handum to Gode clypode* 'with outstretched hands called to God' are taken by some as an absolute and by others as a dative of 'attendant circumstances'. Perhaps they are both. At any rate, such ambiguities are merely terminological.

The Uses of the Infinitives

§205 This section sets out the normal uses of the OE uninflected and inflected infinitives. Exceptional uses of the one in the functions here allotted to the other, however, do occur.

1 The uninflected infinitive is usual after the auxiliaries mentioned in §206 and after *uton* 'let us', *þurfan* 'need', and **durran* 'dare'. The infinitive of a verb of motion is frequently not expressed in such circumstances, e.g. *ær he in wille* 'before he will go in'.

As in MnE, there are circumstances in which either the infinitive without *tō* or a present participle can be used, e.g. *Ic geseah ða englas dreorige wepan and ða sceoccan blissigende on eowerum forwyrde* 'I saw the angels weep bitterly and the demons rejoicing at your destruction'.

On the accusative and infinitive, see §161.

2 The inflected infinitive with *tō* is common in the following functions:

(*a*) To express purpose, e.g. *an wulf wearð asend to bewerigenne þæt heafod* 'a wolf was sent to guard the head' and, with a passive sense, *bindað sceafmælum to forbærnenne* 'bind them in sheaves for burning, to be burnt'. But the simple infinitive also occurs, e.g. *ut eode ahyrian wyrhtan* 'went out to hire workers'.

(*b*) With the verb 'to be' to express necessity or obligation, e.g. *Is eac to witanne* 'It must also be noted'.

(*c*) To complete the sense of a verb, e.g. *and begunnon ða to wyrcenne* 'and then [they] began to work'. But cf. *ða ongan ic ða boc wendan on Englisc* 'then I began to translate the book into English', where the infinitive without *tō* occurs.

(*d*) To complete the sense of a noun, e.g. *anweald to ofsleanne and to edcucigenne* 'power to kill and to restore to life', or of an adjective, e.g. *wæron æþelingas. . . fuse to farenne* 'the nobles were eager to depart'.

(*e*) As the subject, or as the complement, of a sentence, e.g. *to sittanne on mine swyðran healfe . . . nys me inc to syllanne* 'to sit on my right hand is not for me to give to you two'.

The 'Modal' Auxiliaries

Introduction

§206 Some forms of the OE verbs *cunnan, willan, *sculan, magan*, and **mōtan*, still survive as auxiliaries today, viz. 'can', 'will', 'would', 'shall', 'should', 'may', 'might', and 'must'. As in OE, they are followed by the infinitive without 'to'. Their semantic history is a complicated one and even today the uses of some, especially 'shall' and 'will' and 'should' and 'would', cause great confusion to very many foreign speakers of English. Readers of OE too will find difficulties with them, but of a different sort, for the range of meanings they had in OE was wide, just as it is now.

Magan

§207 In *eorðe mæg wið ealra wihta gehwilce* 'earth prevails against every creature', *magan* means 'to prevail against' and has the full force of an independent verb; cf. Hopkins's 'I can no more'. In *þæt he ealle þa tid mihte ge sprecan ge gangan* 'so that all the time he could speak and walk', it means 'to be able', while in *Luke* 16: 2 *ne miht þu leng tunscire bewitan* 'you can no longer hold the stewardship', it means 'to be permitted to'. In these senses, it expresses a shade of meaning which the subjunctive of a simple verb could hardly do. The same is true in *Dream of the Rood* ll. 37–8, where we have a statement of fact 'I could have destroyed all his foes' and not of possibility 'I might have destroyed all his foes'. But this last use – the MnE one – does occur in OE. A striking example is found in *Andreas* ll. 544 ff.

Nænig manna is . . .
ðætte areccan mæg   oððe rim wite . . .

'There is no man . . . [of such a sort] that he may relate or know the number'. The proper mood in such clauses is the subjunctive (see §175.2); hence *wite*. But parallel to it is *āreċċan mæġ* 'may relate, may tell'.

Note
K. R. Brooks, the latest editor of *Andreas*, follows Grein in emending to *mæġe*. Though possible, this does not seem essential.

Thus *magan* has shades of meaning which cannot always be accurately distinguished. Does *Genesis B* ll. 436–7 mean 'what we can win by our own strength' or 'what God will allow us to win'? Consider too *ðu miht* in *Dream of the Rood* l. 78.

When it means 'to be permitted to' *magan* is a rival of **mōtan* 'to be allowed to'; cf. *Luke* 16: 2 quoted above with *Matthew* 20: 15 *ne mot ic don þæt ic wylle?* where the Authorized Version has 'Is it not lawful for me to do what I will?', and *Maldon* ll. 14 and 235 with *Maldon* ll. 83 and 95.

But in the sense of 'to be able to' it frequently comes close to *cunnan*; cf. Cædmon's statement (in the second paragraph of selection 9) *Ne con ic noht singan* 'I do not know how to sing anything' with the angel's reply *Hwæðre þu meaht me singan*[1] 'Yet you can sing to me'. Here, as the Latin original *nescio cantare* suggests, *cunnan* may have its full sense of 'to know how to'. But it comes close to the modern sense of 'to be able to'.

**Mōtan*

§208 The preterite of **mōtan* 'to be allowed to' is *mōste*, the ancestor of MnE 'must'. In *Maldon* l. 30 the present tense *þū mōst* comes close to meaning 'you must'. But it may be a very formal and ceremonious extension of the permissive use, perhaps with ironical overtones: 'The Danes bid me say that they are graciously pleased to allow you to send tribute in exchange for protection'. The sense of 'to be allowed to, may' seems to be the prevailing one for **mōtan* in OE.

Cunnan

§209 For an example of *cunnan* 'to know how to' shading into 'to be able, can' (its MnE sense), see §207 above.

**Sculan*

§210 The most important function of **sculan* is to express necessity or obligation. Thus it must be translated 'must' in *Se byrdesta sceall gyldan* 'The wealthiest must pay', expressing a general obligation, and 'has had to' in *Wanderer* l. 3, where *sceolde* has no future reference at all. In *Maldon* l. 60 too, *sceal* means 'must', but here the reference is more clearly to one specific act which must take place in the future.

Whether **sculan* ever represents the simple future is a matter of some dispute. Cædmon's reply to the comment of the angel quoted at the end of §207 was *Hwæt sceal ic singan?* Some of you may be tempted to translate this 'What shall I sing?' But the Latin has *Quid debeo cantare?* which demands the translation 'What must I (ought I to) sing?' Here then **sculan* clearly does not represent a simple future. And on the whole it will be safer for you to assume that it always has an idea of obligation, except in examples like those

[1] So some MSS. MS T lacks *me*; so some read *þu me aht singan* 'you must sing to me'. But here (i) we might expect an infl. inf. after *aht*; (ii) that *aht* could mean 'must' is uncertain.

discussed in the next two paragraphs. When Ælfric in his grammar equates *lecturus sum cras* with *ic sceal rædan tomerigen*, it might seem a clear case of 'I shall read tomorrow'. But it probably means 'I must read tomorrow', for elsewhere Ælfric equates *osculaturus* with *se ðe wyle oððe sceal cyssan*. This does not mean that *wyle* and *sceal* mean the same thing, but that *osculaturus* has two possible meanings for Ælfric – futurity 'He is going to kiss' (see §211) and obligation 'He has to kiss'. So the OE version of *Matthew* 20: 10 *And þa þe þær ærest comon wendon þæt hi sceoldon mare onfon*, which represents the Latin *Venientes autem et primi, arbitrati sunt quod plus essent accepturi*, is perhaps best translated 'And those who had come there first thought that they ought to receive more'.

**Sculan* can also express what is customary, e.g. *And ealle þa hwile þe þæt lic bið inne, þær sceal beon gedrync and plega* 'And all the time the body is within, there shall be drinking and playing'.

In *ðæs nama sceolde bion Caron* 'whose name is said to be C.', *sceolde* shows that the reporter does not believe the statement or does not vouch for its truth. You will probably meet other examples of this.

Willan

§211 The original function of *willan* seems to have been the expression of wish or intention, e.g. *ic wille sellan* 'I wish to give', *þe þær beon noldon* 'who did not wish to be there', and *he wolde adræfan anne æþeling* 'he wished to expel a princeling'. In these (with the possible exception of the second), there is some future reference. How far *willan* had gone along the road to simple futurity is difficult to determine, but examples like *Hi willað eow to gafole garas syllan* 'They wish to (will) give you spears as tribute',

æghwylc gecwæð,
þæt him heardra nan hrinan wolde

'everyone said that no hard thing would touch him', and *þa Darius geseah, þæt he oferwunnen beon wolde* 'When D. saw that he would be conquered' (note the passive infinitive), come pretty close to it.

Willan, like MnE 'will', is sometimes found 'expressing natural disposition to do something, and hence habitual action' (*OED* s.v. 'will' 8), e.g. *He wolde æfter uhtsange oftost hine gebiddan* 'He would most often pray after matins'.

On paratactic *wolde*, see §185.2 and cf. the *þæt* clause with *willan* in

Geseah ic þa frean mancynnes
efstan elne mycle þæt he me wolde on gestigan

'I saw the Lord of mankind hasten with great zeal in His wish to climb on to me'.

Impersonal Verbs

§212 These are more common in OE than in MnE, but should not cause you much trouble if you notice that the subject 'it' is often not expressed, e.g. *me ðyncð betre* 'it seems better to me' and *hine nanes ðinges ne lyste* lit. 'it pleased him in respect of nothing'. But *hit* does appear, e.g. *hit gelamp* 'it happened'.

XI PREPOSITIONS

§213 The most important prepositions, with their meanings and the cases they govern, are set out below in alphabetical order. For their use in prepositional conjunctions, see §171.

Those marked with a dagger † govern both accusative and dative, the distinction usually being accusative of motion, e.g. *and heo hine in þæt mynster onfeng* 'and she received him into the monastery', and dative of rest, e.g. *on þam huse* 'in that house'. However, this distinction is not always observed.

Prepositions often follow the word they govern, e.g. *him to* 'against them' and *him biforan* 'before him'.

Sometimes words which often occur as prepositions are used without a noun or pronoun, e.g. *þa foron hie to* 'then they went thither' and *het þa in beran segn* 'then [he] ordered [them] to carry in the banner'. Here we have something very similar to the separable prefixes of modern German.

List of Prepositions

§214 (Note: Some prepositions may be followed by the dative or the instrumental. As there is no significance in this variation, the instrumental has not been included in the list.)

æfter		dat. (acc.) 'after, along, according to'
ǣr		dat. (acc.) 'before'
æt		dat. 'at, from, by'; (acc. 'as far as, until')
be		dat. (acc.) 'by, along, alongside, about'
beforan		dat. acc. 'before, in front of'
betweox		dat. acc. 'among, between'
binnan	†	'within, into'
bufan	†	'above, upon'
būtan		dat. acc. 'except, outside, without'
ēac		dat. 'besides, in addition to'
for		dat. acc. 'before (of place), in front of, because of'
fram		dat. 'from, by (of agent)'
ġeond		acc. (dat.) 'throughout'

in	†	'in, into'
innan	†	'in, within'; (occasionally gen.)
mid		dat. acc. 'among, with, by means of'
of		dat. 'from, of'
ofer	†	'above, over, on'
on	†	'in, into, on'
on-ġēan		dat. acc. 'against, towards'
oþ		acc. (dat.) 'up to, until'
tō		gen. 'at, for, to such an extent, so' dat. 'towards, to, at, near' dat. 'as', in the idiom seen in *to frofre* 'as a consolation' and *to menniscum men* 'as a human being' (acc. 'towards')
tō-ġēanes		dat. 'against, towards'
þurh		acc. (dat. gen.) 'through, throughout, by means of'
under	†	'under, beneath'
wiþ		acc. gen. dat. 'towards, opposite, against, along, in exchange for'
ymb(e)		acc. (dat.) 'after, about or concerning'

6

An Introduction to Anglo-Saxon Studies

I SOME SIGNIFICANT DATES

§215 If the Anglo-Saxon period is taken as beginning in 449 and ending in 1066, it lasted for 617 years. It may help you to put this in perspective if you realize that this is roughly the same period of time as that which separates the death of Edward III from the present day, or, to put it in literary terms, the birth of Chaucer from the death of Dylan Thomas.

Note
Where possible, the dates in §216 are taken from *Handbook of British Chronology*, ed. F. M. Powicke and E. B. Fryde (London, Royal Historical Society, 2nd ed., 1961).

§216 See pp. 120–123.

II HISTORY

§217 The Germanic settlements in Britain, which (recent archaeological finds suggest) may have begun at least half a century earlier than the traditional A.D. 449, did not result in the immediate subjugation of the whole island under one Germanic king. Indeed, there is much evidence to suggest a vigorous revival of British fortunes, culminating about the time of the victory of Mons Badonicus (*c.* 490–517), which led to a renewed British predominance in some western and south-midland areas formerly overrun by the invaders. Only with the battles that the Chronicle associates with the West-Saxon leaders Ceawlin, Cuthwulf, Cutha, and Cuthwine (especially Biedcanford 571 and Dyrham 577), was Saxon control re-established in the Chilterns and Cotswolds. Romano-British elements, of course, still survived extensively in the population of Anglo-Saxon England.

The invading English, therefore, lived in independent kingdoms – there were ten south of the Humber in 600 – cut off from one another by geographical barriers and by hostile British. It is in such conditions of isolation that sound-changes flourish, and hence peculiarities which were originally individual or tribal and which would have been eliminated in a larger community flourished unchecked. Thus by *c.* 700, the date of the earliest linguistic records, the four dialects mentioned in §2 – Northumbrian,

Mercian, West-Saxon, and Kentish – can be distinguished in a language which at the time of the invasions appears to have been spoken in much the same way by all those who came to England.

The two hundred or so years after the English victory at the unidentified Biedcanford are not well-documented and the history of the period is often obscure. There was certainly much fighting between the various kingdoms, with now one, now another, temporarily 'top-dog' under some powerful warrior-king, though there was a period of comparative peace during the late seventh and the eighth centuries in which the Northern civilization which produced Bede, Alcuin, and the like, flourished. By 800, however, four great kingdoms survived – Northumbria, Mercia, Wessex, and East Anglia.

Then came the Danes. First they made what might be called 'smash-and-grab' raids in the summer, taking their booty back home with them. In 851 they are recorded as wintering on the Isle of Thanet. In 865 they ravaged Kent. In 867 they moved from East Anglia to York. Over the next few years there was intense activity. One by one, the kingdoms of Northumbria, East Anglia, and Mercia, ceased to exist as independent kingdoms and in 878 Wessex too was nearly extinguished, for in that year King Alfred was taking refuge in Æthelney 'with a small band' while the Danes plundered his kingdom. But Alfred was equal to the challenge. His grasp of the principles of war as revealed by a study of his campaigns against the Danes, and his activities in education, learning, and administration, over the next twenty years until his death in 899, are such that, for some people at any rate, his only rival for the title 'The greatest Englishman of all' is Sir Winston Churchill. The Anglo-Saxon Chronicle has two simple, but revealing, phrases in its account of this period. In 878, it says, the whole of Wessex surrendered to the Danes *buton þam cyninge Ælfrede* 'except King Alfred'. He escaped and rallied his forces. Men flocked to his banner *and his gefægene wærun* 'and were glad of him'.

By 880, then, only Wessex remained of the four kingdoms existing in 800. The subsequent years were a period of uneasy peace in which the Danes settled and ploughed and in which the boundaries of Danelaw were established. The arrival of another great army from France in 892 led to more bitter fighting in which the invaders were helped by those in Northumbria and East Anglia. But gradually Wessex, under Alfred and his successors, won back land from the settled Danes and reconciled them to English rule. In 954 the Scandinavian kingdom of York ceased to exist and the permanent unification of England as one kingdom began. As a result England was able to enjoy a period of comparative peace in the second half of the tenth century in which the great revival of Benedictine monasticism took place, and in which England began to achieve nationhood – a short passage in *The Battle of Maldon* (ll. 51–54) may perhaps contain the beginnings of a sense of patriotism. Nevertheless, in the Laws of Canute we still find a threefold

Date	*Lay*	*Religious*	*Literary*
449	Traditional date of coming of Angles, Saxons, and Jutes.		The legend of Arthur may rest on a British leader who resisted the invaders.
560–616	Æthelbert King of Kent.		*c.* 547 Gildas writes *De Excidio Britanniae*.
c. 563		St. Columba brings Celtic Christianity to Iona.	
597		St. Augustine brings Roman Christianity to Kent.	
616–632	Edwin King of Northumbria.		
c. 625	Earliest possible date for Sutton Hoo ship burial.		
627		Edwin converted to Christianity.	
632	Edwin killed by heathen King Penda of Mercia.		
635		Aidan settles in Lindisfarne, bringing Celtic Christianity.	
635		King Cynegils of Wessex converted.	
641	Oswald King of Northumbria killed by Penda.		
654	Penda killed by Oswy King of Northumbria.		
664		Synod of Whitby establishes supremacy of Roman Christianity.	

664		St. Chad becomes bishop.	
657–680		Hild Abbess of Whitby.	Cædmon uses Germanic alliterative verse for religious subjects during this period.
c. 678		English missions to the continent begin.	
680			Approximate earliest date for composition of *Beowulf*.
c. 700			Date of first linguistic records.
709		Death of Aldhelm, Bishop of Sherborne.	
731			Bede completes *Historia Ecclesiastica Gentis Anglorum*.
735		Death of Bede.	
		Birth of Alcuin.	
757–796	Offa King of Mercia.		
782		Alcuin settles at Charlemagne's court.	
793	Viking raids begin.	Sacking of Lindisfarne.	*fl.* 796 Nennius, author or reviser of *Historia Britonum*.
800	Four great kingdoms remain – Northumbria, Mercia, East Anglia, Wessex.		
780–850			Cynewulf probably flourishes some time in this period.
804		Death of Alcuin.	
851	Danes first winter in England.		
865	Great Danish Army lands in East Anglia.		

Date	*Lay*	*Religious*	*Literary*
867	Battle of York. End of Northumbria as a political power.		
869	King Edmund of East Anglia killed by Danes. East Anglia overrun.		
871	Alfred becomes King of Wessex.		
874	Danes settle in Yorkshire.		
877	Danes settle in East Mercia.		
880	Guthrum and his men settle in East Anglia. Only Wessex remains of the four Kingdoms.		
?886	Boundaries of Danelaw agreed with Guthrum. Alfred occupies London.		The period of the Alfredian translations and the beginning of the Anglo-Saxon Chronicle.
892	Further Danish invasion.		
896	Alfred builds a fleet.		
899	Death of King Alfred.		
899–954	The creation of the English Kingdom.		
c. 909		Birth of Dunstan.	
937	Battle of Brunanburh.		Poem commemorates the battle.
954	The extinction of the Scandinavian kingdom of York.		
959–975	Edgar reigns.		
959		Dunstan Archbishop of Canterbury. The period of the Monastic Revival.	

c. 971			*The Blickling Homilies*.
978 or 979	Murder of King Edward.		
950–1000			Approximate dates of the poetry codices – Junius MS, Vercelli Book, Exeter Book, and *Beowulf* MS.
978 or 979 –1016	Ethelred the Unready reigns.		
988		Death of Dunstan.	
991	Battle of Maldon.		Poem commemorates the battle.
990–992			Ælfric's *Catholic Homilies*.
993–998			Ælfric's *Lives of the Saints*.
1003–1023		Wulfstan Archbishop of York.	
c. 1014			*Sermo Lupi ad Anglos*.
1005– *c.* 1012		Ælfric Abbot of Eynsham.	
1013	Sweyn acknowledged as King of England.		
1014	Sweyn dies.		
1016	Edmund Ironside dies.		
1016–1042	Canute and his sons reign.		
1042–1066	Edward the Confessor.		
1066	Harold King. Battle of Stamford Bridge. Battle of Hastings. William I King.		

division into Wessex, Mercia, and Danelaw, which reflects the divisions of the earlier period.

The subsequent history of Anglo-Saxon England is well-known – the reigns of Ethelred the Unready, of the Danish dynasty, and of Edward the Confessor, were followed by Harold's victory at Stamford Bridge and his defeat at Hastings.

§218 The fortunes of Christianity fluctuated in Anglo-Saxon England, and students of its literature must grasp the implications of this fact, which are discussed in §§243–245. The Christianity of Roman Britain was not accepted by the pagan invaders, who brought with them the Germanic heroic code, which was in many ways no ignoble way of life. St. Columba and his followers brought Celtic Christianity to the north, while St. Augustine and his followers from Rome spread their teaching from the south until in 664 the Synod of Whitby established the supremacy of Rome. But heathenism was never very far away. King Edwin of Northumbria was killed by the pagan Penda, King of Mercia, in 632. Throughout the Anglo-Saxon period, preachers inveighed against paganism. Alcuin asked his famous question 'What has Ingeld to do with Christ?' in 797, in a letter condemning the recitation of heathen poetry to monks. The invading Danes brought their paganism with them. Both King Alfred and King Ethelred stood sponsor at the baptism of some of their foes, and in 1012, during the lifetime of Ælfric and Wulfstan, Ælfeah Archbishop of Canterbury was murdered by drunken Danes. It is therefore possible that any Christian poet writing in Old English between 680 and 850, when most of the extant poetry was probably written, could have been a convert from paganism or the son of a pagan. If he was not either of these, he lived in a society where the battle between the pagan Germanic religions and Christianity had not been finally resolved. Early Christian poetry adapts pagan symbolism to its own use. This crucial ambivalence is seen in the Benty Grange helmet (§244) and in the Sutton Hoo ship burial, which could be a memorial either to the pagan King Rædwald or to one of his early Christian successors.

III ARCHAEOLOGY

Introduction

§219 The belief that Anglo-Saxon civilization was decadent before the Norman Conquest dies hard, despite recent attempts to refute it. But it is without foundation. By 1066, English missionaries had preached Christianity in Scandinavia and, despite two centuries of Danish attacks, political unity had been achieved. The idea of nationhood had developed among the people; in its account of the dispute between Earl Godwine and Edward the Confessor over Count Eustace, the Chronicle observes that 'it was hateful to almost all of them to fight against men of their own race, for there were very few on either side who were worth much, apart from Englishmen. Moreover, they did not wish to put this country at the mercy of foreigners by fighting each other' (MS D, 1052). Despite the wars and rumours of wars of this period, England in 1066 possessed (according to R. W. Chambers)

> a civilization based upon Alfred's English prose as the national official and literary language. English jewellery, metal-work, tapestry and carving were famed throughout Western Europe. English illumination was unrivalled, and so national that the merest novice can identify the work of the Winchester school. Even in stone-carving, those who are competent to judge speak of the superiority of the native English carver over his Norman supplanter. In building upon a large scale England was behind Normandy. But what little is left to us of Eleventh Century Anglo-Saxon architecture shows an astonishing variety. Its mark is 'greater cosmopolitanism, as compared to the more competent, but equally more restricted and traditional architecture of the Normans'.

Unfortunately, space does not permit a full treatment of these points; all that can be done is to provide you with the means of testing for yourself the truth of R. W. Chambers's vividly expressed view that it seems as if 'Eleventh-Century England was getting into the Fifteenth; as if England was escaping from the Dark Ages without passing through the later Middle Ages at all.' A short Bibliography is given first. This is followed by a list of topics accompanied by brief comments and references to the books cited.

Note
The quotations given above are from R. W. Chambers *On the Continuity of English Prose from Alfred to More and his School* (Early English Text Society, 1932).

List of Abbreviated Titles

§220 For convenience, each book is given a brief title which is used in the sections which follow. The first three contain useful Bibliographies covering many of the topics discussed below. See also §258.

The Anglo-Saxons
D. M. Wilson *The Anglo-Saxons* (3rd ed., Penguin, 1981). This includes thirty-eight figures and seventy-nine monochrome illustrations, covering all the topics listed below.

A-S England
P. Hunter Blair *An Introduction to Anglo-Saxon England* (2nd ed., Cambridge, 1977)

Archaeology
The Archaeology of Anglo-Saxon England, ed. David M. Wilson (Methuen, 1976), now available in paperback (Cambridge, 1981)

Architecture

E. A. Fisher *An Introduction to Anglo-Saxon Architecture and Sculpture* (Faber and Faber, 1959)

Art

C. R. Dodwell *Anglo-Saxon Art. A New Perspective* (Manchester, 1982)

Note

David M. Wilson *Anglo-Saxon Art from the Seventh Century to the Norman Conquest* with 285 illustrations, 73 in colour (Thames and Hudson, 1984), can be recommended as an alternative. But it is perhaps less conveniently arranged for the beginner. Its chapter headings are 1. Taste, personalities and survival; 2. The seventh-century explosion; 3. The eighth and ninth centuries; 4. Influences; 5. From Alfred to the Conquest. The Index does not contain main entries under the headings architecture, buildings, carving, dress, embroidery, jewellery, metalwork, sculpture, or weapons.

Beowulf Arch.

Rosemary J. Cramp '*Beowulf* and Archaeology', *Medieval Archaeology* 1 (1957), 57–77

Beowulf Introduction

R. W. Chambers *Beowulf An Introduction with a Supplement by C. L. Wrenn* (3rd ed., Cambridge, 1959)

Everyday Life

R. I. Page *Life in Anglo-Saxon England* (London and New York, 1970)

How They Lived

G. A. Lester *The Anglo-Saxons How They Lived and Worked* (David and Charles, 1976)

Dress

Gale R. Crocker-Owen *Dress in Anglo-Saxon England* (Manchester, 1986)

Jewellery

R. Jessup *Anglo-Saxon Jewellery* (Faber and Faber, 1950)

Bayeux Tapestry

Reproductions of this will be found in

E. Maclagan *The Bayeux Tapestry* (King Penguin, 1949)

Douglas and Greenaway *English Historical Documents Volume II 1042–1189* (Eyre and Spottiswoode, 1953)

F. Stenton and others *The Bayeux Tapestry* (London, 1957)

D. M. Wilson *The Bayeux Tapestry* (London, 1985)

The sections on archaeology are inevitably out of date in some places because many discoveries are not written up until years after they are made. One case in point is the timber material, knowledge of which has expanded enormously in recent years. New information can be found in the Introduction to *The Anglo-Saxons*, in the works listed in §258, in *Anglo-Saxon England*, published annually by Cambridge University Press, and in *Medieval Archaeology*, which each year offers an account of new finds under the heading *Medieval Britain in 19***. Colour slides of manuscripts, jewellery, and so on, can be obtained from Woodmansterne Colourslides, Holywell Industrial Estate, Watford, WD1 8RD, England, or from the museum which houses them.

Weapons and Warfare

§221 See *The Anglo-Saxons*, chapter IV.

It may be of interest to note here how archaeological finds prove the accuracy of the *Beowulf* poet's descriptions of swords, coats-of-mail, helmets, and the like. Thus his mention in ll. 1448–54 of a helmet with chain-mail is confirmed by the discovery in York of the Coppergate helmet, a magnificent piece of Anglo-Saxon craftsmanship in iron and brass with a curtain of mail protecting the neck of the wearer, while the helmet of ll. 1030–4 can be identified as a Romanesque helmet with a solid comb and not the ribbed helmet seen in the Bayeux Tapestry. See further *Beowulf Arch.*, pp. 57–67, and *The Coppergate Helmet* by Dominic Tweddle (York, 1984).

Other points worthy of study are the Danish strategy in the last decade of the ninth century and Alfred's methods of countering it, and the careful way in which the young Beowulf leads his 'platoon' during his journey to Denmark and his stay there. When reading *The Battle of Maldon* you should ask whether Byrhtnoth's decision to let the Danes cross the causeway unmolested was tactically right or the result of *ofermod* (a characteristic attributed only to Byrhtnoth and Satan). (It can scarcely be a misguided expression of the English sense of 'fair play'.)

Life and Dress

§222 Some knowledge of how the Anglo-Saxons dressed, lived, ate, and drank, will help you to realize more clearly that the writers and scribes whose work you read, and the warriors, priests, statesmen, and others, whose lives you study, were human beings like yourself, subject to weariness and pain, and prey to the same emotions as you are. This knowledge can be acquired from *The Anglo-Saxons*, chapter III, from *Dress*, or from *Everyday Life*, which reconstruct life in Anglo-Saxon times. *How They Lived* also gives some valuable insights into the way our ancestors lived, thought, and felt. The Bayeux Tapestry can be studied with profit. Works in Anglo-Saxon which throw light on the more personal and intimate sides of life include the *Leechdoms*, the *Charms*, and the *Riddles*. Ælfric's *Colloquy* (ed. G. N. Garmonsway, 2nd ed., Methuen, 1947) gives a picture of the life and activities of the middle and lower classes of whom we hear little elsewhere. But now and then those who are on the watch will catch momentary glimpses. Thus in the Chronicle for 897 (Parker MS), we find the names of three Frisian sailors killed in a sea-battle. The death of these men, who had been teaching the Anglo-Saxons the art of sea-fighting, is given poignancy by a few lines from the *Maxims* or *Gnomes* of the Exeter Book:

> Welcome is her beloved to the Frisian wife when the ship lies at anchor. His ship has returned and her husband, her own bread-winner, is at home. She welcomes him in, washes his sea-stained garments, gives him new clothes, and grants him on his return what his love demands.

Here are three Frisians whose garments will need no washing and who will be looked for in vain.

Architecture and Buildings

§223 Monochrome plates I and II in *Jewellery* illustrate timber huts and buildings. *Everyday Life* discusses timber huts and halls with illustrations – and supplements the remarks which follow – in chapter IX 'King's Hall, Peasant's Cottage, Town House'. See also *The Anglo-Saxons*, chapter III.

Aerial photographs taken in 1949 led to excavations at Old Yeavering, Northumberland, which revealed an Anglo-Saxon township. A large timber fort dated from the second half of the sixth century. A township outside the fort appeared to have developed in the seventh century. It included a massive timber hall with other smaller halls (one of which may have been a pagan temple later converted to Christian use) and a large timber grandstand for outdoor meetings. The large hall was replaced by an even more ambitious one and the grandstand was enlarged in the reign of King Edwin. The whole township was then destroyed by fire, probably by Cadwallon after Edwin's death in 632. The township was then rebuilt, still in timber, in what may have been Celtic style, and a Christian church was built, around which there grew a large cemetery. This township too was destroyed by fire – perhaps by Penda in 651. The great hall, two smaller halls, and the church, were rebuilt. But towards the end of the seventh century, Yeavering was abandoned in favour of a new site called Melmin, a few miles away.

At Cheddar in Somerset, another Saxon royal residence was excavated in 1960–2. In King Alfred's time, it consisted of a two-storey hall and three smaller buildings, the largest of which was probably a *bur*; see *Beowulf* ll. 140 and 1310. Later kings carried out additions and reconstructions.

The discoveries at Yeavering throw light on the hall in *Beowulf* (see *Beowulf Arch.*, pp. 68–77) and help to fill out the picture given by the poet. Those at Cheddar may serve to illustrate two interesting stories in the Chronicle – the death of King Cynewulf after being trapped in a *bur* which, like that at Cheddar, was separate from the hall, not part of it (selection 6; see note to line 11) and the escape of Archbishop Dunstan, who was left standing alone on a beam when the upper floor of a hall collapsed at Calne, Wiltshire (Laud MS, 978).

On these excavations, see Philip Rahtz *The Saxon and Medieval Palaces at Cheddar* (Oxford, 1979) and B. Hope-Taylor *Yeavering — An Anglo-British centre of early Northumbria* (HMSO, 1977).

Excavations on Cowdery's Down, Basingstoke, Hampshire, in 1978–81 revealed an ancient habitation-site re-used by the Anglo-Saxons but abandoned *c.* 800, and provided well-preserved and detailed evidence for timber architecture of the sixth and seventh centuries A.D.; see *The Archaeological Journal* 140 (1983), 192–261.

§224 Stone was used mainly for churches. But excavations in Northampton in 1981–2 revealed a rectangular stone hall *c.* 37.5 × 11.5 metres, with two rooms subsequently added to the west of the building, increasing its length by 6 metres. Tentatively dated early in the eighth century, it seems to have directly replaced a seventh-century timber hall and possibly decayed or was demolished during the Danish occupation of Northampton in the late ninth and early tenth centuries. See *Current Archaeology* 85 (1982), 38–41. *Architecture* contains a useful introduction to the study of Anglo-Saxon churches and crypts, with plans, photographs, and a bibliography. See also *The Anglo-Saxons*, pp. 50 ff. There are a large number of Saxon churches worth visiting. One which for some reason has proved particularly memorable is that of St. Peter at Bradwell-iuxta-Mare in Essex, which is built mostly of masonry from the nearby Roman fort. A visit to this, to the site of the battle of Maldon on a farm on the R. Blackwater, and to the new nuclear power-station, would make quite an interesting day!

However, wood was used for churches when stone was not readily available. The church at Greenstead, Essex, where (tradition relates) the body of King Edmund of East Anglia rested in 1013 on its way from London to Bury St. Edmunds, is a surviving example of the kind, though its timbers may not date back to Anglo-Saxon times.

Sculpture and Carving

§225 *Architecture* gives an interesting introduction, with illustrations, to works in stone. Survivals include crosses such as those at Ruthwell and Bewcastle, sundials like that at Kirkdale, sepulchral slabs, fonts, and figures like the angels in the Church of St. Lawrence at Bradford-on-Avon. The different types of ornamentation show influences from different countries and civilizations – Celtic, Mediterranean, Northern, and even Eastern.

The carved oak coffin of St. Cuthbert (late seventh-century) and the Franks Casket of whalebone carved with historical and legendary scenes framed with runes (early eighth-century) survive to show that Anglo-Saxon artists worked in media other than stone.

See further *The Anglo-Saxons*, pp. 53 ff., 152 ff., and 158 ff., and *Art*, chapter IV.

Jewellery and Metalwork

§226 A fascinating and well-illustrated account which tells where the jewels can be seen will be found in *Jewellery*. The author writes:

> Side by side with its interest for the archaeologist and the historian, Anglo-Saxon jewellery has a foremost appeal to the artist and the craftsman of today, who find in a contemplation of its design and technique the exercise of something more than a bare academic interest. To the practising jeweller especially its excellence needs no commendation, and to him it has often yielded an inspiration far from that of unalloyed sentiment.

See also *The Anglo-Saxons*, pp. 137 ff. and 161 ff., and *Art*, chapter VII.

To test the truth of this claim, those in a position to do so should view what Anglo-Saxon jewellery they can, especially the Kingston Brooch and the jewels of the Sutton Hoo Treasure in the British Museum (see §230) and the Alfred and Minster Lovell Jewels in the Ashmolean Museum, Oxford. Some of these are shown in colour in *Jewellery*. Other well-known treasures include the Pectoral Cross of St. Cuthbert (in the Cathedral Library, Durham), finger-rings which belonged to King Æthelwulf and to Queen Æthelswith, King Alfred's sister (both in the British Museum), and necklaces of amethyst, gold, or other material. *Jewellery, The Anglo-Saxons*, and *Art*, offer monochrome illustrations. *Art* has colour plates of an ivory crucifix and a chalice.

By viewing these beautiful objects, we are able to see that the love of beauty and craftsmanship we observe in *Beowulf* is no mere artistic pose, but an accurate reflection of the attitude of the people of his time. Like so many of their descendants, they could combine fierceness in battle with love of the beautiful.

Embroidery

§227 'The tapestries', sings the *Beowulf* poet, 'shone gold-embroidered along the walls, many wondrous sights for those among men who gaze upon such.' Unfortunately, none survive. But rich embroideries can be found in the ninth-century chasuble now at Maaseik, Belgium, and in the early tenth-century vestments now among the relics of St. Cuthbert at Durham, which were made to the order of Queen Ælfflæd, King Æthelstan's queen. These include St. Cuthbert's stole, illustrated in colour in *Art*.

Strictly speaking, as Sir Eric Maclagan points out, the Bayeux Tapestry is 'no tapestry at all, the design being embroidered upon the material and not woven into it'. It is very possible that it was made in England within twenty years of the Conquest by English needlewomen working to the order of Bishop Odo of Bayeux.

See further *Art*, chapters V and VI.

Coins

§228 See *Archaeology*, pp. 349–372.

Manuscripts and Runic Inscriptions

§229 On illuminations and decorations, see *The Anglo-Saxons*, pp. 148 ff. and 156 ff., and *Art*, chapter IV and the relevant colour plates.

On the contents and whereabouts of manuscripts, see

N. R. Ker *Catalogue of Manuscripts containing Anglo-Saxon* (Clarendon Press, 1957).

On handwriting, see (in addition to the above)

N. Denholm-Young *Handwriting in England and Wales* (2nd ed., Cardiff, 1964).

On runes, see

R. I. Page *An Introduction to English Runes* (Methuen, 1973).

The Sutton Hoo Ship-Burial

§230 In 1939, the excavation of a barrow at Sutton Hoo, Suffolk, revealed the ship-cenotaph of an East Anglian King. R. L. S. Bruce-Mitford *The Sutton Hoo Ship Burial* (London, 1968, 2nd ed. 1972) gives a useful summary of the finds and contains four colour plates, including one of the great gold buckle (5.2 inches long weighing 14.6 ounces) which is portrayed on the cover of this *Guide*. The importance of this find for students of *Beowulf* has been discussed by Professor Wrenn in *Beowulf Introduction*, pp. 508–523. He summarizes his conclusions thus:

> The Sutton Hoo discoveries, then, have furnished new evidence bearing on the date and genesis of *Beowulf*, clearing away obstacles to the early dating of the poem and affording a possible explanation of why so much Scandinavian subject-matter should appear in an English poem. They have further clarified the blend of Christian and pagan elements in a yet homogeneous work. They have shown that the highly aesthetic approach to treasures in gold and gems and craftsmanship, which appears in *Beowulf* at first sight to be anachronistic, is paralleled at Sutton Hoo: that that joy in such treasures and the power to appreciate them which seemed a sophistication in *Beowulf* shared by its poet with his audience,

had already been demonstrated by the craftsmen of East Anglian Rendlesham in the ship-burial of Sutton Hoo. Much light too has been thrown by comparison of the Sutton Hoo objects on the nature of some of the weapons and armour mentioned in *Beowulf*, as well as on the type of harp which must have accompanied its recitation.

Another article on the same subject by the same author will be found in *Mélanges de Linguistique et de Philologie* (Fernand Mossé in Memoriam) (Paris, 1959). It is reproduced in *An Anthology of Beowulf Criticism*, ed. by Lewis E. Nicholson (University of Notre Dame Press, 1963). On Music and Harps, see this and the relevant passages in *Everyday Life*.

IV LANGUAGE

See first Preliminary Remarks on the Language (§§1–4).

Changes in English

§231 It has already been pointed out in §140 that Old English was in process of changing from an inflected to an uninflected language. It has also been shown in the discussions on syntax that the distinction between subject and object – originally made by the contrast between nominative and accusative endings – was increasingly brought out by word-order and that prepositions more and more took over the function of the oblique cases as the inflexional endings became reduced. These changes in accidence and syntax, and in the pronunciation of unstressed vowels, affected the English language far more fundamentally than the later changes in spelling and in the pronunciation of vowels in stressed syllables.

The primitive Germanic languages developed a stress accent on the first syllable of words in place of the shifting stress of the original IE language which is seen, for example, in classical Greek and which has already been mentioned in §§90 and 105–106. As a result, differences in the pronunciation of unstressed syllables which had been important for making distinctions of meaning gradually disappeared. An important example in the endings of verbs has already been mentioned in §113.3, and there are occasional spellings which suggest that the nom. pl. ending *-as* and the gen. sg. ending *-es* of strong masc. and neut. nouns were not always clearly distinguished in late OE.

Before the case endings finally disappeared, we can see the same job being done twice. In *he ofsloh ge þone cyning ge ða cwene* 'he slew both the king and the queen', we see subject and object distinguished by word-order and case-ending. In *mid ealre þære fierde* 'with the whole army', a preposition is followed by an oblique case. This stage was necessary before one of the two devices doing the same job could disappear. But once they existed together, the disappearance of one of them became very likely, for few human beings like doing the same job twice. The increasing use of, and finally complete reliance on, word-order and prepositions made possible the ultimate disappearance of noun inflexions, apart from the genitive ending *-s* and the distinction between singular and plural. Similarly, new ways were found of distinguishing tense and mood in the verb; see the article by J. M. Wattie mentioned in §256.

The Danish Invasions

§232 These tendencies were already apparent in OE before the influence of the dialects spoken by the Danish invaders of the ninth century could have made itself felt and may well have been more advanced in colloquial OE than in the more conservative forms of the language recorded in the manuscripts. But the Danish invasions and settlements must in fact have hastened the process and perhaps caused it to be more complete than it might otherwise have been. OHG (the ancestor of Modern German) and OE were very similar in their grammatical structure. Yet today, while German has many inflexions and retains the three word-orders S.V., V.S., and S. . . . V., and other typically Germanic grammatical devices such as the distinction between strong and weak forms of the adjective, English has dispensed with them. Why? The Norman Conquest used to be blamed. As we shall see below, it was certainly not without effect here, although its influence on the language was felt more powerfully elsewhere. But the language of the invading Danes was, like Old English, a Germanic language. The roots of many words were similar, but the inflexional endings differed. When a Dane married an Anglo-Saxon woman, it must have been very confusing for their offspring to hear the one say *segls, segli*, where the other said *segles, segle*, or to find that one said *nema nemir nemi* for the present subjunctive singular forms of the verb 'to take' while the other used *nime* for all persons. Some confusion of endings was inevitable as a result of the fixing of the main stress (already mentioned in §231) in all Germanic languages, but this confusion must have been greater in bilingual communities of Danes and Anglo-Saxons.

The Norman Conquest

§233 Since King Ethelred had married a Norman wife in 1002, the influence of French began before the Conquest. But with the Conquest, and its subsequent use as the language of the court and of administration, Norman French became more important. Certain developments already under way in English may have been reinforced by similar tendencies in Norman French and also in Central French, which began to influence English after the accession of the Angevin Henry II in 1154. These are the standardization of word-order as S.V.O. and the loss of inflexions, which resulted in the development of the simple case system of Modern English. The commencement of parallel trends is attested in continental French of the twelfth century, although their completion was long drawn out and varied from region to region. Again, the fact that many French words had plurals in *-s* must have helped the native *-s* ending of *stanas* to oust its rival, the *-n* ending of *naman*, and to become the plural ending of Modern English nouns. But perhaps the most important influences of French were on vocabulary (see §234), on spelling, and on English prose. The French scribes abandoned the conservative English spelling, which often made distinctions which no longer existed, and introduced their own system. As a result it appears that sound-changes which had occurred gradually over the centuries had happened all at once. A similar situation might arise today if English were to be respelt phonetically by Russian scribes who used their own alphabet with the addition of a few English letters. After the Conquest, English prose gradually ceased to be used for official purposes and for history, but was still used for sermons and other religious works. Further reading on this topic is suggested in §259.

Vocabulary

§234 The vocabulary of OE was basically Germanic and the language was less hospitable to borrowings than it is today, frequently preferring to make its own compounds rather than admit foreign words; see §137. But some were admitted. Up to the time of the Norman Conquest, the following groups can be distinguished:

1 Latin
   (*a*) words borrowed in Pr. Gmc. times;
   (*b*) pre-650 borrowings in Britain;
   (*c*) post-650 borrowings in Britain.
2 Greek
   (*a*) direct borrowings, mostly by the Goths;
   (*b*) borrowings through Latin.
3 Celtic.
4 Scandinavian.
5 French.

References to books which deal with this subject will be found in §261. If you do study them, you will find it interesting to note how the words borrowed from the different languages reflect the relationships which existed between the two peoples concerned and so throw light on the history of the period.

Some Questions

§235 If, while studying OE, you consciously note the differences between OE and MnE, you will make your task easier and more interesting. Questions you might like to answer with the help of one of the histories of the language mentioned in §253 are:

1 Where did the *-s* plural of MnE come from? Did French have any influence here? (This has already been touched on in §233.)

2 Where did the *-s* of the MnE genitive singular come from?

3 How did 'of' become a sign of possession, as in 'The mast of the ship'?

4 When did *-eth* disappear as the ending of 3rd sg. pres. ind.?

5 Why do we find in Chaucer the ending *-en* for the pres. ind. pl. when OE has *-að*? Where did this *-en* ending come from?

V LITERATURE

Introduction

§236 As has been pointed out in §218, the Germanic tribes who settled in England in the fifth century brought with them the Germanic heroic code. What we learn of it from Old English literature generally confirms the observations of Tacitus in his *Germania*. The salient points are these. The Germanic warrior was a member of a *comitatus*, a warrior-band. Life was a struggle against insuperable odds, against the inevitable doom decreed by a meaningless fate – *Wyrd*, which originally meant 'what happens'. There is no evidence in their literature that the pagan Anglo-Saxons believed in a life after death like that of Valhalla, the hall in Scandinavian mythology reserved for dead heroes, though there are references to the worship of heathen gods such as Woden, and the practice of placing coins, weapons, and other goods, with the bodies of the dead in both inhumation and cremation burials, suggests a belief in some kind of after-life where they could be used. On this see *The Anglo-Saxons*, pp. 35–6. It is, however, a different kind of immortality which is stressed in their literature. This was *lof*, which was won by bravery in battle and consisted of glory among men, the praise of those still living. These two ideas of *wyrd* and *lof* acquired Christian overtones; see §§244–245. So the reference of passages like those from *Beowulf* which follow is unlikely to be entirely pagan:

Swa sceal man don,
þonne he æt guðe gegan þenceð
longsumne lof; na ymb his lif cearað

'So must a man do when he thinks to win enduring fame in battle; he will show no concern for his life' and

Wyrd oft nereð
unfægne eorl, þonne his ellen deah!

'Fate often spares an undoomed man when his courage is good'.

§237 A pagan warrior brought up in this tradition would show a reckless disregard for his life. Whether he was doomed or not, courage was best, for the brave man could win *lof* while the coward might die before his time. This is the spirit which inspired the code of the *comitatus*. While his lord lived, the warrior owed him loyalty unto death. If his lord were killed, the warrior had to avenge him or die in the attempt. The lord in his turn had the duty of protecting his warriors. He had to be a great fighter to attract men, a man of noble character and a generous giver of feasts and treasures to hold them. So we read in *The Battle of Finnsburh*

Ne gefrægn ic næfre wurþlicor æt wera hilde
sixtig sigebeorna sel gebæran,
ne nefre swanas hwitne medo sel forgyldan
ðonne Hnæfe guldan his hægstealdas

'I have never heard it said that sixty conquering warriors bore themselves better or more worthily in mortal combat, or that any retainers repaid the shining mead better than Hnæf's retainers repaid him'.

The whole code receives one of its last and finest expressions in *The Battle of Maldon*, especially in the oft-quoted lines spoken by the old warrior Byrhtwold:

Hige sceal þe heardra, heorte þe cenre,
mod sceal þe mare, þe ure mægen lytlað

'Courage must be the firmer, heart the bolder, spirit the greater, the more our strength wanes' (or 'our force diminishes'). Here we see a noble manifestation of 'man's unconquerable mind'.

§238 Sometimes a conflict arose between loyalty to *comitatus* and loyalty to kin. The annal for 755 in the Parker MS of the Chronicle tells us of warriors who, in reply to offers of safe-conduct and money from kinsmen in a hostile force, said 'that no kinsman was dearer to them than their lord, and they would never follow his slayer'. This seems to have been the proper attitude. But, as Miss Whitelock points out, the fact that the Laws of Alfred allow a man to fight in defence of a wronged kinsman only if it did not involve fighting against his lord suggests that the claims of kin sometimes overrode the duty to a lord.

§239 A woman given in marriage as a *freoðuwebbe* 'a peace-weaver' to patch up a blood feud was often involved in such a conflict between loyalty to her lord, her husband, on the one hand, and to her family on the other. Freawaru was in this position, Hildeburh may have been; both appear in *Beowulf*. Sigemund's sister Signy was also involved in such a conflict of loyalties, although in her case the feud arose after the marriage. Thus the 'eternal triangle' of Anglo-Saxon literature is based on loyalty rather than on sexual love (though such poems as *The Wife's Lament* and *The Husband's Message* show that such love existed – if we need any assuring on the point). No woman inspired the hero Beowulf, as far as we know. The great love of heroic literature is that of man for man in the noblest sense, the loyalty of warrior to warrior and of warrior to lord. This is not peculiar to the Anglo-Saxons. In the *Chanson de Roland*, Roland's betrothed Aude receives passing mention – even that is perhaps unusual – but Roland's great love is for Charlemagne. Before his last battle, Roland cries to his companion Oliver:

> For his liege lord a man ought to suffer all hardship and endure great heat and great cold and give both his body and his blood. Lay on with thy lance, and I will smite with Durendal, my good sword which the King gave me. If I die here, may he to whom it shall fall say 'This was the sword of a goodly vassal'.

Again, in his book *Island of the Dragon's Blood*, Douglas Botting tells the story of a sixteenth-century battle between the Portuguese and Arabs on the island of Socotra. The Portuguese leader, Tristan da Cunha, offered the Arabs terms. The story goes on:

> But the Arabs replied that they were much obliged to the worthy chief captain for wishing to spare their lives but that, in telling them of their captain's death, he had given them a sufficient reason for declining to receive the favour, for the Fartaquins [Mahri Arabs] were not accustomed to return alive to their land and leave their captain dead on the field, especially as he was the son of their King. Therefore he might do as he pleased for they were not going to yield.

But it is important to grasp that this loyalty is fundamental to much Old English poetry. Of course, the time was not far distant when the interest of writers switched from the 'heroic' love of man for man to the 'romantic' love of man for woman. C. S. Lewis characterizes the change which then came over European literature as a revolution compared to which 'the Renaissance is a mere ripple on the surface of literature'.

§240 Among the members of the *comitatus*, there was an insistence on decorum and etiquette – *cuþe he duguðe þeaw* 'he knew the usages of noble warriors', observes the *Beowulf* poet at one point – a respect for well-tried weapons, a love of precious jewels and beautiful things, joy in ships and in warriors marching, in horse races and beer, and in feasting and music in the hall. There was too a pride in being a well-governed people. The hall was an oasis of comradeship, order, warmth, and happiness, in sharp contrast to the threatening and chaotic world of discomfort and danger which lay outside. Old English poetry is not made up entirely of gloomy moments. Sometimes there is laughter and mirth.

§241 But there is also a great awareness of the transitoriness of life – *þis læne lif* 'this transitory life' sings the poet. Some critics of Old English literature sometimes talk as if this were an idea peculiar to Germanic or Anglo-Saxon paganism. But other peoples have grasped the idea that life is transitory. Numerous passages could be cited from Latin and Greek authors. Rider Haggard quotes a Zulu saying that life is 'as the breath of oxen in winter, as the quick star that runs along the sky, as the little shadow that loses itself at sunset'. A famous passage in The Wisdom of Solomon, chapter V, compares the passing of the things of this earth to the passage of a shadow, of a ship in the waves, and of a bird or an arrow through the air. In James, chapter IV, we read that life is 'a vapour that appeareth for a little time, and then vanisheth away'. You should therefore view with suspicion any comment on such poems as *The Wanderer* and *The Seafarer* which draws unreal distinctions between pagan and Christian elements as a result of failure to realize that the transience of life is a perpetual human theme peculiar to no civilization, age, or culture.

This theme of transience receives frequent expression in Old English poetry. Three fine examples are *The Wanderer* ll. 92–110, *The Seafarer* ll. 80–93, and a passage from the less-known *Solomon and Saturn*:

Lytle hwile   leaf beoð grene;
ðonne hic cft fcalcwiað,   feallað on eorðan
and forweorniað,   weorðað to duste

'For a little while the leaves are green. Then they turn yellow, fall to the earth and perish, turning to dust.' But while the theme is universal, the response is often different. In both *The Wanderer* and *The Dream of the Rood*, the passing of friends is lamented. But whereas in *The Wanderer* the thought provokes the famous response 'Where are they now?', the dreamer who has gazed upon the Cross affirms triumphantly that they live now in Heaven with the King of Glory.

§242 The transitoriness of all joys was brought home with special force to the man without a lord, always a figure of misery in Old English literature. He may have survived his lord because he was a coward who ran away from battle, like the sons of Odda in *The Battle of Maldon*, or by the fortune of war which decreed that he was badly wounded, but not killed, like the two survivors of the fights in the already-mentioned annal for 755. He may even have betrayed his lord, like Ceolwulf, the foolish thane who ruled Mercia as a Danish puppet for a few years after 874. Because of this uncertainty, a lordless man was suspect wherever he went. We can perhaps to some extent conceive his misery if we ponder the state of mind of people who find themselves in one of the following situations today – a trade-unionist expelled from his union and unable to earn money by his only skill; an army officer or an administrator suddenly expelled without compensation from a former colonial territory where he had made his career; a citizen of the West deserting to the East (or vice versa) for ideological reasons; a discharged convict unable to get a job; or a lonely refugee from behind the Iron Curtain who has left dear ones behind him and now exists without hope in a camp for 'displaced persons'.

§243 What joy and hope the coming of Christianity in the sixth century must have brought to such a man! And not to him alone, but also to those safely within a *comitatus*. For even they had little, if any, belief in a personal after-life, and no awareness of what Professor Southern has called 'the personal and secret tie between man and God'. Surrounded by few of the material comforts we take for granted today, liable to sudden attack and without any real hope for the future, they too must have found in Christianity the peace which passeth understanding. Doubtless, the *Beowulf* poet's remark still held:

Forðon sceall gar wesan
monig morgenceald mundum bewunden,
hæfen on handa, nalles hearpan sweg
wigend weccean, ac se wonna hrefn . . .

'For many a spear, cold with the chill of morning, must be grasped with the palms, lifted by the hand. No sound of harp shall wake the warriors, but the dark raven. . .'. But now the warriors could lie down under the protection of the Almighty and could rise with the name of Christ upon their lips.

§244 To be sure, conversion was neither universal nor immediate. But those who experienced it must have been a strange blend of pagan and Christian, combining as they did the fierce courage and pride of paganism with the new hope derived from Christianity – a blend strikingly seen on the Benty Grange helmet which bears both the pagan boar and the Christian Cross. Something of the same (but perhaps in reverse) must, one imagines, be part of the make-up of those elderly Russians of today who were brought up Christians but who have consciously or unconsciously been influenced by the teachings of Marx. In 1961 Mr. Khrushchev was reported as saying that the Soviet Union possessed a 100-megaton bomb 'which, God grant it, we may never have to explode'. Whether this invocation of God was deliberately cynical, the accidental result of thought-habits formed in youth, or proof that he really was a Christian at heart, one cannot say. But the fact that he could call on God will help us to understand why the *Beowulf* poet could say in the same poem both

Wyrd oft nereð
unfægne eorl, þonne his ellen deah!

'Fate often spares an undoomed man when his courage is good' and

Swa mæg unfæge eaðe gedigan
wean ond wræcsið se ðe Waldendes
hyldo gehealdeþ!

'Thus may an undoomed man whom the grace of the Almighty protects easily survive misery and banishment.'

From this it follows that a poem which contains apparently pagan and apparently Christian ideas (as opposed to one which deals with themes common to both, such as the transience of life) need not be a Christian reworking of a pagan poem. Its author may have been a converted pagan, or, like some elderly Russians today, a man who, because he had lived with survivors of a past civilization, could grasp its values imaginatively and appreciate them even while he himself belonged to a new age.[1]

§245 We have heard recently of Roman Catholic missionaries in Africa singing the Mass to the rhythms of a Congo war-chant and of the weaving of native songs and dances into the same church's baptismal ceremony in New Guinea. Missionaries in Anglo-Saxon England similarly 'baptized' pagan institutions, methods, and concepts. The Yeavering excavations give evidence of a pagan temple converted to Christian use. Bede's account of the poet Cædmon tells how, between 657 and 680, Cædmon sang his famous *Hymn* and so used heroic alliterative verse for Christian purposes – a development of great importance for Old English literature. And in *The Seafarer* and other poems, we find the pagan idea of *lof* Christianized – it now consists of praise on earth and life in Heaven and is to be won by fighting against the Devil and by doing good.

If we bear all this in mind, the incongruities to which our attention is so often drawn by critics of Old English poetry will trouble us less. After all, we can today 'thank our lucky stars' and say 'By Jove!' without believing that the stars really influence our lives or that Jupiter will protect us in battle. Similarly, if we find that our own interpretation of *Beowulf* commits us to the view that its author was a passionate believer in Christianity, we need not be deterred by the fact that he speaks of the power of *wyrd*; see §218 and note that the influence of Latin and Christian thought and means of expression is apparent (in varying degrees) in most of the texts in Part Two of this book.

§246 These problems loom large in Old English literature because we know very little about the genesis of most poems. *Cædmon's Hymn* is attributed to Cædmon and four poems – *Fates of the Apostles*, *Elene*, *Juliana*, and *Christ B* – bear Cynewulf's 'signature' in runes. But this does not give us much help, for Cynewulf is little more than a name. The unfortunate fact is that we just do not know for whom, by whom, when, where, or with what aim, most of the poems were written. This inevitably creates difficulties for us when we try to elucidate them and may lead us to criticize a poem for not having a structure which appeals to us or for not being the poem we think it ought to be.

[1] But see D.Whitelock *The Audience of Beowulf* (Oxford, 1951), esp. pp. 22–28.

Poetry

§247 In *An Introduction to Old English Metre*, Alan Bliss makes three points which need stressing here. The first is that 'OE poetry is not at all primitive; on the contrary, it is very highly artificial and sophisticated'. The second is that 'the vocabulary of OE poetry differs widely from that of prose'. The third is that 'OE poetry varies from most other types of poetry in that the metrical patterns are . . . selected from among the patterns which occur most commonly in natural speech'. The metrical unit is the half-line. Two half-lines alliterating together form the alliterative line which originated among the Germanic peoples in prehistoric times, was used for centuries by Old High German, Old Saxon, and other Germanic, poets, as well as by the Anglo-Saxons, and which in England had a glorious flowering in the fourteenth century with such works as *Sir Gawain and the Green Knight* and *Piers Plowman*. See further §267 and Appendix C.

§248 Apart from *The Metres of Boethius* and the Metrical Version of the Psalms found in the Paris Psalter, the bulk of Old English poetry is to be found in four manuscripts, all of which date approximately from the second half of the tenth century. They are the Junius MS, the Vercelli Book, the Exeter Book, and the *Beowulf* MS. Further description of these manuscripts here would be superfluous, but you may find it interesting to answer the following questions:

Why was the Junius MS so-called? And why did some people call it the Cædmon MS? Has it any connexion with Milton?

How did the Vercelli Book become associated with Italy?

Why is the *Beowulf* MS known as Cotton Vitellius A.xv? What happened to it in 1731?

Where can the Exeter Book be seen? How did it get there?

There are, of course, poems which are not found in these four manuscripts. They have been collected in a volume known as *The Anglo-Saxon Minor Poems*, which is referred to in §264.

§249 The extant poems can be roughly classified according to subject matter.

1. Poems treating Heroic Subjects

Beowulf. Deor. The Battle of Finnsburh. Waldere. Widsith.

2. Historic Poems

The Battle of Brunanburh. The Battle of Maldon.

3. Biblical Paraphrases and Reworkings of Biblical Subjects

The Metrical Psalms. The poems of the Junius MS; note especially *Genesis B* and *Exodus. Christ. Judith.*

4. Lives of the Saints

Andreas. Elene. Guthlac. Juliana.

5. Other Religious Poems

Note especially *The Dream of the Rood* and the allegorical poems – *The Phoenix, The Panther*, and *The Whale*.

6. Short Elegies and Lyrics

The Wife's Lament. The Husband's Message. The Ruin. The Wanderer. The Seafarer. Wulf and Eadwacer. Deor might be included here as well as under 1 above.

7. Riddles and Gnomic Verse

8. Miscellaneous

Charms. The Runic Poem. The Riming Poem.

Note

Four poems – *The Fates of the Apostles, Elene, Christ B*, and *Juliana* – contain Cynewulf's 'signature' in runes.

Prose

§250 As has already been pointed out in §182, English prose was far from being a primitive vehicle of expression at the time of the Norman Conquest. You will be able to watch it developing in the Chronicle and elsewhere. One interesting question you may try to answer for yourself is 'Whose prose do you prefer – that of Alfred or Ælfric?'

§251 Old English prose may be said to fall into the seven main divisions set out below.

1. The Anglo-Saxon Chronicle

The surviving manuscripts – lettered A to H – are discussed in *The Anglo-Saxon Chronicle*, ed. Dorothy Whitelock (Eyre and Spottiswoode, 1961), pp. xi–xviii. MS E (The Laud Chronicle) continues until the death of Stephen in 1154. This is, to all intents and purposes, the end of historical writing in English prose until the fifteenth century.

Miss Whitelock observes that 'the confident attribution of the work to Alfred's instigation cannot be upheld'.

2. The Translations of Alfred and his Circle

King Alfred explained his educational policy in his famous Preface to the *Cura Pastoralis*. This is perhaps the first of his translations. He also translated the *De Consolatione Philosophiae* of Boethius and the *Soliloquia* of St. Augustine, and was responsible for a legal code.

Bishop Wærferth of Worcester translated the *Dialogues* of Gregory the Great at Alfred's request. The OE version of Bede's *Ecclesiastical History* has long been attributed to Alfred. Miss Whitelock, in her British Academy Lecture in 1962, finds no evidence for this, but says that it remains a probability that the work was undertaken at Alfred's instigation. The same is true of the OE version of the *Historia adversus Paganos* of Orosius, which incorporates the story of the voyages of Ohthere and Wulfstan.

3. Homiletic Writings

The most important of these are

(*a*) *The Blickling Homilies*, 971.
(*b*) Ælfric's *Catholic Homilies*, 990–2, and *Lives of the Saints*, 993–8.
(*c*) *The Homilies* of Wulfstan, who died in 1023.

4. Other Religious Prose

This includes translations of portions of both the Old and New Testaments, and a version of the Benedictine Office.

5. Prose Fiction

Here we find the story of *Apollonius of Tyre, Alexander's Lętter to Aristotle,* and *The Wonders of the East*. It has been said that these show 'that long before the Conquest the Anglo-Saxons found entertainment in the exotic romanticism of thc East'.

6. Scientific and Medical Writings

7. Laws, Charters, and Wills

7

Select Bibliography

A separate Bibliography is provided for each chapter of Part One; details of the arrangement will be found in the Contents.

For convenience of reference, each section of the Bibliography has been given its own number and the section-numbers of the discussions to which the books relate have been placed in brackets after each heading in the Bibliography.

GENERAL

§252 A useful guide is

Fred C. Robinson *Old English Literature. A Select Bibliography* (Toronto, 1970).

For fuller details see

Stanley B. Greenfield and Fred C. Robinson *A Bibliography of Publications on Old English Literature to the end of 1972* (Toronto, 1980).

Two publications which appear each year deserve mention:

Anglo-Saxon England (Cambridge University Press)
Old English Newsletter (Center for Medieval and Early Renaissance Studies, State University of New York at Binghamton).

Their value will be apparent on inspection. Both offer annual bibliographies.

CHAPTER I
PRELIMINARY REMARKS ON THE LANGUAGE (§§1–4)

§253 An excellent Introduction to Old English will be found in §§1–22 of A. Campbell's *Old English Grammar* (Clarendon Press, 1959, reprinted with corrections 1962).

On the history of the English language generally, the following books can be recommended:

Albert C. Baugh and Thomas Cable *History of the English Language* (3rd ed., Prentice Hall, 1978)

Otto Jespersen *Growth and Structure of the English Language* (10th ed., Basil Blackwell, 1983).

You will not need a dictionary initially, as a Glossary is supplied in this volume. If you are curious, however, you should begin by using

J. R. Clark Hall *A Concise Anglo-Saxon Dictionary* (4th ed., with Supplement by H. D. Meritt, Cambridge, 1960), reprinted in Medieval Academy Reprints for Teaching 14 (Toronto, 1984).

The most complete dictionary is that known as *Bosworth-Toller*. It is published by the Oxford University Press, and consists of a Dictionary and Supplements. The original Dictionary was very deficient in the letters A–G. Here, in particular, you will have to consult both Dictionary and Supplements.

Some have found

J. F. Madden and F. P. Magoun Jr. *A Grouped Frequency Word-List of Anglo-Saxon Poetry* (The Harvard Old English Series, 1967)

a very helpful guide to learning vocabulary. This lists the words which occur in OE poetry, starting with those which are used most frequently. Most of the first 300 words at least are very common in prose texts.

CHAPTER 2
ORTHOGRAPHY AND PRONUNCIATION (§§5–9)
AND CHAPTER 3
INFLEXIONS (§§10–135)

§254 Although A. Campbell's *Old English Grammar* (see §253 above) is too detailed for you to use by itself in your first few months, it may be safely consulted when you are in difficulty. By looking at the Contents (pp. vii–xi) or the Index, you will be able to find full paradigms, lists of examples of strong verbs or anything else you want, and lucid explanations of any difficulty you may encounter.

CHAPTER 4
WORD FORMATION (§§136–138)

§255 Very helpful discussions and lists will be found in chapter IV of Quirk and Wrenn *An Old English Grammar* and in pp. 39–43 of N. Davis *Sweet's Anglo-Saxon Primer*, which are mentioned in §256.

CHAPTER 5
SYNTAX (§§139–214)

§256 The standard work at present is Bruce Mitchell *Old English Syntax* (2 vols., Clarendon Press, 1985). There are plenty of monographs, but many of them are in German and most of those in English are too complicated for the beginner. One which may prove useful is J. M. Wattie's article called 'Tense' in *Essays and Studies* XVI (1930); this deals with the topics discussed in §§195–211. Some articles relevant to texts in this *Guide* will be found in Bruce Mitchell *On Old English* (Basil Blackwell, 1988).

Short but helpful treatments of the syntax will be found in:

N. Davis *Sweet's Anglo-Saxon Primer* (Clarendon Press, 1953 or later)
P. S. Ardern *First Readings in Old English* (New Zealand University Press, 1948)
R. Quirk and C. L. Wrenn *An Old English Grammar* (Methuen, 1955 or later)
G. L. Brook *An Introduction to Old English* (Manchester University Press, 1955).

CHAPTER 6
INTRODUCTION TO ANGLO-SAXON STUDIES (§§215–251)

History (§§215–218)

§257 The following are recommended:

P. Hunter Blair *An Introduction to Anglo-Saxon England* (2nd ed., Cambridge, 1977)
P. Hunter Blair *Roman Britain and Early England 55 BC—AD 871* (Nelson, 1963)
F. M. Stenton *Anglo-Saxon England* (3rd ed., Oxford, 1971)
Dorothy Whitelock (ed.) *English Historical Documents* Volume 1 *c.* 500–1042 (2nd ed., London, 1979)
David Hill *An Atlas of Anglo-Saxon England 700—1066* (Basil Blackwell, 1981)
James Campbell (ed.) *The Anglo-Saxons* (Oxford, 1982)
Christine Fell *Women in Anglo-Saxon England* (London, 1984), now available in paperback (Basil Blackwell, 1986).

Archaeology (§§219–230)

§258 See §220, the section in which each topic is discussed, and

Richard N. Bailey *Viking Age Sculpture in Northern England* (London, 1980)

Rupert Bruce-Mitford, *The Sutton Hoo Ship Burial*

Vol. 1 *Excavations, background, the ship, dating and inventory* (London, 1975)

Vol. 2 *Arms, armour and regalia* (London, 1978)

Vol. 3 *Late Roman and Byzantine silver, hanging-bowls, drinking vessels, cauldrons and other containers, textiles, the lyre, pottery bottle and other items* (Parts I and II, London, 1983)

Rosemary J. Cramp *Early Northumbrian Sculpture* (Jarrow, 1965)

David A. Hinton *A Catalogue of the Anglo-Saxon Ornamental Metalwork 700–1100 in the Department of Antiquities Ashmolean Museum* (Oxford, 1974)

H. M. Taylor and Joan Taylor *Anglo-Saxon Architecture* (3 vols., Cambridge, 1965–78)

David M. Wilson *Anglo-Saxon Ornamental Metalwork 700–1100 in the British Museum* (London, 1964).

Language (§§231–235)

History of English Prose

§259 On the topics mentioned in §233, see

R. W. Chambers *On the Continuity of English Prose from Alfred to More and his School* (Early English Text Society, 1932).[1]

Some of the points he raises are discussed in

N. Davis 'Styles in English Prose of the Late Middle and Early Modern Period' in *Les Congrès et Colloques de l'Université de Liège*, Volume 21 (1961), pp. 165–184.

See also

R. M. Wilson 'English and French in England 1100–1300', *History* 28 (1943), 37–60.

Vocabulary

Word Formation

See §255.

[1] But his suggestion (p. lxxxvi) that the line between OE and ME can be drawn between the Peterborough annals for 1131 and 1132 is not now accepted; see *The Peterborough Chronicle 1070–1154*, ed. Cecily Clark (2nd ed., Oxford, 1970), pp. lii–lxiii.

Changes of Meaning

§260 This is a difficult subject. Chapter VII of Simeon Potter *Modern Linguistics* (Andre Deutsch, 1957) is a useful and helpful introduction. See §4.

Borrowings

§261 See

M. S. Serjeantson *A History of Foreign Words in English* (Routledge and Kegan Paul, 1935)

A. Campbell *Old English Grammar* (see §253 above), chapter X.

Literature (§§236–251)

Topics raised in §§236–246

§262 On the transition from Epic to Romance, see

R. W. Southern *The Making of the Middle Ages* (Hutchinson, 1953), chapter V.

On the heroic way of, and attitudc to, life, see

D. Whitelock *The Beginnings of English Society* (Penguin, 1952)

J. R. R. Tolkien *Beowulf: The Monsters and the Critics* (British Academy Lecture, 1936)

Fred C. Robinson *Beowulf and the Appositive Style* (Knoxville, 1985)

D. Whitelock *The Audience of Beowulf* (Oxford, 1951).

General Criticism

§263 W. P. Ker *Medieval English Literature* (Oxford, 1912) can still be recommended, though its views on *Beowulf* are now generally out of favour. More recent studies of Old English literature include:

E. G. Stanley (ed.) *Continuations and Beginnings* (London, 1966)

Stanley B. Greenfield and Daniel G. Calder *A New Critical History of Old English Literature*. With a survey of the Anglo-Latin background by Michael Lapidge (New York and London, 1986).

Poetry Texts

§264 Good reading editions include those in the Methuen and Manchester series. The standard edition of *Beowulf* remains that of Fr. Klaeber *Beowulf and the Fight at Finnsburg* (D. C. Heath and Company, 3rd ed., 1950). Virtually the entire corpus of Old English poetry is available in *The Anglo-*

Saxon Poetic Records, published by Columbia University Press and Routledge and Kegan Paul. The volumes are

I Junius MS
II Vercelli Book
III Exeter Book
IV Beowulf and Judith
V The Paris Psalter and the Meters of Boethius
VI Anglo-Saxon Minor Poems.

These volumes contain no glossaries and are for the use of scholars rather than of beginners. *A Concordance to the Anglo-Saxon Poetic Records*, edited by Jess B. Bessinger, Jr. and programmed by Philip H. Smith, Jr., was published by Cornell University Press in 1978.

Other editions of poems which have appeared since Robinson's *Bibliography* (see §252 above) include

The Dream of the Rood edited by M. Swanton (Manchester, 1970)
A Choice of Anglo-Saxon Verse selected with an introduction by Richard Hamer (Faber, 1970)
Daniel and Azarias edited by R. T. Farrell (Methuen, 1974)
Finnsburh Fragment and Episode edited by D. K. Fry (Methuen, 1974)
T. A. Shippey *Poems of Wisdom and Learning in Old English* (Cambridge and Totowa, N.J., 1976)
The Battle of Maldon edited by E. V. Gordon with a supplement by D. G. Scragg (Manchester, 1976)
Exodus edited by P. J. Lucas (Methuen, 1977)
The Old English Riddles of the Exeter Book edited by Craig Williamson (Chapel Hill, 1977)
Christ and Satan: A Critical Edition by R. E. Finnegan (Waterloo, 1977)
Genesis A: A New Edition by A. N. Doane (Madison, 1978)
Resignation edited by Lars Malmberg (Durham, 1979)
The Guthlac Poems of the Exeter Book edited by Jane Roberts (Oxford, 1979)
The Old English Rune Poem: A Critical Edition by Maureen Halsall (Toronto, 1981)
The Battle of Maldon edited by D. G. Scragg (Manchester, 1981)
J. R. R. Tolkien *The Old English Exodus: Text Translation and Commentary* edited by Joan Turville-Petre (Oxford, 1981)
The Old English Riming Poem edited by O. D. Macrae-Gibson (Cambridge, 1983)
Old English Minor Heroic Poems edited by Joyce Hill (Durham, 1983)

Appreciation of the Poetry

§265 See §137 and

Alan Bliss 'v. The Appreciation of Old English Poetry' in *An Introduction to Old English Metre* (Basil Blackwell, 1962)

Greenfield and Calder (§263), chapter 5, 'Some Remarks on the Nature and Quality of Old English Poetry'.

The Use of Oral Formulae

§266 The oral nature of Old English poetry has been much discussed of late. But one needs to beware of the notion sometimes advanced that formulaic poetry is necessarily 'oral' and that all poems must be either strictly 'oral' or strictly 'literary'. Lettered or 'literary' poets certainly carried on the techniques of their 'oral' predecessors, and there seems no real reason why one man should not combine the two techniques. On this topic see initially

L. D. Benson 'The Literary Character of Anglo-Saxon Formulaic Poetry', *Publications of the Modern Languages Association* 81 (1966), 334–341

Jeff Opland *Anglo-Saxon Oral Poetry: A Study of the Traditions* (New Haven and London, 1980).

Metre

§267 The best introduction to Old English metre for beginners is C. S. Lewis's 'The Alliterative Metre' in *Rehabilitations and Other Essays* (London, 1939), pp. 117–32. Fuller and more sophisticated but still addressed to students is Alan Bliss, *An Introduction to Old English Metre* (Oxford, 1962). Bliss's 'The Appreciation of Old English Metre', in *English and Medieval Studies: Presented to J. R. R. Tolkien* . . . ed. Norman Davis and Charles L. Wrenn (London, 1962), pp. 27–40 shows how Old English metre relates to Modern English metre. The most recent comprehensive scholarly study of Old English Metre is Geoffrey Russom, *Old English Metre and Linguistic Theory* (Cambridge, 1987), where one can find references to most of the preceding scholarly studies of the subject. In Appendix C below we offer a brief, general introduction to Old English metre.

Prose Texts

§268 Editions and translations of most of the prose texts are available. Important works which have appeared since Robinson's *Bibliography* (see §252 above) include

Ælfric's Catholic Homilies: The Second Series Text edited by Malcolm Godden (Early English Text Society, 1979)

The Old English Orosius edited by Janet Bately (Early English Text Society, 1980)

Vercelli Homilies IX–XXIII edited by Paul E. Szarmach (Toronto, 1981)

Das altenglische Martyrologium herausgegeben von Günter Kotzer (2 Bände, München, 1981)

The Prose Solomon and Saturn and *Adrian and Ritheus* edited by James E. Cross and Thomas D. Hill (Toronto, 1982)

Eleven Old English Rogationtide Homilies edited by Joyce Bazire and James E. Cross (Toronto, 1982)

The Old English Herbarium and Medicina de Quadrupedibus edited by Hubert Jan de Vriend (Early English Text Society, 1984)

The Old English Life of Machutus edited by David Yerkes (Toronto, 1984)

The Anglo-Saxon Chronicle: A Collaborative Edition. General editors David Dumville and Simon Keynes

Vol. 3: MS A edited by J. M. Bately (Cambridge, 1986)

Vol. 4: MS B edited by Simon Taylor (Cambridge, 1983)

Two Voyagers at the Court of King Alfred by Niels Lund, Christine Fell, and others (York, 1984).

Sources

§269 See

G. N. Garmonsway and Jacqueline Simpson *'Beowulf' and its Analogues* (London, 1968), now available in paperback (New York, 1971)

D. G. Calder and M. J. B. Allen *Sources and Analogues of Old English Poetry. The Major Latin Texts in Translation* (Cambridge and Totowa, 1976)

Daniel G. Calder, Robert E. Bjork, Patrick R. Ford and Daniel F. Melia *Sources and Analogues of Old English Poetry II. The Major Germanic and Celtic Texts in Translation* (Cambridge and Totowa, 1983).

APPENDIX A

Strong Verbs

This Appendix, which contains some of the more common strong verbs, is intended to illustrate §§90–109 and 131–134.

As is pointed out in §92, the 3rd pers. sg. pres. ind. is not part of the gradation series. For this reason, these forms are printed in italics in this Appendix.

You will find here further examples of the simplification of endings referred to in §112.2; note

drīehþ : *drēogan* (class II)
cwiþþ : *cweþan* (class V)
and *wierþ* : *weorþan* (class III).

From *bindan* (class III) we find 2nd and 3rd pers. sg. pres. ind. *bintst* and *bint*.

Verbs in which Verner's Law forms occur (see §§105–107) are marked †.

Verbs without Verner's Law forms where they might be expected (see §108) are marked ‡.

When the forms of a verb rhyme with those of the verb before it in the list, the principal parts have been left for you to fill in.[1]

The Appendix is not a complete list of Old English strong verbs. You may find it useful to note down in the appropriate place any new verbs you come across in your reading.

APPENDIX A.1

Class I

Inf.	*3rd Sg. Pres. Ind.*	*1st Pret.*	*2nd Pret.*	*Past Ptc.*
bītan 'bite'	*bītt*	bāt	biton	biten
flītan 'contend'				
slītan 'tear'				
wītan 'blame'				
ġewītan 'go'				

[1] The principle of 'rhyme association' is an important one. Thus most verbs borrowed into English are made weak. But the French borrowing 'strive' became strong through association with verbs like 'drive'. Similarly the Old English weak verb 'wear' became strong through association with the strong verbs 'bear' and 'tear'.

Inf.	3rd Sg. Pres. Ind.	1st Pret.	2nd Pret.	Past Ptc.
wlītan 'behold'				
wrītan 'write'				
bīdan 'await'	*bītt*	bād	bidon	biden
glīdan 'glide'				
rīdan 'ride'				
slīdan 'slide'				
blīcan 'shine'	*blīcþ*	blāc	blicon	blicen
swīcan 'fail'				
drīfan 'drive'	*drīfþ*	drāf	drifon	drifen
belīfan 'remain'				
grīpan 'seize'	*grīpþ*	grāp	gripon	gripen
hrīnan 'touch'	*hrīnþ*	hrān	hrinon	hrinen
scīnan 'shine'				
stīgan 'ascend'	*stīġþ, stīhþ*	stāg[1]	stigon	stigen
hnīgan 'bow to'				
† līþan 'go'	*līþþ*	lāþ	lidon	liden
† scrīþan 'go'				see §108
† snīþan 'cut'				
‡ mīþan 'conceal'	*mīþþ*	māþ	miþon	miþen
‡ rīsan 'rise'	*rīst*	rās	rison	risen
Contracted Verbs (see §103.3)				
† lēon 'lend'	*līehþ*	lāh	ligon	ligen
† tēon 'accuse'				
† þēon 'prosper'[2]				
† wrēon 'cover'				

Note

The following weak verbs are found with *ī* in the infinitive:
ċīdan 'chide', *cwīþan* 'lament', *ġedīgan* 'survive', *līxan* 'gleam', *rīnan* 'rain', and *snīwan* 'snow'.

APPENDIX A.2

Class II

Inf.	3rd Sg. Pres. Ind.	1st Pret.	2nd Pret.	Past Ptc.
bēodan 'command'	*bīett*	bēad	budon	boden
brēotan 'break'	*brīett*	brēat	bruton	broten
flēotan 'float'				

[1] The form *stāh* sometimes occurs as a result of unvoicing of *g*.

[2] Historically a verb of class III. See A. Campbell *Old English Grammar* §739.

	Inf.	*3rd Sg. Pres. Ind.*	*1st Pret.*	*2nd Pret.*	*Past Ptc.*
	ġēotan 'pour'				
	scēotan 'shoot'				
†	ċēosan 'choose'	*ċīest*	ċēas	curon	coren
†	drēosan 'fall'				
†	frēosan 'freeze'				
†	hrēosan 'fall'				
†	lēosan 'lose'				
	crēopan 'creep'	*crīepþ*	crēap	crupon	cropen
	drēogan 'endure'	*drīehþ*	drēag	drugon	drogen
	flēogan 'fly'				
	lēogan 'tell lies'				
	hrēowan 'rue'	*hrīewþ*	hrēaw	hruwon	hrowen
†	sēoþan 'boil'	*sīeþþ*	sēaþ	sudon	soden
	brūcan 'enjoy'	*brȳcþ*	brēac	brucon	brocen
	lūcan 'lock'				
	būgan 'bow'	*bȳhþ*	bēag	bugon	bogen
	dūfan 'dive'	*dȳfþ*	dēaf	dufon	dofen
	scūfan 'shove'				

Contracted Verbs (see §103.4)

†	flēon 'flee'	*flīehþ*	flēah	flugon	flogen
†	tēon 'draw'				

Note

The following weak verbs are found with *ēo* in the infinitive:
frēogan 'love', *nēosan* (*nēosian*) 'seek out', and *sēowan* (*sēowian*) 'sew'.

APPENDIX A.3

Class III

Inf.	*3rd Sg. Pres. Ind.*	*1st Pret.*	*2nd Pret.*	*Past Ptc.*
(*a*) See §95.				
breġdan 'pull'[1]	*britt*[2]	bræġd	brugdon	brogden
streġdan 'strew'				
berstan 'burst'[3]	*birst*	bærst	burston	borsten
(*b*) see §§96–98.				
beorgan 'protect'	*bierhþ*	bearg	burgon	borgen

[1] This verb has been taken as the basic paradigm of class III (see §95) to make explanation easier. Originally it belonged elsewhere; see A. Campbell *Old English Grammar* §736 (b).

[2] Regular forms of 3rd sg. pres. ind. do not seem to be recorded.

[3] See §95 fn. 1.

Inf.	*3rd Sg. Pres. Ind.*	*1st Pret.*	*2nd Pret.*	*Past Ptc.*
ċeorfan 'cut'	*ċierfþ*	ċearf	curfon	corfen
hweorfan 'go'				
sweorcan 'grow dark'	*swiercþ*	swearc	swurcon	sworcen
weorpan 'throw'	*wierpþ*	wearp	wurpon	worpen
† weorþan 'become'	*wierþ*	wearþ	wurdon	worden
feohtan 'fight'	*fieht*	feaht	fuhton	fohten
† fēolan 'press on'[1]		fealh	fulgon	folgen
(*c*) see §§96–97 and 99.				
delfan 'dig'	*dilfþ*	dealf	dulfon	dolfen
helpan 'help'	*hilpþ*	healp	hulpon	holpen
belgan 'be angry'	*bilhþ*	bealg	bulgon	bolgen
swelgan 'swallow'				
meltan 'melt'	*milt*	mealt	multon	molten
sweltan 'die'				
(*d*) see §100.				
ġieldan 'pay'	*ġielt*	ġeald	guldon	golden
ġiellan 'yell'	*ġielþ*	ġeal	gullon	gollen
ġielpan 'boast'	*ġielpþ*	ġealp	gulpon	golpen
(*e*) see §101.				
grimman 'rage'	*grimþ*	gramm	grummon	grummen
swimman 'swim'				
ġelimpan 'happen'	*ġelimpþ*	ġelamp	ġelumpon	ġelumpen
bindan 'bind'	*bint*	band	bundon	bunden
findan 'find'[2]				
grindan 'grind'				
windan 'wind'				
drincan 'drink'	*drincþ*	dranc	druncon	druncen
scrincan 'shrink'				
swincan 'toil'				
onġinnan 'begin'	*onġinþ*	ongann	ongunnon	ongunnen
winnan 'fight'				
singan 'sing'	*singþ*	sang	sungon	sungen
springan 'spring'				
swingan 'flog'				
þringan 'crowd'				
wringan 'wring'				
birnan 'burn'[3]	*birnþ*	barn	burnon	burnen
irnan 'run'[3]				

[1] See §133.2. Forms of 3rd sg. pres. ind. do not seem to be recorded.
[2] In the 1st pret. *funde* is found alongside *fand*; see §109.
[3] Originally *brinnan, rinnan*. But metathesis occurred; see §95 fn. 1.

Inf.	*3rd Sg. Pres. Ind.*	*1st Pret.*	*2nd Pret.*	*Past Ptc.*
(*f*) Exceptional				
friġnan 'ask'	*friġneþ*	fræġn	frugnon	frugnen
murnan 'mourn'	*myrnþ*	mearn	murnon	

Note
The following verbs are weak:
hringan 'ring' and *ġeþingan* 'determine'.
On *bringan* see §123.2.

APPENDIX A.4

Class IV
(See §94 fn. 1)

Inf.	*3rd Sg. Pres. Ind.*	*1st Pret.*	*2nd Pret.*	*Past Ptc.*
beran 'bear'	*birþ*	bær	bǣron	boren
teran 'tear'				
brecan 'break'	*bricþ*	bræc	brǣcon	brocen
cwelan 'die'	*cwilþ*	cwæl	cwǣlon	cwolen
helan 'hide'				
stelan 'steal'				
scieran 'cut'[1]	*scierþ*	scear	scēaron	scoren
niman 'take'[2]	*nimþ*	nam, nōm	nōmon, nāmon	numen
cuman 'come'[2]	*cymþ*	cōm	cōmon	cumen

APPENDIX A.5

Class V
(See §94 fn. 2)

Inf.	*3rd Sg. Pres. Ind.*	*1st Pret.*	*2nd Pret.*	*Past Ptc.*
† cweþan 'say'	*cwiþþ*	cwæþ	cwǣdon	cweden
etan 'eat'	*itt*	ǣt[3]	ǣton	eten
fretan 'devour'				
metan 'measure'	*met*[4]	mæt	mǣton	meten
‡ ġenesan 'survive'	*ġeneseþ*[4]	ġenæs	ġenǣson	ġenesen
sprecan 'speak'	*spricþ*	spræc	sprǣcon	sprecen
specan 'speak'				
wrecan 'avenge'				
tredan 'tread'	*tritt*	træd	trǣdon	treden

[1] See §103.1. [2] See §§103.2 and 109.
[3] See §109. [4] Regular forms do not seem to be recorded.

Inf.	*3rd Sg. Pres. Ind.*	*1st Pret.*	*2nd Pret.*	*Past Ptc.*
wefan 'weave'	*wifþ*	wæf	wǣfon	wefen
ġiefan 'give'[1]	*ġiefþ*	ġeaf	ġēafon	ġiefen
onġietan 'perceive'[1]	*onġiet*	onġeat	onġēaton	onġieten
	Weak Presents (see §116)			
biddan 'ask'	*bitt*	bæd	bǣdon	beden
licgan 'lie'	*liġeþ, līþ*	læġ	lǣgon	leġen
† þicgan 'partake'	*þiġeþ*	þeah[2]	þǣgon	þeġen
sittan 'sit'	*sitt*	sæt	sǣton	seten
	Contracted Verb (see §103.3)			
† sēon 'see'	*siehþ*	seah[2]	sāwon	sewen

APPENDIX A.6

Class VI

Inf.	*3rd Sg. Pres. Ind.*	*1st Pret.*	*2nd Pret.*	*Past Ptc.*
dragan 'draw'	*dræhþ*	drōg	drōgon	dragen
faran 'go'	*færþ*	fōr	fōron	faren
galan 'sing'	*gælþ*	gōl	gōlon	galen
hladan 'load'	*hladeþ*[3]	hlōd	hlōdon	hladen
wadan 'go'	*wadeþ*[3]			
sacan 'quarrel'	*sæcþ*	sōc	sōcon	sacen
scacan 'shake'				
standan 'stand'[4]	*stent*	stōd	stōdon	standen
	Weak Presents (see §116)			
hebban 'lift'	*hefeþ*	hōf	hōfon	hafen
swerian 'swear'	*swereþ*	swōr	swōron	sworen
scieppan 'create'[5]	*scieþþ*	scōp	scōpon	scapen
	Contracted Verbs (see §§103.3 and 108)			
† lēan 'blame'	*liehþ*	lōh, lōg[6]	lōgon	lagen
† slēan 'strike'				slagen, slæġen

[1] See §103.1. [2] See §97.
[3] Regular forms do not seem to be recorded.
[4] See §94 fn. 3. [5] See §103.1. [6] See §108.

APPENDIX A.7

Class VII
(See §104)

Inf.	*3rd Sg. Pres. Ind.*	*1st Pret.*	*2nd Pret.*	*Past Ptc.*
(*a*)				
bannan 'summon'	*benþ*	bēonn	bēonnon	bannen
spannan 'span'				
blāwan 'blow'	*blǣwþ*	blēow	blēowon	blāwen
cnāwan 'know'				
māwan 'mow'				
sāwan 'sow'				
flōwan 'flow'	*flēwþ*	flēow	flēowon	flōwen
grōwan 'grow'				
rōwan 'row'				
spōwan 'succeed'				
fealdan 'fold'	*fielt*	fēold	fēoldon	fealden
healdan 'hold'				
wealdan 'rule'				
feallan 'fall'	*fielþ*	fēoll	fēollon	feallen
weallan 'boil'				
weaxan 'grow'	*wiext*	wēox	wēoxon	weaxen
bēatan 'beat'	*bīett*	bēot	bēoton	bēaten
hēawan 'hew'	*hīewþ*	hēow	hēowon	hēawen
hlēapan 'leap'	*hlīepþ*	hlēop	hlēopon	hlēapen
	Weak Present (see §116)			
wēpan 'weep'	*wēpeþ*	wēop	wēopon	wōpen
(*b*)				
hātan 'command, call'	*hǣtt*	hēt	hēton	hāten
ondrǣdan 'fear'	*ondrǣtt*	ondrēd	ondrēdon	ondrǣden
rǣdan 'advise'[1]				
lǣtan 'let'	*lǣtt*	lēt	lēton	lǣten
slǣpan 'sleep'	*slǣpþ*	slēp	slēpon	slǣpen
	Contracted Verbs (see §108)			
† fōn 'seize'	*fēhþ*	fēng	fēngon	fangen
† hōn 'hang'				

[1] A weak preterite *rǣdde* is also found.

APPENDIX B

Some Effects of *i*-Mutation

The principle of *i*-mutation set forth in §§52–57 explains the relationship among a number of OE (and Modern English) words which otherwise may be unapparent or puzzling. Thus the *e* of the comparative and superlative forms of *old* (i.e. e*lder*, e*ldest*) is explained by the fact that the comparative and superlative suffixes in this adjective were originally *-ira* and *-ist*, the *i* of which caused mutation of the vowel. (See §75 for OE adjectives which follow this pattern.) Similarly, the OE suffix *-þ(o)*, *-þ(u)*, mentioned in §138 as the element that makes feminine abstract nouns out of adjectives, frequently had *i* in the suffix in pre-OE times (*-iþu*) and hence we see the effects of *i*-mutation in nouns formed from these adjectives:

fūl (*foul*) + **-iþ(u)**, by *i*-mutation and subsequent loss of *i* = **fȳlþ** (*filth*)
hāl (*whole, hale*) + **-iþ(u)** = **hǣlþ** (*health*)
lang (*long*) + **-iþ(u)** = **lengþ** (*length*)
slāw (*slow*) + **-iþ(u)** = **slǣwþ** (*sloth*)
strang (*strong*) + **-iþ(u)** = **strengþ** (*strength*)
wrāþ (*wroth, angry*) + **-iþ(u)** = **wrǣþþo** (*wrath*)

Most pervasive, perhaps, is the *i*-mutation in Class 1 weak verbs explained in §117 *Note*. Weak 1 verbs are derived from nouns, adjectives, or from corresponding strong verbs. The following are derived from the nouns indicated:

cuss (*kiss*) + **jan**, by *i*-mutation and subsequent loss of *j* = **cyssan** (*to kiss*)
dōm (*judgment*) + **jan** = **dēman** (*to judge*)
drēam (*joy*) + **jan** = **drīeman** (*to rejoice*)
fær (*journey*) + **jan** = **ferian** (*to carry*)
flēam (*flight*) + **jan** = **(ge)flīeman** (*to put to flight*)
fōda (*food*) + **jan** = **fēdan** (*to feed*)
frōfor (*comfort*) + **jan** = **frēfran** (*to comfort*)
gelēafa (*belief*) + **jan** = **gelīefan** (*to believe*)
heorte (*heart*) + **jan** = **hiertan** (*to hearten*)
lāf (*leaving*) + **jan** = **lǣfan** (*to leave*)
lār (*lore*) + **jan** = **lǣran** (*to teach*)
lēoht (*light*) + **jan** = **līehtan** (*to shine*)
lust (*pleasure*) + **jan** = **lystan** (*to list, desire*)
nama (*name*) + **jan** = **nemnan** (*to name*)

sāl (*rope*) + **jan** = **sǣlan** (*to fasten*)
scrūd (*clothing*) + **jan** = **scrȳdan** (*to clothe*)
searu (*skill*) + **jan** = **sierwan** (*to plot*)
talu (*tale*) + **jan** = **tellan** (*to tell*)
þurst (*thirst*) + **jan** = **þyrstan** (*to thirst after*)
weorc (*work*) + **jan** = **wyrċan** (*to work*)

The following are derived from the adjectives indicated:

beald (*bold*) + **jan** = **bieldan** (*to embolden*)
brād (*broad*) + **jan** = **brǣdan** (*to spread*)
cōl (*cool*) + **jan** = **cēlan** (*to cool*)
cūþ (*known*) + **jan** = **cȳþan** (*to make known*)
eald (*old*) + **jan** = **ieldan** (*to delay*)
feorr (*far*) + **jan** = **fierran** (*to remove*)
full (*full*) + **jan** = **fyllan** (*to fill*)
fūs (*ready*) + **jan** = **fȳsan** (*to prepare*)
ġeorn (*eager*) + **jan** = **ġiernan** (*to be eager, yearn*)
hāl (*whole, hale*) + **jan** = **hælan** (*to heal*)
rūm (*roomy*) + **jan** = **rȳman** (*to make room*)
scearp (*sharp*) + **jan** = **scierpan** (*to sharpen*)
trum (*strong*) + **jan** = **trymman** (*to strengthen*)
wōd (*mad*) + **jan** = **wēdan** (*to be mad*)

The following are derived from strong verbs, imparting to the meaning of the strong verb a causative sense or a transitive function. The vowel of the weak verb is derived from the vowel of the preterite singular or 1st preterite (see §92) of the corresponding strong verb:

cwæl (pret. of **cwelan**, *to die*) + **jan** = **cwellan** (*to kill*)
dranc (pret. of **drincan**, *to drink*) + **jan** = **drenċan** (*to drench*)
fēoll (pret. of **feallan**, *to fall*) + **jan** = **fiellan** (*to fell*)
fōr (pret. of **faran**, *to go*) + **jan** = **fēran** (*to go, lead*)
hwearf (pret. of **hweorfan**, *to turn*) + **jan** = **hwierfan** (*to move about*)
læg (pret. of **licgan**, *to lie*) + **jan** = **lecgan** (*to lay*)
rās (pret. of **rīsan**, *to rise*) + **jan** = **rǣran** (*to rear, raise*) (Verner's Law §§105–108)
sang (pret. of **singan**, *to sing*) + **jan** = **senġan** (*to singe*)
sæt (pret. of **sittan**, *to sit*) + **jan** = **settan** (*to set*)
sprang (pret. of **springan**, *to spring*) + **jan** = **sprenġan** (*to break*)
swæf (pret. of **swefan**, *to sleep*) + **jan** = **swebban** (*to put to sleep, kill*)
swanc (pret. of **swincan**, *to toil*) + **jan** = **swenċan** (*to press hard*)
wand (pret. of **windan**, *to wind*) + **jan** = **wendan** (*to turn around, wend*)
wearp (pret. of **weorpan**, *to throw*) + **jan** = **wierpan** (*to recover*)

APPENDIX C

Metre

with Examples from the Poems in this *Guide*

In order to appreciate fully the often beautiful aural effects of Old English poetry, one must know something about Old English metre, which is fundamentally different from the metres of Modern English verse.[1] In Modern English there are many different metrical forms, such as iambic pentameter ('Sha̽ll Í co̽mpáre the̽e tó a̽ súmme̽r's dáy?'), trochaic tetrameter ('Tíge̽r, tíge̽r, búrni̽ng bríght'), and anapaestic trimeter ('O̽f the̽ béauti̽fu̽l Ánna̽be̽l Lée'), and a poet normally selects one of these metrical forms and uses it exclusively throughout any poem he or she is writing. In Old English there was but one system of versification which was used for all poems. That system consisted of five variations of a basic verse-scheme, and any one of these five types could be used in any verse a poet might write. The system is based upon accent, alliteration, vowel quantity, and specified patterns of unaccented and accented syllables.

ACCENT

Each line of Old English poetry consists of two half-lines or verses:

> rá̄d a̽nd rǽdde̽,   rínc u̽m tǽhte̽
> (*The Battle of Maldon*, l. 18)

The two half-lines are separated by a pause, or caesura, indicated here by a space. Each half-line has two syllables which are accented. That is, in normal speech they would be pronounced with a heavier accent than the other syllables in the line. In this respect Old English and Modern English are much the same. If we translate the above line

> róde a̽nd cóunselle̽d,   táught the̽ sóldi̽ers

and then pronounce it aloud, we will hear immediately that the accented syllables in the Modern English line are *rode*, *coun-*, *taught*, and *sol-*. Only someone totally ignorant of English pronunciation would pronounce the

[1] Accented syllables are marked with ´, unaccented with ×. In citing the conventions of Modern English metre we ignore so-called free verse; a game without rules is beyond systematic analysis.

line ‘r̽ode ánd c̽ounsélled, t̽aught thé s̽oldíers’. Similarly any Anglo-Saxon would know instinctively that *rād*, *rǣd-*, *rinc-*, and *tǣh-* are the heavily accented syllables in the Old English line. The metrical pattern, or ‘scansion’, of both Old English and Modern English lines may be described as ´ × ´ × ‖ ´ × ´ ×.

ALLITERATION

In the Old English line just cited three of the accented syllables alliterate with each other. That is, they all begin with the same sound, *r-*. This is a required, central feature of Old English verse. The two half-lines must be bound together by alliteration: one of the two accented syllables in the first half-line must alliterate with the first accented syllable of the second half-line. It is permissible for both accented syllables in the first half-line to alliterate (as is the case here), and both often do alliterate, but in the second half-line only the first accented syllable may alliterate.

It is only alliteration of accented syllables that counts. Unaccented syllables which happen to alliterate are irrelevant to scansion and should be ignored. An important rule of alliteration in Old English is that *sp-* alliterates only with another syllable beginning with *sp-*. It does not alliterate with *s-*. The same is true of *sc-* and *st-*, each of which alliterates only with syllables beginning with the same consonant cluster. Four lines from *The Battle of Maldon*, ll. 127–37, illustrate this principle:

Stōdon stædefæste;   stihte hī Byrhtnōð,
. . .
Sende ðā se sǣrinc   sūðerne gār,
. . .
hē scēaf þā mid ðām scylde,   þæt se sceaft tōbærst,
and þæt spere sprengde,   þæt hit sprang ongēan.

Any accented syllable beginning with a vowel alliterates with any other accented syllable beginning with a vowel; the vowels do not have to be the same:

ēce dryhten   ōr onstealde
(Cædmon’s *Hymn*, l. 4)

Here the *ē-* of *ēce* alliterates with the *ō-* of *ōr*. Since the prefix *on-* of *onstealde* is unaccented, its alliteration with the accented syllables is fortuitous and irrelevant: it is ignored in scanning the line.

VOWEL QUANTITY

In addition to accent and alliteration, vowel quantity is also functional in Old English versification. Normally the accented syllables in a line are long.

That is, they have a long vowel (as in *rād*, *rǣd-*, *ēc-*) or they have a short vowel followed by two consonants (*rinc-*, *dryht-*, *scyld-*). Also, an accented word consisting of two short syllables may count as one long syllable, this being what is called 'resolved stress'. Thus *spere* in the last of the four lines quoted above from *The Battle of Maldon* is accented as if it were one syllable. Resolved stress is indicated by ´x͜.

THE FIVE TYPES

We have said that each half-line or verse must have two accented syllables. How many unaccented syllables may a verse have, and where may the accented and unaccented syllables fall in relation to each other? The answers to these questions are: (1) a half-line or verse must have at least two unaccented syllables, and it may have more than two, but only in certain specified positions in the verse; and (2) the relative positions of accented and unaccented syllables which are permitted are described in five basic patterns. In a moment we shall examine these five patterns or types, but first it should be noted that in addition to accented syllables and unaccented syllables there are in Old (as in Modern) English also syllables with secondary accent. That is, they are accented more than unaccented syllables but less than accented syllables. Examples of the three levels of accent may be heard in these three sentences: 'Man is mortal'. 'Blindman's buff is a game'. 'He is speaking German'. In the first sentence *man* is accented. In the second sentence *-man* in *blindman* has secondary accent. In the third sentence *-man* in *German* is unaccented. Or again, *-y* in *penny* is unaccented, while *-knife* in *penknife* has secondary accent. *Pen-* in both words is accented. We mark secondary accent with a `.[2]

We are now ready to examine the five accent-patterns, or verse-types, which modern scholars designate A, B, C, D, and E. In any given poem many or all of the five types will be used to shape individual verses, and they occur in any sequence. An A-verse might be followed by a D-verse, which might be followed by a B-verse. Or two or three consecutive verses might all

[2] To some extent accent may be correlated with grammatical categories:
(a) The root syllables of nouns, adjectives, participles, and infinitives are normally accented, while prefixes, suffixes, prepositions, conjunctions, pronouns, and articles are unaccented. This is the case in Modern as well as Old English; note where the accents fall when you say aloud, 'A careful driver was signalling for a turn'.
(b) Adverbs and finite verbs and the second elements of noun or adjective compounds tend to have secondary accent but can sometimes carry primary accent (when the other syllables in their vicinity are all unaccented) and sometimes are unaccented (when the other syllables in their vicinity are all accented).
(c) Some words (such as prepositions and finite verbs) receive primary accent when they are displaced from their normal position in the sentence. Thus *in* in *mā́ðm iͯn héalleͯ* (11*n*, l. 13) is unaccented, but it is accented in *iͯc hiͯm ín wúniͯge* (11*e*, l. 6).

have the same pattern. As long as a verse fits one of the five patterns, it is metrical. In marking the scansion of the five types, × is used where an unaccented syllable is required; ×'s within parentheses, indicate that up to that number of unaccented syllables *may* occur in that position. Following the scansion formula for each verse-type will be half-lines illustrating that type. The source of these examples is identified by the item-number of the poem in this volume from which the line was taken followed by the line number. Line numbers are followed by either *a* or *b* indicating that the verse is either the first or second half-line in the line.

Type A

´ × (× × × ×) ´ ×

gár tō̽ gū́þĕ̽ (12, l. 13a) féor ă̽fȳ́să̽n (12, l. 3a)
fréan tŏ̽ gĕ̽féohtĕ̽ (12, l. 12a) hǽþĕ̽nĕ̽ ǽ̽t híldĕ̽ (12, l. 55a)
rícĕ̽ ǽ̽ftĕ̽r ṓðrŭ̽m (13, l. 10b) rincă̽ manigĕ̽ (18, l. 728b)

Type B

(× × × ×) × ´ × (×) ´

ŏ̽n úrnĕ̽ éard (12, l. 58a) mē̽ séndŏ̽n tō̽ þḗ (12, l. 29a)
mi̽d hi̽s fráncă̽n ŏ̽fscéat (12, l. 77b) ă̽nd þŏ̽nĕ̽ gṓdă̽n fŏ̽rlḗt (12, l. 187b)
ă̽nd tō̽ þǣ̽rĕ̽ híldĕ̽ stṓp (12, l. 8b) þǣ̽t þū̽ mō̽st séndă̽n raðe (12, l. 30b)

Type C

(× × × × ×) × ´ ´ ×

gĕ̽dṓn hǽfdĕ̽ (12, l. 197b) ŏ̽n búrh rídă̽n (12, l. 291b)
þǣ̽t hī̽ fórð ḗodŏ̽n (12, l. 229b) nĕ̽ tō̽ hrǽdwýrdĕ̽ (16, l. 66b)
þŏ̽nnĕ̽ hi̽t ǣ̽ni̽g mǽð wǽrĕ̽ (12, l. 195b) þǣ̽r i̽s blís mýcĕ̽l (14, l. 139b)

As the last example shows, the second of the two accented syllables in type C verses may be short.[3] Other examples: *is nū sǣl cumen* (14, l. 80b), *æt þām wīgplegan* (12, l. 268b), *ne þurfon mē embe Stūrmere* (12, l. 249a). Under special circumstances short accented syllables are permitted in some other verse types.

[3] Note that the other accented syllable in this line (*blis*) is long because when a monosyllable ends with a consonant it is long for purposes of metre, whether the vowel be long or short. Note *grim* in the first example under Type D.

Type D

´(× × ×)´` ×

grím gū́ðplègăͯ (12, l. 61a) hrī́ð hrḗosèndĕͯ (16, l. 102a)

Óffăͯ þŏͯnĕ sǣ̀lidăͯn (12, l. 286a) héaldĕͯ hiͯs hórdcòfăͯn (16, l. 14a)

Other D-verses are a slight variation of this pattern, the final unaccented syllable(s) changing place with the secondary accent:

bórd órd ŏͯnfèng (12, l. 110b) hrī́m hrū́săͯn bònd (17, l. 32a)

éald éntăͯ gĕͯwèorc (16, l. 87a) béarwăͯs blṓstmŭͯm nìmaðͯ (17, l. 48a)

Type E

´` × (×)´

hrī́mcèaldĕͯ sǣ́ (16, l. 4b) ǽschòlt ăͯscḗoc (12, l. 230b)

wǽlræ̀stĕͯ gĕͯcḗas (12, l. 113b) féalaͯ èalrăͯ gĕͯbā́d (14, l. 125b)

wýn èal gĕͯdrḗas (16, l. 36b) wýrd biͯð fùl ăͯrǣ́d (16, l. 5b)[4]

The following mnemonic (a university of Melbourne *macédoine*) may be helpful in the early stages. Each half-line gives the simplest form of one of the types and alliterates on the accented syllables with the letter by which that type is known.

A.	Anna angry	´ × ´ ×	falling-falling
B.	And Byrhtnoth bold	× ´ × ´	rising-rising
C.	In keen conflict	× ´ ´ ×	clashing
D.	Ding down strongly	´ ´ ` ×	falling by stages
	Deal death to all	´ ´ × `	broken fall
E.	Each one with edge	´ ` × ´	fall and rise

ANACRUSIS

Occasionally one or even two unaccented syllables are allowed to come before a line of type A or D, and these syllables are not counted in the scansion of the line but are treated as a kind of extrametrical prelude. Such syllables are called *anacrusis* and are marked off from the verse proper by a vertical bar:

(Type A) (Type D)

gĕͯ|néréd wiͯð nī́ðĕͯ (18, l. 827a) wiͯ|ðhǽfdĕͯ héaþoͯdḕorŭͯm (18, l. 772a)

[4] Here, as in a few other cases, an unaccented syllable is allowed to fall between the first accented syllable and the syllable with secondary accent.

(Type A)	(Type D)
gebíddaþ him tō þyssum bḗacne (14, l. 83a)	behḗold hrḗowcèarig (14, l. 25a)

COMPLEXITY OF ALLITERATIVE METRE

The elaborate regulations for accent, vowel length, alliteration, and verse types, further complicated by anacrusis, resolved stress, and exceptions to certain regulations, all may leave some students of Old English metre wondering whether they are dealing with an impossibly complex prosody or with no systematic prosody at all.[5] Is there any short collocation with two accented syllables that *cannot* be construed as one of the five types if one invokes enough rules and exceptions to rules? If one is tempted toward such scepticism, it may be useful to consider some of the collocations of Old English words which the metrical system *does* exclude. At first glance one might think that a half-line like *in his beorht blōd* 'into his bright blood' would make an excellent Old English verse, but in fact the Anglo-Saxon ear would immediately reject it as prose, for the accent pattern × × ´ ´ is not one of the five types. *Tala tungena* 'utterances of tongues' might at first glance look like an acceptable type A, but it is not. The first accented syllable is short, and, moreover, A-verses never end in two unaccented syllables; only one may occur at the end of an A-verse. *Grimm and glēaw* 'fierce and wise' might seem to be a vigorous and melodious verse to a beginner, but the Old English verse system rejects it because it has only three syllables, and an Old English verse must have at least four. Study the following collocations and see if you can determine why they are not metrical:

> *ne becōm niht* 'nor did night come';
> *folc wæs fūl* 'the people were filthy';
> *gōd is his gār* 'his spear is good';
> *fela fara* 'many journeys';
> *Hygd ne oftēah* 'Hygd did not withhold';
> *scūfað scyldas tō him* 'they push shields to him'.

HYPERMETRIC VERSE

Occasionally Old English poets shift in the course of a poem to an expanded form of verse which we call hypermetric. Hypermetric verses have three rather than two accented syllables in each half-line; they seem to be com-

[5] The analysis of Old English metre presented here is the traditional one first made by Eduard Sievers in the late nineteenth century and generally accepted by later metrical scholars, such as John C. Pope, *The Rhythm of 'Beowulf'* (New Haven, Conn., 1942; rev. ed. 1966). Students should be aware, however, that some metrical theorists have departed from Sievers' system in details or in principles, and their scansions may differ from those presented here.

posed of a regular verse-type with another half-verse added on. These, for example, seem to be A-verses with an additional accented and unaccented syllable at the end:

> Tíl biþ sĕ þĕ his trḗowĕ gĕhéaldĕþ, nĕ scĕal nǽfrĕ his tórn tŏ rýcĕnĕ
> béorn ŏf his brḗostŭm ăcýþăn, némþĕ hĕ ǣr þă bṓtĕ cúnnĕ,
> éorl mid élnĕ gĕfrémmăn. Wél bið þăm þĕ him ā́rĕ sḗcĕð,
> frṓfrĕ tŏ Fæder ŏn héofonŭm, þǣr ŭs éal sĕo fǽstnŭng stóndĕð.
>
> (*The Wanderer*, ll. 112–15)

For more such lines see selections 14, ll. 8–10, 20–4, 30–4, and 39–49. Hypermetric lines usually occur in groups of three or more and must have had some kind of special effect for an Anglo-Saxon audience, but we do not know what that effect was.

RHYME

Rhyme has no functional role in Old English versification. In Modern English, rhyme demarcates the boundaries of verses and provides ornament. In Old English, as we have seen, these functions are served by alliteration. Rhyme was not unknown to the Anglo-Saxons; as incidental ornament it occurs, for example, in selection 12, ll. 42, 309, and 286, in selection 13, ll. 5b and 7b, and in selection 18, ll. 726, 734, 2258, and 3172. In late Old English verse there are signs that rhyme is beginning to displace alliteration as a functional device; see selection 12, l. 271 and note.

Part Two
Prose and Verse Texts

NOTE

The texts are arranged in order of increasing difficulty. The first three selections are normalized throughout, and palatal *ċ* and *ġ* are distinguished from velar *c* and *g*. The fourth selection is not normalized, but a few peculiarities have been removed to ease transition to the unnormalized texts in the remainder of the readings.

I

Practice Sentences

A. Although sometimes pronounced differently from their MnE descendants, many OE words have the same form and the same basic meaning as their MnE counterparts: e.g. *bliss*, *colt*, *dung*, *elm*, *finger*, *fox*, *handle*, *him*, *land*, *mist*, *nest*, *of*, *on*, *rest*, *sprang*, *winter*, *writ*. Indeed, entire sentences can have essentially the same appearance in OE and MnE, although it must be conceded that such sentences can be composed only through a rather artificial selection of words from the OE lexicon:

> Harold is swift. His hand is strong and his word grim. Late in līfe hē went tō his wīfe in Rōme.
>
> Is his inn open? His cornbin is full and his song is writen. Grind his corn for him and sing mē his song.
>
> Hē is dēad. His bed is under him. His lamb is dēaf and blind. Hē sang for mē.
>
> Hē swam west in storm and wind and frost.
>
> Bring ūs gold. Stand ūp and find wīse men.

B. Many other OE words appear strange at first glance, but when pronounced according to the rules set out in §§5–9 they become immediately recognizable as MnE words in earlier dress: e.g. *bæc*, *biscop*, *ċinn*, *diċ*, *disc*, *ecg*, *feðer*, *hecg*, *hwelp*, *lifer*, *piċ*, *ræfter*, *scort*, *þæċ*, *þing*, *þiðer*, *þrescold*, *wecg*, *wofen*. Among the following sentences set out for practice in pronunciation are a number of words which will become recognizable when pronounced correctly.

> Is his þeġn hēr ġīet?
>
> His līnen socc fēoll ofer bord in þæt wæter and scranc.
>
> Hwǣr is his cȳþþ and cynn?
>
> His hring is gold, his disc glæs, and his belt leðer.
>
> Se fisc swam under þæt scip and ofer þone sciellfisc.
>
> His ċicen ran from his horsweġe, ofer his pæð, and in his ġeard.
>
> Se horn sang hlūde: hlysten wē!
>
> Se cniht is on þǣre brycge.

Sēo cwēn went fram þǣre ċiriċe.
Hēo siteþ on þǣre benċe.
God is gōd.
þis trēow is æsc, ac þæt trēow is āc.
Hē wolde begān wiċċecræft, and hē began swā tō dōnne.
Fuhton ġē manlīċe oþþe mānlīċe?
His smiððe is þām smiðe lēof.

C. After studying key paradigms 1, 2, and 4 (p. 4), you should find most of the grammatical relationships in the following sentences readily understandable:

Iċ bræc þone stān.
Se stān is miċel.
Ðæs stānes miċelnes is wundorliċ.
þes stānwyrhta ġeaf þǣm stāne hīw.
Hē slōh þone mann þȳ stāne.
Sēo sunne is swīðe miċel.
þǣr hēo scīnþ, þǣr biþ dæġ.
Niht is þǣre eorðan sceadu betwēonan þǣre sunnan and mancynne.
þis līf is lǣne, and þēos woruld drēoseþ and fealleþ.
Sing þisne song!
Hīe scufon ūt hira scipu and siġldon tō þǣre sǣ.
On þissum dæġe cwealdon wē þone fēond þisses folces.
Iċ ġeman þā naman þāra folca and þissa folca.
His wīfes nama wæs Elizabeþ.
þēos ġiefu is for ūs, and hēo līcaþ ūs.
Se dēaþ is þisses līfes ende, ac sēo sāwol is undēadliċ.
Hīe hine ne dorston þā þing āscian.
Hwæt þyncþ ēow be Crīste? Hwæs sunu is hē?
Hwæs sunu eart þū? And hwæs dohtor eart þū?
Hwȳ ġeworhte God þā yfelan nǣdran?

2

Two Old Testament Pieces

The Bible and its translations have had a profound influence on the English language and on English literature. Among early experiments in rendering Scripture into the vernacular is that of Ælfric, a dedicated scholar and gifted prose stylist who served as Abbot of Eynsham from 1005 until his death. He had serious reservations about the wisdom of translating the Old Testament (see selection 4 below), but on request he did so, rendering the Latin Vulgate version into relatively clean prose marred only occasionally by un-English, Latinate constructions. Readers can compare his work with that of the great King James translation, corresponding excerpts of which are provided on the facing page along with the Latin version for those who might like to compare the Old English with its approximate source. Since the King James translators worked from Greek and Hebrew originals rather than from the Vulgate, the correspondence between the two English versions is inexact.

The text is basically that of Bodleian Library, Oxford, MS Laud Misc. 509, but it has been normalized throughout.

The Fall of Man (Genesis 3: 1–19)

Old English Version

Ēac swelċe sēo nǣdre wæs ġēappre þonne ealle þā ōðre nīetenu þe God ġeworhte ofer eorðan; and sēo nǣdre cwæð tō þām wīfe: 'Hwȳ forbēad God ēow þæt ġē ne ǣten of ǣlcum trēowe binnan Paradīsum?' þæt wīf andwyrde: 'Of þāra trēowa wæstme þe sind on Paradīsum wē etað: and of þæs trēowes wæstme, þe is onmiddan neorxenawange, God bebēad ūs þæt wē ne ǣten, ne wē þæt trēow ne hrepoden þȳ lǣs þe wē swulten.' þā cwæð sēo nǣdre eft tō þām wīfe: 'Ne bēo ġē nāteshwōn dēade, þēah þe ġē of þām trēowe eten. Ac God wāt sōðlīċe þæt ēowre ēagan bēoð ġeopenode on swā hwelċum dæġe swā ġē etað of þām trēowe; and ġē bēoð þonne englum ġelīċe, witende ǣġðer ġe gōd ġe yfel.' þā ġeseah þæt wīf þæt þæt trēow wæs gōd tō etanne, be þām þe hire þūhte, and wlitiġ on ēagum and lustbǣre on ġesihðe; and ġenam þā of þæs trēowes wæstme and ġeǣt, and sealde hire were: hē ǣt þā. And hira bēġra ēagan wurdon ġeopenode: hīe oncnēowon þā þæt hīe nacode wǣron, and sīwodon him fīclēaf and worhton him wǣdbrēċ.

Eft þā þā God cōm and hīe ġehīerdon his stefne, þǣr hē ēode on neorxenawange ofer middæġ, þā behȳdde Adam hine, and his wīf ēac swā dyde, fram Godes ġesihðe onmiddan þām trēowe neorxenawanges. God clipode þā Adam, and cwæð: 'Adam, hwǣr eart þū?'

3 **forbēad . . . þæt ġē ne ǣten** Since OE uses multiple negation for emphasis (§184.4*f*), the negative sense of 'forbade' is here merely reinforced by *ne*. Translate either 'forbade . . . that you should eat' or 'commanded . . . that you should not eat'.

5 **wē etað** literally, 'we eat', but translate 'we do eat'.

6–7 **ne wē þæt trēow ne hrepoden þȳ lǣs þe** 'nor might we touch that tree lest . . .'. As in l. 3, the double negative *ne* conj. (§184.4*d*) . . . *ne* adv. (§184.4*a*) is for emphasis and should not be translated as double negative in Modern English.

8 **Ne bēo ġē** 'You will not be.' For the form and meaning of *bēo* see §§111 and 196. Cf. the form of *bēoð* in l. 10.

12 **gōd tō etanne** 'good to eat'. For this use of the inflected infinitive see §205.2*d*.

be þām þe 'as'. See glossary under *se, þæt, sēo* and §169.

hire þūhte 'it seemed to her'. Impersonal verb (§212).

14 The object of the verbs *ġeǣt, sealde*, and *ǣt* (i.e. 'fruit') is understood (§193.7).

hē ǣt þā 'he ate then'.

16 **him . . . him** Both occurrences mean 'for themselves'. Cf. note to l. 18.

17–18 **þā þā . . . þā** 'when . . . then'. See §151.

18 **hine** 'himself'. In OE the personal pronouns also serve as reflexive pronouns: cf. the second *mē* 'myself' in l. 22.

King James Version

Now the serpent was more subtil than any beast of the field which the Lord
God had made. And he said unto the woman, Yea, hath God said, Ye shall
not eat of every tree of the garden?
2 And the woman said unto the serpent, We may eat of the fruit of the
trees of the garden:
3 But of the fruit of the tree which *is* in the midst of the garden, God
hath said, Ye shall not eat of it, neither shall ye touch it, lest ye die.
4 And the serpent said unto the woman, Ye shall not surely die:
5 For God doth know that in the day ye eat thereof, then your eyes shall
be opened, and ye shall be as gods, knowing good and evil.
6 And when the woman saw that the tree *was* good for food, and that it
was pleasant to the eyes, and a tree to be desired to make *one* wise, she took
of the fruit thereof, and did eat, and gave also unto her husband with her,
and he did eat.
7 And the eyes of them both were opened, and they knew that they *were*
naked; and they sewed fig leaves together, and made themselves aprons.
8 And they heard the voice of the Lord God walking in the garden in the
cool of the day: and Adam and his wife hid themselves from the presence of
the Lord God amongst the trees of the garden.
9 And the Lord God called unto Adam, and said unto him, Where *art*
thou?

Latin Vulgate Version

Sed et serpens erat callidior cunctis animantibus terrae, quae fecerat
Dominus Deus. Qui dixit ad mulierem: Cur praecepit vobis Deus ut non
comederetis de omni ligno paradisi? [2]Cui respondit mulier: De fructu lig-
norum, quae sunt in paradiso, vescimur; [3]de fructu vero ligni, quod est in
medio paradisi, praecepit nobis Deus ne comederemus et ne tangeremus
illud, ne forte moriamur. [4]Dixit autem serpens ad mulierem: Nequaquam
morte moriemini. [5]Scit enim Deus quod in quocumque die comederitis ex
eo, aperientur oculi vestri, et eritis sicut dii scientes bonum et malum.
[6]Vidit igitur mulier quod bonum esset lignum ad vescendum et pulchrum
oculis aspectuque delectabile, et tulit de fructu illius et comedit deditque
viro suo, qui comedit. [7]Et aperti sunt oculi amborum. Cumque cogno-
vissent se esse nudos, consuerunt folia ficus et fecerunt sibi perizomata.
[8]Et, cum audissent vocem Domini Dei deambulantis in paradiso ad
auram post meridiem, abscondit se Adam et uxor eius a facie Domini Dei
in medio ligni paradisi. [9]Vocavitque Dominus Deus Adam et dixit ei: Ubi

Hē cwæð: 'Þīne stefne iċ ġehīerde, lēof, on neorxenawange, and iċ ondrēd mē, for þām þe iċ eom nacod, and iċ behȳdde mē.' God cwæð: 'Hwā sæġde þē þæt þū nacod wǣre, ġif þū ne ǣte of þām trēowe þe iċ þē bebēad þæt þū of ne ǣte?' Adam cwæð: 'Þæt wīf þæt þū mē forġeafe tō ġefēran, sealde mē of þām trēowe, and iċ ǣt.' God cwæð tō þām wīfe: 'Hwȳ dydest þū þæt?' Hēo cwæð: 'Sēo nǣdre bepǣhte mē and iċ ǣt.'

God cwæð tō þǣre nǣdran: 'For þām þe þū þis dydest, þū bist āwierġed betweox eallum nīetenum and wilddēorum. Þū gǣst on þīnum brēoste and etst þā eorðan eallum dagum þīnes līfes. Iċ sette fēondrǣdene betweox þē and þām wīfe and þīnum ofspringe and hire ofspringe; hēo tōbrȳt þīn hēafod and þū sierwst onġēan hire hō.'

Tō þām wīfe cwæð God ēac swelċe: 'Iċ ġemaniġfealde þīne iermða and þīne ġeēacnunga; on sārnesse þū ācenst ċild and þū bist under weres onwealde and hē ġewielt þē.' Tō Adame hē cwæð: 'For þām þe þū ġehīerdest þīnes wīfes stefne and þū ǣte of þǣm trēowe, þe iċ þē bebēad þæt þū ne ǣte, is sēo eorðe āwierġed on þīnum weorce; on ġeswincum þū etst of þǣre eorðan eallum dagum þīnes līfes. Þornas and brēmelas hēo āspryt þē, and þū etst þǣre eorðan wyrta. On swāte þīnes andwlitan þū brȳcst þīnes hlāfes, oð þæt þū ġewende tō eorðan, of þǣre þe þū ġenumen wǣre, for þām þe þū eart dūst and tō dūste wierþst.'

21–2 **iċ ondrēd mē** 'I was afraid.' The *mē* is reflexive and need not be translated in Modern English. (But cf. early Modern English 'fear *thee* not'.)

22 **For þām þe** 'Because' (§§169–170). So also in ll. 28, 36, and 41–2.

29–32 **gǣst . . . etst . . . sette . . . tōbrȳt . . . sierwst** present tense used with future meaning (§196). Several present-tense verbs in the following paragraph (e.g. *ġemaniġfealde*, *ācenst*, *ġewielt*, *etst*, *āspryt*, *brȳcst*) should also be translated as future.

32 **tōbrȳt** The verb ending *-eþ* has disappeared through syncope and assimilation. (See §112.2.) So also in *ġewielt*, *āspryt* in the following paragraph.

39 **hēo** is fem. nom. sg. agreeing in gender with its antecedent, *sēo eorðe*.

40–1 **þīnes hlāfes** The verb *brūcan* takes a genitive object here. See §190.6.

41 **þǣre þe** 'which'. *þe* combines with *þǣre* to form a compound rel. pron. See §162.4.

10 And he said, I heard thy voice in the garden, and I was afraid, because I *was* naked; and I hid myself.

11 And he said, Who told thee that thou *wast* naked? Hast thou eaten of the tree, whereof I commanded thee that thou shouldest not eat?

12 And the man said, The woman whom thou gavest *to be* with me, she gave me of the tree, and I did eat.

13 And the Lord God said unto the woman, What *is* this *that* thou hast done? And the woman said, The serpent beguiled me, and I did eat.

14 And the Lord God said unto the serpent, Because thou hast done this, thou *art* cursed above all cattle, and above every beast of the field; upon thy belly shalt thou go, and dust shalt thou eat all the days of thy life:

15 And I will put enmity between thee and the woman, and between thy seed and her seed; it shall bruise thy head, and thou shalt bruise his heel.

16 Unto the woman he said, I will greatly multiply thy sorrow and thy conception; in sorrow thou shalt bring forth children; and thy desire *shall be* to thy husband, and he shall rule over thee.

17 And unto Adam he said, Because thou hast hearkened unto the voice of thy wife, and hast eaten of the tree, of which I commanded thee, saying, Thou shalt not eat of it: cursed *is* the ground for thy sake; in sorrow shalt thou eat *of* it all the days of thy life;

18 Thorns also and thistles shall it bring forth to thee; and thou shalt eat the herb of the field;

19 In the sweat of thy face shalt thou eat bread, till thou return unto the ground; for out of it wast thou taken: for dust thou *art*, and unto dust shalt thou return.

es? [10]Qui ait: Vocem tuam audivi in paradiso et timui eo quod nudus essem
et abscondi me. [11]Cui dixit: Quis enim indicavit tibi quod nudus esses, nisi
quod ex ligno, de quo praeceperam tibi ne comederes, comedisti?
[12]Dixitque Adam: Mulier, quam dedisti mihi sociam, dedit mihi de ligno,
et comedi. [13]Et dixit Dominus Deus ad mulierem: Quare hoc fecisti? Quae
respondit: Serpens decepit me, et comedi.

[14]Et ait Dominus Deus ad serpentem: Quia fecisti hoc, maledictus es
inter omnia animantia et bestias terrae: super pectus tuum gradieris et
terram comedes cunctis diebus vitae tuae. [15]Inimicitias ponam inter te et
mulierem, et semen tuum et semen illius; ipsa conteret caput tuum, et tu
insidiaberis calcaneo eius. [16]Mulieri quoque dixit: Multiplicabo aerumnas
tuas et conceptus tuos: in dolore paries filios et sub viri potestate eris et
ipse dominabitur tui. [17]Adae vero dixit: Quia audisti vocem uxoris tuae et
comedisti de ligno, ex quo praeceperam tibi ne comederes, maledicta terra
in opere tuo: in laboribus comedes ex ea cunctis diebus vitae tuae. [18]Spinas
et tribulos germinabit tibi, et comedes herbam terrae. [19]In sudore vultus tui
vesceris pane, donec revertaris in terram, de qua sumptus es; quia pulvis
es, et in pulverem reverteris.

Abraham and Isaac (Genesis 22: 1–19)

Old English Version

God wolde þā fandian Abrahames ġehīersumnesse, and clipode his naman, and cwæð him þus tō: 'Nim þīnne āncennedan sunu Īsaac, þe þū lufast, and far tō þām lande *Visionis* hraðe, and ġeoffra hine þǣr uppan ānre dūne.' Abraham þā ārās on þǣre ilcan nihte, and fērde mid twām cnapum tō þām fierlenan lande, and Īsaac samod, on assum rīdende. Þā on þām þriddan dæġe, þā hīe þā dūne ġesāwon þǣr þǣr hīe tō scoldon tō ofslēanne Īsaac, þā cwæð Abraham tō þām twām cnapum þus: 'Anbīdiað ēow hēr mid þām assum sume hwīle. Iċ and þæt ċild gāð unc tō ġebiddenne, and wē siððan cumað sōna eft tō ēow.' Abraham þā hēt Īsaac beran þone wudu tō þǣre stōwe, and hē self bær his sweord and fȳr. Īsaac þā āscode Abraham his fæder: 'Fæder mīn, iċ āscie hwǣr sēo offrung sīe; hēr is wudu and fȳr.' Him andwyrde sē fæder, 'God foresceāwað, mīn sunu, him self þā offrunge.' Hīe cōmon þā tō þǣre stōwe þe him ġesweotolode God, and hē þǣr wēofod ārǣrde on þā ealdan wīsan, and þone wudu ġelōgode swā swā hē hit wolde habban tō his suna bærnette siððan hē ofslæġen wurde. Hē ġeband þā his sunu, and

44 **cwæð him þus tō** 'spoke to him thus'. In OE the preposition can sometimes follow the object (§213).

45 **þām lande *Visionis*** 'the land of Moriah'. The Hebrew name *Moriah* was taken by Biblical commentators to mean 'vision' etymologically, and both the Vulgate and the OE translator preserve this sacral etymology, substituting the Latin word *visionis* for the name itself. For the peculiar use of name-meanings by OE writers, see *Anglia* 86 (1968), 14–58.

48–9 **þā dūne . . . þǣr þǣr hīe tō scoldon tō ofslēanne** 'the mountain where they must (go) to slay'. The verb of motion following *scoldon* is understood (§205.1). For *þǣr þǣr* 'where' see §168, *þǣr* 3.

50 ēow reflexive. OE *anbīdian* takes a reflexive object, but modern 'wait' does not. Therefore ignore *ēow* in translation.

51 **unc** The reflexive pronoun need not be translated.

54 **sīe** 'is, may be'. The present subjunctive form of the verb 'to be' is used here because there is no offering present. Cf. the contrasting use of the indicative in 'hēr *is* wudu and fȳr'. See §156.

55 **foresceāwað** pres. tense with future meaning.

57 **on þā ealdan wīsan** 'in the ancient manner'. The OE translator is concerned to emphasize that human sacrifice, although seemingly condoned by the Old Testament, is no longer an acceptable practice.

59 **ofslæġen wurde** 'had been slain'. For pret. subj. expressing future-in-the-past see §174.

King James Version

And it came to pass after these things, that God did tempt Abraham, and said unto him, Abraham: and he said, Behold, *here* I *am*.

2 And he said, Take now thy son, thine only *son* Isaac, whom thou lovest, and get thee into the land of Mōrīah; and offer him there for a burnt offering upon one of the mountains which I will tell thee of.

3 And Abraham rose up early in the morning, and saddled his ass, and took two of his young men with him, and Isaac his son, and clave the wood for the burnt offering, and rose up, and went unto the place of which God had told him.

4 Then on the third day Abraham lifted up his eyes, and saw the place afar off.

5 And Abraham said unto his young men, Abide ye here with the ass; and I and the lad will go yonder and worship, and come again to you.

6 And Abraham took the wood of the burnt offering, and laid *it* upon Isaac his son; and he took the fire in his hand, and a knife, and they went both of them together.

7 And Isaac spake unto Abraham his father, and said, My father: and he said, Here *am* I, my son. And he said, Behold the fire and the wood: but where *is* the lamb for a burnt offering?

8 And Abraham said, My son, God will provide himself a lamb for a burnt offering: so they went both of them together.

9 And they came to the place which God had told him of; and Abraham built an altar there, and laid the wood in order, and bound Isaac his son, and laid him on the altar upon the wood.

Latin Vulgate Version

Quae postquam gesta sunt, tentavit Deus Abraham et dixit ad eum:
Abraham, Abraham. At ille respondit: Adsum. [2]Ait illi: Tolle filium tuum
unigenitum, quem diligis, Isaac, et vade in terram visionis, atque ibi offeres
eum in holocaustum super unum montium, quem monstravero tibi. [3]Igitur
Abraham de nocte consurgens stravit asinum suum ducens secum duos
iuvenes et Isaac filium suum; cumque concidisset ligna in holocaustum,
abiit ad locum, quem praeceperat ei Deus. [4]Die autem tertio, elevatis
oculis, vidit locum procul, [5]dixitque ad pueros suos: Exspectate hic cum
asino: ego et puer illuc usque properantes, postquam adoraverimus,
revertemur ad vos. [6]Tulit quoque ligna holocausti et imposuit super Isaac
filium suum; ipse vero portabat in manibus ignem et gladium. Cumque
duo pergerent simul, [7]dixit Isaac patri suo: Pater mi. At ille respondit: Quid
vis, fili? Ecce, inquit, ignis et ligna; ubi est victima holocausti? [8]Dixit autem
Abraham: Deus providebit sibi victimam holocausti, fili mi. Pergebant
ergo pariter: [9]et venerunt ad locum, quem ostenderat ei Deus in quo
aedificavit altare, et desuper ligna composuit. Cumque alligasset Isaac
filium suum, posuit eum in altare super struem lignorum [10]extenditque

his sweord ātēah, þæt hē hine ġeoffrode on þā ealdan wīsan. Mid þām þe hē wolde þæt weorc beġinnan, þā clipode Godes engel arodlīċe of heofonum, 'Abraham!' Hē andwyrde sōna. Sē engel him cwæð þā tō: 'Ne ācwele þū þæt ċild, ne þīne hand ne āstreċe ofer his swēoran! Nū iċ oncnēow sōðlīċe þæt þū swīðe ondrǣtst God, nū þū þīnne āncennedan sunu ofslēan woldest for him.'

Þā beseah Abraham sōna underbæc and ġeseah þǣr ānne ramm betweox þām brēmelum be þām hornum ġehæft, and hē āhefde þone ramm tō þǣre offrunge and hine þǣr ofsnāð Gode tō lāce for his sunu Īsaac. Hē hēt þā þā stōwe *Dominus videt*, þæt is 'God ġesiehð', and ġīet is ġesæġd swā, *In monte Dominus videbit*, þæt is 'God ġesiehð on dūne.' Eft clipode se engel Abraham and cwæð, 'Iċ swerie þurh mē selfne, sæġde se Ælmihtiga, nū þū noldest ārian þīnum āncennedan suna, ac þē wæs mīn eġe māre þonne his līf, iċ þē nū bletsie and þīnne ofspring ġemaniġfealde swā swā steorran on heofonum and swā swā sandċēosol on sǣ. Þīn ofspring sceal āgan hira fēonda gatu, and on þīnum sǣde bēoð ealle þēoda ġebletsode for þām þe þū ġehīersumodest mīnre hǣse þus.'

Abraham þā ġeċierde sōna tō his cnapum and fērdon him hām swā mid heofonliċre bletsunge.

60 **ġeoffrode** pret. subj. 'might offer'.
Mid þām þe 'when' (§171).
63 **tō** see note to l. 44.
64–5 **Nū iċ oncnēow . . . nū þū** 'Now I perceive . . . now that thou'. *Nū . . . nū . . .* are correlative conjunctions. See §§150–153.
64 **ondrǣtst** For this form instead of *ondrǣdest*, see §112.2.
67 **ġehæft** see §187(*b*).
69–70 ***Dominus videt*** 'The Lord sees.' ***In monte Dominus videbit*** 'on the mountain the Lord will see'.

10 And Abraham stretched forth his hand, and took the knife to slay his son.

11 And the angel of the LORD called unto him out of heaven, and said, Abraham, Abraham: and he said, Here *am* I.

12 And he said, Lay not thine hand upon the lad, neither do thou any thing unto him: for now I know that thou fearest God, seeing thou hast not withheld thy son, thine only *son* from me.

13 And Abraham lifted up his eyes, and looked, and behold behind *him* a ram caught in a thicket by his horns: and Abraham went and took the ram, and offered him up for a burnt offering in the stead of his son.

14 And Abraham called the name of that place Jehōvahjīreh: as it is said *to* this day, In the mount of the LORD it shall be seen.

15 And the angel of the LORD called unto Abraham out of heaven the second time,

16 And said, By myself have I sworn, saith the LORD, for because thou hast done this thing, and hast not withheld thy son, thine only *son*:

17 That in blessing I will bless thee, and in multiplying I will multiply thy seed as the stars of the heaven, and as the sand which *is* upon the sea shore; and thy seed shall possess the gate of his enemies;

18 And in thy seed shall all the nations of the earth be blessed; because thou hast obeyed my voice.

19 So Abraham returned unto his young men, and they rose up and went together to Beershēba; and Abraham dwelt at Beershēba.

manum et arripuit gladium, ut immolaret filium suum. [11]Et ecce angelus
Domini de caelo clamavit dicens: Abraham, Abraham. Qui respondit:
Adsum. [12]Dixitque ei: Non extendas manum tuam super puerum, neque
facias illi quidquam: nunc cognovi quod times Deum, et non pepercisti
unigenito filio tuo propter me. [13]Levavit Abraham oculos suos viditque
post tergum arietem inter vepres haerentem cornibus, quem adsumens
obtulit holocaustum pro filio. [14]Appellavitque nomen loci illius Dominus
videt. Unde usque hodie dicitur: In monte Dominus videbit.

[15]Vocavit autem angelus Domini Abraham secundo de caelo dicens:
[16]Per memetipsum iuravi, dicit Dominus: quia fecisti hanc rem et non
pepercisti filio tuo unigenito propter me, [17]benedicam tibi et multiplicabo
semen tuum sicut stellas caeli et velut harenam, quae est in litore maris;
possidebit semen tuum portas inimicorum suorum: [18]et benedicentur in
semine tuo omnes gentes terrae quia oboedisti voci meae. [19]Reversusque
est Abraham ad pueros suos, abieruntque Bersabee simul, et habitavit ibi.

3

A Colloquy on the Occupations

Teachers of Latin in the Middle Ages sometimes composed dialogues or colloquies for their pupils to memorize, the assumption being that one learns a foreign language best by actually speaking it. Ælfric, who had already written a Latin *Grammar*, composed a *Colloquy* as a companion piece. He improved on the traditional form considerably, touching his characters with life and giving the exercise dramatic interest. His *Colloquy* is of particular value to modern readers because it offers an informal glimpse of Anglo-Saxon social structure, with representatives of various occupations explaining their function in the society in which they lived. Ælfric provides a series of questions for the Latin teacher to ask, and pupils assuming the roles of the various craftsmen then recite the assigned responses. By rotating pupils in the various roles, the teacher could be sure that each would learn a full range of vocabulary and syntactical structures.

Some time after Ælfric composed his Latin exercise, another Anglo-Saxon translated it into Old English. The charm of Ælfric's work is not wholly lost in this rendering, but as it stands the translation is inappropriate for modern students of Old English to use in learning the language, since it slavishly follows the Latin constructions of the source text, thus producing unnatural, distorted syntax and phrasing. But in 1897 Henry Sweet, one of the greatest modern scholars of Old English, revised the translation into idiomatic prose. The text below is an adaptation and abbreviation of Sweet's version, which was published in his *First Steps in Anglo-Saxon* (Oxford, 1897), pp. 28–38. The text is normalized throughout.

The Monk

Hwelċne cræft canst þū?

Iċ eom munuc.

Hwæt cunnon þās þīne ġefēran?

Sume sind ierþlingas, sume scēaphierdas, sume oxanhierdas, sume huntan, sume fisceras, sume fugleras, sume ċīepemenn, sume scōwyrhtan, sume sealteras, sume bæceras.

The Ploughman

Hwæt seġst þū, ierþling? Hū begǣst þū þīnne cræft?

Lā lēof, þearle iċ swince! Ǣlċe dæġe iċ sceal on dæġrǣd ūtgān. þonne sceal iċ þā oxan tō felda drīfan and tō þǣre sylh ġeocian. Nis nān winter swā stearc þæt iċ dyrre æt hām lūtian: ne dearr iċ for mīnes hlāfordes eġe. Ac þonne iċ þā oxan ġeġeocod hæbbe, and þæt scear and þone culter on þǣre sylh ġefæstnod hæbbe, þonne sceal iċ fulne æcer erian oþþe māre.

Hæfst þū ǣnigne ġefēran?

Ġiese, iċ hæbbe cnapan: sē sceal þā oxan mid gāde þȳwan. Sē is nū hās for ċiele and hrēame.

Hwæt māre dēst þū? Hæfst þū ġīet māre tō dōnne?

Ġiese lēof, miċel iċ hæbbe tō dōnne! Iċ sceal þāra oxena binne mid hīeġe āfyllan, and hīe wæterian, and hira steall feormian.

Ēalā, þæt is miċel ġedeorf!

Ġiese lēof, hit is miċel ġedeorf, for þǣm þe iċ neom frēo.

The Shepherd

Hwæt seġst þū, scēaphierde? Hæfst þū ǣniġ ġedeorf?

Ġiese lēof, iċ hæbbe miċel ġedeorf! On ǣrnemerġen iċ drīfe mīn scēap tō lǣswe. Siþþan stande iċ ofer hīe mid hundum, þȳ lǣs þe wulfas hīe forswelgen. þonne lǣde iċ hīe on ǣfen onġēan tō hira locum. Iċ hīe melce tuwa on dæġe. Iċ macie buteran and ċīese. And iċ eom mīnum hlāforde ġetrīewe.

The Oxherd

Ēalā oxanhierde, hwæt dēst þū?

Lā lēof, iċ swince þearle! þonne se ierþling þā oxan onġeocaþ, þonne lǣde iċ hīe tō lǣswe; and ealle niht iċ stande ofer hīe, waciende for þēofum; and þæs on morgenne iċ hīe betǣċe eft þǣm ierþlinge, wel ġefylde and ġewæterode.

The Hunter

Is þes mann ān of þīnum ġefērum?

Ġiese.

10–11 for mīnes hlāfordes eġe 'for fear of my lord'. See §190.2.

11–12 þonne . . . þonne 'when . . . then'. See §§151–152.

15 sē 'he'. See §§15 and 193.7. When demonstrative *se* is used in place of personal pronoun, it is stressed and the vowel is long.

31 þæs 'afterwards'. A frequent idiomatic meaning of the gen. sg. of *þæt*. See §168 *þæs* 1.

Canst þū ǣniġ þing?

Ānne cræft iċ cann.

Hwelċne cræft canst þū?

Iċ eom hunta.

Hwæs hunta eart þū?

Iċ eom þæs cyninges hunta.

Hū begǣst þū þīnne cræft?

Iċ breġde mē nett, and āsette hīe on ġehæpre stōwe. Þonne ġetyhte iċ mīne hundas þæt hīe þāra wilddēora ēhten, oþ þæt hīe unwærlīċe on þā nett becumen. Þonne hīe þus ġelæht sind, þonne cume iċ tō, and hīe on þǣm nettum ofslēa.

Ne canst þū būtan nettum huntian?

Ġiese, iċ cann būtan nettum huntian.

Hū?

Iċ fō þā wilddēor mid swiftum hundum.

Hwelċ wilddēor ġefēhst þū swīþost?

Iċ ġefō heorotas, and rān, and bāras, and hwīlum haran.

Wǣre þū tōdæġ on huntoþe?

Nese, for þǣm hit is sunnandæġ; ac ġiestrandæġ iċ wæs on huntoþe.

Hwæt ġefēnge þū?

Iċ ġefēng twēġen heorotas and ānne bār.

Hū ġefēnge þū hīe?

Þā heorotas on nettum iċ ġefēng, and þone bār iċ ofsticode.

Hū wǣre þū swā ġedyrstiġ þæt þū bār ofsticodest?

Þā hundas hine bedrifon tō mē, and iċ þǣr fæstlīċe onġēanstōd, and hine fǣrlīċe mid spere ofsticode.

Swīþe ġedyrstiġ wǣre þū þā!

Ne sceal hunta forhtmōd bēon, for þǣm missenlicu wilddēor wuniaþ on wudum.

Hwæt dēst þū ymb þīnne huntoþ?

Iċ selle þǣm cyninge swā hwæt swā iċ ġefō, for þǣm iċ eom his hunta.

Hwæt selþ hē þē?

Hē scrȳtt mē wel and fētt, and hwīlum hē mē hors selþ oþþe bēag, þæt iċ þȳ ġeornor mīnne cræft begā.

42 **Iċ breġde mē nett** 'I weave nets for myself.' Compare modern colloquial English 'I bought me a hat.'

45 **cume iċ tō** 'I come up'. *Tō* here is the adverb.

69 **scrȳtt ... fētt** 'clothes ... feeds'. For the form of the verbs, see §112.2.

70 **þȳ ġeornor** 'the more eagerly'. This use of the instr. *þȳ* is the source of modern phrases like 'the bigger the better' or 'the more the merrier'. See §168 *þȳ*.

The Fisherman

Hwelċne cræft canst þū?

Iċ eom fiscere.

Hwæt beġietst þū of þīnum cræfte?

Bīleofan iċ mē beġiete, and scrūd, and feoh.

Hū ġefēhst þū þā fiscas?

Iċ gā on mīnne bāt, and rōwe ūt on þā ēa, and weorpe mīn nett on þā ēa. Hwīlum iċ weorpe angel ūt mid ǣse, oþþe spyrtan; and swā hwæt swā hīe ġehæftaþ iċ nime.

Hwæt dēst þū gif hit unclǣne fiscas bēoþ?

Iċ weorpe þā unclǣnan ūt, and nime þā clǣnan mē tō mete.

Hwǣr ċīepst þū þīne fiscas?

On þǣre ċeastre.

Hwā byġþ hīe?

Þā ċeasterware. Ne mæġ iċ hira swā fela ġefōn swā iċ sellan mæġe.

Hwelċe fiscas ġefēhst þū?

Ǣlas, and hacodas, and scēotan, and ealle ōþre fiscas þe on þǣm ēam swimmaþ.

For hwȳ ne fiscast þū on sǣ?

Hwīlum iċ dō swā, ac seldon; for þǣm hit is mē miċel rēwett tō þǣre sǣ.

Hwæt ġefēhst þū on þǣre sǣ?

Hæringas, and leaxas, and styrian, and loppestran, and crabban, and fela ōþerra fisca.

Wilt þū hwæl fōn?

Niċ!

For hwȳ?

For þǣm miċel pleoh is þæt man hwæl ġefō. Lǣsse pleoh mē biþ þæt iċ tō þǣre ēa gā mid mīnum bāte þonne iċ mid manigum scipum on hwælhuntoþ fare.

For hwȳ swā?

For þǣm mē is lēofre þæt iċ fisc ġefō þe iċ ofslēan mæġ þonne iċ fisc ġefō þe nealles þæt ān mē selfne ac ēac swelċe mīne ġefēran mid ānum sleġe besenċan mæġ oþþe ofslēan.

74 **mē** See note to l. 42 above.

79 **unclǣne fiscas** Cf. Deuteronomy 14: 10: 'whatsoever [fish] hath not fins and scales ye may not eat; it is unclean unto you'. Some Anglo-Saxons scrupulously observed many of the Mosaic dietary laws.

80 **mē tō mete** 'for my food'. See §191.2.

84 **hira . . . fela** See §190.4.

102 **mē is lēofre** '(it) is more agreeable to me', i.e. 'I prefer'.

103 **nealles þæt ān . . . ac ēac swelċe** 'not only . . . but also'.

And þēah maniġe ġefōþ hwalas, and þǣm frēċennessum ætberstaþ, and miċelne sceatt þanon beġietaþ.

Sōþ þū seġst; ac iċ ne dearr for þǣm iċ eom forhtmōd.

The Fowler

Hwæt seġst þū, fuglere? Hū beswīcst þū þā fuglas?

Iċ hīe on maniġfealde wīsan beswīce: hwīlum mid nettum, hwīlum mid grīnum, hwīlum mid træppum, hwīlum mid līme, hwīlum mid hwistlunge, hwīlum mid hafoce.

Hæfst þū hafocas?

Ġiese.

Canst þū temman hafocas?

Ġiese, iċ cann: hū scolden hīe mē nytte bēon, būtan iċ hīe temman cūþe?

Sele mē hafoc!

Iċ þē selle lustlīċe, ġif þū mē selst swiftne hund. Hwelċne hafoc wilt þū habban, þone māran hwæþer þe þone lǣssan?

Sele mē þone māran! Hū āfētst þū þīne hafocas?

Hīe hīe selfe fēdaþ on wintra ġe ēac swelċe mē, and on lenċtene iċ hīe lǣte tō wuda ætflēogan; and iċ mē nime briddas on hærfest and hīe ġetemme.

For hwȳ lǣtst þū þā ġetemedan hafocas þē ætflēogan?

For þǣm iċ nyle hīe on sumera fēdan, for þǣm þe hīe þearle etaþ.

Ac maniġe fēdaþ þā ġetemedan ofer sumor, þæt hīe hīe eft ġearwe hæbben.

Ġiese, hīe dōþ swā. Ac iċ nyle on swelċum ġeswince mid him bēon, for þǣm iċ cann ōþre ġefōn – nealles ānne, ac maniġe.

The Merchant

Hwæt seġst þū, mangere?

Iċ secge þæt iċ eom swīþe nytt þǣm cyninge, and þǣm ealdormannum, and þǣm weligum, and eallum folce.

Hū?

Iċ āstīge on mīn scip mid mīnum hlæstum, and fare ofer sǣ, and selle mīn þing, and bycge dēorwierþu þing þe on þissum lande

115 **būtan** 'unless'. (So *cūðe* is subjunctive: see §179.5.)

118 **Iċ þē selle** The direct object (*hafoc*) is understood. See note to 2/14.

121 **Hīe hīe selfe fēdaþ** 'They feed themselves.' The first *hīe* is nom., the second acc. (used reflexively).

122 **mē** 'for myself'. Cf. note to l. 42 above.

ācenned ne bēoþ; and iċ hit lǣde tō ēow hider ofer sǣ mid miċlum plēo; and hwīlum iċ þolie forlidennesse, swā þæt mē losiaþ eall mīn þing, and iċ self unēaþe cwic ætberste.

Hwelċ þing lǣtst þū ūs hider ofer sǣ?

Pællas, seoloc, seldcūþ rēaf, wyrtġemang, wīn, ele, elpendbān, dēorwierþe ġimmas, gold, tin, mæstling, ār, seolfor, glæs, and fela ōþerra þinga.

Wilt þū þīn þing hēr on lande sellan wiþ þǣm ilcan weorþe þe þū hīe þǣr ūte mid ġebohtest?

Niċ; hwæt fremede mē þonne mīn ġedeorf? Ac iċ wile hīe wiþ māran weorþe hēr sellan þonne iċ hīe þǣr mid ġebohte, þæt iċ mæġe mē sum ġestrēon beġietan, þe iċ mē mid āfēdan mæġe and mīn wīf and mīn bearn.

The Shoemaker

Þū scōwyrhta, hwæt wyrċst þū ūs tō nytte?

Mīn cræft is ēow swīþe nytt and swīþe nīedbehēfe. Iċ bycge hȳda and fell, and hīe ġearcie mid mīnum cræfte, and wyrċe þǣrof missenliċes cynnes ġescȳ, leþerhosa, þwangas, ġerǣdu, flascan, and fǣtelsas; and ne mæġ ēower nān ofer winter wunian būtan mīnum cræfte.

The Salter

Ēalā þū sealtere, hwæt fremeþ ūs þīn cræft?

Mīn cræft fremeþ ēow eallum þearle. Ne mæġ ēower nān flǣscmetta brūcan būtan mīnum cræfte. Hwelċ mann mæġ swētmetta brūcan būtan sealtes swæcce? Hwā ġefylþ his cleofan and hēdærn būtan mīnum cræfte? Ēowru butere eall ēow losaþ and ēower ċīese būtan iċ hīe mid mīnum cræfte ġehealde. Ne ġē ne magon furþum ēowerra wyrta brūcan būtan mē.

The Baker

Hwæt seġst þū, bæcere? Hwǣm fremeþ þīn cræft?

Būtan mīnum cræfte ǣlċ bēod biþ ǣmettiġ ġeþūht, and būtan

138–9 mē losiaþ eall mīn þing 'all my things are lost to me', i.e. 'I lose everything'.
148 þe . . . mid 'with which'. See §163.3.
150 ūs tō nytte 'of use to us'.
154 ēower nān 'none of you'.
164 biþ . . . ġeþūht 'will seem'.

hlāfe ǣlċ mete biþ tō wlǣttan ġehwierfed. Iċ ġestrangie manna heortan: iċ eom wera mæġen; ġe furþum þā lȳtlingas nyllaþ mē forþolian.

The Cook

Hwæt secge wē be þǣm cōce? Beþurfon wē his cræftes tō āwihte?

Ġif ġē mē of ēowrum ġefērscipe ūtādrīfaþ, ġē etaþ ēowre wyrta grēne and ēowre flǣscmettas hrēawe; ne magon ġē furþum fǣtt broþ habban būtan mīnum cræfte.

Ne reċċe wē be þīnum cræfte: nis hē ūs nā nīedbehēfe, for þǣm wē magon selfe sēoþan þā þing þe tō sēoþanne sind, and brǣdan þā þing þe tō brǣdanne sind.

Ġif ġē mē ūtādrīfaþ and þus dōþ, þonne bēo ġē ealle þēowas, and nān ēower ne biþ hlāford; and þēah hwæþre ġē ne magon etan būtan mīnum cræfte.

Critique of the Occupations

Ēalā munuc, iċ ġesēo þē habban gōde ġefēran and swīþe nytte; hæfst þū ōþre ēac him?

Iċ hæbbe īsensmiþas, goldsmiþas, seolforsmiþas, trēowwyrhtan, and maniġe ōþre.

Hæfst þū wīsne ġeþeahtere?

Ġewisslīċe iċ hæbbe: hū mæġ ūre ġefērscipe bēon ġewissod būtan ġeþeahtere?

Ēalā þū wīsa ġeþeahtere, hwæt seġst þū? Hwelċ þissa cræfta is þē fyrmest ġeþūht?

Iċ þē secge, Godes þēowdōm is mē fyrmest ġeþūht betweox þissum cræftum, swā swā Crīst on his godspelle cwæþ 'Fyrmest sēċaþ Godes rīċe, and þās þing eall ēow bēoþ tōġeīeċed'.

And hwelċ woruldcræft is þē fyrmest ġeþūht?

Eorþtilþ; for þǣm se ierþling fētt ūs ealle.

(Se smiþ seġþ:) Hwanon hæfþ se ierþling scear oþþe culter, oþþe furþum gāde, būtan of mīnum cræfte? Hwanon hæfþ se fiscere angel, oþþe se scōwyrhta āwel, oþþe se sēamere nǣdle būtan of mīnum ġeweorce?

168 **secge wē** See §111.
173 **hē** The masculine pronoun agrees with the gender of its antecedent *cræfte*.
174–5 **tō sēoþanne . . . tō brǣdanne** 'to be boiled . . . to be roasted'.
179 **iċ ġesēo þē habban** 'I see you to have', i.e. 'I see that you have'.
186–7 **is þē . . . geþūht** 'seems to you'.
189–90 Luke 12:31 'But rather seek ye the kingdom of God; and all these things shall be added unto you.'

(Se ġeþeahtere andswaraþ:) Sōþ þū seġst; ac ūs eallum lēofre is mid þǣm ierþlinge tō wīcianne þonne mid þē: for þǣm se ierþling selþ ūs hlāf and drynce; ac þū, hwæt selst þū ūs on þīnre smiþþan būtan īsene spearcan, and bēatendra slecga swēġ and blāwendra bielga?

(Se trēowwyrhta seġþ:) Hwelċ ēower ne notaþ mīnes cræftes, þonne iċ ēow eallum hūs wyrċe and scipu and missenlicu fatu?

(Se smiþ andswaraþ:) Ēalā trēowwyrhta, for hwȳ spriċst þū swā, þonne furþum ān þȳrel þū ne miht dōn būtan mīnum cræfte?

(Se ġeþeahtere seġþ:) Ēalā ġefēran and gōde wyrhtan, uton hrædlīċe ġesēman þās ġeflitu, and sīe sibb and ġeþwǣrnes betweox ēow, and fremme ǣlċ ōþrum on his cræfte! And uton weorþian þone ierþling, of þǣm wē beġietaþ ūs selfum bīleofan and fōdor ūrum horsum! And iċ ġelǣre eallum wyrhtum þisne rǣd: þæt ānra ġehwelċ his cræft ġeornlīċe begā. For þǣm sē þe his cræft forlǣtt, sē biþ fram þǣm cræfte forlǣten. Swā hwelċ swā þū sīe, swā mæssepreōst, swā munuc, swā ċeorl, swā cempa, begā ġeornlīċe þīnne cræft! And bēo þæt þæt þū eart! For þǣm hit is miċel demm and miċel scand ġif man nyle bēon þæt þæt hē is and þæt þæt hē bēon sceal.

207 sīe 'let there be'. Pres. subj. of *bēon* (§127).
209 of þǣm 'from whom' (§162.3).
212–13 Swā hwelċ swā . . . swā . . . swā 'whatsoever . . . whether . . . whether'.
215 þæt þæt 'that which'.

4

Two Characteristic Prose Works by Ælfric

Preface to Genesis

When a medieval scholar like Ælfric read the Bible, he saw behind the literal sense of the words a host of allegorical and typological meanings which had been discerned by biblical commentators from early Christian times to his own day. These meanings make up the 'spiritual sense' (*þæt gāstlice andgit*) as opposed to the literal meaning (*sēo nacede gerecednis*) of the Bible and are one of the means by which medieval Christians reconciled the sometimes bizarre and violent events of the Old Testament with the doctrine of the New. It is therefore understandable that when Ælfric's patron Æthelweard asked him to make the Old Testament available to the laity through translation, the devout scholar was apprehensive. What would the average Christian make of polygamy, human sacrifice, and other Old Testament practices when he read of them without a priest at hand to explain the 'real', spiritual sense of these things? In the Preface below, Ælfric explains these matters in a letter to Æthelweard, giving us a revealing example of how a medieval Christian scholar in Anglo-Saxon England analysed Scripture and applied it to his system of belief. He also makes it clear that he is at heart opposed to translation of the Old Testament (and elsewhere he even has misgivings about translating the New).

Although the prose of Ælfric's Preface is simple and straightforward and therefore seems appropriate as an early reading selection, some students may find the subject-matter unfamiliar and perplexing. Such students may prefer to read selection 7 before selection 4.

The text is that of Bodleian Library MS Laud Misc. 509, except that a few spellings have been normalized to ease transition into the unnormalized texts in the remainder of the reader.

Incipit prefatio Genesis Anglice

Ælfrīc munuc grēt Æðelwærd ealdormann ēadmōdlīce. Þū bǣde mē, lēof, þæt ic sceolde ðē āwendan of Lǣdene on Englisc þā bōc Genesis. Ðā þūhte mē hefigtīme þē tō tīðienne þæs, and þū cwǣde þā þæt ic ne þorfte nā māre āwendan þǣre bēc būton tō Isaace, Abrahames suna, for þām þe sum ōðer man þē hæfde āwend fram Isaace þā bōc oþ ende. Nū þincð mē, lēof, þæt þæt weorc is swīðe plēolic mē oððe ǣnigum men tō underbeginnenne, for þan þe ic ondrǣde, gif sum dysig man þās bōc rǣt oððe rǣdan gehȳrð, þæt hē wille wēnan þæt hē mōte lybban nū on þǣre nīwan ǣ swā swā þā ealdan fæderas leofodon þā on þǣre tīde ǣr þan þe sēo ealde ǣ gesett wǣre, oþþe swā swā men leofodon under Moyses ǣ. Hwīlum ic wiste þæt sum mæssepr ēost, se þe mīn magister wæs on þām tīman, hæfde þā bōc Genesis, and hē cūðe be dǣle Lǣden understandan; þā cwæð hē be þām hēahfædere Iācōbe, þæt hē hæfde fēower wīf – twā geswustra and heora twā þīnena. Ful sōð hē sǣde, ac hē nyste, ne ic þā gīt, hū micel tōdāl ys betweox þǣre ealdan ǣ and þǣre nīwan. On anginne þisere worulde nam se brōðer hys swuster tō wīfe, and hwīlum ēac se fæder tȳmde be his āgenre dehter, and manega hæfdon mā wīfa tō folces ēacan, and man ne mihte þā æt fruman wīfian būton on his siblingum. Gyf hwā wyle nū swā lybban æfter Crīstes tōcyme swā swā men leofodon ǣr Moises ǣ oþþe under Moises ǣ, ne byð se man nā Crīsten, ne hē furþum wyrðe ne byð þæt him ǣnig Crīsten man mid ete.

Þā ungelǣredan prēostas, gif hī hwæt lītles understandað of þām

1 **Incipit . . . Anglice** 'Here begins the preface to Genesis in English.'

2 **grēt** For assimilation of the pres. tense ending -*(e)þ* both here and elsewhere (e.g. *rǣt*, *stynt* below) see §112.2. Writers of letters in OE frequently begin in the third person, as here, and then shift to the first person.

Æðelwærd was a secular patron of Ælfric, a descendant of the house of King Alfred the Great, and the author of a Latin historical work, the *Chronicon Æthelweardi.*

4 **þūhte** Impersonal verb with subject 'it' understood. See also *þincð* in the next sentence; cf. §212.

10 **on þǣre nīwan ǣ** 'in (the time of) the new law' (i.e. the New Testament).

10–11 **þā ealdan fæderas** 'the patriarchs' (of the Old Testament).

11 **þā** 'then'.

12 **wǣre** Subj. follows *ǣr þan þe* (§174.4).

14 **be dǣle** 'in part'.

15–16 **hē hæfde fēower wīf** See Genesis 29: 16–30: 13.

17 **sǣde** Originally *sæġde* (§126), but between a front vowel and *d*, *n*, or *ð* OE *ġ* tends to disappear and the preceding vowel is lengthened. Cf. *foresǣde*, l. 97 below.

20 **mā wīfa** 'more wives (than one)'.

21 **on** 'from among'.

hwā 'someone' (§20).

25 **prēostas . . . hī** The repetition of subject is otiose: see §148 and cf. *hē* (l. 78).

hwæt lītles 'something of a little', i.e. 'a little something'.

Lǣdenbōcum, þonne þincð him sōna þæt hī magon mǣre lārēowas bēon; ac hī ne cunnon swā þēah þæt gāstlice andgit þǣrtō, and hū sēo ealde ǣ wæs getācnung tōweardra þinga, oþþe hū sēo nīwe gecȳþnis æfter Crīstes menniscnisse wæs gefillednys ealra þǣra þinga þe sēo ealde gecȳðnis getācnode tōwearde be Crīste and be hys gecorenum. Hī cweþaþ ēac oft be Pētre, hwī hī ne mōton habban wīf swā swā Pētrus se apostol hæfde, and hī nellað gehīran ne witan þæt se ēadiga Pētrus leofede æfter Moises ǣ oþ þæt Crīst, þe on þām tīman tō mannum cōm and began tō bodienne his hālige godspel and gecēas Pētrum ǣrest him tō gefēran: þā forlēt Pētrus þǣrrihte his wīf, and ealle þā twelf apostolas, þā þe wīf hæfdon, forlēton ǣgþer ge wīf ge ǣhta, and folgodon Crīstes lāre tō þǣre nīwan ǣ and clǣnnisse þe hē self þā ārǣrde. Prēostas sindon gesette tō lārēowum þām lǣwedum folce. Nū gedafnode him þæt hig cūðen þā ealdan ǣ gāstlīce understandan and hwæt Crīst self tǣhte and his apostolas on þǣre nīwan gecȳðnisse, þæt hig mihton þām folce wel wissian tō Godes gelēafan and wel bīsnian tō gōdum weorcum.

Wē secgað ēac foran tō þæt sēo bōc is swīþe dēop gāstlīce tō understandenne, and wē ne wrītað nā māre būton þā nacedan gerecednisse. Þonne þincþ þām ungelǣredum þæt eall þæt andgit bēo belocen on þǣre ānfealdan gerecednisse; ac hit ys swīðe feor þām. Sēo bōc ys gehāten Genesis, þæt ys 'gecyndbōc' for þām þe hēo ys firmest bōca and spricþ be ǣlcum gecinde (ac hēo ne spricð nā be þǣra engla gesceapenisse). Hēo onginð þus: *In principio creauit deus celum et terram*, þæt ys on Englisc, 'On anginne gesceōp God heofenan and eorðan.' Hit wæs sōðlīce swā gedōn, þæt God ælmihtig geworhte on anginne, þā þā hē wolde, gesceafta. Ac swā þēah æfter gāstlicum andgite þæt anginn ys Crīst, swā swā hē self cwæþ tō þām Iūdēiscum: 'Ic eom angin, þe tō ēow sprece.' Þurh þis angin worhte God Fæder heofenan and eorþan, for þan þe hē

27 **þǣrtō** '(pertaining) thereto'.

31 **hwī** '(asking) why'.

35 **him tō gefēran** 'for his companion' (§191.2).

39 **gedafnode** '(it) would befit' (pret. subj.).

40 **hig** An alternate spelling of *hī*, *hīe* 'they'. Since OE *ig* sometimes becomes *ī*, the sound *ī* was sometimes spelled *ig*.

47–8 **feor þām** 'far from that'.

48 **gecynd**, like Latin *genus*, means 'origin' and 'species'.

49–50 **hēo . . . hēo . . . Hēo** The pronoun agrees with the gender of its antecedent *bōc* (§187.2*a*).

50 ***In principio*** . . . 'In the beginning God created Heaven and earth.' Genesis 1:1.

55 **Ic eom angin**, etc. Revelation 1:8, 21:6, 22:13.

gesceōp ealle gesceafta þurh þone Sunu, se þe wæs ǣfre of him ācenned, wīsdōm of þām wīsan Fæder.

Eft stynt on þǣre bēc on þām forman ferse, *Et spiritus dei ferebatur super aquas*, þæt is on Englisc, 'And Godes Gāst wæs geferod ofer wæteru.' Godes Gāst ys se Hālga Gāst, þurh þone gelīffæste se Fæder ealle þā gesceafta þe hē gesceōp þurh þone sunu, and se Hālga Gāst færð geond manna heortan and silð ūs synna forgifenisse, ǣrest þurh wæter on þām fulluhte, and siþþan þurh dǣdbōte; and gif hwā forsihð þā forgifenisse þe se Hālga Gāst sylð, þonne bið his synn ǣfre unmyltsiendlic on ēcnysse. Eft ys sēo hālige þrīnnys geswutelod on þisre bēc, swā swā ys on þām worde þe God cwæð: 'Uton wircean mannan tō ūre ānlīcnisse.' Mid þām þe hē cwæð, 'Uton wircean,' ys sēo þrinnis gebīcnod; mid þām þe hē cwæð, 'tō ūre ānlīcnisse,' ys sēo sōðe ānnis geswutelod; hē ne cwæð nā menifealdlīce tō ūrum ānlīcnissum, ac ānfealdlīce tō ūre ānlīcnisse. Eft cōmon þrī englas tō Abrahame and hē spræc tō him eallum þrīm swā swā tō ānum. Hū clipode Abēles blōd tō Gode būton swā swā ǣlces mannes misdǣda wrēgað hine tō Gode būtan wordum? Be þisum lītlum man mæg understandan hū dēop sēo bōc ys on gāstlicum andgite, þēah þe hēo mid lēohtlicum wordum āwriten sig. Eft Iōsēp, þe wæs geseald tō Ēgipta lande and hē āhredde þæt folc wið þone miclan hunger, hæfde Crīstes getācnunge þe wæs geseald for ūs tō cwale and ūs āhredde fram þām ēcan hungre helle sūsle.

þæt micele geteld þe Moises worhte mid wunderlicum cræfte on þām wēstene, swā swā him God self gedihte, hæfde getācnunge Godes gelaðunge þe hē self āstealde þurh his apostolas mid menigfealdum frætewum and fægerum þēawum. Tō þām geweorce brōhte þæt folc gold and seolfor and dēorwirðe gimstānas and menigfealde mǣrða; sume ēac brōhton gātehǣr, swā swā God bebēad. þæt gold getācnode ūrne gelēafan and ūre gōde ingehygd

58 **wīsdōm** i.e. Christ, the Logos.
Fæder see §60.2.
59–60 ***Et spiritus*** ... 'And the spirit of God was carried over the waters.' Genesis 1:2.
61 **þurh þone** 'through which' (§162.3).
67 **ys** '(it) is' (§193.7).
68 **Uton ... ānlīcnisse** Genesis 1:26. In what follows, Ælfric (who was a grammarian) concentrates on the significance of grammatical number in the scriptural passage.
72 **Eft cōmon þrī englas**, etc. Genesis 18:1–5.
73 **Hū clipode Abēles blōd**, etc. Genesis 4:10.
77 **sig** = *sī*, *sīe* 'may be'. See note to l. 40 above.
79 **þe** The antecedent is *Crīstes*. See §163.4.
81 ff. **geteld** The tabernacle is described in Exodus, chapters 35–9.

þe wē Gode offrian sceolon; þæt seolfor getācnode Godes sprǣca and þā hālgan lāra þe wē habban sceolon tō Godes weorcum; þā gimstānas getācnodon mislice fægernissa on Godes mannum; þæt gātehǣr getācnode þā stīðan dǣdbōte þǣra manna þe heora sinna behrēowsiað. Man offrode ēac fela cinna orf Gode tō lāce binnan þām getelde, be þām ys swīðe menigfeald getācnung; and wæs beboden þæt sē tægel sceolde bēon gehāl ǣfre on þām nȳtene æt þǣre offrunge for þǣre getācnunge þæt God wile þæt wē simle wel dōn oð ende ūres līfes: þonne bið se tægel geoffrod on ūrum weorcum. Nū ys sēo foresǣde bōc on manegum stōwum swīðe nearolīce gesett, and þēah swīðe dēoplīce on þām gāstlicum andgite, and hēo is swā geendebyrd swā swā God self hig gedihte þām wrītere Moise, and wē durron nā māre āwrītan on Englisc þonne þæt Lǣden hæfð, ne þā endebirdnisse āwendan būton þām ānum þæt þæt Lǣden and þæt Englisc nabbað nā āne wīsan on þǣre sprǣce fadunge. Ǣfre se þe āwent oððe se þe tǣcð of Lǣdene on Englisc, ǣfre hē sceal gefadian hit swā þæt Englisc hæbbe his āgene wīsan, elles hit bið swīðe gedwolsum tō rǣdenne þām þe þæs Lǣdenes wīsan ne can. Is ēac tō witanne þæt sume gedwolmen wǣron þe woldon āwurpan þā ealdan ǣ, and sume woldon habban þā ealdan and āwurpan þā nīwan, swā swā þā Iūdēiscan dōð. Ac Crīst self and his apostolas ūs tǣhton ǣgðer tō healdenne þā ealdan gāstlīce and þā nīwan sōðlīce mid weorcum. God gesceōp ūs twā ēagan and twā ēaran, twā nosþirlu and twēgen weleras, twā handa and twēgen fēt, and hē wolde ēac habban twā gecȳðnissa on þissere worulde geset, þā ealdan and þā nīwan, for þām þe hē dēð swā swā hine selfne gewyrð, and hē nǣnne rǣdboran næfð, ne nān man þearf him cweðan tō: 'Hwī dēst þū swā?' Wē sceolon āwendan ūrne willan tō his gesetnissum and wē ne magon gebīgean his gesetnissa tō ūrum lustum.

Ic cweðe nū þæt ic ne dearr ne ic nelle nāne bōc æfter þissere of Lǣdene on Englisc āwendan, and ic bidde þē, lēof ealdorman, þæt

92ff. **fela cinna orf** 'cattle of many kinds'. Leviticus 3:9 specifies that the 'whole rump' of the sacrificial animal must be offered, but Ælfric's spiritual interpretation of the injunction is not in the Bible.

93 **be þām** 'concerning which' (§162.3).

93–4 **wæs beboden** '(it) was commanded' (§212).

101–2 **būton þām ānum þæt** 'except for the one [reason, namely] that'.

102–3 **āne wīsan on . . . fadunge** 'one manner in the disposition of language', i.e. a common word order and idiom. (*Fadunge* 'disposition' is adopted here from one of the other manuscripts of the Preface since the Laud manuscript's *fandunge* 'testing' makes little sense.)

103 **āwent** See note to 2/32 above.

106 **Is** '(It) is'.

106–7 **sume gedwolmen wǣron** 'there were some heretics'.

114 **gewyrð** '(it) pleases' (§212).

þū mē þæs nā leng ne bidde þī lǣs þe ic bēo þē ungehīrsum oððe lēas gif ic dō. God þē sig milde ā on ēcnisse. Ic bidde nū on Godes naman, gif hwā þās bōc āwrītan wylle, þæt hē hig gerihte wel be þǣre bȳsne, for þan þe ic nāh geweald, þēah þe hig hwā tō wōge bringe þurh lēase wrīteras, and hit byð þonne his pleoh nā mīn: mycel yfel dēð se unwrītere, gif hē nele hys wōh gerihtan.

St. Edmund, King and Martyr

The preceding text exemplifies one of the dominant intellectual concerns of Ælfric and his Anglo-Saxon audience – how to understand scriptural narrative in the 'spiritual sense'. The present text exemplifies one of the most popular and most important literary forms in Anglo-Saxon times – the saint's life. Ælfric wrote a series of more than thirty *Lives of Saints* and included more saints' lives in his two series of *Catholic Homilies*. Other Anglo-Saxon writers have left us many more specimens in this genre, some in verse and some in prose. The medieval saint's life was a highly conventional form concerned not so much with presenting actual biography as with supplying inspirational examples of Christian lives well lived and of God's power revealed through the sometimes miraculous accomplishments of His most devoted followers. Since saints' lives often include heathen violence, Christian heroism, and supernatural events, they can be lively and entertaining as well as exemplary. Some of them treat the lives of traditional Christian saints like St. Anthony, St. Sebastian, and St. Andrew, while others deal with the lives of native English saints like St. Oswald, St. Swithun, and St. Æthelthryth.

St. Edmund was a native English saint, a king of East Anglia who was slain by heathen Vikings on 20 November 869. Ælfric's account of St. Edmund is characteristic of the genre: after giving his source for the narrative (ll. 126–36), he describes King Edmund's exemplary qualities – his piety, his charity, and his kindness to his people (ll. 137–46). Then there is a detailed account of his martyrdom, this being the culminating event of his holy life (ll. 147–222). The long, final section of the narrative tells of the disposition of the dead saint's body and of the miracles which occurred before and after his burial. The miracles are carefully recorded because these provide divine verification of Edmund's sainthood. The miracle of

120 þæs gen. obj. of *bidde*: 'ask me for that'.

123–4 þēah þe . . . wrīteras 'although someone might bring it (the book) to error through false scribes'.

the protective wolf, for example, is important witness to the fact that the saint's charismatic power extended even into the animal realm of God's kingdom, a common proof of saintliness. Also, Ælfric explains, the miracles reveal God's power and presence in Anglo-Saxon England, an important domestication of the conventional Christian verities.

At the beginning of his account Ælfric tells us that his source is a Latin narrative by Abbo of Fleury, a French monk who had learned the story on a visit to England and recorded it in his *Passio Sancti Eadmundi.* But Ælfric's Old English rendering is far more than a mechanical translation. He removes Abbo's elaborate rhetorical flourishes, shortens the speeches, and makes the narrative more brisk. His most daring innovation is the prose style he uses. After giving the introduction in sober, utilitarian prose (ll. 126–36), in l. 137 Ælfric shifts into alliterative prose, an ornamental style which he devised early in his career and used in many of his works. Alliterative prose consists of four-stressed units bound by alliteration. Ælfric borrowed these features from Old English poetry, which is composed in long lines with four stresses and alliteration. The difference between Ælfric's prose and Old English verse is that he avoids the distinctive poetic vocabulary characteristic of verse (see §247) and ignores the strictly ordered stress-patterns of verse (see Appendix C). But alliterative prose is sufficiently similar to verse that modern editors usually print it in verse lines like poetry. We decline to follow this practice here for reasons set forth in Bruce Mitchell *Old English Syntax* (Oxford, 1985), II, §§3974–3975, but it may be well to print a few sentences lineated as verse in order to make clear the form that Ælfric is using:

Éadmund se Éadiga   Éastengla cýning
wæs snótor and wúrðful   and wúrðode sýmble
mid ǽþelum þéawum   þone ǽlmihtigan Gód.
He wæs éadmod and geþúngen   and swa ánræd þurhwúnode
þæt he nólde abúgan   to býsmorfullum léahtrum
ne on náþre héalfe   he ne ahýlde his þéawas
ac wæs sýmble gemýndig   þære sóþan láre.
'þu eart to héafodmen gesét?   Ne ahéfe þu ðé
ac béo betwux mánnum   swa swa an mán of hím'.

(ll. 137–43)

Here alliterating sounds are underlined and the four syllables bearing primary stress in each line are marked with an acute accent.

The text presented here is essentially that of British Library MS Cotton Julius E.vii, but a few spellings have been normalized, and occasionally we adopt a reading from one of the other manuscripts.

Sum swȳðe gelǣred munuc cōm sūþan ofer sǣ fram Sancte Benedictes stōwe on Æþelredes cyninges dæge tō Dūnstāne ærcebisceope þrim gēarum ǣr hē forðfērde, and se munuc hātte Abbo. Þā wurdon hī æt sprǣce oþ þæt Dūnstān rehte be Sancte Ēadmunde, swā swā Ēadmundes swurdbora hit rehte Æþelstāne cyninge, þā þā Dūnstān geong man wæs and se swurdbora wæs forealdod man. Þā gesette se munuc ealle þā gereccednysse on ānre bēc and eft, ðā þā sēo bōc cōm tō ūs binnan fēawum gēarum, þā āwende wē hit on Englisc, swā swā hit hēræfter stent. Se munuc þā Abbo binnan twām gēarum gewende hām tō his mynstre and wearð sōna tō abbode geset on þām ylcan mynstre.

Ēadmund se ēadiga, Ēastengla cyning, wæs snotor and wurðful and wurðode symble mid æþelum þēawum þone ælmihtigan God. Hē wæs ēadmōd and geþungen and swā ānrǣd þurhwunode þæt hē nolde ābūgan tō bysmorfullum leahtrum, ne on nāþre healfe hē ne āhylde his þēawas, ac wæs symble gemyndig þǣre sōþan lāre, 'þū eart tō hēafodmen geset? ne āhefe þū ðē, ac bēo betwux mannum swā swā ān man of him'. Hē wæs cystig wǣdlum and widewum swā swā fæder and mid welwillendnysse gewissode his folc symle tō rihtwīsnysse and þām rēþum stȳrde and gesǣliglīce leofode on sōþum gelēafan.

Hit gelamp ðā æt nēxtan þæt þā Deniscan lēode fērdon mid sciphere hergiende and slēande wīde geond land swā swā heora

126–7 **Sancte Benedictes stōwe** The French monastery of Fleury, now called St.-Benoit-sur-Loire.

127–8 **Dūnstāne ærcebisceope** St. Dunstan, who became Archbishop of Canterbury in 959, was an adviser to several Anglo-Saxon kings and a prime mover in the tenth-century monastic reforms which helped revitalize English intellectual life. In making his reforms he sought counsel from the monks at Fleury.

128 **þrim gēarum** For the dative used with expressions of time see §191.3.

se munuc hātte Abbo See §202. Abbo, who became Abbot of Fleury in 988, spent two years in England as an adviser on monastic reform.

129 **wurdon hī æt sprǣce** 'they came into conversation'.

132 **on ānre bēc** i.e. in the *Passio Sancti Eadmundi.*

133 **āwende wē hit** 'we translated it'. See §111 for the form of *āwende.* For *sēo bōc . . . hit* see §187.2(b).

137 According to later sources, Edmund ascended the throne in 855, when he was fourteen years old.

139 **Hē . . . swā ānrǣd þurhwunode** See §167.3.

140–1 **ne on nāþre healfe . . . þēawas** 'neither did he turn away from his good practices' (lit. 'nor did he turn away on either side from his good practices'). The turn of phrase was suggested by Abbo's *nec declinabat ad dexteram, extollendo se de meritis, nec ad sinistram, succumbendo vitiis humanae fragilitatis.*

142–3 **bēo betwux . . . of him** 'be among people as (if you were) one of them' (Ecclesiasticus 32:1).

148 **sciphere** The Scandinavian attack fleets terrorized the Anglo-Saxons and the peoples along the coasts of Europe from approximately 800 to 1050. This particular naval force is discussed at some length in the Anglo-Saxon Chronicle (see piece 7 below), as is Hinguar, the leader. Hinguar and Hubba are the sons of the renowned Viking leader Ragnar Lothbrok ('Shaggy-Britches').

gewuna is. On þām flotan wǣron þā fyrmestan hēafodmen Hinguar and Hubba, geānlǣhte þurh dēofol, and hī on Norðhymbra lande gelendon mid æscum and āwēston þæt land and þā lēoda ofslōgon. Þā gewende Hinguar ēast mid his scipum and Hubba belāf on Norðhymbra lande, gewunnenum sige mid wælhrēownysse. Hinguar þā becōm tō Ēastenglum rowende, on þām gēare þe Ælfred æðeling ān and twentig gēara wæs, se þe, Westsexena cyning, siþþan wearð mǣre; and se foresǣda Hinguar fǣrlīce swā swā wulf on lande bestalcode and þā lēode slōh, weras and wīf and þā unwittigan cild, and tō bysmore tūcode þā bilewitan Crīstenan.

Hē sende ðā sōna syððan tō þām cyninge bēotlic ǣrende þæt hē ābūgan sceolde tō his manrǣdene gif hē rōhte his fēores. Se ǣrendraca cōm þā tō Ēadmunde cyninge and Hingwares ǣrende him arodlīce ābēad: 'Hingwar ūre cyning, cēne and sigefæst on sǣ and on lande, hæfð fela lēoda geweald and cōm nū mid fyrde fǣrlīce hēr tō lande þæt hē hēr wintersetl mid his werode hæbbe. Nū hǣt hē þē dǣlan þīne dīgelan goldhordas and þīnra yldrena gestrēon arodlīce wið hine, and þū bēo his undercyning, gif ðū cwic bēon wylt, for ðan þe ðū næfst þā mihte þæt þū mage him wiðstandan.'

Hwæt þā Ēadmund cyning clypode ǣnne bisceop þe him þā gehendost wæs, and wið hine smēade hū hē þām rēþan Hingware andwyrdan sceolde. Þā forhtode se bisceop for þām fǣrlican gelimpe and for þæs cyninges līfe, and cwæð þæt him rǣd þūhte þæt hē tō þām gebuge þe him bēad Hinguar. Þā swīgode se cyning and beseah tō þǣre eorþan and cwæð þā æt nēxtan cynelīce him tō, 'Ēalā þū bisceop, tō bysmore synd getāwode þās earman landlēoda, and mē nū lēofre wǣre þæt ic on gefeohte fēolle, wið þām þe mīn folc mōste heora eardes brūcan'; and se bisceop cwæð, 'Ēalā þū lēofa cyning, þīn folc līð ofslagen and þū næfst þone fultum þæt þū

150 **geānlǣhte þurh dēofol** See §187.1(b). This emphasizes that they are pagans.

153 **gewunnenum sige** See §191.4. Abbo's Latin has an ablative absolute here.

154–6 **Ælfred . . . Westsexena cyning . . . mǣre** This is King Alfred the Great, who became King of the West Saxons in April of 871, when he was twenty-three years old. For more on King Alfred see p. 119 above.

160 **ābūgan . . . manrǣdene** 'submit to his service', i.e. submit to being an under-king to the pagan Hinguar.

rōhte his fēores 'cared for his life'. See §190.6.

163 **fyrde** Normally *fyrd* is used for the English army and *here* for the Vikings. The unusual use of *fyrd* here to refer to the Vikings may be for the sake of alliteration.

171 **him rǣd þūhte** 'seemed [good] counsel to him', i.e. 'seemed advisable to him'.

172 **þæt hē . . . Hinguar** 'that he should submit to that which Hinguar demanded' of him.

174 **tō bysmore . . . landlēoda** See §202.

175 **wið þām þe** 'provided that', 'so long as'.

feohtan mæge, and þās flotmen cumað and þē cwicne gebindað, būtan þū mid flēame þīnum fēore gebeorge, oððe þū þē swā gebeorge þæt þū būge tō him.' Þā cwæð Ēadmund cyning swā swā hē ful cēne wæs, 'þæs ic gewilnige and gewīsce mid mōde, þæt ic āne ne belīfe æfter mīnum lēofum þegnum þe on heora bedde wurdon mid bearnum and wīfum fǣrlīce ofslagene fram þysum flotmannum. Næs mē nǣfre gewunelic þæt ic worhte flēames, ac ic wolde swīðor sweltan gif ic þorfte for mīnum āgenum earde; and se ælmihtiga God wāt þæt ic nelle ābūgan fram his biggengum ǣfre, ne fram his sōþan lufe, swelte ic, lybbe ic.'

Æfter þysum wordum hē gewende tō þām ǣrendracan þe Hingwar him tō sende and sǣde him unforht, 'Witodlīce þū wǣre wyrðe sleges nū, ac ic nelle āfȳlan on þīnum fūlum blōde mīne clǣnan handa, for ðan þe ic Crīste folgie, þe ūs swā gebȳsnode; and ic blīðelīce wille bēon ofslagen þurh ēow, gif hit swā God forescēawað. Far nū swiþe hraðe and sege þīnum rēþan hlāforde, "Ne ābīhð nǣfre Ēadmund Hingware on līfe, hǣþenum heretogan, būton hē tō Hǣlende Crīste ǣrest mid gelēafan on þysum lande gebūge."'

Þā gewende se ǣrendraca arodlīce āweg and gemētte be wege þone wælhrēowan Hingwar mid eallre his fyrde, fūse tō Ēadmunde, and sǣde þām ārlēasan hū him geandwyrd wæs. Hingwar þā bebēad mid bylde þām sciphere þæt hī þæs cyninges ānes ealle cēpan sceoldon, þe his hǣse forseah, and hine sōna bindan. Hwæt þā Ēadmund cyning, mid þām þe Hingwar cōm, stōd innan his healle, þæs Hǣlendes gemyndig, and āwearp his wǣpnu: wolde geæfenlǣcan Crīstes gebȳsnungum, þe forbēad Petre mid wǣpnum tō winnenne wið þā wælhrēowan Iūdēiscan. Hwæt þā ārlēasan þā Ēadmund gebundon and gebysmrodon huxlīce and bēoton mid sāglum, and swā syððan lǣddon þone gelēaffullan cyning tō ānum eorðfæstum trēowe and tīgdon hine þǣrtō mid heardum bendum,

178 **cumað** Translate present as future. See §196.
þē cwicne gebindað Present with future meaning. See also §187.1(a).

179–80 **þē swā gebeorge . . . būge** 'save yourself by submitting' (lit. 'save yourself in that you submit').

181–2 **'þæs ic . . . þegnum . . .'** This construction is explained in §148.

182 **on heora bedde** 'in their beds'. In OE the singular (*bedde*) is often used when each person in a group has one of the same thing. Cf. the singular *lichaman* in l. 321 below.

187 **swelte ic, lybbe ic** See §178.4.

189–90 **wǣre wyrðe sleges** 'were worthy of death', i.e. 'you deserve to be killed'.

191 **þe ūs swā gebȳsnode** 'who thus set an example for us'.

198 **fūse** 'hastening'. The acc. pl. no doubt refers to Hinguar and his men together.

200 **þæs cyninges ānes** 'only the king'. *Cēpan* takes a genitive object.

201–4 **Hwæt þā Ēadmund . . . gebȳsnungum** See §185.2.

204–5 **Crīstes gebȳsnungum . . . Iūdēiscan** See John 18:10–11.

and hine eft swungon langlīce mid swipum; and hē symble clypode betwux þām swinglum mid sōðum gelēafan tō Hǣlende Crīste; and þā hǣþenan þā for his gelēafan wurdon wōdlīce yrre, for þan þe hē clypode Crīst him tō fultume. Hī scuton þā mid gafelucum, swilce him tō gamenes, tō, oð þæt hē eall wæs beset mid heora scotungum, swilce igles byrsta, swā swā Sebastiānus wæs. Þā geseah Hingwar, se ārlēasa flotman, þæt se æþela cyning nolde Crīste wiðsacan, ac mid ānrǣdum gelēafan hine ǣfre clypode: hēt hine þā behēafdian, and þā hǣðenan swā dydon. Betwux þām þe hē clypode tō Crīste þā gīt, þā tugon þā hǣþenan þone hālgan tō slege and mid ānum swencge slōgon him of þæt hēafod, and his sāwl sīþode gesǣlig tō Crīste. Þǣr wæs sum man gehende, gehealden þurh God behȳd þām hǣþenum, þe þis gehȳrde eall and hit eft sǣde swā swā wē hit secgað hēr.

Hwæt ðā se flothere fērde eft tō scipe and behȳddon þæt hēafod þæs hālgan Ēadmundes on þām þiccum brēmelum þæt hit bebyrged ne wurde. Þā æfter fyrste, syððan hī āfarene wǣron, cōm þæt landfolc tō, þe þǣr tō lāfe wæs þā, þǣr heora hlāfordes līc læg būtan hēafde, and wurdon swīðe sārige for his slege on mōde, and hūru þæt hī næfdon þæt hēafod tō þām bodige. Þā sǣde se scēawere þe hit ǣr geseah, þæt þā flotmen hæfdon þæt hēafod mid him, and wæs him geðūht, swā swā hit wæs ful sōð, þæt hī behȳddon þæt hēafod on þam hōlte forhwega.

Hī ēodon þā ealle endemes to þām wuda, sēcende gehwǣr, geond þȳfelas and brēmelas, gif hī āhwǣr mihten gemētan þæt hēafod. Wæs ēac micel wundor þæt ān wulf wearð āsend þurh Godes wissunge tō bewerigenne þæt hēafod wið þā ōþre dēor ofer dæg and niht. Hī ēodon þā sēcende and symle clypigende, swā swā hit gewunelic is þām ðe on wuda gāð oft, 'Hwǣr eart þū nū, gefēra?', and him andwyrde þæt hēafod, 'Hēr! Hēr! Hēr!', and swā

212 **him tō fultume** See §191.2.

212–13 **scuton . . . tō** 'shot at'. See §213.

213 **him tō gamenes** See §191.2 and §168 p. 86.

214 **Sebastiānus** St. Sebastian was a martyr in the days of Diocletian. When it was discovered that he was a Christian, the Emperor ordered his archers to kill him. Although they shot innumerable arrows into his body and left him for dead, he recovered. Later Diocletian ordered him cudgelled to death. He is always depicted tied to a stake with many arrows protruding from his body.

216 **hēt hine þā behēafdian** See §161.

219 **slōgon him of þæt hēafod** 'struck the head from him', i.e. 'beheaded him'.

220–1 **gehealden þurh God . . . hǣþenum** 'kept hidden from the heathens by God'.

227 **on mōde** modifies *sārige.*

228–9 **se scēawere** i.e. the witness mentioned in ll. 220–2.

230 **wæs him geðūht** '[it] seemed to him'.

234–5 **ān wulf . . . þæt hēafod** See §205.2(a).

236–7 **swā swā hit . . . oft** See §162.1.

gelōme clypode, andswarigende him eallum swā oft swā heora ǣnig clypode, oþ þæt hī ealle becōmon þurh ðā clypunga him tō. þā lǣg se grǣga wulf þe bewiste þæt hēafod and mid his twām fōtum hæfde þæt hēafod beclypped, grǣdig and hungrig, and for Gode ne dorste þæs hēafdes onbyrian ac hēold hit wið dēor. þā wurdon hī ofwundrode þæs wulfes hyrdrǣdenne, and þæt hālige hēafod hām feredon mid him, þancigende þām Ælmihtigan ealra his wundra; ac se wulf folgode forð mid þām hēafde, oþ þæt hī tō tūne cōmon, swylce hē tam wǣre, and gewende eft siþþan tō wuda ongēan. þā landlēoda þā siþþan legdon þæt hēafod tō þām hālgan bodige and bebyrigdon hine swā swā hī sēlost mihton on swylcere hrædinge, and cyrcan ārǣrdon sōna him onuppon.

Eft þā on fyrste, æfter fela gēarum, þā sēo hergung geswāc and sibb wearð forgifen þām geswenctan folce, þā fēngon hī tōgædere and worhton āne cyrcan wurðlīce þām hālgan, for þan ðe gelōme wundru wurdon æt his byrgene æt þām gebedhūse þǣr hē bebyrged wæs. Hi woldon þā ferian mid folclicum wurðmynde þone hālgan līchaman and lecgan innan þǣre cyrcan. þā wæs micel wundor þæt hē wæs eallswā gehāl swilce hē cwic wǣre, mid clǣnum līchaman, and his swūra wæs gehālod, þe ǣr wæs forslagen, and wæs swylce ān seolcen þrǣd embe his swūran rǣd, mannum tō swutelunge hū hē ofslagen wæs. Ēac swilce þā wunda þe þā wælhrēowan hǣþenan mid gelōmum scotungum on his līce macodon, wǣron gehǣlede þurh þone heofonlican God; and hē līð swā ansund oþ þisne andwerdan dæg, andbīdigende ǣristes and þæs ēcan wuldres. His līchama ūs cȳð, þe līð unformolsnod, þæt hē būtan forligre hēr on worulde leofode and mid clǣnum līfe tō Crīste sīþode.

Sum widewe wunode, Ōswyn gehāten, æt þæs hālgan byrgene on gebedum and fæstenum manega gēar syððan, sēo wolde efsian ǣlce gēare þone sanct and his næglas ceorfan sȳferlīce mid lufe and on scrȳne healdan tō hāligdōme on wēofode.

þā wurðode þæt landfolc mid gelēafan þone sanct, and þēodred bisceop þearle mid gifum on golde and on seolfre gegōdode þæt mynster þām sancte tō wurðmynte. þā cōmon on sumne sǣl ungesǣlige þēofas eahte on ānre nihte tō þām ārwurðan hālgan: woldon stelan þā māðmas þe men þyder brōhton, and cunnodon mid cræfte hū hī in cuman mihton. Sum slōh mid slecge swīðe þā hæpsan, sum heora mid fēolan fēolode abūtan, sum ēac underdealf

242 **for Gode** 'because of God'.
249 **swā swā . . . hrædinge** 'as best they could in such haste'.
258–9 **his swūra . . . forslagen** See §197.4.
259 **swylce** 'as it were'.
268 **manega gēar** See §189.2.

þā duru mid spade, sum heora mid hlǣddre wolde unlūcan þæt ēagðȳrl, ac hī swuncon on īdel and earmlīce fērdon swā, þæt se hālga wer hī wundorlīce geband, ǣlcne swā hē stōd strūtigende mid tōle, þæt heora nān ne mihte þæt morð gefremman, ne hī þanon āstyrian, ac stōdon swā oð mergen. Men þā þæs wundrodon hū þā weargas hangodon, sum on hlǣddre, sum lēat tō gedelfe, and ǣlc on his weorce wæs fæste gebunden. Hī wurdon þā gebrōhte tō þām bisceope ealle and hē hēt hī hōn on hēagum gealgum ealle, ac hē næs nā gemyndig hū se mildheorta God clypode þurh his wītegan þās word þe hēr standað: *eos qui ducuntur ad mortem eruere ne cesses* 'þā þe man lǣt tō dēaðe, ālȳs hī ūt symble'; and ēac þā hālgan canōnas gehādodum forbēodað, ge bisceopum ge prēostum, tō bēonne embe þēofas, for þan þe hit ne gebyrað þām þe beoð gecorene Gode tō þegnigenne, þæt hī geþwǣrlǣcan sceolon on ǣniges mannes dēaðe, gif hī bēoð Drihtnes þegnas. Eft þā Ðēodred bisceop scēawode his bēc syððan: behrēowsode mid geōmerunge þæt hē swā rēðne dōm sette þām ungesǣligum þēofum, and hit besārgode ǣfre oð his līfes ende, and þā lēode bæd georne þæt hī him mid fæsten fullīce þrȳ dagas, biddende þone Ælmihtigan þæt hē him ārian sceolde.

On þām lande wæs sum man, Lēofstān gehāten, rīce for worulde and unwittig for Gode, se rād tō þām hālgan mid rīccetere swīðe, and hēt him ætēowian orhlīce swīðe þone hālgan sanct, hwæþer hē gesund wǣre; ac swā hraðe swā hē geseah þæs sanctes līchaman, þā āwēdde hē sōna and wælhrēowlīce grymetode and earmlīce geendode yfelum dēaðe. Þis is ðām gelīc þe se gelēaffulla pāpa Gregōrius sǣde on his gesetnysse be ðām hālgan Laurentie, ðe līð on Rōmebyrig – þæt menn woldon scēawian symle hū hē lāge, ge gōde ge yfele; ac God hī gestilde, swā þæt þǣr swulton on þǣre scēawunge āne seofon menn ætgædere. Þā geswicon þā ōþre to scēawigenne þone martyr mid menniscum gedwylde.

Fela wundra wē gehȳrdon on folclicre sprǣce be þām hālgan Ēadmunde, þe wē hēr nellað on gewrite settan, ac hī wāt gehwā. On

279 **þæt** 'in that'.

282 **þæs** See §148.

285 **hē hēt . . . ealle** See §161.

287 **eos qui . . . cesses** 'Do not fail to release those who are led to death' (Proverbs 24:11).

289–90 **tō bēonne embe** 'to concern themselves with'.

300 **hēt him ætēowian** See §161.

þone hālgan sanct and the **hwæþer** clause are parallel objects of *ætēowian*. See §159.

304 **Laurentie** St. Lawrence was martyred in 258. The story about his body is related in a letter by Gregory the Great (*c.* 540–604).

307 **āne seofon menn ætgædere** 'a band of seven men together'.

310 **ac . . . gehwā** 'for everyone knows them'.

þysum hālgan is swutel, and on swilcum ōþrum, þæt God ælmihtig mæg þone man ārǣran eft on dōmes dæg ansundne of eorþan, se þe hylt Ēadmunde hālne his līchaman oð þone micclan dæg, þēah ðe hē of moldan cōme. Wyrðe is sēo stōw for þām wurðfullan hālgan þæt hī man wurþige and wel gelōgige mid clǣnum Godes þēowum tō Crīstes þēowdōme, for þan þe se hālga is mǣrra þonne men magon āsmēagan.

Nis Angelcynn bedǣled Drihtnes hālgena, þonne on Engla lande licgað swilce hālgan swylce þes hālga cyning, and Cūþberht se ēadiga, and Æþeldrӯð on Ēlig, and ēac hire swustor, ansunde on līchaman, gelēafan tō trymminge. Synd ēac fela ōðre on Angelcynne hālgan þe fela wundra wyrcað (swā swā hit wīde is cūð) þām Ælmihtigan tō lofe, þe hī on gelӯfdon. Crīst geswutelað mannum þurh his mǣran hālgan þæt hē is Ælmihtig God þe macað swilce wundru, þēah þe þā earman Iūdēi hine eallunga wiðsōcen, for þan þe hī synd āwyrgede, swā swā hī wīscton him sylfum. Ne bēoð nāne wundru geworhte æt heora byrgenum, for ðan þe hī ne gelӯfað on þone lifigendan Crīst, ac Crīst geswutelað mannum hwǣr se sōða gelēafa is, þonne hē swylce wundru wyrcð þurh his hālgan wīde geond þās eorðan. Þæs him sӯ wuldor ā mid his heofonlican Fæder and þām Hālgan Gāste. Amen.

312–13 **se þe hylt . . . līchaman** lit. 'He Who keeps his [Edmund's] body whole for Edmund'.

319 **Cūþberht** St. Cuthbert (*c.* 630–687) was bishop of Lindisfarne.

320 **Æþeldrӯð** St. Audrey (*c.* 630–679) and her sister St. Sexburga were daughters of King Anna of East Anglia. Both were abbesses at Ely.

321 **līchaman** For the singular form see note to l. 182 above.

gelēafan tō trymminge 'as a confirmation of the faith'. See §214 s.v. *tō*.

325–6 **for þan þe . . . āwyrgede** 'wherefore they are accursed'. See Matthew 27:25.

5

Alfred the Great's Preface to his Translation of Gregory's *Pastoral Care*

Among the achievements of King Alfred the Great (sketched briefly in §§217 and 251 above), one of the most remarkable was the cultural renaissance he initiated in his realm even while he was leading his nation in a fight for survival against Scandinavian invaders. To save a people militarily without also restoring them culturally was apparently unthinkable to Alfred, and so he conceived and implemented a far-sighted plan for teaching all free Anglo-Saxons literacy in the vernacular and for translating the more important books of the period into English for all to read. In his letter to Bishop Wærferth, which serves as a preface to the King's translation of Pope Gregory the Great's *Cura Pastoralis* (*Pastoral Care*), the first of the important books to be translated, the elements of the programme for cultural revival are set forth, following a moving lament over the decay of learning which Alfred saw in England when he ascended the throne in 871. The prose has the intensity of deep conviction, but its pace is leisurely and aristocratic, its tone rich with nostalgia for the era of England's intellectual preeminence during the lifetime of Bede (673–735).

The text here is based upon that in Hatton MS 20 in the Bodleian Library, although a few unusual spellings (mainly in grammatical endings) have been replaced with more usual spellings from other manuscripts of the preface.

Ælfred kyning hāteð grētan Wǣrferð biscep his wordum luflīce ond frēondlīce; ond ðē cȳðan hāte ðæt mē cōm swīðe oft on gemynd, hwelce wiotan iū wǣron giond Angelcynn, ǣgðer ge

1 **hāteð grētan Wǣrferð biscep** 'commands Bishop Wærferth to be greeted' (§161). For the use of the third person, see note to 4/2 above.

2 **ond** Before nasal consonants *a* often appears as *o* (§103.2). See below such spellings as *lond* (l. 12), *understondan* (l. 15), *mon* (l. 62).

ðē cȳðan hāte '(I) command you to be informed' (§161).

cōm '(it) has come'.

2–3 **mē . . . on gemynd** 'into my mind' (§191.2).

godcundra hāda ge woruldcundra; ond hū gesǣliglica tīda ðā wǣron giond Angelcynn; ond hū ðā kyningas ðe ðone onwald hæfdon ðæs folces Gode ond his ǣrendwrecum hīersumedon; ond hīe ǣgðer ge hiora sibbe ge hiora siodu ge hiora onweald innanbordes gehīoldon, ond ēac ūt hiora ēðel rȳmdon; ond hū him ðā spēow ǣgðer ge mid wīge ge mid wīsdōme; ond ēac ðā godcundan hādas, hū giorne hīe wǣron ǣgðer ge ymb lāre ge ymb liornunga, ge ymb ealle ðā ðīowotdōmas ðe hīe Gode dōn scoldon; ond hū man ūtanbordes wīsdōm ond lāre hieder on lond sōhte; ond hū wē hīe nū sceoldon ūte begietan, gif wē hīe habban sceoldon. Swǣ clǣne hīo wæs oðfeallenu on Angelcynne ðæt swīðe fēawa wǣron behionan Humbre ðe hiora ðēninga cūðen understondan on Englisc oððe furðum ān ǣrendgewrit of Lǣdene on Englisc āreccean; ond ic wēne ðætte nōht monige begiondan Humbre nǣren. Swǣ fēawa hiora wǣron ðæt ic furðum ānne ānlēpne ne mæg geðencean be sūðan Temese ðā ðā ic tō rīce fēng. Gode ælmihtegum sīe ðonc ðætte wē nū ǣnigne onstal habbað lārēowa. Ond for ðon ic ðē bebīode ðæt ðū dō swǣ ic gelīefe ðæt ðū wille, ðæt ðū ðē ðissa woruldðinga tō ðǣm geǣmetige, swǣ ðū oftost mæge, ðæt ðū ðone wīsdōm ðe ðē God sealde ðǣr ðǣr ðū hiene befæstan mæge, befæste. Geðenc hwelc wītu ūs ðā becōmon for ðisse worulde, ðā ðā wē hit nōhwæðer ne selfe ne lufodon, ne ēac ōðrum monnum ne lēfdon; ðone naman ǣnne wē lufodon ðætte wē Crīstne wǣren, ond swīðe fēawa ðā ðēawas.

Ðā ic ðā ðis eall gemunde, ðā gemunde ic ēac hū ic geseah, ǣr ðǣm ðe hit eall forhergod wǣre ond forbærned, hū ðā ciricean

8–9 **him ðā spēow** 'they were successful then' (literally, 'it was successful to them then'; see §212).

10 **hādas, hū giorne hīe wǣron** See note to 4/25.

14 **oðfeallenu** See §201.2.

17 **ðætte** See §155.

19 **tō rīce fēng** 'succeeded to the kingdom'.

22–4 **ðæt ðū ðē . . . befæste** 'that you free yourself, as often as you can, from worldly affairs to the end that you apply the wisdom that God gave you wherever you can apply it'. See §172.A.

24 **wītu** The 'punishments' to which King Alfred refers are the Scandinavian invasions: see §217.

25 **hit** The antecedent is *wīsdōm*. See §187.2, and compare *sīo lār . . . hit* below (ll. 45–6), where natural gender has again displaced grammatical gender.

26 **lēfdon** 'bequeathed, passed on' (taking this to be a non-West-Saxon spelling of *lǣfdon* (l. 35) from *lǣfan* rather than from *līefan* 'allow', as previous editors have assumed). The negligent Christians neither cherished learning themselves nor bothered transmitting it to later generations.

26–7 **ðone naman ǣnne . . . ðā ðēawas** 'we loved only the name that we were Christians, and very few (of us loved) the (Christian) practices'.

29 **forhergod . . . ond forbærned** 'ravaged . . . and burned', i.e. by the Scandinavian invaders (§217).

giond eall Angelcynn stōdon māðma ond bōca gefylda, ond ēac micel mengeo Godes ðīowa; ond ðā swīðe lȳtle fiorme ðāra bōca wiston, for ðǣm ðe hīe hiora nānwuht ongietan ne meahton, for ðǣm ðe hīe nǣron on hiora āgen geðīode āwritene. Swelce hīe cwǣden: 'Ūre ieldran, ðā ðe ðās stōwa ǣr hīoldon, hīe lufodon wīsdōm, ond ðurh ðone hīe begēaton welan ond ūs lǣfdon. Hēr mon mæg gīet gesīon hiora swæð, ac wē him ne cunnon æfter spyrigean. Ond for ðǣm wē habbað nū ǣgðer forlǣten ge ðone welan ge ðone wīsdōm, for ðǣm ðe wē noldon tō ðǣm spore mid ūre mōde onlūtan.'

Ðā ic ðā ðis eall gemunde, ðā wundrade ic swīðe swīðe ðāra gōdena wiotena ðe giū wǣron giond Angelcynn, ond ðā bēc ealla be fullan geliornod hæfdon, ðæt hīe hiora ðā nǣnne dǣl noldon on hiora āgen geðīode wendan. Ac ic ðā sōna eft mē selfum andwyrde, ond cwæð: 'Hīe ne wēndon ðætte ǣfre menn sceolden swǣ recceleāse weorðan ond sīo lār swǣ oðfeallan: for ðǣre wilnunga hīe hit forlēton, ond woldon ðæt hēr ðȳ māra wīsdōm on londe wǣre ðȳ wē mā geðēoda cūðon.'

Ðā gemunde ic hū sīo ǣ wæs ǣrest on Ebriscgeðīode funden, ond eft, ðā hīe Crēacas geliornodon, ðā wendon hīe hīe on heora āgen geðīode ealle, ond ēac ealle ōðre bēc. Ond eft Lǣdenware swǣ same, siððan hīe hīe geliornodon, hīe hīe wendon ealla ðurn wīse wealhstodas on hiora āgen geðīode. Ond ēac ealla ōðra Crīstna ðīoda sumne dǣl hiora on hiora āgen geðīode wendon.

30 **stōdon māðma ond bōca gefylda** 'were full of books and of treasures'.

31–2 **ðā swīðe lȳtle ... wiston** 'they had very little benefit from the books' (literally, 'they knew very little use of the books').

33–4 **Swelce hīe cwǣden** '(It is) as if they had said'. See §177.4 for the meaning of *swelce*.

36 **him ... æfter** See §213.

38–9 **mid ūre mōde** 'with our mind(s)'.

40 **wundrade** Both the gen. pl. *wiotena* and the clause *ðæt hīe ... wendan* are objects of the verb *wundrade*.

45 **for ðǣre wilnunga** 'on purpose, deliberately'.

46–7 **ðȳ ... ðȳ** See §167.7*a*.

48 **ǣ** The Old Testament, or perhaps only the Hexateuch ('the Law'), is meant.

49 **hīe** acc. sg. fem. The antecedent is *ǣ* (l. 48).

49–50 **hīe hīe ... ealle ... ealle** The first *ealle* is acc. sg. fem. modifying the second of the two preceding *hīe*s, whose antecedent is again *ǣ* (l. 48); the second *ealle* is acc. pl. fem. modifying *bēc*. Presumably *ealle ōðre bēc* refers to the remaining books of the Bible.

ðā wendon ... ealle The first *hīe* is nom. pl. referring to *Crēacas*; the second *hīe* is acc. fem. sg. referring to *ǣ* (l. 48). *Ealle* is acc. fem. sg. modifying the second *hīe*.

51 **siððan hīe hīe geliornodon, hīe hīe wendon ealla** 'after they (*Lǣdenware*) had learned them (*bēc*), they translated them all'. On the repetition of the subject (*Lǣdenware ... hīe*), see §148.

Forðȳ mē ðyncð betre, gif īow swǣ ðyncð, ðæt wē ēac sume bēc, ðā ðe nīedbeðearfosta sīen eallum monnum tō wiotonne, ðæt wē ðā on ðæt geðīode wenden ðe wē ealle gecnāwan mægen, ond gedōn, swǣ wē swīðe ēaðe magon mid Godes fultume, gif wē ðā stilnesse habbað, ðætte eall sīo giogud ðe nū is on Angelcynne frīora monna, ðāra ðe ðā spēda hæbben ðæt hīe ðǣm befēolan mægen, sīen tō liornunga oðfæste, ðā hwīle ðe hīe tō nānre ōðerre note ne mægen, oð ðone first ðe hīe wel cunnen Englisc gewrit ārǣdan. Lǣre mon siððan furður on Lǣdengeðīode ðā ðe mon furðor lǣran wille ond tō hīerran hāde dōn wille.

Ðā ic ðā gemunde hū sīo lār Lǣdengeðīodes ǣr ðissum āfeallen wæs giond Angelcynn, ond ðēah monige cūðon Englisc gewrit ārǣdan, ðā ongan ic ongemang ōðrum mislicum ond manig-fealdum bisgum ðisses kynerīces ðā bōc wendan on Englisc ðe is genemned on Lǣden *Pastoralis*, ond on Englisc 'Hierdebōc', hwīlum word be worde, hwīlum andgit of andgiete, swǣ swǣ ic hīe geliornode æt Plegmunde mīnum ærcebiscepe, ond æt Assere mīnum biscepe, ond æt Grimbolde mīnum mæsseprīoste, ond æt Iōhanne mīnum mæssepreōste. Siððan ic hīe ðā geliornod hæfde, swǣ swǣ ic hīe forstōd, ond swǣ ic hīe andgitfullīcost āreccean meahte, ic hīe on Englisc āwende; ond tō ǣlcum biscepstōle on mīnum rīce wille āne onsendan; ond on ǣlcre bið ān æstel, se bið on fiftegum mancessa. Ond ic bebīode on Godes naman ðæt nān mon ðone æstel from ðǣre bēc ne dō, ne ðā bōc from ðǣm mynstre – uncūð hū longe ðǣr swǣ gelǣrede biscepas sīen, swǣ swǣ nū, Gode ðonc, welhwǣr siendon. Forðȳ ic wolde ðætte hīe ealneg æt ðǣre stōwe wǣren, būton se biscep hīe mid him habban wille, oððe hīo hwǣr tō lǣne sīe, oððe hwā ōðre bī write.

54–61 **Forðȳ . . . ārǣdan** See §172.B for a detailed analysis of this sentence.

55 **ðæt wē** Otiose restatement of *ðæt wē* in l. 54. See §148.

60 **ðā hwīle ðe . . . ne mægen** 'as long as they are competent for no other employment'.

69 **hīe** acc. sg. fem. The antecedent is *Hierdebōc*.

70–2 **Plegmunde . . . Assere . . . Grimbolde . . . Iōhanne** These are scholars whom King Alfred brought in from outside Wessex to help implement the cultural revival he sought for his people. Plegmund was a Mercian who became Archbishop of Canterbury in 890. Asser, a Welshman, became bishop of Sherborne and wrote a Latin biography of King Alfred. Grimbold was a Frankish priest who was ultimately canonized, and John (*Iōhannes*) a continental Saxon whom King Alfred established as abbot of a new monastery at Athelney in Somerset.

75–6 **se bið on fiftegum mancessa** 'it will be worth fifty mancuses'. This use of *on* is an idiom. for the gen. pl. *mancessa*, see §194.2.

78 **uncūð** '(it is) unknown'.

79–81 **Forðȳ ic . . . bī write** 'Therefore I have desired that they (the book and the æstel) always remain at that place, unless the bishop wants to have them (or it, i.e. the book) with him, or it (the book) is on loan somewhere, or someone is making a copy (from it).'

6

Cynewulf and Cyneheard

This account appears in the Anglo-Saxon Chronicle, a year-by-year record of important events in the kingdom. (See the next selection for details.) The entry for the year 755 contains a narrative which exemplifies one of the cardinal virtues of Germanic society in the heroic age: unswerving loyalty to one's sworn leader, even when that loyalty is in conflict with claims of kinship. (See §§236–240.) For a contemporary audience, the violence and tragedy of the feud between Cynewulf and Cyneheard would have been transcended by the reassuring fact that the ideal prevailed: on both sides men made the heroic choice, and they chose right. The narration is so swift and breathless, the selection of detail so adroit, that some scholars have felt that the chronicler was recording a saga refined by many retellings in oral tradition. Supporting this view (and complicating the modern reader's task in following the narrative) is the tale's spontaneous syntax and free word-order, which require close attention to grammatical endings if the sentences are to be construed accurately. Readers should also be wary of the unusual spellings of some verb endings (*wǣron*, *-un*, *-an*; *locude* for *locode*; and the subjunctives *ūþon* and *ēodon* in lines 29 and 33, where we would expect *-en* for *-on*). See §113.3 for such spelling variations.

The text is that of Corpus Christi College, Cambridge, MS 173 except in line 29, where we adopt *cȳþde*, the reading of most manuscripts, for *cȳðdon* of our manuscript. For historical information about persons and places mentioned and chronological disturbances, see Whitelock's work cited in §251.1.

755. Hēr Cynewulf benam Sigebryht his rīces ond Westseaxna wiotan for unryhtum dǣdum, būton Hamtūnscīre; ond hē hæfde

1 Hēr i.e. 'in this year': the chronicler uses an adverb of place rather than of time because he is referring to the dated slot in the manuscript where he is making his entry.

Sigebryht King of the West Saxons before Cynewulf, his kinsman, deposed him.

1–2 **Cynewulf . . . ond Westseaxna wiotan** is the compound subject of the sentence. The verb *benam* is singular because in OE verbs normally agree only with that part of a compound subject which precedes them: see §§149.1 and 187.3*c*.

þā oþ hē ofslōg þone aldormon þe him lengest wunode. Ond hiene þā Cynewulf on Andred ādrǣfde, ond hē þǣr wunade oþ þæt hiene ān swān ofstang æt Pryfetes flōdan; ond hē wræc þone aldormon Cumbran. Ond se Cynewulf oft miclum gefeohtum feaht uuiþ Bretwālum. Ond ymb XXXI wintra þæs þe hē rīce hæfde, hē wolde ādrǣfan ānne æþeling se was Cyneheard hāten; ond se Cyneheard wæs þæs Sigebryhtes brōþur. Ond þā geāscode hē þone cyning lȳtle werode on wīfcȳþþe on Merantūne, ond hine þǣr berād ond þone būr ūtan beēode ǣr hine þā men onfunden þe mid þām kyninge wǣrun.

Ond þā ongeat se cyning þæt, ond hē on þā duru ēode ond þā unhēanlīce hine werede oþ hē on þone æþeling lōcude, ond þā ūt rǣsde on hine ond hine miclum gewundode; ond hīe alle on þone cyning wǣrun feohtende oþ þæt hīe hine ofslægenne hæfdon. Ond þā on þæs wīfes gebǣrum onfundon þæs cyninges þegnas þā unstilnesse, ond þā þider urnon swā hwelc swā þonne gearo wearþ ond radost. Ond hiera se æþeling gehwelcum feoh ond feorh

3 **þā** acc. sg. fem., agreeing in gender with its antecedent *Hamtūnscīre*.
þe him lengest wunode 'who had dwelt with him longest', i.e. who had remained faithful to him longer than the rest.

4 **Andred** A large forest which extended from Kent into Hampshire (the area now called the Weald).

5 **Pryfetes flōdan** 'the stream at Privett' (in Hampshire).

5–6 **þone aldormon Cumbran** This is the loyal *aldormon* slain by Sigebryht (l. 3).

6–7 **Bretwālum** Britons (probably Cornishmen) descended from the original inhabitants of England before the Anglo-Saxon invasion (§217).

7 **Ond ymb XXXI wintra þæs þe** . . . literally 'And after 31 winters from that in which . . .'.
wintra i.e. 'years'. The Anglo-Saxons reckoned years in terms of winters. For the case of *wintra* see §194.2; cf. §190.4. The passage of many years in the course of this 'annal' shows that this is not a normal chronicle entry (which would record only the events of the year just ended) but rather is an independent tale which the chronicler has interpolated into his sequence of yearly reports. The *Chronicle* records the death of Cynewulf in the annal dated 784: apparently XXXI is an error for XXIX. The 784 entry reads as follows: *Hēr Cyneheard ofslōg Cynewulf cyning, ond hē þǣr wearþ ofslægen ond lxxxiiii monna mid him.*

10 **lȳtle werode** See §192.2.
on wīfcȳþþe on Merantūne i.e. visiting a mistress in Merton.

11 **būr** i.e. the apartment where the lady receives the King. The *būr* stands inside the stronghold (*burh*) but is separate from the main hall, where the King's retinue is housed. The entire compound is surrounded by a wall and is entered through *gatu* (ll. 27, 36) in the wall. The *būr* is entered through a *duru* (l. 13).

14 **æþeling** i.e. Cyneheard.

17 **on þæs wīfes gebǣrum** 'from the woman's outcries'.

18–19 **urnon . . . ond radost** literally, 'they ran, whoever became ready and quickest', i.e. each ran to the King as quickly as he could get ready.

19 **hiera . . . gehwelcum** 'to each of them (i.e. the King's men)'.

gebēad, ond hiera nǣnig hit geþicgean nolde; ac hīe simle feohtende wǣran oþ hīe alle lǣgon būtan ānum Bryttiscum gīsle, ond sē swīþe gewundad wæs.

Þā on morgenne gehīerdun þæt þæs cyninges þegnas þe him beæftan wǣrun, þæt se cyning ofslægen wæs. Þā ridon hīe þider, ond his aldormon Ōsrīc, ond Wīferþ his þegn, ond þā men þe hē beæftan him lǣfde ǣr, ond þone æþeling on þǣre byrig mētton þǣr se cyning ofslægen læg (ond þā gatu him tō belocen hæfdon) ond þā þǣrto ēodon. Ond þā gebēad hē him hiera āgenne dōm fēos ond londes, gif hīe him þæs rīces ūþon, ond him cȳþde þæt hiera mǣgas him mid wǣron, þā þe him from noldon. Ond þā cuǣdon hīe þæt him nǣnig mǣg lēofra nǣre þonne hiera hlāford, ond hīe nǣfre his banan folgian noldon. Ond þā budon hīe hiera mǣgum þæt hīe gesunde from ēodon. Ond hīe cuǣdon þæt tæt ilce hiera gefērum geboden wǣre þe ǣr mid þām cyninge wǣrun. Þā cuǣdon hīe þæt hīe hīe þæs ne onmunden 'þon mā þe ēowre gefēran þe mid þām cyninge ofslægene wǣrun.' Ond hīe þā ymb þā gatu feohtende

20–1 **simle feohtende wǣran** i.e. 'kept on fighting'.

21 **gīslc** Presumably the hostage was taken in the course of Cynewulf's wars with the Britons (ll. 6–7).

26 **ǣr** Here as elsewhere *ǣr* combined with pret. tense signals the pluperfect (§197.4): 'and the men that he had left behind him'.

27 **þā gatu . . . hæfdon** Cyneheard's men 'had locked the gates (leading in) to them', i.e. had locked themselves in the compound. Or, alternatively, one could read, 'had locked the gates against them (King Cynewulf's men)'.

28 **hiera āgenne dōm** Cyneheard offers to let King Cynewulf's men name their own price for allowing him to assume the kingship. (Giving enemies 'their own judgment of compensation' is a common Germanic idiom and practice.)

30 **þā þe him from noldon** 'who did not want (to go) from him' (§205.1).

30 **cuǣdon hīe** 'they (Cynewulf's men) said'.

32 **Ond þā budon hīe** 'And then they (Cynewulf's men) offered'.

33 **ēodon** subj. 'might go'.

33–4 **Ond hīe cuǣdon . . . geboden wǣre** 'And they (Cyneheard's men) said that the same (thing) had been offered to their (Cynewulf's men's) comrades'.

34–5 **þā cuǣdon . . . onmunden** 'Then they (Cyneheard's men) said that they would not pay attention to that (offer of safe passage).' *Onmunan* with refl. pron. (*hīe*) takes a gen. obj. (*þæs*).

35 **þon mā þe** '(any) more than (did)'. The mid-sentence shift into direct discourse is characteristic of vivid oral narrative.

C. T. Onions, in earlier editions of Henry Sweet's *Anglo-Saxon Reader*, provided the following dialogue to clarify the rapid shifts of speaker in the foregoing passage:

> *Cyneheard*. I offer you your own choice of money and land if you will grant me the kingship; and there are kinsmen of yours with us who will not leave me (us). *Osric*. No kinsman of ours is dearer to us than our liege lord, and we will never follow his slayer. We offer a safe exit to those of them who come out. *Cyneheard*. The same offer was made to your comrades who were with the king before. We pay no more regard to the offer than your comrades did who were killed along with the king.

36 **Ond hīe** 'And they (i.e. Cynewulf's men)'.

wǣron oþ þæt hīe þǣrinne fulgon ond þone æþeling ofslōgon ond þā men þe him mid wǣrun, alle būtan ānum, se wæs þæs aldormonnes godsunu; ond hē his feorh generede, ond þēah hē wæs oft gewundad.

Ond se Cynewulf rīcsode XXXI wintra and his līc līþ æt Wintanceastre, ond þæs æþelinges æt Ascanmynster; ond hiera ryhtfæderencyn gǣþ tō Cerdice.

37 **oþ þæt hīe** 'until they (i.e. Cynewulf's men)'.

38–9 **þæs aldormonnes** presumably Osric, mentioned in l. 25.

39 **ond hē his feorh generede** The *hē* refers to the godson.

43 **Cerdice** the putative founder of the kingdom and royal line of the West Saxons.

7

Selections from the Anglo-Saxon Chronicle

Around A.D. 890, during the reign of King Alfred the Great, Anglo-Saxon scholars compiled a year-by-year record of important events from antiquity to their own day. Copies of this Chronicle were distributed throughout the realm, and the annual record of happenings in England was continued by various hands in various places, sometimes only a short while after the events occurred. This annalistic activity at times approaches genuine historical writing and constitutes an important stage in the development of a narrative prose independent of Latin models. The following selections suggest the nature both of the Chronicle's prose style and of the events it portrays at one dark period in England's history. Norsemen were waging a war of conquest in the land, and the English King, Æthelred the Unready, adopted the disastrous policy of paying the invaders Danegeld rather than rallying his troops for defence, as King Alfred had done in an earlier time of trial (see §217). The leading men of the realm, moreover, were often untrustworthy, and the nation was demoralized. One Anglo-Saxon leader named Brihtnoth, whose death is noted briefly in the entry for 991, rejected the prevailing pusillanimity of his times and made a desperate stand against the invaders rather than pay Danegeld. His valour and that of his men is extolled in a moving heroic poem, *The Battle of Maldon*, which appears below as selection 12.

The entries are drawn from several manuscripts of the Chronicle, and some have been abbreviated. The words *tobrocon* (l. 39), *gefeordon* (l. 50), *se* (l. 52), and *beodon* (l. 74) have been normalized to *tōbrocen*, *gefērdon*, *sēo*, and *bēodan*.

980. Hēr on þȳs gēare wæs Æþelgār abbod tō bisceope gehālgod on vi nōnas Mai tō þām bisceopstōle æt Sēolesigge. And on þām

1 Hēr See 6/1 n.

2 vi nōnas Mai i.e. May 2nd. (Latin terms are used by some chroniclers in reckoning time.) Note here and elsewhere in this text (e.g. ll. 10, 24, 63) the use of Roman numerals.

ylcan gēare wæs Sūðhamtūn forhergod fram scipherige, and sēo burhwaru mǣst ofslegen and gehæft. And þȳ ilcan gēare wæs Tenetland gehergod; and þȳ ilcan gēare wæs Lēgeceasterscīr gehergod fram norðscipherige.

981. Hēr on þīs gēare wæs Sancte Petroces stōw forhergod, and þȳ ilcan gēare wæs micel hearm gedōn gehwǣr be þām sǣriman ǣgþer ge on Defenum ge on Wēalum.

982. Hēr on þȳs gēare cōmon ūpp on Dorsǣtum iii scypu wīcinga and hergodon on Portlande. þȳ ilcan gēare forbarn Lundenbyrig. And on þām ylcan gēare forðfērdon twēgen ealdormenn, Æþelmǣr on Hamtūnscīre and Ēadwine on Sūðseaxum.

.....

988. Hēr wæs Wecedport geheregod, and Goda, se Defenisca þegen, ofslagen, and mycel wæl mid him. Hēr gefōr Dūnstān arcebisceop, and Æðelgār bisceop fēng æfter him tō arcestōle, and hē lȳtle hwīle æfter þǣm lyfode – būtan i gēare and iii mōnþas.

.....

990. Hēr Sigerīc wæs gehālgod tō arcebisceope, and Ēadwine abbod forðfērde, and Wulfgār abbod fēng tō þām rīce.

991. Hēr wæs Gypeswīc gehergod, and æfter þām swīðe raðe wæs Brihtnōð ealdorman ofslægen æt Mǣldūne. And on þām gēare man gerǣdde þæt man geald ǣrest gafol Deniscan mannum for þām mycclan brōgan þe hī worhtan be þām sǣriman. þæt wæs ǣrest x þūsend punda. þæne rǣd gerǣdde Sīrīc arcebisceop.

992. Hēr Ōswald se ēadiga arcebisceop forlēt þis līf and gefērde þæt heofonlice, and Æðelwine ealdorman gefōr on þām ilcan gēare. Ðā gerǣdde se cyng and ealle his witan þæt man gegaderode þā scipu þe āhtes wǣron tō Lundenbyrig. And se cyng þā betǣhte þā fyrde tō lǣdene Ealfrīce ealdorman and þorode eorl and Ælfstāne bisceop and Æscwīge bisceop, and sceoldan cunnian gif hī muhton þone here āhwǣr ūtene betræppen. Ðā sende se

12 Lundenbyrig nom. sg. Since *burg* is declined like *bōc* (§58), the normal nom. sg. form is *-burg*, not *-byrig*. But in the Chronicle and elsewhere the form with *i*-mutation occasionally appears as a nominative singular.

16 fēng ... tō arcestōle 'succeeded to the archiepiscopal see after him'.

19 fēng tō þām rīce 'succeeded to the office (of abbot)'.

22 man gerǣdde ... gafol 'advice was given so that tribute was first paid'.

Deniscan A late spelling of *Deniscum* (§65). The Anglo-Saxons used *Denisc* loosely to refer to any and all of the Scandinavian peoples who were invading them. The Vikings at Maldon seem to have been mainly Norwegians.

28 āhtes 'of any value' (gen. sg. of *āwiht*).

29 tō lǣdene Properly, *tō lǣdenne* 'for leading' i.e. 'as leaders'.

29–30 Ealfrīce ealdorman ... Æscwīge bisceop The names of these leaders are, correctly, in the dative case, but their titles are uninflected.

ealdorman Ælfrīc and hēt warnian þone here, and þā on þēre nihte ðe hī on ðone dæi tōgædere cumon sceoldon, ðā sceōc hē on niht fram þǣre fyrde, him sylfum tō mycclum bismore. And se here þā ætbærst, būton ān scip þǣr man ofslōh. And þā gemǣtte se here ðā scipu of Ēastenglum and of Lunden, and hī ðǣr ofslōgon mycel wæl and þæt scip genāmon eall gewǣpnod and gewǣdod, þe se ealdorman on wæs.

993. Hēr on ðissum gēare wæs Bæbbanburh tōbrocen and mycel herehūðe þǣr genumen; and æfter þām cōm tō Humbran mūðe se here and þǣr mycel yfel gewrohtan ǣgðer ge on Lindesīge ge on Norðhymbran. Þā gegaderode man swīðe mycele fyrde, and þā hī tōgædere gān sceoldan, þā onstealdon þā heretogan ǣrest þone flēam – þæt wæs Frǣna and Godwine and Friðegist. On þysum ilcan gēare hēt se cyng āblendan Ælfgār Ælfrīces sunu ealdormannes.

994. Hēr on þisum gēare cōm Anlāf and Swegen tō Lundenbyrig on Nativitas sancte Marie mid iiii and hundnigontigum scipum, and hī ðā on ðā burh festlīce feohtende wǣron, and ēac hī mid fȳre ontendan woldon. Ac hī þār geferdon māran hearm and yfel þonne hī ǣfre wēndon þæt heom ǣnig burhwaru gedōn sceolde. Ac sēo hālige Godes mōdor on ðām dæge hire mildheortnisse þǣre burhware gecȳðde and hī āhredde wið heora fēondum. And hī þanon fērdon, and wrohton þæt mǣste yfel þe ǣfre ǣnig here dōn mihte on bærnette and hergunge and on manslihtum ǣgðer be ðām sǣriman on Ēastseaxum and on Centlande and on Sūðseaxum and

32 **Ælfrīc** This treacherous Ælfric (whose name is spelled *Ealfrīce* in l. 29) was ealdorman of Hampshire. He has no connection with Abbot Ælfric, author of the *Colloquy*, Biblical translations, and other works.

hēt warnian (§161).

32–3 **on þēre nihte ðe hī on ðone dæi** 'in the night before the day on which they'. (A day was regarded as going with the previous night.)

35 **ān scip . . . ofslōh** literally 'one ship where one destroyed', i.e. 'one ship which was destroyed'.

36 **hī** The antecedent of *hī* is the collective noun *here* (l. 35).

40 **herehūðe** partitive gen. with *micel*.

41 **gewrohtan** A late spelling of *gewrohton*. The Chronicler first thinks of *here* as a unit (*cōm*) and then pluralizes (*gewrohtan*) as he thinks of it as many men. See §187.3*b*, and cf. ll. 61–2 below (*cōm . . . nāmon*).

45 **hēt . . . āblendan Ælfgār** (§161) This blinding of the son was presumably in retribution for Ælfric's treachery.

47 **Anlāf and Swegen** Since it precedes the compound subject, *cōm* is singular. (Anlāf is King Olaf Tryggvason of Norway, who ultimately converted his countrymen to Christianity; Swegen is Sweyn Forkbeard, King of Denmark and conqueror of England in 1013. His son Canute was King of England and Denmark 1016–35.)

48 **Nativitas sancte Marie** '(the day of) the Nativity of Saint Mary', i.e. September 8th.

49 **hī** (preceding *mid*) acc. sg. fem. (antecedent is *burh*).

on Hamtūnscīre. And æt nȳxtan nāman heom hors and ridon swā wīde swā hī woldon and unāsecgendlice yfel wircende wǣron. Þā gerǣdde se cyng and his witan þæt him man tō sende and him gafol behēte and metsunge wið þon þe hī þǣre hergunge geswicon. And hī þā þet underfēngon, and cōm þā eall se here tō Hamtūne and þǣr wintersetle nāmon. And hī man þǣr fǣdde geond eall Westseaxna rīce, and him man geald fēos xvi þūsend punda.

. . . . .

1011. Hēr on þissum gēare sende se cyning and his witan tō ðām here, and gyrndon friðes, and him gafol and metsunge behēton wið þām ðe hī hiora hergunge geswicon. Hī hæfdon þā ofergān (i) Ēast-engle and (ii) Ēastsexe and (iii) Middelsexe and (iiii) Oxena-fordscīre and (v) Grantabricscīre and (vi) Heortfordscīre and (vii) Buccingahamscīre and (viii) Bedefordscīre and (ix) healfe Huntadūnscīre and micel (x) on Hāmtūnscīre, and be sūþan Temese ealle Kentingas and Sūðsexe and Hǣstingas and Sūðrige and Bearrocscīre and Hamtūnscīre and micel on Wiltūnscīre.

Ealle þās ungesǣlða ūs gelumpon þuruh unrǣdas, þæt man nolde him ā tīman gafol bēodan oþþe wið gefeohtan; ac þonne hī mǣst tō yfele gedōn hæfdon, þonne nam mon frið and grið wið hī. And nā þē lǣs for eallum þissum griðe and gafole hī fērdon ǣghweder flocmǣlum, and heregodon ūre earme folc, and hī rȳpton and slōgon.

57 **nāman heom** Late spellings of *nāmon him*. For the function of the pronoun see note to 3/42.

58 **unāsecgendlice** a late form of acc. pl. neut. *-licu*.

73 **unrǣdas** See below, p. 241 n. 1.

þæt 'in that'.

74 **him** i.e. the Danes.

ā tīman 'in time'.

75 **mǣst tō yfele** 'the most for harm', i.e. 'the most to (our) injury'.

8

Bede's Account of the Conversion of King Edwin

Saint Bede the Venerable – scientist, historian, philologist, and one of the Church Fathers – lived in the north of England from *c.* 673 to 735. His important work as a theologian earned him a place in the fourth heaven of Dante's *Paradiso*, but it is his work as a historian that has established his reputation among modern readers. At a time when most 'historical' writing was a mish-mash of fact and fiction, Bede's *Ecclesiastical History of the English People* (written, like virtually all his works, in Latin) maintained a high standard of accuracy, order, and verification of sources. It is also well written and has sustained the interest of readers both during and after the Middle Ages.

Sometime in the reign of King Alfred the Great (871–899), Bede's *History* was translated into Old English. The translation is vigorous and at times even eloquent, but one can also detect in it the struggle of a vernacular artist trying (not always successfully) to free himself from the alien syntax of his source text and to establish a native English prose style. All these features are present in the following excerpt from the Old English Bede, which recounts how Christianity was brought to the pagan Anglo-Saxons of Northumbria in 625. The first missionary work took place in 597 in Kent, and it is from there that Bishop Paulinus travelled to the court of King Edwin of Northumbria in hopes of persuading the ruler and his *witan* to renounce their pagan beliefs and accept Christianity. At the point where our excerpt begins, Paulinus has just succeeded in converting Edwin, but the King explains that he must put the matter before his *witan* before he can commit his subjects to the new faith. The deliberations of his advisers, which Bede records with deft and unobtrusive art, give us a remarkable glimpse of that pivotal moment in history when the warrior society of Anglo-Saxon England began to abandon Germanic paganism for the religion newly brought from Rome.

The text is basically that of Corpus Christi College, Oxford, MS 279 up to *-bedo* in l. 47 and of Bodleian Library MS Tanner 10 for the rest, but we have occasionally adopted a simpler reading from another manuscript when the base text is problematic, and in l. 56 we read *þā þe* for the various and conflicting readings of the manuscripts.

þā se cyning þā þās word gehȳrde, þā andswarode hē him and cwæð, þæt hē ǣghwæþer ge wolde ge sceolde þām gelēafan onfōn þe hē lǣrde; cwæð hwæþere, þæt hē wolde mid his frēondum and mid his wytum gesprec and geþeaht habban, þæt gif hī mid hine þæt geþafian woldan, þæt hī ealle ætsomne on līfes willan Crīste gehālgade wǣran. þā dyde se cyning swā swā hē cwæð, and se bisceop þæt geþafade.

þā hæfde hē gesprec and geþeaht mid his witum and syndriglīce wæs fram him eallum frignende hwylc him þūhte and gesawen wǣre þēos nīwe lār and þǣre godcundnesse bīgong þe þǣr lǣred wæs. Him þā andswarode his ealdorbisceop, Cēfi wæs hāten: 'Geseoh þū, cyning, hwelc þēos lār sīe þe ūs nū bodad is. Ic þē sōðlīce andette þæt ic cūðlīce geleornad hæbbe, þæt eallinga nāwiht mægenes ne nyttnesse hafað sīo ǣfæstnes þe wē oð ðis hæfdon and beēodon, for ðon nǣnig þīnra þegna nēodlicor ne gelustfullīcor hine sylfne underþēodde tō ūra goda bīgange þonne ic, and nōht þon lǣs monige syndon þā þe māran gefe and fremsumnesse æt þē onfēngon þonne ic, and in eallum þingum māran gesynto hæfdon. Hwæt, ic wāt, gif ūre godo ǣnige mihte hæfdon, þonne woldan hīe mē mā fultumian, for þon ic him geornlīcor þēodde ond hȳrde. For þon mē þynceð wīslic, gif þū gesēo þā þing beteran and strangran þe ūs nīwan bodad syndon, þæt wē þām onfōn.'

þæs wordum ōþer cyninges wita and ealdormann geþafunge

1 **him** i.e. Bishop Paulinus, who has just explained to the King his obligation to accept Christianity.

5 **woldan** Here and elsewhere the scribe (who made this copy in the eleventh century) uses *-an* instead of *-en* for the subj. pl. ending: cf. *wǣran* (l. 6) and *woldan* (l. 20). He also uses *-an* for *-on*: *sprǣcan* (l. 38), *beēodan* (l. 43). These spellings are characteristic of the late Old English period.

9–10 **hwylc him . . . wǣre** literally 'how seemed to them and was seen (by them)'. The Latin word *videretur* 'seemed' is translated with two roughly synonymous expressions (*þūhte* and *gesawen wǣre*). This practice is common in the Old English Bede and is symptomatic of the translator's awkwardness in dealing with his Latin source. Cf. *hæfdon and beēodon* (l. 15) and *sōhte ond āhsode* (l. 53).

11 **Cēfi wæs hāten** See §186.1. (Cefi's title *ealdorbisceop* means he was a *pagan* high priest.)

19 **godo** = *godu* nom. pl. neut. Pagan gods are neuter, while the Christian God is masculine.

24 **þæs wordum . . . wita** 'To that one's words another counsellor of the King'.

sealde, and tō þǣre sprǣce fēng and þus cwæð: 'þyslīc mē is gesewen, þū cyning, þis andwearde līf manna on eorðan tō wiðmetenesse þǣre tīde þe ūs uncūð is: swylc swā þū æt swǣsendum sitte mid þīnum ealdormannum and þegnum on wintertīde, and sīe fȳr onǣlæd and þīn heall gewyrmed, and hit rīne and snīwe and styrme ūte; cume ān spearwa and hrædlīce þæt hūs þurhflēo, cume þurh ōþre duru in, þurh ōþre ūt gewīte. Hwæt, hē on þā tīd þe hē inne bið ne bið hrinen mid þȳ storme þæs wintres; ac þæt bið ān ēagan bryhtm and þæt lǣsste fæc, ac hē sōna of wintra on þone winter eft cymeð. Swā þonne þis monna līf tō medmiclum fæce ætȳweð; hwæt þǣr foregange, oððe hwæt þǣr æfterfylige, wē ne cunnun. For ðon gif þēos nīwe lār ōwiht cūðlicre ond gerisenlicre brenge, þæs weorþe is þæt wē þǣre fylgen.' þeossum wordum gelīcum ōðre aldormen and ðæs cyninges geþeahteras sprǣcan.

þā gēn tōætȳhte Cēfi and cwæð, þæt hē wolde Paulīnus þone bisceop geornlīcor gehȳran be þām Gode sprecende þām þe hē bodade. þā hēt se cyning swā dōn. þā hē þā his word gehȳrde, þā clypode hē and þus cwæð: 'Geare ic þæt ongeat, þæt ðæt nōwiht wæs þæt wē beēodan; for þon swā micle swā ic geornlīcor on þām bīgange þæt sylfe sōð sōhte, swā ic hit lǣs mētte. Nū þonne ic openlīce ondette, þæt on þysse lāre þæt sylfe sōð scīneð þæt ūs mæg þā gyfe syllan ēcre ēadignesse and ēces līfes hǣlo. For þon ic þonne nū lǣre, cyning, þæt þæt templ and þā wīgbedo, þā ðe wē būton wæstmum ǣnigre nytnisse hālgodon, þæt wē þā hraþe forlēosen ond fȳre forbærnen.' Ono hwæt, hē þā se cyning openlīce ondette þām biscope ond him eallum, þæt hē wolde fæstlīce þām dēofolgildum wiðsacan ond Crīstes gelēafan onfōn.

Mid þȳ þe hē þā se cyning from þǣm foresprecenan biscope sōhte ond āhsode heora hālignesse þe hēo ǣr biēodon, hwā ðā

25 **tō þǣre sprǣce fēng** 'took up the discussion', i.e. 'took the floor'.

25–6 **mē is gesewen** 'seems to me' (literally 'is seen by me').

27 **swylc swā** (more usually *swylce swā*) + subj. means 'as if'. The poignant simile introduced here is the subject of Wordsworth's sixteenth Ecclesiastical Sonnet, but the poet misconstrues the terms of the comparison. The anonymous counsellor compares the flight of a sparrow through a hall with the life of men on earth (*þis andwearde līf manna on eorðan*). Wordsworth thinks the comparison is with 'the human Soul . . . / While in the Body lodged, her warm abode'.

37 **þæs weorþe is þæt wē** 'it is worthy of that, (namely) that we . . .'. The pleonastic *þæs* anticipates the following clause (§148).

37–8 **þeossum wordum gelīcum** 'in words like these'.

41 **hē** i.e. Cefi.

43–4 **swā micle swā ic geornlīcor . . . swā ic . . . lǣs** 'the more eagerly I . . . the less I', literally 'by so much as I more eagerly . . . so I less'.

48 **þæt wē þā** *þæt* conj. repeats the first *þæt* in l. 47; *þā* is a recapitulatory pronoun (§148).

52–3 **biscope . . . heora hālignesse** 'high priest . . . of their religion' (i.e. Cefi).

53 **hēo** nom. pl. refers to Edwin's pagan subjects.

wīgbed ond þā hergas þāra dēofolgilda mid heora hegum þe hēo ymbsette wǣron, hēo ǣrest āīdligan ond tōweorpan scolde, þā ondsworede hē: 'Efne ic. Hwā mæg þā nū, þā þe ic longe mid dysignesse beēode, tō bysene ōðerra monna gerisenlecor tōweorpan, þonne ic seolfa þurh þā snytro þe ic from þǣm sōðan Gode onfēng?' Ond hē ðā sōna from him āwearp þā īdlan dysignesse þe hē ǣr beēode, ond þone cyning bæd þæt hē him wǣpen sealde ond stōdhors þæt hē meahte on cuman ond dēofolgyld tōweorpan, for þon þām biscope heora hālignesse ne wæs ālȳfed þæt hē mōste wǣpen wegan ne elcor būton on mȳran rīdan. þā sealde se cyning him sweord þæt hē hine mid gyrde ond nom his spere on hond ond hlēop on þæs cyninges stēdan ond tō þǣm dēofulgeldum fērde. þā ðæt folc hine þā geseah swā gescyrpedne, þā wēndon hēo þæt hē teola ne wiste, ac þæt hē wēdde. Sōna þæs þe hē nēalēhte tō þǣm herige, þā scēat hē mid þȳ spere þæt hit sticode fæste on þǣm herige, ond wæs swīðe gefēonde þǣre ongytenesse þæs sōðan Godes bīgonges. Ond hē ðā hēht his gefēran tōweorpan ealne þone herig ond þā getimbro, ond forbærnan. Is sēo stōw gȳt ætēawed gū þāra dēofulgilda nōht feor ēast from Eoforwīcceastre begeondan Deorwentan þǣre ēa, ond gēn tō dæge is nemned Gōdmundingahām, þǣr se biscop þurh ðæs sōðan Godes inbryrdnesse tōwearp ond fordyde þā wīgbed þe hē seolfa ǣr gehālgode.

Ðā onfēng Ēadwine cyning mid eallum þǣm æðelingum his þēode ond mid micle folce Crīstes gelēafan ond fulwihte bæðe þȳ endlyftan gēare his rīces.

55 **hēo** recapitulatory pronoun (§148).

56 **þā . . . þā þe** 'those (pagan things) . . . which'.

57 **ōðerra monna** gen. pl. Translate 'for other men'.

67 **teola ne wiste** 'did not perceive well', i.e. 'was not in his right mind'.

Sōna þæs þe 'Immediately after', i.e. 'As soon as'. For *þæs þe*, see §168 *þæs* (*þe*) and §174.2.

71–2 **Is sēo stōw . . . dēofulgilda** 'The place formerly of the idols is still pointed out.'

9

Bede's Account of the Poet Cædmon

Cædmon is the first English poet whose name is known to us. Yet, to say that English poetry begins with him would be misleading, for when Cædmon's Anglo-Saxon forebears migrated from the Continent to the British Isles, they brought with them a well-developed poetic tradition shaped by centuries of oral improvisation in the Germanic north. Not only was this tradition rich with legends and characters, but it also included a highly formalized poetic diction and an intricate system of versification. In the normal course of Christianization this tradition would have been displaced by new subjects and new styles derived from Christian Latin poetry, for medieval missionaries were usually anxious and intolerant in the presence of established pagan traditions. But the ancient Germanic style survived in England, for it was demonstrated soon after the conversion that the old heroic tradition of poetry could be put in the service of Christian themes. The result of this wedding of Christian matter with pagan Germanic style is that unique blend of Christian and heroic elements which characterizes so much Old English poetry, such as *The Dream of the Rood*, *Andreas*, *Exodus*, and *The Fates of the Apostles*.

Bede's account in his *Ecclesiastical History* of how the illiterate cattle-herd Cædmon suddenly began singing of Christian subjects in the old heroic measure seems to capture that moment in history when two cultures began to merge. To the Anglo-Saxons, Cædmon's miracle was his instantaneous acquisition of the power of poetic composition through the agency of a divinely inspired dream. Modern readers familiar with the widely documented folk-motif of men suddenly acquiring poetic powers through a dream may dismiss Bede's story as essentially fabulous, but the nine-line *Hymn* itself attests to a minor miracle of literary history that cannot be denied: in these polished verses Cædmon demonstrated that the ancient heroic style was not incompatible with Christian doctrine and hence was worthy of preservation. The old Germanic poets had hailed Woden with such terms as 'Father of Armies' (cf. Old Norse *Herja-faðir* in the *Edda*) and Cædmon skilfully adapts the formula to make it reflect the Christian term for God, 'Father of

Glory' (Ephesians 1:17): *Wuldorfæder*. Kings were referred to as 'guardians of the realm' in traditional Anglo-Saxon poetry (cf. *Brytenrīces weard* and *rīces weard* in other Old English poems) and Cædmon appropriates the term for Christian poetry by altering it to *heofonrīces Weard.* The metre and the dignity of the phrases remain intact; only the spiritual quality has been changed. Through such expedients as these the ancient style was saved from disrepute and extinction, so that even poets who wished to treat subjects not specifically Christian (such as the poets of *Finnsburg*, *Maldon*, or *The Battle of Brunanburh*) were free to do so without reproach from the Christian establishment. And monastic scribes did not hesitate to preserve poems written in the old measure, thus making it possible for us to read today specimens of the earliest English poetry which would otherwise have been lost forever.

The text of the Old English Bede presented here is that of the Bodleian Library MS Tanner 10, although we have occasionally adopted a reading from one of the other manuscripts when these seemed preferable to Tanner, most notably in lines 32, 35, 36, 47, and 69.

In ðeosse abbudissan mynstre wæs sum brōðor syndriglīce mid godcundre gife gemǣred ond geweorðad, for þon hē gewunade gerisenlice lēoð wyrcan, þā ðe tō ǣfæstnisse ond tō ārfæstnisse belumpen, swā ðætte, swā hwæt swā hē of godcundum stafum þurh bōceras geleornode, þæt hē æfter medmiclum fæce in scopgereorde mid þā mǣstan swētnisse ond inbryrdnisse geglængde ond in Engliscgereorde wel geworht forþbrōhte. Ond for his lēoþsongum monigra monna mōd oft tō worulde forhogdnisse ond tō geþēodnisse þæs heofonlican līfes onbærnde wǣron. Ond ēac swelce monige ōðre æfter him in Ongelþēode ongunnon ǣfæste lēoð wyrcan; ac nǣnig hwæðre him þæt gelīce dōn meahte, for þon hē nales from monnum ne þurh mon gelǣred wæs, þæt hē þone lēoðcræft leornade, ac hē wæs godcundlīce gefultumed ond þurh Godes gife þone songcræft onfēng. Ond hē for ðon nǣfre nōht lēasunge ne īdles lēoþes wyrcan meahte, ac efne þā ān þā ðe tō ǣfæstnesse belumpon, ond his þā ǣfestan tungan gedafenode singan.

1 **ðeosse abbudissan** Abbess Hild, the woman in charge of the monastic community where Cædmon was a brother. Cf. ll. 49, 61.

9 **geþēodnisse** 'joining' of the heavenly life. This very awkward sense is probably the result of confusion (by the translator or a scribe) between Latin *appetitum* 'longing' (which is what Bede wrote in the Latin version) and *appictum*, past participle of *appingo* 'join'. 'Longing for the heavenly life' is what Bede intended.

16–17 **his þā ǣfestan ... singan** '(it) befitted that pious tongue of his to sing' (§212).

Wæs hē se mon in weoruldhāde geseted oð þā tīde þe hē wæs gelȳfdre ylde, ond hē nǣfre nǣnig lēoð geleornade. Ond hē for þon oft in gebēorscipe, þonne þǣr wæs blisse intinga gedēmed, þæt hēo ealle sceolden þurh endebyrdnesse be hearpan singan, þonne hē geseah þā hearpan him nēalēcan, þonne ārās hē for scome from þǣm symble ond hām ēode tō his hūse. Þā hē þæt þā sumre tīde dyde, þæt hē forlēt þæt hūs þæs gebēorscipes ond ūt wæs gongende tō nēata scipene, þāra heord him wæs þǣre neahte beboden, þā hē ðā þǣr in gelimplicre tīde his leomu on reste gesette ond onslēpte, þā stōd him sum mon æt þurh swefn ond hine hālette ond grētte ond hine be his noman nemnde: 'Cedmon, sing mē hwæthwugu.' Þā ondswarede hē ond cwæð: 'Ne con ic nōht singan; ond ic for þon of þeossum gebēorscipe ūt ēode, ond hider gewāt, for þon ic nāht singan ne cūðe.' Eft hē cwæð, se ðe mid hine sprecende wæs: 'Hwæðre þū meaht mē singan.' Þā cwæð hē: 'Hwæt sceal ic singan?' Cwæð hē: 'Sing mē frumsceaft.' Þā hē ðā þās andsware onfēng, þā ongon hē sōna singan in herenesse Godes Scyppendes þā fers ond þā word þe hē nǣfre gehȳrde, þāra endebyrdnes þis is:

Nū wē sculon herigean   heofonrīces Weard,
Meotodes meahte   ond his mōdgeþanc,
weorc Wuldorfæder,   swā hē wundra gehwæs,
ēce Drihten,   ōr onstealde.
Hē ǣrest sceōp   eorðan bearnum
heofon tō hrōfe,   hālig Scyppend.
Þā middangeard   monncynnes Weard,
ēce Drihten,   æfter tēode
fīrum foldan,   Frēa ælmihtig.

Þā ārās hē from þǣm slǣpe, ond eal þā þe hē slǣpende song fæste in gemynde hæfde, ond þǣm wordum sōna monig word in þæt ilce gemet Gode wyrðes songes tōgeþēodde. Þā cōm hē on

19–28 **Ond hē ... nemnde** See §153. For the semantic distinction between *þonne* and *þā*, see §168 *þonne* 2.

20 **þonne þǣr ... gedēmed, þæt** 'whenever it was deemed (that there was) cause for merriment there, (namely) that ...'. The sense of the Latin is different: 'whenever it would be decided, for the sake of merriment, that ...'. The Old English translator mistook the Latin ablative *causā* for a nominative.

hēo 'they'. So also in ll. 55, 101, 104, 106, 107, and 114.

25 **þāra heord** 'the care of which'.

32 **þū meaht mē singan** 'thou canst sing to me'. See §207 and fn.

45 **eal þā þe** 'all those (things) which'.

47 **Gode wyrðes songes** 'of song dear to God'. Since this sentence tells us that Cædmon immediately added more verses to the nine lines he composed in his dream (and presumably sang this completed version to the Abbess and her scholars), we should regard the text which we now call 'Cædmon's Hymn' as only a fragment, the opening lines of a much longer poem in praise of the Creator.

morgenne tō þǣm tūngerēfan, þe his ealdormon wæs; sægde him hwylce gife hē onfēng. Ond hē hine sōna tō þǣre abbudissan gelǣdde ond hire þā cȳðde ond sægde. Þā hēht hēo gesomnian ealle þā gelǣredestan men ond þā leorneras, ond him ondweardum hēt secgan þæt swefn ond þæt lēoð singan, þæt ealra heora dōme gecoren wǣre, hwæt oððe hwonon þæt cuman wǣre. Þā wæs him eallum gesegen, swā swā hit wæs, þæt him wǣre from Drihtne sylfum heofonlic gifu forgifen. Þā rehton hēo him ond sægdon sum hālig spell ond godcundre lāre word; bebudon him þā, gif hē meahte, þæt hē in swinsunge lēoþsonges þæt gehwyrfde. Þā hē ðā hæfde þā wīsan onfongne, þā ēode hē hām tō his hūse, and cwōm eft on morgenne, ond þȳ betstan lēoðe geglenged him āsong ond āgeaf þæt him beboden wæs.

Ðā ongan sēo abbudisse clyppan ond lufigean þā Godes gife in þǣm men; ond hēo hine þā monade ond lǣrde þæt hē woruldhād ānforlēte ond munuchād onfēnge; ond hē þæt wel þafode. Ond hēo hine in þæt mynster onfēng mid his gōdum, ond hine geþēodde tō gesomnunge þāra Godes þēowa, ond hēht hine lǣran þæt getæl þæs hālgan stǣres ond spelles. Ond hē eal þā hē in gehȳrnesse geleornian meahte mid hine gemyndgade, ond swā swā clǣne nēten eodorcende in þæt swēteste lēoð gehwerfde. Ond his song ond his lēoð wǣron swā wynsumu tō gehȳranne þætte þā seolfan his lārēowas æt his mūðe wreoton ond leornodon. Song hē ǣrest be middangeardes gesceape ond bī fruman moncynnes ond eal þæt stǣr Genesis (þæt is sēo ǣreste Moyses booc); ond eft bī ūtgonge Israhēla folces of Ǣgypta londe ond bī ingonge þæs gehātlandes ond bī ōðrum monegum spellum þæs hālgan gewrites canōnes bōca, ond bī Crīstes menniscnesse ond bī his þrōwunge ond bī his ūpāstīgnesse in heofonas ond bī þæs Hālgan Gāstes cyme ond þāra apostola lāre; ond eft bī þǣm dæge þæs tōweardan dōmes ond bī fyrhtu þæs tintreglican wiites ond bī swētnesse þæs heofonlecan rīces hē monig lēoð geworhte. Ond swelce ēac ōðer monig be þǣm godcundan fremsumnessum ond dōmum hē geworhte. In eallum

51 **him ondweardum** 'with them present', i.e. 'in their presence'.

52–3 **þæt ealra . . . cuman wǣre** 'so that it might be determined by the judgement of them all what (that poetic skill was) or whence it had come'. The Old English is awkward and unidiomatic because the translator is following his Latin source too slavishly.

59–60 **ond þȳ . . . wæs** 'and sang and gave back to them what had been dictated to him, adorned with the best poetry'.

66 **eal þā** 'all those things which'.

67 **mid hine gemyndgade** 'remembered within himself', i.e. 'mulled over'.

67–8 **swā swā . . . eodorcende** Biblical commentators explain that the ruminating animals of Leviticus 11:3 symbolize pious men meditating on God.

69–70 **þā seolfan his lārēowas** 'the same ones his teachers', i.e. 'his very teachers'.

þǣm hē geornlīce gēmde þæt hē men ātuge from synna lufan ond māndǣda, ond tō lufan ond tō geornfulnesse āwehte gōdra dǣda; for þon hē wæs se mon swīþe ǣfæst ond regollecum þēodscipum ēaðmōdlīce underþēoded. Ond wið þǣm þā ðe in ōðre wīsan dōn woldon, hē wæs mid welme micelre ellenwōdnisse onbærned; ond hē for ðon fægre ænde his līf betȳnde ond geendade.

For þon þā ðǣre tīde nēalǣcte his gewitenesse ond forðfōre, þā wæs hē, fēowertȳnum dagum ǣr, þæt hē wæs līchomlicre untrymnesse þrycced ond hefgad, hwæðre tō þon gemetlīce þæt hē ealle þā tīd meahte ge sprecan ge gongan. Wæs þǣr in nēaweste untrumra monna hūs, in þǣm heora þēaw wæs þæt hēo þā untrumran ond þā ðe æt forðfōre wǣron inlǣdan sceoldon, ond him þǣr ætsomne þegnian. Þā bæd hē his þegn on ǣfenne þǣre neahte þe hē of worulde gongende wæs þæt hē in þǣm hūse him stōwe gegearwode þæt hē gerestan meahte. Þā wundrode se þegn for hwon hē ðæs bǣde, for þon him þūhte þæt his forðfōr swā nēah ne wǣre; dyde hwæðre swā swā hē cwæð ond bibēad. Ond mid þȳ hē ðā þǣr on reste ēode, ond hē gefēonde mōde sumu þing mid him sprecende ætgædere ond glēowiende wæs, þe þǣr ǣr inne wǣron, þā wæs ofer middeneaht þæt hē frægn hwæðer hēo ǣnig hūsl inne hæfdon. Þā ondswarodon hēo ond cwǣdon: 'Hwylc þearf is ðē hūsles? Ne þīnre forþfōre swā nēah is, nū þū þus rōtlīce ond þus glædlīce tō ūs sprecende eart.' Cwæð hē eft: 'Berað mē hūsl tō.' Þā hē hit þā on honda hæfde, þā frægn hē hwæþer hēo ealle smolt mōd ond būton eallum incan blīðe tō him hæfdon. Þā ondswaredon hȳ ealle ond cwǣdon þæt hēo nǣnigne incan tō him wiston, ac hēo ealle him swīðe blīðemōde wǣron; ond hēo wrixendlīce hine bǣdon þæt hē him eallum blīðe wǣre. Þā ondswarade hē ond cwæð: 'Mīne brōðor, mīne þā lēofan, ic eom swīðe blīðemōd tō ēow ond tō eallum Godes monnum.' Ond swā wæs hine getrymmende mid þȳ heofonlecan wegneste ond him ōðres līfes ingong gegearwode. Þā gȳt hē frægn, hū nēah þǣre tīde wǣre þætte þā brōðor ārīsan scolden ond Godes lof rǣran ond heora ūhtsong singan. Þā ondswaredon hēo: 'Nis hit feor tō þon.' Cwæð hē:

87 **nēalǣcte** '(it) drew near' (§212).

88 **þæt hē wæs** In a clumsy effort to control the sentence the translator introduces these three redundant words (§148). Ignore them when rendering into modern English.

89 **tō þon gemetlīce þæt** 'to that (extent) moderately that', i.e. 'sufficiently moderately that'.

92 **æt forðfōre** 'at (the point of) death'.

99 **þe** The antecedent is *him* in l. 98. See §163.4.

104–5 **smolt mōd ... hæfdon** 'had a serene and friendly spirit without any rancour toward him'.

106 **nǣnigne incan ... wiston** 'felt no rancour toward him'.

'Teala: wuton wē wel þǣre tīde bīdan.' Ond þā him gebæd ond hine gesegnode mid Crīstes rōdetācne, ond his hēafod onhylde tō þām bolstre, ond medmicel fæc onslēpte, ond swā mid stilnesse his līf geendade. Ond swā wæs geworden þætte swā swā hē hlūttre mōde ond bilwitre ond smyltre wilsumnesse Drihtne þēode, þæt hē ēac swylce swā smylte dēaðe middangeard wæs forlǣtende, ond tō his gesihðe becwōm. Ond sēo tunge, þe swā monig hālwende word in þæs Scyppendes lof gesette, hē ðā swelce ēac þā ȳtmæstan word in his herenisse, hine seolfne segniende ond his gāst in his honda bebēodende, betȳnde. Ēac swelce þæt is gesegen þæt hē wære gewis his seolfes forðfōre, of þǣm wē nū secgan hȳrdon.

121–4 **Ond sēo tunge ... betȳnde** The awkward change of subject from *sēo tunge* to *hē* is the result of a mistranslation, the Latin ablative *illāque linguā* having been mistaken for a nominative. The Anglo-Saxon translator ought to have written *mid þǣre tungan*: 'And with the tongue that had composed so many salutary words ... he then concluded his last words', etc.

124–5 **is gesegen ... of þǣm wē** 'it is seen from what we'.

10

The Goths and Boethius: Prose and Verse from the Introduction to King Alfred's Boethius Translation

Among the works which King Alfred the Great translated into Old English as part of his educational programme (see selection 5 above and §251.2) was the philosophical treatise *De consolatione philosophiae* by the Roman consul Boethius. One of the most popular writings of the entire Middle Ages, the *Consolation* was composed after its author had been falsely accused of treason and imprisoned by Theodoric, King of the Ostrogoths and ruler in Rome. The injustice which occasioned Boethius's search for consolation and the pathos of his subsequent murder give the work a special force and immediacy, and so it is not surprising that King Alfred prefaced his translation with an account of the historical background of Boethius's fate: the invasion of Rome by the Goths, Theodoric's rise to power, and the imprisonment and execution of the philosopher. Nor is it surprising that this prefatory material should be recounted first in prose and then in poetry, for much of the Latin *Consolatio* itself is written in verse, and the Old English translator has left both prose and poetic renditions of each verse passage. The existence of these dual versions of the same material affords the modern student an excellent means of becoming acquainted with the form and style of Old English poetry. In the selection which follows (containing King Alfred's preface to his translation) one sees some of the most prominent features which differentiate the language of Old English poetry from that of Old English prose: the fondness for apposition, complicated syntax, colourful compounds like *sincgeofa* and *wēalāf*, and a wealth of poetic synonyms for concepts like warrior and war.

The text for the prose (*a*) is from Bodleian Library MS 180 (except that *miđ* [l. 2], *and* [l. 3], *gelæst* [l. 9], and *arwyrđa wæs on* [l. 26] have been changed to *mid*, *hī þā*, *gelǣste*, and *ārwyrđa on*). The text for the verse (*b*) is from Bodleian Library MS Junius 12, except that *Gotene* [l. 5], *ealla* [l. 12], *Godena* [l. 38], *weorđmynđa* [l. 51], and *hererine* [l. 71] have been changed to *Gotena*, *ealle*, *Gotena*, *weorðmynda*, and *hererinc*.

(a)

On ðǣre tīde ðe Gotan of Sciððiu mǣgðe wið Rōmāna rīce gewin ūp āhōfon and mid heora cyningum, Rǣdgōta and Eallerīca wǣron hātne, Rōmāne burig ābrǣcon, hī þā eall Ītālia rīce þæt is betwux þām muntum and Sicilia þām ēalonde in anwald gerehton; and þā æfter þām foresprecenan cyningum þēodrīc fēng tō þām ilcan rīce. Se þēodrīc wæs Amulinga. Hē wæs Crīsten, þēah hē on þām Arriāniscan gedwolan þurhwunode. Hē gehēt Rōmanum his frēondscipe, swā þæt hī mōstan heora ealdrihta wyrðe bēon, ac hē þā gehāt swīðe yfele gelǣste, and swīðe wrāðe geendode mid manegum māne. þæt wæs, tō ēacan ōðrum unārīmedum yflum, þæt hē Iōhannes þone pāpan hēt ofslēan.

þā wæs sum consul, þæt wē heretoha hātað, Bōētius wæs gehāten, se wæs in bōccræftum and on woruldþēawum se rihtwīsesta. Sē þā ongeat þā manigfealdan yfel þe se cyning Ðēodrīc wið þǣm crīstenandōme and wið þām Rōmaniscum witum dyde. Hē þā gemunde þāra ēðnessa and þāra ealdrihta þe hī under þām cāserum hæfdon, heora ealdhlāfordum. þā ongan hē smēagan and leornigan on him selfum hū hē þæt rīce þām unrihtwīsan cyninge āferran mihte and on ryhtgelēaffulra and on rihtwīsra anwealde gebringan. Sende þā dīgellīce ǣrendgewritu tō

2–3 **Rǣdgōta . . . hātne** '(who) were called Rædgota and Alaric'. See §186. The Anglo-Saxon writer is here telescoping (and confusing) actual events. The heathen Goth Radagaesius (*Rædgota*) was killed in battle five years before Alaric led his troops into Rome.

4 **in anwald gerehton** 'subjugated'.

4–5 The Anglo-Saxon writer here skips over many years and several reigns. Theodoric did not become King of Italy until A.D. 493 – more than eighty years after the death of Alaric.

5 **foresprecenan** The ending *-an* stands here for dat. pl. *-um*; see §65; cf. *gesceapþēotan* 11(g)/4.

8 **heora ealdrihta wyrðe bēon** 'be in possession of their ancient rights', i.e. 'regain their ancient rights'.

11 **Iōhannes . . . ofslēan** In 525 Theodoric had Pope John I cast into prison, where he languished and soon died.

12–13 **Bōētius wæs gehāten** '(who) was named Boethius'.

14 **Sē þā ongeat** 'he then perceived'.

16–17 **hī under . . . ealdhlāfordum** *cāserum* and *ealdhlāfordum* are in apposition: 'they had under the emperors, their ancient lords'.

17–19 **þā ongan hē . . . āferran mihte** 'then he began to study and take thought within himself as to how he might remove the kingdom from the unrighteous king'. Actually Boethius denied that he had betrayed the King in this way, but his enemies claimed that he had written treasonous letters to the eastern emperor Justin I.

þām kāsere tō Constentinopolim, þǣr is Crēca hēahburg and heora cynestōl, forþām se kāsere wæs heora ealdhlāfordcynnes. Bǣdon hine þæt hē him tō heora crīstendōme and tō heora ealdrihtum gefultumede. þā þæt ongeat se wælhrēowa cyning Ðēodrīc, þā hēt hē hine gebringan on carcerne and þǣrinne belūcan. þā hit ðā gelomp þæt se ārwyrða on swā micelre nearanessa becōm, þā wæs hē swā micle swīðor on his mōde gedrēfed swā his mōd ǣr swīðor tō þām woruldsǣlþum gewunod wæs; and hē þā nānre frōfre beinnan þām carcerne ne gemunde, ac hē gefēoll niwol ofdūne on þā flōr, and hine āstrehte swīðe unrōt, and ormōd hine selfne ongan wēpan and þus singend cwæð.

(b)

Hit wæs gēara iū,   ðætte Gotan ēastan
of Sciððia   sceldas lǣddon,
þrēate geþrungon   þēodlond monig;
setton sūðweardes   sigeþēoda twā.
Gotena rīce   gēarmǣlum wēox.
Hæfdan him gecynde   cyningas twēgen,
Rǣdgōd and Alerīc;   rīce geþungon.
þā wæs ofer Muntgīop   monig ātyhted
Gota gylpes full,   gūðe gelysted,
folcgewinnes;   fana hwearfode
scīr on sceafte;   scēotend þōhton
Ītālia   ealle gegongan,
lindwīgende.   Hī gelǣstan swuā
efne from Muntgīop   oð þone mǣran wearoð,
þǣr Sīcilia   sǣstrēamum in
ēglond micel,   ēðel mǣrsað.
Ðā wæs Rōmāna   rīce gewunnen,
ābrocen burga cyst;   beadurincum wæs
Rōm gerȳmed;   Rǣdgōt and Alerīc
fōron on ðæt fæsten;   flēah cāsere
mid þām æþelingum   ūt on Crēcas.

(*a*) 22–4 **Bǣdon hine þæt . . . gefultumede** 'bade him that he should assist them (to return) to their Christianity and their ancient laws'. 'Their Christianity' is the orthodox Christianity that the Romans were practising when the Arian Christian, Theodoric, conquered them. Late in his reign he began to persecute them.

24–5 **hēt hē hine . . . belūcan** Active infinitives to be translated as passive: 'he commanded him to be brought to prison and to be locked up therein'. See §161.

26–8 **wæs hē swā micle swīðor . . . gewunod wæs** 'he was so much the more troubled in his mind in as much as his mind had previously been accustomed to earthly blessings'.

Ne meahte þā sēo wēalāf wīge forstandan
Gotan mid gūðe; giōmonna gestrīon
sealdon unwillum ēþelweardas,
hālige āðas. Wæs gehwæðeres waa.
þēah wæs magorinca mōd mid Crēcum,
gif hī lēodfruman læstan dorsten.
Stōd þrāge on ðām; þēod wæs gewunnen
wintra mænigo, oððæt wyrd gescrāf
þæt þe þēodrīce þegnas and eorlas
hēran sceoldan. Wæs se heretēma
Crīste gecnōden; cyning selfa onfēng
fulluhtþēawum. Fægnodon ealle
Rōmwara bearn and him recene tō
friðes wilnedon. Hē him fæste gehēt,
þæt hȳ ealdrihta ǣlces mōsten
wyrðe gewunigen on þǣre welegan byrig,
ðenden God wuolde, þæt hē Gotena geweald
āgan mōste. Hē þæt eall ālēag.
Wæs þǣm æþelinge Arriānes
gedwola lēofre þonne Drihtnes ǣ.
Hēt Iōhannes, gōdne pāpan,
hēafde behēawan; næs ðæt hærlic dǣd!
Ēac þā wæs unrīm ōðres mānes,
þæt se Gota fremede gōdra gehwilcum.
Ðā wæs rīcra sum on Rōme byrig
āhefen heretoga, hlāforde lēof,
þenden cynestōle Crēacas wīoldon.
þæt wæs rihtwīs rinc; næs mid Rōmwarum
sincgeofa sēlla siððan longe;
hē wæs for weorulde wīs, weorðmynda georn,
beorn bōca glēaw. Bōītius

(*b*) 4 **sigeþēoda twā** i.e. Rædgota's army and Alaric's.

25 **Wæs gehwæðeres waa** 'It was an affliction (to the Romans) in both respects'; (to have to give both their wealth and their sacred oaths to the conquerors).

26–7 **þēah wæs . . . dorsten** The conquered Romans looked to the Greeks in the Eastern Empire (in Constantinople) for rescue from their Gothic invaders. Under duress they had given 'holy vows' for allegiance to the Goths (l. 25a), 'Yet the heart of the (Roman) warriors was with the Greeks if they would dare to help the leader of the people (i.e. the exiled Roman emperor).'

28 **Stōd þrāge on ðām** 'it remained thus for a time'.

31–2 **Wæs . . . Crīste gecnōden** 'was committed to Christ'.

34–5 **and him . . . wilnedon** 'and soon petitioned for peace from him'.

48 **þenden . . . wīoldon** 'while the Greeks controlled the throne'. Theodoric's predecessor, Odowacer, had acknowledged the overlordship of the eastern emperor in Constantinople, as had Theodoric when he became king, but Theodoric's relations with the Greek emperor became strained in the closing years of his reign.

se hæle hātte; sē þone hlīsan geþāh.
Wæs him on gemynde mǣla gehwilce
yfel and edwit þæt him elðēodge
kyningas cȳðdon; wæs on Crēacas hold,
gemunde þāra āra and ealdrihta,
þe his eldran mid him āhton longe,
lufan and lissa. Angan þā listum ymbe
ðencean þearflīce, hū hē ðider meahte
Crēcas oncerran, þæt se cāsere eft
anwald ofer hī āgan mōste.
Sende ǣrendgewrit ealdhlāfordum
dēgelīce, and hī for Drihtne bæd
ealdum trēowum, ðæt hī æft tō him
cōmen on þā ceastre, lēte Crēca witan
rǣdan Rōmwarum, rihtes wyrðe
lēte þone lēodscipe. Đā þā lāre ongeat
Đēodrīc Amuling and þone þegn oferfēng,
hēht fæstlīce folcgesīðas
healdon þone hererinc; wæs him hrēoh sefa,
ege from ðām eorle. Hē hine inne hēht
on carcerne clūstre belūcan.
Þā wæs mōdsefa miclum gedrēfed
Bōētius. Brēac longe ǣr
wlencea under wolcnum; hē þȳ wyrs meahte
þolian þā þrāge, þā hīo swā þearl becōm.
Wæs þā ormōd eorl, āre ne wēnde,
ne on þām fæstene frōfre gemunde;
ac hē neowol āstreaht niðer ofdūne
fēol on þā flōre; fela worda spræc
forþōht ðearle; ne wēnde þonan ǣfre
cuman of ðǣm clammum. Cleopode tō Drihtne
geōmran stemne, gyddode þus.

58 **þe his eldran . . . longe** 'that his elders long had among themselves'.

64–5 **hī for Drihtne . . . trēowum** 'asked them for the sake of God, (and because of their) ancient beliefs'.

66–8 **lēte Crēca . . . lēodscipe** 'let Greek senators worthy of rule, let that nation have control over the Romans'.

71–2 'his (Boethius') mind was troubled, (in him was) fear of the leader (Theodoric)'.

72–3 **Hē hine . . . belūcan** 'He commanded him to be locked in a prison, in a cell.' *Hine* is the object of *belūcan*. See §161.

76–7 **hē þȳ wyrs . . . becōm** 'the worse he was able to endure so harsh a time when it befell'.

84 The lament which follows is the first of the Latin metres of Boethius, translated into OE.

11

Riddles

Riddles are popular in most cultures, and their presence in the Bible (e.g. Judges 14:14) and in Greek tragedy reminds us that they are more than a children's game. In the Old English period scholars like Aldhelm and Symphosius composed verse riddles in polished Latin hexameters, and the anonymous vernacular riddles presented here are sometimes based upon Latin originals. Indeed, since the Latin riddles are accompanied by their solutions (as the Old English are not), this correspondence between Latin and vernacular riddles has sometimes helped scholars to solve some knottier enigmas among the latter.

The Old English verse riddles fall into two basic types. In one type the riddler speaks in his own voice (*Ic seah, Wiga is*) describing the subject of the riddle and asking the reader to guess the answer. The description is in vague, metaphorical, deliberately misleading language with much anthropomorphizing of animals and inanimate objects. In the second type, which is equally mystifying and indirect in expression, the subject of the riddle describes itself (*Ic eom, Ic wæs*) and asks to be identified. The idea of inanimate objects speaking about themselves was not unfamiliar to Anglo-Saxons, for when they inscribed a weapon or piece of jewellery to mark possession, they often put the statement in the first person singular, as if the object itself were speaking. Thus the inscription on the King Alfred Jewel says, 'Ælfred mec het gewyrcan' ('Alfred had me made'), while another says, 'Ædred mec ah, Eanred mec agrof' ('Ædred owns me, Eanred engraved me'). This habit of mind culminates in one of the grandest achievements of Old English poetry, *The Dream of the Rood* (selection 14 below), in which the cross on which Christ died recounts with agony and awe the grim details of the crucifixion. Indeed, two of the riddles printed below (texts *n* and *o*) appear to have 'cross' as their solution and so may be seen as seed stages of *The Dream of the Rood*.

The subjects of the riddles presented here are various: farm implements, weapons, animals and insects, items of food or drink, the Bible, the natural world. Casual and intimate, they are brief meditations on familiar objects. They are often light but rarely humorous, and sometimes the riddlers seem to forget their primary purpose of creating a puzzle as they become absorbed in the curiosities and quaint perplexities which become apparent in the objects around us when we reflect on them. They explore paradoxes both in the object described and in the language describing the objects. Thoughtful probings of both the milieu and the language, the riddles reveal quirks and moods of the Anglo-Saxons quite unlike anything we find in their other poetry.

The riddles presented here have been selected from the Exeter Book, a tenth-century manuscript which contains some of the best poetry left by the Anglo-Saxons. It is a rich poetic miscellany containing nearly a hundred verse riddles and more than thirty different poems including *The Wife's Lament*, *The Wanderer*, and *The Seafarer*, all three of which appear below (selections 15, 16, and 17).

(*a*)

Wer sæt æt wīne   mid his wīfum twām
ond his twēgen suno   ond his twā dohtor,
swāse gesweostor,   ond hyra suno twēgen,
frēolico frumbearn;   fæder wæs þǣr inne
þāra æþelinga   ǣghwæðres mid,
ēam ond nefa.   Ealra wǣron fīfe
eorla ond idesa   insittendra.

(*b*)

Wiht cwōm gongan   þǣr weras sǣton
monige on mæðle,   mōde snottre;
hæfde ān ēage   ond ēaran twā,
ond twēgen fēt,   twelf hund hēafda,
hrycg ond wombe   ond honda twā,
earmas ond eaxle,   ānne swēoran
ond sīdan twā.   Saga hwæt ic hātte.

Riddle a The solution is 'Lot and his offspring'. Genesis 19:30–8 tells how Lot's two daughters, after an incestuous union with their father, each gave birth to a son. The riddle explores the complicated, overlapping kinship relations which resulted. Emendations: *Wer* for MS *wær* (l. 1), *hyra* for *hyre* (l. 3).

6 **ēam ond nefa** This refers to the sons in relation to each other. Since Lot is the father both of the daughters and their two sons, his four offspring are siblings. Therefore each son is both uncle and nephew to the other.

Riddle b The solution is 'one-eyed garlic pedlar'. Emendation: *hrycg* for MS *hryc* (l. 5).

(*c*)

Moððe word fræt. Mē þæt þūhte
wrǣtlicu wyrd, þā ic þæt wundor gefrægn,
þæt se wyrm forswealg wera gied sumes,
þēof in þȳstro, þrymfæstne cwide
ond þæs strangan staþol. Stælgiest ne wæs
wihte þȳ glēawra, þe hē þām wordum swealg.

(*d*)

Hrægl mīn swīgað, þonne īc hrūsan trede,
oþþe þā wīc būge, oþþe wado drēfe.
Hwīlum mec āhebbað ofer hæleþa byht
hyrste mīne ond þēos hēa lyft,
ond mec þonne wīde wolcna strengu
ofer folc byreð. Frætwe mīne
swōgað hlūde ond swinsiað,
torhte singað, þonne ic getenge ne bēom
flōde ond foldan, fērende gǣst.

Riddle c Since the first word identifies the subject of the poem, this is not a riddle so much as an exploration of a paradox: the insect devours learning but is none the wiser for it. The whimsical meditation is enhanced by delicate puns on words like *(for)swelgan* (which can mean 'understand' as well as 'consume') and *cwide* (which can mean 'morsel' as well as 'statement').

5 **þæs strangan staþol** 'the (very) foundation of that mighty (utterance)', i.e. the vellum on which the *cwide* is written. *Staþol* could also refer to the intellectual content of the statement (cf. *staþolung* 'ordinance').

5–6 **ne ... swealg** 'was not a whit the wiser in that he had swallowed (comprehended) those words'. For the *þȳ ... þe* construction, see §167(*a*) and §177.3.

Riddle d The solution is 'swan'. The Anglo-Saxons believed that when the swan was aloft the feathers in its wings produced music. In typical riddling fashion the poet refers to the swan's feathers with vague, metaphorical words like *hrægl* 'raiment', *hyrst* 'equipment', and *frætwe* 'trappings'.

5 **wolcna strengu** 'The strength of the skies' is the wind.

(*e*)

Nis mīn sele swīge, ne ic sylfa hlūd
ymb dryhtsele; unc dryhten scōp
sīþ ætsomne. Ic eom swiftra þonne hē,
þrāgum strengra, hē þreohtigra.
Hwīlum ic mē reste; hē sceal rinnan forð.
Ic him in wunige ā þenden ic lifge;
gif wit unc gedǣlað, mē bið dēað witod.

(*f*)

Ic eom weorð werum, wīde funden,
brungen of bearwum ond of bēorghleoþum,
of denum ond of dūnum. Dæges mec wǣgun
feþre on lifte, feredon mid liste
under hrōfes hlēo. Hæleð mec siþþan
baþedan in bydene. Nū ic eom bindere
ond swingere, sōna weorpe
esne tō eorþan, hwīlum ealdne ceorl.
Sōna þæt onfindeð, se þe mec fēhð ongēan
ond wið mægenþisan mīnre genǣsteð,
þæt hē hrycge sceal hrūsan sēcan,
gif hē unrǣdes ǣr ne geswīceð.
Strengo bistolen, strong on sprǣce,
mægene binumen, nāh his mōdes geweald,
fōta ne folma. Frige hwæt ic hātte,
ðe on eorþan swā esnas binde,
dole æfter dyntum be dæges lēohte.

Riddle e The solution is 'fish in the river'. The poet delights in the paradox of the silent, versatile fish in the rushing stream, which, though seemingly insubstantial, is essential to the fish's life and will survive its death. Emendations: *ymb dryhtsele*; *unc dryhten scōp* for MS *ymb unc . . . dryht scop* (l. 2), *swiftra* for *swistre* (l. 3), *rinnan* for *yrnan* (l. 5).

1 *Eom* is understood before *ic*.

Riddle f The solution is 'mead', an alcoholic beverage made from honey. Emendations: *bēorghleoþum* (l. 2) for MS *burghleoþum*, *weorpe* for *weorpere* (l. 7), *esne* for *efne* (l. 8).

3 **Dæges** 'by day'. See §190.5.

4 **feþre** The wings of the bees who gather the honey from which mead is made and bring it to the hive (*under hrōfes hlēo*).

17 **be dæges lēohte** i.e. the morning after.

(*g*)

Ic þā wiht geseah wǣpnedcynnes.
Geoguðmyrþe grǣdig him on gafol forlēt
ferðfriþende fēower wellan
scīre scēotan on gesceapþēotan.
Mon maþelade, se þe mē gesægde:
'Sēo wiht, gif hīo gedȳgeð, dūna briceð;
gif hē tōbirsteð, bindeð cwice.'

(*h*)

Agob is mīn noma eft onhwyrfed;
ic eom wrǣtlic wiht on gewin sceapen.
þonne ic onbūge, ond mē on bōsme fareð
ǣtren onga, ic bēom eallgearo
þæt ic mē þæt feorhbealo feor āswāpe.
Siþþan mē se waldend, se mē þæt wite gescōp,
leoþo forlǣteð, ic bēo lengre þonne ǣr,
oþþæt ic spǣte spilde geblonden
ealfelo āttor þæt ic ǣr gegēap.
Ne tōgongeð þæs gumena hwylcum,
ǣnigum ēaþe þæt ic þǣr ymb sprice,
gif hine hrīneð þæt me of hrife flēogeð,
þæt þone māndrinc mægne gecēapaþ,
fullwer fæste fēore sīne.
Nelle ic unbunden ǣnigum hȳran
nymþe searosǣled. Saga hwæt ic hātte.

Riddle g The solution is 'bull calf' or 'young ox'. In related contemporary Latin riddles, the poets make much of the calf's drinking milk from the 'four fountains' of the mother. Emendation: *Geoguðmyrþe* for MS *geoguð myrwe* (l. 2).

2 him on gafol 'as a gift to himself'.

6–7 i.e. while alive the bull will break the ground by pulling a plough through it, while the dead bull's hide will provide leather thongs that can tie people up. The shift from the grammatical gender of *wiht* in l. 6 to the logical gender of a bull in l. 7 may be intentionally mystifying.

Riddle h The solution 'bow' is spelled backwards in the first word in the riddle. (This reverse spelling of *boga* was corrupted to *agof* by an inattentive scribe.) The riddler speaks first of the arrow as it passes into the bosom of the arched bow as the bowman takes aim (ll. 2–5) and then of the arrow's flight to its target after it is released (ll. 6–9). Emendations besides *Agob* are *on* for MS *of* (l. 3), *gegēap* for *geap* (l. 9), and *fullwer* for *full wer* (l. 14).

2 on gewin sceapen A characteristic riddler's double meaning: the bow is created in the toil and strife of the arrowsmith's shop; it is also given its (arched) shape in the course of battle when the bowman bends it.

5 þæt ic mē . . . āswāpe 'that I may remove that mortal danger (the arrow) far from me'.

6 se mē . . . gescōp 'who caused me that pain' (i.e. by bending the bow).

11 The noun clause *þæt ic . . . sprice* is the subject of the verb *tōgongeð*.

(*j*)

Ic wæs wǣpen, wiga. Nū mec wlonc þeceð
geong hagostealdmon golde ond sylfore,
wōum wīrbogum. Hwīlum weras cyssað;
hwīlum ic tō hilde hlēoþre bonne
wilgehlēþan; hwīlum wycg byreþ
mec ofer mearce; hwīlum merehengest
fereð ofer flōdas frætwum beorhtne;
hwīlum mægða sum mīnne gefylleð
bōsm bēaghroden; hwīlum ic on bordum sceal,
heard, hēafodlēas, behlȳþed licgan;
hwīlum hongige hyrstum frætwed,
wlitig on wāge, þǣr weras drincað,
frēolic fyrdsceorp. Hwīlum folcwigan
on wicge wegað, þonne ic winde sceal
sincfāg swelgan of sumes bōsme;
hwīlum ic gereordum rincas laðige
wlonce tō wīne; hwīlum wrāþum sceal
stefne mīnre forstolen hreddan,
flȳman fēondsceaþan. Frige hwæt ic hātte.

Riddle j The subject of the riddle, a horn, is described variously as a weapon and fighter (while still growing on the animal's head), as an ornamented drinking horn, and as a wind instrument (used to summon warriors to battle or to the wine-drinking, or to sound the alarm after a robbery). Emendations: *on* supplied in ll. 9 and 14; *wrāþum* for MS *wraþþum* (l. 17).

3 **Hwīlum weras cyssað** Supply *mec*. Men kiss the horn when they put their lips to it either to blow it or drink from it.

6–7 **hwīlum . . . beorhtne** Again, *mec* is understood.

9–10 **hwīlum . . . licgan** 'at times I must lie on the tables, hard, headless, plundered' – presumably plundered of its contents (mead) after its lid ('head') has been removed.

13–14 **Hwīlum . . . wegað** *Mec* is understood.

(*k*)

Mec on þissum dagum dēadne ofgēafon
fæder ond mōdor; ne wæs mē feorh þā gēn,
ealdor in innan. Þā mec ān ongon,
welhold mēge, wēdum þeccan,
hēold ond freoþode, hlēosceorpe wrāh
swā ārlīce swā hire āgen bearn,
oþþæt ic under scēate, swā mīn gesceapu wǣron,
ungesibbum wearð ēacen gǣste.
Mec sēo friþemǣg fēdde siþþan,
oþþæt ic āwēox, wīddor meahte
sīþas āsettan. Hēo hæfde swǣsra þȳ lǣs
suna ond dohtra, þȳ hēo swā dyde.

Riddle k The cuckoo leaves its egg in the nest of other birds and flies away, leaving the foster mother to hatch and feed the fledgling along with her own brood. As the young cuckoo gains strength, it often evicts the fledglings who were hatched with it. The subject of this riddle became a legendary example of ingratitude, as in the Fool's observation in *King Lear* I. iv. 235: 'The Hedgesparrow fed The Cuckoo so long that it had it head bit off by it young.' Emendations: *ofgēafon* for MS *ofgeafum* (l. 1), *ān* supplied in l. 3, *þeccan* for *weccan* (l. 4), *swā ārlīce* for *nearlice* (l. 6).

1 **on þissum dagum** 'in these days', i.e. 'recently'.

dēadne The egg is only apparently dead, of course.

7 **swā mīn gesceapu wǣron** 'as was my destiny'.

8 **ungesibbum** ... **gǣste** 'among (nestlings) unrelated to me I became great with life'.

11–12 **Hēo hæfde swǣsra þȳ lǣs** ... **þȳ hēo swā dyde** A correlative use of the instrumental *þȳ*: '*by so much* as she did so ... she had *so much* the fewer of her own dear ones.' This idiom survives in MnE 'the bigger they come, the harder they fall' and 'the more the merrier'. The word *the* in these constructions is a survival of OE *þȳ*. Cf. 12/312–13.

(*l*)

Ic seah wrǣtlice   wuhte fēower
samed sīþian;   swearte wǣran lāstas,
swaþu swīþe blacu.   Swift wæs on fōre,
fuglum framra;   flēag on lyfte,
dēaf under ȳþe.   Drēag unstille
winnende wiga   se him wegas tǣcneþ
ofer fǣted gold   fēower eallum.

(*m*)

Wiga is on eorþan   wundrum ācenned
dryhtum tō nytte,   of dumbum twām
torht ātyhted,   þone on tēon wigeð
fēond his fēonde.   Forstrangne oft
wīf hine wrīð;   hē him wel hēreð,
þēowaþ him geþwǣre,   gif him þegniað
mægeð ond mæcgas   mid gemete ryhte,
fēdað hine fægre;   hē him fremum stēpeð
līfe on lissum.   Lēanað grimme
þām þe hine wloncne   weorþan lǣteð.

Riddle l The solution is two fingers and a thumb writing with a quill pen. Emendations: *flēag on* for *fleotgan* (l. 4) and *wegas* for *wægas* (l. 6).

4 **fuglum framra** 'more swift among the birds', i.e. swifter *in the air* (when the hand darts from the writing surface to the inkwell and back again) than it is when moving across the vellum page, writing. Perhaps also with a glance back at the time when the quill was a feather in the wing of a living bird flying through the air. See §191.5.

5 **under ȳþe** i.e. into the ink. **Drēag** 'persevered'.

7 **fǣted gold** 'ornamented gold' (of the illuminated manuscript page).

Riddle m The solution is 'fire'. Emendations: *forstrangne* for MS *fer strangne* (l. 4), and *þām* supplied in l. 10.

3–4 **þone on ... fēonde** 'which foe bears against foe to his injury'. A reference, apparently, to the use of fire in warfare.

5–7 **hē him wel ... mæcgas** 'he obeys them well, compliant, he serves them, if women and men serve him ...'.

(*n*)

Ic seah in healle, þǣr hæleð druncon,
on flet beran fēower cynna,
wrǣtlic wudutrēow ond wunden gold,
sinc searobunden, ond seolfres dǣl
ond rōde tācn, þæs ūs tō roderum ūp
hlǣdre rǣrde, ǣr hē helwara
burg ābrǣce. Ic þæs bēames mæg
ēaþe for eorlum æþelu secgan;
þǣr wæs hlin ond āc ond se hearda īw
ond se fealwa holen: frēan sindon ealle
nyt ætgædre; naman habbað ānne,
wulfhēafedtrēo; þæt oft wǣpen abǣd
his mondryhtne, māðm in healle,
goldhilted sweord. Nū mē þisses gieddes
ondsware ȳwe, se hine on mēde
wordum secgan hū se wudu hātte.

Riddle n The solution appears to be 'cross', although some details of the riddle remain obscure. In early Christian tradition the cross was thought to have been made from four different kinds of wood, the specific kinds varying from one authority to another. (See W. O. Stevens *The Cross in the Life and Literature of the Anglo-Saxons* Yale Studies in English 22 (New Haven, 1904), p. 10; reprinted in *The Anglo-Saxon Cross* with a new preface by Thomas D. Hill (New Haven, 1977), pp. 14–15.) Ceremonial crosses were ornamented with gold, silver, and jewels. See *The Dream of the Rood* below. Emendations: *healle* for MS *heall* (l. 1), *āc* for *acc* (l. 9).

2–3 **fēower . . . wudutrēow** 'wondrous forest-wood of four different kinds'.

5–6 **rōde tācn . . . rǣrde** 'the sign of the cross of the One (who) raised for us a ladder to the heavens'. Following *þæs* the relative *þe* is either understood or has been omitted by a scribe.

6–7 **ǣr hē . . . ābrǣce** i.e. the harrowing of Hell.

12 **wulfhēafedtrēo** 'outlaw-tree', i.e. 'gallows'. The Anglo-Saxons regularly referred to the cross as gallows.

12–14 **þæt oft . . . sweord** 'that often wards off from his lord (owner) a weapon . . .'. An obscure sentence referring perhaps to the cross's power of protecting the believer from hostile attack.

15 **se hine on mēde** 'he who takes it upon himself' or 'he who presumes'.

(*o*)

Ic eom lēgbysig, lāce mid winde,
bewunden mid wuldre, wedre gesomnad,
fūs forðweges fȳre gebysgad,
bearu blōwende, byrnende glēd.
Ful oft mec gesīþas sendað æfter hondum,
þæt mec weras ond wīf wlonce cyssað.
Þonne ic mec onhæbbe, hī onhnīgaþ tō mē
monige mid miltse; þǣr ic monnum sceal
ȳcan ūpcyme ēadignesse.

(*þ*)

Ic wæs fǣmne geong, feaxhār cwene,
ond ǣnlic rinc on āne tīd;
flēah mid fuglum ond on flōde swom,
dēaf under ȳþe dēad mid fiscum,
ond on foldan stōp; hæfde ferð cwicu.

Riddle o This too is conjectured to be a riddle about the cross, or more specifically about *ān bēam*, the Old English words which can mean 'a cross', 'a tree', and 'a log'. Emendation: *hī onhnīgaþ* for MS *ond hi on hin gaþ* (l. 7).

2 **bewunden mid wuldre** 'girded with splendour' (probably with reference to foliage).

3 **fūs forðweges** 'ready for the way hence'. Usually this phrasing means 'ready for death', and this is the log's fate when afflicted by fire.

5 **sendað æfter hondum** 'pass from hand to hand'.

8–9 **þǣr ic ... ēadignesse** 'there I shall increase the ascendancy of happiness among men'.

Riddle þ The solution is unknown. Scholars have suggested answers – 'cuttlefish', 'swan', 'water', 'siren', 'writing', 'ship's figurehead', etc. – but none satisfies all the conditions set forth in the poem. Emendation: *ferð* for MS *forð* (l. 5).

2 **on āne tīd** 'at the same time', 'all at once'.

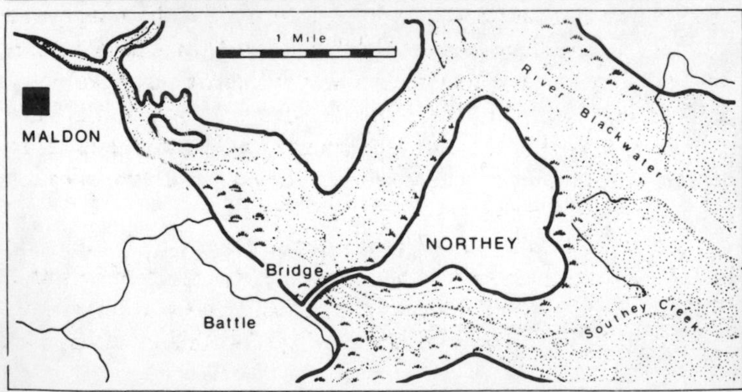

Plan of the Battle of Maldon in 991. From David Hill *An Atlas of Anglo-Saxon England* (Basil Blackwell, 1981), p. 64.

12

The Battle of Maldon

In August of the year 991 marauding Vikings sailed up the river Blackwater (then called 'Pante') and beached their ships on an island not far from the town of Maldon. The English ealdorman, Byrhtnoth, called out the local levy and, combining with this force the warriors from his own personal retinue, marched to the river-bank across from the island and confronted the Viking army. The ensuing battle (which is reported in the Anglo-Saxon Chronicle entry for 991 printed above on p. 197) is the subject of the poem which we are about to read.

The Battle of Maldon is the story of a military disaster suffered by the English in the course of their long and losing struggle against Scandinavian invaders. (Since 980 the Viking fleets had been raiding Southampton, Thanet, and elsewhere, and in the second decade of the eleventh century they seized the English throne.) The Anglo-Saxon king who presided over this prolonged humiliation of the English was Æthelræd (dubbed by later chroniclers 'the Unready'[1]), whose reign seems to have been characterized by demoralization in the military and, if a famous sermon by Archbishop Wulfstan is to be believed, in the populace as a whole. It is against this unhappy background that the battle of Maldon is fought by the Englishmen and celebrated by the poet. The poem is about how men bear up when things go wrong. The fighting men at Maldon, no less than those at Balaklava and Dunkirk, triumph in this test of character in a manner of which Englishmen have always been especially proud. The Anglo-Saxons who fight to the bitter end are portrayed by the poet as glorious in defeat, and their valour redeems the honour of their country. The poet of course idealizes the actual battle; his verses are poetry, not history.

To understand the action of the poem, and especially the action in ll. 62–99, one must have some idea of the geography of the battle. (See map on p. 224, which shows the site which most scholars agree to be the likeliest location of the battle.) The Vikings occupy the

[1] The name *Æðelræd* means 'noble counsel'. The sobriquet *unræd* means 'no counsel', i.e. 'folly'. 'Unready' is an inaccurate modernization of *unræd*.

island now called Northey, and Byrhtnoth's Anglo-Saxons array themselves across the water along the river-bank. At high tide the island is completely surrounded by water, but when the tide recedes (l. 72), an elevated road or causeway (called a *bricg* in ll. 74 and 78) is exposed, thus providing access to the island from the mainland. When the two armies first confront each other, the tide is in and the causeway is submerged (ll. 64–71). When the tide goes out, the Vikings begin to file across the causeway to the mainland, but the Anglo-Saxons block their progress from the narrow passageway to the shore (ll. 72–83). Seeing that they are at a serious disadvantage, the Vikings ask Byrhtnoth to order his troops to stand back and allow the invaders free passage to the shore (ll. 84–8). Byrhtnoth rashly agrees to give the enemy this advantage (ll. 89–95), and the battle begins.

Many of the English participants in the battle are named in the poem. (The poet seems to know nothing of the individual identities of the Vikings.) Extant documents from the period allow us to identify some of those mentioned, and it is to be assumed that all were actual Englishmen who were known to the poet's audience. Modern readers need to concern themselves with only the most important of these: the hero of the poem, Byrhtnoth (about whom a great deal is known), and his king, Æthelræd the Unready. We should also bear in mind the names of the cowardly sons of Odda: Godric, Godwig, and Godwine. Any other persons named in the poem can be assumed to be members of the Anglo-Saxon defending force – most likely members of Byrhtnoth's personal retinue, since the *fyrd*-men are generally left anonymous.

The Old English manuscript leaves containing *The Battle of Maldon* were destroyed by fire in 1731. Fortunately, a man named David Casley made a copy of the poem a few years before the fire and this copy is the basis for the present edition, except that modern conventions of punctuation, capitalization, word-division, verse-lineation, and long-vowel marking are introduced, and the following emendations are adopted: *tō hige* for MS *t hige* (l. 4), *þā* for *þ* (l. 5), *þām* for *þætam* (l. 10), *wīge* for *w . . . . ge* (l. 10), *randas* for *randan* (l. 20), *hilde* for *. . ulde* (l. 33), *wē* for *þe* (l. 61), *feohte* for *fohte* (l. 103), *grimme gegrundene* for *gegrundene* (l. 109), *wearð* for *weard* (l. 113), *wearð* for *wærd* (l. 116), *gestandan* for *ge stundan* (l. 171), *Geþancie* for *ge þance* (l. 173), *wearð* for *wurdon* (l. 186), *mearh* for *mear* (l. 188), *ærndon* for *ærdon* (l. 191), *Godwine* for *godrine* (l. 192), *þearfe* for *þære* (l. 201), *forlǣtan* for *for lætun* (l. 208), *ǣgðer* for *ægder* (l. 224), *wrǣce* for *wrece* (l. 257), *lǣge* for *lege* (l. 279), *crincgan* for *crintgan* (l. 292), *Forð þā* for *forða* (l. 297), *sunu* for *suna*

(l. 298), *geþrange* for *geþrang* (l. 299), *oðþæt* for *od þæt* (l. 324), *gūðe* for *gude* (l. 325).

brocen wurde.
Hēt þā hyssa hwæne hors forlǣtan,
feor āfȳsan, and forð gangan,
hicgan tō handum and tō hige gōdum.
þā þæt Offan mǣg ǣrest onfunde,
þæt se eorl nolde yrhðo geþolian,
hē lēt him þā of handon lēofne flēogan
hafoc wið þæs holtes, and tō þǣre hilde stōp;
be þām man mihte oncnāwan þæt se cniht nolde
wācian æt þām wīge, þā hē tō wǣpnum fēng.
Ēac him wolde Ēadrīc his ealdre gelǣstan,
frēan tō gefeohte, ongan þā forð beran
gār tō gūþe. Hē hæfde gōd geþanc
þā hwīle þe hē mid handum healdan mihte
bord and brād swurd; bēot hē gelǣste
þā hē ætforan his frēan feohtan sceolde.
Ðā þǣr Byrhtnōð ongan beornas trymian,
rād and rǣdde, rincum tǣhte
hū hī sceoldon standan and þone stede healdan,
and bæd þæt hyra randas rihte hēoldon
fæste mid folman, and ne forhtedon nā.
þā he hæfde þæt folc fægere getrymmed,
hē līhte þā mid lēodon þǣr him lēofost wæs,

1 The opening lines of the poem are lost. They must have told how the Anglo-Saxon leader Byrhtnoth heard of the Vikings' arrival, gathered his troops, and led them to the river shore where they could challenge the invaders.

2 The subject of *Hēt* is Byrhtnoth, referred to as *se eorl* in l. 6. Cf. §161.

4 **hicgan . . . gōdum** 'to give thought to their hands and to virtuous courage', i.e. to think about courage and about the handiwork through which they can display that courage.

5–6 For the anticipatory *þæt* see §148.

7 **handon** = *handum*. *-on* for *-um* appears again in l. 23 (*lēodon*), l. 129 (*Denon*), l. 270 (*hwīlon*), 306 (*wordon*), etc. This is a feature of late Old English.

14 **þā hwīle þe** 'while, as long as' (so also in ll. 83, 235, and 272).

17–24 In ll.17–21 Byrhtnoth gives elementary instructions to the members of the *fyrd* (ll. 140, 221), the home guard consisting of civilians who answer the call to arms when the local leader summons them in an emergency. In ll. 24–4 Byrhtnoth dismounts among his personal retinue of professional fighting men (*heorðwerod*), 'where it was most agreeable to him' (*þār him lēofost wæs*).

20 **hēoldon** = *hēolden* The subjunctive plural ending of verbs is invariably spelled *-on* in this poem rather than *-en*: e.g. *forgyldon* (l. 32), *dǣlon* (l. 33), *gangon* (l. 56), *syllon* (l. 61), *ēodon* (l. 229). This coalescence in spelling is characteristic of late Old English.

þǣr hē his heorðwerod   holdost wiste.
Þā stōd on stæðe,   stīðlīce clypode
wīcinga ār,   wordum mǣlde,
se on bēot ābēad   brimlīþendra
ǣrænde tō þām eorle,   þǣr hē on ōfre stōd:
'Mē sendon tō þē   sǣmen snelle,
hēton ðē secgan   þæt þū mōst sendan raðe
bēagas wið gebeorge; and ēow betere is
þæt gē þisne gārrǣs   mid gafole forgyldon,
þon wē swā hearde   hilde dǣlon.
Ne þurfe wē ūs spillan,   gif gē spēdaþ tō þām;
wē willað wið þam golde   grið fæstnian.
Gyf þū þat gerǣdest,   þe hēr rīcost eart,
þæt þū þīne lēoda   lȳsan wille,
syllan sǣmannum   on hyra sylfra dōm
feoh wið frēode,   and niman frið æt ūs,
wē willaþ mid þām sceattum   ūs tō scype gangan,
on flot fēran,   and ēow friþes healdan.'
Byrhtnōð maþelode,   bord hafenode,
wand wācne æsc,   wordum mǣlde,
yrre and ānrǣd   āgēaf him andsware:
'Gehȳrst þū, sǣlida,   hwæt þis folc segeð?
Hī willað ēow tō gafole   gāras syllan,
ǣttrynne ord   and ealde swurd,
þā heregeatu   þe ēow æt hilde ne dēah.
Brimmanna boda,   ābēod eft ongēan,
sege þīnum lēodum   miccle lāþre spell,
þæt hēr stynt unforcūð   eorl mid his werode,
þe wile gealgean   ēþel þysne,
Æþelrēdes eard,   ealdres mīnes,
folc and foldan.   Feallan sceolon
hǣþene æt hilde.   Tō hēanlic mē þinceð
þæt gē mid ūrum sceattum   tō scype gangon
unbefohtene,   nū gē þus feor hider
on ūrne eard   in becōmon.
Ne sceole gē swā sōfte   sinc gegangan;

30 **hēton ðē secgan** Cf. 5/1, 10(*a*)/72–3, etc., and ll. 62 and 101 below. Cf. §161.
31 **wið** 'in exchange for'. Cf. ll. 35, 39.
31–3 **betere . . . þon . . .** See §168 *þonne* 3(*c*). (*þon* = *þonne*.)
34 **gif gē . . . tō þām** 'If you are sufficiently rich for that (i.e. for the purpose of paying us off).'
38 **on hyra . . . dōm** 'according to their own stipulation'. Cf. 6/28.
50 **miccle lāþre spell** 'a much more unpleasant report (than they expect)'.

ūs sceal ord and ecg   ǣr gesēman,
grim gūðplega,   ǣr wē gofol syllon.'
  Hēt þā bord beran,   beornas gangan,
þæt hī on þām ēasteðe   ealle stōdon.
Ne mihte þǣr for wætere   werod tō þām ōðrum;
þǣr cōm flōwende   flōd æfter ebban,
lucon lagustrēamas.   Tō lang hit him þūhte,
hwænne hī tōgædere   gāras bēron.
Hī þǣr Pantan strēam   mid prasse bestōdon,
Ēastseaxena ord   and se æschere.
Ne mihte hyra ǣnig   ōþrum derian,
būton hwā þurh flānes flyht   fyl genāme.
Se flōd ūt gewāt;   þā flotan stōdon gearowe,
wīcinga fela,   wīges georne.
Hēt þā hæleða hlēo   healdan þā bricge
wigan wīgheardne,   se wæs hāten Wulfstān,
cāfne mid his cynne,   þæt wæs Cēolan sunu,
þe ðone forman man   mid his francan ofscēat
þe þǣr baldlīcost   on þā bricge stōp.
þǣr stōdon mid Wulfstāne   wigan unforhte,
Ælfere and Maccus,   mōdige twēgen,
þā noldon æt þām forda   flēam gewyrcan,
ac hī fæstlīce   wið ðā fȳnd weredon,
þā hwīle þe hī wǣpna   wealdan mōston.
þā hī þæt ongēaton   and georne gesāwon
þæt hī þǣr bricgweardas   bitere fundon,
ongunnon lytegian þā   lāðe gystas,
bǣdon þæt hī ūpgangan   āgan mōston,
ofer þone ford faran,   fēþan lǣdan.
  Ðā se eorl ongan   for his ofermōde
ālȳfan landes tō fela   lāþere ðēode.
Ongan ceallian þā   ofer cald wæter

60–1 **ǣr . . . ǣr . . .** 'first . . . before . . .'.

66 **lucon lagustrēamas** i.e. the rising tide submerges the causeway, completely encircling the island.

67 **hwænne** 'when, until'. See §159, note 2.

71 **hwā** 'someone'. Cf. 5/81.

81 **flēam gewyrcan** 'flee, yield'.

89–90 **ofermōde** 'pride' The national pride and manly defiance which Byrhtnoth has expressed so eloquently in his answer to the Viking messenger (ll. 45–61) has been carefully noted by the invaders, who play on Byrhtnoth's *ofermōd* to persuade him to grant them free access to 'too much land' (*landes tō fela*). The poet acknowledges that Byrhtnoth makes a tactical error here, but at a time when many Anglo-Saxons are seen as cowardly, he probably half admires this display of rash pride.

Byrhtelmes bearn (beornas gehlyston):
'Nū ēow is gerȳmed, gāð ricene tō ūs,
guman tō gūþe; God āna wāt
hwā þǣre wælstōwe wealdan mōte.'
Wōdon þā wælwulfas (for wætere ne murnon),
wīcinga werod, west ofer Pantan,
ofer scīr wæter scyldas wēgon,
lidmen tō lande linde bǣron.
þǣr ongēan gramum gearowe stōdon
Byrhtnōð mid beornum; hē mid bordum hēt
wyrcan þone wīhagan, and þæt werod healdan
fæste wið fēondum. þā wæs feohte nēh,
tīr æt getohte. Wæs sēo tīd cumen
þæt þǣr fǣge men feallan sceoldon.
þǣr wearð hrēam āhafen, hremmas wundon,
earn ǣses georn; wæs on eorþan cyrm.
Hī lēton þā of folman fēolhearde speru,
grimme gegrundene gāras flēogan;
bogan wǣron bysige, bord ord onfēng.
Biter wæs se beadurǣs, beornas fēollon
on gehwæðere hand, hyssas lāgon.
Wund wearð Wulfmǣr, wælræste gecēas,
Byrhtnōðes mǣg; hē mid billum wearð,
his swustersunu, swīðe forhēawen.
þǣr wearð wīcingum wiþerlēan āgyfen.
Gehȳrde ic þæt Ēadweard ānne slōge
swīðe mid his swurde, swenges ne wyrnde,
þæt him æt fōtum fēoll fǣge cempa;
þæs him his ðēoden þanc gesǣde,
þām būrþēne, þā hē byre hæfde.
Swā stemnetton stīðhicgende
hysas æt hilde, hogodon georne
hwā þǣr mid orde ǣrost mihte
on fǣgean men feorh gewinnan,
wigan mid wǣpnum; wæl fēol on eorðan.
Stōdon stædefæste; stihte hī Byrhtnōð,
bæd þæt hyssa gehwylc hogode tō wīge
þe on Denon wolde dōm gefeohtan.

92 **Byrhtelmes bearn** i.e. Byrhtnoth.

115 **swustersunu** The relationship between a man and his sister's son was peculiarly close in Germanic society (Tacitus comments on it in *Germania*), and so this opening scene of killing and vengeance reveals the Anglo-Saxons' adherence to ancient traditions of loyalty, both familial and military. Note that it is Byrhtnoth's personal chamberlain (*būrþegn*) who instantly avenges his leader's heavy loss.

Wōd þā wīges heard, wǣpen ūp āhōf,
bord tō gebeorge, and wið þæs beornes stōp.
Ēode swā ānrǣd eorl tō þām ceorle,
ǣgþer hyra ōðrum yfeles hogode.
Sende ðā se sǣrinc sūþerne gār,
þæt gewundod wearð wigena hlāford;
hē scēaf þā mid ðām scylde, þæt se sceaft tōbærst,
and þæt spere sprengde, þæt hit sprang ongēan.
Gegremod wearð se gūðrinc; hē mid gāre stang
wlancne wīcing, þe him þā wunde forgeaf.
Frōd wæs se fyrdrinc; hē lēt his francan wadan
þurh ðæs hysses hals, hand wīsode
þæt hē on þām fǣrsceaðan feorh gerǣhte.
Ðā hē ōþerne ofstlīce scēat,
þæt sēo byrne tōbærst; hē wæs on brēostum wund
þurh ðā hringlocan, him æt heortan stōd
ǣtterne ord. Se eorl wæs þē blīþra,
hlōh þā, mōdi man, sǣde Metode þanc
ðæs dægweorces þe him Drihten forgeaf.
Forlēt þā drenga sum daroð of handa,
flēogan of folman, þæt sē tō forð gewāt
þurh ðone æþelan Æþelrēdes þegen.
Him be healfe stōd hyse unweaxen,
cniht on gecampe, se full cāflīce
brǣd of þām beorne blōdigne gār,
Wulfstānes bearn, Wulfmǣr se geonga,
forlēt forheardne faran eft ongēan;
ord in gewōd, þæt sē on eorþan læg
þe his þēoden ǣr þearle gerǣhte.
Ēode þā gesyrwed secg tō þām eorle;

130 **wīges heard** evidently refers to some Viking, while *þæs beornes* (l. 131) refers to Byrhtnoth. The transition is so abrupt here that we might suspect the loss of a line or two introducing the Viking who is *wīges heard* 'bold in battle'.

134 **sūþerne gār** 'spear of southern make'. Vikings prized weapons produced in lands to the south of them, such as England and France.

135 **wigena hlāford** Byrhtnoth.

136–7 With a thrust of his shield Byrhtnoth knocks away the spear that the Viking had hurled into his body. Specifically, his shield breaks the spear-shaft in such a way that it 'forced out' (*sprengde*) the spear, which 'sprang back' (*sprang ongēan*) from the wound.

142 **feorh gerǣhte** 'reached the life'. That is, Byrhtnoth's hand guided the spear so that it reached (and thus extinguished) the life in the Viking. The phrase is strikingly Homeric. Cf. l. 226.

143 **Ðā hē . . . scēat** 'Then he (Byrhtnoth) swiftly pierced another (Viking).'

157 **sē** refers to the Viking who had wounded Byrhtnoth.

159 **gesyrwed secg** The 'armoured warrior' is yet another Viking.

hē wolde þæs beornes   bēagas gefecgan,
rēaf and hringas   and gerēnod swurd.
þā Byrhtnōð bræd   bill of scēðe,
brād and brūneccg,   and on þā byrnan slōh.
Tō raþe hine gelette   lidmanna sum,
þā hē þæs eorles   earm āmyrde.
Fēoll þā tō foldan   fealohilte swurd;
ne mihte hē gehealdan   heardne mēce,
wǣpnes wealdan.   þā gȳt þæt word gecwæð
hār hilderinc,   hyssas bylde,
bæd gangan forð   gōde gefēran;
ne mihte þā on fōtum leng   fæste gestandan.
Hē tō heofenum wlāt:
'Geþancie þē,   ðēoda Waldend,
ealra þǣra wynna   þe ic on worulde gebād.
Nū ic āh, milde Metod,   mǣste þearfe
þæt þū mīnum gāste   gōdes geunne,
þæt mīn sāwul tō ðē   sīðian mōte
on þīn geweald,   þēoden engla,
mid friþe ferian.   Ic eom frymdi tō þē
þæt hī helscēaðan   hȳnan ne mōton.'
Ðā hine hēowon   hǣðene scealcas
and bēgen þā beornas   þe him big stōdon,
Ælfnōð and Wulmǣr   bēgen lāgon,
ðā onemn hyra frēan   feorh gesealdon.
Hī bugon þā fram beaduwe   þe þǣr bēon noldon.
þǣr wearð Oddan bearn   ǣrest on flēame,
Godrīc fram gūþe,   and þone gōdan forlēt
þe him mænigne oft   mēarh gesealde;
hē gehlēop þone eoh   þe āhte his hlāford,
on þām gerǣdum   þe hit riht ne wæs,
and his brōðru mid him   bēgen ærndon,
Godwine and Godwīg,   gūþe ne gȳmdon,
ac wendon fram þām wīge   and þone wudu sōhton,
flugon on þæt fæsten   and hyra fēore burgon,

172 The second half of this line is missing. A few words may be lost, but since there are other metrical irregularities in the poem (e.g. in ll. 45, 75, 183, 271) it is also possible that this is a feature of the later, looser style of *The Battle of Maldon*.

173 **Geþancie þē** '(I) thank Thee.'

179 **Ic eom frymdi tō þē** 'I am suppliant to Thee', i.e. 'I beg Thee.'

180 **hī** acc. sg. fem. referring to *sāwul* (l. 177).

190 **þe hit riht ne wæs** Either 'as it was not right (to do)' (see §168 s.v. *þe* 6), or 'which was not right' (assuming *þe hit* to be a compound relative introducing an adjective clause). Or *þe* may be a scribal error for *þēah* or *þēh* 'although', but in that case one might expect the subjunctive.

and manna mā þonne hit ǣnig mǣð wǣre,
gyf hī þā geearnunga ealle gemundon
þe hē him tō duguþe gedōn hæfde.
Swā him Offa on dæg ǣr āsǣde
on þām meþelstede, þā hē gemōt hæfde,
þæt þǣr mōdelīce manega sprǣcon
þe eft æt þearfe þolian noldon.
  Þā wearð āfeallen þæs folces ealdor,
Æþelrēdes eorl; ealle gesāwon
heorðgenēatas þæt hyra heorra læg.
Þā ðǣr wendon forð wlance þegenas,
unearge men efston georne;
hī woldon þā ealle ōðer twēga,
līf forlǣtan oððe lēofne gewrecan.
Swā hī bylde forð bearn Ælfrīces,
wiga wintrum geong, wordum mǣlde,
Ælfwine þā cwæð, hē on ellen spræc:
'Gemunu þā mǣla þe wē oft æt meodo sprǣcon,
þonne wē on bence bēot āhōfon,
hæleð on healle, ymbe heard gewinn;
nū mæg cunnian hwā cēne sȳ.
Ic wylle mīne æþelo eallum gecȳþan,
þæt ic wæs on Myrcon miccles cynnes;
wæs mīn ealda fæder Ealhelm hāten,
wīs ealdorman, woruldgesǣlig.
Ne sceolon mē on þǣre þēode þegenas ætwītan
þæt ic of ðisse fyrde fēran wille,
eard gesēcan, nū mīn ealdor ligeð
forhēawen æt hilde. Mē is þæt hearma mǣst;
hē wæs ǣgðer mīn mǣg and mīn hlāford.'

198 **Swā him . . . āsǣde** 'Thus Offa had told him (earlier) in the day.' Evidently Byrhtnoth had called a meeting (*gemōt* l. 199) earlier that day to plan strategy with his *heorðwerod*, who had vowed to support him loyally in the field, as was their solemn obligation. See §237.

203–4 **ealle . . . heorðgenēatas** Byrhtnoth's personal retainers (*heorðgenēatas*), who would have been fighting close by him, could all see that their leader had fallen. Members of the *fyrd* fighting at a greater distance could not see this (ll. 239–42).

212 **Gemunu þā mǣla** '(I) remember the occasions.' Unexpressed subjects are entirely permissible in Old English when they can be readily inferred from the context (see §193.7), but their repeated use in direct discourse here (173, 212, 215) is probably a stylistic device aimed at suggesting the hurried speech of men talking to one another during the rush of battle.

215 **nū mæg . . . sȳ** 'now (one) can find out who is brave'. Cf. preceding note.

221 **fyrde** The aristocrat Ælfwine, kinsman of Byrhtnoth, identifies himself with the *fyrd*, the common militia. Distinctions between upper-class retainers and the levy are forgotten as aristocracy of rank is superseded by an aristocracy of courage.

þā hē forð ēode, fǣhðe gemunde,
þæt hē mid orde ānne gerǣhte
flotan on þām folce, þæt sē on foldan læg
forwegen mid his wǣpne. Ongan þā winas manian,
frȳnd and gefēran, þæt hī forð ēodon.
Offa gemǣlde, æscholt āscēoc:
'Hwæt þū, Ælfwine, hafast ealle gemanode
þegenas tō þearfe, nū ūre þēoden līð,
eorl on eorðan. Ūs is eallum þearf
þæt ūre ǣghwylc ōþerne bylde
wigan tō wīge, þā hwīle þe hē wǣpen mæge
habban and healdan, heardne mēce,
gār and gōd swurd. Ūs Godrīc hæfð,
earh Oddan bearn, ealle beswicene.
Wēnde þæs formoni man, þā hē on mēare rād,
on wlancan þām wicge, þæt wǣre hit ūre hlāford;
forþan wearð hēr on felda folc tōtwǣmed,
scyldburh tōbrocen. Ābrēoðe his angin,
þæt hē hēr swā manigne man āflȳmde!'
Lēofsunu gemǣlde and his linde āhōf,
bord tō gebeorge; hē þām beorne oncwæð:
'Ic þæt gehāte, þæt ic heonon nelle
flēon fōtes trym, ac wille furðor gān,
wrecan on gewinne mīnne winedrihten.
Ne þurfon mē embe Stūrmere stedefæste hælæð
wordum ætwītan, nū mīn wine gecranc,
þæt ic hlāfordlēas hām sīðie,
wende fram wīge, ac mē sceal wǣpen niman,
ord and īren.' Hē ful yrre wōd,
feaht fæstlīce, flēam hē forhogode.
Dunnere þā cwæð, daroð ācwehte,
unorne ceorl, ofer eall clypode,
bæd þæt beorna gehwylc Byrhtnōð wrǣce:
'Ne mæg nā wandian se þe wrecan þenceð
frēan on folce, ne for fēore murnan.'
þā hī forð ēodon, fēores hī ne rōhton;
ongunnon þā hīredmen heardlīce feohtan,
grame gārberend, and God bǣdon

239 **þæs** gen. obj. of *wēnan* anticipating the *þæt* clause in l. 240. See §148.
242 **Ābrēoðe his angin** 'Damn his behaviour!'
255–9 The brief, simple speech of Dunnere befits his status as a 'simple churl' (*unorne ceorl*), and yet its mere appearance here puts him in the company of the noblest men in the region, all now united in common loyalty to the code of honour which requires that fighting men avenge their slain leader or die in the attempt.

þæt hī mōston gewrecan hyra winedrihten
and on hyra fēondum fyl gewyrcan.
Him se gȳsel ongan geornlīce fylstan;
hē wæs on Norðhymbron heardes cynnes,
Ecglāfes bearn, him wæs Æscferð nama.
Hē ne wandode nā æt þām wīgplegan,
ac hē fȳsde forð flān genehe;
hwīlon hē on bord scēat, hwīlon beorn tǣsde,
ǣfre embe stunde hē sealde sume wunde,
þā hwīle ðe hē wǣpna wealdan mōste.
Þā gȳt on orde stōd Ēadweard se langa,
gearo and geornful, gylpwordum spræc
þæt hē nolde flēogan fōtmǣl landes,
ofer bæc būgan, þā his betera leg.
Hē bræc þone bordweall and wið þā beornas feaht,
oðþæt hē his sincgyfan on þām sǣmannum
wurðlīce wrec, ǣr hē on wæle lǣge.
Swā dyde Æþerīc, æþele gefēra,
fūs and forðgeorn, feaht eornoste.
Sībyrhtes brōðor and swīðe mænig ōþer
clufon cellod bord, cēne hī weredon;
bærst bordes lærig, and sēo byrne sang
gryrelēoða sum. Þā æt guðe slōh
Offa þone sǣlidan, þæt hē on eorðan fēoll,
and ðǣr Gaddes mǣg grund gesōhte.
Raðe wearð æt hilde Offa forhēawen;
hē hæfde ðēah geforþod þæt hē his frēan gehēt,
swā hē bēotode ǣr wið his bēahgifan
þæt hī sceoldon bēgen on burh rīdan,
hāle tō hāme, oððe on here crincgan,
on wælstōwe wundum sweltan;
hē læg ðegenlīce ðēodne gehende.

271 'Ever and anon he gave one (of the Vikings) a wound.' Since *st-* alliterates only with *st-* in the Germanic verse system, this line lacks alliteration altogether, but, like l. 282, it has rhyme to link the two half-lines. These lines anticipate the Middle English period, when rhyme displaces alliteration almost completely.

277 **Hē bræc þone bordweall** 'He penetrated the wall of shields.' Apparently Eadweard broke through the phalanx of the Vikings and fought individually with enemy warriors until he was overwhelmed and slain.

283 **cellod** occurs nowhere else, and its meaning is obscure. It is evidently an adjective describing the shield (*bord*).

285–6 **þā æt gūðe . . . sǣlidan** 'Then Offa struck that Viking in the fight so that he fell to the earth.' What Viking? It has been reasonably suggested that a line or two has been lost between ll. 283 and 284, telling us who it was whose shield's rim was broken (l. 284), and this person would be *þone sǣlidan* of l. 286.

Đā wearð borda gebræc. Brimmen wōdon,
gūðe gegremode; gār oft þurhwōd
fǣges feorhhūs. Forð þā ēode Wīstān,
þurstānes sunu, wið þās secgas feaht;
hē wæs on geþrange hyra þrēora bana,
ǣr him Wīgelines bearn on þām wæle lǣge.
þǣr wæs stīð gemōt; stōdon fæste
wigan on gewinne, wīgend cruncon,
wundum wērige. Wæl fēol on eorþan.
Ōswold and Ēadwold ealle hwīle,
bēgen þā gebrōþru, beornas trymedon,
hyra winemāgas wordon bǣdon
þæt hī þǣr æt ðearfe þolian sceoldon,
unwāclīce wǣpna nēotan.
Byrhtwold maþelode, bord hafenode
(se wæs eald genēat), æsc ācwehte;
hē ful baldlīce beornas lǣrde:
'Hige sceal þē heardra, heorte þē cēnre,
mōd sceal þē māre, þē ūre mægen lȳtlað.
Hēr līð ūre ealdor eall forhēawen,
gōd on grēote. Ā mæg gnornian
se ðe nū fram þīs wīgplegan wendan þenceð.
Ic eom frōd fēores; fram ic ne wille,
ac ic mē be healfe mīnum hlāforde,
be swā lēofan men, licgan þence.'
Swā hī Æþelgāres bearn ealle bylde,
Godrīc tō gūþe. Oft hē gār forlēt,
wælspere windan on þā wīcingas,
swā hē on þām folce fyrmest ēode,
hēow and hȳnde, oðþæt hē on hilde gecranc.
Næs þæt nā se Godrīc þe ðā gūðe forbēah

* * *

300 'before the son of Wigelin lay down in the carnage'. (The same use of reflexive pronoun with *licgan* appears in ll. 318–19 and need not be translated.) *Wīgelines bearn* seems clearly to refer to Wistan, but how can he be the son both of *þurstān* (l. 298) and *Wīgelin*? A metronymic would be very unusual – even in a poem like *Maldon*, which seems to be addressed to an audience which knew the poem's characters and their families. It has been conjectured that Wistan's father may have been known by two different names, but it is also possible that lines introducing a new character have been lost.

312–13 'Our resolve must be so much the firmer, our hearts so much the bolder, our courage so much the greater, by so much as our (physical) strength diminishes.' See §168 *þȳ* l.; cf. 11(*k*)/11–12 note.

325 The closing lines of the poem are lost. We know from other accounts of the battle that the Vikings were victorious.

13
The Ruin

'Where are those who lived before us?' In every age and culture people have raised this haunting question, especially when prompted to such thoughts by an ancient ruin or some other relic of the past. In both their poetry and their prose the Anglo-Saxons were very given to reflection on former civilizations and the people who built them, so much so that their language had a word for such meditation: *dūstscēawung* 'contemplation of the dust'. This theme occurs often as an incidental motif in longer works (e.g. *The Wanderer* ll. 73–110 and *Beowulf* ll. 2255–66), but *The Ruin* is an entire poem devoted to the depiction of an ancient ghost town and to the thoughts which the scene evokes.

The poet draws no explicit moral from his description of Roman ruins. He records rather the simple wonder with which the scene fills him: wonder at the ingenuity of the people who built the city, and wonder at the power of *wyrd* 'fate' which has laid it all waste. Although the poem is for the most part an admiring catalogue of artefacts and architecture, the objects described are all closely associated with the people who had made and used them. The poet marvels at how the builders conceived of such structures, he imagines how the inhabitants filled the city with life and joy, he muses over the fact that their gaze had fallen on the very objects he is studying, and he reflects on the powerful fate (*wyrd sēo swīþe*) that has swept them all into oblivion. Buildings and people alike have fallen (*crungon*, *gecrong*) and though the artefacts have survived their creators, their deteriorated state bears eloquent witness to the perishability of everything on earth. The transience of earthly things is emphasized by the repeated contrast between the ruins the poet sees and the city in its prime, which the poet re-creates with lively imagination. His details are so persuasive that some scholars have thought they could identify the city he describes as the Roman city of Bath, where thermal springs were skilfully channelled into stone baths much like those described in ll. 38–46. But other sites have also been suggested, and it could well be that the scene is a composite of various Roman ruins that the poet had seen.

The poem survives in the Exeter Book (see selection 11,

Riddles). Damage done to the later pages of the book have left *The Ruin* something of a ruin itself. Aside from a tentative reconstruction of l. 12, no effort is made to restore the damaged verses. Losses in the text are indicated by series of dots. Emendations include normalization of *þæs* to *þes* in ll. 9 and 30, deletion of *torras* (mechanically repeated from l. 3) in l. 4 following *hrīmgeat*, and the change of MS *geheapen* to *gehēawen* (l. 12), *secgrof* to *secgrōfra* (l. 26), *rof* to *hrōf* (l. 31), and *gefrætweð* to *gefrætwed* (l. 33).

Wrǣtlic is þes wealstān;   wyrde gebrǣcon
burgstede burston;   brosnað enta geweorc.
Hrōfas sind gehrorene,   hrēorge torras,
hrīmgeat berofen   hrīm on līme
scearde scūrbeorge   scorene, gedrorene,
ældo undereotone.   Eorðgrāp hafað
waldendwyrhtan,   forweorone, geleorene,
heard gripe hrūsan,   oþ hund cnēa
werþēoda gewitan.   Oft þes wāg gebād
ræghār ond rēadfāh   rīce æfter ōþrum,
ofstonden under stormum;   stēap gēap gedrēas.
Wunað gīet se wealstān   wederum gehēawen
fel on . . . .
grimme gegrunden   . . . .
. . . . scān   hēo . . . .
. . . . g orþonc   ǣrsceaft . . . .
. . . . g   lāmrindum bēag
mōd mo . . . .   yne swiftne gebrægd
hwætrēd in hringas,   hygerōf gebond
weallwalan wīrum   wundrum tōgædre.

1–2 **wyrde . . . burston** 'the fates broke, smashed the city'.

enta geweorc 'the work of giants'. The Anglo-Saxons used this expression to refer to the impressive stone buildings left by the Romans. Cf. *Wanderer* l. 87.

3–5 **Hrōfas sind . . . gedrorene** The verb *sind* should be carried over, in both singular and plural senses, in the ensuing verses: 'The roofs are fallen, the towers [are] in ruins, the frosty gate [is] despoiled. . . .'

6–7 **undereotone** and **forweorone** are past participles with *-on-* for *-en-*, a rare but attested spelling.

9 **gewitan** = *gewiton* '[shall] have passed away'. See §198.

9–11 **Oft þes wāg . . . stormum** 'Often this wall, red-stained and grey with lichen, unmoved beneath the storms, has survived kingdom after kingdom.'

11 **stēap . . . gedrēas** *stēap* and *gēap* modify *wāg* (cf. l. 9), the understood subject of *gedrēas*.

13–18 It is best to skip over the fragmentary words and phrases, of which little sense can be made. Resume in l. 18 with *swiftne gebrægd.*

18–20 **swiftne gebrægd . . . tōgædre** '. . . put together (*gebrægd*, past ptc.) a swift, quick plan in rings; one strong in intelligence (*hygerōf*) bound the wall-braces together marvellously with wires.'

Beorht wǣron burgræced, burnsele monige,
hēah horngestrēon, hereswēg micel,
meodoheall monig mondrēama full,
oþþæt þæt onwende wyrd sēo swīþe.
Crungon walo wīde, cwōman wōldagas,
swylt eall fornōm secgrōfra wera;
wurdon hyra wīgsteal wēstenstaþolas,
brosnade burgsteall. Bētend crungon
hergas tō hrūsan. Forþon þās hofu drēorgiað,
ond þes tēaforgēapa tigelum sceādeð
hrōstbēages hrōf. Hryre wong gecrong
gebrocen tō beorgum, þǣr iū beorn monig
glædmōd ond goldbeorht gleoma gefrætwed,
wlonc ond wīngāl wīghyrstum scān;
seah on sinc, on sylfor, on searogimmas,
on ēad, on ǣht, on eorcanstān,
on þās beorhtan burg brādan rīces.
Stānhofu stōdan, strēam hāte wearp
wīdan wylme; weal eall befēng
beorhtan bōsme, þǣr þā baþu wǣron,
hāt on hreþre. þæt wæs hȳðelic.
Lēton þonne gēotan ....
ofer hārne stān hāte strēamas
un ....
.þþæt hringmere hāte ....
.... þǣr þā baþu wǣron.
þonne is ....
.... re; þæt is cynelic þing,
hūse .... burg .....

27 **wurdon ... wēstenstaþolas** 'their sanctuaries (place of idols) became waste places'. *Wīgsteal* could also mean 'war places', but a possible Biblical source in Amos 6:9 ('and the sanctuaries of Israel shall be laid waste') has been suggested, and this would support the meaning 'places of idols, sanctuaries'.

28–9 **Bētend ... hrūsan** 'The tenders (i.e. repairmen), the armies fell to the earth.' *Hergas* could also mean 'idols, temples', and reference could be to the *wīgsteall* of l. 27: 'The tenders, the idols, fell to the earth.'

30–1 **ond þes tēaforgēapa ... hrōf** 'and this red-curved roof of the vault splits from the tiles'.

32 **gebrocen tō beorgum** 'broken into rubble-heaps'.

34 **wīghyrstum scān** 'shone in his war-trappings'. (The subject is *beorn monig* 'many a warrior'.)

38–9 **strēam hāte ... wylme** 'the flowing water threw out heat, a great billow'.

40 **beorhtan bōsme** 'within its bright bosom', i.e. in the interior of the encircling wall that holds the hot bath-water.

41 **hāt on hreþre** 'hot to the core', i.e. 'very hot'.

42–3 **Lēton þonne ... strēamas** 'They let the hot streams gush over the grey stone.' From here to the end the text is too fragmentary to translate, except for l. 48b.

14

The Dream of the Rood
or
A Vision of the Cross

This, the earliest dream-vision poem in the English language, is the central literary document for understanding that resolution of competing cultures which was the presiding concern of the Christian Anglo-Saxons. The Germanic heroic tradition which the Anglo-Saxons brought with them to England celebrated courage, mastery, and aggressive action. The Christian outlook which the Anglo-Saxons in due course adopted stressed virtues like loving kindness and self-sacrifice. (See §§218, 236–246.) Finding a proper adjustment of the two competing ideals was a constant spiritual struggle. The poet of *The Dream of the Rood* discovered in the central event of Christian history an opportunity for using his people's native poetic tradition to encompass and naturalize the alien ideals of the new faith. In so far as the crucifixion required great courage of the Saviour, it offered the poet ample opportunity for displaying how the heroic diction of Old English poetry could serve to extol Christ's passion, especially since early Christianity perceived Christ in more heroic terms than later Christianity was to do: he was a warrior-king doing battle with the Devil (as one can readily see by reading the sources and analogues of the poem in D. G. Calder and M. J. B. Allen's *Sources and Analogues of Old English Poetry* (Cambridge, 1976), pp. 53–8). But there is a gentle, passive side to the character of Christ that is absent from the pagan heroic ethos. Under provocation he turns the other cheek. He forgives his tormentors. He accepts physical defeat for the sake of spiritual victory. He allows his adversaries to kill him. The poet of *The Dream of the Rood* accommodates the intermingled passivity and heroism of Christ by his daring and imaginative device of giving human characteristics and the power of speech to the inanimate cross on which Christ died. Possibly this literal personification of the cross was suggested to him by the Old English verse riddles, where various inanimate objects are made to speak out and describe their essential qualities. (See especially riddles *n* and *o* above.) The example of the riddles would have been reinforced by

Classical rhetorical exercises in prosopopoeia, which were prescribed in the schools. Whatever the source of the device, the poet uses it to portray a cross which is the passive, plangent sufferer in the crucifixion while Christ is left to be active and heroic – a figure reminiscent of the awesome Byzantine mosaics of Christ the King and also of Germanic heroes like Beowulf.

On a literary level the poem resolves not only the pagan–Christian tensions within Anglo-Saxon culture but also current doctrinal discussions concerning the nature of Christ, who was both God and man, both human and divine. But throughout its imaginative poeticizing of theological issues, *The Dream of the Rood* remains a thoroughly Germanic poem with an exciting plot, vivid martial imagery which makes heroic all that happens, startling effects such as the gory, talking cross whose drops of blood surrealistically congeal into beautiful gems and then become blood again. The characterization of the cross is also quintessentially Germanic: it presents itself as a loyal retainer (all creatures on earth being members of God's retinue) who is forced by his very loyalty to become the instrument of his beloved Lord's execution.

That this poem gripped the imagination of its Anglo-Saxon audience is suggested by the fact that a large, ornamented Anglo-Saxon stone cross in the town of Ruthwell has been inscribed with excerpts from *The Dream of the Rood* written in the ancient runic alphabet of the Germanic peoples (§229). Each passage quoted is from portions of the poem spoken by the animate cross. One of the passages, quoted here in the Northumbrian dialect of the inscription (slightly restored), may be compared with ll. 44–5 of the poem:

Ahof ic riicnæ kyninc
heafunæs hlafard hælda ic ni dorstæ

A silver reliquary cross in Brussels is also inscribed with verses which echo lines spoken by the cross in *The Dream of the Rood*.[1] The poem and the idea of a speaking cross evidently met with cordial responsiveness in the imaginations of the Anglo-Saxons.

Like virtually all Old English poems, *The Dream of the Rood* has no title in its original manuscript (The Vercelli Book), its present title being an invention of modern scholars. It has also been called *A Vision of the Cross*, which is perhaps more suitable. Following are emendations which have been adopted in the text which follows: *hwæt* for MS *hæt* (l. 2), *eaxl* for *eaxle* (l. 9), *geweorðod* for *geweorðode* (l. 15), *bewrigen* for *bewrigene* (l. 17), *Wealdendes* for *wealdes* (l. 17),

[1] Rod is min nama; geo ic ricne cyning bær byfigynde, blode bestemed. Cf. ll. 44 and 48.

sorgum for *surgum* (l. 20), *ǣnigum* for *nænigum* (l. 47), *sorgum* supplied in l. 59, *grēotende* for *reotende* (l. 70), *stefn* for *syððan* (l. 71), *holtwudu* for *holmwudu* (l. 91), *lǣnan* for *lǣnum* (l. 109), *anforht* for *unforht* (l. 117), *þām* for *þan* (l. 122), *mē* for *he* (l. 142).

Hwæt, ic swefna cyst   secgan wylle,
hwæt mē gemǣtte   tō midre nihte,
syðþan reordberend   reste wunedon.
þūhte mē þæt ic gesāwe   syllicre trēow
on lyft lǣdan   lēohte bewunden,
bēama beorhtost.   Eall þæt bēacen wæs
begoten mid golde;   gimmas stōdon
fægere æt foldan scēatum,   swylce þǣr fīfe wǣron
uppe on þām eaxlgespanne.   Behēoldon þǣr engel Dryhtnes ealle
fægere þurh forðgesceaft;   ne wæs ðǣr hūru fracodes gealga,
ac hine þǣr behēoldon   hālige gāstas,
men ofer moldan   and eall þēos mǣre gesceaft.
Syllic wæs se sigebēam,   and ic synnum fāh,
forwundod mid wommum.   Geseah ic wuldres trēow

1–2 **swefna cyst** in l. 1 and the clause introduced by *hwæt* in l. 2 are parallel objects of the verb *secgan*: 'to tell the best of dreams, (to tell) what . . .'. See §159.

2 **mē gemǣtte** 'came to me in a vision', i.e. 'I dreamed' *gemǣtan* (like *þūhte* in l. 4) is an impersonal verb with dative of person. See §212.

4 **syllicre** is often said to be an absolute comparative ('exceedingly rare'), but some comparative meaning can also be implicit: 'a rarer tree (than all the others)'. Cf. ll. 90–4 below.

5 **on lyft lǣdan** 'lifted into the air'. The infinitive following *gesāwe* has a passive sense. See §161. So also *þenian* following *geseah* in l. 52.

8 **foldan scēatum** Either 'at the surface of the earth' (i.e. at the foot of the cross) or 'at the corners of the earth', the cross being seen as extending across the sky to four points on the horizon. With this verse begins the first of several groups of hypermetric lines which appear periodically throughout this poem (in ll. 8–10, 20–3, 30–4, 39–43, 46–9, 59–69, 75, and 133) and occasionally in other poems as well (e.g. *The Wanderer*, ll. 111–15, *The Seafarer*, ll. 106–9). Obviously some special effect was achieved by shifting from normal to hypermetric verses, but we cannot be sure what that effect was. The hypermetric verses seem to be systematic variations on the regular verse-types, most of them being expanded A-verses. The effect of hypermetric verses was exclusively aural and not visual, since the Anglo-Saxons wrote poetry continuously across the page from margin to margin just like prose and did not lineate their poems into separate verses.

9–10 **Behēoldon . . . forðgesceaft** 'All those fair by eternal decree gazed on the angel of the Lord (i.e. Christ or possibly the cross) there.' 'Those fair by eternal decree' are the *hālige gāstas* of l. 11 – the loyal angels who were predestined to remain in Heaven. Line 9b is long even for a hypermetric line and therefore has often been emended. But since it makes sense as it stands and none of the emendations is entirely satisfactory, we retain the manuscript reading.

11 **hine** refers to the nearest masculine antecedent, *gealga* 'the cross'.

wǣdum geweorðod wynnum scīnan,
gegyred mid golde; gimmas hæfdon
bewrigen weorðlīce Wealdendes trēow.
Hwæðre ic þurh þæt gold ongytan meahte
earmra ǣrgewin, þæt hit ǣrest ongan
swǣtan on þā swīðran healfe. Eall ic wæs mid sorgum gedrēfed;
forht ic wæs for þǣre fægran gesyhðe; geseah ic þæt fūse
bēacen
wendan wǣdum and blēom: hwīlum hit wæs mid wǣtan
bestēmed,
beswyled mid swātes gange, hwīlum mid since gegyrwed.
Hwæðre ic þǣr licgende lange hwīle
behēold hrēowcearig Hǣlendes trēow,
oð ðæt ic gehȳrde þæt hit hlēoðrode;
ongan þā word sprecan wudu sēlesta:
'þæt wæs gēara iū – ic þæt gȳta geman –
þæt ic wæs āhēawen holtes on ende,
āstyred of stefne mīnum. Genāman mē ðǣr strange fēondas,
geworhton him þǣr tō wǣfersȳne, hēton mē heora wergas
hebban;
bǣron mē þǣr beornas on eaxlum, oð ðæt hīe mē on beorg
āsetton;
gefæstnodon mē þǣr fēondas genōge. Geseah ic þā Frēan
mancynnes
efstan elne micle, þæt hē mē wolde on gestīgan.
þǣr ic þā ne dorste ofer Dryhtnes word
būgan oððe berstan, þā ic bifian geseah
eorðan scēatas. Ealle ic mihte
fēondas gefyllan, hwæðre ic fæste stōd.

15 **wǣdum geweorðod** 'adorned with garments'. 'Garments' is a poetic reference to the gold and jewelled adornments. In l. 22 it refers to these and the blood covering the cross as well.

19 **earmra ǣrgewin** 'ancient hostility of wretched ones', i.e. those who crucified Christ. *Ǣrgewin* and the following *þæt* clause are parallel objects of *ongytan*.

20 **on þā swīðran healfe** 'on the right side'. According to Christian tradition, it was Christ's right side that the centurion pierced with a spear.

31 **geworhton ... wǣfersȳne** 'they made (me) into a spectacle for themselves there'. This refers to the Romans' use of crosses for the public (and ignominious) execution of felons.

33 **gefæstnodon ... genōge** 'Enemies enough (i.e. many enemies) secured me there.'

34 **þæt hē ... gestīgan** '(in) that he wanted to ascend onto me', i.e. 'in his wish to ascend onto me'. See §211.

36–7 **þā ic bifian ... scēatas** 'when I saw the surface of the earth tremble'. Matthew 27:51 says that the earth trembled at the crucifixion.

37–8 **Ealle ... gefyllan, hwæðre ...** 'I was able to fell (i.e. could have felled) all the adversaries, but... '.

Ongyrede hine þā geong hæleð – þæt wæs God ælmihtig! –
strang and stīðmōd; gestāh hē on gealgan hēanne,
mōdig on manigra gesyhðe, þā hē wolde mancyn lȳsan.
Bifode ic þā mē se beorn ymbclypte; ne dorste ic hwæðre būgan tō eorðan,
feallan tō foldan scēatum, ac ic sceolde fæste standan.
Rōd wæs ic ārǣred; āhōf ic rīcne Cyning,
heofona Hlāford; hyldan mē ne dorste.
þurhdrifan hī mē mid deorcan næglum; on mē syndon þā dolg gesīene,
opene inwidhlemmas; ne dorste ic hira ǣnigum sceððan.
Bysmeredon hīe unc būtū ætgædere; eall ic wæs mid blōde bestēmed,
begoten of þæs guman sīdan siððan hē hæfde his gāst onsended.
'Feala ic on þām beorge gebiden hæbbe
wrāðra wyrda: geseah ic weruda God
þearle þenian. þȳstro hæfdon
bewrigen mid wolcnum Wealdendes hrǣw,
scīrne scīman; sceadu forð ēode,
wann under wolcnum. Wēop eal gesceaft,
cwīðdon Cyninges fyll: Crīst wæs on rōde.
Hwæðere þǣr fūse feorran cwōman
tō þām Æðelinge; ic þæt eall behēold.
Sāre ic wæs mid sorgum gedrēfed, hnāg ic hwæðre þām secgum tō handa
ēaðmōd, elne mycle. Genāmon hīe þǣr ælmihtigne God,
āhōfon hine of ðām hefian wīte; forlēton mē þā hilderincas
standan stēame bedrifenne; eall ic wæs mid strǣlum forwundod.
Ālēdon hīe ðǣr limwērigne; gestōdon him æt his līces hēafdum;
behēoldon hīe ðǣr heofenes Dryhten, and hē hine ðǣr hwīle reste,
mēðe æfter ðām miclan gewinne. Ongunnon him þā moldern wyrcan
beornas on banan gesyhðe, curfon hīe ðæt of beorhtan stāne;

49 **begoten** 'drenched' modifies *ic* in l. 48.

51–2 See note to l. 5 above.

54 **scīrne scīman** 'the bright radiance' is in apposition with *wealdendes hrǣw*.

57 **fūse** 'eager ones'. In view of John 19: 38–9, the eager ones would appear to be Joseph of Arimathea and Nicodemus, who came to claim the body of Jesus.

59 **þām secgum tō handa** 'to the hands of the men'. Poss. dat. See §191.2.

62 **strǣlum** 'with arrows'. The cross is referring to the hostile nails of l. 46.

63 **gestōdon . . . hēafdum** 'they positioned themselves at his body's head'. Dat. pl. *hēafdum* with singular meaning is an Old English idiom. Cf. *brēostum* in l. 118.

66 **banan** 'of the slayer'. The cross refers to itself as Christ's slayer.

gesetton hīe ðǣron sigora Wealdend. Ongunnon him þā
sorhlēoð galan
earme on þā ǣfentīde, þā hīe woldon eft sīðian,
mēðe fram þām mǣran þēodne; reste hē ðǣr mǣte weorode.
Hwæðere wē ðǣr grēotende gōde hwīle
stōdon on staðole; stefn up gewāt
hilderinca; hrǣw cōlode,
fæger feorgbold. Þā ūs man fyllan ongan
ealle tō eorðan; þæt wæs egeslic wyrd!
Bedealf ūs man on dēopan sēaþe; hwæðre mē þǣr Dryhtnes
þegnas,
frēondas gefrūnon,
gyredon mē golde and seolfre.
'Nū ðū miht gehȳran, hæleð mīn se lēofa,
þæt ic bealuwara weorc gebiden hæbbe,
sārra sorga. Is nū sǣl cumen
þæt mē weorðiað wīde and sīde
menn ofer moldan and eall þēos mǣre gesceaft,
gebiddaþ him tō þyssum bēacne. On mē Bearn Godes
þrōwode hwīle; for þan ic þrymfæst nū
hlīfige under heofenum, and ic hǣlan mæg
ǣghwylcne ānra þāra þe him bið egesa tō mē.
Iū ic wæs geworden wita heardost,
lēodum lāðost, ǣr þan ic him līfes weg
rihtne gerȳmde, reordberendum.
Hwæt, mē þā geweorþode wuldres Ealdor
ofer holtwudu, heofonrīces Weard,
swylce swā hē his mōdor ēac, Marīan sylfe,
ælmihtig God for ealle menn
geweorðode ofer eall wīfa cynn.
'Nū ic þē hāte, hæleð mīn se lēofa,
þæt ðū þās gesyhðe secge mannum;
onwrēoh wordum þæt hit is wuldres bēam,
se ðe ælmihtig God on þrōwode

69 **mǣte werode** 'with little company'. Germanic understatement meaning 'alone'. So also in l. 124.

70 **wē** i.e. the three crosses.

76 The second half of this line is lost, but the sense is clear: the cross was buried, and then many years later St. Helena recovered it and adorned it as a precious relic.

79–80 **þæt ic bealuwara . . . sārra sorga** 'that I have suffered distress from dwellers in iniquity, from sore sorrows'. *Bealuwara* and *sorga* are parallel genitives dependent on *weorc*.

86 **þāra þe . . . tō mē** 'of those in whom is fear of me'. See §162.1 and 2.

92 **swylce swā** 'just as'.

98 **se ðe . . . þrōwode** 'on which almighty God suffered'. See §163.1.

for mancynnes manegum synnum
and Adomes ealdgewyrhtum.
Dēað hē þǣr byrigde; hwæðere eft Dryhten ārās
mid his miclan mihte mannum tō helpe.
Hē ðā on heofenas āstāg. Hider eft fundaþ
on þysne middangeard mancynn sēcan
on dōmdæge Dryhten sylfa,
ælmihtig God and his englas mid,
þæt hē þonne wile dēman, se āh dōmes geweald,
ānra gehwylcum, swā hē him ǣrur hēr
on þyssum lǣnan līfe geearnaþ.
Ne mæg þǣr ǣnig unforht wesan
for þām worde þe se Wealdend cwyð:
frīneð hē for þǣre mænige hwǣr se man sīe,
se ðe for Dryhtnes naman dēaðes wolde
biteres onbyrigan, swā hē ǣr on ðām bēame dyde.
Ac hīe þonne forhtiað, and fēa þencaþ
hwæt hīe tō Crīste cweðan onginnen.
Ne þearf ðǣr þonne ǣnig anforht wesan
þe him ǣr in brēostum bereð bēacna sēlest;
ac ðurh ðā rōde sceal rīce gesēcan
of eorðwege ǣghwylc sāwl,
sēo þe mid Wealdende wunian þenceð.'
Gebæd ic mē þā tō þām bēame blīðe mōde,
elne mycle, þǣr ic āna wæs
mǣte werede. Wæs mōdsefa
āfȳsed on forðwege, feala ealra gebād
langunghwīla. Is mē nū līfes hyht
þæt ic þone sigebēam sēcan mōte
āna oftor þonne ealle men,
well weorþian. Mē is willa tō ðām
mycel on mōde, and mīn mundbyrd is
geriht tō þǣre rōde. Nāh ic rīcra feala
frēonda on foldan, ac hīe forð heonon
gewiton of worulde drēamum, sōhton him wuldres Cyning;

107–9 **þæt hē þonne . . . geearnaþ** 'in that He who has power of judgement wishes to pass judgement then on each of those even as he shall have earned for himself (while) here in this transitory life'. *Ǣrur* with the present (with future meaning) *geearnaþ* yields a future perfect in meaning. Similarly *ǣr . . . bereð* in l. 118.

124–6 **Wæs mōdsefa . . . langunghwīla** '(My) mind was inspired with longing (*āfȳsed*) for the way hence (to the next world), it has experienced in all (*ealra*) many periods of longing (for the next life).'

129–30 **Mē is willa . . . on mōde** 'The desire for that is intense in my heart.'

133 **him** This reflexive dative (with *sōhton*) need not be translated.

lifiaþ nū on heofenum mid Hēahfædere,
wuniaþ on wuldre; and ic wēne mē
daga gehwylce hwænne mē Dryhtnes rōd,
þe ic hēr on eorðan ǣr scēawode,
on þysson lǣnan līfe gefetige,
and mē þonne gebringe þǣr is blis mycel,
drēam on heofonum, þǣr is Dryhtnes folc
geseted tō symle, þǣr is singāl blis;
and mē þonne āsette þǣr ic syþþan mōt
wunian on wuldre, well mid þām hālgum
drēames brūcan. Sī mē Dryhten frēond,
se ðe hēr on eorðan ǣr þrōwode
on þām gealgtrēowe for guman synnum;
hē ūs onlȳsde, and ūs līf forgeaf,
heofonlicne hām. Hiht wæs genīwad
mid blēdum and mid blisse, þām þe þǣr bryne þolodan.
Se Sunu wæs sigorfæst on þām sīðfate,
mihtig and spēdig, þā hē mid manigeo cōm,
gāsta weorode, on Godes rīce,
Anwealda ælmihtig, englum tō blisse
and eallum ðām hālgum þām þe in heofonum ǣr
wunedon on wuldre, þā heora Wealdend cwōm,
ælmihtig God, þǣr his ēðel wæs.

135–8 **ic wēne mē . . . gefetige** 'I look forward each day to (the time) when the cross of the Lord . . . will fetch me.' The *mē* in l. 135 is reflexive and need not be translated. On *hwænne* introducing a clause, see §159 note 2.

144 **Sī mē Dryhten frēond** 'May the Lord be a friend to me.' Cf. ll. 131–2.

146 **for guman synnum** 'for men's sins'. *Guman* is a late gen. pl. (for *gumena*).

148–9 **Hiht wæs genīwad . . . þolodan** This sentence refers to Christ's harrowing of hell when, following the crucifixion, he descended to the nether regions and rescued from the burning fires all good people who had died since the creation.

150–6 These verses refer to Christ's ascension into heaven with all the souls he had rescued in the harrowing. The ascension actually takes place forty days later.

153 **englum tō blisse** 'to the delight of the angels'.

15

The Wife's Lament

The Wife's Lament is a woman's account of how she became estranged from her young husband through the machinations of his relatives. Forced to live alone in a settlement far away from him, she suffers pitifully, yearning for him day and night. The details of the plot are somewhat sketchy, the poet's main attention being on the speaker's sadness and love-longing. It has been conjectured that the woman speaking in the poem was a character known to the audience from other narratives and that by knowing her story beforehand they would have been better able to understand what is going on in *The Wife's Lament*. It is true that we are told nothing about why her husband originally had to leave her and make a sea journey, about why and how his relatives persuaded him to reject her, or about the identities of any of the principal characters. But the general sequence of actions is fairly clear in the poem as it is presented here. Her husband leaves, and the wife, smitten with longing for him, joins him (ll. 6–10). His kinsmen, who want to separate the couple from each other, get the husband to send her back to his homeland where he orders her to live in a cave or hovel in the midst of a forbidding grove of trees (ll. 11–32). (Sad recollections of their former devotion to one another contrasted with the husband's hostile state of mind at present intervene at ll. 18–22.) Lines 32–41 are a poignant account of the abandoned wife's longing and sorrow. The final section (ll. 42–53) seems to be the wife's speculations as to the husband's present circumstances and her assurances to herself that he must feel as sad as she when he recalls their former life together. She closes with a gnomic observation about the suffering of parted lovers.

Since thousands of lines of Old English poetry deal primarily with women (e.g. *Elene*, *Judith*, *Juliana*), it is not surprising to find in *The Wife's Lament* a concern with exploring the psychology of a suffering woman. Yet some scholars have doubted that this is a woman's monologue and try to interpret it as the lament of a man, much like *The Wanderer*. Such interpretations have to begin by altering or explaining away the grammatical endings in *gēomorre* (l. 1) and *mīnre sylfre* (l. 2), which make it clear that the speaker is feminine. Other interpretations have sought to introduce a love-triangle by suggesting that some of the speaker's references to her lord and lover are to one man (her husband) and others are to another (her lover). Yet other scholars have suggested that the monologue is spoken by the Heavenly Bride (i.e. the Church), who is commanded by Christ to remain in this world of sorrow until the Second Coming. Another suggests it is a voice from the grave. The narrative is sufficiently cryptic and the language of Old English poetry sufficiently flexible that a case can be made for a variety of different situations in the poem. As in much literary interpretation, the only available curb to ever more ingenious speculations about *The Wife's Lament* is common sense.

The text here is that of the Exeter Book, except that modern conventions of punctuation, capitalization, word-division, verse-lineation, and long-vowel marking are introduced, and the following emendations are adopted: *āwēox* for MS *weox* in l. 3, *hycgendne* for *hycgende* in l. 20, *nǣfre* for *no* in l. 24, *sceal* for *seal* in l. 25, and *sittan* for *sittam* in l. 37.

Ic þis giedd wrece   bī mē ful geōmorre,
mīnre sylfre sīð.   Ic þæt secgan mæg,
hwæt ic yrmþa gebād,   siþþan ic ūp āwēox,
nīwes oþþe ealdes,   nō mā þonne nū.
Ā ic wīte wonn   mīnra wræcsīþa.
Ǣrest mīn hlāford gewāt   heonan of lēodum
ofer ȳþa gelāc;   hæfde ic ūhtceare
hwǣr mīn lēodfruma   londes wǣre.
Ðā ic mē fēran gewāt   folgað sēcan,
wineleās wræcca,   for mīnre wēaþearfe,
ongunnon þæt þæs monnes   māgas hycgan
þurh dyrne geþōht,   þæt hȳ tōdǣlden unc,
þæt wit gewīdost   in woruldrīce
lifdon lāðlicost,   ond mec longade.

2 **sīð** is acc. sing., parallel with *giedd*. 'I narrate this poem, . . . (narrate) my own experience' lit. '[the] experience of mine of self' – a strange pattern rare in OE.

8 **hwǣr . . . wǣre** '(as to) where in the land my leader of men might be'. *Londes* (like *nīwes oþþe ealdes* in l. 4) is adverbial genitive (§190.5).

9–10 **Ðā . . . wēaþearfe** 'When, because of my woeful need, I set out, a friendless stranger, to visit the retinue'. Her husband, who has just been described as 'a leader of men' (*lēodfruma*, l. 8) is travelling with his retainers, and it is this group that she must seek out when she goes to visit him.

11–14 'The man's kinsmen began plotting that they would separate us, so that we two have lived most miserably, most far apart, and longing has afflicted me.'

Hēt mec hlāford mīn herheard niman,
āhte ic lēofra lӯt on þissum londstede,
holdra frēonda, for þon is mīn hyge geōmor.
Ðā ic mē ful gemæcne monnan funde,
heardsǣligne, hygegeōmorne,
mōd mīþendne, morþor hycgendne
blīþe gebǣro. Ful oft wit bēotedan
þæt unc ne gedǣlde nemne dēað āna
ōwiht elles; eft is þæt onhworfen,
is nū swā hit nǣfre wǣre,
frēondscipe uncer. Sceal ic feor ge nēah
mīnes felalēofan fǣhðu drēogan.
  Heht mec mon wunian on wuda bearwe,
under āctrēo in þām eorðscræfe.
Eald is þes eorðsele, eal ic eom oflongad,
sindon dena dimme, dūna ūphēa,
bitre burgtūnas, brērum beweaxne,
wīc wynna lēas. Ful oft mec hēr wrāþe begeat
fromsīþ frēan. Frӯnd sind on eorþan,
lēofe lifgende, leger weardiað,
þonne ic on ūhtan āna gonge
under āctrēo geond þās eorðscrafu.
þǣr ic sittan mōt sumorlangne dæg;
þǣr ic wēpan mæg mīne wræcsīþas,
earfoþa fela; forþon ic ǣfre ne mæg
þǣre mōdceare mīnre gerestan,
ne ealles þæs longaþes þe mec on þissum līfe begeat.
  Ā scyle geong mon wesan geōmormōd,

15 OE *eard niman* means 'to take up an abode', so *herheard niman* means 'to take up (my) abode in a *herh*'. *Herh* (or *hearh*) refers either to a grove or a part of a pagan sanctuary or temple grounds. In view of l. 27b, it probably means 'grove' here.

18 'Then I found the man (who had been) very suitable to me. . . .'

22–3 **ne . . . ōwiht** 'naught, nothing': 'that naught but death alone should separate us'.

24 'it is now as if it had never been'.

27 **Heht mec mon** 'I was commanded (by my husband).'

32 **mec hēr wrāþe begeat** 'took hold of me cruelly here', i.e. 'caused me pain'.

34 **leger weardiað** 'occupy their bed', i.e. 'are in bed together'.

39–41 **Forþon . . . longaþes** 'Therefore I can never rest from that sorrow of mine nor from all that longing.'

42–52 Here the speaker seems to speculate over what might be the present state of her estranged spouse and to assure herself that whatever his circumstances he will certainly be sharing her sorrow over their separation.

42–3 **Ā scyle . . . geþōht** 'It may be that the young man must always be sorrowful (and) his heart's thought stern.' The subjunctive *scyle* suggests that she is only speculating about his state of mind, but the shift to indicative *sceal* indicates certainty ('at the same time he *must* have a cheerful demeanour along with his

heard heortan geþōht,   swylce habban sceal
blīþe gebǣro,   ēac þon brēostceare,
sinsorgna gedreag.   Sȳ æt him sylfum gelong
eal his worulde wyn,   sȳ ful wīde fāh
feorres folclondes,   þæt mīn frēond siteð
under stānhliþe   storme behrīmed,
wine wērigmōd,   wætre beflōwen
on drēorsele,   drēogeð se mīn wine
micle mōdceare;   hē gemon tō oft
wynlicran wīc.   Wā bið þām þe sceal
of langoþe   lēofes ābīdan.

---

breast- cares'), since she has observed at first hand in ll. 20–1 that this is a characteristic of the young man.

45–7 Sȳ . . . sȳ . . . .The two subjunctives are used correlatively to introduce alternative speculations: 'Whether he is dependent (solely) upon himself for all his joy in the world, or whether he is outlawed far from his remote inheritance so that my dear one sits . . . .'

50–1 drēogeð . . . mōdceare 'that lover of mine will experience great sorrow at heart'. This is the main clause upon which the preceding subordinate clauses depend.

16

The Wanderer

The Wanderer is one of several great meditative poems from the Exeter Book. It is a dramatic monologue briefly introduced by the Christian poet and briefly concluded by him with a terse exhortation to seek comfort in God the Father. The monologue itself is spoken by a heroic-age nobleman whose assessment of life's meaning shows no awareness of Christian enlightenment. The only outside forces of which he has knowledge are fate, the forces of nature, and a 'creator of men' (*ælda scyppend*, l. 85) whose only action in the poem is to lay waste all that men have made. The wanderer who speaks the monologue is in the worst possible circumstances for an Anglo-Saxon warrior in the heroic age: he is a retainer who has lost his lord and comrades and who therefore finds himself with no place in society, no identity in a hostile world. He is man *in extremis*, alone with his memories and naked to his enemies. This plight moves him to strenuous and painful reflection.

He begins by acknowledging the noble precept that a suffering man must bear up silently and, indeed, all that he says is spoken *on mōde* 'in his mind', i.e. 'silently to himself' (l. 111). He is *āna* (l. 8), and what we hear are his inmost thoughts. The depth of his feeling for his dead lord and lost comrades is dramatized by the unceasing sorrow that seems to attend his vain wanderings, and by his reveries of the past, which at times lead to hallucinatory illusions that his dead friends have returned and which leave him even deeper in sadness after his return to reality. At l. 58 he begins to move from his personal sorrow into a sense of the sorrowful state of the entire world, where all is transient and meaningless. Like the sparrow in Bede's story of the conversion of Edwin (8, ll. 24–38), men leave the hall at the end of life (l. 61) and pass into darkness and oblivion. With poetic imagination he evokes and laments a ruined city (ll. 75–110) and concludes with the hopeless observation that 'all the foundation of this earth will become empty'. He has summoned the full range of heroic-age wisdom to his meditation on existence, and the conclusion to which this wisdom brings him is that all is empty and without meaning. When his thoughts have run their course, the Christian poet returns and offers his terse comment: our only security lies with the Father in Heaven; we must seek consolation from Him.

Some modern readers have found a troubling imbalance in the monologue and authorial comment. The wanderer's hopeless situation and despairing scrutiny of the meaning of existence seem too briefly answered by the Christian poet's assertion that all our hope is in God the Father. But this assertion is in fact all that is needed since the wanderer's philosophizing – strong in feeling, high in dignity, and wisely reflective – demonstrates its own impotence before the transience and sorrow of the world. The poet can safely assume that if such an eloquent inquirer as the wanderer can find no more satisfying answer than 'eal þis eorþan gesteal īdel weorþeð' (l. 110), then the Christian invitation to consolation requires no elaboration. This after all is the logic of the nameless nobleman who counselled King Edwin to accept Christianity: if our pagan faith offers nothing more than the meaninglessness of a sparrow's flight through a hall, then let us turn to the God whom Paulinus is proclaiming.

Later Christian poets have followed a similar course in presenting the superiority of Christianity to a noble but unavailing pagan alternative. Throughout the five books of *Troilus* Chaucer involves his readers in the beauties and disasters of love in the pagan Classical world, only to end with the brief but moving palinode exhorting his readers, 'Repeyreth hom fro worldly vanyte!' An even closer parallel is Samuel Johnson's *The Vanity of Human Wishes*, in which the poet gives eloquent expression throughout most of the poem to the Juvenalian commentator who surveys the world with stoic insight and learns from his survey nothing more than that helpless man must 'roll darkling down the torrent of his fate'. At this point the poet as Christian moralist interrupts with the command 'Enquirer cease!' and closes the poem with the solemn observation that only Christian faith offers hope and meaning to man. In all these poems it is the powerful and unavailing pagan perspective that moves the reader and makes the Christian's point, so that no Christian insistence is needed. And yet each poet leaves us permanently fascinated by the outlook he deftly rejects: Chaucer's Homeric milieu, Johnson's Roman stoicism, and the pre-Christian creed of the Anglo-Saxon wanderer.

The following emendations have been adopted: *healde* for MS *healdne* (l. 14), *mīnne* for *mine* (l. 22), *waþema* for *waþena* (l. 24), *frēondlēasne* for *freond lease* (l. 28), *wenian* for *weman* (l. 29), *mōdsefa* for *mod sefan* (l. 59), *weorþan* for *wearþan* (l. 64), *ealre* for *ealle* (l. 74), *deorce* for *deornce* (l. 89), *hrūsan* for *hruse* (l. 102).

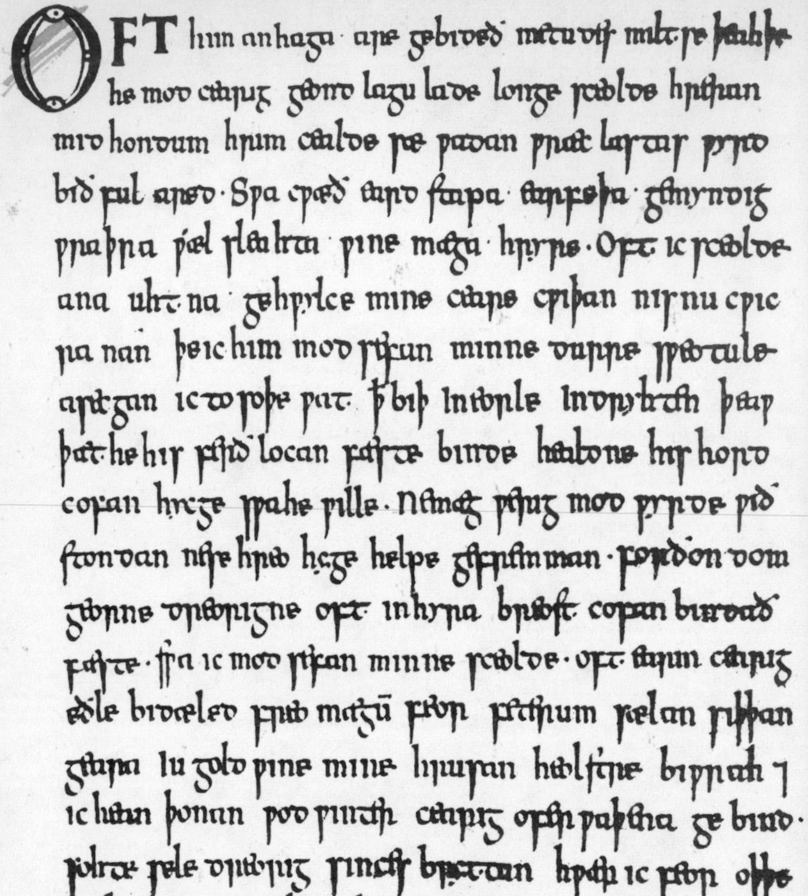

OFT him anhaga are gebideð metudes miltse þeah þe
he modcearig geond lagu lade longe sceolde hreran
mid hondum hrimcealde sæ wadan wræclastas wyrd
bið ful aræd. Swa cwæð eardstapa earfeþa gemyndig
wraþra wælsleahta winemæga hryre. Oft ic sceolde
ana uhtna gehwylce mine ceare cwiþan nis nu cwic
ra nan þe ic him modsefan minne durre sweotule
asecgan ic to soþe wat þ biþ in eorle indryhten þeaw
þæt he his ferðlocan fæste binde healde his hord
cofan hycge swa he wille. Ne mæg werig mod wyrde wið
stondan ne se hreo hyge helpe gefremman. Forðon dom
georne dreorigne oft in hyra breostcofan bindað
fæste. swa ic modsefan minne sceolde. oft earmcearig
eðle bidæled freomægū feor feterum sælan siþþan
geara iu goldwine minne hrusan heolstre biwrah ⁊
ic hean þonan wod wintercearig ofer waþema gebind.
sohte sele dreorig sinces bryttan hwær ic feor oþþe
neah findan meahte þone þe in meoduhealle mine
wisse oþþe mec freondleasne frefran wolde weman mid
wynnum. wat se þe cunnað hu sliþen bið sorg to gefe
ran þam þe him lyt hafað leofra geholena. warað hi
ne wræclast nales wunden gold ferðloca freorig

Facsimile of the opening page of *the Wanderer*, from the Exeter Book, folio 76b, lines 1–33a. Reproduced by kind permission of the Dean and Chapter of Exeter Cathedral.

Oft him ānhaga āre gebīdeð,
metudes miltse, þēah þe hē mōdcearig
geond lagulāde longe sceolde
hrēran mid hondum hrīmcealde sǣ,
wadan wræclāstas. Wyrd bið ful ārǣd!
Swā cwæð eardstapa, earfeþa gemyndig,
wrāþra wælsleahta, winemǣga hryre:
'Oft ic sceolde āna ūhtna gehwylce
mīne ceare cwīþan. Nis nū cwicra nān
þe ic him mōdsefan mīnne durre
sweotule āsecgan. Ic tō sōþe wāt
þæt biþ in eorle indryhten þēaw,
þæt hē his ferðlocan fæste binde,
healde his hordcofan, hycge swā hē wille.
Ne mæg wērig mōd wyrde wiðstondan,
ne se hrēo hyge helpe gefremman.
Forðon dōmgeorne drēorigne oft
in hyra brēostcofan bindað fæste;
swā ic mōdsefan mīnne sceolde,
oft earmcearig, ēðle bidǣled,
frēomǣgum feor feterum sǣlan,
siþþan gēara iū goldwine mīnne
hrūsan heolstre biwrāh, ond ic hēan þonan
wōd wintercearig ofer waþema gebind,
sōhte seledrēorig sinces bryttan,
hwǣr ic feor oþþe nēah findan meahte
þone þe in meoduhealle mīne wisse,
oþþe mec frēondlēasne frēfran wolde,

1–5 **Oft him ānhaga . . . ful ārǣd!** Because *gebīdeð* can mean both 'waits for' and 'experiences', this sentence has been variously interpreted. We suggest: 'The solitary man always waits for prosperity, for the favour of fate, although he, sad at heart, has long had to stir the ice-cold sea with his hands, traverse throughout the water-ways the paths of an exile. Fate is wholly inexorable!' *Oft* literally means 'often', but in poetry is frequently an understatement for 'always'. The pronoun *him* (l. 1) is dative of interest: 'for himself'.

7 **winemǣga hryre** (= **hryra**) 'of the deaths of kinsmen'. This is but one of several attempts by scholars to interpret the grammar of *hryre*.

9–11 **Nis nū . . . āsecgan** See §163.2.

11 **tō sōþe** 'for a truth', 'truly'.

14 **hycge . . . wille** 'think as he will', 'whatever he may want to think'.

17 **drēorigne** 'sorrowful (mind)', with *hyge* understood from l. 16.

22–3 **siþþan gēara iū . . . biwrāh** 'since years ago I concealed (i.e. buried) my lord in earth's darkness'. The subject of *biwrāh* is *ic*, understood from l. 19.

25 **sōhte seledrēorig** 'sad for the lack of a hall, I sought'. See §159.

27 **mīne wisse** 'might know of my own (i.e. my origins or people)'. Only if a lord has prior knowledge of the man's tribal affiliations will he be willing to accept the wanderer into his retinue.

wenian mid wynnum.   Wāt se þe cunnað
hū slīþen bið   sorg tō gefēran
þām þe him lȳt hafað   lēofra geholena:
warað hine wræclāst,   nales wunden gold,
ferðloca frēorig,   nalæs foldan blǣd.
Gemon hē selesecgas   ond sincþege,
hū hine on geoguðe   his goldwine
wenede tō wiste.   Wyn eal gedrēas!
Forþon wāt se þe sceal   his winedryhtnes
lēofes lārcwidum   longe forþolian:
ðonne sorg ond slǣp   somod ætgædre
earmne ānhogan   oft gebindað,
þinceð him on mōde   þæt hē his mondryhten
clyppe ond cysse   ond on cnēo lecge
honda ond hēafod,   swā hē hwīlum ǣr
in gēardagum   giefstōlas brēac.
Ðonne onwæcneð eft   winelēas guma,
gesihð him biforan   fealwe wēgas,
baþian brimfuglas,   brǣdan feþra,
hrēosan hrīm ond snāw   hagle gemenged.
þonne bēoð þȳ hefigran   heortan benne,
sāre æfter swǣsne.   Sorg bið genīwad
þonne māga gemynd   mōd geondhweorfeð;
grēteð glīwstafum,   georne geondscēawað
secga geseldan;   swimmað oft on weg.

29–30 **Wāt se þe cunnað . . . gefēran** 'He who knows (at first hand) how cruel is sorrow for a companion . . . understands.'

32 **warað hine wræclāst** 'the path of an exile claims him'.

37–44 **Forþon wāt . . . brēac** The long sentence in ll. 39–44 is the direct object of *wāt* (l. 37): 'He who must long forgo his beloved lord's counsels knows (that) when sorrow and sleep both together constrain the wretched solitary, it seems to him . . .'.

43–4 **swā hē hwīlum . . . brēac** 'just as from time to time he used to make use of the throne in days of old'. (*giefstōlas* is a late spelling of gen. sg. *giefstōles*.) 'Making use of the throne' by embracing the lord, placing hand and head on his knees, etc. is evidently a ritual confirming the close ties between the lord and his retainer.

46–7 **gesihð him biforan . . . brimfuglas** 'sees before him the fallow waves (sees) the seabirds bathing', etc.

51–3 **þonne māga gemynd . . . geseldan** Either 'whenever the memory of kinsmen passes through his mind, he greets joyfully (and) eagerly scrutinizes the companions of men' or 'whenever the mind passes through the memory of kinsmen, it greets joyfully (and) eagerly scrutinizes the companions of men'. *Secga geseldan* (and the *flēotendra ferð* of l. 54) appear to refer both to the birds the wanderer sees when he is awake and to the remembered kinsmen, whom he imagines he sees before him in his dreams and reveries.

53 **swimmað oft on weg** 'they always drift away'. Just as in the next line *nō . . . fela* means (by ironic understatement) 'none', here *oft* 'often' means 'always'. Cf. l. 1 above.

Flēotendra ferð nō þǣr fela bringeð
cūðra cwidegiedda. Cearo bið genīwad
þām þe sendan sceal swīþe geneahhe
ofer waþema gebind wērigne sefan.
Forþon ic geþencan ne mæg geond þās woruld
for hwan mōdsefa mīn ne gesweorce
þonne ic eorla līf eal geondþence,
hū hī fǣrlīce flet ofgēafon,
mōdge maguþegnas. Swā þes middangeard
ealra dōgra gehwām drēoseð ond fealleþ;
forþon ne mæg weorþan wīs wer, ǣr hē āge
wintra dǣl in woruldrīce. Wita sceal geþyldig,
ne sceal nō tō hātheort ne tō hrædwyrde,
ne tō wāc wiga ne tō wanhȳdig,
ne tō forht ne tō fægen, ne tō feohgīfre
ne nǣfre gielpes tō georn, ǣr hē geare cunne.
Beorn sceal gebīdan, þonne hē bēot spriceð,
oþþæt collenferð cunne gearwe
hwider hreþra gehygd hweorfan wille.
Ongietan sceal glēaw hæle hū gǣstlic bið,
þonne ealre þisse worulde wela wēste stondeð,
swā nu missenlīce geond þisne middangeard
winde biwāune weallas stondaþ,
hrīme bihrorene, hryðge þā ederas.
Wōriað þā wīnsalo, waldend licgað
drēame bidrorene, duguþ eal gecrong,
wlonc bī wealle. Sume wīg fornōm,

58–9 **Forþon ic geþencan . . . gesweorce** 'Wherefore I cannot think for all this world why my mind does not grow dark.' The highly metaphorical *modsefa . . . gesweorcan* 'mind darken' obviously means more than simply 'become sad', since the speaker has been sad ever since his wanderings began. Probably 'despair' or 'lose the light of reason' or something equally critical is intended.

61 **flet ofgēafon** lit. 'left the floor (of the meadhall)', i.e. 'died'.

66–9 **ne sceal . . . geare cunne** 'must not be wrathful at all, nor precipitate of speech', etc. Although the literal sense is that a wise man 'must not be too wrathful, nor too precipitate in speech', etc., it is obvious that these are qualities to be avoided altogether. The use of *tō* 'too' here seems to be a rhetorical expression growing out of the Anglo-Saxons' predilection for understatement rather than absolute assertion. (An infinitive meaning 'be' should be understood following each *sceal*, this omission being characteristic of gnomic utterances in Old English.)

70–2 'Whenever he makes a vow, a stout-hearted warrior must wait until he knows precisely where the thoughts of his heart will tend.' Both here and in l. 69 the speaker is warning against rash vows (*gielp*, *bēot*) uttered in public, since a man would earn contempt if he failed to carry out what he boasted he would do.

73 **bið** 'it will be'.

80–4 **Sume wīg fornōm** 'War destroyed several' is followed by a description of the fate met by the corpses of individual members of the slain (*sumne* being acc. sg.

ferede in forðwege, sumne fugel oþþær
ofer hēanne holm, sumne se hāra wulf
dēaðe gedǣlde, sumne drēorighlēor
in eorðscræfe eorl gehȳdde.
Ȳþde swā þisne eardgeard ælda scyppend
oþþæt burgwara breahtma lēase
eald enta geweorc īdlu stōdon.
Se þonne þisne wealsteal wīse geþōhte
ond þis deorce līf dēope geondþenceð,
frōd in ferðe, feor oft gemon
wælsleahta worn, ond þās word ācwið:
"Hwǣr cwōm mearg? Hwǣr cwōm mago? Hwǣr cwōm
māþþumgyfa?
Hwǣr cwōm symbla gesetu? Hwǣr sindon seledrēamas?
Ēalā beorht bune! Ēalā byrnwiga!
Ēalā þēodnes þrym! Hū sēo þrāg gewāt,
genāp under nihthelm, swā hēo nō wǣre.
Stondeð nū on lāste lēofre duguþe
weal wundrum hēah, wyrmlīcum fāh.
Eorlas fornōman asca þrȳþe,
wǣpen wælgīfru, wyrd sēo mǣre,
ond þās stānhleoþu stormas cnyssað,
hrīð hrēosende hrūsan bindeð,
wintres wōma, þonne won cymeð,
nīpeð nihtscūa, norþan onsendeð
hrēo hæglfare hæleþum on andan."
Eall is earfoðlic eorþan rīce,
onwendeð wyrda gesceaft weoruld under heofonum.
Hēr bið feoh lǣne, hēr bið frēond lǣne,
hēr bið mon lǣne, hēr bið mǣg lǣne,

---

masc.). The bird of prey which carries off the body (piecemeal) and the wolf are a familiar motif in Old English battle poetry. Cf. 12/106–7.

86–7 **oþþæt burgwara . . . stōdon** 'until the ancient works of giants stood empty, devoid of the revelry of their (erstwhile) inhabitants'.

87 **enta geweorc** Cf. 13/2 and note.

88 **Se** 'He who'. See §164.

92–3 **Hwǣr cwōm** 'where has gone'; loosely, 'what has become of'. This haunting lament on the transience of earthly things may be based on *ubi sunt* passages in Latin sermons, as has been suggested, but such a universal sentiment hardly needs a specific source.

97 **on lāste lēofre duguþe** lit. 'in the track of the dear retinue', i.e. 'after (the departure, i.e. death of) the dear retinue'.

99–100 **Eorlas** is acc. pl. masc.; **þrȳþe, wǣpen,** and **wyrd** are nom., parallel subjects of *fornōman*.

107 **onwendeð . . . heofonum** 'the operation of the fates changes the world under the heavens'.

eal þis eorþan gesteal   īdel weorþeð!'
  Swā cwæð snottor on mōde,   gesæt him sundor æt rūne.
Til biþ se þe his trēowe gehealdeþ,   ne sceal nǣfre his torn tō rycene
beorn of his brēostum ācȳþan,   nemþe hē ǣr þā bōte cunne,
eorl mid elne gefremman.   Wel bið þām þe him āre sēceð,
frōfre tō Fæder on heofonum,   þǣr ūs eal sēo fæstnung stondeð.

114 **Wel bið . . . sēceð 'Well is it for the one who seeks mercy for himself.'**

17

The Seafarer

Ever since the Anglo-Saxons migrated by ship from the Continent to the isle of Britain, Englishmen seem to have been more aware than most people of the importance and fascination of the sea and seafaring. One aspect of the seafaring life which has always captured the attention of people everywhere is the paradoxical state of mind called 'sea fever' – that irresistible call of the sea felt by experienced seamen who may on some occasions complain bitterly about the pains and trials of sea travel, but will sign on for another voyage when the opportunity presents itself. Poems and novels in many periods have treated this subject, but none has done so more convincingly than the Old English poetic monologue *The Seafarer*, which searches so deeply the thoughts and feelings of one Anglo-Saxon sailor that the poet Ezra Pound claims to have discovered in this work 'the English national chemical'.

But impressive as it is in its treatment of the physical and psychological rigours of seafaring life, the poem is about much more than that. Indeed, most of the latter half of the monologue does not mention the sea but rather is concerned with the impermanence of earthly riches and worldly fame and the importance of fixing one's attention on the world to come, where judgement will be severe and the rewards will be lasting. The juxtaposition of the seafarer's account of his involvement with the sea and his concerns for the future life is startling, but it is not incomprehensible. First he describes dramatically his sufferings at sea while men on land live in comfort, but he simultaneously expresses his disdain for the landlubber's life and his preference for the trials and challenges of seafaring. But then (ll. 64–6) his thoughts shift from considerations of sea voyages to his ultimate goal of union with the Lord in Heaven. To achieve this higher goal, one must forgo the pomps and joys of earthly existence and the fleeting benefits of gold and worldly goods at large. Just as the seafaring man is willing to deny himself the pleasures of life on land in order to take up the hard challenges of the sea, the devout Christian must be willing to renounce the pleasures of the flesh in order to arrive at his heavenly destination. Once this analogy is perceived, the vividness and force of the early description of the seafarer's lot take on in retrospect larger dimensions. The movingly expressed catalogue of pleasures that the seafarer renounces (ll. 44–7) seem on second thought like the determined exercise in self-abnegation that a Christian might practise on taking holy orders. The undefined cares which are hot in the seafarer's heart in l. 11 are echoed in ll. 64–6 when he speaks of the joys of the Lord being 'hotter' than transitory earthly existence. (And we may be reminded of Luke 24:32: 'did not our heart burn within us, while he [the Lord] talked with us by the way . . . ?') Key words like *dryhten* and *lond* take on second meanings as the initial monologue of the seafarer is placed in juxtaposition with this broader conception of man's voyage through life to an ultimate destination. Scholars have detected artful symmetries and subtle allegories at work in *The Seafarer*, but perhaps the poet's strongest statement is the question implicit in the simple analogy he has established: if we can all accept the fact that seafaring men will forgo the pleasures of life on land for the obscure enticements of a dangerous ocean journey, is it unreasonable for Christianity to require renunciation of some earthly delights for the goal of eternal salvation?

As the notes below will indicate, *The Seafarer* presents some difficulties in syntax and thought transition, partly because of its strong feeling and sometimes passionate insistence. But its hard realism combined with lofty otherworldliness repays the effort required to read the poem. The following emendations have been adopted: *hleahtre* for MS *hleahtor* (l. 21), *ne ǣnig* for *nǣnig* (l. 25), *frēfran* for *feran* (l. 26), *gewītan* for *gewita* (l. 52), *sēftēadig* for *efteadig* (l. 56), *hwælweg* for *wælweg* (l. 63), *stondað* for *stondeð* (l. 67), *tīddege* for *tide ge* (l. 69), *bið* for *þæt* (l. 72), *fremum* for *fremman* (l. 75), *blǣd* for *blæð* (l. 79), *nearon* for *næron* (l. 82), *mon* for *mod* (l. 109), *lufan* supplied in l. 112, *swīþre* for *swire* (l. 115), *wē* for *se* (l. 117).

Mæg ic be mē sylfum sōðgied wrecan,
sīþas secgan, hū ic geswincdagum
earfoðhwīle oft þrōwade,
bitre brēostceare gebiden hæbbe,
gecunnad in cēole cearselda fela,
atol ȳþa gewealc. þǣr mec oft bigeat
nearo nihtwaco æt nacan stefnan,

2 **geswincdagum** 'in days of hardship'.

5 **cearselda fela** 'many a house of care'. The ship has often been a sorrowful abode for the seafarer.

6–7 **mec oft bigeat . . . stefnan** 'the anxious nightwatch often held me at the ship's prow'.

þonne hē be clifum cnossað. Calde geþrungen
wǣron mīne fēt, forste gebunden,
caldum clommum, þǣr þā ceare seofedun
hāt'ymb heortan; hungor innan slāt
merewērges mōd. þæt se mon ne wāt
þe him on foldan fægrost limpeð,
hū ic earmcearig īscealdne sǣ
winter wunade wræccan lāstum,
winemǣgum bidroren,
bihongen hrīmgicelum; hægl scūrum flēag.
þǣr ic ne gehȳrde būtan hlimman sǣ,
īscaldne wǣg. Hwīlum ylfete song
dyde ic mē tō gomene, ganetes hlēoþor
ond huilpan swēg fore hleahtre wera,
mǣw singende fore medodrince.
Stormas þǣr stānclifu bēotan, þǣr him stearn oncwæð
īsigfeþera; ful oft þæt earn bigeal,
ūrigfeþra; ne ǣnig hlēomǣga
fēasceaftig ferð frēfran meahte.
Forþon him gelȳfeð lȳt, se þe āh līfes wyn
gebiden in burgum, bealosīþa hwōn,
wlonc ond wīngāl, hū ic wērig oft
in brimlāde bīdan sceolde.
Nāp nihtscūa, norþan snīwde,
hrīm hrūsan bond, hægl fēol on eorþan,

11 **hāt'** The correct nom. pl. fem. form (modifying *ceare*) is *hāte*, but here the *-e* is elided before the vowel of *ymb*.

12–14 **þæt se mon . . . hū ic . . .** 'The man whom it befalls most pleasantly on land does not know that, (namely) how I . . . ' etc. *þæt* anticipates the noun clause introduced by *hū*. See §148.

13 **þe him.** See §162.2.

15 **winter** 'in the winter' (adverbial acc.). The object of *wunade* is *sǣ* (l. 14).

16 A half-line appears to be missing, but the sense is unimpaired.

18 **ic ne gehȳrde būtan** 'I heard nought but'.

19–20 **ylfete song . . . tō gomene** 'I made the song of the wild swan (serve) for my entertainment.'

23 **him** i.e. the storms.

24 **þæt** is object of *bigeal* and refers to the clamour of the storms and the tern (l. 23) according to most scholars, but the construction is odd. Alternatively, *þæt* could be explained as referring to the eagle, although *earn* is usually masc.

27 **Forþon** The usual meanings of *forþon* 'therefore', 'because' do not always serve well in *The Seafarer*, and it has been suggested that in this poem (as in a few other places) it may sometimes have the meaning 'indeed' or even 'and yet'.

27–9 **him gelȳfeð lȳt . . . hū ic . . .** 'he who has experienced joy of life in the cities (and) few baleful journeys little believes how I . . .'. *Āh* in l. 27 is used as an auxiliary verb with past ptc. *gebiden*; *wyn* and *hwōn* are parallel objects of *āh gebiden*.

corna caldast. Forþon cnyssað nū
heortan geþōhtas, þæt ic hēan strēamas,
sealtȳþa gelāc sylf cunnige;
monað mōdes lust mǣla gehwylce
ferð tō fēran, þæt ic feor heonan
elþēodigra eard gesēce.
Forþon nis þæs mōdwlonc mon ofer eorþan,
ne his gifena þæs gōd, ne in geoguþe tō þæs hwæt,
ne in his dǣdum tō þæs dēor, ne him his dryhten tō þæs
hold,
þæt hē ā his sǣfōre sorge næbbe,
tō hwon hine dryhten gedōn wille.
Ne biþ him tō hearpan hyge ne tō hringþege,
ne tō wīfe wyn ne tō worulde hyht,
ne ymbe ōwiht elles, nefne ymb ȳða gewealc,
ac ā hafað longunge se þe on lagu fundað.
Bearwas blōstmum nimað, byrig fægriað,
wongas wlitigað, woruld ōnetteð;
ealle þā gemoniað mōdes fūsne

33–5 **Forþon cnyssað nū . . . cunnige** 'And yet the thoughts of my heart are pressing (me) now that I myself should explore the high seas, the tumult of the salt waves.' But since the seafarer has already been to sea, some have argued that *sylf* means 'alone'.

37 **ferð** is acc., direct object of *monað*.

38 **elþēodigra eard** 'land of foreigners', i.e. 'foreign lands'. Some have argued that this could mean 'Heaven', *elþēodig* referring to those who are pilgrims on earth and regard Heaven as their true home. See Hebrews 11: 13–16.

39 **nis þæs . . . mon** 'there is no man so proud in spirit'. The repeated *þæs* (or *tō þæs*) in ll. 40–1 means 'so' also. See §168 *þæs . . . þæt* note 2.

40 **ne his . . . gōd** 'nor so fortunate in his gifts'.

41–3 **dryhten . . . dryhten** The first *dryhten* seems clearly to refer to the seafarer's earthly lord; the second one could have the same reference ('that he does not always have concern as to what his lord might be willing to do for him [in return for his services as a seafarer]'). But the sentence could also refer to what rewards on earth or in the next life the Lord may have in store for him. The ambiguity is probably deliberate since this is where the poet begins to make his transition between the seafarer's account of his experiences and Christian exhortation. Since Old English scribes did not capitalize the first letter of terms for the Deity (as is regularly done in Modern English), the play on the secular and religious meanings of *dryhten* was easy.

44–6 **Ne biþ him . . . gewealc** 'His thought is not for the harp nor for the ring-taking, nor his pleasure in a woman nor his delight in the world, nor (is his thought) about anything else but the rolling of the waves.' This description of how the seafarer willingly forgoes the delights of the land for a higher, harder goal establishes the analogy between the self-abnegation of seamen and that required of Christians.

48–9 **Bearwas . . . wlitigað** *Bearwas* 'groves' may be taken as the subject of *fægriað* and *wlitigað* as well as of *nimað*. But since it is odd to say that *bearwas* ('groves', 'woods') beautify cities, some have preferred to take *fægriað* and *wlitigað* as intransitive: 'the cities grow fair, the meadows become beautiful'.

50–1 **gemoniað . . . tō sīþe** 'urge (the one) eager of spirit, (urge) the mind to the journey'.

sefan tō sīþe þām þe swā þenceð
on flōdwegas feor gewītan.
Swylce gēac monað geōmran reorde,
singeð sumeres weard, sorge bēodeð
bitter in brēosthord. Þæt se beorn ne wāt,
sēftēadig secg, hwæt þā sume drēogað
þe þā wræclāstas wīdost lecgað.
  Forþon nū mīn hyge hweorfeð ofer hreþerlocan,
mīn mōdsefa mid mereflōde
ofer hwæles ēþel hweorfeð wīde,
eorþan scēatas, cymeð eft tō mē
gīfre ond grǣdig, gielleð ānfloga,
hweteð on hwælweg hreþer unwearnum
ofer holma gelagu. Forþon mē hātran sind
Dryhtnes drēamas þonne þis dēade līf,
lǣne on londe. Ic gelȳfe nō
þæt him eorðwelan ēce stondað.
Simle þrēora sum þinga gehwylce
ǣr his tīddege tō twēon weorþeð;
ādl oþþe yldo oþþe ecghete
fǣgum fromweardum feorh oðþringeð.
Forþon bið eorla gehwām æftercweþendra
lof lifgendra lāstworda betst,
þæt hē gewyrce, ǣr hē on weg scyle,

51 **þām þe swā þenceð** 'by which (he [*mōdes fūs*]) intends': the *seþe* relative (§162.4) with an unexpressed subject.

58 **Forþon** 'and yet'. (Alternatively, one can take this *Forþon* as correlative with the *forþon* in l. 64: 'Indeed . . . because . . .'.) In this sentence the mind of the speaker leaves his body and ranges like a bird over land and sea, locates his goal, and then returns to urge him on to his destination.

58–61 **hyge** and **mōdsefa** are parallel subjects of *hweorfeð*; **ēþel** and **scēatas** are parallel objects of *ofer*. **ofer hreþerlocan** 'beyond my breast'.

66 **on londe** Two senses are simultaneously operative here: 'land (as opposed to sea)' and 'earth (as opposed to heaven)'.

67 **þæt him . . . stondað** 'that worldly goods will endure forever'. The *him* is apparently reflexive and need not be translated.

68 **þinga gehwylce** 'in every circumstance', i.e. 'invariably'.

69 **tō twēon weorþeð** 'arises as an uncertainty', i.e. 'hangs in the balance'. Until the end of his days (*ǣr his tīddege*) a man can never be sure when age, sickness, or death might take his life from him.

72–80 Having mentioned the certainty of death, the poet seems at first to cite the traditional Germanic-heroic view that earning fame after death through valorous deeds in life is the best course for a man. But he Christianizes this admonition by specifying that the deeds should be in Christian action against the devil and that the fame that counts is fame in Heaven, which will earn him the joy of eternal life. Cf. Milton's *Lycidas*, ll. 78–84.

72–4 **bið eorla . . . hē gewyrce** 'for every man the best of reputations after death (*lāstworda*) will be the praise of posterity (*æftercweþendra*), of the living, (will be) that he should bring it about . . .'.

fremum on foldan wið fēonda nīþ,
dēorum dǣdum dēofle tōgēanes,
þæt hine ælda bearn æfter hergen,
ond his lof siþþan lifge mid englum
āwa tō ealdre, ēcan līfes blǣd,
drēam mid dugeþum.

Dagas sind gewitene,
ealle onmēdlan eorþan rīces;
nearon nū cyningas ne cāseras
ne goldgiefan swylce iū wǣron,
þonne hī mǣst mid him mǣrþa gefremedon
ond on dryhtlīcestum dōme lifdon.
Gedroren is þēos duguð eal, drēamas sind gewitene,
wuniað þā wācran ond þās woruld healdaþ,
brūcað þurh bisgo. Blǣd is gehnǣged,
eorþan indryhto ealdað ond sēarað,
swā nū monna gehwylc geond middangeard.
Yldo him on fareð, onsӯn blācað,
gomelfeax gnornað, wāt his iūwine,
æþelinga bearn, eorþan forgiefene.
Ne mæg him þonne se flǣschoma, þonne him þæt feorg losað,
ne swēte forswelgan ne sār gefēlan,
ne hond onhrēran ne mid hyge þencan.
þēah þe græf wille golde strēgan
brōþor his geborenum, byrgan be dēadum
māþmum mislicum, þæt hine mid wille,
ne mæg þǣre sāwle þe biþ synna ful
gold tō gēoce for Godes egsan,
þonne hē hit ǣr hӯdeð þenden hē hēr leofað.

80–100 This declaration of the demise of the past (heroic) age, though somewhat tinged with regret (e.g. ll. 85, 87–9), is concerned primarily to emphasize the transience of worldly glory as contrasted with the eternal life in Heaven.

84 **þonne hī . . . gefremedon** 'when they performed the greatest of glorious deeds among themselves'.

88 **brūcað þurh bisgo** 'live in (it) by toil'.

97–102 **þēah þe græf . . . hēr leofað** 'Although a brother may wish to strew the grave with gold for his born (brother), bury (him) among the dead with various treasures, which he wishes (to go) with him, gold, when he hides it here while he lives on earth previously, cannot (be) of help before the terrible power of God to the soul that is full of sin.' *þæt* (l. 99) is a neut. sg. relative pron. agreeing with *gold* (l. 97). The familiar Christian admonition against hoarding gold and burying lavish treasures with the dead is here introduced to stress that man is beyond earthly help when he faces Judgement.

Micel biþ se Meotudes egsa,   for þon hī sēo molde oncyrreð;
se gestaþelade   stīþe grundas,
eorþan scēatas   ond ūprodor.
Dol biþ se þe him his Dryhten ne ondrǣdeþ;   cymeð him se dēað unþinged.
Ēadig bið se þe ēaþmōd leofaþ;   cymeð him sēo ār of heofonum,
Meotod him þæt mōd gestaþelað,   forþon hē in his meahte gelȳfeð.
Stīeran mon sceal strongum mōde,   ond þæt on staþelum healdan,
ond gewis wērum,   wīsum clǣne;
scyle monna gehwylc   mid gemete healdan
lufan wiþ lēofne   ond wið lāþne bealo,
þēah þe hē hine wille fȳres   fulne . . . .
oþþe on bǣle   forbærnedne
his geworhtne wine.   Wyrd biþ swīþre,
Meotud meahtigra   þonne ǣnges monnes gehygd.
Uton wē hycgan   hwǣr wē hām āgen,
ond þonne geþencan   hū wē þider cumen,
ond wē þonne ēac tilien,   þæt wē tō mōten
in þā ēcan   ēadignesse,
þǣr is līf gelong   in lufan Dryhtnes,
hyht in heofonum.   þæs sȳ þām Halgan þonc,
þæt hē ūsic geweorþade,   wuldres Ealdor,
ēce Dryhten,   in ealle tīd.

Amen.

103 **for þon hī sēo molde oncyrreð** 'before which the earth turns (itself) aside'. Revelation 20: 11 'him . . . from whose face the earth and the heaven fled away' may lie behind this.

108 'The Lord establishes that (good) spirit in him, because he believes in His (the Lord's) power.'

110 **ond gewis . . . clǣne** 'and (keep it) steadfast in (its) pledges, pure in (its) ways'.

111–12 'each man should hold in moderation his affection toward a friend and his enmity toward a foe.'

113–15 **þēah þe hē . . . wine.** This seems to continue the sense of what precedes, but l. 113 is metrically defective, and the lines are probably corrupt: 'although he may wish him (the *lāþne* of l. 112) full of fire (in hell?) or his friend (i.e. the friend of the enemy?) consumed on a funeral pyre'.

117–18 These lines return the religious exhortation to the original seafaring imagery.

119 **þæt wē tō mōten** 'that we may (proceed) thither'.

18

Beowulf

Beowulf is the first great English heroic poem, and yet its subject is not England but men and women from Germanic legend and history. It takes place in Northern Europe before Christianity had reached that part of the world. The poet, who wrote centuries later than the time of the poem's action, was a Christian and may even have been a churchman, but he claimed for his subject pre-Christian nations living in and around the lands from which the Anglo-Saxons had originally migrated to England. He admires the characters he describes, especially the hero Beowulf, but there is poignancy in his admiration, for he knows that these brave and eloquent people were ignorant of the revelation generally believed to be essential for Christian salvation.

The poem describes how a powerful warrior from the land of the Geats (a Scandinavian people dwelling in southern Sweden) travels to Denmark to do battle with a man-eating ogre who is killing King Hrothgar's thanes in a series of nocturnal attacks. Beowulf rids the Danes of their tormentor and returns to Geatland, where he puts his great strength at the service of his own people in their wars with hostile neighbours. Eventually, he becomes King of the Geats, and years later, when he is an old man, he gives his life in the course of slaying a dragon that had threatened to destroy the nation. His people bury him amid forebodings of disaster, for the Geats will not be able to withstand their enemies without Beowulf's strong supporting hand.

Beowulf is our most sustained demonstration of the power and range of Old English poetry. In the excerpts printed here readers will recognize several of the themes and strains encountered individually in the preceding poetic texts: appreciative descriptions of valour in battle, stirring speeches, elegiac reflections on man and his world, love of the past, and a keen sense of the transience of things.[1]

[1] The emendations and reconstructions required in these passages from *Beowulf* are extensive and so are relegated to this footnote. 'MS' refers to MS Cotton Vitellius A.XV in the British Museum; 'A' and 'B' refer to the two transcripts of the manuscript known as the Thorkelin transcripts. Textual details and complexities

(*a*) *Beowulf's Fight with Grendel*

For twelve years the monster Grendel has left his watery abode at night and come to the royal hall Heorot to seize and devour some warriors of King Hrothgar's. On the occasion described in this selection the Geatish champion Beowulf and his fourteen comrades are awaiting Grendel's attack. The monster stalks across the moor, tears open the door to the hall and gobbles down one of the Geatish warriors before Beowulf can do battle with him. The two then fight, and after the fray the Danes and Geats follow Grendel's tracks to the mere and then return to Heorot. Along the way one of King Hrothgar's thanes celebrates Beowulf's courage by reciting a poem about Sigemund, son of Wæls, Sigemund being the ideal Germanic hero and a worthy figure with whom to compare Beowulf.

Cōm on wanre niht
scrīðan sceadugenga.   Scēotend swǣfon,
þā þæt hornreced   healdan scoldon –
ealle būton ānum.   þæt wæs yldum cūþ,
þæt hīe ne mōste,   þā metod nolde,
se scynscaþa   under sceadu bregdan;

---

are avoided here. For a thorough description of the manuscript readings, see *The Nowell Codex*, ed. Kemp Malone, Early English Manuscripts in Facsimile, vol. 12 (Copenhagen, 1963).

The emendations and reconstructions are as follows: *scynscaþa* for MS *synscaþa* (l. 707), *æthrān* for MS *hran* (l. 722), *hē gebolgen* for MS . . . *bolgen* (l. 723), *scēata* for MS *sceat/ta* (l. 752), *wæs* for MS *he wæs* (l. 765), *betlīc* for MS *hetlic* (l. 780), *hrōf* for B *hr* (l. 836), *Sigemundes* for MS *sige munde* (l. 875), *hwæþer* for MS *hwæþre* (l. 1314), *nǣgde* for AB *hnægde* (l. 1318), *æþeling ǣrgōd* for MS *ærgod* (l. 1329), *nēodlaðum* for MS *neod laðu* (l. 1320), *hwæder* for MS *hwæþer* (l. 1331), *gefægnod* for MS *ge frægnod* (l. 1333), *onlīcnes* for MS *onlic næs* (l. 1351), *nemdon* for MS *nemdod* (l. 1354), *standeð* for MS *stanðeð* (l. 1362), *hafelan beorgan* for MS *hafelan* (l. 1372), *sinnigne* for MS *fela sinnigne* (l. 1379), *wundnum* for MS *wun/dini* (l. 1382), *mōstan* for MS *mæstan* (l. 2247), *fȳra* for MS *fyrena* (l. 2250), *þāra* for MS *þana* (l. 2251), *þis līf ofgeaf* for MS *þis ofgeaf* (l. 2251), *feormie* for MS *fe . r* . . . (l. 2253), *scēoc* for MS *seoc* (l. 2254), *twelfe* for MS *twelfa* (l. 3170), *ceare* for illegible space in MS (l. 3171), *ond cyning* for MS *cyning* (l. 3171), *lǣded* for illegible space in MS (l. 3177), *wyruldcyninga* for MS *wyruldcyning* (l. 3180).

702–3 **Cōm** . . . **scrīðan** The threefold announcement of Grendel's approach to Heorot is each time expressed using *cōm* plus an infinitive: *cōm* . . . *scrīðan* 'came gliding', *cōm* . . . *gongan* 'came striding' (ll. 710–11), *Cōm* . . . *sīðian* 'came stalking' (l. 720).

703 **sceadugenga** 'walker in darkness', i.e. Grendel (who always attacks at night).

706–7 **þæt hīe** . . . **bregdan** 'that the demonic foe might not fling them beneath the shades when the ruler did not wish (it)', i.e. Grendel could not kill them without the consent of a higher power.

ac hē wæccende   wrāþum on andan
bād bolgenmōd   beadwa geþinges.
Ðā cōm of mōre   under misthleoþum
Grendel gongan;   Godes yrre bær;
mynte se mānscaða   manna cynnes
sumne besyrwan   in sele þām hēan.
Wōd under wolcnum   tō þæs þe hē wīnreced,
goldsele gumena   gearwost wisse
fǣttum fāhne.   Ne wæs þæt forma sīð,
þæt hē Hrōþgāres   hām gesōhte;
nǣfre hē on aldordagum   ǣr ne siþðan
heardran hǣle,   healðegnas fand!
Cōm þā tō recede   rinc sīðian
drēamum bedǣled.   Duru sōna onarn
fȳrbendum fæst,   syþðan hē hire folmum æthrān;
onbrǣd þā bealohȳdig,   ðā hē gebolgen wæs,
recedes mūþan.   Raþe æfter þon
on fāgne flōr   fēond treddode,
ēode yrremōd;   him of ēagum stōd
ligge gelīcost   lēoht unfæger.
Geseah hē in recede   rinca manige,
swefan sibbegedriht   samod ætgædere,
magorinca hēap.   Þā his mōd āhlōg:
mynte þæt hē gedǣlde,   ǣr þon dæg cwōme,
atol āglǣca   ānra gehwylces
līf wið līce,   þā him ālumpen wæs
wistfylle wēn.   Ne wæs þæt wyrd þā gēn,
þæt hē mā mōste   manna cynnes
ðicgean ofer þā niht.   Þrȳðswȳð behēold
mǣg Higelāces   hū se mānscaða
under fǣrgripum   gefaran wolde.
Ne þæt se āglǣca   yldan þōhte,
ac hē gefēng hraðe   forman sīðe

708 **hē** i.e. Beowulf.

709 **geþinges** 'result, outcome' (object of *bād*, which takes gen.).

714 **tō þæs þe** 'to (the point) where, until'.

715 **wisse** 'knew', i.e. 'recognized'.

718–19 **nǣfre hē . . . fand!** 'Never did he before nor after in the days of his life find hall-thanes (and) worse luck!'

722 **hire** i.e. the door (object of *æthrān*).

726 **him of ēagum stōd** 'from his eyes shone forth' (poss. dat.; see §191.2).

731 **mynte þæt hē gedǣlde** 'he intended to sever' (lit., 'he intended that he should sever').

734 **Ne wæs . . . gēn** 'It was not by any means destined.'

738 **under . . . wolde** 'would proceed with his sudden grips'.

740 **forman sīðe** 'at the first opportunity'.

slǣpendne rinc, slāt unwearnum,
bāt bānlocan, blōd ēdrum dranc,
synsnǣdum swealh; sōna hæfde
unlyfigendes eal gefeormod,
fēt ond folma. Forð nēar ætstōp,
nam þā mid handa higeþīhtigne
rinc on ræste, rǣhte ongēan
fēond mid folme; hē onfēng hraþe
inwitþancum ond wið earm gesæt.
Sōna þæt onfunde fyrena hyrde,
þæt hē ne mētte middangeardes,
eorþan scēata on elran men
mundgripe māran; hē on mōde wearð
forht on ferhðe; nō þȳ ǣr fram meahte.
Hyge wæs him hinfūs, wolde on heolster flēon,
sēcan dēofla gedræg; ne wæs his drohtoð þǣr
swylce hē on ealderdagum ǣr gemētte.
Gemunde þā se gōda, mǣg Higelāces,
ǣfensprǣce, uplang āstōd
ond him fæste wiðfēng; fingras burston;
eoten wæs ūtweard, eorl furþur stōp.
Mynte se mǣra, þǣr hē meahte swā,
wīdre gewindan ond on weg þanon
flēon on fenhopu; wiste his fingra geweald
on grames grāpum. þæt wæs gēocor sīð,
þæt se hearmscaþa tō Heorute ātēah.
Dryhtsele dynede; Denum eallum wearð,
ceasterbūendum, cēnra gehwylcum,
eorlum ealuscerwen. Yrre wǣron bēgen,
rēþe renweardas. Reced hlynsode.
þā wæs wundor micel, þæt se wīnsele
wiðhæfde heaþodēorum, þæt hē on hrūsan ne fēol,

745 **fēt ond folma** '(including) the feet and hands'.

748–9 **fēond** i.e. Grendel. **hē onfēng ... gesæt** 'he (Beowulf) received (him, i.e. Grendel) quickly with hostile purpose and sat up against (Grendel's) arm'. Beowulf seizes Grendel in an arm-lock.

750 **fyrena hyrde** 'master of crimes', i.e. Grendel.

752–3 **on elran ... māran** 'a greater handgrip in (any) other man'.

754 **nō þȳ ... meahte** 'none the sooner could he (get) away', i.e. 'yet he could not (get) away'.

756–7 **ne wæs his ... gemētte** 'nor was his experience there such as (§168 *swelce* 2) he had ever before met with in the days of his life'.

760 **him** i.e. Grendel.

762 **se mǣra** i.e. Grendel.

þǣr hē meahte swā 'if he (Grendel) could (do) so'.

764 **wiste his ... geweald** 'he (Grendel) realized the control of his fingers (was)'.

769 **ealuscerwen** '?terror'. A mysterious word, recorded only here.

fæger foldbold; ac hē þæs fæste wæs
innan ond ūtan īrenbendum
searoþoncum besmiþod. Þǣr fram sylle ābēag
medubenc monig mīne gefrǣge
golde geregnad, þǣr þā graman wunnon.
Þæs ne wēndon ǣr witan Scyldinga,
þæt hit ā mid gemete manna ǣnig
betlīc ond bānfāg tōbrecan meahte,
listum tōlūcan, nymþe līges fæþm
swulge on swaþule. Swēg ūp āstāg
nīwe geneahhe: Norð-Denum stōd
atelīc egesa, ānra gehwylcum
þāra þe of wealle wōp gehȳrdon,
gryreléoð galan Godes andsacan,
sigelēasne sang, sār wānigean
helle hæfton. Hēold hine fæste
se þe manna wæs mægene strengest
on þǣm dæge þysses līfes.
Nolde eorla hlēo ǣnige þinga
þone cwealmcuman cwicne forlǣtan,
ne his līfdagas lēoda ǣnigum
nytte tealde. Þǣr genehost brægd
eorl Bēowulfes ealde lāfe,
wolde frēadrihtnes feorh ealgian,
mǣres þēodnes, ðǣr hīe meahton swā.
Hīe þæt ne wiston, þa hīe gewin drugon,
heardhicgende hildemecgas,
ond on healfa gehwone hēawan þōhton,
sāwle sēcan: þone synscaðan
ǣnig ofer eorþan īrenna cyst,

773 **hē** i.e. the hall.
þæs 'so' (§168 *þæs* 2).

776 **mīne gefrǣge** 'as I have heard say'. Infrequently the poet enters the narrative in the first person.

778–9 **þæs . . . þæt** Anticipatory pronoun followed by noun clause (§148). *þæs* is object of *wēndon*, which takes gen.

786–8 **Godes andsacan . . . helle hæfton** i.e. Grendel. Cf. l. 711. The monster's screams of pain are described with grim irony as an unhappy song.

788 **Hēold hine fæste** '(Beowulf) held him (Grendel) firmly.'

791–2 **Nolde eorla hlēo . . . forlǣtan** 'The protector of men (Beowulf) did not want to let the murderous visitor go alive by any means.' But the monster does break away (ll. 819–21). It is important to notice that although he is 'the strongest of men in that day of this life' (ll. 789–90), Beowulf is subject to human limitations.

794–5 **Þǣr genehost . . . lāfe** 'A warrior of Beowulf's in abundance brandished his ancient heirloom there', i.e. 'Many a warrior brandished his sword.'

800–1 **ond on healfa . . . sēcan** 'and intended to slash away on every side, to get (i.e. kill) the soul (of Grendel)'.

gūðbilla nān   grētan nolde;
ac hē sigewǣpnum   forsworen hæfde,
ecga gehwylcre.   Scolde his aldorgedāl
on ðǣm dæge   þysses līfes
earmlic wurðan,   ond se ellorgāst
on fēonda geweald   feor sīðian.
Ðā þæt onfunde   se þe fela ǣror
mōdes myrðe   manna cynne,
fyrene gefremede   – hē fāg wið God –
þæt him se līchoma   lǣstan nolde,
ac hine se mōdega   mǣg Hygelāces
hæfde be honda;   wæs gehwæþer ōðrum
lifigende lāð.   Līcsār gebād
atol ǣglǣca;   him on eaxle wearð
syndolh sweotol,   seonowe onsprungon,
burston bānlocan.   Bēowulfe wearð
gūðhrēð gyfeþe;   scolde Grendel þonan
feorhsēoc flēon   under fenhleoðu,
sēcean wynlēas wīc;   wiste þē geornor
þæt his aldres wæs   ende gegongen,
dōgera dægrīm.   Denum eallum wearð
æfter þām wælrǣse   willa gelumpen.
Hæfde þā gefǣlsod   se þe ǣr feorran cōm,
snotor ond swȳðferhð,   sele Hrōðgāres,
genered wið nīðe.   Nihtweorce gefeh,
ellenmǣrþum.   Hæfde Ēast-Denum
Gēatmecga lēod   gilp gelǣsted,
swylce oncȳþðe   ealle gebētte,
inwidsorge,   þe hīe ǣr drugon
ond for þrēanȳdum   þolian scoldon,
torn unlȳtel.   Þæt wæs tācen sweotol,
syþðan hildedēor   hond ālegde,
earm ond eaxle   – þǣr wæs eal geador
Grendles grāpe –   under gēapne hrōf.

801–5 Grendel's invulnerability to weapons seems to be explained here as the result of his having laid a spell on them, but the meaning of *forsworen* is uncertain.

805–8 **Scolde** 'had to' is to be construed with both *wurðan* and *sīðian*.

810–11 **mōdes myrðe . . . gefremede** *myrðe* and *fyrene* are parallel gen. pl. nouns with *-e* for *-a* (cf. 16/7 note): 'had done to the race of men afflictions of spirit, crimes'.

811 **hē fāg wið God** 'he (who was) hostile towards God'. This phrase is parallel with and specifies *se þe* (l. 809).

817–18 **seonowe . . . bānlocan** 'the sinews sprang asunder, the joints broke (apart)', that is, Grendel's arm was torn from his body.

822–3 **his aldres . . . dægrīm** 'the number of his days, the end of his life, had run out'.

Đā wæs on morgen   mīne gefrǣge
ymb þā gifhealle   gūðrinc monig;
fērdon folctogan   feorran ond nēan
geond wīdwegas   wundor scēawian,
lāþes lāstas.   Nō his līfgedāl
sārlīc þūhte   secga ǣnegum
þāra þe tīrlēases   trode scēawode,
hū hē wērigmōd   on weg þanon,
nīða ofercumen,   on nicera mere
fǣge ond geflȳmed   feorhlāstas bær.
Đǣr wæs on blōde   brim weallende,
atol ȳða geswing   eal gemenged,
hāton heolfre,   heorodrēore wēol;
dēaðfǣge dēog,   siððan drēama lēas
in fenfreoðo   feorh ālegde,
hǣþene sāwle;   þǣr him hel onfēng.
Þanon eft gewiton   ealdgesīðas
swylce geong manig   of gomenwāþe,
fram mere mōdge   mēarum rīdan,
beornas on blancum.   Đǣr wæs Bēowulfes
mǣrðo mǣned;   monig oft gecwæð,
þætte sūð ne norð   be sǣm twēonum
ofer eormengrund   ōþer nǣnig
under swegles begong   sēlra nǣre
rondhæbbendra,   rīces wyrðra.
Nē hīe hūru winedrihten   wiht ne lōgon,
glædne Hrōðgār,   ac þæt wæs gōd cyning.
Hwīlum heaþorōfe   hlēapan lēton,
on geflit faran   fealwe mēaras,
ðǣr him foldwegas   fægere þūhton,
cystum cūðe.   Hwīlum cyninges þegn,
guma gilphlæden,   gidda gemyndig,
se ðe ealfela   ealdgesegena
worn gemunde,   word ōþer fand
sōðe gebunden;   secg eft ongan

837 **mīne gefrǣge** See l. 776 note.

847 **Đǣr wæs . . . weallende** 'There the water was surging with blood.' The men from far and near have followed Grendel's tracks back to the mere where he has his abode.

850 **dēaðfǣge dēog** 'the one doomed to death (i.e. Grendel) had been concealed'. The meaning of *dēog*, which occurs only here, is uncertain.

861 **rīces wyrðra** 'more worthy of a kingdom', i.e. 'more worthy of being a king'. This high praise leads naturally to the reassurance that they intended no dispraise of their own king (who had been unable to protect them from Grendel).

867 **cystum cūðe** 'known for their good qualities' refers to *foldwegas* nom. pl.

870–1 **word ōþer . . . gebunden** '(the king's thane) found other words faithfully

sīð Bēowulfes snyttrum styrian,
ond on spēd wrecan spel gerāde,
wordum wrixlan; wēlhwylc gecwæð,
þæt hē fram Sigemundes secgan hȳrde
ellendǣdum, uncūþes fela,
Wælsinges gewin, wīde sīðas,
þāra þe gumena bearn gearwe ne wiston,
fǣhðe ond fyrena, būton Fitela mid hine,
þonne hē swulces hwæt secgan wolde,
ēam his nefan, swā hīe ā wǣron
æt nīða gehwām nȳdgesteallan;
hæfdon ealfela eotena cynnes
sweordum gesǣged. Sigemunde gesprong
æfter dēaðdæge dōm unlȳtel,
syþðan wīges heard wyrm ācwealde,
hordes hyrde; hē under hārne stān,
æþelinges bearn āna genēðde
frēcne dǣde, ne wæs him Fitela mid;
hwæþre him gesǣlde, ðæt þæt swurd þurhwōd
wrǣtlicne wyrm, þæt hit on wealle ætstōd,
dryhtlic īren; draca morðre swealt.
Hæfde āglǣca elne gegongen,
þæt hē bēahhordes brūcan mōste
selfes dōme; sǣbāt gehlēod,
bær on bearm scipes beorhte frætwa,
Wælses eafera; wyrm hāt gemealt.

---

bound together', 'other' meaning perhaps new words for this occasion. *Gebunden* seems to refer to the alliterative linking together of words in Old English verse.

872 **sīð . . . styrian** 'to engage Beowulf's undertaking skilfully'. Some such sense as 'engage' is implied, because the thane does not narrate the hero's achievement but rather celebrates it by telling other heroic stories, exalting Beowulf's victory to the status of the greatest victories of Germanic legend, such as Sigemund's slaying of the dragon.

874–97 The first part of the thane's account of Sigemund's adventures describes his expeditions with his nephew Fitela (ll. 874–84). The details of this activity are to be found in the Old Norse *Volsungasaga*, chapters 3–8. Sigemund's dragon fight (ll. 884–97) is the event renowned in Germanic legend at large, only in other accounts the dragon is slain by Sigemund's son Siegfried. Indeed, it is possible that this passage says the same, since *wīges heard . . . hē* (ll. 886–7) could refer to Siegfried. The Middle High German *Nibelungenlied* is the most famous of the accounts of Siegfried, but he is also prominent in Scandinavian literature.

879 **būton Fitela mid hine** 'except for Fitela (who was) with him'.

891 **þæt hit . . . ætstōd** 'so that it (the sword) stuck into the wall'. The dragon is pinned to the wall.

893 **Hæfde . . . gegongen** 'By his valour the combatant (i.e. Sigemund or Siegfried) had brought it about.'

895 **selfes dōme** 'according to (his own) judgement', i.e. 'to his heart's content'.

897 **wyrm hāt gemealt** 'the hot dragon was consumed (? in its own fire)'.

(*b*) *Beowulf Consoles Hrothgar for Æschere's Death*

The night after Beowulf's victory over Grendel, the Danes are surprised by another monstrous visitant: Grendel's mother comes to Heorot and slays Hrothgar's favourite thane, Æschere, in vengeance for her son's death. Beowulf, who has lodged in a separate building some distance from the royal hall, is brought to the King, and Hrothgar tells him of Æschere's death. He also describes to Beowulf the eerie lair where Grendel and his mother live, and this description (ll. 1357–79) is one of the most famous passages in all Old English literature. As if appalled by his own account of the monsters' dwelling place, he asks almost despairingly whether the hero will consider challenging this second monster. Beowulf's answer (ll. 1383–96) is the finest statement we have of the Germanic heroic ethos.

þā wæs frōd cyning,
hār hilderinc   on hrēon mōde,
syðþan hē aldorþegn   unlyfigendne,
þone dēorestan   dēadne wisse.
Hraþe wæs tō būre   Bēowulf fetod,
sigorēadig secg.   Samod ǣrdæge
ēode eorla sum,   æþele cempa
self mid gesīðum   þǣr se snotera bād
hwæþer him alwalda   ǣfre wille
æfter wēaspelle   wyrpe gefremman.
Gang ðā æfter flōre   fyrdwyrðe man
mid his handscale   – healwudu dynede –
þæt hē þone wīsan   wordum nǣgde
frēan Ingwina,   frægn gif him wǣre
æfter nēodlaðum   niht getǣse.
Hrōðgār maþelode,   helm Scyldinga:
'Ne frīn þū æfter sǣlum!   Sorh is genīwod
Denigea lēodum.   Dēad is Æschere,
Yrmenlāfes   yldra brōþor,
mīn rūnwita   ond mīn rǣdbora,
eaxlgestealla,   ðonne wē on orlege
hafelan weredon,   þonne hniton fēþan,

1309 **þone dēorestan . . . wisse** 'knew the dearest one (to be) dead'.

1312 **eorla sum** 'a certain one of the warriors' or perhaps 'the important warrior' (i.e. Beowulf).

1313–14 **bād hwæþer** 'waited (to find out) whether'.

eoferas cnysedan. Swylc scolde eorl wesan,
æþeling ǣrgōd, swylc Æschere wæs!
Wearð him on Heorote tō handbanan
wælgǣst wǣfre; ic ne wāt hwæder
atol ǣse wlanc eftsīðas tēah,
fylle gefægnod. Hēo þā fǣhðe wræc,
þe þū gȳstran niht Grendel cwealdest
þurh hǣstne hād heardum clammum,
forþan hē tō lange lēode mīne
wanode ond wyrde. Hē æt wīge gecrang
ealdres scyldig, ond nū ōþer cwōm
mihtig mānscaða, wolde hyre mǣg wrecan,
ge feor hafað fǣhðe gestǣled,
þæs þe þincean mæg þegne monegum,
se þe æfter sincgyfan on sefan grēoteþ,
hreþerbealo hearde; nū sēo hand ligeð,
se þe ēow wēlhwylcra wilna dohte.
Ic þæt londbūend, lēode mīne,
selerǣdende secgan hȳrde,
þæt hīe gesāwon swylce twēgen
micle mearcstapan mōras healdan,
ellorgǣstas. Ðǣra ōðer wæs,
þæs þe hīe gewislīcost gewitan meahton,
idese onlīcnes; ōðer earmsceapen
on weres wæstmum wræclāstas træd,
næfne hē wæs māra þonne ǣnig man ōðer;
þone on gēardagum Grendel nemdon
foldbūende; nō hīe fæder cunnon,
hwæþer him ǣnig wæs ǣr ācenned

1330 **Wearð him . . . handbanan** 'became his slayer in Heorot'.

1340 **ge feor . . . gestǣled** 'and has avenged the hostility far (i.e. thoroughly)'.

1341 **þæs þe** 'as'. See §177.2 (*f*).

1343 **hreþerbealo hearde** acc. sg., object of *hafað . . . gestǣled* (l. 1340).

1343–4 **nū sēo hand . . . dohte** 'now the hand lies low which did well by you as regards all good things'. Grammatically *sēo þe* rather than *se þe* (l. 1344) is required to agree with *sēo hand*, but the poet was no doubt thinking of the man rather than the feminine hand.

1347 **swylce twēgen** 'two such', i.e. Grendel and his mother.

1349–51 **Ðǣra ōðer . . . ōðer** 'One of them . . . the other.'

1350 **þæs þe hīe gewislīcost** 'as well as they'. See §177.2 (*f*).

1351–2 **idese onlīcnes . . . on weres wæstmum** 'the likeness of a woman (i.e. of a woman's shape) . . . in a man's shape'.

1353 **næfne** 'except that'. See §179.5.

1355–7 **nō hīe fæder . . . gāsta** 'they do not know whether they had any father born of mysterious demons'. Earlier in the poem the poet explains that the Grendelkin are the offspring of Cain, but the Danes, who know nothing of the Bible, are ignorant as to the monsters' parentage.

dyrnra gāsta. Hīe dȳgel lond
warigeað wulfhleoþu, windige næssas,
frēcne fengelād, ðǣr fyrgenstrēam
under næssa genipu niþer gewīteð,
flōd under foldan. Nis þæt feor heonon
mīlgemearces, þæt se mere standeð;
ofer þǣm hongiað hrinde bearwas,
wudu wyrtum fæst wæter oferhelmað.
þǣr mæg nihta gehwǣm nīðwundor sēon,
fȳr on flōde. Nō þæs frōd leofað
gumena bearna, þæt þone grund wite.
Đēah þe hǣðstapa hundum geswenced,
heorot hornum trum holtwudu sēce,
feorran geflȳmed, ǣr hē feorh seleð,
aldor on ōfre, ǣr hē in wille,
hafelan beorgan; nis þæt hēoru stōw!
þonon ȳðgeblond ūp āstīgeð
won tō wolcnum, þonne wind styreþ
lāð gewidru, oð þæt lyft drysmaþ,
roderas rēotað. Nū is se rǣd gelang
eft æt þē ānum. Eard gīt ne const,
frēcne stōwe, ðǣr þū findan miht
sinnigne secg; sēc gif þū dyrre!
Ic þē þā fǣhðe fēo lēanige,
ealdgestrēonum, swā ic ǣr dyde,
wundnum golde, gyf þū on weg cymest.'
Bēowulf maþelode, bearn Ecgþēowes:
'Ne sorga, snotor guma! Sēlre bið ǣghwǣm,
þæt hē his frēond wrece, þonne hē fela murne.
Ūre ǣghwylc sceal ende gebīdan

1357–76 The landscape described here is at once vivid and mysterious. There is a mere or pool surrounded by sheer cliffs with overhanging trees. A waterfall descends into the mere, and concealed behind this waterfall is a cave where Grendel and his mother live. The cave can be reached only by diving into the water and swimming under the waterfall. The Old Norse *Grettissaga*, which tells a story much like that of Beowulf's fight with the Grendelkin, describes the setting with precision.

1362 mīlgemearces 'in measurement by miles'. See §190.5.

1366 fȳr on flōde The fire in the water would be the fire burning in the cave of the Grendelkin (which Beowulf later sees), but to the Danes it is an inexplicable glimmering on the surface of the water.

1366–7 þæs . . . þæt See §168 *þæs . . . þæt* and note 1.

1370–1 ǣr hē feorh . . . wille 'he will sooner give up his life, his spirit, on the shore before he will (go) in'.

1376–7 Nū is se rǣd . . . ānum 'Now the remedy is again dependent upon you alone.'

worolde līfes; wyrce se þe mōte
dōmes ǣr dēaþe; þæt bið drihtguman
unlifgendum æfter sēlest.
Ārīs, rīces weard, uton hraþe fēran,
Grendles māgan gang scēawigan.
Ic hit þē gehāte: nō hē on helm losaþ,
ne on foldan fæþm, ne on fyrgenholt,
ne on gyfenes grund, gā þǣr hē wille!
Ðȳs dōgor þū geþyld hafa
wēana gehwylces, swā ic þē wēne tō.'
Āhlēop ðā se gomela, gode þancode,
mihtigan drihtne, þæs se man gespræc.

(*c*) *The Lament of the Last Survivor*

The last thousand lines of *Beowulf* describe the hero's final battle with a fire-breathing dragon. He is an old man and, having no progeny, the last of his line. The profoundly elegiac tone of this final section of the poem is established by the poet just after the section gets under way. He describes an unnamed man who is the sole survivor of his people, a people who lived in an earlier age long before the time of the poem's action. Since there is no one left to carry on the tribe's history, the heroic ideal of fame as the one means of survival beyond death is rendered meaningless. Having no other use for the treasures of his nation, he decides to bury them, and as there is no one to whom he can address his lament, he addresses it to the earth which is receiving the people's treasure. The speech prefigures the end of *Beowulf*, where the Geatish nation buries a treasure hoard with their slain king (selection 18(d) following). Compare selection 13.

'Heald þū nū, hrūse, nū hæleð ne mōstan,
eorla ǣhte! Hwæt, hyt ǣr on ðē
gōde begēaton. Gūðdēað fornam,
feorhbealo frēcne fȳra gehwylcne

(*b*) 1387–8 **wyrce . . . dēaþe** 'let him who is able achieve fame before death'. This is the ruling ideal of the Germanic heroic ethos.

1392–4 **hē . . . hē** Grammatical gender: masc. *hē* agrees with the antecedent *māgan* (l. 1391).

1395–6 **geþyld . . . gehwylces** 'have patience in each of your afflictions'.

1397–8 **gode þancode . . . gespræc.** See §163.5.

(*c*) 2247 **nū hæleð ne mōstan** For *nū* see §168 *nū* 2.

lēoda mīnra þāra ðe þis līf ofgeaf,
gesāwon seledrēam. Nāh, hwā sweord wege
oððe feormie fǣted wǣge,
dryncfæt dēore; duguð ellor sceōc.
Sceal se hearda helm hyrstedgolde,
fǣtum befeallen; feormynd swefað,
þā ðe beadogrīman bȳwan sceoldon;
ge swylce sēo herepād, sīo æt hilde gebād
ofer borda gebræc bite īrena,
brosnað æfter beorne. Ne mæg byrnan hring
æfter wīgfruman wīde fēran,
hæleðum be healfe. Næs hearpan wyn,
gomen glēobēames, ne gōd hafoc
geond sæl swingeð, ne se swifta mearh
burhstede bēateð. Bealocwealm hafað
fela feorhcynna forð onsended!'

(*d*) *Beowulf's Funeral*

The aged King Beowulf was successful in his fight with the dragon: the creature that had threatened to destroy the Geatish nation was himself destroyed by Beowulf's hand. But in the course of the fight Beowulf received a mortal wound. The poet describes the hero's suffering and death and records his speeches of farewell to his people. The Geats cremate his body in an impressive pagan ceremony, and then we are told in the present selection how they bury his ashes and bid him farewell. The sadness of his funeral is deepened by the people's awareness that with King Beowulf gone the entire nation faces certain destruction by their surrounding enemies, who had been kept at bay only by the protective power of their king. With Beowulf's fall the nation will fall.

Geworhton ðā Wedra lēode
hlǣw on hōe, se wæs hēah ond brād,

(*c*) 2252 **gesāwon seledrēam** Assuming that the *ge*- prefix gave perfective meaning to the verb *sāwon* here, we can translate '(who) had seen the last of joys in the hall'.

Nāh, hwā sweord wege 'I do not have anyone who can bear the sword.' Cf. 12/212 note.

2255–6 **Sceal . . . befeallen** 'Must (be) . . . deprived of'.

2258 **ge swylce** 'and likewise'.

2261 **æfter wīgfruman** 'along with the war-leader'. The corselet is personified and described as a companion of the man.

2262 **Næs** (= *Ne ealles*) 'by no means (is there)'.

wǣglīðendum wīde gesȳne,
ond betimbredon on tȳn dagum
beadurōfes bēcn, bronda lāfe
wealle beworhton, swā hyt weorðlīcost
foresnotre men findan mihton.
Hī on beorg dydon bēg ond siglu,
eall swylce hyrsta swylce on horde ǣr
nīðhēdige men genumen hæfdon;
forlēton eorla gestrēon eorðan healdan,
gold on grēote, þǣr hit nū gēn lifað
eldum swā unnyt swā hit ǣror wæs.
Þā ymbe hlǣw riodan hildedēore,
æþelinga bearn, ealra twelfe,
woldon ceare cwīðan, ond kyning mǣnan,
wordgyd wrecan, ond ymb wer sprecan;
eahtodan eorlscipe ond his ellenweorc
duguðum dēmdon, swā hit gedēfe bið,
þæt mon his winedryhten wordum herge,
ferhðum frēoge, þonne hē forð scile
of līchaman lǣded weorðan.
Swā begnornodon Gēata lēode
hlāfordes hryre, heorðgenēatas;
cwǣdon þæt hē wǣre wyruldcyninga
mannum mildust ond monðwǣrust,
lēodum līðost ond lofgeornost.

3161–2 **swā hyt . . . mihton** 'as splendidly as the very wise men were able to devise it'.

3164 **eall swylce hyrsta** 'all such treasures as'.

on horde 'from the hoard'.

3176 **ferhðum frēoge** 'cherish (him) in (his) heart'. For the dat. pl. *ferhðum* see 14/63 note.

A Note on the Punctuation of Old English Poetry

One thing at least is certain about OE prosaists and poets, scribes and *scops*: they knew nothing of modern punctuation. Yet today modern punctuation is invariably used in OE texts presented to beginners and is probably the norm in scholarly editions. Why? The main reason appears to be the 'inadequacy' of the punctuation of OE manuscripts. This is less true of the prose, where some texts at any rate can be and have been presented with manuscript punctuation, than of the poetry where (as a glance at the facsimile of lines 1–33a of *The Wanderer* printed on page 254 will show) the punctuation can be almost non-existent. But there are good grounds for believing that the use of modern punctuation can distort both the syntax and the meaning of OE texts. The paragraphs which follow deal only with the poetry. But – *mutatis mutandis* – much that is said holds for the prose. Those interested can read further in *Review of English Studies* 31 (1980), 385–413.

A comparison of recordings of various great actors performing such passages as Hamlet's soliloquy 'To be, or not to be' or King Lear's outburst 'Ay, every inch a King' will reveal differences in stress, intonation, and timing, and in the arrangement of breath-groups and sense-groups. At least six contexts can be detected in which different interpretations were or may have been available to a *scop* performing an OE poem.

The first two are the result of the fact that *se* can be a demonstrative meaning 'that one, he', or a relative pronoun meaning 'who' (see §162.3) and that words such as *þa* and *þær* can be adverbs meaning 'then' and 'there' or conjunctions meaning 'when' and 'where' (see §168). The Anglo-Saxons would have distinguished these when speaking, but today we have no way of deciding which we have in any given context. Thus, in selection 12 we cannot be certain whether *þa* in line 5 means 'then' or 'when' or whether *be þam* in line 9 means 'by that' or 'by which'. So we do not know whether we have one sentence or two or three in lines 5–10, which are printed here with no punctuation apart from the initial capital and the final full stop:

þa þæt Offan mæg ærest onfunde
þæt se eorl nolde yrhðo geþolian
he let him þa of handon leofne fleogan
hafoc wið þæs holtes and to þære hilde stop
be þam man mihte oncnawan þæt se cniht nolde
wacian æt þam wige þa he to wæpnum feng.

With the text printed in this way, we can feel that lines 5–10 form a verse paragraph and can see that, if we do not translate, the grammatical questions posed above are not significant. But modern editors, using modern punctuation and thinking in terms of modern sentences rather than of OE verse paragraphs, have to make arbitrary decisions by putting either a comma or a semi-colon (or full stop) after *geþolian* in line 6 and *stop* in line 8. We could signal these ambiguities by using a double comma in these places.

The third of the six contexts referred to above can be illustrated from selection 18(*b*) from *Beowulf*, lines 1392–4:

Ic hit þe gehate: no he on helm losaþ,
ne on foldan fæþm, ne on fyrgenholt,
ne on gyfenes grund, ga þær he wille!

There is a similarity between this and the first two contexts in that we cannot be sure whether *ga þær he wille* is independent of, or subordinate to, what goes before 'Let her go where she will' or '. . . no matter where she intends to go'; see §178.4. (For *he* 'she', see the note on the line.) This difficulty could be similarly resolved by using ,, after *grund*.

We turn now to parentheses, which – it is increasingly being realized – play an important part in the construction of the OE verse paragraph. Space prevents a full exposition of this problem. But we may note that in selection 14 (*The Dream of the Rood*) line 39b *þæt* cannot be a relative pronoun referring to *geong hæleð* – that would require *se* – and that the line is therefore not an apologetic aside 'by the way, he was God Almighty' but a triumphant affirmation:

– þæt wæs God ælmihtig! –

In the verse selections in this *Guide*, the problem of the possible parenthesis is perhaps best illustrated from selection 16 (*The Wanderer*), where both line 50b *sorg bið geniwad* and line 55b *cearo bið geniwad* have been taken as parenthetic. But the punctuation of this poem, especially lines 37–57, must be left for discussion in class or tutorial.

The fifth of our six contexts involves the *apo koinou* construction, seen in its most simple form in a sentence like 'I went out beagling is my favourite pastime', where *beagling* is a common element or *koinon* to two sentences 'I went out beagling' and 'Beagling is my favourite pastime.' Much of the magic and mystery of OE poetry will be lost to the reader insensitive to such constructions. The *koinon* can be a noun, an adjective, a verb, a phrase, or a principal or subordinate clause. Simple examples include two passages from selection 18, viz. 18*a*/753–4 *he on mode wearð // forht on ferhðe* (the *koinon* is *wearð forht*) and 18*b*/1357–8 *Hie dygel lond // warigeað wulfhleoþu* (*warigeað*). Rather more elaborate perhaps is *Andreas* 474:

Ic wille þe,
eorl unforcuð, anre nu gena
bene biddan, þeah ic þe beaga lyt,
sincweorðunga, syllan mihte,
fætedsinces, wolde ic freondscipe,
þeoden þrymfæst, þinne, gif ic mehte,
begitan godne

'And now again, noble warrior, I wish to ask a favour of you, although I can give you few rings, few precious things, little beaten gold, I would (if I could) win your gracious friendship, O glorious prince', where the speaker's poverty makes him both reluctant to ask and fearful of a refusal. When you read lines 49–57 of selection 16, we would urge you to disregard the punctuation and to bear in mind the possibility of taking line 53a *secga geseldan apo koinou*. Similarly, when reading lines 162–8a of selection 12, you could ask yourself such questions as: When and how did the seaman hinder Byrhtnoth? What happened as a result of Byrhtnoth's injury? Why did it happen? If you do, you will see a relationship of time, cause, and effect, in a series of clauses which make a verse paragraph and of which only one – that in line 165 – need be taken as subordinate.

Finally, we turn to what for want of a better term can be called 'enjambment of sense' – the continuation of the sense beyond the end of a (half-) line seen in the *Andreas* passage quoted above, where the sequence *freondscipe . . . þinne . . . godne* gives dramatic emphasis: 'friendship . . . your friendship . . . your gracious friendship', and perhaps in line 151 of selection 12, *The Battle of Maldon*, where

þurh ðone æþelan Æþelredes þegen

can be translated 'through the noble thane of Æthelred', but is better rendered 'through that noble one, the thane of Æthelred'. After patient work with grammar and glossary, we may translate lines 7–8 of the passage from selection 12 printed in the third paragraph of this note thus: 'then he let the dear hawk fly from his hands towards the wood, and advanced to the battle.' But if we take it word by word, it reads: 'he let from him then from hands the dear one fly, the hawk towards the wood, and advanced to the battle.' This version restores to us what has been called 'the excitement of the momentary riddle' experienced by Anglo-Saxon hearers.

Much more could be said about OE poetry, with its technique of repetition with variation and advance, well demonstrated in lines 113–15 of selection 12, where the first half-line summarizes the contents of the three lines, with Wulfmær being identified in the next two first half-lines as a relation and then as a very close relation of Byrhtnoth, and the nature of his wound – fatal, with swords, cruelly cut down – being explained in the three second half-lines. But, as Chaucer said, *shortly for to maken is the best*.

Glossary

Abbreviations are the same as those on p. xvii except that within entries case, number, and gender are indicated with a single initial letter (nsm = nominative singular masculine, gpf = genitive plural feminine, isn = instrumental singular neuter, etc.) and verb classes are identified with a simple numeral, Roman for strong verbs and Arabic for weak, or else with *anom.* for anomalous verbs and *pret. pres.* for preterite present verbs. Thus if an entry word is followed by m. or f., this means it is a masculine noun or a feminine noun. If it is followed by II, this means it is a second-class strong verb, while a 2 would mean it was a second-class weak verb. In analysing verb forms we use an Arabic numeral to indicate person and s or p to indicate singular or plural (3p = third person plural). When verb forms are indicative, no mood is specified, but subjunctives and imperatives are marked subj and imp respectively. Where it seems helpful to do so, we indicate in parentheses the section in the *Guide* where the word or its general type is discussed. Following are abbreviations used in addition to, or instead of, those listed on p. xvii:

anom.	anomalous	pers. n.	personal name
compar.	comparative degree	p ptc	past participle
corr.	correlative	refl.	reflexive object
imp s	imperative singular	superl.	superlative degree
imp p	imperative plural	w.a.	with accusative object
interj.	interjection	w.d.	with dative object
interr.	interrogative	w.g.	with genitive object
MnE	Modern English	w.i.	with instrumental object
num.	numeral	w. refl.	with reflexive object

The letter *æ* follows *a*, *þ/ð* follows *t*. The prefix *ġe-* is ignored in alphabetizing words, so that *ġe***munan** appears under *m*. Occurrences of words are cited by text number and line: 3/25 refers to text number 3 (*A Colloquy on the Occupations*), line 25.

Probably the most difficult element of Old English vocabulary for the beginner is the considerable number of compound conjunctions like **mid þām þe** and **for þon**. Students will find it helpful to familiarize themselves with the list of conjunctions in §§168 and 171 before reading the texts or using the glossary.

This revised glossary was prepared in collaboration with Roy Michael Liuzza of Tulane University and Philip Rusche of Yale University.

ā adv. *forever, always* 4/121, 4/330, 11(e)/6, 12/315, 15/5, 15/42, āwa 17/79, etc.; *ever* 18(a)/779 [archaic MnE aye]

ābǣdan 1 *repel, ward off* pres 3s ābǣd (= ābǣdeð) 11(n)/12

Abbo pers. n. *Abbo* ns 4/128, 4/134

abbod m. *abbot* ns 7/1, 7/19; ds abbode 4/136

abbudisse f. *abbess* ns 9/61; gs abudissan 9/1; ds 9/49

ābēag see **ābūgan**

Abēl pers. n. *Abel* gs Abēles 4/73

ābēodan II *announce, deliver (a message)* imp s ābēod 12/49; pret 3s ābēad 4/162, 12/27

ābīdan I w.g. *await* inf 15/53 [MnE abide]

ābīhð see **ābūgan**

āblendan 1 *blind* inf 7/45

Abraham pers. n. *Abraham* ns 2/46, 2/52; as 2/53, 2/71; gs Abrahames 2/43, 4/6

ābrecan IV *storm, sack* pret 3p ābrǣcon 10(a)/3; subj 3s ābrǣce 11(n)/7; p ptc ābrocen 10(b)/18

ābrēoðan II *fail, come to naught* pret subj 3s ābrēoðe 12/242 (see note)

ābūgan II *yield, give way* inf 4/140, 4/160, etc.; pres 3s ābīhð 4/194; pret 3s ābēag 18(a)/775

abūtan adv. *about, around* 4/277

ac conj. *but, however, but on the contrary* 1/13, 1/33, 2/9, 2/73, 3/11, etc.

āc f. *oak* ns 1/13, acc 11(n)/9

ācennan 1 *bring forth, give birth to, produce* pres 2s ācenst 2/34; p ptc ācenned 3/137, 4/58, 11(m)/1, 18(b)/1356

ācsian 2 *ask* pret 3s āhsode 8/53
āctrēo n. *oak tree* ds 15/28, 15/36
ācwealde see **ācwellan**
ācweccan 1 *shake, brandish* pret 3s ācwehte 12/255, 12/310 [MnE quake]
ācwellan 1 *kill* imp s ācwele 2/63; pret 3s ācwealde 18(a)/886
ācweðan V *utter* pres 3s ācwið 16/91
ācȳþan 1 *make known* inf 16/113
Adam pers. n. *Adam* ns 2/18, 2/20, 2/24; as 2/20; gs Adomes 14/100
ādl f. *sickness, disease* ns 17/70
ādrǣfan 1 *drive out, exile* inf 6/8; pret 3s ādrǣfde 6/4
āfaran VI *depart* p ptc npm āfarene 4/225
āfeallan VII *fall off, fall* (*in death*) p ptc āfeallen (*decayed*) 5/64, 12/202
āfēdan 1 *feed* inf 3/148; pres 2s āfētst 3/120
āferran see **āfierran**
āfētst see **āfēdan**
āfierran 1 *remove* inf **āferran** 10(a)/19
āflȳman 1 *put to flight, cause to flee* pret 3s āflȳmde 12/243
āfȳlan 1 *defile, stain* inf 4/190
āfyllan 1 *fill up* inf 3/19
āfȳsan 1 *impel* inf 12/3 (*drive away*); p ptc āfȳsed 14/125
āgan pret. pres. *possess, own, have* inf 2/76, 10(b)/39, 10(b)/62, 12/87; pres 1s āh 12/175; 3s 14/107, 17/27; subj 3s āge 16/64; 1p āgen 17/117; pret 1s āhte 15/16; 3s 12/189; 3p āhton 10(b)/58. With negative: pres 1s nāh *do not have* 4/123, 14/131; 3s 11(f)/14 [MnE owe]
āġeaf see **āġiefan**
āgen see **āgan**
āgen adj. *own* asm āgenne 6/28; dsm āgenum 4/185; asn āgen 5/33, 11(k)/6; asf āgene 4/105; dsf āgenre 4/20
āġiefan V *give back* pret 3s āgeaf 9/60, 12/44; p ptc āgyfen 12/116.
āglǣca m. *combatant, belligerent* ns 18(a)/732, 18(a)/739, 18(a)/893; ǣglǣca 18(a)/816
agob see **boga**
āgyfen see **āġiefan**
āh see **āgan**
āhāfen see **āhebban**
āhēawan VII *cut down* p ptc āhēawen 14/29
āhebban VI, 1 *raise, lift up, wage* (*war*) imp s āhefe 4/142; pres 3p āhebbað 11(d)/3; pret 1s āhof 14/44; 3s āhefde 2/67, āhof 12/130, 12/244; 1p āhofon 12/213; 3p 10(a)/2, 14/61; p ptc āhafen 12/106, āhefen 10(b)/47
āhlēapan VII *leap up* pret 3s āhlēop 18(b)/1397
āhlēop see **āhlēapan**
āhliehhan VI *laugh at, deride, exult* pret 3s āhlōg 18(a)/730
āhlōg see **āhliehhan**
āhof see **āhebban**
āhofon see **āhebban**
āhreddan 1 *rescue, save* pret 3s **āhredde** 4/79, 7/53
āhsode see **ācsian**
āhte see **āgan**
āhtes see **āwiht**
āhton see **āgan**
āhwǣr adv. *anywhere* 4/233, 7/31
āhyldan 1 *deviate from* pret 3s āhylde 4/141
āīdliġan 2 *render useless, profane* inf 8/55
aldor see **ealdor**
aldordagum see **ealdordæg**
aldorman see **ealdormann**
aldorþeġn see **ealdorþeġn**
ālēag see **ālēogan**
ālecgan 1 *lay down* pret 3s ālegde 18(a)/834, 18(a)/851 (*give up*), 3p ālēdon 14/63 (see note to 4/17)
ālēogan II *leave unfulfilled* pret 3s ālēag 10(b)/39
Aleric see **Ealleric**
ālimpan III *befall, come to pass* p ptc ālumpen 18(a)/733
alle see **eall**
alwalda m. *all-ruler, the Lord* ns 18(b)/1314
ālȳfan 1 *permit, allow* inf 12/90; p ptc ālȳfed 8/62
ālȳsan 1 *release* imp s ālȳs 4/288
Amuling pers. n. *Amuling* ns 10(b)/69; gp Amulinga 10(a)/6
āmyrran 1 *wound* pret 3s āmyrde 12/165 [MnE mar]
ān adj. (§§83, 193.4, 194) *a, an, one, only* nsm 3/33, 4/143, 11(b)/3, 11(k)/3, āne, āna *alone* 4/181, 12/94, 14/123, 14/128, 15/22, 15/35, 16/8; asm ānne 2/66, 3/36, 3/56, 5/18 (ānne ānlēpne *a single one*) ǣnne 4/168, 5/26, etc.; gsm ānes 4/200; dsm ānum 3/104, 4/74, 6/21, etc.; asn 3/205, 5/16; dsn ānum 4/103, 4/207; asf āne 4/253, 5/75, 11(p)/2; dsf ānre 2/46, 4/132, 4/274; npm āne 4/307 (see note); apn ān 9/16; gp ānra (ānra gehwelc *each one*) 3/210, 14/108; as pron. asm ānne 12/117, 12/226
anbīdian 2 *wait, abide* pres ptc andbīdigende (w.g.) 4/263; imp p **anbīdiað** (w. refl. ēow) 2/50
āncenned adj. *only begotten* asm āncennedan 2/44, 2/65; dsm 2/73
and conj. *and* 1/2, 1/3, 1/5, 2/2, 2/5, etc.; ond 5/2, 5/4, etc.
anda m. *malice, hostility* ds andan 16/105, 18(a)/708
andbīdigende see **anbīdian**
andettan 1 *confess* pres 1s andette 8/13, ondette 8/45; pret 3s 8/50

andġit n. *meaning, sense* ns 4/46; as 4/27; ds andgite 4/54, andgiete 5/69.
andġitfullīċe adv. *clearly, intelligibly* superl. andgitfullīcost 5/73
andsaca m. *enemy, adversary* as ondsacan 18(a)/786
andswarian 2 *answer* pres ptc andswarigende 4/239; pres 3s andswaraþ 3/197, 3/204; pret 3s andswarode 8/1, ondsworede 8/56, ondswarede 9/29, ondswarade 9/108; 3p ondswarodon 9/101, ondswaredon 9/114
andswaru f. *answer* as andsware 9/33, 12/44, ondsware 11(n)/15
andweard adj. *present* asm andwerdan 4/263; nsn andwearde 8/26
andwlita m. *face* gs andwlitan 2/40
andwyrdan 1 (w.d.) *answer* inf 4/170; pret 1s andwyrde 5/43; 3s 2/4, 2/55, 2/62, 4/238; p ptc geandwyrd 4/199
ānfeald adj. *simple, onefold* dsf ānfealdan 4/47
ānfealdlīce adv. *in the singular* 4/71
ānfloga m. *solitary flier* ns 17/62
anforht adj. *very frightened, terrified* nsm 14/117
ānforlǣtan VII *abandon, renounce* pret subj 3s ānforlēte 9/63
angel m. *hook* as 3/77, 3/195 [MnE angle]
Angelcynn n. *the English people, England* ns 4/318; as 5/3, 5/30; ds Angelcynne 4/321, 5/14, 5/58
anġinn n. *beginning* ns angin 4/55, 12/242 (see note); ds anginne 4/18, 4/51
ānhaga m. *solitary one, one who dwells alone* ns 16/1
ānhoga m. *solitary one, one who contemplates alone* as ānhogan 16/40
Anlāf pers. n. *Olaf* ns 7/47
*ġe***ānlǣċan** 1 *unite* p ptc npm geānlǣhte 4/150
ānlēpe adj. *single* asn ānlēpne 5/18
ānlīcnes f. *image* ds ānlīcnisse 4/68, 4/70; dp ānlīcnissum 4/71. See **onlīcnes**
ānne see **ān**
ānnis f. *oneness, unity* ns 4/70
ānrǣd adj. *resolute* nsm 4/139, 12/44, 12/132; dsm ānrǣdum 4/216
ānre see **ān**
ansund adj. *whole, uncorrupted* nsm 4/263; asm ansundne 4/312; np ansunde 4/320
anwald see **onweald**
anwealda m. *ruler, Lord* ns 14/153
apostol m. *apostle* ns 4/32; np apostolas 4/36; gp apostola 9/78
ār n. *copper* as 3/142 [MnE ore]
ār m. *messenger* ns 12/26
ār f. *mercy, favour, prosperity* ns 17/107; as āre 16/1, 16/114; gs 10(b)/78; gp āra 10(b)/57
ār f. *oar*
ārās see **ārīsan**
ārǣdan 1 *read* inf 5/61, 5/66; p ptc ārǣd *predetermined, inexorable* 16/5
ārǣran 1 *raise, erect, establish* inf 4/312; pret 3s ārǣrde 2/57, 4/38; 3p ārǣrdon 4/250; p ptc ārǣred 14/44
arċebiscop m. *archbishop* ns arcebisceop 7/16, 7/24, 7/25; ds ærcebiscepe 4/127, 5/70, arcebisceope 7/18
arċestōl m. *archiepiscopal see* ds arcestōle 7/16
āreċċean 1 *translate, render* inf 5/17, 5/73
ārfæstnis f. *piety* ds ārfæstnisse 9/3
ārian 2 w.d. *spare, pardon* inf 2/72, 4/297
ārīsan I *arise* inf 9/113; imp s ārīs 18(b)/1390; pret 3s ārās 2/46, 9/22, 9/45, 14/101
ārlēas adj. *dishonourable* nsm ārlēasa 4/215; dsm ārlēasan 4/199; npm 4/205
ārlīċe adv. *honourably, kindly* 11(k)/6
arodlīċe adv. *quickly* 2/62, 4/162, 4/165, 4/197
Arriān pers. n. *Arius* gs Arriānes 10(b)/40
Arriānisc adj. *Arian* dsm Arriāniscan 10(a)/7
ārweorðe adj. *honourable* dsm ārwurðan 4/274; as noun nsm ārwyrða 10(a)/26
āsǣde see **āsecgan**
asca see **æsc**
Ascanmynster n. *Axminster* as 6/42
āsceacan VI *shake* pret 3s āsceōc 12/230
āsceōc see **āsceacan**
āscian 2 *ask* inf 1/34; pres 1s āscie 2/54; pret 3s āscode 2/54
*ġe***āscian** 2 *learn by asking, learn of, discover* pret 3s geāscode 6/9
*ġe***āscode** see *ġe***āscian**
āsecgan 3 *say, tell* inf 16/11; pret 3s āsǣde 12/198
āsendan 1 *send* p ptc āsend 4/234
āsettan 1 *set, set up* inf 11(k)/11 (sīþas āsettan *to set out on journeys*); pres 1s āsette 3/42, subj 3s 14/142; pret 3p āsetton 14/32
āsingan III *sing, recite* pret 3s **āsong** 9/59
āsmēagan 1 *imagine, understand* inf 4/317
āsong see **āsingan**
āspryttan 1 *sprout, bring forth* pres 3s āspryt 2/39
assa m. *ass* dp assum 2/48, 2/50
āstāg see **āstīgan**
āstandan VI *stand up, get up* pret 3s āstōd 18(a)/759
āstealde see **āstellan**
āstellan 1 *establish* pret 3s **āstealde** 4/83
āstīgan I *proceed, ascend* pres 1s āstīge 3/135, 3s āstīgeð 18(b)/1373; pret 3s āstāg 14/103, 18(a)/782
āstōd see **āstandan**

āstreaht see **āstreċċan**
āstreċċan I *stretch out, extend* imp s āstreċe 2/63; pret 3s āstrehte (w. refl.) 10(a)/30; p ptc āstreaht 10(b)/80
āstyrian I *remove, move* inf 4/282; p ptc āstyred 14/30 [MnE stir]
āswāpan VII *sweep away, remove* pres 1s āswāpe 11(h)/5
ātēah see **ātēon**
ateliċ adj. *horrible, dreadful* nsm 18(a)/784
ātēon II *draw, unsheathe* pret 3s ātēah 2/60, 18(a)/766 (sið . . . ātēah *took a journey*); subj 3s ātuge 9/81
atol adj. *terrible, hateful* nsm 18(a)/732, 18(a)/816, nsn 18(a)/848, 18(b)/1332, asn 17/6
attor n. *venom* as 11(h)/9
ātuge see **ātēon**
ātyhtan I *produce, entice* p ptc ātyhted 10(b)/8, 11(m)/3
āð m. *oath* ap āðas 10(b)/25
āwa see **ā**.
āwearp see **āweorpan**
āweaxan VII *grow up* pret 1s āweox 11(k)/10, 15/3.
āweċċan I *awaken, arouse* pret subj 3s āwehte 9/82
āwēdan I *go mad* pret 3s āwēdde 4/302
āweg see **onweg**
āwel m. *awl* as 3/195
āwendan I *translate, change, distort* inf 4/3, 4/5, 4/101 (*change*); pres 3s āwent 4/103; pret 1s āwende 5/74; 1p āwende 4/133; p ptc āwend 4/6
āweorpan III *throw away, discard* inf āwurpan 4/108; pret 3s āwearp 4/203, 8/59
āweox see **āweaxan**
āwēstan I *lay waste, ravage* pret 3p āwēston 4/151
āwierġan I *curse, damn* p ptc āwierġed 2/29, 2/37, npm āwyrgede 4/326
āwiht n. *aught, anything* gs āhtes 7/28 (see note); ds 3/168 (to āwihte *at all*)
āwrītan I *write* inf 4/100, 4/122 (*copy*); p ptc āwriten 4/77, np āwritene 5/33
āwurpan see **āweorpan**
āwyrgede see **āwierġan**
ǣ f. *law, scripture* ns 4/12, 4/28, 5/48, 10(b)/41; as 4/40; ds 4/10, 4/12, 4/23
æcer m. *cultivated field* as 3/13 [MnE acre]
ǣdre f. *vein* dp ēdrum 18(a)/742
ǣfæst adj. *pious* nsm 9/83; asf ǣfæstan 9/16; apn ǣfæste 9/11
ǣfæstnes f. *religion* ns 8/14; ds ǣfæstnisse 9/3, ǣfæstnesse 9/16
ǣfen m. *evening* as 3/25; ds ǣfenne 9/93
*ġe***æfenlǣcan** I *imitate* inf 4/204
ǣfenspræc f. *evening speech* as ǣfenspræce 18(a)/759
ǣfentīd f. *evening-time* as ǣfentīde 14/68 [archaic MnE eventide]
ǣfre adv. *forever, always, ever* 4/57, 4/66, 4/186, 4/216, 4/295, 5/44, 7/54, etc.
æft see **eft**
æfter adv. *afterwards* 9/43, 17/77
æfter prep. w.d. *after, according to* 4/22, 4/33, 4/54, 5/36, etc.; w.a. *with longing for* 16/50
æftercweðende m. pl. (pres ptc) *those speaking after (a man's death)* gp æftercweðendra 17/72
æfterfylġan I *follow, come after* pres subj 3s æfterfylige 8/35
ǣġhwǣm see **ǣġhwā**
ǣġhwā pron. *every one, everything* dsm ǣghwǣm 18(b)/1384
ǣġhwæþer see **ǣġðer**
ǣġhwæðres see **ǣġðer**
ǣġhweder adv. *in all directions* 7/77
ǣġhwylc pron. *each* nsm 12/234, 18(b)/1386, as ǣghywlcne ānra *every one* 14/86; as adj. nsf 14/120
ǣglǣca see **āglǣca**
ǣġðer pron. *each, both* ns 12/133, 12/224; gs ǣghwæðres 11(a)/5; **ǣġðer ġe . . . ġe** *both . . . and* 2/11, 4/37, 5/37, 7/9, etc., **ǣġhwæþer ġe . . . ġe** 8/2 [MnE either]
Ǣgypta see **Ēgipte**
ǣht f. *possessions, property* as ǣht 13/36; ap ǣhta 4/37, ǣhte 18(c)/2248
ǣl m. *eel* ap ǣlas 3/87
ǣlċ pron., adj. *each, every* nsm 3/164, 4/283; asn ǣlcne 4/280; gsm ǣlces 4/74; dsm ǣlcum 5/74; ism ǣlce 3/8; gsn ǣlces 10(b)/36; dsn ǣlcum 2/3, 4/49; isn ǣlce 4/269; dsf ǣlcre 5/75
ælde m. pl. *men* gp ælda 16/85, 17/77; dp yldum 18(a)/705, eldum 18(d)/3168
ældo see **yldu**
Ælfere pers. n. *Ælfere* ns 12/80
Ælfgār pers. n. *Ælfgar* as 7/45
Ælfnoð pers. n. *Ælfnoth* ns 12/183
Ælfred pers. n. *Ælfred* ns 4/154, 5/1
Ælfrīc see **Ealfrīc**
Ælfrīc pers. n. *Ælfric* gp Ælfrīces 12/209
Ælfstān pers. n. *Ælfstan* ds **Ælfstāne** 7/30
Ælfwine pers. n. *Ælfwine* ns 12/211, vs 12/231
ælmihtig adj. *almighty* nsm 2/72 (se Ælmihtiga *the Almighty*), 4/53, 4/186, 4/311, 14/93, (se Ælmihtiga *the Almighty*) 2/72, 4/186, 14/98, etc.; asm ælmihtigne 14/60, ælmihtigan 4/138, 4/296; dsm Ælmihtigan 4/245, 4/323, ælmihtegum 5/20
*ġe***ǣmetiġan** 2 *free, empty, disengage* pres subj 2s geǣmetige 5/22
ǣmettig adj. *empty* nsm 3/164
ænde see **ende**

ǣniġ adj. *any* nsm 4/24, 4/239, 7/54, etc.; asm ǣnigne 5/20; gsm ǣniges 4/291, ǣnges 17/116; dsm ǣniġum 11(h)/11, 11(h)/15, etc.; asn ǣnig 3/22, 3/35, 9/100, etc.; as pron., nsm 14/110, 14/117, 18(a)/779; hyra ǣnig *any of them* 12/70; isn ǣnige þinga *in any way, by any means* 18(a)/791; as noun 18(b)/1356

ǣnliċ adj. *unique, solitary, beautiful* nsm 11(p)/2

ǣnne see **ān**

ǣr adv. *before, previously* (§§168, 197.4) 5/34, 6/26, 8/75, 9/88, 10(b)/75, 11(f)/12, 11(h)/7, etc.; compar: see **ǣror**; superl: see **ǣrest**; conj. *before* 4/128, 6/11, 11(n)/6, 12/279, 12/300, etc.; w. subj. *rather than* 12/61, *before* 17/74; prep. w.d.i. *before* 17/69; **ǣr þan** (or **þǣm**) (**ðe**) *before* 4/11, 5/28 14/88 [MnE ere]

ǣrænde see **ǣrende**

ǣrċebiscop see **ārċebiscop**

ǣrdæg m. *daybreak, early morning* ds ǣrdæge 18(b)/1311

ǣrende n. *message* as 4/159, 4/161, ǣrænde 12/28 [MnE errand]

ǣrendġewrit n. *letter* as 5/16, 10(b)/63; ap ǣrendgewritu 10(a)/18 [MnE errand, writ]

ǣrendraca m. *messenger, minister* ns 4/160, 4/197; ds ǣrendracan 4/198; dp ǣrendwrecum 5/6

ǣrendwrecum see **ǣrendraca**

ǣrest adj. *first* nsf ǣreste 9/72, 15/6 [archaic MnE erst, erst(while)]

ǣrest adv. *first* 4/35, 4/64, 4/195, 5/48, 7/22, 9/40, etc., ǣrost 12/124, etc.

ǣrġewin n. *ancient hostility* as 14/19

ǣrgōd adj. *good from old times, very good* nsm 18(b)/1329

ǣrist mfn. *resurrection* gs ǣristes 4/263

ærnan I *run, gallop* pret 3p ærndon 12/191

ǣrnemerġen m. *early morning* ds 3/23

ǣror adv. *earlier* ǣrur 14/108, ǣror 18(a)/809, 18(d)/3168

ǣrsceaft n. *ancient work* ns 13/16

ǣr þan þe, ǣr ðǣm ðe see **ǣr**

ǣs n. *bait, food* ds ǣse 3/77; *carrion* ds ǣse 18(b)/1332, gs ǣses 12/107

æsc m. *ash* (*tree*) ns 1/13; *ash* (*spear*) as 12/43, 12/310; gp asca 16/99; dp æscum 4/151

Æscferð pers. n. *Æscferth* ns 12/267

Æschere pers. n. *Æschere* ns 18(b)/1323, 18(b)/1329.

æschere m. *army in ships, viking army* ns 12/69

æscholt n. *spear made of ash* as 12/230

Æscwīġ pers. n. *Æscwig* ds Æscwīge 7/30

æstel m. *pointer used to keep one's place as one reads* ns 5/75

æt prep. w.d. *at, from* 3/10, 4/21, 4/129 (*into*), 5/70, 9/27 (*to*), etc.

*ġe***ǣt** see *ġe***etan**

ætberstan III *escape* pres 1s ætberste 3/139; 3p ætberstaþ 3/105; pret 3s ætbærst 7/35

ætēawed see **atȳwan**

ǣten see **etan**

ætēowian see **ætȳwan**

ætflēogan II *fly away* inf 3/122, 3/124

ætforan prep. w.d. *in front of, before* 12/16

ætgædere adv. *together* 4/307, 9/99, 14/48, ætgædre 11(n)/11; somod ætgædre *together* 16/39, 18(a)/729

æthrīnan I w.g. or d. *touch* pret 3s æthrān 18(a)/722

ætsomne adv. *together* 8/5, 9/93, 11(e)/3

ætstandan VI *stand fixed, stop* pret 3s ætstōd 18(a)/891

ætsteppan VI *step forth* pret 3s ætstōp 18(a)/745

ætstōd see **ætstandan**

ætstōp see **ætsteppan**

ætren see **ættryne**

ætterne see **ættryne**

ættryne adj. *poisoned, fatal, deadly* nsm ætren 11(h)/4, ætterne 12/146; asm ættrynne 12/47

ætwītan I w.d. *reproach* inf 12/220, 12/250

ætȳwan I *appear, show* inf ætēowian 4/300; pres 3s ætyweð 8/35; p ptc æteawed 8/71

Æþeldrȳð pers. n. *Æthelthryth* ns 4/320

æðele adj. *noble* nsm 12/280, 18(b)/1312; æþela 4/215; asm æðelan 12/151; dpm æþelum 4/138

Æþelgār pers. n. *Æthelgar* ns 7/1, 7/16; gs Æþelgāres 12/320

æþeling m. *prince, atheling* ns 4/155, 6/19, 18(b)/1329; as 6/8, 6/14; gs æþelinges 6/42, 18(a)/888; ds æþelinge 10(b)/40, 14/58; gp æþelinga 11(a)/5, 17/93, 18(d)/3170; dp æðelingum 8/76, 10(b)/21

Æþelmǣr pers. n. *Æthelmær* ns 7/13 [MnE Elmer]

æþelo n. pl. *origin, descent, noble lineage* ap 12/216, æþelu 11(n)/8

Æþelred pers. n. *Æthelred* gs Æþelredes 4/127, 12/53, 12/151, 12/203

Æþelstān pers. n. *Æthelstan* ds Æþelstāne 4/130

Æðelwine pers. n. *Æthelwine* ns 7/26

Æþeriċ pers. n. *Ætheric* ns 12/280

*ġe***bād** see *ġe***bīdan**

baldlīce adv. *boldly* 12/311; superl. baldlīcost 12/78

bana m. *slayer* ns 12/299; gs banan 14/66, ds 6/32 [MnE bane]

*ġe***band** see *ġe***bindan**

bānfāg adj. *adorned with bone* asn 18(a)/780

bānloca m. *joint, body* np bānlocan 18(a)/818, ap 18(a)/742

bār m. *wild boar* as 3/56, 3/58, 3/59; ap bāras 3/51

bāt m. *boat* as 3/76; ds bāte 3/99

bāt see **bītan**

baþian 2 *bathe* inf 16/47; pret 3p baþedan 11(f)/6

baþu see **bæð**

Bæbbanburh f. *Bamburgh (Northumberland)* ns 7/39

bæc n. *back* as 12/276 (ofer bæc *away, to the rear*)

bæcere m. *baker* ns 3/162; np bæceras 3/6

bæd see **biddan**

bǣde see **biddan**

bǣl n. *fire, funeral pyre* ds bǣle 17/114

bær see **beran**

*ġe***bǣre** n. *outcry* dp gebærum 6/17

bærnett n. *burning* ds bærnette 2/58, 7/55

*ġe***bǣro** n. *demeanour* as 15/44; is 15/21

bǣron see **beran**

bærst see **berstan**

bæð n. *bath* ds bæðe 8/77; np baþu 13/40, 13/46

be prep. w.d. *about, concerning* 1/35, 3/168, 3/173, 4/31, etc., bī 9/72, etc.; *near, by* 12/152, 12/318, 12/319, big 12/182; be þām *through that* 12/9; be þām þe *as, according as* 2/12; be sūðan see **sūðan**

bēacen n. *beacon, sign, portent, symbol* ns 14/6, as 14/21, as bēcn 18(d)/3160 (*monument*); ds bēacne 14/83; gp bēacna 14/118

bēad see **bēodan**

*ġe***bēad** see *ġe***bēodan**

beadogrīma m. *war-mask, helmet* as beadogrīman 18(c)/2257

beadu m. *battle* ds beaduwe 12/185; gp beadwa 18(a)/709

beadurǣs m. *rush of battle, onslaught* ns 12/111

beadurinc m. *warrior* dp beadurincum 10(b)/18

beadurōf adj. *bold in battle* gsm beadurōfes 18(d)/3160

bēag see **būgan**

bēag m. *ring* (*of precious metal used for money or ornaments*) as 3/70, bēg (as plural) 18(d)/3163, ap bēagas 12/31, 12/160 [MnE (through Yiddish) bagel]

bēaggifa m. *ring-giver, lord* as bēahgifan 12/290

bēaghroden adj. *adorned with rings* nsf 11(j)/9

bēahhord n. *ring-hoard, treasure* gs bēahhordes 18(a)/894

bealo n. *harm, injury, ruin* as (?) 17/112 [MnE bale]

bealocwealm m. *baleful death* ns 18(c)/2265

bealohȳdig adj. *intending evil, hostile* nsm 18(a)/723

bealosīþ m. *painful journey, bitter experience* gp bealosīþa 17/28

bealuware m. pl. *dwellers in iniquity, evildoers* gp bealuwara 14/79

bēam m. *tree, log, cross* ns 14/97; gs bēames 11(n)/7; ds bēame 14/114, 14/122; gp bēama 14/6 [MnE beam]

bearm m. *bosom, lap* on bearm scipes *in the hold of a ship* as 18(a)/896

bearn n. *child, son* ns 12/92, 12/155, 12/186, 12/209, 12/238, etc.; np 10(b)/34, 17/77; ap 3/148, 11(k)/6, 17/93; gp bearna 18(b)/1367; dp bearnum 4/183, 9/40 [MnE bairn]

Bearrocscīr f. *Berkshire* as Bearrocscīre 7/72

bearu m. *grove* ns 11(o)/4; ds bearwe 15/27; np bearwas 17/48, 18(b)/1363; dp bearwum 11(f)/2

bēatan VII *beat, pound* pres ptc gpm bēatendra 3/200; pres 3s bēateð 18(c)/2265; pret 3p bēoton 4/206, bēotan 17/23

beæftan prep. w.d. *behind* 6/24

bebēad see **bebēodan**

bebēodan II (w.d. of person) *command, commend* pres ptc bebēodende 9/124; pres 1s bebīode 5/21, 5/76; pret 1s bebēad 2/24, 2/37; 3s 2/6, 4/87, 4/200, bibēad 9/97; 3p bebudon 9/56; p ptc beboden 4/94, 9/25, 9/60

bebīode see **bebēodan**

beboden see **bebēodan**

bebudon see **bebēodan**

bebyrgan 1 *bury* pret 3p bebyrigdon 4/249; p ptc bebyrged 4/225, 4/255

bēċ see **bōc**

beclyppan 1 *clasp* p ptc beclypped 4/242

bēcn see **bēacen**

becōm see **becuman**

becuman IV *come* pres subj 3p becumen 3/44; pret 3s becwōm 9/121, becōm 4/154, 10(a)/26, 10(b)/77 (*befell*); 2p becōmon 12/58; 3p 4/240, 5/24 (*befell*), 12/58 [MnE become]

becwōm see **becuman**

*ġe***bed** n. *prayer* dp gebedum 4/268

bedǣlan 1 w.d. *deprive* p ptc bedǣled 4/318, 18(a)/721; bidǣled 16/20

bedd n. *bed* ds bedde 4/182

Bedefordscīr f. *Bedfordshire* as Bedefordscīre 7/69

bedelfan III *bury* pret 3s bedealf 14/75

*ġe***bedhūs** n. *chapel, oratory* ds gebedhūse 4/254

bedrīfan I *drive, chase* pret 3p bedrifon 3/60; *cover over, sprinkle* p ptc asm bedrifenne 14/62

beēode see **begān**
befæstan 1 *apply, use* inf 5/24, pres subj 2s befæste 5/24
befeallan VII *fall* p ptc befeallen *deprived, bereft* 18(c)/2256
befēng see **befōn**
befēolan III (§133.2) w.d. *apply oneself* inf 5/59
beflōwan VII *flow around, surround by water* p ptc beflowen 15/49
befōn VII *enclose* pret 3s befēng 13/39
began see **beġinnan**
begān anom. (§128) *practise, perform, surround* inf 1/14; imp s begā 3/213; pres 2s begǣst 3/7, 3/41; subj 1s begā 3/70; 3s 3/211; pret 1s beēode 8/57, 3s 6/11, etc.; 1p beēodon 8/15, beēodan 8/43; 3p biēodon 8/53
begǣst see **begān**
beġeat see **beġietan**
beġēaton see **beġietan**
bēġen m. (§84) *both* np 12/183, 12/191, 12/291, 12/305, 18(a)/769; ap 12/182; gp bēgra 2/14
beġeondan prep. w.d. *beyond* 8/72, begiondan 5/17
beġēotan II *drench, cover* p ptc nsn begoten 14/7 (*covered*); nsm 14/49
beġietan V *get, gain, acquire, lay hold of* inf 3/148, 5/13; pres 1s begiete 3/74; 2s begietst 3/73; 1p begietaþ 3/209; pret 3s begeat 15/32, 15/41, bigeat 17/6; 3p begēaton 5/35, 18(c)/2249
beġinnan III *begin* inf 2/61; pret 3s began 1/14, 4/34
beġiondan see **beġeondan**
begnornian 2 *lament, bemoan* pret 3p begnornodon 18(d)/3178
begong m. *circuit, compass, region* as 18(a)/860
beġoten see **beġēotan**
bēgra see **bēġen**
behātan VII *promise* pret 3p behēton 7/65; subj 3s behēte 7/60
behēafdian 2 *behead* inf 4/216
behealdan VII *behold, gaze at, watch over* pret 1s behēold 14/25, 14/58, 3s 18(a)/736; 3p behēoldon 14/9, 14/11, 14/64
behēawan VII *cut off* inf behēawan 10(b)/43
behēte see **behātan**
behionan prep. w.d. *on this side of* 5/15
behlȳþan 1 *strip, despoil* p ptc behlȳþed 11(j)/10
behrēowsian 2 *repent* pres 3p behrēowsiað 4/92; pret 3s behrēowsode 4/293
behrīman 1 *cover with frost* p ptc behrīmed 15/48
behȳdan 1 *hide, conceal* pret 1s behȳdde 2/22; 3s 2/18; 3p behȳddon 4/223, 4/231; p ptc behȳd 4/220
beinnan adv. *within* 10(a)/26
belāf see **belīfan**
*ġe***belgan** III *enrage* p ptc gebolgen 18(a)/723
belīfan I *remain behind, survive* pres 1s belīfe 4/182; pret 3s belāf 4/152
belimpan III *pertain* pret 3p belumpen 9/4, belumpon 9/16
belocen see **belucan**
belt m. *belt* ns 1/4
belūcan II *contain, lock shut* inf 10(a)/25, 10(b)/73; p ptc belocen 4/47, 6/27
belumpen (= belumpon) see **belimpan**
benam see **beniman**
benċ f. *bench* ds bence 1/11, 12/213
bend mfn. *bond, chain* dp bendum 4/208
Benedict pers. n. *Benedict* gs Benedictes 4/126
beniman IV *deprive* pret 3s benam (w.a. of person and g. of thing) 6/1
benn f. *wound* np benne 16/49
bēo see **bēon**
bēod m. *table* ns 3/164
bēodan II *command, offer* inf 7/74; pres 3s bēodeð (*announce*) 17/54; pret 3s bēad 4/172; 3p budon 6/32
*ġe***bēodan** II *offer* pret 3s gebēad 6/20, 6/28; p ptc geboden 6/34
bēon anom. (§127) *be* inf 3/63, 3/115, 3/130, etc.; infl inf (tō) bēonne 4/289; imp s bēo 3/214, 4/142, 4/166; pres 1s eom 2/22, 3/2, 3/40, etc., bēom 11(d)/8, 11(h)/4; 2s eart 1/36, 2/20, 2/42, 3/39, bist 2/28, 2/35; 3s is 1/1, 1/3, 1/4, 2/5, 2/37, 4/17 (ys), etc.; biþ 1/23, 3/98, 3/177, 4/66, etc.; byð 4/23; 2p bēoð 2/10, bēo 2/8, 3/176; 3p sind 2/4, 3/44, sindon 4/38, siendon 5/79, syndon 8/17, bēoð 2/9, 2/76, 3/79, 3/137, 3/190, 4/290; subj 2s sīe 3/212; 3s sīe 2/54, 3/207, 5/20, 8/12, 8/29, etc., sī 14/144, sȳ 4/330, 12/215, bēo 4/47; 3p sīen 5/55; pret 1s wæs 3/53; 2s wǣre 2/42, 3/52, 3/59, 3/62; 3s wæs 1/31, 2/1, 2/12, 2/73, etc., was 6/8; 3p wǣron 2/16, 4/107, 4/225, 5/18, 7/58, etc.; wǣrun 6/12, 6/16, 6/24, wǣran 11(i)/2; subj 2s wǣre 2/23, 4/189; 3s 4/12, 4/175, 4/257, 4/301, 5/29, 6/34, 8/10, 9/97, etc.; 3p wǣren 5/80, wǣran 8/6. With negative: pres 1s neom 3/21; 3s nis 3/9, 3/173, 4/318, 9/114, 11(e)/1; 3p nearon 17/82; pret 3s næs 4/184, 4/286, 10(b)/43, 12/325; subj 3s nǣre 6/31; 3p nǣren 5/18, nǣron 5/33
beorg m. *mound of stone* as 14/32 (*hill, mountain*), 18(d)/3163; ds beorge 14/50; dp beorgum 13/32
*ġe***beorg** n. *defence* ds gebeorge (*peace*) 12/31, 12/131, 12/245
beorgan III w.d. *save, protect* inf 18(c)/1372; pret 3p burgon 12/194

*ġe***beorgan** III (w.d.) *save, protect* pres subj 2s gebeorge 4/179

beorghliþ n. *mountain-slope* dp beorghleoþum 11(f)/2

beorht adj. *bright* npn 13/21; nsf 16/94; asm beorhtne 11(j)/7; asf beorhtan 13/37; dsm 13/40, 14/66; apf beorhte 18(a)/896; superl. beorhtost 14/6

beorn m. *man, warrior* ns 10(b)/52, 13/32, 14/42, 16/70, 16/113, 17/55; as 12/270; gs beornes 12/131, 12/160; ds beorne 12/154, 12/245, etc.; np beornas 12/92, 12/111, 14/32, etc.; ap beornas 12/17, 12/62, 12/182, etc.; gp beorna 12/257; dp beornum 12/101

*ġe***bēorscipe** m. *feast, beer party* gs gebēorscipes 9/24; ds gebēorscipe 9/20, 9/30

bēot n. *vow, boast, threat* as 12/15, 12/27 (on bēot *threateningly*) 12/213, 16/70

bēotan see **bēatan**

bēotian 2 *vow* pret 3s bēotode 12/290; 1p bēotedan 15/21

bēotlic adj. *boastful, threatening* asn 4/159

bēoton see **bēatan**

Bēowulf pers. n. *Beowulf* ns 18(b)/1310, 18(b)/1383; gs Bēowulfes 18(a)/795, 18(a)/856, 18(a)/872; ds Bēowulfe 18(a)/818

bepǣċan 1 *deceive* pret 3s bepǣhte 2/27

berād see **berīdan**

beran IV *carry, bear, bring* inf 2/52, 11(n)/2, 12/12, 12/62; imp p berað 9/104; pres 3s bereð 14/118, byreð 11(d)/6, 11(j)/5; pret 3s bær 2/53, 18(a)/711, 18(a)/846, etc.; 3p bǣron 12/99, 14/32; subj 3p bēron 12/67

berēofan II *destroy, ravage* p ptc berofen 13/4

berīdan I *ride up to, overtake* pret 3s berād 6/11

berofen see **berēofan**

berstan III *burst, fall apart* inf 14/36; pret 3s bærst 12/284; 3p burston 13/2 (transitive: *smashed, broke*), 18(a)/760, 18(a)/818

besārgian 2 *regret* pret 3s besārgode 4/295

beseah see **besēon**

besenċan 1 *cause to sink, drown* inf 3/104

besēon V *look* pret 3s beseah 2/66, 4/173

besettan 1 *cover, beset* p ptc beset 4/213

besmiþian 2 *fasten* p ptc besmiþod 18(a)/775

bestalcode see **bestealcian**

bestandan VI *stand alongside* pret 3p bestōdon 12/68

bestealcian 2 *move stealthily, stalk* pret 3s bestalcode 4/157

bestēman 1 *make wet, drench* p ptc bestēmed nsm 14/48, nsn 14/22

beswīcan I *ensnare, deceive* pres 1s beswīce 3/109; 2s beswīcst 3/108; p ptc apm beswicene 12/238

beswillan 1 *drench, soak* p ptc beswyled nsn 14/23

besyrwan 1 *ensnare, entrap* inf 18(a)/713

*ġe***bētan** 1 *improve, remedy* pret 3s gebētte 18(a)/830

betǣċan 1 *entrust, deliver* pres 1s betǣċe 3/31; pret 3s betǣhte 7/28

betǣhte see **betǣċan**

bētend m. *tender, rebuilder, restorer* np 13/28

betera adj. (compar. of gōd; cf. §76) *better* nsn betre 5/54, nsm betera (as noun *the better* [*one*]) 12/276; nsn betere 12/31; apn beteran 8/22

betimbran 1 *build* pret 3p betimbredon 18(d)/3159

betliċ adj. *excellent, splendid* asn 18(a)/780

betræppan 1 *entrap* inf 7/31

betre see **betera**

betst adj. (superl. of gōd; cf. §76) *best* nsn 17/73 (as noun); isn betstan 9/59

betwēonan prep. w.d. *between* 1/24

betweox, betwux prep. w.d. *between, among* 2/29, 2/31, 2/67, 3/188, 3/207, 4/17, betwux 4/142, 4/210, 10(a)/3; betwux þām þe *while* 4/217 [MnE betwixt]

betȳnan 1 *close, conclude* pret 3s betȳnde 9/86, 9/124

beþurfan pret. pres. w.g. *need* pres 1p beþurfon 3/168

beweaxan VII *grow over* p ptc npm beweaxne 15/31

bewerian 2 *protect* infl. inf. (tō) bewerigenne 4/235

bewindan III *wind around, envelop* p ptc bewunden 11(o)/2, 14/5

bewiste see **bewitan**

bewitan pret pres *guard* pret 3s bewiste 4/241

beworhton see **bewyrcan**

bewrēon I *cover* pret 3s biwrāh 16/23; p ptc bewrigen 14/17, 14/53

bewunden see **bewindan**

bewyrcan 1 *build around, surround* pret 3p beworhton 18(d)/3161

bī see **be**

bibēad see **bebēodan**

*ġe***bīcnian** 2 *signify, indicate* p ptc gebīcnod 4/69

bīdan I w.g. *await* inf 9/115, 17/30 (*remain*); pret 3s bād 18(a)/709, 18(b)/1313 (*remain*) [MnE bide]

*ġe***bīdan** I w.g. *await, experience* inf 16/70, 18(b)/1386; pres 3s gebīdeð 16/1; pret 1s gebād 12/174, 14/125, 15/3; 3s 13/9, 18(a)/815, 18(c)/2258; p ptc gebiden 14/50, 14/79, (w.a.) 17/4, 17/28

bidǣled see **bedǣlan**

biddan V *ask, bid* pres ptc biddende 4/296; pres 1s bidde 4/121; subj 2s 4/120; pret 2s bǣde 4/2; 3s bæd 4/295, 8/60, 10(b)/64, 12/20, 12/128, 12/170, 12/257; 3p bǣdon 9/108,

10(a)/22, 12/87, 12/262, 12/306; subj 3s bǣde (w.g.) 9/96 [MnE bid]

*ġe***biddan** V *pray* infl inf (to) gebiddenne 2/51; pres 3p gebiddaþ (w. refl. d.) 14/83; pret 1s gebæd (w. refl. d.) 14/122; 3s 9/115

bidrēosan II *deprive* p ptc bidroren nsm 17/16; npm bidrorene 16/79

bidroren see **bidrēosan**

bielg m. *bellows, leather bag* gp bielga 3/201 [MnE belly]

biēodon see **begān**

bifian 2 *shake, tremble* inf 14/36; pret 1s bifode 14/42

biforan prep. w.d. *in front of* 16/46 [MnE before]

big see **be**

bigang see **bigong**

bigeal see **bigiellan**

*ġe***bīgean** 1 *bend* inf 4/116

biġeat see **beġietan**

biġgeng m. *worship, service* dp biggengum 4/186

biġiellan III *scream round about, yell against* pret 3s bigeal 17/24

bīgong m. *worship* ns 8/10; gs bīgonges 8/70; ds bīgange 8/16, 8/44

bihōn VII *hang around* (*with*) p ptc w.i. bihongen 17/17

bihongen see **bihōn**

bihrēosan II *cover* p ptc npm bihrorene 16/77

bīleofa m. *sustenance, food* as bīleofan 3/74, 3/209

bilewit adj. *innocent* isn bilwitre 9/119; ap bilewitan 4/158

bill n. *sword* as 12/162; dp billum 12/114

bilwitre see bilewit

*ġe***bind** n. *binding, commingling* as 16/24, 16/57

bindan III *bind* inf 4/201; pres 1s binde 11(f)/16; 3s bindeð 11(g)/7, 16/102; 3p bindað 16/18; subj 3s binde 16/13; pret 3s bond 17/32; p ptc gebunden apn 18(a)/871

*ġe***bindan** III *bind, hold fast* pres 3p gebindað 4/178, 16/40; pret 3s ġeband 2/59, 4/280, gebond 13/19; 3p gebundon 4/206; p ptc gebunden 4/284, npm 17/9

bindere m. *binder* ns 11(f)/6

biniman IV *deprive* p ptc binumen 11(f)/14

binn f. *bin, manger* as binne 3/18

binnan prep. w.d. *within, in* 2/3, 4/92, 4/133

binumen see **biniman**

biscepstōl m. *episcopal see* ds biscepstōle 5/74, bisceopstōle 7/2

biscop m. *bishop, high priest* ns bisceop 4/170, 4/272, 4/293, 7/16, 7/30 (see note), 8/7; as biscep 5/1, bisceop 4/168, 8/40; ds biscepe 5/70, bisceope 4/285, 7/1, biscope 8/50, 8/52; dp bisceopum 4/289

bisgu f. *occupation, concern, care* as 17/88; dp bisgum 5/67 [MnE busy]

bismor see **bysmor**

bīsnian 2 *set an example, instruct by example* inf 4/42

*ġe***bīsnian** 2 *set an example* pret 3s gebȳsnode 4/191

*ġe***bīsnung** f. *example* dp gebȳsnungum 4/204

bistelan IV *deprive of* p ptc bistolen 11(f)/13

bītan I *bite* pret 3s bāt 18(a)/742

bite m. *bite, cut* as 18(c)/2259

biter adj. *bitter, grim, fierce* nsm 12/111; gsm biteres 14/114; asf bitre 17/4, bitter 17/55; npm bitre 15/31; apm bitere 12/85

biþ see **bēon**

biwāune see **biwāwan**

biwāwan VII *blow upon* p ptc npm biwāune 16/76

biwrāh see **bewrēon**

blācian 2 *grow pale* pres 3s blācað 17/91

blanca m. *white (or grey) horse* dp blancum 18(a)/856

*ġe***blandan** VII *taint, infect, corrupt* p ptc geblonden 11(h)/8

blāwan VII *blow* pres ptc gpm blāwendra 3/200

blæc adj. *black* npn blacu 11(l)/3

blǣd m. *glory, wealth* ns 16/33, 17/79, 17/88; dp blēdum (*blessings*) 14/149

blēdum see **blǣd**

blēo n. *colour* dp blēom 14/22

bletsian 2 *bless* pres 1s bletsie 2/74; p ptc gebletsode 2/77

bletsung f. *blessing* ds bletsunge 2/79

bliss f. *bliss, joy, happiness* ns blis 14/139, 14/141; ds blisse 14/149, 14/153, gs 9/20 (*merriment*)

blīðe adj. *friendly, cheerful* asn 9/105, 15/44; isn 14/122, 15/21; np 9/108; compar. blīðra *happier* nsm 12/146 [MnE blithe]

blīðelīce adv. *gladly* 4/192

blīðemōd adj. *friendly* nsm 9/109; np blīðemōde 9/107

blōd n. *blood* ns 4/73, as 18(a)/742; ds blōde 4/190, 14/48, on blōde *bloody* 18(a)/847

blōdiġ adj. *bloody* asm blōdigne 12/154

*ġe***blonden** see *ġe***blandan**

blōstma m. *blossom* dp blōstmum 17/48

blōwan VII *bloom* pres ptc nsm blōwende 11(o)/4 [MnE blow 'blossom']

bōc f. *book* ns 4/44, 4/133, booc 9/72; as 4/3; gs bēc 4/5; ds 4/67, 4/132, 4/293; ap 5/41, 5/50; gp bōca 4/49, 5/30, 9/75, 10(b)/52

bōccræft m. *literature, scholarship* dp bōccræftum 10(a)/13 [MnE book-craft]

bōcere m. *scholar* ap bōceras 9/5

boda m. *messenger* ns 12/49

bodian 2 *preach* infl inf (tō) bodienne 4/34;

pret 3s bodade 8/41, p ptc bodad 8/12, 8/22 [MnE bode]
bodig n. *body* ds bodige 4/228, 4/248
boga m. *bow* nsm agob (reverse spelling) 11(h)/1; np bogan 12/110
*ġe***bohte** see *ġe***bycgan**
*ġe***bohtest** see *ġe***bycgan**
Boētius pers n. *Boethius* ns 10(a)/12, Boītius 10(b)/52; gs Boētius 10(b)/75
bolgenmōd adj. *enraged* ns 18(a)/709
bolster n. *pillow* ds bolstre 9/117 [MnE bolster]
bond see **bindan**
*ġe***bond** see *ġe***bindan**
bonnan VII *summon* pres 1s bonne 11(j)/4
bord n. *board, side of a ship* as 1/2; *shield* ns 12/110; as 12/15, 12/42, 12/131, etc.; ap 12/62, 12/283; gs bordes 12/284; gp borda 12/295, 18(c)/2259; dp bordum 11(j)/9 (*tables*), 12/101
bordweall m. *shield-wall* as 12/277
*ġe***boren** m. (p ptc) *one born in the same family, brother* ds geborenum 17/98
bōsm m. *bosom* as 11(j)/9; ds bōsme 11(h)/3, 11(j)/15, 13/40
bōt f. *remedy* as bōte 16/113 [MnE boot 'compensation']
brād adj. *broad, wide, spacious* ns 18(d)/3157; asn 12/15, 12/163; gsn brādan 13/37
bræc see **brecan**
*ġe***bræc** n. *crashing* ns 12/295, as 18(c)/2259
*ġe***brǣcon** see *ġe***brecan**
brǣd see **breġdan**
brǣdan 1 *roast, broil* inf 3/174; infl inf (tō) brǣdanne 3/175
brǣdan 1 *spread* inf 16/47
*ġe***bræġd** see *ġe***breġdan**
brēac see **brūcan**
breahtm m. *noise, revelry* gp breahtma 16/86
brecan IV *break* pres 3s briceð 11(g)/6; pret 1s bræc 1/17; 3s 12/277; p ptc brocen 12/1
*ġe***brecan** V *shatter, smash* pret 3p gebrǣcon 13/1; p ptc gebrocen 13/32
breġdan III *weave, knit, braid* pres 1s breġde 3/42; *pull, drag, fling, draw* (*a sword*) inf 18(a)/707, pret 3s brǣd 12/154, 12/162, brægd 18(a)/794
*ġe***breġdan** III *weave together, conceive* pret 3s gebrægd 13/18
brēmel m. *bramble, brier* ap brēmelas 2/39, 4/233; dp brēmelum 2/67, 4/224
brenġan 1 *bring* pres subj 3s brenge 8/37
brēost n. *breast* ds brēoste 2/30; dp (w. sg. meaning) brēostum 12/144, 14/118, 16/113
brēostcearu f. *grief of heart* as brēostceare 15/44, 17/4
brēostcofa m. *heart* ds brēostcofan 16/18
brēosthord n. *inmost feelings* as 17/55
brēr m. *brier* dp brērum 15/31
Bretwālas m. pl. *the Britons* dp Bretwālum 6/7
briceð see **brecan**
bricg f. *bridge, causeway* as bricge 12/74, 12/78; ds brycge 1/9
bricgweard m. *guardian of the bridge* ap bricgweardas 12/85
bridd m. *young bird* ap briddas 3/122
Brihtnōð pers. n. *Brihtnoth* ns 7/21. See also **Byrhtnōð**
brim n. *sea, water* ns 18(a)/847
brimfugol m. *seabird* ap brimfuglas 16/47
brimlād f. *sea-way, path of ocean* ds brimlāde 17/30
brimlīðend m. *seafarer, Viking* gp brimlīðendra 12/27
brimmann m. *seafarer, Viking* np brimmen 12/295; gp brimmanna 12/49
bringan 1 *bring* pres 3s bringeð 16/54; subj 3s bringe 4/124; pret 3s brōhte 4/85; 3p brōhton 4/86, 4/275; p ptc brungen 11(f)/2
*ġe***bringan** 1 *bring* inf 10(a)/20, 10(a)/25; pres subj 3s gebringe 14/139; p ptc npm gebrōhte 4/284
brocen see **brecan**
*ġe***brocen** see *ġe***brecan**
brōga m. *terror* ds brōgan 7/23
brōhte, brōhton see **bringan**
brond m. *burning, fire* gp bronda 18(d)/3160 [MnE brand]
brosnian 2 *decay* pres 3s brosnað 13/2, 18(c)/2260; pret 3s brosnade 13/28
broþ n. *broth* as 3/172
*ġe***brōðru** see **brōðor**
brōðor m. (§60) *brother* ns brōðor 12/282, 17/98, 18(b)/1324, brōðer 4/19, 9/1, brōþur 6/9; np 9/109, 9/113, brōðru 12/191, gebrōðru 12/305
brūcan II (w.g.) *enjoy, use, benefit from, eat* inf 3/158, 3/159, 3/162, 4/176, 14/144, 18(a)/894; pres 2s brȳcst 2/40; 3p brūcað 17/88; pret 3s brēac 10(b)/75, 16/44 [MnE brook]
brūneccg adj. *with shining blade* asn 12/163
brungen see **bringan**
brycge see **bricg**
brȳcst see **brūcan**
bryhtm m. *blink* ns 8/33
bryne m. *burning, fire* as 14/149
brytta m. *bestower, one who gives* as bryttan 16/25
Bryttisc adj. *British* dsm Bryttiscum 6/21
būan 1 *inhabit, dwell* pres 1s būge 11(d)/2
Buccingahamscīr f. *Buckinghamshire* as Buccingahamscīre 7/69
budon see **bēodan**
būgan II *bend, turn away, submit* inf 12/276,

14/36, 14/42; pres subj 2s būge 4/180; pret 3s bēag 13/17; 3p bugon 12/185
ġe**būgan** II *submit, yield* pres subj 3s gebūge 4/196; pret subj 3s gebuge 4/172
būge see **būan**
ġe**bunden** see ġe**bindan**
bune f. *goblet, cup* ns 16/94
būr m. *chamber, cottage* as 6/11; ds būre 18(b)/1310 [MnE bower]
burg f. *stronghold, enclosure* as burh 7/49, 12/291, burig 10(a)/3, burg 11(n)/7, 13/37 (*city*); ds byrig 6/26, 10(b)/37, 10(b)/46; ap byrig 17/48; gp burga 10(b)/18; dp burgum 17/28 [MnE borough]
burgon see **beorgan**
burgræced n. *city building* np 13/21
burgsteall n. *city* ns 13/28
burgstede m. *city* as 13/2, burhstede 18(c)/2265 (*courtyard pavement*)
burgtūn m. *protecting hedge* np burgtūnas 15/31
burhwaru f. *citizenry, population* ns 7/4, 7/51; ds burhware 7/53; gp burgwara 16/86
buriġ see **burg**
burnsele m. *bathing hall* np 13/21
būrþēn m. *servant of the bower, chamberlain* ds būrþēne 12/121
burston see **berstan**
būtan prep. w.d. *without, except, but, only* 3/46, 3/47, 3/158, 3/160, būton 4/45, 4/75, 6/2, etc., 7/17 (w.a. *only*); conj (§179.5) w. ind. *except, only* 4/5, 4/21, w. subj. *unless* 3/115, 3/161, 4/179, 4/195, 12/71, etc.
butere f. *butter* ns 3/160; as buteran 3/26
būton see **būtan**
būtū n. dual *both* acc. 14/48
bycgan 1 *buy* pres 1s bycge 3/136, 3/151; 3s bygþ 3/83
ġe**bycgan** 1 *buy* pret 1s gebohte 3/147; 2s gebohtest 3/145
byden f. *tub* ds bydene 11(f)/6
byht n. *dwelling* ap 11(d)/3
byldan 1 *encourage, embolden* pret 3s bylde 12/169, 12/209, 12/320; pres subj 3s bylde 12/234
byldu f. *arrogance, boldness* ds bylde 4/200
ġe**byrað** see ġe**byrian**
byre m. *opportunity* as 12/121
byreð see **beran**
byrġan 1 *bury* inf 17/98
byrġen f. *burial place, grave* ds byrgene 4/254, 4/267; dp byrgenum 4/327
Byrhtelm pers. n. *Byrhtelm* gs Byrhtelmes 12/92
Byrhtnōð pers. n. *Byrhtnoth* ns 12/17, 12/42, 12/101, etc.; as 12/257; gs Byrhtnōðes 12/114. See also **Brihtnōð**
Byrhtwold pers. n. *Byrhtwold* ns 12/309

ġe**byrian** 1 *befit, be proper to* pres 3s gebyrað 4/290
byriġ see **burg**
byriġan 1 *taste* pret 3s byrigde 14/101
byrnan III *burn* pres ptc nsf byrnende 11(o)/4
byrne f. *corselet, coat of mail* ns 12/144, 12/284; as byrnan 12/163; gs 18(c)/2260 [MnE byrnie]
byrnwiga m. *mailed warrior* ns 16/94
byrst f. *bristle* np byrsta 4/214
bȳsen f. *exemplar, original, example* ds bȳsne 4/123, bȳsene 8/57
bysiġ adj. *busy* npm bysige 12/110
bysiġian 2 *afflict, occupy, trouble* p ptc gebysgad 11(o)/3 [MnE (to) busy]
bysmerian 2 *mock, revile* pret 3p bysmeredon 14/48
ġe**bysmerian** 2 *mock* pret 3p gebysmrodon 4/206
bysmor m. *disgrace* ds bysmore 4/158 (tō bysmore *shamefully*), bismore 7/34
bysmorful adj. *shameful* dp bysmorfullum 4/190
ġe**bȳsnode** see ġe**bīsnian**
ġe**bȳsnungum** see ġe**bīsnung**
bȳwan 1 *polish, adorn, prepare* inf 18(c)/2257

cāf adj. *brave, quick, vigorous* asm cāfne 12/76
cāfliċe adv. *bravely, boldly* 12/153
cald n. (*the*) *cold* is calde 17/8
cald adj. *cold* asn 12/91, dp caldum 17/10; superl. caldast nsn 17/33
ġe**camp** m. *battle* ds gecampe 12/153
cann see **cunnan**
canōn m. *canon* gs canōnes 9/74; np canōnas 4/288
canst see **cunnan**
carcern n. *prison, dungeon* as carcerne 10(a)/25; ds 10(a)/29, 10(b)/73
care see **cearo**
cāsere m. *emperor* ns 10(b)/20, 10(b)/61, kāsere 10(a)/22; ds kāsere 10(a)/21; np cāseras 17/82; dp cāserum 10(a)/17 [MnE caesar]
ceallian 2 *call out, shout* inf 12/91
ġe**ċēapian** 2 *buy* pres 3s geceāpaþ 11(h)/13
cearo f. *care, trouble, sorrow* ns 16/55; as ceare 16/9, 18(d)/3171; np ceare 17/10
cearseld n. *abode of care* gp cearselda 17/5
ġe**ċēas** see ġe**ċēosan**
ċeaster f. *town* as ceastre 10(b)/66, ds 3/82 [MnE (Win)chester, (Man)chester, etc.]
ċeasterbūend m. *city-dweller* dp ceasterbūendum 18(a)/768
ċeasterware f. pl. *city-dwellers* np 3/84
Cedmon pers. n. *Cædmon* ns 9/28
Cēfi pers. n. *Cefi* ns 8/11, 8/39

cellod adj. see note to 12/283
cempa m. *warrior, champion* ns 3/213, 12/119, 18(b)/1312
cēne adj. *keen, brave* nsm 4/162, 4/181, 12/215, gpm cēnra 18(a)/768; compar. cēnre nsf 12/312
cēne adv. *boldly, bravely* 12/283
Centland n. *Kent* ds Centlande 7/56
cēol m. *keel, ship* ds ceole 17/5
Cēola pers. n. *Ceole* gs Cēolan 12/76
ceorfan III *carve, hew out* inf 4/269; pret 3p curfon 14/66
ċeorl m. *peasant, yeoman, free man of the lowest rank* ns 3/213, 12/256; as 11(f)/8; ds ceorle 12/132 [MnE churl]
*ġe***ċēosan** II *choose* pret 3s gecēas 4/35, 12/113; p ptc nsn gecoren 9/53 (*decided*), npm gecorene 4/290, dpm gecorenum (*chosen ones, disciples*) 4/31
cēpan 1 (w.g.) *seize* inf 4/201
Cerdiċ pers. n. *Cerdic* ds Cerdice 6/43
ċicen n. *chicken* ns 1/6
ċiele m. *chill, cold* ds 3/16
ċīepan 1 *sell* pres 2s cīepst 3/81
ċīepemann m. *merchant* np cīepemenn 3/5
*ġe***ċierran** 1 *return* pret 3s gecierde 2/79
ċīese m. *cheese* ns 3/161; as 3/26
ċild n. *child* ns 2/51; as 2/63; ap 2/34, 4/158
*ġe***cinde** see *ġe***cynd**
cinn see **cynn**
ċiriċe f. *church* as cyrcan 4/250, 4/253; ds 4/256, cirice 1/10; np ciricean 5/29
clammum see **clomm**
clǣne adj. *clean, pure* dsm clǣnum 4/258; nsn clǣne 9/67; asn 17/110; dsn clǣnum 4/265; apm clǣnan 3/80; dpm clǣnum 4/315; apf clǣnan 4/191
clǣne adv. *utterly, entirely* 5/14 [MnE clean]
clǣnnis f. *purity, cleanness* ds clǣnnisse 4/38
cleofa m. *cellar, pantry* as cleofan 3/159
clēofan II *split, cleave* pret 3p clufon 12/283
cleopode see **clipian**
clif n. *cliff* dp clifum 17/8
clipian 2 *call, summon, cry out* pres ptc clypigende 4/236; pret 3s clipode 2/20, 2/43, 2/61, 2/71, 4/73, clypode 4/168, 4/209, 4/286, 8/42, 12/25, 12/256, cleopode 10(b)/83 [archaic MnE clepe, yclept]
clomm m. *grip, fetter* dip clommum 17/10, clammum 10(b)/83, 18(b)/1335
clūstor n. *prison* ds clūstre 10(b)/73
clypiġende see **clipian**
clyppan 1 *embrace* inf 9/61; pres subj 3s clyppe 16/42 [MnE clip]
clypode see **clipian**
clypung f. *shout, calling out* ap clypunga 4/240
cnapa m. *servant, boy* as cnapan 3/15; dp cnapum 2/47, 2/50, 2/78 [MnE knave]
*ġe***cnāwan** VII *understand* inf 5/56 [MnE know]
cnēo n. *knee* as 16/42; *generation* gp cnēa 13/8
cniht m. *boy, youth, squire, servant* ns 1/9, 12/9, 12/153 [MnE knight]
cnōdan VII *to be committed (to)* p ptc gecnōden 10(b)/32
cnossian 2 *toss, dash, drive* pres 3s cnossað 17/8
cnyssan 1 *dash against, batter* pres 3p cnyssað 16/101, 17/33 (fig. *urge, press*); pret 3p cnysedan (*clashed*) 18(b)/1328
cōc m. *cook* ds **cōce** 3/167
cōlian 2 *cool* pret 3s cōlode 14/72
collenferð adj. *stout-hearted* nsm 16/71
cōm see **cuman**
cōmen see **cuman**
cōmon see **cuman**
con (= **cann**) see **cunnan**
const see **cunnan**
Constentinopolim f. *Constantinople* ds 10(a)/21
consul m. *consul* ns 10(a)/12
*ġe***coren** see *ġe***ċēosan**
corn n. *kernel, grain* gp corna 17/33 [MnE corn]
crabba m. *crab* ap crabban 3/93
*ge***cranc** see *ge***cringan**
cræft m. *trade, skill, force* ns 3/151, 3/163; as 3/1, 3/7, 3/41, etc.; gs cræftes 3/168; ds cræfte 3/73, 3/151, 3/155, 4/81, 4/276 [MnE craft]
Crēacas m. pl. *the Greeks, Greece* npm 5/49, 10(b)/48; ap Crēacas 10(b)/56, Crēcas 10(b)/21, Crēcas 10(b)/61; gp Crēca 10(a)/21, 10(b)/66; dp Crēcum 10(b)/26
crincgan III *fall, perish* inf 12/292; pret 3p cruncon 12/302, crungon 13/25, 13/28 [MnE cringe]
*ġe***cringan** III *fall, perish* pret 3s gecranc 12/250, 12/324, gecrang 18(b)/1337, gecrong 13/31 (*fell to*), 16/79
Crīst pers. n. *Christ* ns 4/33, 4/323, 4/328, 14/56; as 4/212, 4/328; gs Crīstes 4/29, 4/204, 4/210, 8/77; ds Crīste 1/35, 4/30, 4/191, 4/195, 4/266, 8/5, 10(b)/32, 14/116
Crīsten adj. *Christian* nsm 4/23, 10(a)/6; np Crīstne 5/27; ap Crīstenan 4/158; npf Crīstna 5/53
crīstendōm m. *Christendom, Christianity* ds crīstendōme 10(a)/23, crīstenandōme 10(a)/15
*ġe***crong** see *ġe***cringan**
crungon see **crincgan**
cuǣdon see **cweðan**
culter m. *coulter, a cutting blade on a plough* as 3/12, 3/193

cuman IV *come* inf 4/276, 8/61, cumon 7/33, etc.; pres 1s cume 3/45; 2s cymest 18(b)/1382; 3s cymeð 8/34, 16/103, 17/61, etc.; 1p cumað 2/52; 3p 4/178; subj 3s cume 8/30; 1p cumen 17/118, pret 3s cōm 2/17, 4/34, 4/126, 4/202, 7/40, etc., cwōm 9/58, 11(b)/1, etc.; 3p cōmon 2/56, 4/72, 4/246, 4/273, 7/10, cwōman 13/25, etc.; subj. 3s cōme 4/314, cwōme 18(a)/731; 3p cōmen 10(b)/66; p ptc cuman 9/53, cumen 12/104, 14/80
Cumbra pers. n. *Cumbra* as Cumbran 6/6
cumon see **cuman**
cunnan pret. pres. *know, know how to, can* pres 1s cann, 3/36, 3/47, 3/115, 3/130, con 9/29; 2s canst 3/1, 3/35, 3/37, const 18(b)/1377, etc.; 3s can 4/106; 1p cunnon 5/36, cunnun 8/36; 3p cunnon 3/3, 4/27, etc.; subj 3s cunne 16/69 (*have knowledge*), 16/71, 16/113; 3p cunnen 5/61; pret 1s cūðe 9/31; 3s 4/14; 1p cūðon 5/47; 3p 5/65; subj 1s cūþe 3/116; 3p cūðen 4/40, 5/15
cunnian 2 *try, find out* inf 7/30, 12/215; pres 3s cunnað 16/29 (*knows at first hand*); subj 1s cunnige 17/35; pret 3p cunnedon 4/275 (*tried to discover*); p ptc gecunnad 17/5 (*experienced, came to know*)
curfon see **ceorfan**
cūð adj. *familiar, well known* ns 4/322, 18(a)/705; npm cūðe 18(a)/867; gpn cūðra 16/55 [MnE (un)couth]
Cūþberht pers. n. *Cuthbert* ns 4/319
cūþe see **cunnan**
cūðlić adj. *certain* comp. as cūðlicre 8/36
cūðlīċe adv. *clearly* 8/13
cūðon see **cunnan**
cwalu f. *death* ds cwale 4/79
cwǣde see **cweðan**
cwæð see **cweðan**
cwealdon see **cwellan**
cwealmcuma m. *murderous visitor* as cwealmcuman 18(a)/792
cwellan 1 *kill* pret 2s cwealdest 18(b)/1334, 1p cwealdon 1/29 [MnE quell]
cwēn f. *woman, queen* ns 1/10.
cwene f. *woman* ns 11(p)/1
cweðan V *say* inf 14/116; pres 1s cweðe 4/118; 3s cwyþ 14/111; 3p cweþaþ 4/31; pret 1s cwæð 5/44; 2s cwǣde 4/4; 3s cwæð 2/2, 2/7, 2/20, 2/21, 2/44, 3/189, etc.; 3p cuǣdon 6/30, 6/34, cwǣdon 9/106 etc.; subj 3p cwǣden 5/34 [archaic MnE quoth]
*ġe***cweðan** V *speak, utter* pret 3s gecwæð 12/168, 18(a)/857, 18(a)/874
cwic adj. *alive* nsm 3/139, 4/166, 4/257; asm cwicne 4/178, 18(a)/792; asn cwicu 11(p)/5; apm cwice 11(g)/7; gpm cwicra 16/9 [MnE quick]
cwide m. *statement, saying* as 11(c)/4
cwideġiedd n. *spoken utterance* gp cwidegiedda 16/55
cwīðan 1 *bewail, lament* inf 16/9, 18(d)/3171; pret 3p cwīðdon 14/56
cwōm see **cuman**
cyme m. *coming* ds 9/76
cymeð see **cuman**
*ġe***cynd** n. *species, kind, origin, lineage* ds gecinde 4/49
*ġe***cyndbōc** f. *book of origin*, i.e. *book of Genesis* ns 4/48
*ġe***cynde** adj. *proper, lawful* apm 10(b)/6 [MnE kind]
cynelić adj. *noble* nsn 13/48
cynelīce adv. *regally* 4/173
cynerīċe n. *kingdom* gs kynerīces 5/67
cynestōl m. *royal seat, throne* ns 10(a)/22; ds cynestōle 10(b)/48
Cynewulf pers. n. *Cynewulf* ns 6/1, 6/4, 6/6, etc.
cyng see **cyning**
cyning m. *king* ns kyning 5/1, cyng 7/27, 7/45, cyning 4/137, 4/319, 8/1, 8/76, 10(a)/14, 10(a)/24, 18(a)/863, 18(b)/1306; as 4/207, 6/10, 8/60, etc., kyning 18(d)/3171; gs cyninges 3/40, 4/127, 4/200, 6/17, etc.; ds cyninge 3/66, 3/132, 4/130, 10(a)/19, kyninge 6/12; np cyningas 17/82, kyningas 5/5; ap cyningas 10(b)/6, kyningas 10(b)/56; dp cyningum 10(a)/2, etc.
cynn n. *kin, family, kind, race* ns 1/3; as 14/94; gs cynnes 3/153, 12/217, 12/266, 18(a)/712, 18(a)/735, etc.; ds cynne 12/76, 18(a)/810; gp cynna 11(n)/2, cinna 4/92
ċyrċan see **ċiriċe**
cyrm m. *cry, uproar* ns 12/107
cyssan 1 *kiss* pres 3p cyssað 11(j)/3, 11(o)/6; subj 3s cysse 16/42
cyst f. *best* ns 10(b)/18, 18(a)/802, as 14/1; dp cystum 18(a)/867 (*good quality, excellence*)
cystig adj. *generous* nsm 4/143
cȳðan 1 *reveal, make known, inform* inf 5/2; pres 3s cȳð 4/264; pret 3s cȳþde 6/29, 9/50; 3p cȳðdon (*manifested toward*) 10(b)/56
*ġe***cȳðan** 1 *show, make known, declare* inf 12/216; pret 3s gecȳðde 7/53
*ġe***cȳþnis** f. *testament* ns 4/29; ds gecȳðnisse 4/41; ap gecȳðnissa 4/112
cȳþþ f. *kinfolk* ns 1/3 [MnE kith (and kin)]

*ġe***dafenian** 2 (impersonal verb (§212) w.d.) *befit* pret 3s gedafenode 9/17; subj gedafnode 4/39
dagas see **dæġ**
daroð m. *spear* as 12/149, 12/255
dǣd f. *deed* ns 10(b)/43; as dǣde 18(a)/889; gp dǣda 9/82; dp dǣdum 6/2, 17/41, 17/76
dǣdbōt f. *penitence, penance* as dǣdbōte 4/65

dæġ m. *day* ns 1/23, etc.; as dæg 4/236, 4/263, 4/312, 4/313, 12/198, 15/37, dæi 7/33; gs dæges 11(f)/3 (as adv.), 11(f)/17; ds dæge 1/29, 2/10, 2/48, 3/26, etc., tō dæge *today* 8/73; np dagas 17/80; ap 4/296; gp daga 14/136; dp dagum 2/38, 11(k)/1, etc.

dæġrǣd n. *dawn* as 3/8

dæġrīm n. *number of days* ns 18(a)/823

dæġweorc n. *day's work* gs dægweorces 12/148

dæi see **dæġ**

dǣl m. *part, portion* as 5/42, 5/53, 11(n)/4, 16/65; ds dǣle 4/14 [MnE deal]

dǣlan I *share* inf 4/165; pres subj 1p dǣlon 12/33 [MnE deal]

*ġe***dǣlan** I *part, separate* pres 1p gedǣlað 11(e)/7; pret 3s gedǣlde (*shared*) 16/83; subj 3s 15/22, 18(a)/731

dēad adj. *dead* nsm 11(p)/4, 18(b)/1323; nsn dēade 17/65; asm dēadne 11(k)/1, 18(b)/1309; np dēade 2/8; dp (as noun) dēadum 17/98

dēaf see **dūfan**

dēagan VII *conceal, be concealed* pret 3s dēog 18(a)/850

dēah see **dugan**

dearr see **durran**

dēaþ m. *death* ns 1/33, 11(e)/7, 15/22, 17/106, as 14/101; gs dēaðes 14/113; ds dēaðe 4/288, 4/292, 4/303, 9/120, 16/83, 18(b)/1388

dēaðdæġ m. *death-day* ds dēaðdæge 18(a)/885

dēaðfæġe adj. *fated to die, doomed* ns 18(a)/850

*ġe***dēfe** adj. *fitting, seemly* nsm 18(d)/3174

Defenas m. pl. *Devon, the people of Devon* dp Defenum 7/9

Defenisc adj. *Devonian, from Devon* nsm Defenisca 7/14

degelīċe see **dēogollīċe**

dehter see **dohtor**

*ġe***delf** n. *digging* ds gedelfe 4/283

dēman I *judge, deem* inf 14/107; pret 3p dēmdon 18(d)/3174 (*praised*); p ptc gedēmed 9/20

demm m. *misfortune, loss* ns 3/214

Dene m. pl. *Danes* dp Denum 12/129 (*vikings*), 18(a)/767, 18(a)/823; gp Denigea 18(b)/1323

Denisc adj. *Danish* np Deniscan 4/147; dp 7/22

denu f. *valley* np dena 15/30; dp denum 11(f)/3

dēofol m.n. *the devil* as 4/150; ds dēofle 17/76; gp dēofla 18(a)/756

dēofolġild n. *idol* as dēofolgyld 8/61; gp dēofolgilda 8/54; dp dēofolgildum 8/51, dēofulgeldum 8/65

dēog see **dēagan**

dēogol adj. *secret, hidden, mysterious* asn dȳgel 18(b)/1357; apm dīgelan 4/165

dēogollīce adv. *secretly* dēgelīce 10(b)/64, dīgellīce 10(a)/20

dēop adj. *deep, profound* nsf 4/44, 4/75; dsm dēopan 14/75

dēope adv. *deeply, profoundly* 16/89

dēoplīċe adv. *profoundly, deeply* 4/98

dēor n. *wild animal* ap 4/235, 4/243 [MnE deer]

dēor adj. *bold, brave* nsm 17/41; dipf dēorum 17/76

deorc adj. *dark* asn deorce 16/89; dpm deorcan 14/46

dēore adj. *dear, precious, beloved* asn 18(c)/2254; superl. asm dēorestan 18(b)/1309

*ġe***deorf** n. *toil, hardship* ns 3/20, 3/21, 3/146; as 3/22, 3/23

Deorwente f. *the Derwent River* ds Deorwentan 8/73

dēorwierþe adj. *valuable, costly* apm 3/142, dēorwirðe 4/85; apn dēorwierþu 3/136 [archaic MnE dearworth]

derian I w.d. *harm* inf 12/70

dēst see **dōn**

dēð see **dōn**

dīgelan see **dēogol**

dīgellīċe see **dēogollīċe**

*ġe***dihtan** I *direct* pret 3s gedihte 4/82

dim adj. *gloomy* npf dimme 15/30 [MnE dim]

disc m. *dish* ns 1/4

dō see **dōn**

dōgor n. *day* dis 18(b)/1395; gp dōgra 16/63, dōgera 18(a)/823

dohte see **dugan**

dohtor f. (§60) *daughter* ns 1/36, np 11(a)/2; ds dehter 4/20; gp dohtra 11(k)/12

dol adj. *foolish* nsm 17/106; apm dole 11(f)/17 (*dazed*)

dolg n. *wound* np 14/46

dōm m. *judgment* as 4/294, 6/28, 12/38; gs dōmes 4/312, 9/77, 14/107; ds dōme 9/52, 18(a)/895; dp dōmum 9/80; poet. *glory, reputation, fame* ns 18(a)/885, as 12/129; gs dōmes 18(b)/1388; ds dōme 17/85 [MnE doom]

dōmdæġ m. *day of judgment* ds dōmdæge 14/105 [MnE doom(s)day]

dōmgeorn adj. *eager for glory* npm dōmgeorne 16/17

dōn anom. (§128) *do, make, take* inf 3/205, 5/63 (*promote*), etc.; infl inf (tō) dōnne 1/14, 3/17; pres 1s dō 3/90; 2s dēst 3/17, 3/28, 3/65, 3/79; 3s dēð 4/113; 2p dōþ 3/176; 3p 3/129, 4/108; subj 2s dō 5/21; 3s 5/77; 1p 4/96; pret 1s dyde 17/20; 2s dydest 2/26, 2/28; 3s dyde

2/19, 8/6, 9/24, etc.; 3p dydon 4/217; p ptc gedōn 4/52, 12/197

*ġe***dōn** anom. (§128) *do* inf 7/51, 17/43; pres subj 1p 5/56

Dorsǣte m. pl. *Dorset, men of Dorset* dp Dorsǣtum 7/10

dorste see **durran**

dorston see **durran**

dōþ see **dōn**

draca m. *dragon* ns 18(a)/892 [archaic MnE drake]

*ġe***dræg** n. *tumult, (noisy) company* as 18(a)/756, gedreag 15/45 (*multitude*)

drēag see **drēogan**

*ġe***dreag** see *ġe***dræg**

drēam m. *joy, delight* ns 14/140, 17/80; gs drēames 14/144; ds drēame 16/79; np drēamas 17/65, 17/86; gp drēama 18(a)/850; dp drēamum 14/133, 18(a)/721 [MnE dream]

*ġe***drēas** see *ġe***drēosan**

drēfan 1 *stir up, disturb* pres 1s drēfe 11(d)/2

*ġe***drēfan** 1 *trouble, afflict* p ptc gedrēfed nsm 10(a)/27, 10(b)/74, 14/20, 14/59

dreng m. (*Viking*) *warrior* gp drenga 12/149

drēogan II *suffer, perform, be engaged in* inf 15/26; pres 3s drēogeð 15/50; 3p drēogað 17/56; pret 3s drēag 11(l)/5; 3p drugon 18(a)/798, 18(a)/831

drēorgian 2 *grow desolate* pres 3p drēorgiað 13/29

drēoriġ adj. *sad* asm drēorigne 16/17 [MnE dreary]

drēoriġhlēor adj. *sad-faced* nsm 16/83

drēorsele m. *desolate hall, hall of sorrow* ds 15/50

drēosan II *decline* pres 3s drēoseþ 1/26, 16/63

*ġe***drēosan** II *collapse, perish* pret 3s gedrēas 13/11, 16/36 (*perish*); p ptc gedroren nsf 17/86; npf gedrorene 13/5

drīfan I *drive* inf 3/9; pres 1s drīfe 3/23

drihten m. *lord, the Lord* ns 9/39, 12/148, dryhten 11(e)/2, 14/101, etc.; as 14/64, 17/106; gs Drihtnes 4/292, 4/318, 10(b)/41, dryhtnes 14/9, 14/35, 14/75, 14/113, 14/136, 14/140, 17/65, 17/121; ds Drihtne 9/54, 9/119, 10(b)/64, 10(b)/83, 18(b)/1398

drincan III *drink* pres 3p drincað 11(j)/12; pret 3s dranc 18(a)/742 3p druncon 11(n)/1

drohtoð m. *course, way of life* ns 18(a)/756

*ġe***drorene** see *ġe***drēosan**

druncon see **drincan**

dryht f. *multitude, men* dp dryhtum 11(m)/2

dryhten see **drihten**

dryhtguma m. *retainer, warrior* ds drihtguman 18(b)/1388

dryhtliċ adj. *lordly, magnificent* nsn 18(a)/892; superl. dsm dryhtlicestum 17/85

dryhtsele m. *retainer's hall, splendid hall* ns 18(a)/767

drynce m. *drink* as 3/199

dryncfæt n. *drinking vessel, cup* as 18(c)/2254

drysmian 2 *become gloomy* pres 3s drysmaþ 18(b)/1375

dūfan II *dive* pret 1s dēaf 11(l)/5, 11(p)/4

dugan pret. pres. w.d. *be of use* pret 3s dēah 12/48, dohte 18(b)/1344

duguð f. *advantage, benefit* ds duguðe 12/197; dip duguðum 18(d)/3174 (*power, excellence, glory*)

duguð f. *troop of seasoned retainers, mature men* ns 16/79, 17/86, 18(c)/2254; ds duguþe 16/97; dp dugeþum (*heavenly host*) 17/80

dumb adj. *dumb* dpm dumbum 11(m)/2

dūn f. *hill, down, mountain* as dūne 2/48; ds 2/46, 2/71; np dūna 15/30; ap 11(g)/6; dp dūnum 11(f)/3

Dunnere pers. n. *Dunnere* ns 12/255

Dūnstān pers. n. *Dunstan* ns 4/129, 4/131, 7/15; ds Dūnstāne 4/127

durran pret. pres. *dare* pres 1s dearr 3/10, 3/107; 1p durron 4/100; subj 1s dyrre 3/10, durre 16/10; 2s dyrre 18(b)/1379; pret 1s dorste 14/35, 14/42, 14/45, etc.; 3s 4/243; 3p dorston 1/34; subj. 3p dorsten 10(b)/27

duru f. *door* ns 18(a)/721; as 4/278, 6/13, 8/31

dūst n. *dust* ns 2/42; ds dūste 2/42

*ġe***dwola** m. *heresy* ns 10(b)/41; ds gedwolan 10(a)/7

*ġe***dwolmann** m. *heretic* np gedwolmen 4/106

*ġe***dwolsum** adj. *misleading* nsn 4/105

*ġe***dwyld** n. *heresy* ds gedwylde 4/308

dyde see **dōn**

dydon see **dōn**

*ġe***dygan** 1 *survive* pres 3s gedygeð 11(g)/6

dȳgel see **dēogol**

dynnan 1 *resound* pret 3s dynede 18(a)/767, 18(b)/1317

dynt m. *blow* dp dyntum 11(f)/17 [MnE dint]

dyrne adj. *secret* asm 15/12; gpm dyrnra 18(b)/1357

dyrre see **durrran**

*ġe***dyrstiġ** adj. *daring, bold* nsm 3/59, 3/62

dysiġ adj. *ignorant, foolish* nsm 4/9 [MnE dizzy]

dysiġnes f. *folly* as dysignesse 8/59; ds 8/57 [MnE dizziness]

ēa f. *river* as 3/76, 3/77; ds 3/99, 8/73; dp ēam 3/88

ēac adv. *also, and* 4/19, 4/31, 4/234, 4/277, 7/49, 14/92, etc.; prep. w.d.i. *in addition to, besides* 3/180, 10(b)/44, 12/11; **ēac swā** *likewise, also* 2/19; **ēac swelce (swā), swelce**

ēac (*cont.*)
ēac *also, moreover* 2/1, 2/33, 3/103, 3/121, 4/260, 9/79, ēac swylce 9/120; **ēac þon** *moreover, besides* 15/44; **ne ēac** *nor even* 5/25 [archaic MnE eke]
ēaca m. *increase* ds ēacan 4/20; **tō ēacan** (w.d.) *in addition to* 10(a)/10
ēacen adj. *increased, endowed, great* nsm 11(k)/8
*ġe***ēacnung** f. *child-bearing, increase* ap ġeēacnunga 2/34
ēad n. *wealth* as 13/36
ēadiġ adj. *blessed* nsm 17/107, ēadiga 4/33, 4/137, 4/320, 7/25
ēadiġnes f. *blessedness, bliss* as ēadignesse 17/120, gs 8/46, 11(o)/9
ēadmōd adj. *humble* nsm 4/139
ēadmōdlīċe adv. *humbly* 4/2
Ēadmund pers. n. *Edmund* ns 4/137, 4/168, 4/194; as 4/206; gs Ēadmundes 4/130; ds Ēadmunde 4/129, 4/313
Ēadrīc pers. n. *Eadric* ns 12/11
Ēadweard pers. n. *Edward* ns 12/117, 12/273
Ēadwine pers. n. *Eadwine* ns 7/13, 7/18, 8/76 [MnE Edwin]
Ēadwold pers. n. *Eadwold* ns 12/304
eafora m. *offspring, son* ns eafera 18(a)/897
ēage n. *eye* as 11(b)/3; gs ēagan 8/33; np ēagan 2/9, 2/15; ap 4/111; dp ēagum 2/13, 18(a)/726
ēagðӯrl n. *window* as 4/279
eahte num. *eight* npm 4/271
eahtian 2 *esteem, praise* pret 3p eahtodan 18(d)/3173
eal see **eall**
ēalā interj. *oh, lo* 3/20, 3/28, 3/156, 3/179, etc.
eald adj. *old, ancient* nsm 12/310, 15/29, ealda 12/218 (see **fæder**); asm ealdne 11(f)/8; nsf ealde 4/11, 4/28; asf ealdan 2/57, 2/60, 4/40, ealde 18(a)/795; npm ealdan 4/11 (see **fæder**); npn eald 16/87; apn ealde 12/47; ipm ealdum 10(b)/65; compar. yldra 18(b)/1324
ealdes adv. *long ago* 15/4
ealdġeseġen f. *old tradition* gp ealdgesegena 18(a)/869
ealdġesīð m. *old comrade or retainer* np ealdgesīþas 18(a)/853
ealdġestrēon n. *ancient treasure* dp ealdgestrēonum 18(b)/1381
ealdġewyrht n. or f. *deed of old, former action* dp ealdgewyrhtum 14/100
ealdhlāford m. *lord from old times* dp ealdhlāfordum 10(a)/17, 10(b)/63
ealdhlāfordcynn n. *hereditary lordship, race of ancient kings* gs ealdhlāfordcynnes 10(a)/22
ealdian 2 *grow old* pres 3s ealdað 17/89
ealdor m. *leader, prince* ns 12/202, 12/222, 12/314, 14/90, 17/123; gs ealdres 12/53; ds ealdre 12/11 [MnE alder(man)]
ealdor n. *life, age* ns 11(k)/3; as aldor 18(b)/1371; gs ealdres 18(b)/1338, aldres 18(a)/822; ds ealdre 17/79 (āwa tō ealdre *for ever*)
ealdorbisceop m. *high-priest* ns 8/11
ealdordagas m. pl. *days of life* dp aldordagum 18(a)/718, ealdordagum 18(a)/757
ealdorġedǣl n. *separation from life, death* ns aldorgedāl 18(a)/805
ealdorman m. *nobleman, ruler* ns 4/119, 7/21, 7/29 (see note), aldormon 6/25, etc.; as ealdormann 4/2, aldormon 6/3, 6/6; gs ealdormannes 7/45; np ealdormenn 7/12, aldormen 8/38; dp ealdormannum 3/133, 8/28 [MnE alderman]
ealdorþeġn m. *chief thane* as aldorþegn 18(b)/1308
ealdriht n. *ancient right* gp ealdrihta 10(a)/8, 10(a)/16, 10(b)/36, 10(b)/57; dp ealdrihtum 10(a)/23
ealfela adj. *very much, a great many* as 18(a)/869, 18(a)/883
ealfelo adj. *entirely harmful, dire* asn 11(h)/9
Ealfrīc pers. n. *Ælfric* ns Ælfrīc 7/32; gs Ælfrīces 7/45; ds Ealfrīce 7/29
ealgian 2 *defend* inf 18(a)/796
*ġe***ealgian** 2 *defend* inf gealgean 12/52
Ealhelm pers. n. *Ealhelm* ns 12/218
eall adj. *all* nsm 7/61; asm ealne 8/70; gsm ealles 15/41; nsn eall 14/6; asn 4/221, 5/30, 14/58, 14/94; nsf 3/160, 14/12, 14/55, eal 15/46, etc.; asf ealle 3/30, 4/132, 5/50, 9/89, 10(b)/12; dsf eallre 4/198; npm ealle 3/176, 4/200, 4/232, 4/240, 4/285, 7/27, 11(n)/10, 14/128, alle 6/15; apm 3/87, 3/192, 5/11, 7/71, 12/320, 14/37, etc.; gpm ealra 11(a)/6; dpm eallum 4/239, 11(l)/7, 12/233; npn ealle 2/1, eall 3/138, 3/190; apn eal 9/45; dpn eallum 2/29; gpn ealra 4/29, 4/245, 14/125; npf ealle 2/76; apf ealle 4/62, ealla 5/41; gpf ealra 12/174; as pron. nsn eal 18(a)/835; asn eall 12/256, 13/26, 13/39; npm ealle 14/9
eall adv. *all, entirely, completely* 4/213, 7/37, 12/314, 14/20, 14/48, 14/82, eal 15/29
Eallerīca pers. n. *Alaric* ns Eallerīca 10(a)/2; as Alerīc 10(b)/7
eallġearo adj. *entirely ready, eager* nsf 11(h)/4
eallswā adv. *just as* 4/257 (eallswā . . . swilce *just as . . . as if*)
eallunga adv. *utterly* 4/325, eallinga 8/13
ealneġ adv. *always* 5/79
ēalond n. *island* ds ēalonde 10(a)/4
ealra see **eall**
ealuscerwen f. *dispensing of ale, distress, terror* ns 18(a)/769 (see note)
ēam m. *uncle* ns 11(a)/6, 18(a)/881

eard m. *homeland, country* as 12/53, 12/58, 12/222, 17/38, 18(b)/1377; gs eardes 4/176; ds earde 4/185
eardġeard m. *city, dwelling place* as 16/85
eardstapa m. *wanderer* ns 16/6
ēare n. *ear* ap ēaran 4/111, 11(b)/3
earfeða see **earfoð**
earfoð n. *hardship* gp earfoða 15/39, earfeþa 16/6
earfoðhwīl f. *time of hardship* as earfoðhwīle 17/3
earfoðliċ adj. *full of trouble, fraught with hardship* nsn 16/106
earh adj. *cowardly* nsn 12/238 [MnE eerie]
earm m. *arm* as 12/165, 18(a)/749, 18(a)/835; ap earmas 11(b)/6
earm adj. *poor, wretched* asm earmne 16/40; asn earme 7/77; npm earme 14/68, earman 4/174, 4/325; as noun gp earmra 14/19
earmceariġ adj. *wretched and troubled* nsm 16/20, 17/14
earmliċ adj. *miserable, pitiable* ns 18(a)/807
earmlīċe adv. *miserably, wretchedly* 4/279, 4/302
earmsceapen adj. *wretched, miserable* nsm 18(b)/1351
earn m. *eagle* ns 12/107, 17/24
*ġe***earnian** 2 *earn, deserve* pres 3s geearnaþ 14/109
*ġe***earnung** f. *favour, act deserving gratitude* ap geearnunga 12/196
eart see **beon**
ēast adv. *east* 4/152, 8/72
ēastan adv. *from the east* 10(b)/1
Ēastdene m. pl. *the Danes* dp Ēastdenum 18(a)/828
Ēastengle m. pl. *East Anglia* ap 7/66; gp Ēastengla 4/137; dp Ēastenglum 4/154, 7/36
ēasteð n. *riverbank* ds ēasteðe 12/63
Ēastseaxe m. pl. *Essex, the East Saxons* ap Ēastsexe 7/67; dp Ēastseaxum 7/56; gp Ēastseaxena 12/69
ēaðe adv. *easily* 5/57, 11(h)/11, 11(n)/8
ēaðmōd adj. *humble* nsm 14/60, 17/107
ēaðmōdlīċe adv. *humbly* 9/84
eaxl f. *shoulder* as eaxle 18(a)/835, ds 18(a)/816; ap eaxle 11(b)/6; dp eaxlum 14/32
eaxlġespann n. *crossbeam, intersection* ds eaxlgespanne 14/9
eaxlġestealla m. *shoulder-companion, comrade* ns 18(b)/1326
ebba m. *ebb-tide* ds ebban 12/65
Ebriscġeðiode n. *the Hebrew language* ds 5/48
ēċe adj. *eternal, everlasting* nsm 9/39, 9/43, 17/124; dsm ēcan 4/80; gsn ēces 8/46, ēcan 4/264, 17/79; asf ēcan 17/120; gsf ēcre 8/46; as adv. *eternally* 17/67
ecg f. *edge, sword* ns 12/60; gp ecga 18(a)/805
ecghete m. *deadly hatred, violence* ns 17/70
Ecglāf pers. n. *Ecglaf* gp Ecglāfes 12/267
Ecgþēow pers. n. *Ecgtheow* gs Ecgþēowes 18(b)/1383
ēċnis f. *eternity* ds on ēcnysse *forever and ever* 4/66, ecnisse 4/121
ēċre see **ēċe**
edor m. *building* np ederas 16/77
ēdrum see **ǣdre**
edwit n. *reproach, disgrace* ns 10(b)/55
efne adv. *even, only* 8/56, 9/15, 10(b)/14
efsian 2 *cut* (*the hair*) inf 4/268
efstan 1 *hasten* inf 14/34; pret 3p efston 12/206
eft adv. *again, afterwards, thereupon, back* 2/7, 2/17, 2/52, 2/71, 3/31, 3/126, 5/49, etc., æft 10(b)/65; **eft ongean** *in reply, back again* 12/49, 12/156; **eft onhwyrfed** *reversed, backwards* 11(h)/1
eftsīð m. *journey back, return* ap eftsīðas tēah *returned* 18(b)/1332
eġe m. *fear, terror* ns 2/73, 10(b)/72, ds 3/11
eġesa m. *awe, terror* ns 14/86, 18(a)/784, egsa 17/103; ds egsan 17/101
eġesliċ adj. *fearful, awesome, dreadful* nsf 14/73
Ēgipte m. pl. *Egyptians* gp Ēgipta 4/77, Ǣgypta 9/73
ēġlond n. *island* ns 10(b)/16
ēhtan 1 w.g. *chase, pursue* pres subj 3p ēhten 3/43
elcor adv. *otherwise* 8/63
eldran see **ieldran**
eldum see **ælde**
ele m. *oil* as 3/141
Ēlig f *Ely* ds Ēlig 4/320
Elizabeþ pers. n. *Elizabeth* ns 1/31
ellen n. *courage, strength* ds elne 16/114, 18(a)/893; is elne mycle *with great zeal* 14/34, 14/60, 14/123, on ellen *valiantly* 12/211
ellendǣd f. *deed of valour* dp ellendǣdum 18(a)/876
ellenmǣrþu f. *fame for courage, heroic deed* dp ellenmǣrþum 18(a)/828
ellenweorc n. *valorous deed* ap 18(d)/3173
ellenwōdnis f. *zeal* gs ellenwōdnisse 9/85
elles adv. *otherwise, else* 4/105, 15/23, 17/46
ellor adv. *elsewhither* 18(c)/2254
ellorgǣst m. *spirit from elsewhere, alien spirit* ns ellorgāst 18(a)/807; ap ellorgǣstas 18(b)/1349
elne see **ellen**
elpendbān n. *ivory, elephant bone* as 3/141
elra adj. *another* dsm elran 18(a)/752
elþēodiġ adj. *alien, foreign* as noun: np elðēodge 10(b)/55; gp elþēodigra 17/38
embe see **ymbe**

ende m. *end, conclusion* ns 1/33, 18(a)/822; as 4/7, 4/96, 4/295, 18(b)/1386; ds 14/29 (on ende *from the edge*) is ænde 9/86

endebyrdan 1 *arrange, dispose* p ptc geendebyrd 4/99

endebyrdnes f. *order, succession, sequence* ns 9/35; as endebirdnisse 4/101, endebyrdnesse 9/21

endemes adv. *together* 4/232

*ġe*endian 2 *end, complete* pret 3s geendode 4/303 (ended his life), 10(a)/9; geendade 9/86

endlyfta adj. *eleventh* isn endlyftan 8/78

engel m. *angel* ns 2/61, 2/71; as 14/9; np englas 4/72, 14/106; dp englum 2/11, 14/153, 17/78; gp engla 4/50, 12/178

Engle m.pl. *the English* gp Engla 4/318

Englisc adj., noun *English* ns 4/102; as 4/3, 4/51, 4/134, 5/16, 5/61, etc.

Engliscġereord n. *the English language* ds Engliscgereorde 9/7

ent m. *giant* gp enta 13/2, 16/87

ēode see **gān**

ēodon see **gān**

eodorcan 1 *chew the cud* pres ptc nsn eodorcende 9/68

eofor m. *boar, figure of a boar* np eoferas 18(b)/1328

Eoforwīċċeaster f. *York* ds Eoforwīcceastre 8/72

eoh m. *horse* as 12/189

eom see **bēon**

eorcanstān m. *jewellery, precious stone* as 13/36

eorl m. *nobleman* ns 7/29, 10(b)/78, 12/6, 12/51, 12/89, etc.; gs eorles 12/165; ds eorle 10(b)/72, 12/28, 12/159, 16/12; np eorlas 10(b)/30; ap 16/99; gp eorla 11(a)/7, 16/60, 17/72, 18(b)/1312; dp eorlum 11(n)/8, 18(a)/769 [MnE earl]

eorlscipe m. *nobility* as 18(d)/3173

eormengrund m. *spacious ground, earth* as 18(a)/859

eornoste adv. *earnestly, determinedly* 12/281

eorðe f. *earth* as eorðan 2/30, 4/52, 4/56, 4/330, 12/126, 12/286, 12/303, etc.; gs 1/24, 2/40, 9/40, 14/37, etc.; ds 2/2, 2/38, 2/40, etc.

eorðfæst adj. *firmly rooted in the earth* dsn eorðfæstum 4/208 [MnE earthfast]

eorþgrāp f. *grip of earth* ns 13/6

eorþscræf n. *cave, grave* ds eorðscræfe 15/28, 16/84; ap eorðscrafu 15/36

eorþsele m. *cave, barrow* ns 15/29

eorþtilþ f. *farming, earth-tilling* ns 3/192

eorþweġ m. *earthly way* ds eorðwege 14/120

eorþwela m. pl. *worldly prosperity* np eorþwelan 17/67

eoten m. *giant* ns 18(a)/761; gp eotena 18(a)/883

ēow see **ġē**

ēower *of you* see **ġē**

ēower poss adj. *your* nsm 3/161; dsm ēowrum 3/170; nsf ēowru 3/160; npm ēowre 6/35; npn ēowre 2/9; apf ēowre 3/170; gpf ēowerra 3/162

erian 1 *plough* inf 3/13

esne m. *man* as 11(f)/8; ap esnas 11(f)/16

etan V *eat* infl inf (tō) etanne 2/12; pres 2s etst 2/30, 2/39; 1p etað 2/5; 2p 2/10, 3/170; 3p 3/126; subj 3s ete 4/24; 2p eten 2/8; pret 1s ǣt 2/25, 2/27; 2s æte 2/36, 3s æt 2/14; subj 2s ǣte 2/23, 2/24, 2/37; 1p ǣten 2/6; 2p ǣten 2/3

*ġe*etan V *eat, devour* pret 3s ġeǣt 2/14

ēþel m. *homeland, territory* ns 14/156; as 5/8, 10(b)/16, 12/52, 17/60; ds ēðle 16/20

ēþelweard m. *defender of the homeland* np ēþelweardas 10(b)/24

ēðnis f. *ease, comfort* gp ēðnessa 10(a)/16

*ġe*fadian 2 *arrange, phrase* inf 4/104

fadung f. *arrangement, order (of words)* ds fadunge 4/103

fāh adj. *stained, guilty, outcast* nsm 14/13, 15/46, 16/98 (*decorated*), fāg 18(a)/811 (*in a state of feud with*); asm fāgne 18(a)/725, fāhne 18(a)/716

fana m. *banner* ns 10(b)/10 [MnE (weather)vane]

fandian 2 w.g. *test* inf 2/43

far see **faran**

faran VI *go, travel, advance* inf 12/88, 12/156, 18(a)/865; imp s far 2/45, 4/193; pres 1s fare 3/135; 3s færð 4/63, fareð 11(h)/3, 17/91 (him on fareð *overtakes him*); subj 1s fare 3/100; pret 3p fōron 10(b)/20 [MnE fare]

*ġe*faran VI *proceed, act, die* inf 18(a)/738; pret 3s gefōr 7/15, 7/26

fatu see **fæt**

fæc n. *interval* ns 8/33; as 9/117; ds fæce 8/34, 9/5

fæder m. (§60) *father* ns 2/54, 2/55, 4/56, 4/144, 11(a)/4, 11(k)/2, etc.; as 2/54, etc.; ds 4/58, 4/330, 16/115; np ealdan fæderas *patriarchs* 4/11; nsm ealda fæder *grandfather* 12/218

fǣġe adj. *fated, doomed to die* nsm 12/119, 18(a)/846; dsm fǣgean 12/125; npm fǣge 12/105; as noun gsm fǣges 12/297, dsm fǣgum 17/71 [archaic MnE fey]

fæġen adj. *rejoicing, happy* nsm 16/68 [MnE fain]

fæġer adj. *beautiful, pleasant* nsn 14/73, 18(a)/773; dsf fægran 14/21; ism fægre 9/86; npm

fægere 14/8, 14/10, 18(a)/866, dpm fægerum 4/84 [MnE fair]
fæġere adv. *pleasantly, well* fægre 11(m)/8; *properly, with care* fægere 12/22
fæġernis f. *beauty, excellent feature* ap fægernissa 4/90 [MnE fairness]
fæġnian 2 *rejoice* pret 3p fægnodon 10(b)/33
*ġe***fæġnian** 2 *make glad* p ptc gefægnod 18(b)/1333
fæġrian 2 *make or become beautiful, adorn* pres 3p fægriað 17/48
fæġrost adv. superl. *most happily, most pleasantly* 17/13
fǣhðo f. *feud, battle, enmity* as fǣhðe 12/225, 18(a)/879, 18(b)/1333, 18(b)/1340, 18(b)/1380, fǣhðu 15/26
fælsian 2 *cleanse, purge* p ptc gefælsod 18(a)/825
fǣmne f. *maiden, woman* ns 11(p)/1
fǣrgripe m. *sudden grip, sudden attack* dp fǣrgripum 18(a)/738
fǣrlic adj. *sudden* dsn færlican 4/170
fǣrlīċe adv. *quickly, suddenly* 3/61, 4/156, 4/163, 16/61
fǣrsceaða m. *sudden attacker, Viking* ds fǣrsceaðan 12/142
færð see **faran**
fæst adj. *fast, firm, fixed* nsm 18(b)/1364, nsf 18(a)/722
fæstan 1 *fast, abstain from food* pret subj 3p fæsten 4/296
fæste adv. *firmly, fast* 4/284, 8/68, 9/46, 10(b)/35, 11(h)/14, 12/21, 12/103, etc.
fæsten see **fæstan**
fæsten n. *stronghold, fortress* as 10(b)/20, 12/194; ds fæstene 10(b)/79
fæsten n. *fast, abstinence from food* dp fæstenum 4/268
fæstlīċe adv. *steadfastly, firmly, steadily* 3/60, 8/50, 10(b)/70, 12/82, 12/254, festlīce 7/49
fæstnian 2 *fasten, establish* (*truce*) inf 12/35; p ptc gefæstnod 3/12
*ġe***fæstnian** 2 *fasten* pret 3p gefæstnodon 14/33
fæstnung f. (*place of*) *stability, permanence* ns 16/115
fæt n. *vessel, utensil* ap fatu 3/203 [MnE vat]
fǣt n. *gold ornament, ornamental plate* dp fǣtum 18(c)/2256, fǣttum 18(a)/716
fǣted adj. *ornamented, plated* asn 11(l)/7, 18(c)/2253
fǣtels m. *pouch, bag* ap fǣtelsas 3/154
fǣtt adj. *fat, rich* asn 3/171
fæðm m. *embrace* ns 18(a)/781, as 18(b)/1393 (*interior*) [MnE fathom]
fēa adv. *little* 14/115
feaht see **feohtan**
feala see **fela**
feallan VII *fall, fall in battle* inf 12/54, 12/105, 14/43; pres 3s fealleþ 1/26, 16/63; pret 3s fēoll 1/2, 12/119, 12/166, 12/286, fēol 10(b)/81, 12/126, 12/303, etc.; 3p fēollon 12/111; subj 1s fēolle 4/175
*ġe***feallan** VII *fall* pret 3s gefēoll 10(a)/27
fealohilte adj. *golden-hilted* nsn 12/166
fealu adj. *tawny, dark* nsm fealwe 11(n)/10, apm 16/46, 18(a)/865 [MnE fallow]
fēasceaftiġ adj. *wretched, desolate* asn 17/26
fēawe pl. adj. *few* np fēawa 5/14, 5/18, 5/27, etc.; dp fēawum 4/133
feaxhār adj. *grey-haired* nsf 11(p)/1
*ġe***fecgan** 2 *fetch, carry off* inf 12/160.
fēdan 1 *feed* inf 3/125; pres 3s fētt 3/69, 3/192; 3p fēdaþ 3/121, 3/127, 11(m)/8; pret 3s fēdde 11(k)/9, fǣdde 7/62
*ġe***fēhst** see **ġefōn**
fēhð see **fōn**
fela pron. (usually w.g.: see §190.4) *many* 3/84 (hira ... fela *many of them*), 3/94, 3/142, etc.
felalēof adj. *dearly loved* gsm felalēofan 15/26
*ġe***fēlan** 1 *feel* inf 17/95
feld m. (§§61, 62) *field* ds felda 3/9, 12/241
fell n. *skin* ap 3/152
fenfreoðo f. *refuge in the fens* ds 18(a)/851
fēng see **fōn**
*ġe***fēng** see *ġe***fōn**
fenġelād n. *fen-path, tract of swamp* as 18(b)/1359
fengon see **fōn**
fenhlið n. *fen slope, marshy tract* ap fenhleoþu 18(a)/820
fenhop n. *retreat in the fen* ap fenhopu 18(a)/764
feoh n. *money* ns 16/108; as 3/74, 6/19, 12/39; gs fēos 6/28, 7/63; ds fēo 18(b)/1380 [MnE fee]
feohġīfre adj. *greedy, avaricious* nsm 16/68
*ġe***feoht** n. *battle, fight* ds gefeohte 4/175, 12/12; dp gefeohtum 6/6
feohtan III *fight* inf 4/178, 12/16, 12/261; pres ptc feohtende 6/16, 6/21, 7/49, etc.; pret 3s feaht 6/6, 12/254, 12/277, 12/281, etc.; 2p fuhton 1/15
*ġe***feohtan** III *fight, achieve by fighting* inf 7/74, 12/129
feohte f. *battle, fight* ns 12/103
fēol see **feallan**
fēolan III *penetrate* pret 3p fulgon 6/37
fēole f. *file* ds fēolan 4/277
fēolheard adj. *hard as a file* apn fēolhearde 12/108
fēolian 2 *file* pret 3s fēolode 4/277
fēoll see **feallan**
*ġe***fēoll** see *ġe***feallan**

fēolode see **fēolian**

*ġe***fēon** V *rejoice* pres ptc gefēonde (w.g. or i. *rejoicing in*) 8/69, 9/98; pret 3s gefeh 18(a)/827

fēond m. (§59) *enemy* ns 11(m)/4, 18(a)/725; as 1/28, 18(a)/748; ds fēonde 11(m)/4; np fēondas 14/30, 14/33; ap fȳnd 12/82, fēondas 14/38; gp fēonda 2/77, 17/75, 18(a)/808; dp fēondum 7/53, 12/103, 12/264 [MnE fiend]

fēondrǣden f. *enmity* as fēondrǣdene 2/31

fēondsceaþa m. *enemy, robber* ap fēondsceaþan 11(j)/19

feor adj. *far* nsn 4/48 (w.d. *far from*), 8/72, 9/114, etc.; gsn feorres 15/47

feor adv. *far* 11(h)/5, 12/3, 12/57, 15/25, 16/21, 16/26, etc.

fēore see **feorh**

feorg see **feorh**

feorgbold n. *life-house, dwelling of the soul, body* ns 14/73

feorh n. *life* ns 11(k)/2, feorg 17/94, as feorh 6/19, 6/39, 12/125, 12/142, 12/184, etc.; gs fēores 4/160, 12/260, 12/317; ds fēore 4/179, 12/194, 12/259; is 11(h)/14

feorhbealo n. *threat to life, deadly evil* ns 18(c)/2250, as 11(h)/5

feorhcynn n. *race of men* gp feorhcynna 18(c)/2266

feorhhūs n. *life-house, body* as 12/297

feorhlāst m. *bloody track* ap feorhlāstas 18(a)/846

feorhsēoc adj. *mortally wounded* nsm 18(a)/820

feormian 2 *clean* inf 3/19; pres subj 3s feormie 18(c)/2253

*ġe***feormian** 2 *consume, eat up* p ptc gefeormod 18(a)/744

feormynd m. *cleanser, polisher* np 18(c)/2256

feorran adv. *from afar* 14/57, 18(a)/825, 18(a)/839, 18(b)/1370

fēos see **feoh**

fēower num. *four* ap 4/16, 11(g)/3, 11(l)/1, 11(l)/7, 11(n)/2

fēowertȳne num. *fourteen* dpm fēowertȳnum 9/88

*ġe***fēra** m. *companion, comrade* ns 4/238, 12/280; as gefēran 3/14, 8/70; ds 2/25, 4/35, 16/30; np 3/3, 3/206, 6/35; ap 3/103, 3/179, 12/170, 12/229; dp gefērum 3/33, 6/33

fēran 1 *set out, proceed, go, fare* inf 12/41, 12/221, 15/9, 17/37, etc.; pres ptc nsm fērende 11(d)/9; pret 3s fērde 2/47, 4/223, 8/65; 3p fērdon 2/78 (w. refl. obj.), 4/147, 4/279, 7/54, 18(a)/839

*ġe***fēran** 1 *reach by travel, attain, meet with* pret 3s gefērde 7/25; 3p gefērdon 7/50

feredon see **ferian**

fērende see **fēran**

ferhðe see **ferð**

ferian 1 *go* inf 12/179

ferian 2 *carry* inf 4/255; pres 3s fereð 11(j)/7; pret 3s ferede 16/81; 3p feredon 4/245, 11(f)/4; p ptc geferod 4/60 [MnE ferry]

fers n. *verse* ds ferse 4/59; ap fers 9/35

*ġe***fērscipe** m. *fellowship, community* ns 3/184; ds 3/170

ferð n. *spirit, mind* ns 16/54; as 11(p)/5, 17/26, 17/37; ds ferðe 16/90, ferhðe 18(a)/754; dp (w. sg. meaning) ferhðum 18(d)/3176

ferðfriþende adj. *life-sustaining* apm 11(g)/3

ferðloca m. *breast, heart* ns 16/33; as ferðlocan 16/13

festlice see **fæstlice**

fēt see **fōt**

feter f. *fetter* dp feterum 16/21

fetian 2 *fetch* pres sub 3s gefetiġe 14/138; p ptc fetod 18(b)/1310

fētt see **fēdan**

fēða m. *foot-troop, infantry* as fēðan 12/88, np 18(b)/1327

feðer f. *feather* np feþre 11(f)/4; ap feþra 16/47

fīclēaf n. *figleaf* ap 2/16

fierlen adj. *far off, distant* dsn fierlenan 2/47

fīf num. *five* npm fīfe 11(a)/6, 14/8

fīfteġ num. *fifty* dp fīftegum 5/76

*ġe***fillednys** f. *fulfilment* ns 4/29

findan III *find, meet* inf 16/26, 18(b)1378, 18(d)/3162 (*devise*); pret 1s funde 15/18; 3s fand 18(a)/719, 18(a)/870; 3p fundon 12/85; p ptc funden 5/48, 11(f)/1

finger m. *finger* np fingras 18(a)/760; gp fingra 18(a)/764

fiorm f. *use, benefit* as fiorme 5/31

fīras m. pl. *people, human beings* gp fȳra 18(c)/2250; dp fīrum 9/44

firmest see **fyrmest**

first m. *period of time, time* as 5/61; ds fyrste 4/225, 4/251

fīrum see **fīras**

fisc m. *fish* ns 1/5; as 3/102, 3/103; np fiscas 3/79; ap 3/75, 3/81, 3/86, 3/87; gp fisca 3/94; dp fiscum 11(p)/4

fiscere m. *fisherman* ns 3/72, 3/195; np fisceras 3/5

fiscian 2 *fish, catch fish* pres 2s fiscast 3/89

Fitela pers. n. *Fitela* ns 18(a)/879, 18(a)/889

flān m. *arrow, missile* as 12/269; gs flānes 12/71

flasce f. *flask, leather bottle* ap flascan 3/153

flǣschoma m. *covering of flesh, body* ns 17/94

flǣscmete m. *meat* ap flǣscmettas 3/171; gp flǣscmetta 3/158 [MnE fleshmeat]

flēag see **flēogan**

flēam m. *flight* as 7/44, 12/81, 12/254; qs flēames 4/184; ds flēame 4/179, 12/186

flēogan II *fly* inf 12/7, 12/109, 12/150, 12/275 (*flee*); 3s flēogeð 11(h)/12; pret 1s flēah 11(p)/3; 3s flēag 11(l)/4, 17/17

flēon II *flee* inf 12/247, 18(a)/755, 18(a)/764, 18(a)/820; pret 3s flēah 10(b)/20; 3p flugon 12/194

flēotend m. *swimmer, seafarer* (*seabird*) gp flēotendra 16/54

flet n. *floor, hall* as 11(n)/2, 16/61

*ġe***flit** n. *dispute, rivalry, contest* as 18(a)/865; ap geflitu 3/207

flocmǣlum adv. *in* (*armed*) *bands* 7/77 [archaic MnE flockmeal]

flōd m. *body of water, stream, tide* ns 12/65, 12/72, 18(b)/1361; ds flōde 11(d)/9, 11(p)/3, 18(b)/1366, flōdan 6/5; ap flōdas 11(j)/7 [MnE flood]

flōdwegas m. pl. *paths of the ocean* ap 17/52 [MnE floodways]

flōr m. *floor* as 18(a)/725; as flōr 10(a)/30, flōre 10(b)/81; ds 18(b)/1316

flot n. *sea* as 12/41

flota m. *ship, seaman, Viking* as 12/227; ds flotan 4/149; np 12/72

flothere m. *sea-army, Viking band* ns 4/223

flotman m. *sailor, Viking* ns 4/215; np flotmen 4/178, 4/229; dp flotmannum 4/183

flōwan VII *flow* pres ptc flōwende nsm 12/65

flugon see **flēon**

flyht m. *flight* as 12/71

flȳman 1 *put to flight* inf 11(j)/19; p ptc geflȳmed 18(a)/846, 18(b)/1370

fōdor n. *fodder, food* as 3/209

folc n. *folk, people, nation* ns 4/86, 4/176, 8/66, 12/45, 12/241, 14/140; as 4/78, 4/144, 7/77, 11(d)/6, 12/22, 12/54; gs folces 1/29, 4/20, etc.; ds folce 3/133, 4/39, 4/252, 12/227, etc.; is 8/77; gp folca 1/30

folcġesīð m. *companion of the people, warrior* ap folcgesīðas 10(b)/70

folcġewinn n. *battle* gs folcgewinnes 10(b)/10

folclic adj. *vernacular, public* dsn folclicum 4/255; dsf folclicre 4/309

folclond n. *country* gs folclondes 15/47 [MnE folkland]

folctoga m. *leader of the people, chief* np folctogan 18(a)/839

folcwiga m. *warrior* np folcwigan 11(j)/13

foldbold n. *building* ns 18(a)/773

foldbūend m. *earth-dweller, man* np foldbūende 18(b)/1355

folde f. *earth, ground* as foldan 9/44, 12/54, 18(b)/1361; gs 14/8, 14/43, 16/33, 18(b)/1393; ds 11(d)/9, 11(p)/5, 12/166, 12/227, 14/132, 17/13, 17/75

foldweġ m. *way, path* np foldwegas 18(a)/866

folgað m. *retinue* as 15/9

folgian 2 w.d. *follow* inf 6/32; pres 1s folgie 4/191; pret 3s folgode 4/246; 3p folgodon 4/37

folme f. *hand* ds folme 18(a)/748; ds folman 12/21, 12/108, 12/150; dp folmum 18(a)/722; ap folma 18(a)/745; gp 11(f)/15

fōn VII *catch, seize* inf 3/95; pres 1s fō 3/49; 3s fēhð 11(f)/9 (fēhð ongean *struggles against*); **fōn tō rīce** *succeed to the kingdom* (or *the office*, etc.) pret 1s fēng 5/19; 3s 7/16, 8/25 (see note), 10(a)/5, 12/10; 3p fengon 4/252 (fengon tōgædere *joined together*)

*ġe***fōn** VII *catch* inf 3/84, 3/130; pres 1s gefō 3/51, 3/66, 3/102, 3/103; 2s gefēhst 3/50, 3/75, 3/86, 3/92; 3p gefōþ 3/105; subj 3s gefō 3/98; pret 1s gefēng 3/56, 3/58; 2s gefēnge 3/55, 3/57; 3s gefēng 18(a)/740

for prep. w.d.a.i. *for, because of, before* 1/32, 2/65, 2/68, 3/10, 3/16, 4/298 (*with respect to*), 7/76 (*in spite of*), 9/8, etc.; **for hwon** *why* 9/95–6; **for hwȳ** *why* 3/89, 3/101, 3/124; **for þǣm,** *because* 3/53, 3/63, 3/66, 3/90, 3/98, 3/102, 3/107, 3/125; **for þǣm þe, for ðān þe** *because* 2/22, 2/28, 2/36, 2/42, 2/77, 3/21, 3/125, 4/6, 4/166; **for ðon (ðe)** *therefore, because, and so, wherefore* 4/325, 5/21, 8/15, 8/61, 9/96; **for ðȳ** *therefore, because.* See §169

fōr f. *journey, course* ds fōre 11(l)/3

*ġe***fōr** see *ġe***faran**

foran tō adv. *beforehand, in advance* 4/44

forbarn see **forbeornan**

forbærnan 1 *burn, burn up* inf 8/71; pres subj 1p forbærnen 8/49; p ptc forbærned 5/29, asm forbærnedne 17/114

forbēad see **forbēodan**

forbēah see **forbūgan**

forbēodan II (w.d. of person) *forbid* pres 3p forbēodaþ 4/289; pret 3s forbēad 2/3, 4/204

forbeornan III *burn down* pret 3s forbarn 7/11

forbūgan II *flee from* pret 3s forbēah 12/325

ford m. *ford* as 12/88; ds forda 12/81

fordōn anom. (§128) *destroy* pret 3s fordyde 8/75 [MnE fordo]

fore prep. w.d. *for, in place of* 17/21, 17/22

forealdian 2 *grow old* p ptc forealdod *elderly* 4/131

foregangan VII *precede* pres subj 3s foregange 8/35

foresceāwian 2 *provide, preordain* pres 3s foresceāwað 2/55, 4/193

foresecgan 3 *mention before* p ptc nsm foresǣda (*aforementioned*) 4/156; nsf 4/97, nsm 4/156

foresnotor adj. *very wise, very clever* npm foresnotre 18(d)/3162

foresprecan V *say before* p ptc dsm foresprecenan (*aforementioned*) 8/52, dpm 10(a)/5
forġēafe see **forġiefan**
forġiefan V *give* pret 2s forgēafe 2/25; 3s forgēaf 12/139, 12/148, 14/147; p ptc forgifen 4/252, 9/55, ap forgiefene 17/93 [MnE forgive]
forġifenis f. *forgiveness* as forgifenisse 4/65
forgyldan III *buy off* pres subj 2p forgyldon 12/32
forheard adj. exceedingly hard asm forheardne 12/156
forhēawan VII *cut down* p ptc forhēawen 12/115, 12/223, 12/288, 12/314
forherġian 2 *ravage* p ptc forhergod 5/29, 7/3, 7/7
forhicgan 2 *despise, scorn* pret 3s forhogode 12/254
forhogdnis f. *contempt* ds forhogdnisse 9/8
forht adj. *afraid* nsm 14/21, 16/68, 18(a)/754
forhtian 2 *fear* pres 3p forhtiað 14/115; pret 3s forhtode 4/170; subj 3p forhtedon 12/21
forhtmōd adj. *timorous* nsm 3/63, 3/107
forhwega adv. *somewhere* 4/231
for hwon see **for**
for hwȳ see **for**
forlǣtan VII *abandon, neglect, forsake, let (go)* inf 12/2, 12/208, 18(a)/792; pres ptc forlǣtende 9/120; pres 3s forlǣtt 3/211, forlǣteð 11(h)/7; pret 3s forlēt 4/35, 7/25, 9/24, 11(g)/2, 12/149, 12/156, 12/187, etc.; 3p forlēton 4/37, 5/46, 14/61, 18(d)/3166; p ptc forlǣten 3/212, 5/37
forlēosan II *destroy* pres subj 1p forlēosen 8/49 [MnE p ptc forlorn]
forlēt see **forlǣtan**
forlidennes f. *shipwreck* as forlidennesse 3/138
forliġer n. *fornication, wantonness* ds forligre 4/265
forma adj. *first* nsm 18(a)/716, asm forman 12/77; ds 4/59, 18(a)/740 [MnE form(er), forem(ost)]
formoni adj. *very many (a)* nsm 12/239
forniman IV *take away* pret 3s fornōm 13/26, 16/80, fornam 18(c)/2249; 3p fornōman 16/99
fornōm see **forniman**
fōron see **faran**
forsēon V *reject, despise* pres 3s forsihð 4/65; pret 3s forseah 4/201
forsihð see **forsēon**
forslēan VI *cut through* p ptc forslagen 4/259
forst m. *frost* is forste 17/9
forstandan VI *understand, withstand* inf 10(b)/22; pret 1s forstōd 5/73
forstelan IV *rob, steal* p ptc asn forstolen 11(j)/18 (as noun: *that which has been stolen*)
forstōd see **forstandan**
forstrang adj. *very strong* asm forstrangne 11(m)/4
forswelgan III *devour, eat* inf 17/95; pret 3s forswealg 11(c)/3; pres subj 3p forswelgen 3/25
forswerian VI w.d. *make useless by a spell* p ptc forsworen 18(a)/804 [MnE forswear]
forð adv. *forth, forward* 4/246, 11(e)/5, 12/3, 12/12, 12/170, etc.; to forð *too deeply, too successfully* 12/150
for þan þe see **for**
for þǣm see **for**
for þǣm þe see **for**
forþbringan 1 *produce, bring forth* pret 3s forþbrōhte 9/7
forðencan 1 *despair* p ptc forðōht *in despair* 10(b)/82
forðfēran 1 *die* pret 3s forðfērde 4/128, 7/19; 3p forðfērdon 7/12
forðfōr f. *forth-faring, death* ns 9/96; gs forðfōre 9/88, 9/125; ds 9/92; forþfōre 9/102
forðġeorn adj. *eager to advance* nsm 12/281
forðġesceaft f. *eternal decree* as 14/10
forðian 2 *carry out, accomplish* p ptc geforðod 12/289
forðōht see **forðencan**
forþolian 2 *do without, dispense with* inf 3/167, 16/38
for þon see **for**
forðweġ m. *the way forth, departure* gs forðweges 11(o)/3, ds forðwege 16/81, 14/125
forðȳ adv. *therefore* 5/54, 5/79
forwegan V *carry off, kill* p ptc forwegen 12/228
forweorone see **forweosan**
forweosan I *perish* p ptc apm forweorone 13/7
forwundian 2 *wound sorely* p ptc forwundod 14/14, 14/62
fōt m. *foot* gs fōtes 12/247; np fēt 17/9; ap 4/112, 11(b)/4, 18(a)/745; gp fōta 11(f)/15; dp fōtum 4/241, 12/119, 12/171
fōtmǣl n. *space of a foot* as 12/275
fracod adj. *vile, wicked* as noun gsm fracodes 14/10
fram prep w.d. *from, by* 1/10, 2/19, 3/212, 7/3, etc.
fram adv. see **from**
framra adj. see **from**
franca m. *spear* as francan 12/140; ds 12/77
*ġe***frǣġe** n. *information through hearsay* is mīne gefrǣge *as I have heard say* 18(a)/776, 18(a)/837

fræġn see **friġnan**
Fræna pers. n. *Fræna* ns 7/44
fræt see **fretan**
frætwan 1 *ornament, adorn* p ptc frætwed 11(j)/11
*ġe***frætwan** 1 *adorn* p ptc gefrætwed 13/33
frætwe f. pl. *ornaments* np 11(d)/6; ap frætwa 18(a)/896; dp frætewum 4/84; ip frætwum 11(j)/7
frēa m. *lord, master, the Lord* ns 9/44; as frēan 12/184, 12/259, 14/33, 18(b)/1319; gs 15/33; ds 11(n)/10, 12/12, 12/16, 12/289
frēadryhten m. *lord* gs frēadryhtnes 18(a)/796
frēċennes f. *danger, harm* dp frēcennessum 3/105
frēcne adj. *daring, dangerous, audacious* nsn 18(c)/2250, asn 18(b)/1359, asf 18(a)/889, 18(b)/1378
frēfran 1 *console, comfort* inf 16/28, 17/26
fremman 1 *accomplish, perpetrate, advance, benefit* pres 3s fremeþ 3/156, 3/163; subj 3s fremme 3/208; pret 3s fremede 10(b)/45; subj 3/146
*ġe***fremman** 1 *bring about, provide, do* inf 4/281, 16/16, 16/114, 18(b)/1315; pret 3s gefremede 18(a)/811; 3p gefremedon 17/84
fremsumnes f. *benefit* ap fremsumnesse 8/17; dp fremsumnessum 9/80
fremu f. *beneficial action, good deed* dip fremum 11(m)/8, 17/75
frēo adj. *free* nsm 3/21; gpm frīora 5/58
frēod f. *friendship, peace* as frēode 12/39
frēoġan 2 *love* pres subj 3s frēoge 18(d)/3176
frēoliċ adj. *free, noble, beautiful* nsn 11(j)/13; npn frēolico 11(a)/4
frēomæġ m. *noble kinsman* dp frēomægum 16/21
frēond m. (§59) *friend, lover* ns 14/144, 15/47, 16/108; as 18(b)/1385; np frȳnd 15/33, frēondas 14/76; ap frȳnd 12/229; gp frēonda 14/132, 15/17; dp frēondum 8/3
frēondlēas adj. *friendless* asm frēondlēasne 16/28
frēondlīċe adv. *lovingly, in friendly fashion* 5/2
frēondscipe m. *friendship, love* ns 15/25; as 10(a)/8
frēoriġ adj. *frozen* nsm 16/33
freoþian 2 *care for, protect* pret 3s freoþode 11(k)/5
fretan V *eat up, devour* pret 3s fræt 11(c)/1 [MnE fret]
friġnan III *ask, inquire* pres ptc frignende 8/9; imp s frige 11(f)/15, 11(j)/19, frīn 18(b)/1322; pres 3s frīneð 14/112; pret 3s frægn 9/100, 9/104, etc.
*ġe***friġnan** III *find out, learn by asking* pret 1s gefrægn 11(c)/2; 3p gefrūnon 14/76
frīn see **friġnan**
frīneð see **friġnan**
frīora see **frēo**
frið m. *peace* as 7/75, 12/39; gs friðes 7/65, 10(b)/35, 12/41; ds friðe 12/179
Friðeġist pers. n. *Frithegist* ns 7/44
friþemæġ f. *protective woman* ns 11(k)/9
frōd adj. *old, wise, experienced* nsm 12/140, 12/317, 16/90, 18(b)/1306, etc.
frōfor f. *consolation, solace* as frōfre 16/115; gs 10(a)/28, 10(b)/79
from adj. *active, swift, strong* comp. nsm framra 11(l)/4
from adv. *away* 6/33, fram 12/317, 18(a)/754
from prep. see **fram**
fromsīþ m. *departure* ns 15/33
fromweard adj. *about to depart, passing away* dsm fromweardum 17/71
fruma m. *beginning* ds fruman 4/21, 9/71
frumbearn n. *first-born* np 11(a)/4
frumsceaft f. *first creation* as 9/33
*ġe***frunon** see *ġe***friġnan**
frymdi adj. *desiring, requesting, entreating* nsm 12/179 (ic eom frymdi tō þē *I beseech you*)
frȳnd see **frēond**
fuglere m. *fowler* ns 3/108; np fugleras 3/5
fugol m. *bird* ns fugel 16/81; ap fuglas 3/108; dp fuglum 11(l)/4, 11(p)/3 [MnE fowl]
fuhton see **feohtan**
fūl adj. *foul, vile* dsn fūlum 4/190
ful adv. *very, completely* 4/181, 11(o)/5, 12/253, 12/311, 15/1, 15/18, 15/21, etc., full 12/153
fulgon see **fēolan**
full adj. *full, entire, completed, filled* nsm 10(b)/9; nsf 13/23, 17/100; asm fulne 3/13, 17/113; asn ful 4/16; **be fullan** *completely* 5/42
fullīce adv. *entirely, fully* 4/296
fulluht see **fulwiht**
fulluhtþēaw m. *rite of baptism* dp fulluhtþēawum 10(b)/33
fullwēr m. *complete atonement* as 11(h)/14
fulne see **full**
fultum m. *help, support* as 4/177; ds fultume 4/212, 5/57
fultumian 2 *help, support* inf 8/20; p ptc gefultumed 9/14
*ġe***fultumian** 2 *help* pret subj gefultumode 10(a)/24
fulwiht m. f. *baptism* gs fulwihte 8/77; ds fulluhte 4/64
funde see **findan**
funden see **findan**
fundian 2 *set out* pres 3s fundaþ 14/103, 17/47
furþum adv. *even* 3/162, 3/166, 4/24, 5/16, etc.

furþur adv. *further* 5/62, 18(a)/761, furðor 5/62, 12/247
fūs adj. w.g. *eager, ready* (*for death or battle*) nsm 11(o)/3, 12/281; asm fūsne 17/50; asn fūse 14/21; apm 4/198; as noun npm fūse (*hastening ones*) 14/57
fyl m. *fall, death* as 12/71, 12/264, fyll 14/56
fylġan 1 w.d. *follow* pres subj 1p fylgen 8/37
fyllan 1 *fill, satisfy* p ptc apm gefylde 3/32
fyllan 1 *fell, cut down* inf 14/73
*ġe***fyllan** 1 *fill, replenish* pres 3s gefylleð 11(j)/8, gefylþ 3/159; p ptc npf gefylda 5/30
*ġe***fyllan** 1 *fell, kill, strike down* inf 14/38
fyllo f. *fill, plenty, feast* ds fylle 18(b)/1333
fylstan 1 w.d. *help* inf 12/265
fȳnd see **fēond**
fȳr n. *fire* ns 2/55, 8/29; as 2/53, 18(b)/1366; gs fȳres 17/113; ds fȳre 7/49; is 8/49, 11(o)/3
fȳra see **fīras**
fȳrbend f. *band forged with fire* dp fȳrbendum 18(a)/722
fyrd f. *national army, the English levy* as fyrde 7/29, 7/42; ds 4/163, 4/198, 7/34, 12/221
fyrdrinc m. *warrior* ns 12/140
fyrdsceorp n. *war-ornament* ns 11(j)/13
fyrdwyrðe adj. *distinguished in war* nsm 18(b)/1316
fyren f. *crime, wickedness, sin* gp fyrena 18(a)/750, fyrene 18(a)/811; ap 18(a)/879
fyrgenholt n. *mountain-wood* as 18(b)/1393
fyrgenstrēam m. *mountain stream* ns 18(b)/1359
fyrhtu f. *horror, fear* dsf 9/78 [MnE fright]
fyrmest adj. (superl. of forma) *foremost, first* nsm 3/187, 3/188, 3/191, 12/323; nsf firmest 4/49; npm fyrmestan 4/149
fyrmest adv. *first of all* 3/189
fyrst see **first**
fȳsan 1 *send forth, shoot* pret 3s fȳsde 12/269

gād f. *goad* as gāde 3/194; ds 3/15
Gadd pers. n. *Gadd* gp gaddes 12/287
*ġe***gaderian** 2 *gather* pret 3s gegaderode 7/27, 7/42, etc.
gafeluc m. *spear, missile* dp gafelucum 4/212
gafol n. *tribute* as 7/22, 7/59, 7/65, 11(g)/2 (him on gafol *as a gift to himself*), gofol 12/61; ds gafole 7/76, 12/32, 12/46
galan VI *sing, sound* inf 14/67, 18(a)/786 [MnE (nightin)gale]
gamen see **gomen**
gamol adj. *old, aged, ancient* nsm gomela 18(b)/1397
gān anom. (§128) *go, walk* inf 7/43, 12/247; imp p gāð 12/93; pres 1s gā 3/76; 2s gǣst 2/29; 3s gǣþ 6/43; 1p gāð (w. refl. unc) 2/51; 3p 4/237; subj 1s gā 3/99; 3s 18(b)/1394; pret 1s ēode 9/30; 3s 2/17, 6/13, 9/23, etc.; 3p ēodon 4/232, 4/236, 6/28, etc.; subj 3p 6/33, 12/229
ganet m. *gannet* gs ganetes 17/20
gang m. *flow* ds gange 14/23; *track* as 18(b)/1391 [MnE gang, gang(ster)]
gangan see **gongan**
*ġe***gangan** see *ġe***gongan**
gār m. *spear* ns 12/296; as 12/13, 12/134, 12/154, etc.; ds gāre 12/138; ap gāras 12/46, 12/67, 12/109 [MnE gar(fish)]
gārberend m. *spear-bearer, warrior* np 12/262
gārrǣs m. *storm of spears, battle* as 12/32
gāst m. *spirit, soul, angel* ns 4/61, gǣst 11(d)/9; as 9/123, 14/49; gs Gāstes 9/76; ds gāste 4/331, 12/176, gǣste 11(k)/8; np gāstas 14/11 (*souls, angels*); gp gāsta 14/152, 18(b)/1357 [MnE ghost]
gāstliċ adj. *spiritual* asn gāstlice 4/27; dsn gāstlicum 4/54 [MnE ghostly]
gāstlīċe adv. *spiritually, in the spiritual sense* 4/40, 4/44
gātehǣr n. *goat-hair* as 4/86
gatu see **ġeat**
gāð see **gān**
gǣst see **gān**
gǣst see **gāst**
gǣstliċ adj. *spectral, terrifying* nsn 16/73
gǣþ see **gān**
ġe conj. *and* 3/121, 3/166; **(ǣġðer) ġe . . . ġe** *both . . . and* 2/11, 4/289, 5/37, etc.
ġē pron. (§21) *ye, you* np 1/15, 2/3, 2/8, 2/10, 3/161, 3/170, etc.; gp ēower 3/154, 3/177, 3/202; dp ēow 1/35, 2/3, 2/50 (refl.), 2/52, 3/137, 3/157, 3/190, īow 5/54
ġēac m. *cuckoo* ns 17/53
ġeador adv. *together* 18(a)/835
ġeaf see **ġiefan**
ġeald see **ġieldan**
ġealga m. *gallows, cross* ns 14/10; as gealgan 14/40; dp gealgum 4/285
ġealgean see *ġe***ealgian**
ġealgtrēo n. *gallows-tree, cross* ds gealgtreowe 14/146
ġēap adj. *deceitful* comp ns gēappre 2/1
ġēap adj. *spacious, wide* nsm 13/11; asm gēapne 18(a)/836
*ġe***ġēap** see *ġe***ġēopan**
ġēar n. *year* as 7/17; ds geare 4/154, 7/21, 7/47, 7/64, etc.; is 4/269, 7/1, 7/7, 7/10, 8/78; ap gēar 4/268; gp gēara 4/155; dp gēarum 4/128, etc.
ġēara adv. *long ago* 10(b)/1, 14/28 (gēara iu *years ago, very long ago*), 16/22 [archaic MnE (days of) yore]
ġearcian 2 *prepare* pres 1s gearcie 3/152
ġeard m. *yard, enclosure* as 1/6

ġēardagas m. pl. *days gone by* dp gēardagum 16/44, 18(b)/1354

ġeare adv. *readily* 8/42; *clearly* 16/69, gearwe 16/71; gearwe ne . . . *not at all* 18(a)/878; superl. gearwost nsm 18(a)/715

ġēarmǣlum adv. *year by year* 10(b)/5

ġearo adj. *ready, prepared* nsm 6/18, 12/274; npm gearowe 12/72, 12/100; apm gearwe 3/128

ġearwe see **ġearo** and **ġeare**

*ġe***ġearwian** 2 *prepare* pret subj 2s gegearwode 9/95

ġeat n. *gate* ap gatu 2/76, 6/27, 6/36

Gēatas m. pl. *the Geats* gp Gēata 18(d)/3178

Gēatmæcgas m. pl. *men of the Geats* gp Gēatmecga 18(a)/829

ġefe see **ġiefu**

ġēman 1 *take heed* pret 3s gēmde 9/81

ġēn adv. *yet* 8/39, 11(k)/2, 18(a)/734, 18(d)/3167

ġeō adv. *formerly, of old* iū 5/3, 10(b)/1, 13/32, 14/28 (see **ġēara**), 14/87, giū 5/41, gū 8/71, etc.

ġēoc f. *help* ds gēoce 17/101

ġeocian 2 *yoke* inf 3/9; p ptc gegeoced 3/11

ġēocor adj. *grievous, sad* nsm 18(a)/765

ġeofon m. or n. *sea, ocean* gs gyfenes 18(b)/1394

ġeoguðe see **gioguð**

ġeoguðmyrþ f. *delight of the young* (*i.e. milk*) gs geoguðmyrþe 11(g)/2

ġeōmerunge see **ġeōmorung**

ġeōmor adj. *sad* nsm 15/17; dsf geōmorre 15/1, geōmran 17/53; dsm geōmran 10(b)/84

ġeōmormōd adj. *sad-minded, serious* nsm 15/42

ġeōmorung f. *sadness* ds geōmerunge 4/293

ġeond prep. w.a. *through, throughout* 4/63, 4/148, 4/233, 4/330, 7/62, 15/36, 16/3, giond 5/3, 5/30, etc. [MnE (be)yond]

ġeondhweorfan III *pervade, visit every part* pres 3s geondhweorfeð 16/51

ġeondscēawian 2 *survey, examine every part* pres 3s geondscēawað 16/52

ġeondþenċean 1 *meditate on, ponder every part* pres 1s geondþence 16/60; 3s geondþenceð 16/89

ġeong adj. *young* nsm 4/131, 11(j)/2, 12/210, 14/39, 15/42, etc.; nsf 11(p)/1; as noun nsm geonga 12/155

*ġe***ġēopan** II *take to oneself, receive, swallow* pret 1s gegēap 11(h)/9

ġeorn adj. w.g. *eager* nsm 10(b)/51, 12/107, 16/69; npm georne 12/73, giorne 5/10

ġeorne adv. *eagerly, zealously, readily* 4/295, 12/123, 12/206, 12/84, 16/52; compar. geornor 3/70, 18(a)/821

ġeornful adj. *eager* nsm 12/274

ġeornfulnes f. *desire* ds geornfulnesse 9/82 [MnE yearnfulness]

ġeornlīċe adv. *eagerly, zealously* 3/211, 9/81, 12/265; comp geornlīcor 8/20, 8/40, 8/43

ġēotan II *pour* inf 13/42

ġidda see **ġiedd**

ġiedd n. *word, speech, riddle* as 15/1, gied 11(c)/3; gs gieddes 11(n)/14; gp gidda 18(a)/868

ġieddian 2 *sing, recite* pret 3s gyddode 10(b)/84

ġiefan V *give* pret 3s geaf 1/20

ġiefstōl m. *throne* gs giefstolas 16/44

ġiefu f. *gift* ns 1/32, gifu 9/55; as gyfe 8/46, gife 9/14, 9/49, etc.; ds 9/2; ap gefe 8/17; gp gifena 17/40 (see note); dp gifum 4/272

ġieldan III *pay, render* pret 3s geald 7/22, 7/63 [MnE yield]

ġiellan III *cry out* pres 3s gielleð 17/62 [MnE yell]

ġielpes see **ġylp**

ġiernan 1 *entreat, beg for* pret 3p gyrndon (w.g.) 7/65 [MnE yearn]

ġiese adv. *yes* 3/15, 3/18, 3/21, 3/113, etc.

ġiestrandæġ m. *yesterday* ns 3/53

ġiet adv. *yet, still* 1/1, 2/70, gīt 4/17, gȳt 8/71, etc., gȳta 14/28; þā gȳt *still* 4/218, 12/168, etc.

ġif conj. *if* 2/23, 3/79, 3/118, 3/170, 4/9, gyf 4/21, etc.

ġife see **ġiefu**

ġifeðe adj. *given, granted by fate* nsm gyfeþe 18(a)/819

ġifheall f. *gift-hall* as gifhealle 18(a)/838

ġifre adj. *greedy, ravenous* nsm 17/62

ġifum see **ġiefu**

ġilp see **ġylp**

ġilphladen adj. *covered with glory, proud* nsm 18(a)/868

ġimm m. *gem* gimmas np 14/7, 14/16; ap 3/142

ġimstān m. *jewel* ap gimstanas 4/85 [MnE gemstone]

ġioguð f. *young people, youth* ns 5/58; ds geoguðe 16/35, 17/40

ġiōmonn m. *man of yore* gp giōmonna 10(b)/23

ġiond see **ġeond**

ġiorne see **ġeorn**

ġīsl m. *hostage* ns gȳsel 12/265; ds gīsle 6/21

ġit see **ġiet**

ġiū see **ġeō**

glæd adj. *kind, gracious* asm glædne 18(a)/863 [MnE glad]

glædlīċe adv. *joyfully* 9/103 [MnE gladly]

glædmōd adj. *joyous* nsm 13/33
*ġe***glængde** see **glengan**
glæs n. *glass* ns 1/4, as 3/142
glēaw adj. *wise, clear-sighted* nsm 10(b)/52, 16/73; comp nsm glēawra 11(c)/6
glēd f. *ember, burning coal* ns 11(o)/4 [MnE gleed]
glengan 1 *adorn* pret 3s geglængde 9/7, p ptc geglenged 9/59
glēobēam m. *harp* gs glēobēames 18(c)/2263
gleomu f. *splendour* ds gleoma 13/33
glēowian 2 *make merry, joke* pres ptc glēowiende 9/99
glīwstafum adv. *joyfully* 16/52
gnornian 2 *mourn, feel sorrow* inf 12/315; pres 3s gnornað 17/92
gōd adj. *good* nsm 1/12, 17/40, gōda 18(a)/758 (as noun); asm gōdne 10(b)/42, gōdan 12/187 (as noun); dsm gōdum 12/4; asn gōd 12/13; asf gōde 4/89, 14/70 (gōde hwīle *a long while*); npm 3/206, 4/306; apm 3/179; gpm gōdena 5/41, gōdra 10(b)/45; gpf gōdra 9/82; dpn gōdum 4/42
God m. *God* ns 1/12, 1/37, 2/2, 2/3, 2/55, 4/52, etc.; as 2/64, etc.; gs Godes 2/19, 2/61, 3/188, etc.; ds Gode 2/68, 4/242, 4/291, 4/299, 5/11, etc.
god n. (*pagan*) *god* np godo 8/19; gp goda 8/16
gōd n. *good, goodness, goods* as 2/11; gs gōdes 12/176; dp gōdum 9/64
Goda pers. n. *Goda* ns 7/14
godcund adj. *divine, religious* gsf godcundre 9/56; dsf 9/2; npm godcundan 5/10; gpm godcundra 5/4; dpm godcundum 9/4; dpf godcundan 9/80
godcundlīċe adv. *divinely* 9/13
godcundnes f. *divinity, Godhead* gs godcundnesse 8/10
*ġe***gōdian** 2 *endow* pret 3s gegōdode 4/272
Gōdmundingahām m. *Goodmanham* (*Yorkshire*) ns 8/73
Godrīc pers. n. *Godric* ns 12/187, 12/237, 12/321, 12/325
godspell n. *gospel* as godspel 4/35; ds godspelle 3/189
godsunu m. *godson* ns 6/39
Godwig pers. n. *Godwig* ns 12/192
Godwine pers. n. *Godwin* ns 7/44; 12/192
gofol see **gafol**
gold n. *gold* ns 1/4, 16/32, 17/101; as 3/142, 4/87, 11(l)/7, 11(n)/3, 14/18; ds golde 4/272, 12/35, 14/7, 14/16, 14/77, 17/97, etc.; is 11(j)/2
goldbeorht adj. *bright with gold* nsm 13/33
goldġiefa m. *gold-giver, lord* np goldgiefan 17/83
goldhilted adj. *gold-hilted* asn 11(n)/14
goldhord m. *hoard of gold, treasure* ap goldhordas 4/165
goldsele m. *gold-hall* as 18(a)/715
goldsmiþ m. *goldsmith* ap goldsmiþas 3/181
goldwine m. *generous lord* ns 16/35; as 16/22
gomela see **gamol**
gomelfeax adj. *hoary-haired* as noun nsm 17/92
gomen n. *entertainment, pastime, sport, mirth* ns 18(c)/2263; gs gamenes 4/213; ds gomene 17/20 [MnE game]
gomenwāþ f. *joyous journey* ds gomenwāþe 18(a)/854
gongan VII *go, walk* inf 9/90, 11(b)/1, 18(a)/711, gangan 12/3, 12/40, 12/62, 12/170; pres ptc gongende 9/24, 9/94; pres 1s gonge 15/35; subj 2p gangon 12/56; pret 3s gang 18(b)/1316
*ġe***gongan** VII *get, obtain, overrun* inf 10(b)/12, gegangan 12/59; p ptc gegongen 18(a)/822, 18(a)/893
Gota m. *Goth* ns 10(b)/9, 10(b)/45; np Gotan 10(a)/1, 10(b)/1; ap 10(b)/23; gp Gotena 10(b)/5, 10(b)/38
gram adj. *fierce, hostile* gsm grames 18(a)/765; npm grame 12/262; graman 18(a)/777; as noun dpm gramum 12/100
Grantabriċscir f. *Cambridgeshire* as Grantabricscire 7/68
grāp f. *grasp, claw* gs grāpe 18(a)/836; dp grāpum 18(a)/765
grǣdiġ adj. *greedy* nsm 4/242, 17/62, nsf 11(g)/2
græf n. *grave* as 17/97
grǣg adj. *grey* nsm grǣga 4/241
Gregōrius pers. n. *Gregory* ns 4/304
gremian 2 *enrage* p ptc nsm gegremod 12/138; npm gegremode 12/296
Grendel pers. n. *Grendel* ns 18(a)/711, 18(a)/819; as 18(b)/1334, 18(b)/1354; gs Grendles 18(a)/836, 18(b)/1391
grēne adj. *green, raw* apf 3/171
grēot n. *dirt, dust* ds grēote 12/315, 18(d)/3167
grēotan II *weep* pres ptc grēotende np 14/70; pres 3s grēoteþ 18(b)/1342
grēt see **grētan**
grētan 1 *greet, approach, touch* inf 5/1, 18(a)/803 (*harm*); pres 3s grēt 4/2, grēteð 16/52; pret 3s grētte 9/27
grim adj. *fierce* nsm 12/61 [MnE grim]
grimme adv. *grimly, fiercely* 11(m)/9, 12/109, 13/14
grīn n. *snare* dp grīnum 3/110
grindan III *grind, sharpen* p ptc gegrunden 13/14; apm gegrundene 12/109
gripe m. *grasp* ns 13/8
grið n. *truce* as 7/75, 12/35, ds griðe 7/76

grund m. *ground, earth, bottom* as 12/287, 18(b)/1367, 18(b)/1394; ap grundas 17/104

ġe **grundene** see **grindan**

grymetian 2 *roar, rage* pret 3s grymetode 4/302

gryreleōð n. *song of terror, terrible song* as 18(a)/786; gp gryreleōða 12/285

ġū see **ġeō**

guma m. *man* ns 16/45, 18(a)/868, 18(b)/1384; gs guman 14/49; np 12/94; gp gumena 11(h)/10, 18(a)/715, 18(a)/878, 18(b)/1367, guman 14/146 (see note)

gūð f. *war, battle* as gūðe 12/325; gs 10(b)/9, 12/192; ds 10(b)/23, 12/13, 12/94, 12/187, etc.

gūðbill n. *war-sword* gp gūðbilla 18(a)/803

gūðdēað m. *death in battle* ns 18(c)/2249

gūðhrēð n. *glory in battle* ns 18(a)/819

gūðplega m. *the game of battle, conflict* ns 12/61

gūðrinc m. *warrior* ns 12/138, 18(a)/838

ġyddode see **ġieddian**

ġyf see **ġif**

ġyfe see **ġiefu**

ġyfenes see **ġeofon**

ġyfeþe see **ġifeþe**

ġylp m. *boasting, pride* as gilp 18(a)/829; gs gylpes 10(b)/9, gielpes 16/69 [MnE yelp]

ġylpword n. *boasting word* dp gylpwordum 12/274

gȳman 1 w.g. *care about or for* pret 3p gȳmdon 12/192

Ġypeswīċ m. *Ipswich* ns 7/20

gyrdan 1 *gird* pret 3s gyrde 8/64

gyrndon see **ġiernan**

gyrwan 1 *adorn, prepare, dress* pret 3p gyredon 14/77; p ptc gegyred 14/16, gegyrwed 14/23

ġȳsel see **ġīsl**

gyst m. *stranger* np gystas 12/86 [MnE guest]

ġystran adv. *yesterday* 18(b)/1334

ġȳt(a) see **ġiet**

habban 3 *have, hold* inf 2/58, 3/119, 3/172, 4/112 (*keep*) etc.; pres 1s hæbbe 3/11, 3/12, 3/15, 3/23, 8/13; 2s hæfst 3/14, 3/17, 3/22, 3/112, 3/180, hafast 12/231; 3s hæfþ 3/193, 4/101, 4/163, etc., hafað 8/14, 13/6 etc.; 1p habbað 5/37, etc.; subj 3s hæbbe 4/104, 4/164; 3p hæbben 3/128, 5/59; pret 3s hæfde 4/6, 4/14, 6/7, 8/8, etc.; 1p hæfdon 8/15; 3p 4/20, 4/36, 4/229, 6/16, etc., hæfdan 10(b)/6; subj 8/19, 9/101. With negative: pres 2s næfst 4/167, 4/177; 3s næfð 4/114; 3p nabbað 4/102; subj 3s næbbe 17/42; pret 3p næfdon 4/228

hacod m. *pike* ap hacodas 3/87 [MnE haked]

hād m. *office, order* as 18(b)/1335 (*manner*); ds hāde 5/63; np hādas 5/10; gp hāda 5/4 [MnE (mother)hood, (child)hood]

hādian 2 *ordain* p ptc *ordained (ones), clerics* dpm gehādodum 4/289

ġe **hādodum** see **hādian**

hafast see **habban**

hafela m. *head* as hafelan 18(b)/1327, ds 18(b)/1372

hafenian 2 *raise aloft* pret 3s hafenode 12/42, 12/309

hafoc m. *hawk* ns 18(c)/2263; as 3/117, 3/118, 12/8; ds hafoce 3/111; ap hafocas 3/112, 3/114, 3/120, 3/124

hagle see **hægl**

hagostealdmon m. *bachelor, warrior* ns 11(j)/2

hāl adj. *safe, unhurt* asm hālne 4/313; npm hāle 12/292 [MnE hale, whole]

ġe **hāl** adj. *whole, intact* nsm 4/94, 4/257

hālettan 1 *hail* pret 3s hālette 9/27

hālgian 2 *consecrate* pret 1p hālgodon 8/48; p ptc gehālgod 7/1, gehālgade 8/6, gehālgode 8/75 [MnE hallow]

hālian 2 *heal* p ptc gehālod 4/258

hāliġ adj. *holy* nsm 9/41, Hālga 4/63, 4/280; asm hālgan 4/256, 4/300; gsm 4/224; dsm 4/304, 4/331; asn hālige 4/34, 4/244, hālig 9/56; gsn hālgan 9/66, 9/74; dsn 4/248, 4/309; nsf hālige 7/52; npm 14/11, hālgan 4/288; apm 10(b)/25; apf hālgan 4/89; as noun m. *saint* ns hālga 4/316, 4/319; as hālgan 4/218; gs 4/267; ds 4/253, 4/274, 4/299, 4/314; Hālgan (*God*) 17/122; np 4/322; ap 4/324; gpm hālgena 4/318, dpm hālgum 14/143, 14/154

hāliġdōm m. *relics* ds hāligdome 4/270

hāliġnes f. *religion* gs hālignesse 8/53, 8/62 [MnE holiness]

ġe **hālod** see **hālian**

hals m. *neck* as 12/141

hālwende adj. *salutary, salvific* apn 9/121

hām adv. *homewards, home* 2/78, 4/135, 4/244, 9/23, 12/251

hām m. *home* as 14/148, 17/117, 18(a)/717, ds (or locative) hām 3/10, hāme 12/292

Hamtūn m. *Southampton* ds Hamtūne 7/61

Hamtūnscīr f. *Hampshire* as Hamtūnscīre 7/72; ds 6/2, 7/13, 7/57

Hāmtūnscīr f. *Northamptonshire* ds Hāmtūnscīre 7/70

hand f. *hand* ns 12/141, 18(b)/1343; as 2/63, 12/112, hond 8/64, 17/96, 18(a)/834; ds handa 12/149, 14/59, 18(a)/746, honda 9/104, 9/123, 18(a)/814; ap handa 4/111, 4/191, honda 11(b)/5, 16/43; dp handum 12/4, 12/14, hondum 11(o)/5, 16/4, handon 12/7

handbona m. *slayer with the hand* ds handbanan 18(b)/1330

handscalu f. *hand-troop, companions* ds handscale 18(b)/1317

hangian 2 *hang* pres 1s hongige 11(j)/11; 3p hongiað 18(b)/1363; pret 3p hangodon 4/283

hār adj. *hoary, grey, grey-haired* nsm 12/169, 18(b)/1307, hāra 16/82; asm hārne 13/43, 18(a)/887

hara m. *hare* ap haran 3/51

hās adj. *hoarse* nsm 3/16

hāt n. *heat* ds hāte 13/38 (see note)

hāt adj. *hot* nsm hāt 18(a)/897; dsm hāton 18(a)/849; npn 13/41; npf 17/11; npm hāte 13/43, 13/45; compar. **hātra** npm hātran 17/64

*ġe***hāt** n. *promise* ap 10(a)/9

hātan VII *command, order, call, name* pres 1s hāte 5/2, 14/95; 3s hǣt 4/164, hāteð 5/1; 1p hātað 10(a)/12; pass. hātte 1s 11(f)/15, 11(h)/16, 11(j)/19 (**hwæt ic hātte** *what I am called*); 3s 4/128, 4/300, 10(b)/53, 11(b)/7, 11(n)/16; pret 3s hēt 2/52, 2/69 (*named*), 4/216, 4/285, 7/32, 9/52, etc., hēht 8/70, 9/50, 9/65, 10(b)/70, etc.; 3p hēton 12/30, 14/31; p ptc gehāten 4/48, 4/267, 4/298, 10(a)/13, hāten 6/8, 12/75, 12/218, np hātne 10(a)/3 [archaic MnE hight]

*ġe***hātan** VII *promise, vow* pres 1s gehāte 12/246, 18(b)/1392; pret 3s gehēt 10(a)/7, 10(b)/35, 12/289

hātheort adj. *angry, impulsive* nsm 16/66 [MnE hotheart(ed)]

*ġe***hātland** n. *promised land* gs gehātlandes 9/73

hātte see **hātan**

hæbbe see **habban**

hæfde see **habban**

hæfdon see **habban**

hæfst see **habban**

hæft m. *captive* asm hæfton 18(a)/788

*ġe***hæftan** 1 *catch, hold captive* pres 3p gehæftaþ 3/78; p ptc asm gehæft 2/67; nsf 7/4

hæfþ see **habban**

hæġl m. *hail* ns 17/17, 17/32; ds hagle 16/48

hæġlfaru f. *hailstorm* as hæglfare 16/105

hǣlan 1 *heal, save* inf 14/85; p ptc npf gehǣlede 4/262

hæle m. *warrior, man* ns 10(b)/53, 16/73

Hǣlend m. *Saviour* (*lit. Healer*) gs Hǣlendes 4/203, 14/25; ds Hǣlende 4/195, 4/210

hæleþ m. *hero, warrior* ns 14/39, 14/78, 14/95; np 11(f)/5, 11(n)/1, 12/214, 18(c)/2247, hælæð 12/249; gp hæleða 11(d)/3, 12/74; dp hæleþum 16/105, 18(c)/2262

hǣlo f. *luck* as hǣle 18(a)/719; *salvation* gs 8/46 [obs. MnE heal]

*ġe***hæp** adj. *suitable* dsf gehæpre 3/42 [MnE hap(py)]

hæpse f. *hasp, door-fastener* as hæpsan 4/277

hærfest m. *autumn* as 3/122 [MnE harvest]

hǣring m. *herring* ap hǣringas 3/93

hærliċ adj. *noble* nsf 10(b)/43

hǣs f. *behest, command* as hǣse 4/201; gs 2/77

hǣste adj. *violent* asm hǣstne 18(b)/1335

Hǣstingas m. pl. *Hastings* (*Sussex*) ap 7/71

hǣt see **hātan**

hǣþen adj. *heathen* dsm hǣþenum 4/194, 4/221; npm hǣðene 12/181; asf hǣþene 18(a)/852; as noun npm hǣþenan 4/211, 4/217, 4/218, 4/261, hǣþene 12/55

hǣþstapa m. *heath-stalker, stag* ns 18(b)/1368

hē, hēo, hit pron (§18) *he, she, it* pl. *they* nsm hē (*he*) 1/14, 1/21, 1/35, 2/14, etc.; asm hine (*him*) 1/34, 2/18 (refl.), 2/45, 3/60, 3/61, 6/14 (refl.), etc., hiene 5/23, 6/3, etc.; gsm his 1/1, 1/2, 1/3, 1/31, etc.; dsm him 2/55, 2/56, 2/62, etc.; nsn hit (*it*) 3/21, 3/53, etc.; asn 2/58, 4/130, 4/294, etc.; nsf hēo (*she*) 1/11, 1/23, 1/32, 2/26, 2/32, hīo 5/81; asf hīe 5/49, 5/80, hī 4/315, etc.; gsf hire (*her*) 2/14, 2/32, 7/52, etc.; dsf 2/12, 9/50, etc.; np hīe (*they*) 1/28, 1/34, 2/15, 2/17, 2/48, 2/49, 2/56, 3/42, 3/43, 3/121, hī 4/26, 4/129, 7/49, hig 4/40, 4/41, hēo 9/55, 9/104, 9/106, etc.; ap hīe (*them*) 3/19, 3/25, 3/26, 3/30, 3/121 (refl.), 3/123, 3/161, hī 4/310, 7/53; gp hira (*their*) 1/28, 2/14, 2/76, 3/84, heora 4/148, 4/226, hiora 5/7, 5/18, 7/66, hiera 6/19, hyra 11(a)/3; dp him (*them*) 2/16, 3/180, 4/143, 5/36, heom 7/57, etc.

hēa see **hēah**

hēafod n. *head* as 2/32, 4/219, 4/223, 4/238, 9/116, 16/43; gs hēafdes 4/243; ds hēafde 4/227, 4/246, 10(b)/43; dp hēafdum 14/63 (w. ds meaning: see note); gp hēafda 11(b)/4

hēafodlēas adj. *headless* nsm 11(j)/10

hēafodman m. *leader* ds hēafodmen 4/142; np 4/149 [MnE headman]

hēagum see **hēah**

hēah adj. *high* nsm 16/98, 18(d)/3157, nsn 13/22; nsf hēa 11(d)/4; asm hēanne 14/40, 16/82; dsm hēan 18(a)/713; apm hēan 17/34; dpm hēagum 4/285; compar. **hīerra** (§75) dsm hīerran 5/63

hēahburg f. *chief city* ns 10(a)/21

hēahfæder m. *patriarch* ds hēahfædere 4/15; 14/134 (*God the father*)

healdan VII *keep, observe, hold, stand firm* inf 4/270, 12/14, 12/19, 12/41 (w.d. of person and g. of thing), 12/74, etc., healdon 10(b)/71; infl inf (tō) healdenne 4/109; pres 3s hylt 4/313; 3p healdaþ 17/87; subj 3s healde 16/14; pret 3s hēold 4/243, 11(k)/5 (*foster, cherish*), 18(a)/788; 3p hīoldon 5/34 (*occupied*); subj 3p hēoldon 12/20

*ġe***healdan** VII *hold, maintain, preserve* inf 12/167; pres 3s gehealdeþ 16/112, subj 1s gehealde 3/161; pret 3p gehīoldon 5/8; p ptc gehealden 4/220
healf adj. *half* asf healfe 7/69
healf f. *side* (w.d. of person) as healfe 14/20; ds 4/140, 12/152, 12/318, 18(c)/2262; gp healfa 18(a)/800
heall f. *hall* ns 8/29; ds healle 4/203, 11(n)/1, 11(n)/13, 12/214
healðegn m. *hall-thane* ap healðegnas 18(a)/719
healwudu m. *wood of a hall* ns 18(b)/1317
hēan adj. *dejected, wretched* nsm 16/23
hēanliċ adj. *humiliating, shameful* nsn 12/55
hēanne see **hēah**
hēap m. *band, troop, company* as 18(a)/730 [MnE heap]
heard adj. *hard, resolute, bitter, fierce, brave* nsm 11(j)/10, 12/130, 13/8, 15/43, 18(a)/886, hearda 11(n)/9, 18(c)/2255; asn hearde 18(b)/1343, heard 12/214; asm heardne 12/167, 12/236; asf hearde 12/33; gsn heardes 12/266; dp heardum 4/208; dpm 18(b)/1335; compar. **heardra** nsm 12/312, heardran asf 18(a)/719; superl. **heardost** nsn 14/87
heardhicgende adj. *brave-minded* npm 18(a)/799
heardlīċe adv. *fiercely* 12/261 [MnE hardly]
heardsǣliġ adj. *unfortunate, unhappy, ill-fated* asm heardsǣligne 15/19
hearm m. *damage, harm, grief, sorrow* ns 7/8, as 7/50; gp hearma 12/223
hearmscaþa m. *pernicious enemy* ns 18(a)/766
hearpe f. *harp* as hearpan 9/22, gs 18(c)/2262, ds 9/21, 17/44
heaþodēor adj. *brave in battle* dpm heaþodēorum 18(a)/772
heaþorōf adj. *brave in battle* npm heaþorōfe 18(a)/864
hēawan VII *hew, cut down, kill* inf 18(a)/800; pret 3s hēow 12/324; 3p hēowon 12/181; p ptc gehēawen 13/12
hebban VI *raise up, lift* inf 14/31 [MnE heave]
hēdærn n. *storeroom* as 3/160
hefian see **hefiġ**
hefiġ adj. *heavy, oppressive* dsn hefian 14/61; compar. npf hefigran 16/49
hefiġan 2 *weigh down, burden* p ptc hefgad 9/89
hefiġtīme adj. *burdensome, troublesome* nsn 4/4
heġe m. *fence, enclosure* dp hegum 8/54 [MnE hedge]
hēht see **hātan**
hell f. *hell* ns hel 18(a)/852; gs helle 4/80, 18(a)/788
helm m. *protection, cover, helmet* ns 18(b)/1321 (*lord*), 18(c)/2255, as 18(b)/1392
help f. *help* as helpe 16/16; ds 14/102
helsceaða m. *thief from hell, devil* np helsceaðan 12/180
helwaru f. pl. *inhabitants of hell* gp helwara 11(n)/6
*ġe***hende** prep. w.d. *near to* 12/294; adv. gehende *nearby* 4/220, superl. gehendost 4/169
hēo see **hē**
heofon m. *heaven* as 9/41, heofenan 4/52, 4/56; gs heofenes 14/64; ap heofonas 9/76, 14/103; gp heofona 14/45; dp heofonum 2/62, 2/75, 12/172, 14/85, 14/134, etc.
heofonliċ adj. *heavenly* asm heofonlicne 14/148, heofonlican 4/262; dsm 4/330; asn heofonlice 7/26; gsn heofonlican 9/9, heofonlecan 9/78; isn heofonlecan 9/111; nsf heofonlic 9/55; dsf heofonlicre 2/79
heofonrīċe n. *kingdom of heaven* gs heofonrīces 9/36, 14/91
heold see **healdan**
heolfor m. or n. *blood, gore* ds heolfre 18(a)/849
heolstor m. *darkness, hiding-place* as 18(a)/755, ds heolstre 16/23 [MnE holster]
heom (= **him**) see **hē**
heonon adv. *hence, from here* 12/246, 14/132, 15/6, 17/37, 18(b)/1361
heora (= **hira**) see **hē**
heord f. *care, custody* ns 9/25 [MnE herd]
hēore adj. *safe, pleasant, good* nsf hēoru 18(b)/1372
heorodrēor m. *battle-blood* ds heorodrēore 18(a)/849
heorot m. *deer, stag* ns 18(b)/1369; ap heorotas 3/51, 3/56, 3/58 [MnE hart]
Heorot m. *Heorot* ds Heorute 18(a)/766, Heorote 18(b)/1330
heorra m. *lord* ns 12/204
heorte f. *heart* ns 12/312; as heortan 17/11; ds 12/145; gs 15/43, 16/49, 17/34; ap 3/166, 4/63
Heortfordscīr f. *Hertfordshire* as Heortfordscīre 7/68
heorðġenēat m. *hearth-companion, retainer* np heorðgenēatas 12/204, 18(d)/3179
heorðwerod n. *body of household retainers* as 12/24
hēow see **hēawan**
hēr adv. *here* 1/1, 2/50, 2/54, 3/144, etc.
hēran see **hīeran**
hēræfter adv. *hereafter* (i.e. *in the following pages*) 4/134
here m. *invading army* ns 7/34, 7/41; as 7/31; ds 12/292
hereġeatu f. *heriot, war-equipment* as 12/48

herehūð f. *booty, plunder* gs herehūðe 7/40
herenes f. *praise* ds herenesse 9/34, herenisse 9/123
herepād f. *coat of mail* ns 18(c)/2258
hererinc m. *soldier, hero* as 10(b)/71
hereswēg m. *noise of an army, martial sound* ns 13/22
heretēma m. *ruler* ns 10(b)/31
heretoga m. *military leader, commander* ns 10(b)/47, heretoha 10(a)/12; ds heretogan 4/194; np 7/43
hēreð see **hīeran**
herġas see **heriġ**
herġen see **heriġean**
herġian 2 *ravage* pres ptc npm herġiende 4/148; pret 3p hergodon 7/11, heregodon 7/77; p ptc gehergod 7/5, 7/20, geheregod 7/14 [MnE harry]
herġung f. *ravaging, harrying* ns 4/251; ds hergunge 7/55, 7/60
herheard m. *abode in a grove* as 15/15
heriġ m. *pagan sanctuary, fane* as 8/71; ds herige 8/68; np hergas 13/29; ap 8/54
heriġean 1 *praise* inf 9/36; pres subj 3s herge 18(d)/3175, 3p hergen 17/77
hēt see **hātan**
hī see **hē**
hicgan 3 *think, plan, be intent upon* inf 12/4 (see note), hycgan 15/11, 17/117; pres ptc asm hycgendne 15/20; pres subj 3s hycge 16/14
hider adv. *hither* 3/137, 3/140, 12/57, 14/103, hieder 5/12
hīe see **hē**
hieder see **hider**
hīeg n. *hay* ds hīege 3/19
hiene (= **hine**) see **hē**
hiera see **hē**
hīeran 1 (w.d.) *obey, hearken to, hear* inf hēran 10(b)/31, hȳran 11(h)/15; 3s hēreð 11(m)/5; pret 1s hȳrde 8/21, 18(b)/1346; 1p hȳrdon 9/125; 3s hȳrde 18(a)/875
*ġe***hīeran** 1 *hear* inf gehīran 4/32, gehȳran 8/40, 14/78; infl inf (tō) gehȳranne 9/69; pres 2s gehȳrst 12/45; 3s gehȳrð 4/9; pret 1s gehīerde 2/21, gehȳrde 12/117, 14/26, 17/18; 2s gehīerdest 2/36; 3s gehȳrde 4/221, 8/1, 8/41, etc.; 3p gehīerdon 2/17, gehīerdun 6/23, gehȳrdon 4/309, 18(a)/785
hierdebōc f. *shepherd book* as 5/68
hīerran see **hēah**
hīersumian 2 *be obedient, obey* pret 3p hīersumedon 5/6
*ġe***hīersumian** 2 *obey* pret 2s gehīersumodest (w.g.) 2/77
*ġe***hīersumnes** f. *obedience* gs gehīersumnesse 2/43
hig (= **hīe**) see **hē**
hige m. *mind, heart, courage, thought* ns 12/312, hyge 15/17, 16/16, 17/44, 17/58, 18(a)/755; ds 12/4, 17/96
Higelāc see **Hygelāc**
higeþīhtig adj. *strong-hearted, determined* asm higeþīhtigne 18(a)/746
hiht see **hyht**
hild f. *battle* as hilde 12/33; ds 11(j)/4, 12/8, 12/48, 12/55, 12/123, etc.
hildedēor adj. *brave in battle* nsm 18(a)/834; npm hildedēore 18(d)/3169
hildemecg m. *warrior* np hildemecgas 18(a)/799
hilderinc m. *warrior* ns 12/169, 18(b)/1307; np hilderincas 14/61; gp hilderinca 14/72
hine see **hē**
hinfūs adj. *eager to get away* nsm 18(a)/755
Hinguar pers. n. *Hingwar* ns 4/149, 4/151; as 4/198; gs Hingwares 4/161; ds Hingware 4/169, 4/194
hīo (= **hīe**) see **hē**
*ġe***hioldon** see *ġe***healdan**
hiora see **hē**
hira see **hē**
*ġe***hīran** see *ġe***hīeran**
hire see **hē**
hīredmann m. *retainer, warrior* np hīredmen 12/261
his see **hē**
hit see **hē**
hīw n. *shape, form* as 1/20 [MnE hue]
*ġe***hladan** VI *load* pret 3s gehleōd 18(a)/895
hlāf m. *bread* as 3/199; gs hlāfes 2/41; ds hlāfe 3/165 [MnE loaf]
hlāford m. *lord, master* ns 3/177, 6/31, 12/135, 12/189, etc.; as 14/45; gs hlāfordes 3/11, 4/226, 18(d)/3179; ds hlāforde 3/27, 4/193, 10(b)/47, 12/318
hlāfordlēas adj. *lordless, without a lord* nsm 12/251
hlǣder f. *ladder* as hlǣdre 11(n)/6; ds hlæddre 4/278, 4/283
hlæst m. *load, freight* dp hlæstum 3/135
hlǣw m. *mound, barrow, cave* as 18(d)/3157, 18(d)/3169
hleahtor m. *laughter* ds hleahtre 17/21
hlēapan VII *leap, gallop* inf 18(a)/864; pret 3s hlēop 8/65
*ġe***hlēapan** VII *leap upon, mount* pret 3s gehlēop 12/189
hlēo n. *protection, shelter, protector* ns 12/74, 18(a)/791; as 11(f)/5
hlēomæg m. *protecting kinsman* gp hlēomæga 17/25
hlēop see **hlēapan**
hlēosceorp n. *protecting garment* ds hlēosceorpe 11(k)/5
hlēoðor n. *sound, cry, voice* as 17/20; is hlēoþre 11(j)/4

hlēoðrian 2 *make a noise, speak* pret 3s hlēoðrode 14/26
hliehhan VI *laugh, exult* pret 3s hlōh 12/147
hlīfian 2 *tower, rise up* pres 1s hlīfige 14/85
hlimman III *roar, resound* inf 17/18
hlin m. *maple* ns 11(n)/9
hlīsa m. *fame, reputation* as hlīsan 10(b)/53
hlōh see **hliehhan**
hlūd adj. *loud* nsm 11(e)/1
hlūde adv. *loud, loudly* 1/8, 11(d)/7
hlūttor adj. *pure* isn hlūttre 9/118
hlynsian 2 *resound* pret 3s hlynsode 18(a)/770
hlystan 1 *listen* pres subj 1p hlysten 1/8
*ġe***hlystan** 1 *listen* pret 3p gehlyston 12/92
hnāg see **hnīgan**
hnǣgan 1 *bring low, humble* p ptc gehnǣged 17/88
hnīgan I *bow down* pret 1s hnāg 14/59
hnītan I *strike, clash together* pret 3p hniton 18(b)/1327
hō see **hōh**
hof n. *building* np hofu 13/29
hogian 2 *think, give thought, intend* pret 3s hogode 12/133; 3p hogodon 12/123; subj 3s hogode 12/128 [Late WS for hicgan]
hōh m. *heel* ds hō 2/32; *promontory* ds hōe 18(d)/3157
*ġe***hola** m. *confidant, close friend* gp geholena 16/31
hold adj. *loyal, friendly, gracious* nsm 10(b)/56, 17/41; gpm holdra 15/17; superl. holdost asn 12/24
holen m. *holly* ns 11(n)/10
holm m. *sea* as 16/82; gp holma 17/64
holt n. *wood, forest* gs holtes 12/8, 14/29; ds holte 4/231
holtwudu m. *tree of the forest, forest* as 14/91, 18(b)/1369
hōn VII *hang, be hanged* inf 4/285
hond see **hand**
hongiað see **hangian**
hongige see **hangian**
hord n. *hoard, treasure* gs hordes 18(a)/887; ds horde 18(d)/3164
hordcofa m. *heart* as hordcofan 16/14
horn m. *horn* ns 1/8; dp hornum 2/67, 18(c)/1369
horngestrēon n. *abundance of gables* ns 13/22
hornreced adj. *gabled house* as 18(a)/704
hors n. *horse* as 3/69, 12/2; dp horsum 3/210
horsweġ m. *bridle path, horseway* ds horsweġe 1/6
hraðe adj. *quick* superl. radost 6/19
hraðe adv. *quickly, soon* 2/45, 4/193, 4/301, 8/48, raðe 7/20, 12/30, 12/164, 12/288, etc. [MnE rath(er), archaic MnE rathe]
hræding f. *haste* ds hrædinge 4/249
hrædlīċe adv. *forthwith, swiftly* 3/207, 8/30
hrædwyrde adj. *hasty of speech* nsm 16/66
hrægl n. *dress, garment* ns 11(d)/1 [archaic MnE rail]
hræw n. *corpse* ns 14/72, as 14/53
hrēam m. *shouting* ns 12/106; ds hrēame 3/16
hrēaw adj. *raw* apm hrēawe 3/171
hreddan 1 *save, rescue* inf 11(j)/18
hremm m. *raven* np hremmas 12/106
hrēoh adj. *troubled* nsm hrēoh 10(b)/71, hrēo 16/16; asf 16/105 (*fierce*); dsn hrēon 18(b)/1307
hrēoriġ adj. *ruinous* npm hrēorge 13/3
hrēosan II *fall* inf 16/48; pres ptc nsf hrēosende 16/102; p ptc npm gehrorene 13/3
hrēowcearig adj. *sorrowful, troubled* nsm 14/25
hrepian 2 *touch* pret subj 1p hrepoden 2/7
hrēran 1 *set in motion, stir* inf 16/4
hreþer n. *heart* as 17/63; ds hreþre 13/41; gp hreþra 16/72
hreðerbealo n. *distress* as 18(b)/1343
hreðerloca m. *enclosure of the heart, breast* as hreðerlocan 17/58
hrif n. *belly, womb* ds hrife 11(h)/12
hrīm m. *frost* ns 13/4, 17/32; as 16/48; is hrīme 16/77 [archaic MnE rime]
hrīmceald adj. *ice-cold* asf hrīmcealde 16/4
hrīmġeat n. *frosty gate* ns 13/4
hrīmġicel m. *icicle* dp hrīmgicelum 17/17
hrīnan I *touch* 3s hrīneð 11(h)/12; p ptc hrinen 8/32
hrinde adj. *covered with frost* nsm 18(b)/1363
hring m. *ring* ns 1/4, 18(c)/2260 (*ring-mail, armour*); ap hringas 12/161, 13/19
hringloca m. *ring-mail shirt, corselet* ap hringlocan 12/145
hringmere m. *circular pool* as 13/45
hringþegu f. *receiving of rings* (*by a retainer from his lord*) ds hringþege 17/44
hrīð f. *snowstorm* ns 16/102
hrōf m. *roof* ns 13/31, as 18(a)/836; gs hrōfes 11(f)/5; ds hrōfe 9/41; np hrōfas 13/3
hrōstbēag m. *circle formed by inner roofwork, ceiling-vault* gs hrōstbēages 13/31
*ġe***hrorene** see **hrēosan**
Hrōðgār pers. n. *Hrothgar* ns 18(b)/1321; as 18(a)/863; gs Hrōðgāres 18(a)/717, 18(a)/826 [MnE Roger]
hrūse f. *earth* ns 18(c)/2247; as hrūsan 11(d)/1, 11(f)/11, 13/29, 16/102, 17/32, 18(a)/772; gs 13/8, 16/23
hrycg m. *back* as 11(b)/5, is hrycge 11(f)/11 [MnE ridge]
hryre m. *ruin, fall* ns 13/31, as 18(d)/3179; gp 16/7 (see note)
hrȳðig adj. *snow-swept, exposed to storms* npm hrȳðge 16/77

hū adv. *how* 3/7, 3/41, 3/48, 3/57, 3/75, etc.; conj. 4/169, 4/199, 4/260, 16/30, 16/35, 16/61, etc.
Hubba pers. n. *Hubba* ns 4/150, 4/152
huilpe f. *curlew* gs huilpan 17/21 [dialectal MnE whaup]
Humbre f. *the Humber River* gs Humbran 7/40; ds Humbre 5/15
hund m. *dog* as 3/118; ap hundas 3/43; dp hundum 3/24, 3/49, 18(b)/1368 [MnE hound]
hund num. *hundred* ns 11(b)/4, 13/8
hundnigontiġ num. *ninety* dp hundnigontigum 7/48
hungor m. *hunger, famine* ns hungor 17/11; as hunger 4/78; ds hungre 4/80
hungrig adj. *hungry* nsm 4/242
hunta m. *huntsman* ns 3/38, 3/39, 3/40, etc.; np huntan 3/5
Huntadunscīr f. *Huntingdonshire* as Huntadunscīre 7/70
huntian 2 *hunt* inf 3/46, 3/47
huntoþ m. *hunting, game* as 3/65 (*game*); ds (on) huntoþe (*on a*) *hunt* 3/52, 3/54
hūru adv. *certainly, especially* 4/228, 14/10
hūs n. *house* ns 9/91; as 3/202, 8/30, 9/24; ds hūse 9/23, 9/94
hūsl n. *Eucharist, the consecrated bread and wine for Holy Communion* as 9/100, 9/103; gs hūsles 9/102
huxlīċe adv. *shamefully* 4/206
hwā, hwæt pron. (§20) *who, what, someone, something* ns hwā 2/23, 3/83, 3/159, 4/21 (*someone*), 4/65 (*someone*), 8/56, etc.; as hwæne 12/2 (*each one*); gs hwæs 1/36, 3/39; nsn hwæt 1/35, 8/35; asn 3/3, 3/7, 3/17, 3/22, 3/28, 3/55, 3/65, 3/66 (see **swā**), 3/73, 3/78 (see **swā**), 3/92, 4/25 (*something*), 4/40, etc.; dsn hwǣm 3/163; isn hwon 9/96 (see **for**), 17/43 (to hwon *to what, as to what*); hwȳ *why* 1/37, 2/2, 2/26, hwī 4/31, for hwȳ (see **for**)
*ġe***hwā** pron. *each, everyone* nsm 4/310; gsn gehwæs 9/38; dsm gehwām 16/63, 17/72
hwanon adv. *whence* 3/193, 3/194, hwonon 9/53
hwæder see **hwider**
hwæl m. *whale* as 3/95, 3/98; gs hwæles 17/60; ap hwalas 3/105
hwælhuntoþ m. *whale-hunt* as 3/100
hwælweg m. *path of the whale, the sea* as 17/63
hwæne pron. see **hwā**
hwænne conj. *until the time when* 12/67, 14/136
hwǣr adv. *where* 1/3, 2/20, 3/81, 5/81 (*somewhere*), etc.; conj. 2/54, 4/328, 15/8, 16/26
*ġe***hwǣr** adv. *everywhere* 4/232, 7/8
hwæs see **hwā**
*ġe***hwæs** see *ġe***hwā**
hwæt interj. *lo!* 4/168, 4/201, 4/223, 8/19, 8/31, 12/231, 14/1, 18(c)/2248
hwæt pron. see **hwā**
hwæt adj. *vigorous, quick, active* nsm 17/40
hwæthwugu pron. *something* as 9/28
hwætrēd m. *ingenuity, quick design* as 13/19
hwæðer conj. *whether* 4/300, 9/100, 18(b)/1314, 18(b)/1356, hwæþer 9/104. See **hwæþer þe**
*ġe***hwæðer** indef. adj. *either* nsm 18(a)/814, asf gehwæðere 12/112
hwæþere adv., conj. *however, nevertheless, yet, but* 8/3, hwæðre 9/11, 9/32, 9/89, 14/18, 14/38, 14/42, etc.
*ġe***hwæðeres** adv. *in both respects* 10(b)/25
hwæþer þe conj. *or* 3/119
hwæþre see **hwæþere**
hwearfian 2 *wave* pret 3s hwearfode 10(b)/10
hwelċ interrogative pron. and adj. *which, what, what kind of* nsm 3/186, 3/212 (swa hwelc swa *whatsoever*); asm hwelcne 3/1, 3/37, 3/71, 3/118; dsm hwelcum (see **swa**) 2/10; dsm hwylcum 11(h)/10 (each, any); swā hwelc(um) (... swā) swā *whoever* see **swā**; nsf hwylc 8/9 (*of what sort*), hwelc 8/12, hwylc 9/101; asf hwylce 9/49; npn hwelc 5/24; apn 3/50, 3/140
*ġe***hwelċ** pron., adj., *each* nsm 3/211 (ānra gehwelc *each one*), gehwylc 12/128, 12/257; dsm gehwelcum 6/19, gehwilcum 10(b)/45, gehwylcum 14/108; ism gehwylce 14/136, 16/8, 17/36, 17/68
hweorfan III *turn, go* inf 16/72; pres 3s hweorfeð 17/58, 17/60
*ġe***hwerfde** see *ġe***hwierfan**
hwettan 1 *whet, incite* pres 3s hweteð 17/63
hwī see **hwā**
hwider adv. *whither, in which direction* 16/72, hwæder 18(b)/1331
hwierfan 1 *turn, change* p ptc gehwierfed 3/165
*ġe***hwierfan** 1 *turn* pret 3s gehwerfde 9/68; subj 3s gehwyrfde 9/57
hwīl f. *time, while* as hwīle 2/51, 7/17, etc.; dp hwīlum *sometimes* 3/51, 3/69, 3/77, 3/90, 3/109, 3/110, 3/111, 4/12 (*once, at one time*), 4/19, hwīlon 12/270, etc.; ðā hwīle ðe conj. *while, as long as* 5/60, 12/14, 12/83, 12/235, etc.
hwīlon see **hwīl**
hwīlum see **hwīl** [archaic MnE whilom]
hwistlung f. *whistling* ds hwistlunge 3/111
hwon see **hwā**
hwōn adj. (as noun) *little, few* as (w.g.) 17/28
hwonon see **hwanon**

hwȳ see **hwā**
hwylc see **hwelc**
hwylce see **hwelc**
*ġe***hwyrfde** see *ġe***hwierfan**
hycgan see **hicgan**
hycgendne see **hicgan**
hȳd f. *hide, skin* ap hȳda 3/151
hȳdan I *hide, hoard* pres 3s hȳdeð 17/102
*ġe***hȳdan** I *conceal* pret 3s gehȳdde 16/84
*ġe***hygd** f. *thought, intention* ns 16/72, 17/116
hyge see **hige**
hygegeōmor adj. *sad at heart* asm hygegeōmorne 15/19
Hygelāc pers. n. *Hygelac* gs Higelāces 18(a)/737, 18(a)/758, Hygelāces 18(a)/813
hygerōf adj. *resolute* as noun nsm 13/19
hyht m. *hopeful joy, bliss* ns 14/126, 17/45, 17/122, hiht 14/148
hyldan I *bow, bend* inf 14/45 (w. refl.)
hylt see **healdan**
hȳnan I *injure, lay low, kill* inf 12/180; pret 3s hȳnde 12/324
hȳra see **hē**
hȳran see **hīeran**
*ġe***hȳran** see *ġe***hīeran**
hȳrde see **hīeran**
hyrde m. *guardian, keeper* ns 18(a)/750, as 18(a)/887 [MnE (cow)herd, (shep)herd]
*ġe***hȳrde** see *ġe***hīeran**
*ġe***hȳrdon** see *ġe***hīeran**
hyrdrǣden f. *guardianship* ds hyrdrǣdenne 4/244
*ġe***hȳrnes** f. *hearing* ds gehȳrnesse 9/66
hyrst f. *ornament, trapping* np hyrste 11(d)/4; ap hyrsta 18(d)/3164; ip hyrstum 11(j)/11
hyrstedgold n. *fairly-wrought gold* ds hyrstedgolde 18(c)/2255
*ġe***hȳrð** see *ġe***hīeran**
hys (= **his**) see **hē**
hyse m. *warrior, youth* ns 12/152; gs hysses 12/141; np hyssas 12/112, hysas 12/123; ap hyssas 12/169; gp hyssa 12/2, 12/128
hȳþelic adj. *convenient* nsn 13/41

Iācōb pers. n. *Jacob* ds **Iācōbe** 4/15
iċ pron. (§21) *I* ns 1/17, 1/30, 2/21, 2/22, 3/2, 3/23, etc.; as mē 2/25, 2/72, 3/103, mec 16/28, 17/6; gs mīn (*of me*) 2/73; ds mē 2/25, 2/27, 3/74 (*for myself*), 3/80, 3/122
īdel adj. *idle, worthless, vain* nsm 16/110; gs īdles 9/15; asf īdlan 8/59; npn īdlu 16/87; on īdel *in vain* 4/279
ides f. *woman* gs idese 18(b)/1351; gp idesa 11(a)/7
ieldran m. pl. (§75) *elders, ancestors* np 5/34, eldran 10(b)/58; gp yldrena 4/165
iermðu f. *misery* ap iermða 2/34
ierþling m. *ploughman, farmer* ns 3/7, 3/29, 3/192; as 3/209; ds ierþlinge 3/32, 3/198; np ierþlingas 3/4 [MnE earthling]
īewan I *disclose, show* pres subj 3s ȳwe 11(n)/15
igl m. *hedgehog* gs igles 4/214
ilca adj., pron. *same, the same* asn ilce 6/33, 9/47; dsn ilcan 3/144, 4/136, 7/26, 7/45, 10(a)/5, ylcan 7/3, 7/12; isn ilcan 7/4, 7/8; dsf 2/46 [MnE ilk]
in prep. w.d. *in*, w.a. *into* (§213) w.d. 9/5, 9/7, 9/34, 9/61, 9/90, etc.; w.a. 1/2, 9/10, 9/46, 9/64, 9/76, etc.
in adv. *in, inside* 12/58, 12/157, 18(b)/1371
inbryrdnes f. *inspiration* as inbryrdnesse 8/74, inbryrdnisse 9/6
inca m. *rancour* as incan 9/106; ds 9/105
indryhten adj. *very noble, aristocratic* nsm 16/12
indryhto f. *nobility* ns 17/89
inġehygd f. *intention, conscience* as 4/87
ingong m. *immigration, entry* as 9/111; ds ingonge 9/73
Ingwine m. pl. *the Danes* gp Ingwina 18(b)/1319
inlǣdan I *bring in* inf 9/92
innan prep. (w.d.) *within* 4/202, 4/256
innan adv. *from within* 17/11, 18(a)/774; in innan *inside* 11(k)/3
innanbordes adv. *at home, within the nation* 5/8
inne adv. *inside, within* 8/32, 9/99, 11(a)/4, 10(b)/72
insittende adj. *sitting within* as noun: gpm insittendra 11(a)/7
intinga m. *cause* ns 9/20
inwidhlemm m. *malicious wound* np inwidhlemmas 14/47
inwidsorh f. *evil care or sorrow* as inwidsorge 18(a)/831
inwitþanc m. *hostile purpose* dp inwitþancum 18(a)/749
Iōhannes pers. n. *John* as 10(a)/11, 10(b)/42
Iōsēp pers. n. *Joseph* ns 4/77
īow (= **ēow**) see **ġē**
īren n. (*iron*) *sword* ns 12/253, 18(a)/892; gp īrenna 18(a)/802, īrena 18(c)/2259
īrenbend f. *iron band* dp īrenbendum 18(a)/774
irnan III *run* inf rinnan (*hasten, flow*) 11(e)/5; pret 3s ran 1/6; 3p urnon 6/18
is see **bēon**
Īsaac pers. n. *Isaac* ns 2/47, 2/53; as 2/44, 2/52, 2/69; ds Īsaace 4/5
īsceald adj. *ice-cold* asm īscealdne 17/14, īscaldne 17/19
īsen adj. *iron* ap īsene 3/200
īsensmiþ m. *blacksmith* ap īsensmiþas 3/181
īsigfeþera adj. *having icy feathers* nsm 17/24

Israhēlas m. pl. *Israelites* gp Israhēla 9/73
Ītālia m. pl. *the Italians, Italy* ap 10(b)/12; gp 10(a)/3
iū see **ġeō**
Iūdēi m. pl. *Jews* np 4/325
Iūdēiscan adj. pl. *Jewish (people), the Jews* np 4/108; ap 4/205; dp Iūdēiscum 4/55
iūwine m. *friend (or lord) of former days* ap 17/92
īw m. *yew* ns 11(n)/9

kāsere see **cāsere**
Kentingas m. pl. *Kent* ap 7/71
kynerīċes see **cynerīċe**
kyning see **cyning**

lā interj. *lo! oh!* 3/8, 3/29
lāc n. *sacrifice, offering* ds lāce 2/68, 4/92
*ġe***lac** n. *rolling, tumult* as 15/7, 17/35
lācan VII *sport, contend, fight* pres 1s lāce 11(o)/1
lāf f. *remnant, heirloom, inheritance* as lāfe 18(a)/795, 18(d)/3160; ds tō lāfe wæs *was left* 4/226
lāge see **licgan**
lāgon see **licgan**
lagu m. *sea, water* as 17/47
*ġe***lagu** n. pl. *expanse (of ocean)* ap 17/64
lagulād f. *sea-way* ap lagulāde 16/3
lagustrēam m. *water, river* np lagustrēamas 12/66
*ġe***lamp** see *ġe***limpan**
lāmrind f. *crust of mud* dp lāmrindum 13/17
land n. *land, country* as 4/148, lond 5/12, 18(b)/1357; gs londes 6/29, 15/8, landes 12/90, 12/275; ds lande 2/45, 2/47, 3/136, 4/77, etc.
landbūend m. pl. *earth-dwellers, inhabitants* ap londbūend 18(b)/1345
lang adj. *long, tall* nsm langa 12/273; asf lange 14/24 (lange hwīle *a long time*); nsn tō lang *too long (a time)* 12/66; compar. nsf lengre 11(h)/7
*ġe***lang** see *ġe***long**
lange adv. *long, for a long time* longe 5/78, 8/56, 10(b)/50, 10(b)/58, etc., lange 18(b)/1336; compar. leng *longer* 4/120, 12/171; superl. lengest 6/3
langlice adv. *for a long time* 4/209
langoþ m. *longing* gs longaþes 15/41; ds langoþe 15/53
langung f. *longing, yearning* as longunge 17/47
langunghwīl f. *time of longing, time of spiritual desire* gp langunghwīla 14/126
lār f. *teaching, doctrine* ns 5/45, 5/64, 8/10; as lāre 5/10, 10(b)/68; gs 4/141, 9/56; ds 4/37, 9/77; ap lāra 4/89 [MnE lore]
lārcwide m. *counsel* dp lārcwidum 16/38
lārēow m. *teacher* np lārēowas 4/26, 9/70; gp lārēowa 5/20; dp lārēowum 4/39
lāst m. *track* np lāstas 11(l)/2; ap 18(a)/841; ds on lāste (see note) 16/97; dp lastum 17/15
lāstword n. *reputation left behind* gp lāstworda 17/73
lāð adj. *hateful* nsm 18(a)/815; gsm lāþes 18(a)/841; dsf lāðere 12/90; npm lāðe 12/86; apm lāð 18(b)/1375; as noun asm lāþne 17/112; compar. lāðre asn 12/50; superl. lāðost nsm 14/88 [MnE loathe(some)]
laðian 2 *invite, summon* pres 1s laðige 11(j)/16
lāðlicost adv. (superl. of **lāðlice**) *in most wretched fashion* 15/14
lāðost see **lāð**
lāðre see **lāð**
*ġe***laðung** f. *church, congregation* gs gelaðunge 4/83
Laurentius pers. n. *Lawrence* ds Laurentie 4/304
læċċan 1 *capture, catch* p ptc gelæht 3/44 [colloquial MnE latch (onto)]
lǣdan 1 *lead, bring, lift* inf 12/88, 14/5 (see note); infl inf (tō) lǣdene 7/29 (see note); pres 1s lǣde 3/25, 3/30, 3/137; 2s lǣtst 3/140; 3s lǣt 4/288; pret 3p lǣddon 4/207, 10(b)/2; p ptc lǣded nsm 18(d)/3177
*ġe***lǣdan** 1 *lead* pret 3s gelǣdde 9/50
Lǣden n. *Latin* ns 4/101, 4/102; as 4/14, 5/68; gs Lǣdenes 4/106; ds Lǣdene 4/3, 5/16
Lǣdenbōc f. *Latin book* dp Lǣdenbōcum 4/26
Lǣdenġeðīode n. *the Latin language* as 5/62; gs Lǣdengeðīodes 5/64
Lǣdenware m. pl. *the Romans* npm 5/50
lǣfan 1 *leave, bequeath* pret 3s lǣfde 6/26; 3p lēfdon 5/26, lǣfdon 5/35
lǣg see **licgan**
lǣgon see **licgan**
*ġe***læht** see **læċċan**
lǣn n. *loan* ds lǣne 5/81
lǣne adj. *temporary, transitory* nsm 16/108, 16/109 (twice); nsn 1/26, 16/108, 17/66; dsn lǣnan 14/109, 14/138
lǣran 1 *teach, advise* inf 5/62, 9/65; pres 1s lǣre 8/47; subj 3s lǣre 5/61; pret 3s lǣrde 8/3, 9/62, 12/311; p ptc lǣred 8/10
*ġe***lǣran** 1 *teach, advise, urge* pres 1s gelǣre 3/210; p ptc nsm gelǣred 4/126, npm gelǣrede 5/78, gelǣred 9/12; superl apm gelæredestan *most learned* 9/51
*ġe***lǣredestan** see *ġe***lǣran**
lǣrig m. *rim of a shield* ns 12/284
lǣs adv. *less* 8/44, 11(k)/11; nōht þon lǣs *nevertheless* 8/17; þȳ lǣs þe *lest* 2/7, 3/24, 4/120
lǣs f. *pasture* ds lǣswe 3/24, 3/30

lǣssa adj. (compar. of lȳtel; cf. §76) *less, smaller* asm lǣssan 3/119; nsn lǣsse 3/98
lǣsst adj. (superl. of lȳtel; cf §76) adj. *least, smallest* nsn lǣsste 8/33
lǣstan 1 w.d. *follow* inf 10(b)/27, 18(a)/812 (*do service, avail*) [MnE last]
*ġe***lǣstan** 1 *perform, carry out, continue, stand by, support* inf 12/11 (w.d.); pret 3s gelǣste 10(a)/9, 12/15; 3p gelǣstan 10(b)/13; p ptc gelǣsted 18(a)/829
lǣswe see **lǣs**
lǣt see **lǣdan**
lǣtan VII *let, allow* pres 1s lǣte 3/122; 2s lǣtst 3/124; 3s lǣteð 11(m)/10; pret 3s lēt (*cause*, w. verb of motion) 12/7, 12/140; 3p lēton 12/108, 13/42, 18(a)/864; subj 3s lēte 10(b)/66, 10(b)/68
lǣtst see **lǣdan**
lǣwede adj. *unlearned, lay* dsn lǣwedum 4/39 [MnE lewd]
*ġe***lēafa** m. *belief, faith* ns 4/329; as gelēafan 4/87; gs 4/321; ds 4/42, 4/146, 4/195, 8/2, 8/77
*ġe***lēafful** adj. *faithful* nsm gelēaffulla 4/303; asm gelēaffullan 4/207
leahtor m. *sin, vice* dp leahtrum 4/140
lēan VI *blame, find fault with* pret 3p lōgon 18(a)/862
lēanian 2 w.d. *repay, reward* pres 1s lēanige 18(b)/1380, 3s lēanað 11(m)/9
lēas adj. (w.g.) *devoid of, without* nsm 18(a)/850; nsn 15/32; npn lease 16/86 [MnE (home)less, (bottom)less, etc.]
lēas adj. *false* nsm 4/121
lēasung f. *lying, fable, fiction* gs lēasunge 9/15
lēat see **lūtan**
leax m. *salmon* ap leaxas 3/93 [MnE (through Yiddish) lox]
lecgan 1 *lay, place* inf 4/256; pres 3p lecgað 17/57; subj 3s lecge 16/42; pret 3p legdon 4/248
lēfdon see **lǣfan**
lēgbysig see **līgbysig**
legdon see **lecgan**
Lēġeċeasterscīr f. *Cheshire* ns 7/5
leġer n. *bed* ap 15/34 [MnE lair)]
lencten m. *spring* ds lenctene 3/121 [MnE lent]
*ġe***lendan** 1 *land, arrive* pret 3p gelendon 4/151
leng see **lange**
lengest see **lange**
lengre see **lange**
lēod m. *man, member of a tribe or nation, prince* ns 18(a)/829
lēode f. or m. pl. *people* np 4/147, 18(d)/3156, 18(d)/3178; ap lēoda 4/151, 12/37, lēode 4/157, 4/295, 18(b)/1336, 18(b)/1345; gp lēoda 4/163, 18(a)/793; dp lēodum 12/23, 12/50, 14/88, 15/6, 18(b)/1323, 18(d)/3182, lēodon 12/23
lēodfruma m. *leader of a people, lord* ns 15/8; ds lēodfruman 10(b)/27
lēodon see **lēode**
lēodscipe m. *nation* as 10(b)/68
lēof adj. *beloved, dear, pleasant, agreeable*, (*in direct address*) *sir, sire* ns 2/21, 3/8, 3/18, 3/21, 3/23, 3/29, 4/3, lēofa 4/177, 14/78, etc.; asm lēofne 12/7, 12/208, 17/112 (as noun); gsm lēofes 15/53 (as noun), 16/38; dsm lēofan 12/319; dsf lēofre 16/97; npm lēofan 9/109, lēofe 15/34 (as noun); gpm lēofra 15/16 (as noun), 16/31; dpm lēofum 4/182; compar. lēofre *more agreeable, preferable* nsn 3/102, 3/197, 4/175; nsm 10(b)/41 lēofra *dearer* 6/31; superl. lēofost *most pleasing, most agreeable* nsm 12/23 [archaic MnE lief]
leofað see **libban**
leofede see **libban**
leofode see **libban**
leofodon see **libban**
Lēofstān pers. n. *Leofstan* ns 4/298
Lēofsunu pers. n. *Leofsunu* ns 12/244
lēoht n. *light* ns 18(a)/727; ds lēohte 11(f)/17, 14/5
lēohtlīċ adj. *apparently easy, unimportant* dpn lēohtlicum 4/76
leomu see **lim**
*ġe***lēoran** II *depart* p ptc apm geleorene 13/7
leornere m. *scholar* ap leorneras 9/51 [MnE learner]
leornian 2 *learn, study* inf leornigan 10(a)/18; pret 3s leornade 9/13; 3p leornodon 9/70
*ġe***leornian** 2 *learn* inf 9/67; pret 1s geliornode 5/70; 3s geleornode 9/5, geleornade 9/19; 3p geliornodon 5/49; p ptc geliornod 5/42, geleornad 8/13
lēoð n. *song, poem, poetry* ns 9/69; as 9/19, 9/52, etc.; gs lēoþes 9/15; is lēoðe 9/59; ap lēoð 9/3, 9/11, 9/79
lēoðcræft m. *poetic art* as 9/13
leoþo see **liþ**
lēoþsong m. *song, poem, poetry* gs lēoþsonges 9/57; dp lēoþsongum 9/8
lēt see **lǣtan**
lēte see **lǣtan**
lēton see **lǣtan**
*ġe***lettan** 1 *hinder, prevent* pret 3s gelette 12/164
leðer m. *leather* ns 1/4
leþerhose f. *leather gaiter* ap leþerhosa (*leggings*) 3/153
libban 3 *live* inf lybban 4/10, 4/22; pres ptc asm lifigendan 4/328; npm lifgende 15/34, lifigende 18(a)/815, gp lifgendra 17/73;

libban (*cont.*)
pres 3s lifað 18(d)/3167, leofað 17/102, 17/107, 18(b)/1366; 3p lifiaþ 14/134; subj 1s lybbe 4/187, lifge 11(e)/6; 3s 17/78; pret 3s leofede 4/33, leofode 4/146, 4/265, lyfode 7/17; 1p lifdon 15/14; 3p leofodon 4/11, 4/22, lifdon 17/85

līc n. *body* ns 4/226, 6/41; gs līces 14/63; ds līce 4/261, 18(a)/733

*ġe***līċ** adj. (w.d.) *like, similar to* nsn 4/303; np gelīce 2/11; dp gelīcum 8/38

*ġe***līċe** adv. (w.d.) *like* 9/11; superl. gelīcost *just like, most like unto* nsn 18(a)/727

licgan V *lie, lie dead* inf 11(j)/10, 12/319; pres ptc licgende nsm 14/24; pres 3s līþ 4/177, 4/262, 4/304, 6/41, 12/232, 12/314, ligeð 12/222, 18(b)/1343; 3p licgað 4/319, 16/78; pret 3s læg 4/226, 4/240, 6/27, 12/157, 12/204, 12/227, leg 12/276, etc.; 3p lǣgon 6/21, lāgon 12/112, 12/183; subj 3s lāge 4/305, lǣge 12/279, 12/300

līchama m. *body* ns 4/264, līchoma 18(a)/812; as līchaman 4/256, 4/301; ds 4/258, 4/313, 4/321, 18(d)/3177

līchomliċ adj. *bodily* ds līchomlicre 9/88

līcian 2 *please* pres 3s līcaþ 1/32 [MnE like]

līcsār n. *bodily pain, wound* as 18(a)/815

lidmann m. *sailor, Viking* np lidmen 12/99; gp lidmanna 12/164

*ġe***līefan** 1 *believe, trust in* pres 1s gelīefe 5/21, gelȳfe 17/66; 3s gelȳfeð (w. refl. d.) 17/27, 17/108; 3p gelȳfað 4/327; pret 3p gelȳfdon 4/323

līf n. *life* ns 1/26, 2/73, 8/26, 8/34, etc.; as 7/25, 9/86, 9/118, etc.; gs līfes 1/33, 2/30, 2/39, 4/295, 8/5, etc.; ds līfe 4/171, 4/194 (on līfe *alive*), 4/265, 11(m)/9, 14/109, 14/138, 15/41

līfdagas m. pl. *life-days, life* ap 18(a)/793

lifdon see **libban**

*ġe***līffæstan** 1 *bring to life* pret 3s gelīffæste 4/61

lifge see **libban**

līfgedǣl n. *parting from life, death* ns 18(a)/841

lifgende see **libban**

lifiaþ see **libban**

lifte see **lyft**

līg m. *flame, fire* gs līges 18(a)/781; ds ligge 18(a)/727

līgbysig adj. *beset by flames, flammable* nsm lēgbysig 11(o)/1

ligeð see **licgan**

līhtan 1 *alight, dismount* pret 3s līhte 12/23

lim n. *limb* ap leomu 9/26

līm m. *sticky material, birdlime* ds līme 3/110, 13/4 (*cement*)

*ġe***limp** n. *occurrence, misfortune* ds gelimpe 4/171

limpan III (impers. w.d.) *befall, happen* pres 3s limpeð 17/13

*ġe***limpan** III *befall* pret 3s gelamp 4/147, gelomp 10(a)/26; 3p gelumpon 7/73; p ptc gelumpen 18(a)/824

*ġe***limpliċ** adj. *suitable* isf gelimplicre 9/26

limwērig adj. *weary of limb, exhausted* asm limwērigne 14/63

lind f. *shield* (*of linden-wood*) as linde 12/244; ap 12/99

Lindesīġ f. *Lindsey* ds Lindesīge 7/41

lindwīgend m. *warrior* np lindwigende 10(b)/13

līnen adj. *linen, made of flax* nsn 1/2

*ġe***liornod** see *ġe***leornian**

liornung f. *learning* as liornunga 5/11; ds 5/60

liss f. *kindness, joy* gp lissa 10(b)/59; dp lissum 11(m)/9

list f. *art, skill, cunning* ds liste 11(f)/4; dp listum 10(b)/59, 18(a)/781

lītel see **lȳtel**

līþ see **licgan**

liþ n. *limb* ap leoþo 11(h)/7

līþe adj. *gentle, kind* superl līðost nsm 18(d)/3182 [MnE lithe]

loc n. *enclosure, sheepfold* dp locum 3/26 [MnE lock]

lōcian 2 *look* pret 3s lōcude 6/14

lōcude see **lōcian**

lof n. *praise* ns 17/73, 17/78; as 9/122; ds lofe 4/323

lofgeorn adj. *eager for praise, eager for fame* superl lofgeornost nsm 18(d)/3182

*ġe***lōgian** 2 *place, put, arrange* pres subj 3s gelōgige 4/315; pret 3s gelōgode 2/58

lōgon see **lēan**

*ġe***lōme** adj. *frequent* dpf gelōmum 4/261; adv. gelōme *frequently* 4/239, 4/253

*ġe***lomp** see *ġe***limpan**

lond see **land**

londbūend see **landbūend**

londstede m. *country* ds 15/16

*ġe***long** adj. *belonging to, dependent on* nsn 17/121, nsf 15/45, nsm gelang 18(a)/1376

longaþes see **langoþ**

longe see **lange**

longian 2 impers. w.a. *afflict with longing* pret 3s longade 15/14

longunge see **langung**

loppestre f. *lobster* ap loppestran 3/93

losian 2 *escape, be lost, perish* pres 3s losaþ 3/160 (*spoil, go bad*), 17/94, 18(b)/1392; 3p losiaþ 3/138 [MnE lose]

lūcan II *lock, join, enclose* pret 3p lucon 12/66

lufian 2 *love* inf lufigean 9/61; pres 2s lufast 2/45; pret 1p lufodon 5/25, 5/26

luflīċe adv. *affectionately* 5/1 [obs MnE lovely]
lufu f. *love* gs lufan 10(b)/59; ds lufan 9/81, 9/82, 17/121; ds lufe 4/187, 4/269
*ġe***lumpon** see *ġe***limpan**
Lunden f. *London* ds 7/36
Lundenbyriġ f. *London* ns 7/12 (see note); ds 7/28, 7/47
lust m. *desire* ns 17/36; dp lustum 4/117 [MnE lust]
lustbǣre adj. *desirable, pleasant* nsn 2/13
*ġe***lustfullīċe** adv. *willingly* compar. gelustfullīcor 8/16
lustlīċe adv. *gladly, willingly* 3/118 [MnE lust(i)ly]
lūtan II *bend, stoop* pret 3s lēat 4/283
lūtian 2 *skulk, lurk* inf 3/10
lybban see **libban**
*ġe***lȳfað** see *ġe***līefan**
*ġe***lȳfdon** see *ġe***līefan**
*ġe***lȳfed** adj. *advanced* gsf gelȳfdre 9/19
*ġe***lȳfeð** see *ġe***līefan**
lyfode see **libban**
lyft f. *air, sky* ns 11(d)/4, 18(b)/1375; ds lyfte 11(l)/4, lifte 11(f)/4; as on lyft *in the air, aloft* 14/5
lȳsan 1 *release, redeem, ransom* inf 12/37, 14/41
*ġe***lysted** adj. *desirous of* nsm 10(b)/9
lȳt noun indecl. w.g. *few, little* as 15/16, 16/31; as adv. 17/27
lytegian 2 *use guile, deceive* inf 12/86
lȳtel adj. *little* asf lȳtle 7/17; gsn lītles 4/25; isn lȳtle 6/10; dpn lītlum 4/75 (used substantively: *little things*)
lȳtlian 2 *diminish, grow less* pres 3s lȳtlað 12/313
lȳtling m. *child* np lȳtlingas 3/165 [MnE dialect littling]

mā adj., noun, adv. *more* as (indeclinable noun) 5/47, 18(a)/735; np 12/195; ap 4/20; adv. 8/20, 15/4, þon mā þe *any more than* 6/35 [archaic MnE mo]
macian 2 *make* pres 1s macie 3/26; pres 3s macað 4/324; pret 3p macodon 4/262
Maccus pers. n. *Maccus* ns 12/80
māga m. *relative, kin* gs māgan 18(b)/1391
magan pret. pres. *be able, can, be competent* pres 1s mæg 3/84, 3/102, etc.; 2s miht 3/205; 3s mæg 3/104, 3/154, 3/184, 4/75, etc.; 1p magon 3/174, 5/57; 2p 3/162, 3/171; 3p 4/26, 4/317; subj 1s mæge 3/85, 3/148; 2s 4/178, 5/23; mage 4/167; 1p mægen 5/56; 3p 5/60; pret 1s meahte 5/74, 14/18, mihte 14/37; 3s meahte 9/12, 9/15, etc., mihte 4/21, 7/55, etc.; 3p mihton 4/41, 4/249, 4/276, meahton 5/32, etc.; subj 3s meahte 9/57, mihte 4/281; 3p mihten 4/233, muhton 7/31 [MnE may]
māge f. *kinswoman* ns mēge 11(k)/4
magister m. *teacher* ns 4/13 [MnE master]
mago m. *young man, youth* ns 16/92
magon see **magan**
magorinc m. *warrior* gp magorinca 10(b)/26, 18(a)/730
maguþegn m. *young retainer* np maguþegnas 16/62
man see **mann**
man indefinite pron. *one, they* ns 3/98, 3/215, 4/21, 4/75, mon 5/61, etc.
*ġe***man** see *ġe***munan**
mān n. *crime* gs mānes 10(b)/44; ds māne 10(a)/10
mancess m. *mancus* (*a gold coin worth 30 silver pence*) gp mancessa 5/76
mancynn n. *mankind* as 14/104, mancyn 14/41; gs mancynnes 14/33, 14/99, monncynnes 9/42; ds mancynne 1/25
māndǣd f. *evil deed* gp māndǣda 9/82
māndrinc m. *evil drink, poison, deadly drink* as 11(h)/13
manega see **maniġ**
mangere m. *merchant* ns 3/131 [MnE (fish)monger]
manian 2 *exhort, urge, admonish* inf 12/228; pres 3s monað 17/36, 17/53; pret 3s monade 9/62
*ġe***manian** 2 *exhort, urge, remind* pres 3p gemoniað 17/50; p ptc apm gemanode 12/231
maniġ adj., pron. *many, many a* (w.sg. noun) nsm mænig 12/282; asm mænigne 12/188, manigne 12/243; asn monig 10(b)/3; dsn manegum 10(a)/10; np manega 4/20, 12/200, manige 3/127, monige 5/17, 8/17, 9/10, 11(b)/2, etc.; ap manige 3/130, 3/182; apn manega 4/268, monig 9/46, 9/79, mænigo 10(b)/29; gp monigra 9/8; dpn manigum 3/99; dpf manegum 14/99; gp manigra 14/41
maniġeo see **menigu**
maniġfeald adj. *manifold, various* nsf menigfeald 4/93; apf manigfealde 3/109, menigfealde 4/86; apm manigfealdan 10(a)/14; dpm menigfealdum 4/83; dpf manigfealdum 5/66
*ġe***maniġfealdan** 1 *multiply, increase* pres 1s gemanigfealde 2/33, 2/74
manlīċe adv. *manfully, nobly* 1/15
mānlīċe adv. *wickedly* 1/15
mann m. *person, man* ns 3/33, 3/158, man 4/143, 4/288, mon 5/77, etc.; as man 4/312, mann 1/21, mannan 4/68, mon 9/12, monnan 15/18; gs mannes 4/74, 4/292; ds men 4/8, 9/62; np 4/22, 4/275, 4/282, 6/25,

mann (*cont.*)
menn 4/307, 5/44; ap men 9/81; gp manna 3/165, 4/63, 8/26, monna 5/58, 8/34, etc.; dp mannum 4/34, 4/142, 4/260, monnum 5/26, 9/12, 11(o)/8, etc.

manrǣden f. *service, tribute* ds manrǣdene 4/160

mānscaða m. *wicked ravager, evil-doer* ns 18(a)/712, 18(a)/737, 18(b)/1339

mansliht m. *manslaughter, slaying* dp manslihtum 7/55

māra adj. (compar. of micel §76) *more, larger* asm māran 3/119, 3/120, 7/50, 18(a)/753; nsn māre 12/313; asn māre 2/73, 3/13, 3/17, 4/5, 4/45; dsn māran 3/147; asf māran 8/17, 8/18

Maria pers. n. *Mary* as Marian 14/92

martyr m. *martyr* as 4/308

maðelian 2 *speak, make a speech* pret 3s maðelode 12/42, 12/309, 18(b)/1321, 18(b)/1383, maþelade 11(g)/5

māðm m. *treasure* as 11(n)/13; ap māðmas 4/275; gp māðma 5/30; dp māðmum 17/99

māþþumgyfa m. *giver of treasure* ns 16/92

*ġe***mæc** adj. *suitable* asm gemæcne 15/18

mæcg m. *man* np mæcgas 11(m)/7

mǣg m. *kinsman* ns 6/31, 12/5, 12/114, 12/224, 12/287, 16/109, etc.; as 18(b)/1339; np mǣgas 6/29, māgas 15/11; gp māga 16/51; dp mǣgum 6/32

mæg see **magan**

mæġen n. *strength, power* ns 3/166, 12/313; gs mægenes 8/14; ds mægene 11(f)/14, 18(a)/789; is mægne 11(h)/13 [MnE (might and) main]

mæġenþise f. *force, violence* ds mægenþisan 11(f)/10

mǣġð f. *tribe, nation* ds mǣgðe 10(a)/1

mæġð f. *maiden, woman* np mægeð 11(m)/7; gp mægða 11(j)/8

mǣl n. *time, occasion* ap mǣla 12/212; gp 10(b)/54, 17/36

mǣlan 1 *speak* pret 3s mǣlde 12/26, 12/43, 12/210 [MnE (black)mail]

*ġe***mǣlan** 1 *speak* pret 3s gemǣlde 12/230, 12/244

Mǣldūn m. *Maldon* ds Mǣldūne 7/21

mǣnan 1 *speak of, relate, bemoan* inf 18(d)/3171; p ptc mǣned 18(a)/857

mæniġ see **maniġ**

mæniġe see **meniġu**

mǣran 1 *make famous* p ptc gemǣred 9/2

mǣre adj. *famous, illustrious, glorious, notorious* nsm 4/156, 18(a)/762 (as noun); dsm 14/69; nsf 14/12, 14/82, 16/100; asm mǣran 10(b)/14; gsm mǣres 18(a)/797; np mǣre 4/26; apm mǣran 4/324; compar. mǣrra nsm 4/316

mǣrsian 2 *proclaim, mark out* pres 3s mǣrsað 10(b)/16

mǣrðu f. *glorious thing, fame, glory* ns mǣrðo 18(a)/857; ap mǣrða 4/86; gp mǣrþa 17/84

mæssepreost m. *mass-priest* ns 3/213, 4/13; ds mæsseprioste 5/71

mǣst adj. *most, greatest* asn mǣste 7/54; asf mǣstan 9/6, mǣste 12/175

mǣst adv. *mostly* 7/4

mǣst n. *most, greatest* ns 12/223; as 7/75, 17/84

mæstling m. *brass* as 3/142

*ġe***mǣtan** 1 (impers. w.d. of person) *dream* pret 3s gemǣtte 14/2

mǣte adj. *small, limited* isn 14/69 (see note), 14/124

*ġe***mǣtte** see *ġe***mǣtan,** *ġe***mētan**

mǣð f. *propriety, fitness* ns 12/195

mæðel n. *assembly* ds mæðle 11(b)/2

mǣw m. *mew, seagull* as 17/22

mē see **iċ**

meahte (n.) see **miht**

meahte (v.) see **magan**

meahtigra see **mihtig**

mearc f. *boundary, region, border* ap mearce 11(j)/6

mearcstapa m. *wanderer in the wasteland, border-haunter* ap mearcstapan 18(b)/1348

mearg see **mearh**

mearh m. *horse* ns 18(c)/2264, mearg 16/92; as mearh 12/188; ds mēare 12/239; ap mēaras 18(a)/865; dp mēarum 18(a)/855 [MnE mare]

mec see **iċ**

mēċe m. *sword* as 12/167, 12/236

mēdan 1 *presume* (?) pres subj 3s mēde 11(n)/15

medmiċel adj. *moderate, brief* asn 9/117; dsn medmiclum 8/34, 9/5

medobenċ f. *mead-bench* ns medubenc 18(a)/776

medodrinc m. *mead* ds medodrince 17/22

mēge see **māge**

melcan III *milk* pres 1s melce 3/26

*ġe***meltan** III *melt* pret 3s gemealt 18(a)/897

men see **mann**

*ġe***mengan** 1 *mingle* p ptc gemenged 16/48, 18(a)/848

menġeo see **meniġu**

menifealdliċe adv. *in the plural* 4/71 [MnE manifoldly]

meniġfeald see **maniġfeald**

meniġu f. *multitude* ns mengeo 5/31; ds mænige 14/112, manigeo 14/151

menn see **mann**

mennisc adj. *human* dsn menniscum 4/308

menniscnis f. *incarnation* ds menniscnisse

4/29, menniscnesse 9/75 [MnE mannishness]

meodo m. *mead* ds 12/212

meodoheall f. *mead-hall* ns 13/23; ds meoduhealle 16/27

meotod m. *creator* ns 17/108, meotud 17/116, metod 18(a)/706, 12/175; gs meotodes 9/37, metudes 16/2, meotudes 17/103; ds metode 12/147

Merantūn m. *Merton* ds Merantūne 6/10

mere m. *pool, lake* ns 18(b)/1362; as 18(a)/845; ds 18(a)/855 [MnE mer(maid)]

mereflōd m. *sea-tide, ocean* ds mereflōde 17/59

merehengest m. *sea-horse (ship)* ns 11(j)/6

merewēriġ adj. *sea-weary* gs merewērges 17/12 (as noun)

mergen see **morgen**

*ġe***met** n. *measure, metre* as 9/47; mid gemete *with moderation, in proper measure* 11(m)/7, 17/111, 18(a)/779 (*in any way*)

mētan 1 *meet, encounter* pret 1s mētte 8/44; 3s 18(a)/751; 3p mētton 6/26

*ġe***mētan** 1 *meet, find* inf 4/233; pret 3s gemētte 4/197, 18(a)/757, gemǣtte 7/35

mete m. *food* ns 3/165; ds 3/80 [MnE meat]

*ġe***metlīċe** adv. *moderately* 9/89

metod see **meotod**

metsung f. *provisions* as metsunge 7/60, 7/65

mētte see **mētan**

mētton see **mētan**

mēðe adj. *weary, tired* nsm 14/65, npm 14/69

meðelstede m. *meeting-place, assembly* ds meþelstede 12/199

micclan see **micel**

miccle adv. *much* 12/50

miċel adj. *great, large, much* nsm 1/18, 3/214; asm micelne 3/106, miclan 4/78, micclan 4/313; gsm miccles 12/217; dsm mycclum 7/34; ism micle 8/77, 14/34 (elne micle *with great zeal*), etc.; nsn 3/20, 3/21, 3/98, 4/17, etc.; asn 3/23, mycel 7/15, 7/36, 7/39, etc.; dsn miclum 3/137; isn micle 8/43; nsf 1/22, 3/214; asf 15/51; gsf micelre 9/85; dpn miclum 6/6 [MnE dialect mickel]. See **miccle, miclum**

miċel n. *much, a great part* as 3/18, 7/70, 7/72

miċelnes f. *size* ns 1/19

miclum adv. *greatly, severely* 6/15, 10(b)/74

mid prep. w.d.a.i. *with, amid, by means of* 2/47, 2/50, 2/79, 3/15, 4/24, etc.; as adv. *in attendance, at the same time* 11(a)/5, 14/106; **mid þām þe** *when* 2/60, 4/69, 4/202; **mid þȳ** (þe) *when* 8/52, 9/97

midd adj. *middle, mid* dsf midre 14/2

middanġeard m. *world, middle earth* ns 16/62; as 9/42, 9/120, 14/104, 16/75, 17/90; gs middangeardes 9/71, 18(a)/751

middæġ m. *midday, noon* as 2/18

Middelseaxe m. pl. *Middlesex* ap Middelsexe 7/67

middeneaht f. *midnight* as 9/100

mid þām þe see **mid**

mid þȳ see **mid**

miht f. *power, might* as mihte 4/167, 8/19, meahte 9/37, 17/108; ds mihte 14/102

miht (v.) see **magan**

mihte (n.) see **miht**

mihte (v.) see **magan**

mihten see **magan**

mihtiġ adj. *mighty, powerful* nsm 14/151, 18(b)/1339; dsm mihtigan 18(b)/1398; compar. meahtigra nsm 17/116

mihton see **magan**

milde adj. *merciful, kind* nsm 4/121; nsm 12/175; superl. mildust nsm 18(d)/3181 [MnE mild]

mildheort adj. *merciful* nsm mildheorta 4/286 [MnE mildheart(ed)]

mildheortnes f. *mercy, pity* as mildheortnisse 7/52 [MnE mildheart(ed)ness]

mīlġemearc n. *measure by miles* gs milgemearces 18(b)/1362

milts f. *mercy, favour, reverent joy* as miltse 16/2; ds 11(o)/8

mīn poss. adj. *my, mine* nsm 2/54, 2/55; asm mīnne 3/70, 3/76, etc.; gsm mīnes 3/11; dsm mīnum 3/27, 3/172; isn mīne gefrǣge *as I have heard tell* 18(a)/776, 18(a)/837; asn mīn 3/76, 3/135; nsf mīn 14/130; gsf mīnre 2/77; dsf 11(j)/18; npm mīne 9/109; apm 3/43, 3/103; dpm mīnum 3/135; npn mīn 3/138; apn 3/23, 3/135, 3/149; apf mīne 4/190

mīn (pron.) see **iċ**

mine 16/27 see note

misdǣd f. *misdeed* np misdǣda 4/74

misliċ adj. *various* apf mislice 4/90; dpm mislicum 17/99; dpf 5/66

missenliċ adj. *various, manifold* gsn missenlices 3/153; npn missenlicu 3/63; apn 3/203

missenlīċe adv. *in various places* 16/75

misthliþ n. *misty hill, cover of darkness* dp misthleoþum 18(a)/710

mīþan 1 *conceal* pres ptc asm mīþendne 15/20

mōd n. *spirit, courage, mind* ns 10(b)/26, 12/313, 13/18, 16/15, 16/51, 18(a)/730; as 9/104, 15/20, 17/12, 17/108; gs mōdes 11(f)/14, 17/36, 17/50, 18(a)/810; ds mōde 4/181, 4/227, 5/39, 10(a)/27, 11(b)/2, 14/130, 16/41, 16/111, 17/109, 18(a)/753, 18(b)/1307; is 9/98, 9/119, 14/122; np 9/8 [MnE mood]

mōdceariġ adj. *troubled in thought* nsm 16/2

mōdcearu f. *grief of heart* as mōdceare 15/51; gs 15/40
mōdġeþanc m. *conception, purpose* as 9/37
mōdiġ adj. *brave, courageous* nsm 14/41, mōdi 12/147, mōdega 18(a)/813; npm mōdige 12/80, mōdge 16/62, 18(a)/855
mōdiġlīċe adv. *boldly, bravely* mōdelice 12/200 [MnE moodily]
mōdor f. *mother* ns 7/52, 11(k)/2; as 14/92
mōdsefa m. *heart, spirit* ns 10(b)/74, 14/124, 16/59, 17/59; as mōdsefan 16/10, 16/19
mōdwlonc adj. *proud of heart, spirited* nsm 17/39
molde f. *earth* ns 17/103; as moldan 14/12, 14/82; ds 4/314
moldern n. *earth-house, sepulchre* as 14/65
*ġe*mon see *ġe***munan**
monade see **manian**
monað see **manian**
mōnað m. *month* ap mōnþas 7/17
mondrēam m. *joy of men, revelry, festivity* gp mondrēama 13/23
mondryhten m. *liege lord* as 16/41; ds mondryhtne 11(n)/13
*ġe***moniað** see *ġe***manian**
moniġ see **maniġ**
monn see **mann**
monnan see **mann**
monncynnes see **mancynn**
mōnþas see **mōnað**
monðwǣre adj. *gentle, kind* superl. monðwǣrust nsm 18(d)/3181
mōr m. *moor, marsh, wasteland* ds mōre 18(a)/710; ap mōras 18(b)/1348
morgen m. *morning* as 18(a)/837, mergen 4/282; ds morgenne 3/31, 6/23, 9/48, 9/59 [MnE morn]
morð n. *crime* as 4/281
morþor n. *crime, murder* as 15/20; ds morðre 18(a)/892
mōste see **mōtan**
*ġe***mōt** n. *meeting, council, encounter* ns 12/301; as 12/199
mōtan pret. pres. *may, be allowed to* pres 1s mōt 14/142; 2s mōst 12/30; 3p mōton 4/31; subj 1s mōte 14/127; 1p mōten 17/119, 3p mōton 12/180; pret 3s mōste 8/62, 12/272, 18(a)/706, 18(a)/735; 3p mōston 12/83; subj 3s mōste 4/176, 10(b)/39, 10(b)/62; 3p mōstan 10(a)/8, 12/87, 12/263, mōsten 10(b)/36
moððe f. *moth* ns 11(c)/1
Moyses pers. n. *Moses* gs 4/12, 9/72, Moises 4/23
muhton see **magan**
*ġe***munan** pret. pres. *remember* pres 1s geman 1/30, 14/28, gemunu 12/212; 3s gemon 15/51, 16/34, 16/90; pret 1s gemunde 5/28, 5/40; 3s 10(a)/16 (w.g.), 10(a)/29, 10(b)/57, 10(b)/79, 12/225, 18(a)/758, 18(a)/870; subj 3p gemundon 12/196
mundbyrd f. *protection, hope of protection* ns 14/130
mundgripe m. *hand-grip* as 18(a)/753
munt m. *mountain* dp muntum 10(a)/4 [MnE mount]
Muntġiop m. *the Alps* as 10(b)/8; ds 10(b)/14
munuc m. *monk* ns 3/179, 3/213, 4/2, etc.
munuchād m. *monastic orders* as 9/63 [MnE monkhood]
murnan III *mourn, care about* inf 12/259; pres subj. 3s murne 18(b)/1385; pret 3p murnon 12/96
mūð m. *mouth* as mūþan 18(a)/724; ds mūðe 7/40, 9/70
mycclan see **miċel**
myċel see **miċel**
*ġe***mynd** n. *mind, remembrance* as 5/3, 16/51; ds gemynde 9/46, 10(b)/54
*ġe***myndgian** 2 *remember* pret 3s gemyndgade 9/67
*ġe***myndig** adj. w.g. *mindful* nsm 4/141, 4/203, 4/286, 16/6, 18(a)/868
mynster n. *church, monastery* as 4/273, 9/64; ds mynstre 4/135, 5/77, 9/1 [MnE (West)minster]
myntan 1 *intend, think* pret 3s mynte 18(a)/712, 18(a)/731, 18(a)/762
Myrce m. pl. *the Mercians* dp Myrcum 12/217
myre f. *mare* ds myran 8/63
myrðu f. *disturbance, trouble, affliction* gp myrðe 18(a)/810

nā adv. *no, by no means, not at all, never* 3/173, 4/5, 4/23, etc., nō 15/4, 16/54, etc.; nā þē lǣs *nevertheless* 7/76
nabbað see **habban**
naca m. *boat, ship* gs nacan 17/7
nacod adj. *naked* nsm 2/22, 2/23; asf nacedan (*bare, literal*) 4/45; np nacode 2/15
nāh see **āgan**
nāht see **nānwuht**
nalæs see **nealles**
nales see **nealles**
nam see **niman**
*ġe***nam** see *ġe***niman**
nama m. *name* ns 1/31, 12/267, noma 11(h)/1; as naman 2/44, 11(n)/11; ds 4/122, 5/76, 14/113 (see note), noman 9/28; ap naman 1/30
*ġe***namon** see *ġe***niman**
nān (= ne ān) pron., adj. *none, not one, not any, no* nsm 3/10, 3/154, 3/177, etc.; asm nǣnne 4/114, 5/42; nsn nān 18(a)/803; asf nāne 4/118; gsf nānre 10(a)/28; npn nāne 4/326
nānwuht pron. *nothing* as 5/32, nōht 9/15, 9/29, nāht 9/31

nāp see **nīpan**
nāteshwōn adv. *not at all* 2/8
nāþer adj. *neither* dsf nāþre 4/140
nāwiht n. *nothing* ns nōwiht 8/42; as 8/14 [MnE naught]
næbbe see **habban**
nǣdl f. *needle* as nǣdle 3/195
nǣdre f. *snake, serpent* ns 2/1, 2/2, 2/27; ds nǣdran 2/28; as nǣdran 1/37 [MnE (a)n adder]
næfdon (= **ne hæfdon**) see **habban**
næfne see **nefne**
nǣfre adv. *never* 4/184, 4/195, 6/31, 9/15, 9/19, 9/35, etc.
næfst (= **ne hæfst**) see **habban**
næfð (= **ne hæfð**) see **habban**
nǣgan I *accost, address* pret 3s nǣgde 18(b)/1318
nægl m. *nail, fingernail* ap næglas 4/269; dp næglum 14/46
nǣnig pron. *none, no one* ns 6/20, 6/31, 8/15, 9/11, etc.; as 9/19
nǣnne see **nān**
nǣren (= **ne wǣren**) see **bēon**
næs (= **ne wæs**) see **bēon**
næs adv. *by no means* 18(c)/2262
næss m. *headland, bluff* ap næssas 18(b)/1358; gp næssa 18(b)/1360
*ġe***nǣstan** I *contend, grapple* pres 3s genǣsteð 11(f)/10
ne adv., conj. *not, nor* 1/34, 2/3, 3/63, 3/84, 3/161 (ne . . . ne *nor*), 4/23, 4/24, etc.
nēah adv. *near* 15/25, 16/26, nēh 12/103; comp. nēar 18(a)/745; predicate adj. *near, imminent* 9/96, 9/112; superl. nīehstra dsn nēxtan 4/147, nȳxtan 7/57 (æt nēxtan *at last, eventually*) [MnE nigh]
*ġe***neahhe** adv. *often, very, frequently* 16/56, 18(a)/783, genehe 12/269; superl. genehost 18(a)/794
neahte see **niht**
nēalēcan I *draw near* inf 9/22; pret 3s nēalēhte 8/67, nēalǣcte 9/87
nealles adv. *not at all* nales 9/12, 16/32, nalæs 16/33, nealles (þæt) ān . . . ac *not only . . . but* 3/103, 3/130
nēan adv. *from near, near* 18(a)/839
nearo adj. *narrow, close, anxious* nsf 17/7
nearolīċe adv. *densely* 4/98 [MnE narrowly]
nearon see **bēon**
nearones f. *distress, strait* ds nearanessa 10(a)/26 [MnE narrowness]
nēat n. *cattle, neat* gp nēata 9/25
*ġe***nēat** m. *retainer, comrade* ns 12/310
nēawest f. *neighbourhood* ds nēaweste 9/90
nefa m. *nephew* ns 11(a)/6; ds nefan 18(a)/881
nefne conj. *except, but* 17/46, næfne 18(b)/1353. See **nemne**
nēh see **nēah**
*ġe***nehe** see *ġe***neahhe**
*ġe***nehost** see *ġe***neahhe**
nele (= **ne wile**) see **willan**
nellað (= **ne willað**) see **willan**
nemnan I *call, name* pret 3s nemnde 9/28; 3p nemdon 18(b)/1354; p ptc genemned 5/68, nemned 8/73
nemne conj. *except* 15/22. See **nefne**
nemþe see **nymþe**
nēodlaðu f. *desire* (or *urgent summons?*) dp nēodlaðum 18(b)/1320
nēodlīċe adv. *diligently* compar. nēodlīcor 8/15
neom (= **ne eom**) see **bēon**
neorxenawang m. *Paradise* gs neorxenawanges 2/19; ds neorxenawange 2/6, 2/18, 2/21
nēotan II w.g. *use, make use of* inf 12/308
neowol adj. *prostrate* nsm 10(b)/80, niwol 10(a)/29
*ġe***nerian** I *save, protect* pret 3s generede 6/39; p ptc genered 18(a)/827
nese adv. *no* 3/53
nēten see **nīeten**
nett n. *net* as 3/76; ap 3/42, 3/44; dp nettum 3/45, 3/46, 3/109, etc.
*ġe***nēþan** I *venture* (*on*) pret 3s genēðde 18(a)/888
nēxtan see **nēah**
niċ adv. *no, not I* 3/96, 3/146
nicor m. *sea-monster* gp nicera 18(a)/845
nīedbehēfe adj. *necessary* nsm 3/151, 3/173
nīedbeðearf adj. *necessary, essential* superl. npf nīedbeðearfosta 5/55
nīehst see **nēah**
nīeten n. *beast, cattle* ns nēten 9/67; ds nytene 4/94; np nietenu 2/1
niht f. *night* ns 1/24, 18(b)/1320; as 3/30, 4/236, 7/33 (on niht *by night*), 18(a)/736; gs neahte 9/93; ds nihte 2/46, 4/274, 7/32, 14/2, neahte 9/25, niht 18(a)/702, 18(b)/1334; gp nihta 18(b)/1365
nihthelm m. *cover of night* as 16/96
nihtscūa m. *shadow of night* ns 16/104, 17/31
nihtwaco f. *night-watch* ns 17/7
nihtweorc n. *night-work* ds nihtweorce 18(a)/827
niman IV *take* inf 12/39, 12/252, 15/15; imp s nim 2/44; pres 1s nime 3/78, 3/80, 3/122; 3p nimað 17/48; pret 3s nam 4/18, 7/75, nom 8/64, etc.; 3p naman 7/57, namon 7/62; p ptc genumen 2/41, 7/40
*ġe***niman** IV *take, seize* pret 3s genam 2/13; 3p genamon 7/37, 14/30, 14/60; subj 3s gename 12/71; p ptc genumen nsm 18(d)/3165
*ġe***nip** n. *darkness, mist* ap genipu 18(b)/1360

nīpan I *grow dark* pres 3s nīpeð16/104; pret 3s nāp 17/31
*ġe***nīpan** I *grow dark* pret 3s genāp 16/96
nis (= **ne is**) see **bēon**
nīþ m. *hatred, malice, trouble, affliction* as 17/75; ds nīðe 18(a)/827; gp nīða 18(a)/845, 18(a)/882
niþer adv. *downwards* 10(b)/80, 18(b)/1360 [MnE nether]
nīðhedig adj. *hostile* npm nīðhedige 18(d)/3165
nīðwundor n. *fearful wonder, portent* as 18(b)/1365
*ġe***nīwad** see **nīwian**
nīwan adv. *newly* 8/22
nīwe adj. *new* nsm 18(a)/783, nsf 4/28, 8/10; dsf nīwan 4/10, 4/18
nīwes adv. *recently* 15/4
nīwian 2 *restore, renew* p ptc genīwad nsm 14/148; nsf 16/50, 16/55, genīwod 18(b)/1322
niwol see **neowol**
nō see **nā**
*ġe***nōg** adj. *enough* npm genōge 14/33 (*many*)
nōht adv. *not, not at all* 5/17, 8/72, nāwiht 8/14; **nōht þon lǣs** *nevertheless* 8/17
nōht see **nānwuht**
nōhwæðer conj. *neither* 5/25 (nōhwæðer ne . . . ne *neither . . . nor*)
nolde (= **ne wolde**) see **willan**
noldest (= **ne woldest**) see **willan**
noldon (= **ne woldon**) see **willan**
nom see **niman**
noman see **nama**
norð adv. *northwards* 18(a)/858
norðan adv. *from the north* 16/104, 17/31
Norðdene m. pl. *the Danes* dp Norðdenum 18(a)/783
Norðhymbre m. pl. *Northumbria* gp Norðhymbra 4/150, 4/153; dp Norðhymbran 7/42, Norðhymbron 12/266
norðsciphere m. *northern fleet, attack fleet of the Northmen* ds norðscipherige 7/6
nosþyrl n. *nostril* ap nosþirlu 4/111
notian 2 w.g. *use, enjoy* pres 3s notaþ 3/202
notu f. *employment* ds note 5/60
nōwiht see **nāwiht**
nū adv., conj. *now that, now* adv. 2/64, 2/74, etc.; conj. 2/64 (nū . . . nū *now . . . now that*), 2/72, 12/57, etc.
*ġe***numen** see **niman**
nȳdġesteall a m. *comrade in battle* np nȳdgesteallan 18(a)/882
nyle (= **ne wyle**) see **willan**
nymþe conj. *unless, except* 11(h)/16, 18(a)/781, nemþe 16/113
nyste (= **ne wyste**) see **witan**
nytene see **nieten**
nytnisse see **nyttnes**
nytt adj. *useful* nsm 3/132, 3/151; npm nytte 3/115; apm 3/179, 18(a)/794; npn nyt 11(n)/11
nytt f. *use, utility* ds nytte 3/150, 11(m)/2
nyttnes f. *usefulness, benefit* gs nyttnesse 8/14, nytnisse 8/48
nȳxtan see **nēah**

Odda pers. n. *Odda* gs Oddan 12/186, 12/238
of prep. w.d. *from* 2/3, 2/14, 2/25, 3/33 (*of*), 4/3, etc.
ofdūne adv. *down* 10(a)/27, 10(b)/80
ofer prep. w.d.a. *over, after* 1/2, 1/5, 2/2, 2/18, 2/64, 3/24, etc., *contrary to* 14/35; ofer bæc see **bæc**
ōfer m. *river-bank, shore* ds ōfre 12/28, 18(b)/1371
ofercuman IV *overcome* p ptc ofercumen 18(a)/845
oferfēng see **oferfōn**
oferfōn VII *seize* pret 3s oferfēng 10(b)/69
ofergān anom. (§128) *overrun* p ptc ofergān 7/66 [MnE overgo]
oferhelmian 2 *overhang, overshadow* pres 3s oferhelmað 18(b)/1364
ofermōd n. *pride, arrogance, overconfidence* ds ofermōde 12/89
Offa pers. n. *Offa* ns 12/198, 12/230, 12/286, 12/288; gs Offan 12/5
offrian 2 *offer* inf 4/89; pret 3s offrode 4/93
*ġe***offrian** 2 *sacrifice, offer up* imp s geoffra 2/45; pret subj 3s geoffrode 2/60; p ptc geoffrod 4/97
offrung f. *offering, sacrifice* ns 2/54; as offrunge 2/56; ds 2/69
ofġiefan V *abandon* pret 3s ofgeaf 18(c)/2251; 3p ofgēafon 11(k)/1, 16/61
oflongian 2 *seize with longing* p ptc oflongad 15/29
ofscēotan II *shoot, kill with a missile* pret 3s ofscēat 12/77
ofslagen see **ofslēan**
ofslægen see **ofslēan**
ofslēan VI *slay, destroy* inf 2/65, 3/102, 10(a)/10; infl inf (tō) ofslēanne 2/49; pres 1s ofslēa 3/45, pret 3s ofslōg 6/3, ofslōh 7/35; 3p ofslōgon 4/151, 6/37, 7/36; p ptc ofslagen 2/59, 4/177, 4/192, 4/260, 7/15, ofslægen 6/24, 6/27, 7/21, ofslegen 7/4, asm ofslægenne 6/16, npm ofslagene 4/183
ofslegen see **ofslēan**
ofslōg see **ofslēan**
ofsnāð see **ofsnīðan**
ofsnīðan I *slaughter* pret 3s ofsnāð 2/68
ofspring m. *offspring* ns 2/75; as 2/74; ds ofspringe 2/31
ofstang see **ofstingan**
ofstician 2 *stab to death* pret 1s ofsticode 3/58, 3/61; 2s ofsticodest 3/59

ofstingan III *stab to death* pret 3s ofstang 6/5
ofstlīċe adv. *quickly* 12/143
ofstondan VI *remain standing* p ptc ofstonden 13/11
oft adv. *often* 4/237, 5/2, 6/6, etc.; compar. oftor 14/128; superl. oftost 5/22
ofwundrian 2 *be astonished* p ptc npm ofwundrode 4/244
on adv. *on, onward* 8/61, 17/91
on prep. w.d.a. *on, onto, upon, in, into* w.d. (*on, in*) 1/9, 1/11, 1/29, 2/4, 2/9, 2/17, 2/21, 3/26 (*during*), 4/132, 6/17 (*from*), etc.; w.a. (*onto, upon, into*) 3/44, 3/76, 3/122, 6/15 (*against*), etc.
onarn see **onirnan**
onǣlan 1 *kindle* p ptc onǣlæd 8/29 [archaic MnE anneal]
onbærnan 1 *kindle, inspire* p ptc npm onbærnde 9/9, onbærned 9/85
onbreġdan III *swing open* pret 3s onbrǣd 18(a)/723
onbūgan II *bend* pres 1s onbūge 11(h)/3
onbyriġan 1 w.g. *taste* inf 14/114, onbyrian 4/243
oncierran 1 *turn* inf oncerran 10(b)/61; pres 3s oncyrreð (w. refl.: *change direction, turn aside*) 17/103
oncnāwan VII *recognize, perceive, acknowledge* inf 12/9; pret 1s oncnēow 2/64; 3p oncnēowon 2/15
oncnēow see **oncnāwan**
oncnēowon see **oncnāwan**
oncweðan V w.d. *answer* pret 3s oncwæð 12/245, 17/23
oncyrreð see **oncierran**
oncȳðð f. *grief, distress* as oncȳþðe 18(a)/830
ond see **and**
ondette see **andettan**
ondrǣdan VII *be afraid, dread* pres 1s ondrǣde 4/9; 2s ondrǣtst 2/64; 3s ondrǣdeþ 17/106; pret 1s ondrēd (w. refl.) 2/22
ondrēd see **ondrǣdan**
ondswarodon see **andswarian**
ondsworede see **andswarian**
ondweard adj. *present* dp ondweardum 9/51
onemn prep. w.d.a. *alongside* 12/184
ōnettan 1 *hasten on, be active* pres 3s ōnetteð 17/49
onfēng see **onfōn**
onfēngon see **onfōn**
onfindan III *discover, realize* pres 3s onfindeð 11(f)/9; pret 3s onfunde 12/5, 18(a)/750, 18(a)/809; 3p onfundon 6/17; subj 3p onfunden 6/11
onfōn VII w.d.a. *receive, accept, take up* inf 8/2, 8/51; pres subj 1p 8/23; pret 1s onfēng 8/59; 3s 8/76, 9/14, etc.; 3p onfēngon 8/18; subj 3s onfēnge 9/63; p ptc asf onfongne 9/58
onga m. *arrow, dart* ns 11(h)/4
ongan see **onġinnan**
onġēan prep. w.d.a. *against* 2/32, 11(f)/9, 12/100
ongēan adv. *again, back* 3/25, 4/247, 12/49, 12/137, 12/156, 18(a)/747 (*out*)
ongēanstandan VI *stand opposite, withstand* pret 1s ongēanstōd 3/60
onġeat see **onġietan**
Ongelþēod f. *the English people, England* ds Ongelþēode 9/10
onġemang prep. w.d. *among* 5/66
onġeocian 2 *unyoke* pres 3s ongeocaþ 3/29
onġietan V *understand, perceive* inf 5/32, 16/73, ongytan 14/18; pret 1s ongeat 8/42; 3s 6/13, 10(a)/14, 10(a)/24, 10(b)/68; 3p ongēaton 12/84
onġinnan III *begin* pres 3p onginð 4/50; subj 3p onginnen 14/116; pret 1s ongan 5/66; 3s 9/61, 10(a)/17, 10(a)/30, 12/12, 12/17, 12/89, 12/91, ongon 11(k)/3, angan 10(b)/59, etc.; 3p ongunnon 9/11, 12/86, 12/261, 14/65, 14/67, 15/11
ongon see **onġinnan**
ongunnon see **onġinnan**
ongyrwan 1 *unclothe, strip* pret 3s ongyrede 14/39
onġytan see **onġietan**
onġytenes f. *knowledge* gs ongytenesse 8/69
onhæbbe see **onhebban**
onhebban VI *raise up, exalt* pres 1s (w. refl.) onhæbbe 11(o)/7
onhnīgan I *bend, bow down* pres 3p onhnīgað 11(o)/7
onhrēran 1 *stir, move* inf 17/96
onhweorfan III, 3 *change* p ptc onhworfen 15/23
onhworfen see **onhweorfan**
onhwyrfan 1 *turn around* p ptc onhwyrfed 11(h)/1
onhwyrfed see **onhwyrfan**
onhyldan 1 *lower, incline* pret 3s onhylde 9/116
onirnan III *give way, spring open* pret 3s onarn 18(a)/721
onlīcnes f. *image* ns onlīcnes 18(b)/1351. See **ānlīcnes**
onlūtan II *bow, incline, bend down* inf 5/39
onlȳsan 1 *liberate, redeem* pret 3s onlȳsde 14/147
onmēdla m. *pomp, magnificence* np onmēdlan 17/81
onmiddan prep. w.d. *in the middle of* 2/5, 2/19 [MnE amid]
onmunan pret. pres. w.g. *pay attention to* pret subj 3p onmunden 6/35

onmunden see **onmunan**
ono hwæt interj. *lo and behold!* 8/49
onsendan 1 *send, send forth* inf 5/75; pres 3s onsendeð 16/104; p ptc onsended 14/49, 18(c)/2266
onslēpan 1 *fall asleep* pret 3s onslēpte 9/26, 9/117
onspringan III *spring asunder* pret 3p onsprungon 18(a)/817
onstal m. *supply* as 5/20
onstellan 1 *institute, set the example for, establish* pret 3s onstealde 9/39; 3p onstealdon 7/43
onsȳn f. *appearance, face* ns 17/91
ontendan 1 *kindle, burn* inf 7/50
onuppon prep (w.d.) *above* 4/250
onwæcnan VI *awaken* pres 3s onwæcneð 16/45
onweald m. *authority, power, jurisdiction, command* as onwald 5/5, anwald 10(a)/4, 10(b)/62; ds onwealde 2/35, anwealde 10(a)/20
onweġ adv. *away* 16/53, āweg 4/197
onwendan 1 *change* pres 3s onwendeð 16/107; pret 3s onwende 13/24
onwrēon 1 *reveal, disclose* imp. s onwrēoh 14/97
open adj. *open* npm opene 14/47
openian 2 *open* p ptc npn geopenode 2/15
openlīċe adv. *openly* 8/45, 8/49
*ġe***openode** see **openian**
ōr n. *beginning* as 9/39
ord m. *point, spear, vanguard* ns 12/60, 12/69, 12/146, 12/157, etc.; as 12/47, 12/110; ds orde 12/124, 12/226, 12/273
orf n. *cattle, livestock* as 4/92
orhlīċe adv. *insolently* 4/300
orlege n. *war, battle, strife* ds orlege 18(b)/1326
ormōd adj. *despondent, sad* nsm 10(a)/30, 10(b)/78
orþonc m. *skill, intelligence* ns 13/16
Ōsrīċ pers. n. *Osric* ns 6/25
Ōswold pers. n. *Oswold* ns 12/304
Ōswyn pers. n. *Oswyn* ns 4/267
oð prep. w.a. *up to, as far as, until* 4/7, 4/96, 4/282, 4/295, 5/61, etc.; conj. *until* 6/3, oþ þæt *until* 3/43, 4/33, 4/129, etc.
oðberan IV *carry away* pret 3s oþbær 16/81
ōðer adj., pron. *other, another, next* nsm 4/6, etc.; asm ōþerne 12/143; dsm ōþrum 3/208, 12/70, 12/64, 12/133, 18(a)/814; dsn 13/10; gsn ōðres 9/111; asf ōðre 9/84; ōþre ... ōþre *one ... the other* 8/31; npm ōþre 4/307, 4/321; ōðre 9/10; apm ōþre 3/87, 3/130, 3/180; gpm ōþerra 3/94, 8/57; dpm ōðrum 4/311, 5/26; npn ōðre 2/1; apn 4/235, ōðer 9/79; gpn ōþerra 3/143; dpn ōðrum 10(a)/10; npf ōðra 5/52; apf ōðre 5/50; asn ōðer twēga *one of two things* 12/207
oðfæstan 1 *set (to a task)* p ptc np oðfæste 5/60
oðfeallan VII *fall away, decline* p ptc oðfeallan 5/45; nsf oðfeallenu 5/14
ōðre see **ōðer**
oþþe conj. *or* 1/15, 3/13, 3/69, 3/77, 3/104, 4/9, etc.
oðþringan III *wrest away* pres 3s oðþringeð 17/71
ōwiht pron. *anything* nsn 15/23; as 8/36, 17/46. See **āwiht** [MnE aught]
oxa m. *ox* ap oxan 3/9, 3/11, 3/29; gp oxena 3/18
oxanhierde m. *oxherd* ns 3/28; np oxanhierdas 3/4
Oxenafordscīr f. *Oxfordshire* as Oxenafordscīre 7/67

pāpa m. *pope* ns 4/303; as pāpan 10(a)/11, 10(b)/42
Pante f. *the river Blackwater in Essex* as Pantan 12/68, 12/97
Paradīsus m. *Paradise* ds Paradīsum 2/3, 2/5
Paulīnus pers. n. *Paulinus* as 8/39
pæll m. *purple garment, silk robe* ap pællas 3/141 [MnE pall]
pæð m. *path* as 1/6
Petroces stōw f. *Padstow (Cornwall)* ns 7/7
Pētrus pers. n. *Peter* ns 4/32, 4/33; as Pētrum 4/35; ds Pētre 4/31, 4/204
pleoh n. *danger, risk* ns 3/98, 4/124; ds plēo 3/138
plēoliċ adj. *dangerous* nsn 4/8
Portland n. *Portland (Dorset)* ds Portlande 7/11
prass m. *array, military force* ds prasse 12/68
prēost m. *priest* np prēostas 4/25, 4/38; dp prēostum 4/289
pund n. *pound* gp punda 7/24, 7/63

rā m. *roebuck* ap rān 3/51 [MnE roe]
rād see **rīdan**
*ġe***rād** adj. *skilful, apt* asn gerāde 18(a)/873
radost see **hraðe**
ramm m. *ram* as 2/66
ran see **irnan**
rān see **rā**
rand m. *shield-boss, shield* ap randas 12/20
randhæbbend m. *shield-bearer, warrior* gp rondhæbbendra 18(a)/861
raðe see **hraðe**
rǣċan 1 *reach (out)* pret 3s rǣhte 18(a)/747
*ġe***rǣċan** 1 *touch, reach, wound* pret 3s gerǣhte 12/142, 12/158, 12/226
rǣd see **rēad**
rǣd m. *advice* ns 4/171, 18(b)/1376; as 3/210, 7/24

rǣdan 1 *read* inf 4/9; infl inf (tō) rǣdenne 4/105; pres 3s rǣt 4/9; *instruct, give counsel, rule* inf 10(b)/67; pret 3s rǣdde 12/18

*ġe***rǣdan** 1 *decide* pres 2s gerǣdest 12/36; pret 3s gerǣdde 7/22, 7/24, 7/27, 7/59

rǣdbora m. *advisor* ns 18(b)/1325; as rǣdboran 4/114

Rǣdgōd pers. n. *Radagaisus* ns Rǣdgōt 10(b)/19, Rǣdgōta 10(a)/2; as 10(b)/7

*ġe***rǣdu** n. pl. *harness, trappings* ap 3/153; dp gerǣdum 12/190

rǣghār adj. *grey with lichen* nsm 13/10

rǣhte see **rǣċan**

*ġe***rǣhte** see *ġe***rǣċan**

rǣran 1 *lift up, offer up* inf 9/113; pret 3s rǣrde 11(n)/6 (*raised*) [MnE rear]

rǣsan 1 *rush* pret 3s rǣsde 6/15

ræste see **rest**

rǣt see **rǣdan**

rēad adj. *red* nsm rǣd 4/259

rēadfāh adj. *stained with red* nsm 13/10

rēaf n. *garment, raiment* as 12/161; ap (*armour*) 3/141

reċċan 1 (w.g.) *care about, care* pres 1p recce 3/173; pret 3s rōhte 4/160; 3p rōhton 12/260 [archaic MnE reck]

reċċan 1 *explain, relate* pret 3s rehte 4/129, 4/130; 3p rehton 9/55

*ġe***reċċan** 1 *wield, control* pret 3p gerehton 10(a)/4

*ġe***reċċednyss** see *ġe***reċednis**

reċċelēas adj. *negligent, careless* npm reccelēase 5/45 [MnE reckless]

reced m. *building, hall* ns 18(a)/770; gs recedes 18(a)/724; ds recede 18(a)/720, 18(a)/728

*ġe***reċednis** f. *narrative* as gerecednisse 4/46, gereccednysse 4/132; ds 4/47

recene adv. *quickly* 10(b)/34, ricene 12/93, rycene 16/112

*ġe***reġnad** adj. *ornamented, decorated* nsm 18(a)/777; asn gerēnod 12/161

regollic adj. *regular, according to (monastic) rule* dpm regollecum 9/83

rehton see **reċċan**

*ġe***rēnod** see *ġe***reġnad**

renweard m. *guardian of the house* np renweardas 18(a)/770

reord f. *voice* ds reorde 17/53

*ġe***reord** n. *speech, voice* dp gereordum 11(j)/16

reordberend m. *speech-bearer, man* np 14/3; dp reordberendum 14/89

rēotan II *weep* pres 3p rēotað 18(b)/1376

rest f. *rest, resting place* as reste 9/98, 14/3; ds 9/26, ræste 18(a)/747

restan 1 *rest, lie, remain* pres 1s reste (w. refl.) 11(e)/5; pret 3s reste 14/64 (w. refl.), 14/69

*ġe***restan** 1 *rest* inf 9/95, 15/40

rēþe adj. *fierce, cruel, furious* asm rēðne 4/294; dsm rēþan 4/169, 4/193; npm 18(a)/770; dpm rēþum 4/145

rēwett n. *rowing* ns 3/90

rīċċeter n. *arrogance* ds rīccetere 4/299

rīċe n. *kingdom, reign* ns 10(b)/5; as 3/190, 6/7, 7/63, 10(a)/3, 10(a)/18, 13/10, 14/119, etc.; gs rīces 6/1, 6/29, 8/78, 13/37, 17/81, 18(a)/861, 18(b)/1390; ds rīce 5/19, 5/75, 10(a)/1, 10(a)/5, 10(b)/7, 16/106 [MnE (bishop)ric, German Reich]

rīċe adj. *powerful, great* nsm 4/298; asm rīcne 14/44; npm 10(b)/7; gp rīcra 10(b)/46 (as noun), 14/131; superl. rīcost *most powerful, noblest, richest* nsm 12/36

ricene see **recene**

rīcost see **rīċe**

rīcsian 2 *reign* pret 3s rīcsode 6/41

rīdan I *ride* inf 8/63, 12/291, 18(a)/855; pres ptc rīdende 2/48; pret 3s rād 4/299, 12/18, 12/239; 3p ridon 6/24, 7/57, riodan 18(d)/3169

rīdende see **rīdan**

ridon see **rīdan**

riht adj. *fitting, right* nsn 12/190; asm rihtne 14/89; dsn ryhte 11(m)/7

riht n. *justice, right* gsm rihtes 10(b)/67

*ġe***rihtan** 1 *correct* inf 4/125; pres subj 3s gerihte 4/122; p ptc nsf geriht 14/131 (*directed*) [MnE right]

rihte adv. *properly, correctly* 12/20

rihtġelēaffull adj. *orthodox* gpm ryhtgelēaffulra 10(a)/19

rihtwīs adj. *righteous, upright* nsm 10(b)/49; gpm rihtwīsra 10(a)/19; superl. rihtwīsesta nsm 10(a)/14

rihtwīsnys f. *righteousness* ds rihtwīsnysse 4/145

rīnan 1 *rain* pres subj 3s rīne 8/29

rinc m. *man, warrior* ns 10(b)/49, 11(p)/2, 18(a)/720; as 18(a)/741, 18(a)/747; ap rincas 11(j)/16; gp rinca 18(a)/728; dp rincum 12/18

rinnan see **irnan**

riodan see **rīdan**

*ġe***risenliċ** adj. *suitable, proper, honourable* apn gerisenlice 9/3; compar. asn gerisenlicre 8/36

*ġe***risenlīċe** adv. *fittingly* compar. gerisenlecor 8/57

rōd f. *rood, cross* ns 14/44, 14/136; as rōde 14/119; gs 11(n)/5; ds 14/56, 14/131 [MnE rood]

rōdetācn n. *sign of the cross* ds rōdetācne 9/116 [MnE rood token]

rodor m. *sky, heaven* np roderas 18(b)/1376; dp roderum 11(n)/5

rōhte see **reċċan**
rōhton see **reċċan**
Rōm f. *Rome* ns 10(b)/19; ds Rōme 10(b)/46
Rōmane pl. *Romans* gp 10(a)/1, 10(b)/17, Rōmane 10(a)/3; dp Rōmanum 10(a)/7
Rōmanisc adj. *Roman* dp Rōmaniscum 10(a)/15
Rōmeburg f. *Rome* ds Romebyrig 4/305
Rōmwara pl. *Romans* gp 10(b)/34; dp Rōmwarum 10(b)/49, 10(b)/67
rondhæbbendra see **randhæbbend**
rōtlīċe adv. *cheerfully* 9/102
rōwan VII *row* pres ptc rōwende 4/154; pres 1s rōwe 3/76
rūn f. *consultation, secret meditation* ds rūne 16/111
rūnwita m. *confidant, trusted counsellor* ns 18(b)/1325
rycene see **recene**
ryhte see **riht**
ryhtfæderencyn n. *direct paternal ancestry* ns 6/42
rȳman 1 *extend* pret 3p rȳmdon 5/8
*ġe***rȳman** 1 *open* (*a way*) pret 1s gerȳmde 14/89; p ptc gerȳmed 10(b)/19, 12/93 (ēow is gerȳmed *passage is granted to you*)
rȳpan 1 *plunder* pret 3p rȳpton 7/78

saga see **secgan**
sāgol m. *cudgel, staff* dp sāglum 4/207
same see **swā**
samed see **samod**
samod adv. *too, at the same time* 2/47, 18(a)/729, samed 11(l)/2, somod 16/39; prep w.d. *simultaneously with* 18(b)/1311
sanct m. *saint* as 4/269, 4/271, 4/300; gs sancte 4/126, 7/7, 7/48, sanctes 4/301; ds sancte 4/129, 4/273
sandċēosol m. *sand, grains of sand* as 2/75
sang see **singan**
sang see **song**
sār n. *pain, wound* as 17/95, 18(a)/787
sār adj. *sore, painful, grievous* npf sāre 16/50; gpf sārra 14/80
sāre adv. *sorely, grievously* 14/59
sārig adj. *sorrowful* npm sārige 4/227 [MnE sorry]
sārliċ adj. *painful, sad* nsn 18(a)/842
sārnes f. *pain* ds sārnesse 2/34 [MnE soreness]
*ġe***sawen** see *ġe***sēon**
sāwol f. *soul* ns 1/33, sāwul 12/177, sāwl 4/219, 14/120; as sāwle18(a)/801, 18(a)/852; ds 17/100
sǣ f. and m. *sea* as 4/126, 16/4, 17/14, 17/18; ds 1/28, 2/75, 3/89, 3/91; dp sǣm 18(a)/858
sǣbāt m. *sea-boat, ship* as 18(a)/895
sǣd n. *seed, offspring* ds sǣde 2/76
sǣde see **secgan**
sǣfōr f. *sea-voyage* ds sǣfōre 17/42
sǣġan 1 *lay low, slay* p ptc gesǣged 18(a)/884
*ġe***sæġd** see **secgan**
sæġde see **secgan**
*ġe***sæġde** see **secgan**
sǣl m. or f. *time, occasion* ns 14/80; as 4/273; *happiness, joy* dp sǣlum 18(b)/1322
sæl n. *hall* as 18(c)/2264
sǣlan 1 *bind, fasten* inf 16/21
*ġe***sǣlan** 1 *befall, chance, turn out favourably* pret 3s gesǣlde 18(a)/890
sǣlida m. *sailor, Viking* ns 12/45; as sǣlidan 12/286
*ġe***sǣlig** adj. *blessed* nsf 4/219 [MnE silly]
*ġe***sǣliġliċ** adj. *blessed, happy* npf gesǣliglica 5/4
*ġe***sǣliġlīċe** adv. *blessedly, happily* 4/145
sǣmann m. *sailor, Viking* np sǣmen 12/29; dp sǣmannum 12/38, 12/278
sǣrima m. *coast* ds sǣriman 7/8, 7/23, 7/56 [MnE sea rim]
sǣrinc m. *sea-going warrior, Viking* ns 12/134
sǣstrēam m. *ocean current* dp sǣstrēamum 10(b)/15
sæt see **sittan**
scān see **scīnan**
scand f. *shame, disgrace* ns 3/215
sceacan VI *flee, hasten away* pret 3s sceōc 7/33, 18(c)/2254 [MnE shake]
scead n. *shade* ap sceadu 18(a)/707
sceādan VII *part* pres 3s sceādeð 13/30
sceadu f. *shadow, shade, darkness* ns 1/24, 14/54
sceadugenga m. *walker in darkness* ns 18(a)/703
scēaf see **scūfan**
sceaft m. *staff, shaft* ns 12/136; ds sceafte (*staff*) 10(b)/11
*ġe***sceaft** f. *creation, creature* ns 14/12, 14/55, 14/82, 16/107 (wyrda gesceaft *ordained course of events*); ap gesceafta 4/53, 4/62
sceal see **sculan**
scealc m. *man, warrior* np scealcas 12/181
scēap n. *sheep* ap 3/24
*ġe***sceap** n. *creation* ds gesceape 9/71; np gesceapu 11(k)/7 (*destiny, fate*)
*ġe***sceapþēote** f. *appointed channel* dp gesceapþēotan 11(g)/4
sceapen see **scieppan**
*ġe***sceapenis** f. *creation* ds gesceapenisse 4/50
scēaphierde m. *shepherd* ns 3/22; np scēaphierdas 3/4
scear n. *ploughshare* as 3/12, 3/193
sceard adj. *cut, mutilated, chipped* npf scearde 13/5
scēat m. *surface, region* ap scēatas 14/37, 17/

61, 17/105; ds scēate 11(k)/7 (*fold, bosom*); gp scēata 18(a)/752; dp scēatum 14/8, 14/43

scēat see **scēotan**

sceatt m. *money, payment* as 3/106; dp sceattum 12/40, 12/56 [MnE (through Old Norse) scot(free)]

scēawere m. *observer* ns 4/229

scēawian 2 *see, behold, look at* inf 4/305, 18(a)/840, scēawigan 18(b)/1391; infl inf (tō) scēawigenne 4/308; pret 1s scēawode 14/137; 3s 4/293 (w.d.), 18(a)/843 [MnE show]

scēawung f. *viewing, examination* ds scēawunge 4/307 [MnE showing]

sceld see **scield**

sceōc see **sceacan**

sceolde see **sculan**

sceole see **sculan**

sceolon see **sculan**

sceōp see **scieppan**

sceōta m. *trout* ap sceōtan 3/87 [MnE shoat]

scēotan II *thrust, shoot, throw* inf 11(g)/4; pret 3s scēat 8/68, 12/143, 12/270; 3p scuton 4/212 (scuton . . . tō *shot at*)

scēotend m. *warrior, bowman* np 10(b)/11, 18(a)/703

scēð f. *sheath* ds scēðe 12/162

sceððan VI *injure* inf 14/47 [MnE (through Old Norse) scathe]

scield m. *shield* ds scylde 12/136; ap sceldas 10(b)/2, scyldas 12/98

sciellfisc m. *shellfish* as 1/5

scieppan VI *create* pret 3s sceōp 9/40, scōp 11(e)/2; p ptc sceapen 11(h)/2 [MnE shape]

*ġe***scieppan** VI *create* pret 3s gesceōp 4/51, 4/110, gescōp 11(h)/6

scieppend m. *creator* ns Scyppend 9/42, 16/85; gs Scyppendes 9/34, 9/122

scieran IV *rend, tear* p ptc npf scorene 13/5 [MnE shear]

scile see **sculan**

scīma m. *light, radiance* as scīman 14/54

scīnan I *shine* inf 14/15; pres 3s scīnþ 1/23, scīneð 8/45; pret 3s scān 13/15, 13/34

scīnþ see **scīnan**

scip n. *ship* as 1/5, 3/135, 7/37; gs scipes 18(a)/896; ds scipe 4/223, scype 12/40, 12/56; np scypu 7/10; ap scipu 1/28, 3/203, 7/28; dp scipum 3/100, 4/152, 7/48

scipen n. *shed* ds scipene 9/25

sciphere m. *fleet, naval attack force* ds 4/148, 4/200, scipherige 7/3

scīr adj. *gleaming, resplendent* nsm 10(b)/11; asn 12/98; asm scīrne 14/54; apm scīre 11(g)/4 [MnE sheer]

Sciððia f. *Scythia* gs Sciððiu 10(a)/1, Sciððia 10(b)/2

scoldon see **sculan**

scomu f. *shame* ds scome 9/22

scōp see **scieppan**

*ġe***scōp** see *ġe***scieppan**

scopgereord n. *poetic language* ds scopgereorde 9/6

scorene see **scieran**

scotung f. *missile, shooting* dp scotungum 4/213, 4/261

scōwyrhta m. *shoemaker* ns 3/150, 3/195; np scōwyrhtan 3/6

*ġe***scrāf** see *ġe***scrīfan**

scranc see **scrincan**

*ġe***scrīfan** I *ordain* pret 3s gescrāf 10(b)/29 [MnE shrive]

scrincan III *shrink* pret 3s scranc 1/2

scrīþan I *glide, move, wander* inf 18(a)/703

scrūd n. *clothing* as 3/74 [MnE shroud]

scrȳdan 1 *clothe* pres 3s scrȳtt 3/69

scrȳn n. *chest, coffer* ds scrȳne 4/270 [MnE shrine]

scrȳtt see **scrȳdan**

scūfan II *shove, push* pret 3s scēaf 12/136, 3p scufon 1/28

sculan pret. pres. *must, have to, ought to* pres 1s sceal 3/8, 3/9, 3/13; 3s sceal 3/15, 3/63, 3/216, etc.; 1p sculon 9/36; 2p sceole 12/59; 3p sceolon 4/291, 12/54, 12/220; subj 3s scyle 15/42, 17/111, 17/74 (on weg scyle *must depart*), scile 18(d)/3176; pret 1s sceolde 4/3, 17/30; 3s 4/160, 8/2, 12/16, etc.; 3p scoldon 2/49 (*had to* [*go*]), sceoldon 4/201, 12/19, 12/105, 12/291, etc; subj 3s sceolde 4/297, 7/51; 3p scolden 3/115, 9/113, sceoldon 5/13, sceoldan 7/30 (*ought to have*), sceoldon 7/33, etc.; sceolden 9/21 [MnE shall]

scūr m. *shower, storm* dp scūrum 17/17

scūrbeorg f. *protection from storms* (*i.e. buildings*) np scūrbeorge 13/5

scuton see **scēotan**

*ġe***scȳ** n. pl. *shoes, footwear* ap 3/153

scyld see **scield**

scyldiġ adj. w.g. *guilty* ns ealdres scyldig *having forfeited his life* 18(b)/1338

Scyldingas m. pl. *descendants of Scyld, i.e. the Danes* gp Scyldinga 18(a)/778, 18(b)/1321

scyldburh f. *wall of shields* ns 12/242

scyle see **sculan**

scynscaþa m. *demonic foe, hostile demon* ns 18(a)/707

scyp see **scip**

scyppend see **scieppend**

scypu see **scip**

*ġe***scyrpan** 1 *accoutre, equip* p ptc asn gescyrpedne 8/66

se, þæt, sēo dem. pron., def. art. (§16) m. n. f. *that, the, he, she, it, who, which* (§162.3) nsm se 1/5, 1/8, 1/9, 1/18, 1/33, 2/55, 3/15 (*he*),

se, þæt, sēo (*cont.*) etc.; asm þone 1/5, 1/17, 1/29, 2/52, 3/12, þæne 7/24; gsm þæs 1/19, 3/40, etc.; dsm þǣm 1/20, 3/66; ism þȳ 8/32; nsn þæt 2/4, 2/11, tæt 6/33, etc.; asn 1/2, 1/5, 1/13, 2/6, þet 7/61, þat 12/36, etc.; gsn þæs 2/5, 4/105, 6/29, *after, afterward* 3/31, 6/7, etc.; dsn þām 2/2, 2/10, 2/12 (be þām þe *as*), 4/39, 4/101; isn þȳ 2/7 (þȳ lǣs þe *lest*), 3/24, 3/70 (see note), 9/60, þan 4/8, þon 6/35 (see note), 9/114, etc., þē (w. compar.) *the, by that* 12/146, 12/312, 12/313; nsf sēo 1/10, 1/33, 2/1, 2/2, 2/26, sīo 5/45; asf þā 2/30, 2/56, 3/76, 6/3; gsf þǣre 1/24, etc.; dsf 1/9, 1/11, 1/24, 1/28, 2/41 (þǣre þe *which*), 3/9, þēre 7/32; np þā 3/60, 3/166, etc.; ap 1/30, 3/9, 3/11, 3/29, 3/44, 3/49, 3/58, 3/75, 3/80, 3/108, 8/48, etc.; gp þāra 1/30, 2/4, 3/18, 3/43, þǣra 4/29, etc.; dp þām 2/67, 4/145, 4/237, þǣm 3/87, 3/105, etc.

seah see **sēon**

*ġe***seah** see *ġe***sēon**

sealde see **sellan**

sealt n. *salt* gs sealtes 3/159

sealtere m. *salter, salt-maker* ns 3/156; np sealteras 3/6

sealtȳþ f. *salt seawave, ocean wave* gp sealtȳþa 17/35

sēamere m. *tailor* ns 3/195

sēarian 2 *grow sere, wither, fade* pres 3s sēarað 17/89

searobunden adj. *cunningly fastened* asn 11(n)/4

searogim m. *precious stone* ap searogimmas 13/35

searosǣled adj. *skilfully bound* nsf 11(h)/16

searoþonc m. *ingenuity, skill* dp searoþoncum 18(a)/775

sēaþ m. *pit* ds sēaþe 14/75

Sebastianus pers. n. *Sebastian* 4/214

sēċan 1 *seek, search for, visit* inf 11(f)/11, 14/104, 14/127 (*resort to*), 15/9, 18(a)/756, 18(a)/801, sēcean 18(a)/821; pres ptc sēcende 4/232, 4/236; imp s sēc 18(b)/1379; imp p sēcaþ 3/190; pres 3s sēceð 16/114; subj 3s sēce 18(b)/1369; pret 1s sōhte 8/44, 16/25; 3s 5/12, 8/53; 3p sōhton 12/193, 14/133

*ġe***sēċan** 1 *seek* inf 12/222, 14/119; pres subj 1s gesēce 17/38; pret 3s gesōhte 12/287, 18(a)/717

secg m. *man, warrior* ns 12/159, 17/56, 18(a)/871, 18(b)/1311; as 18(b)/1379; ap secgas 12/298; gp secga 16/53, 18(a)/842; dp secgum 14/59

secgan 3 *say, tell* inf 9/52, 11(n)/8, 11(n)/16, 12/30, 14/1, 15/2, 17/2, 18(a)/875, etc.; imp s saga 11(b)/7, 11(h)/16, sege 4/193, 12/50; pres 1s secge 3/132; 2s segst 3/7, 3/22, 3/107, 3/108, 3/197; 3s segþ 3/193, segeð 12/45; 1p secge 3/168, secgað 4/44, 4/222; subj 2s secge 14/96; pret 3s sægde 2/23, 2/72, sǣde 4/17, 4/189, 4/199, 12/147, etc.; 3p sægdon 9/55; p ptc gesægd 2/70

*ġe***secgan** 3 *say* pret 3s gesægde 11(g)/5, gesǣde (þanc gesǣde *gave thanks*) 12/120

secgrōf adj. *sword-valiant, brave* gpm secgrōfra 13/26

sefa m. *heart* ns 10(b)/71; as sefan 16/57, 17/51; ds 18(b)/1342

sēftēadig adj. *blessed with comfort* nsm 17/56

sege see **secgan**

*ġe***seġen** see *ġe***sēon**

seġnian 2 *bless, cross* (*oneself*) pres ptc segniende 9/123

*ġe***seġnian** 2 *bless, cross* (*oneself*) pret 3s gesegnode (w. refl.) 9/116

segst see **secgan**

segþ see **secgan**

*ġe***selda** m. *companion* ap geseldan 16/53

seldcūþ adj. *rare* apn 3/141

seldon adv. *seldom* 3/90

sele m. *hall, house* ns 11(e)/1; as 18(a)/826; ds 18(a)/713

seledrēam m. *revelry in the hall* as 18(c)/2252; np seledrēamas 16/93

seledrēorig adj. *sad at the loss of a hall* nsm 16/25

selerǣdend m. *counsellor in the hall* ap selerǣdende 18(b)/1346

selesecg m. *retainer* ap selesecgas 16/34

sēlest adj. (superl. of gōd; cf. §76) *best* nsm sēlesta 14/27; asn w.g. sēlest 14/118; nsn 18(b)/1389; adv. sēlost 4/249

self pron., adj. *self, himself, herself, etc., same, very* nsm 2/53, 2/56, 4/38, 4/83, seolfa 8/58, 8/75, sylfa 11(e)/1; asm selfne 2/72, 3/103 (*myself*), sylfne 8/16, seolfne 9/123; gsm seolfes 9/125; dsm selfum 5/43, sylfum 7/34, 9/55, 17/1; asf sylfe 14/92; gsf sylfre 15/2; nsn sylfe 8/45; asn 8/44; npm selfe 3/174 (*ourselves*), 5/25 (*ourselves*), seolfan 9/69; apm selfe 3/121; gpm sylfra 12/38; dpm sylfum 4/326

sēlla see **sēlra**

sellan 1 *give, sell* inf 3/84, 3/144, syllan 8/46, 12/38, 12/46; imp s sele 3/117, 3/120; pres 1s selle 3/66, 3/118, 3/136; 2s selst 3/118, 3/199; 3s selþ 3/68, 3/69, 3/199, silð 4/63, sylð 4/65, seleð 18(b)/1376 (*give up*); subj 1p syllon 12/61; pret 3s sealde 2/14, 2/25, 5/23, 8/63, etc.; 3p sealdon 10(b)/24; subj 3s sealde 8/60; p ptc geseald 4/77

*ġe***sellan** 1 *give, give up* pret 3s gesealde 12/188; pret 3p gesealdon 12/184

sēlost see **sēlest**
sēlra adj. (compar. of gōd; cf. §76) *better* nsm 18(a)/860, sēlla 10(b)/50; nsn sēlre 18(b)/1384
selþ see **sellan**
*ġe***sēman** 1 *reconcile, settle* (*a dispute*) inf 3/207, 12/60
sendan 1 *send* inf 12/30, 16/56; pres 3p sendað 11(o)/5; pret 3s sende 4/159, 4/189, 7/31, 10(a)/20, 10(b)/63, 12/134; 3p sendon 12/29; subj 3s sende 7/59
sēo see **se**
*ġe***sēo** see *ġe***sēon**
seofen num. *seven* np 4/307
seofian 2 *lament, sigh* pret 3p seofedun 17/10
seolcen adj. *silken, made of silk* nsm 4/259
Sēolesīġ f. *Selsey* (*Sussex*) ds Sēolesigge 7/2
seolfa see **self**
seolfne see **self**
seolfor n. *silver* as 3/142, 4/85, sylfor 13/35; gs seolfres 11(n)/4; ds seolfre 4/272; is 14/77, sylfore 11(j)/2
seolforsmiþ m. *silversmith* ap seolforsmiþas 3/181
seoloc m. *silk* as 3/141
sēon V *look, see* inf 18(b)/1365; pret 1s seah 11(l)/1, 11(n)/1, 3s 13/35
*ġe***sēon** V *see* inf gesion 5/36; imp s geseoh 8/12; pres 1s gesēo 3/179; 3s gesiehð 2/69, 2/71, gesihð 16/46; subj 2s gesēo 8/21; pret 1s geseah 5/28, 11(g)/1, 14/14, 14/21, 14/33, etc.; 3s 2/11, 2/66, 4/214, 4/301, 8/66, etc.; 3p gesāwon 2/48, 12/84, 12/203; subj 1s gesāwe 14/4; p ptc gesawen 8/9, gesewen 8/26, is gesegen *seems* 9/124, wæs gesegen *seemed* 9/54
seonu f. *sinew* np seonowe 18(a)/817
sēoþan II *boil* inf 3/174; infl inf (tō) sēoþanne 3/174 [MnE seethe]
*ġe***set** n. *seat* np gesetu 16/93
*ġe***setnis** f. *decree, narrative* ds gesetnysse 4/304; ap gesetnissa 4/116; dp gesetnissum 4/116
*ġe***sett** see **settan**
settan 1 *set, put, establish, appoint, set out, go, set down, compose* inf 4/310; pres 1s sette 2/30; pret 3s 4/294; 3p setton 10(b)/4; p ptc gesett 4/12, 4/98, geset 4/113, 4/136, 4/142, geseted 9/18, 14/141; npm gesette 4/39
*ġe***settan** 1 *set, put, compose* pret 3s gesette 4/132, 9/26, 9/122; 3p gesetton 14/67
*ġe***sewen** see *ġe***sēon**
sī see **bēon**
sibb f. *peace, concord* ns 3/207, 4/252; as sibbe 5/7
sibbeġedriht f. *band of kinsmen* as 18(a)/729
sibling m. *kinsman, sibling* dp siblingum 4/21
Sībyrht pers. n. *Sibyrht* gs Sībyrhtes 12/282
Siċilia f. *Sicily* ns 10(b)/15; ds 10(a)/4
sīde f. *side* ds sīdan 14/49, ap 11(b)/7
sīde adv. *widely* 14/81 (wīde and sīde *far and wide*)
sīe see **bēon**
*ġe***siehð** see *ġe***sēon**
sīen see **bēon**
siendon see **bēon**
*ġe***siene** adj. *visible* nsn gesyne 18(d)/3158; npn gesiene 14/46
sierwan 1 *contrive, plot* pres 2s sierwst 2/32
siġ (= **sīe**) see **bēon**
siġe m. *victory* ds 4/153
siġebēam m. *tree of victory, cross* ns 14/13; as 14/127
Siġebryht pers. n. *Sigebryht* as 6/1
siġefæst adj. *victorious* nsm 4/162
siġelēas adj. *without victory, in defeat* asm sigelēasne 18(a)/787
Siġemund pers. n. *Sigmund* gs Sigemundes 18(a)/875; ds Sigemunde 18(a)/884
Siġerīċ pers. n. *Sigeric* ns 7/18, Sīrīc 7/24
siġeþēod f. *victorious nation* np sigeþēoda 10(b)/4
siġewǣpen n. *weapon of victory* dp sigewǣpnum 18(a)/804
siġlan 1 *sail* pret 3p sigldon 1/28
siġle n. *jewel, brooch, necklace* ap siglu 18(d)/3163
sigor m. *victory* gp sigora 14/67
sigorēadig adj. *victorious* nsm 18(b)/1311
sigorfæst adj. *triumphant, victorious* nsm 14/150
*ġe***sihð** f. *sight, vision, presence* ds gesihðe 2/13, 2/19, 9/121, gesyhðe 14/21, 14/41, 14/66, as 14/96
silð see **sellan**
simle adv. *always* 4/95, 6/20, 17/68, symble 4/138, 4/141, 4/288, symle 4/144, 4/236, 4/305
sīn poss. pron. *his, her, its* isn sīne 11(h)/14
sinc n. *treasure* as 11(n)/4, 12/59, 13/35; gs sinces 16/25; ds since 14/23
sincfāg adj. *decorated with treasure, richly adorned* nsm 11(j)/15
sincġeofa see **sincġyfa**
sincġyfa m. *one who gives treasure, lord* ns sincgeofa 10(b)/50; as sincgyfan 12/278; ds 18(b)/1342; as 12/278
sincþegu f. *receiving of treasure* as sincþege 16/34
sind see **bēon**
sindon see **bēon**
singāl adj. *perpetual, everlasting* nsf 14/141
singan III *sing, resound* inf 9/17, 9/21, etc.; pres ptc singend nsm 10(a)/31; asm singende 17/22; imp s sing 1/27, 9/28; pres

singan (*cont.*)
3s singeþ 17/54, 3p singað 11(d)/8; pret 3s sang 1/8, song 9/45, 9/70, etc.
sinnig adj. *sinful* asm sinnigne 18(b)/1379
sinsorg f. *constant sorrow* gp sinsorgna 15/45
sīo see **se**
siodu m. *morality* as 5/7
*ġe***sīon** see *ġe***sēon**
Sīrīc see **Siġerīc**
siteþ see **sittan**
sittan V *sit* inf 15/37; pres 3s siteþ 1/11, 15/47; subj 2s sitte 8/28; pret 3s sæt 11(a)/1, 3p sǣton 11(b)/1
*ġe***sittan** V. *sit* pret 3s gesæt 16/111, 18(a)/749 (*sat up*)
sīð m. *journey, fate, lot, venture* ns 18(a)/765, 18(a)/716 (*time, occasion*); as 11(e)/3, 15/2, 18(a)/872; ds sīþe 17/51, 18(a)/740 (*time*); ap sīþas 11(k)/11, 17/2, 18(a)/877
*ġe***sīþ** m. *companion* np gesīþas 11(o)/5; dp gesīþum 18(b)/1313
sīðfæt m. *journey, expedition* ds sīðfate 14/150
sīðian 2 *travel* inf 11(l)/2, 12/177, 14/68, 18(a)/720, 18(a)/808; pres subj 1s sīðie 12/251; pret 3s sīþode 4/219, 4/266
siððan adv. *afterwards, later* 2/51, 3/24, 4/64, 4/156, 5/62, syððan 4/159, 4/268, etc.; conj. *after, since, when* 2/59, 15/3, syðþan 14/3, etc.
sīwian 2 *sew, stitch together* pret 3p sīwodon 2/16
slāt see **slītan**
slǣp m. *sleep* ns 16/39; ds slǣpe 9/45
slǣpan VII *sleep* pres ptc slǣpende 9/45; asm slǣpendne 18(a)/741
slēan VI *strike, beat, attack* pres ptc slēande 4/148; pret 3s slōh 1/21, 4/157, 4/276, 12/163, 12/285; 3p slōgon 4/219, 7/78; subj 3s slōge 12/117 [MnE slay]
slecg m. *sledge-hammer* ds slecge 4/276; gp slecga 3/200
sleġe m. *blow, stroke, slaughter* gs sleges 4/190; ds slege 3/104, 4/218, 4/227
slītan I *tear, rend* pret 3s slāt 17/11, 18(a)/741 [MnE slit]
slīðen adj. *cruel* nsf 16/30
slōgon see **slēan**
slōh see **slēan**
smēagan 1 *contrive, reflect, investigate* inf 10(a)/17; pret 3s smēade 4/169
smiþ m. *blacksmith* ns 3/193, 3/204; ds smiðe 1/16
smiððe f. *smithy* ns 1/16; ds smiþþan 3/199
smolt adj. *peaceful, serene* asn 9/104
smylte adj. *serene* ism 9/120; dsf smyltre 9/119
snāw m. *snow* as 16/48
snell adj. *keen, bold* npm snelle 12/29
snīwan 1 *snow* pres subj 3s snīwe 8/29; pret 3s snīwde 17/31
snottor adj. *wise* nsm 16/111, snotor 4/137, 18(a)/826, 18(b)/1384, snotera 18(b)/1313; npm snottre 11(b)/2
snytro f. *wisdom* as 8/58; dp snyttrum 18(a)/872
socc m. *sock* ns 1/2
sōfte adv. *easily* 12/59
sōhte see **sēċan**
*ġe***somnian** 2 *gather, assemble* inf 9/50; p ptc gesomnad 11(o)/2
*ġe***somnung** f. *community* ds gesomnunge 9/65
somod see **samod**
sōna adv. *immediately* 2/52, 2/62, 2/78, 4/26, etc. [MnE soon]
song m. *song, cry* ns song 9/68; as song 1/27, 17/19, sang 18(a)/787; gs songes 9/47
songcræft m. *poetic art* as 9/14
sorg f. *sorrow, grief, trouble* ns 16/30, 16/39, 16/50, sorh 18(b)/1322; as sorge 17/42, 17/54; gp sorga 14/80; dp sorgum 14/20, 14/59
sorgian 2 *sorrow, grieve, care* imp s sorga 18(b)/1384
sorh see **sorg**
sorhlēoþ n. *song of sorrow, dirge* as 14/67
sōþ adj. *true* nsm sōða 4/328; gsm sōðan 8/69; dsm 8/58, sōþum 4/146, 4/210; nsn sōð 4/230; gsf sōþan 4/141; dsf 4/187 [archaic MnE sooth]
sōþ n. *truth* as 3/107, 3/197, 4/16, etc.; tō sōþe *as a fact* 16/11 [archaic MnE (for)sooth]
sōðe adv. *truly, faithfully* 18(a)/871
sōðgied m. *lay of truth, story about actual events* as 17/1
sōðlīċe adv. *truly* 2/9, 2/64, 4/52, etc. [archaic MnE soothly]
spadu f. *shovel, spade* ds spade 4/278
spǣtan 1 *spit* pres 1s spǣte 11(h)/8
spearca m. *spark* ap spearcan 3/200
spearwa m. *sparrow* ns 8/30
spēd f. *means, opportunity, wherewithal* as on spēd *successfully* 18(a)/873; ap spēda 5/59
spēdan 1 *be prosperous, be wealthy* pres 2p spēdað 12/34 [MnE speed]
spēdiġ adj. *successful* nsm 14/151
spell n. *story, message* as 9/56, 12/50, spel 18(a)/873; gs spelles 9/66; dp spellum 99/74
spēow see **spōwan**
spere n. *spear* as 8/64, 12/137; ds 3/61; is 8/68; ap speru 12/108
spild m. *destruction* ds spilde 11(h)/8
spillan 1 *destroy* inf 12/34
spor n. *track, trail* ds spore 5/38 [MnE spoor]
spōwan VII *succeed* (impersonal, w.d.) pret 3s spēow 5/9

sprǣċ f. *utterance, speech, language* gs sprǣċe 4/104; ds 4/129, 4/309, 8/25, 11(f)/13; ap sprǣca 4/88

sprǣcan (= **sprǣcon**) see **sprecan**

ġesprec n. *conference, discussion* as 8/4

sprecan V *speak, say* inf 9/90, 14/27, 18(d)/3172; pres ptc sprecende 8/40, 9/31, 9/99, etc.; pres 1s sprece 4/55, sprice 11(h)/11; 2s spricst 3/204; 3s spricð 4/49, spriceð 16/70; pret 3s spræc 4/72, 10(b)/81, 12/211, 12/274; 1p sprǣcon 12/212; 3p sprǣcan 8/38, sprǣcon 12/200, 12/212

ġesprecan V *say* pret 3s gespræc 18(b)/1398

sprengan 1 *break, cause to spring or quiver* pret 3s sprengde 12/137

spricst see **sprecan**

springan III *spring (away)* pret 3s sprang 12/137

ġespringan III *spring forth, arise* pret 3s gesprong 18(a)/884

spyriġean 1 *follow, follow in the footsteps of* inf 5/37

spyrte f. *basket, eel basket* as spyrtan 3/77

stafum see **stæf**

stān m. *stone* ns 1/18; as 1/17, 13/43, 18(a)/887; gs stānes 1/19; ds stāne 1/20, 14/66; is 1/21

stānclif n. *rocky cliff, crag* ap stānclifu 17/23

standan VI *stand, remain* inf 12/19, 14/43, 14/62; pres 1s stande 3/24, 3/30; 3s stent 4/134, stynt 4/59, 12/51, standeð 18(b)/1362, stondeð 16/74, 16/97, 16/115; 3p standað 4/287, stondaþ 16/76, 17/67; pret 1s stōd 14/38; 3s 4/202, 4/280, 10(b)/28, 12/25, 12/28, 12/145, etc., stōd him . . . æt *appeared to him* 9/27; 1p stōdon 14/71; 3p 4/282, 5/30, 12/63, 12/72, 12/79, 12/100, etc.

ġestandan VI *stand up* inf 12/171; pret 3p gestōdon 14/63 (w. refl., see note)

stang see **stingan**

stānhliþ n. *cliff* ds stānhliþe 15/48; ap stānhleoþu 16/101

stānhof n. *stone building* np stānhofu 13/38

stānwyrhta m. *stone-mason* ns 1/20

ġestaðelian 2 *establish, make steadfast* pres 3s gestaþelað 17/108; pret 3s gestaþelade 17/104

staðol m. *fixed position* as 11(c)/5 (*foundation*); ds staðole 14/71; dp staðelum *in place* 17/109

stædefæste see **stedefæst**

stæf m. *letter* dp stafum 9/4 [MnE staff]

stǣlan 1 *avenge* p ptc gestǣled 18(b)/1340

stælgiest m. *thievish guest, thieving stranger* ns 11(c)/5

stǣr n. *history* as 9/72; gs stǣres 9/66

stæð n. *bank, shore* ds stæðe 12/25

ġesteal n. *foundation* ns 16/110

steall m. *stall* as 3/19

stēam m. *moisture* ds stēame 14/62 [MnE steam]

stēap adj. *high* nsm 13/11 [MnE steep]

stearc adj. *severe* nsm 3/10 [MnE stark]

stearn m. *tern* ns 17/23

stēda m. *stallion* as stēdan 8/65 [MnE steed]

stede m. *place, position* as 12/19 [MnE stead]

stedefæst adj. *steadfast, unyielding* npm stedefæste 12/249; stædefæste 12/127

stefn m. *trunk, stem, root* ds stefne 14/30

stefn f. *voice* ns 14/71; as stefne 2/17, 2/21, 2/36; is 11(j)/18; stemne 10(b)/84

stefna m *prow or stern of a ship* ds stefnan 17/7

stelan IV *steal* inf 4/275

stemn see **stefn**

stemnettan 1 *stand firm* pret 3p stemnetton 12/122

stent see **standan**

steorra m. *star* ap steorran 2/74

stēpan 1 w.d. *exalt* pres 3s stēpeð 11(m)/8

steppan VI *step, advance* pret 1s stōp 11(p)/5; 3s 12/8, 12/78, 12/131, 18(a)/761

stician 2 *stick* pret 3s sticode 8/68

stīeran 1 w.d. *steer, control, punish* inf 17/109; pret 3s stȳrde 4/145

ġestīgan I *climb up, mount, ascend* inf 14/34; pret 3s gestāh 14/40

stihtan 1 *direct, command, exhort* pret 3s stihte 12/127

ġestillan 1 *restrain, stop* pret 3s gestilde 4/306

stilnes f. *peace* as stilnesse 5/57; ds 9/117 [MnE stillness]

stingan III *stab, pierce* pret 3s stang 12/138 [MnE sting]

stīð adj. *stern, firm, hard* nsn 12/301; as stīðan 4/91; apm stīþe 17/104

stīðhicgende adj. *firm of purpose, resolute* npm 12/122

stīðlīċe adv. *sternly, loudly* 12/25

stīðmōd adj. *resolute, brave* nsm 14/40

stōd see **standan**

stōdhors n. *stallion* as 8/61 [MnE studhorse]

stōdon see **standan**

stondaþ see **standan**

stōp see **steppan**

storm m. *storm* ds storme 15/48, is 8/32; np stormas 16/101, 17/23; dp stormum 13/11

stōw f. *place* ns 4/314, 8/71, 18(b)/1372; as stōwe 2/69, 18(b)/1378; ds stōwe 2/53, 2/56, 3/42, etc.; ap stōwa 5/34; dp stōwum 4/97 [MnE stow]

strang adj. *strong* nsm 14/40, strong 11(f)/13; gsm strangan 11(c)/5; dsm strongum 17/109; npm strange 14/30; compar. nsm strengra 11(e)/4; apn strangran 8/22; superl. strengest nsm 18(a)/789

*ge***strangian** 2 *strengthen* pres 1s gestrangie 3/165
strǣl m. or f. *arrow* dp strǣlum 14/62
strēam m. *river* ns 13/38; as 12/68; ap strēamas 13/43, 17/34 (*sea*) [MnE stream]
strēġan 1 *strew, spread* inf 17/97
strengra see **strang**
strengu f. *strength, power* ns 11(d)/5; ds strengo 11(f)/13
*ġe***strēon** n. *wealth, profit, treasure* as 3/148, 4/165, 18(d)/3166, gestrīon 10(b)/23
strong see **strang**
strutian 2 *struggle* pres ptc strutigende 4/280 [MnE strut]
stund f. *time, short while* as stunde 12/271
Stūrmere m. *village of Sturmer (Essex)* as 12/249
stynt see **standan**
stȳrde see **stīeran**
styria m. *sturgeon* ap styrian 3/93
styrian 1 *stir up* inf 18(a)/872 (*treat of, engage*); pres 3s styreþ 18(b)/1374
styrman 1 *storm* pres subj 3s styrme 8/30
sulh f. *plough* ds sylh 3/9, 3/12
sum pron., adj. (§193.4) *a certain, some* nsm 4/6, 4/126, 4/220, 9/1, 10(a)/12, 10(b)/46, 12/149, 12/164, etc.; asm sumne 4/273, 5/53, 16/81, 16/82, etc.; gsm sumes 11(c)/3, 11(j)/15; nsn sum 17/68; asn 3/148, 9/55, 12/285, sume 2/50; nsf sum 4/267, 11(j)/8; asf sume 12/271; dsf sumre 9/23; npm sume 3/4, 3/5, 3/6, 17/56 (þā sume *those particular ones*); apm 16/80; apf 5/54
sumor m. *summer* as 3/127; gs sumeres 17/54; ds sumera 3/125
sumorlang adj. *long as in summer* asm sumorlangne 15/37
*ġe***sund** adj. *unharmed, whole, uncorrupted* nsm 4/301; npm gesunde 6/33 [MnE (safe and) sound]
sundor adv. *apart* 16/111 [MnE (a)sunder]
sunnandæġ m. *Sunday* ns 3/53
sunne f. *sun* ns 1/22; ds sunnan 1/24
sunu m. *son* ns 1/35, 1/36, 12/76, 12/298, 14/150; as 2/44, 2/59, 2/65, 2/69, 4/57, 7/45; gs suna 2/58; ds 2/73, 4/6; np suno 11(a)/2, 11(a)/3; gp suna 11(k)/12
sūsl f. *torment* gs sūsle 4/80
sūð adv. *south(wards)* 18(a)/858
sūðan adv. *from the south* be sūðan *south of* 4/126, 5/19, 7/70
sūðerne adj. *southern, of southern design* asm 12/134
Sūðhamtūn m. *Southampton* ns 7/3
Sūðriġe pl. *Surrey* ap 7/71
Sūðseaxe m. pl. *Sussex, the South Saxons* ap Sūðsexe 7/71; dp Sūðseaxum 7/13, 7/56
sūðweardes adv. *southwards* 10(b)/4
swā adv. (§168 s. v. swā) *thus, so* 1/14, 2/70, 3/10, 3/59, 3/101, swǣ 5/14, 5/78 (*such*); swǣ same *likewise, similarly* 5/51; conj. *as* 3/84 (swā fela ... swa *as many as*), 4/239 (swā oft swā *as often as*), 15/24 (w. subj. *as if*), 7/58 (swā wīde swā *as far as*); ēac swā *likewise, also* 2/19; swā hwæt swā *whatsoever* 3/66, 3/77, 9/4; swā hwelc swā *whoever* nsm 6/18; swā hwelc swā ... swā ... swā *whatsoever... whether... or* 3/212; swā hwelcum ... swā *whatsoever* 2/9; swā swā *just as* 2/58, 2/75, 3/189, 4/10, 4/22, etc.; swā þēah *however* 4/27
*ge***swāc** see *ge***swīcan**
swam see **swimman**
swān m. *swineherd* ns 6/5
swāse see **swǣs**
swāt m. *sweat* gs swātes (*blood*) 14/23; ds swāte 2/40
swaþu see **swæð**
swaþul m. or n. *flame, heat* ds swaþule 18(a)/782
swǣ see **swā**
swæcc m. *taste, flavour* ds swæcce 3/159
swǣs adj. *beloved* asm swǣsne 16/50; npf swāse 11(a)/3; gpm swǣsra 11(k)/11
swǣsendu n. pl. *banquet* dp swǣsendum 8/27
swǣtan 1 *bleed* inf 14/20 [MnE sweat]
swæð n. *track, swath* as 5/36; np swaþu 11(l)/3
swealg see **swelgan**
sweart adj. *dark, black* npm swearte 11(l)/2 [MnE swart]
swefan V *sleep, sleep in death* inf 18(a)/729; pres 3p swefað 18(c)/2256; pret 3p swǣfon 18(a)/703
swefn n. *dream* as 9/27, 9/52; gp swefna 14/1
swēġ m. *sound, din* ns 18(a)/782; as 3/200, 17/21
Sweġen pers. n. *Swein* ns 7/47
sweġl n. *sky, heaven* gs swegles 18(a)/860
swelċ adj. *such* dsn swelcum 3/129; dsf swylcere 4/249; dpm swilcum ōðrum *in other such* 4/311; apn swilce 4/324, swylce 4/329; swylc ... swylc *such... as* nsm 18(b)/328–9; npm swilce ... swylce 4/319; pron. *such* gsn swulces 18(a)/880; rel. pron. *such as* npm 17/83
swelċe adv. *likewise* swylce 14/8, 15/43; ēac swelce, swelce ēac *also, likewise* 2/1, 2/33, 3/103, 3/121, 9/79, ēac swilce 4/260; conj. *as if* 5/33, swilce 4/212, 4/257; *like* swilce 4/214, swylce 4/259; swylce swā *just as* 14/92
swelgan III w.d. *swallow, imbibe* inf 11(j)/15; pret 3s swealg 11(c)/6, swealh 18(a)/743; sub 3s swulge 18(a)/782
sweltan III *die, perish* inf 4/185, 12/293; pres

subj 1s swelte 4/187; pret 3s swealt 18(a)/892; 3p swulton 4/306; subj 1p swulten 2/7
swencan 1 *press hard, harass, afflict* p ptc geswenced 18(b)/1368, dsn geswenctan 4/252
sweng m. *blow, stroke* gs swenges 12/118; ds swencge 4/219
swēora m. *neck* ns swūra 4/258; as swēoran 2/64, 11(b)/6; ds swūran 4/259
*ġe***sweorcan** III *grow dark, become obscured* pres subj 3s gesweorce 16/59
sweord n. *sword* ns swurd 12/166, 18(a)/890; as sweord 2/53, 2/59, 8/64, 11(n)/14, swurd 12/15, 12/161, etc.; ds swurde 12/118; ap swurd 12/47; dp sweordum 18(a)/884
sweostor f. (§60) *sister* ns swustor 4/320; as swuster 4/19; np gesweostor 11(a)/3 (see §138 Prefixes, ġe-); ap geswustra 4/16
sweostersunu m. *sister's son* ns swustersunu 12/115
sweotol adj. *clear, manifest* nsn 18(a)/817, 18(a)/833, swutel 4/311
*ġe***sweotolian** 2 *reveal, show* pres 3s geswutelað 4/323, 4/328; pret 3s gesweotolode 2/56; p ptc geswutelod 4/67, 4/70
sweotolung f. *manifestation, evidence* ds swutelunge 4/260
sweotule adv. *openly* 16/11
swerian VI *swear* pres 1s swerie 2/72
swēte adj. *sweet* asn 17/95 (as noun); superl. asn swēteste 9/68
swētmete m. *sweetmeat* gp swētmetta 3/159
swētnis f. *sweetness* as swētnisse 9/6; ds swētnesse 9/78
*ġe***swīcan** 1 *cease, desist* pres 3s geswiceð 11(f)/12; pret 3s geswāc 4/251; 3p geswicon 4/307; subj. 7/60, 7/66
swift adj. *swift* nsm 11(l)/3, swifta 18(c)/2264; asm swiftne 3/118, 13/18; dpm swiftum 3/49; compar. nsf swiftre 11(e)/3
swīge adj. *silent, still* nsm 11(e)/1
swīgian 2 *be quiet, fall silent* pres 3s swīgað 11(d)/1; pret 3s swīgode 4/172
swilċe see **swelċe**
swimman III *swim* pres 3p swimmaþ 3/88, 16/53; pret 1s swom 11(p)/3, 3s swam 1/5
*ġe***swinc** n. *toil, hardship* ds geswince 3/129; dp geswincum 2/38 [archaic MnE swink]
swincan III *labour, toil, struggle* pres 1s swince 3/8, 3/29; pret 3p swuncon 4/279
*ġe***swincdagas** m. pl. *days of toil* dp geswincdagum 17/2
*ġe***swing** n. *vibration, swirl, surf* ns 18(a)/848
swingan III *beat, fly* pres 3s swingeð 18(c)/2264; pret 3p swungon 4/209
swingel f. *blow, stroke* dp swinglum 4/210
swingere m. *beater, scourger* ns 11(f)/7
swinsian 2 *sing, sound melodiously* pres 3p swinsiað 11(d)/7
swinsung f. *melody* ds swinsunge 9/57
swipu f. *whip, scourge* dp swipum 4/209
swīþ adj. *mighty* nsf swīþe 13/24; compar. swīþre nsf 17/115; asf swīðran 14/20
swīðe adv. *very, exceedingly* 1/22, 3/62, 3/151, 3/179, 4/7, 4/193, 4/276 (*mightily*), 4/299 (*fiercely*), 11(l)/3, 12/115 (*cruelly*), etc.; swīðe swīðe *very much* 5/40; compar. swīðor *more, rather* 4/185; superl. swīþost 3/50 (*especially*)
swīðferhð adj. *strong-minded, brave* nsm 18(a)/826
swīðran see **swīðe**
swōgan VII *resound, make a noise* pres 3p swōgað 11(d)/7 [MnE sough]
swom see **swimman**
swuā see **swā**
swulge see **swelgan**
swulten see **sweltan**
swungon see **swingan**
swūra sec **swēora**
swurd see **sweord**
swurdbora m. *swordbearer* ns 4/130, 4/131
swuster see **sweostor**
swustersunu see **sweostersunu**
*ġe***swustra** see **sweostor**
swutel see **sweotol**
*ġe***swutelað** see *ġe***sweotolian**
*ġe***swutelod** see *ġe***sweotolian**
swutelunge see **sweotolung**
swylce see **swelċe**
swylt m. *death* ns 13/26
sȳ (= **sīe**) see **bēon**
sȳferlīċe adv. *neatly, cleanly* 4/269
*ġe***syhðe** see *ġe***sihð**
sylf see **self**
sylfor see **seolfor**
sylh see **sulh**
syll f. *sill, floor* ds sylle 18(a)/775
syllan see **sellan**
syllic adj. *marvellous, wondrous* nsm 14/13; compar. syllicre asn 14/4 (see note)
symbel n. *feast* ds symble 9/23, symle 14/141; gp symbla 16/93
symble, symle see **simle**
syndolh n. *very great wound* ns 18(a)/817
syndon see **bēon**
syndriġlīċe adv. *individually, separately, especially* 8/8, 9/1 [archaic MnE sundrily]
*ġe***syne** see *ġe***siene**
synn f. *sin* gp synna 4/63, 9/81, 17/100; dp synnum 14/13, 14/99, 14/146
synscaða m. *malefactor, miscreant* as synscaðan 18(a)/801
synsnǣd f. *huge* or *sinful gobbet* dp synsnǣdum 18(a)/743

*ġe***syntu** f. *prosperity* as gesynto 8/19
*ġe***syrwed** adj. *armed* nsm 12/159
syððan see **siððan**

tācn n. *sign, token* ns tācen 18(a)/833; as tācn 11(n)/5
*ġe***tācnian** 2 *prefigure, betoken* pret 3s getācnode 4/30, 4/87, 4/88
*ġe***tācnung** f. *prefiguration, signification, type* ns 4/28; as getācnunge 4/78 [MnE tokening]
tam adj. *tame* nsm 4/247
*ġe***tāwian** 2 *harass, mistreat* p ptc npm getāwode 4/174
tǣċan 1 *teach, show, direct* pres 3s tǣcð 4/103; pret 3s tǣhte 4/41, 12/18; 3p tǣhton 4/109
tǣcnan 1 *point out, signify, direct* pres 3s tǣcneð 11(l)/6
tæġel m. *tail* ns 4/94
tǣhte see **tǣċan**
*ġe***tæl** n. *account, sequence* as 9/65
tǣsan 1 *lacerate, tear apart* pret 3s tǣsde 12/270 [MnE tease]
*ġe***tǣse** adj. *agreeable* nsf 18(b)/1320
tæt (= **þæt**) see **sē**
tēaforgēap adj. *red-curved* nsm tēaforgēapa 13/30
tēah see **tēon**
teala adv., interj. *well* 9/115, teola 8/67
*ġe***teld** n. *tabernacle* ns 4/81; ds getelde 4/93
tellan 1 *account, reckon, consider* pret 3s tealde 18(a)/794 [MnE tell]
Temese f. *the Thames* ds 5/19, 7/71
temman 1 *tame* inf 3/114, 3/116; p ptc apm getemedan 3/124, 3/127
*ġe***temman** 1 *tame* pres 1s getemme 3/123
templ n. *temple* as 8/47
Tenetland n. *Thanet* ns 7/5
*ġe***tenge** adj. w.d. *near to, resting on* nsm 11(d)/8
teola see **teala**
tēon n. *injury, harm* as 11(m)/3
tēon 2 *adorn* pret 3s tēode 9/43
tēon II *draw, drag, take* (*a trip or journey*) pret 3s tēah 18(b)/1332; 3p tugon 4/218
tīd f. *time* ns 12/104; as 8/31, 9/90, 11(p)/2 (on āne tīd *at the same time*), 17/124, tīde 9/18; gs tīde 8/27, 9/115; ds 4/11, 9/23, 9/87, 9/112 np tīda 5/4 [MnE tide]
tīddeg m. *span of life, final hour* ds tīddege 17/69
tīgan 1 *tie, fasten* pret 3p tīgdon 4/208
tiġel f. *tile* dp tigelum 13/30
til adj. *good* nsm 16/112
tilian 2 *strive, endeavour* pres subj 1p tilien 17/119
tīma m. *time* ds tīman 4/14, 4/34, 7/74
*ġe***timbre** n. *building, structure* ap getimbro 8/71
tin n. *tin* as 3/142
tintreġliċ adj. *tormenting* gsn tintreglican 9/78
tīr m. *glory* ns 12/104
tīrlēas adj. *inglorious, vanquished* gsm tīrlēases 18(a)/843
tīðian 2 (w.d. of person and g. of thing) *grant* infl inf (tō) tīðienne 4/4
tō prep. w.d. *to, into, for, as a* 1/28, 2/2, 2/7, 2/25, 2/68, 3/9, 3/150 (tō nytte *of use*), 4/5, 4/92 (tō lace *as an offering*), 7/1, 8/34, 12/10 (fōn tō *take up*), etc.; adv. cume . . . tō *arrive* 3/45, 4/213 (scuton . . . tō *shot at*); with the infl inf (§205.2), 2/12 (tō etanne *for eating, to eat*), 2/49, 2/51, 3/17, etc.; as adv. *thither* 17/119
tō adv. *too* 12/55, 12/66, 12/90, etc.
tōætȳcan 1 *add* pret 3s tōætȳhte 8/39
tōætȳhte see **tōætȳcan**
tōberstan III *break apart, shatter* pres 3s tōbirsteð 11(g)/7; pret 3s tōbærst 12/136, 12/144
tōbrecan IV *destroy, break open, shatter* inf 18(a)/780; p ptc tōbrocen 7/39, 12/242
tōbrȳtan 1 *crush* pres 3s tōbrȳt 2/32
tōcyme m. *coming, advent* ds 4/22
tōdāl n. *distinction, difference* ns 4/17
tōdæġ adv. *today* 3/52
tōdǣlan 1 *part, separate* pret 3p subj tōdǣlden 15/12
tōgædere adv. *together* 4/252, 7/33, 7/43, 12/67, tōgædre 13/20
tōġēanes prep. w.d. *against* 17/76
tōġeīeċan 1 *increase, add to* p ptc tōgeīeced 3/190
tōġeþēodan 1 *add* pret 3s tōgeþēodde 9/47
tōgongan VII w.g. *pass away* (impers.) pres 3s tōgongeð 11(h)/10
*ġe***toht** n. *battle* ds getohte 12/104
tōl n. *tool* ds tōle 4/281
tōlūcan II *pull asunder, destroy* inf 18(a)/781
torht adj. *bright, splendid* nsm 11(m)/3
torhte adv. *brightly, splendidly* 11(d)/8
torn n. *resentment, grief, affliction* as 16/112, 18(a)/833
torr m. *tower* np torras 13/3
tōtwǣman 1 *divide, break up* p ptc tōtwǣmed nsn 12/241
tōweard adj. *coming, future* gsm tōweardan 9/77; gpn tōweardra 4/28 [MnE toward]
tōwearde adv. *beforehand, in advance* 4/30
tōwearp see **tōweorpan**
tōweorpan III *throw down, demolish* inf 8/55, 8/57, 8/61, 8/70; pret 3s tōwearp 8/74
træppe f. *trap* træppum 3/110
tredan V *tread on, trample* pres 1s trede 11(d)/1; pret 3s træd 18(b)/1352
treddian 2 *step, go* pret 3s treddode 18(a)/725

trēow n. *tree* ns 1/13, 2/12; as 2/6, 14/4, 14/14, 14/17, 14/25, etc.; gs trēowes 2/5; ds trēowe 2/3, 2/8, 2/10, etc.; gp trēowa 2/4
trēow f. *faith, trust* as trēowe 16/112; dp trēowum 10(b)/65 (*beliefs*) [MnE tru(th)]
trēowwyrhta m. *carpenter* ns 3/202; ap trēowwyrhtan 3/181
*ġe***trīewe** adj. *faithful* nsm 3/27 [MnE true]
trodu f. *track, footprint* ap trode 18(a)/843
trum adj. *strong* nsm 18(b)/1369
trym n. *step, pace* as 12/247
trymedon see **trymian**
trymian 1 *array, draw up, encourage* inf 12/17; pret 3p trymedon 12/305; p ptc getrymmed asn 12/22
*ġe***trymman** 1 *strengthen* pres ptc getrymmende 9/110 [MnE trim]
*ġe***trymmed** see **trymian**
trymming f. *confirmation* ds trymminge 4/321
tūcian 2 *mistreat, torment* pret 3s tūcode 4/158
tugon see **tēon**
tūn m. *town, village* ds tūne 4/246
tunge f. *tongue* ns 9/121; as tungan 9/16
tūnġerēfa m. *town reeve, overseer of an estate* ds tūngerēfan 9/48
tuwa adv. *twice* 3/26
twā see **twēġen**
twām see **twēġen**
twēġen num. (§84) *two* npm 7/12, 11(a)/2, 11(a)/3, 12/80; apm 3/56, 10(b)/6, 11(b)/4, 18(b)/1347; dpm twām 2/47, 2/50, 4/241, 11(m)/2; dpn 4/135, 11(a)/1; gpn twēga 12/207; npf twā 10(b)/4, 11(a)/2; apf 4/16, 11(b)/3, 11(b)/5, 11(b)/7 [archaic MnE twain]
twelf num. *twelve* npm 4/36, 11(b)/4, twelfe 18(d)/3170
twentig num. *twenty* npm 4/155
twēo m. *doubt, uncertainty* ds twēon 17/69 (tō twēon weorþeð *becomes an occasion for uncertainty*)
twēone num. *two* dp be sǣm twēonum *between the seas, on earth* 18(a)/858
*ġe***tyhtan** 1 *train, urge on, incite* pres 1s getyhte 3/43
tȳman 1 *propagate, beget offspring* pret 3s tȳmde 4/19 [MnE teem]
tȳn num. *ten* dpm 18(d)/3159

þā adv. *then* (§151 and §168 s. v. þonne) 2/7, 2/11, 2/13, 2/15, 2/20, 2/46, 2/49, 2/56, 2/59, 2/61, 4/4, etc.; conj. *when* 8/66, 15/9, þā þā *when* 2/17, 4/130, etc.; þā . . . þā *then. . . when* 2/48, *when . . . then* 5/28, 5/40, 8/1, 9/23, 9/33, 9/57, etc.; þā gȳt *still* 12/168, 12/273
þā pron. see **se**
þafian 2 *consent to* pret 3s þafode 9/63
*ġe***þafian** 2 *consent to, approve* inf 8/5; pret 3s geþafade 8/7
*ġe***þafung** f. *assent* as geþafunge 8/24
*ġe***þāh** see *ġe***þicgan**
þan see **þon**
þanc see **þonc**
*ġe***þanc** n. *thought, intention* as 12/13
*ġe***þancie** see *ġe***þoncian**
þancigende see **þoncian**
þancode see **þoncian**
þanon adv. *thence, therefrom* 3/106, 4/281, 7/54, 18(a)/763, 18(a)/844, 18(a)/853, þonan 10(b)/82, 16/23, 18(a)/819, 18(b)/1373
þār see **þǣr**
þās see **þes**
þǣm, þām see **se**
þǣne (= **þone**) see **se**
þǣr adv., conj. (§152, §168) adv. *there* 2/46, 2/57, 3/60, 3/145, etc.; conj. *where* 2/17, 4/254, 6/26, etc.; þǣr . . . þǣr *where. . . there* 1/23; þǣr þǣr *there where, where* 2/49, *wherever* 5/23
þǣra see **se**
þǣre see **se**
þærfe see **þearfe**
þǣrinne adv. *therein* 6/37, 10(a)/25
þǣrof adv. *thereof, from that* 3/152
þǣron adv. *therein* 14/67
þǣrrihte adv. *immediately* 4/36
þǣrtō adv. *thereto* 4/27, 4/208, 6/28
þæs adv. (g. s. of þæt) *afterwards, therefore* 3/31 (þæs on morgenne *next morning*), 4/330; conj. 6/7 (þæs þe *after*)
þæs pron. see **se**
þæt conj. *that, so that* 2/3, 2/6, 2/9, 2/23, 2/37, 2/60, 2/64, 3/43, 3/59, 8/68, 10(b)/30 (þæt þe), etc.
þæt pron. see **se**
þætte (= **þæt þe**) conj. (§155) *that* ðætte 5/17, 5/26, etc.
þe indeclinable relative particle (§162) *which, who, that* 2/1, 2/4, 2/5, 2/22, 2/36, 2/45 (whom), 2/56, 3/87, etc.; *as* 12/313; sē þe *he who* 3/211; þe him *to whom* 16/10, 17/13
þē see **þū**
þē (= **þȳ**, isn of **se**) see **se**
þēah adv. *though, yet, however, nevertheless* 3/105, 4/98, 6/39, etc.; swā þēah *however* 4/27; conj. þēah (þe) *although* 2/8, 4/313
þēah hwæþre adv. *moreover, nevertheless* 3/177
*ġe***þeaht** n. *counsel, deliberation* as 8/4
*ġe***þeahtere** m. *counsellor, adviser, manager* ns 3/185, 3/197; as 3/183; np geþeahteras 8/38
þearf f. *need, stress, danger* ns 9/101, 12/233; as þearfe 12/175, ds 12/232, 12/307, þærfe 12/201
þearf see **þurfan**

þearflīċe adv. *profitably, with good effect* 10(b)/60

þearl adj. *severe* nsf 10(b)/77

þearle adv. *severely, exceedingly* 3/8, 3/29, 3/125 (*ravenously*), 3/157 (*greatly*), 4/272, 10(b)/82, 12/158, 14/52 (*violently*)

þēaw m. *custom, practice* ns 9/91, 16/12; ap ðēawas 4/141, 5/27; dp þēawum 4/84, 4/138

þeċċan I *cover* inf 11(k)/4; pres 3s þeceð 11(j)/1

þeġen see **þeġn**

þeġenlīce adv. *loyally, nobly* 12/294

þeġn m. *nobleman, thane, retainer, warrior* ns 1/1, 6/25, 18(a)/867, þegen 7/15; as þegn 9/93, 10(b)/69, þegen 12/151; ds þegne 18(b)/1341; np þegnas 4/292, 6/17, 10(b)/30, 14/75 (*disciples*), þegenas 12/205, 12/220, ap 12/232; gp þegna 8/15; dp þegnum 4/182, 8/28

þeġnian 2 w.d. *serve* inf 9/93; infl inf (tō) þegnigenne 4/291; pres 3p þegniað 11(m)/6

*ġe***þencan** see *ġe***þenċean**

þenċean 1 *think, intend* inf 10(b)/60, þencan 17/96; pres 1s þence 12/319; 3s þenceð 12/258, 12/316, 14/121, 17/51; 3p þencaþ 14/115; pret 3s þōhte 18(a)/739; 3p þōhton 10(b)/11, 18(a)/800

*ġe***þenċean** 1 *think, ponder, consider* inf 5/19, geþencan 16/58, 17/118; imp s. geðenc 5/24; pret 3s geþōhte 16/88

þenden conj. *while* 10(b)/38, 10(b)/48, 11(e)/6, 17/102

þenian 1 *stretch out* inf 14/52 (see note) [MnE thin]

ðēning f. *divine service* ap ðēninga 5/15

þēod f. *people, nation* ns 10(b)/28; gs þēode 8/77; ds þēode 12/90, 12/220; np þēoda 2/76, ðīoda 5/53, gp þēoda 12/173

*ġe***þēodan** 1 *join* pret 3s geþēodde 9/64

þēodde see **þēowan**

*ġe***þēode** n. *language* as geðīode 5/33, 5/52, etc.; gp geðēoda 5/47

þēoden m. *prince, lord* ns 12/120, 12/232, 12/178; as 12/158; gs þēodnes 16/95, 18(a)/797; ds þēodne 12/294, 14/69

þēodland n. *nation* as þēodlond 10(b)/3

*ġe***þēodnis** f. *joining* ds geþēodnisse 9/9

þēodred pers. n. *Theodred* ns 4/271, 4/292

þēodrīċ pers. n. *Theodoric* ns 10(a)/5, 10(a)/15, 10(a)/24, 10(b)/69; ds þēodrīce 10(b)/30

þēodscipe m. *discipline* dp þēodscipum 9/83

þēof m. *thief* ns 11(c)/4; np þēofas 4/274; ap 4/290; dp þēofum 3/31, 4/294

*ġe***þēon** III *flourish* pret 3p geþungon 10(b)/7; p ptc geþungen 4/139 (*virtuous*)

þēos see **þes**

ðeosse (= **ðisse**) see **þes**

þeossum (= **þissum**) see **þes**

þēow m. *slave, servant* np þēowas 3/176; gp ðīowa 5/31, þēowa 9/65; dp þēowum 4/315

þēowan 1 w.d. *serve* pret 1s þēodde 8/21, 3s þēode 9/119

þēowdōm m. *service* ns 3/188; ds þēowdōme 4/316

þēowian 2 w.d. *serve* pres 3s þēowaþ 11(m)/6

þēre (= **þǣre**) see **se**

þes m., **þēos** f., **þis** n. dem. pron. *this* **þās** pl. *these* (§17) nsm þes 1/20, 3/33; asm þisne 1/27, 3/210, þysne 12/52; dsm þissum 1/29; nsn þis 1/13, 4/303; asn 2/28, 4/55, etc.; gsn þisses 1/29, 1/32; dsn þissum 3/136, 5/64, þisum 7/47; isn þȳs 7/1, þīs 7/7; nsf þēos 1/32; asf þās 4/9; gsf þisere 4/18, þisre 4/67, ðeosse 9/1; dsf þissere 4/112; ðisse 5/25, þysse 8/45; gsf þisse 16/74; np þās 3/3, 7/73; ap 16/91, 16/101; gp þissa 1/30, 3/186, 5/22; dp þisum 4/75, þyssum 4/183, 4/188, þeossum 8/37

þet (= **þæt**) see **se**

þicce adj. *thick, dense* dpm þiccum 4/224

þicgan V *receive, take, eat* inf ðicgean 18(a)/736

*ġe***þicgan** V *receive, gain* pret 3s geþāh 10(b)/53

*ġe***þicgean** V *accept* inf 6/20

þider adv. *thither* 6/18, 10(b)/61, 17/118, þyder 4/275

þīn poss. adj. *thy, thine* asm þīnne 2/44, 2/65, 2/74, 3/7, 3/41, 3/65; gsm þīnes 2/40; dsm þīnum 2/31, 3/73; asn þīn 2/32; gsn þīnes 2/30, 2/36, 2/39; dsn þīnum 2/30, 2/73; asf þīne 2/21, 2/63; dsf þīnre 3/199; npm þīne 3/3; apm 3/81, 3/120; gpm þīnra 8/15, 4/165; dpm þīnum 3/33; apn þīn 3/144; apf þīne 2/33

þinċeð see **þynċan**

þīnen f. *handmaid* ap þīnena 4/16

þing n. *thing* ns 13/48; as 3/35; np 3/139, 3/190; ap 1/34, 3/136, 3/139, 8/21, 9/98; gp þinga 3/143, 4/30, 17/68 (þinga gehwylce *in all circumstances*), 18(a)/791 (ǣnige þinga *in any way, by any means*); dp þingum 8/18

*ġe***þinge** n. *result, issue* gs geþinges 18(a)/709

ðīod see **þēod**

*ġe***þīode** see *ġe***þēode**

þīow see **þēow**

þīowotdōm m. *service* ap ðīowotdōmas 5/11

þis see **þes**

þisere see **þes**

þissa see **þes**

þisse see **þes**

*ġe***þōht** m. *thought* ns 15/43, as 15/12, np geþōhtas 17/34

*ġe***þōhte** see *ġe***þenċean**
þōhton see **þenċean**
þolian 2 *suffer, endure* inf 10(b)/77, 12/201, 12/307, 18(a)/832; pres 1s þolie 3/138; pret 3p þolodan 14/149
*ġe***þolian** 2 *endure, tolerate* inf 12/6
þon adv. *than* 12/33
þon i. s. of **þæt** (see **se**) *the* (used with comparatives) 8/17; **for þon** see **for**; **wið þon þe** see **wiþ**
þonan see **þanon**
þonc m. w.d. of person and g. of cause *thanks* (*for*) ns 5/20, 5/79, 17/122; as þanc 12/120, 12/147
þoncian 2 w.d. of person and g. of cause *thank* pret 3s þancode 18(b)/1397
*ġe***þoncian** 2 w.d. of person and g. of cause *thank, give thanks to* pres ptc þancigende 4/245; pres 1s geþancie 12/173
þone see **se**
þonne adv. *then* (§§151–152, 168 s.v. þonne) 2/10, 3/9, 3/12, 3/25, 3/30, 3/42, 3/44, 3/146, etc.; conj. *when, whenever* 3/11, 3/30, 3/44, 3/205, 4/318, 4/329, etc.; conj. w. compar. (§177) *than* 2/1, 2/73, 3/99, 3/146, 3/198, 4/316, 8/18, 11(h)/7, 12/195, etc.
þorfte see **þurfan**
þorn m. *thorn* ap þornas 2/39
þorod pers. n. *Thorod* ds þorode 7/29
þrāg f. *time, interval* ns 16/95; as þrāge 10(b)/77; ds þrāge *for a time* 10(b)/28; dp þrāgum *sometimes, at times* 11(e)/4
*ġe***þrang** n. *throng, crowd* ds geþrange 12/299
þrǣd m. *thread* ns 4/259
þrēanȳd f. *distress, sad necessity* dp þrēanȳdum 18(a)/832
þrēat m. *host, troop* is þrēate 10(b)/3 [MnE threat]
þreohtig adj. *enduring* compar. nsm þreohtigra 11(e)/4
þridda num. *third* dsm þriddan 2/48
þrīe num. *three* ap þrȳ 4/296; gp þrēora 12/299, 17/68 (þrēora sum *one of three things*); dp þrim 4/73, 4/128
þrim see **þrīe**
*ġe***þringan** III *oppress, pinch, constrict* pret 3p geþrungon 10(b)/3; p ptc geþrungen npm 17/8
þrīnnys f. *trinity* ns 4/67 [archaic MnE threeness]
þrōwian 2 *suffer* pret 1s þrōwode 17/3; 3s 14/84, 14/98, 14/145
þrōwung f. *passion, suffering* ds þrōwunge 9/75
*ġe***þrungen** see *ġe***þringan**
þrȳ see **þrīe**
þryċċan 1 *oppress* p ptc þrycced 9/89
þrym m. *majesty, glory* ns 16/95
þrymfæst adj. *glorious* nsm 14/84; asm þrymfæstne 11(c)/4
þrȳð f. pl. *power, force* np 16/99
þrȳðswȳð adj. *strong, mighty* nsm 18(a)/736
þū pron. *thou, you* ns 1/36, 2/20, 2/23, 2/24, 2/26, 2/40, 3/1, 3/7, etc.; as þē 2/35, 2/74, 3/179, 4/142; ds þē 2/23, 2/24, 2/31, 2/37, 2/39, 2/74, 3/68, 3/124 (*from you*), 4/4 (*for you*)
*ġe***þūht** see **þynċan**
þūhte see **þynċan**
*ġe***þungon** see *ġe***þēon**
þurfan pret. pres. *need* pres 3s þearf 4/115, 14/117; 1p þurfe 12/34; 3p þurfon 12/249; pret 1s þorfte 4/5, 4/185
þurh prep. *through, by, by means of* 2/72, 4/64, etc., þuruh 7/73, 9/21 (*in*), 9/27 (*in*)
þurhdrīfan I *pierce, drive through* pret 3p þurhdrifan 14/46
þurhflēon II *fly through* pres subj 3s þurhflēo 8/30
þurhwadan VI *pierce, pass through* pret 3s þurhwōd 12/296, 18(a)/890
þurhwunian 2 *persist, remain* pret 3s þurhwunode 4/139, 10(a)/7
þurstān pers. n. *Thurston* gs þurstānes 12/298
þuruh see **þurh**
þus adv. *thus, in this way, as follows* 2/44, 2/50, 2/77, 3/44, 3/176, etc.
þūsend num. *thousand* ns 7/24, 7/63
þwang m. *thong, strap* ap þwangas 3/153
*ġe***þwǣre** adv. *gently, obediently* 11(m)/6
*ġe***þwǣrlǣcan** 1 *be a party to, assent to* inf 4/291
*ġe***þwǣrnes** f. *concord, tranquillity* ns 3/207
þȳ see **se**
þȳ lǣs þe see **lǣs**
þyder see **þider**
þȳfel m. *bush* ap þȳfelas 4/233
*ġe***þyld** f. *patience* as 18(b)/1395
*ġe***þyldiġ** adj. *patient* nsm 16/65
þynċan 1 (impersonal verb [§212] w.d.) *seem* inf þincean 18(b)/1341; pres 3s þyncþ 1/35, þincð 4/7, 4/26, þynceð 8/21, þinceð 12/55, 16/41; pret 3s þūhte 2/12, 4/4, 9/96, 11(c)/1, 12/66, 14/4, 18(a)/842; 3p þūhton 18(a)/866; p ptc geþūht 3/164 (biþ geþūht *will seem*), 3/187 (is geþūht *seems*), 3/191, 4/230 [archaic MnE (me)thinks]
þȳrel n. *hole* as 3/205 [MnE (nos)tril]
þyslīċ adj. *such* nsn 8/25
þȳstro n. *darkness, shadow* ds 11(c)/4, np 14/52
þȳwan 1 *drive, urge, goad* inf 3/15

ūhta m. or f. *period just before dawn* ds ūhtan 15/35; gp ūhtna 16/8
ūhtcearu f. *grief before dawn* as ūhtceare 15/7
ūhtsong m. *matins* as 9/113

unārīmed adj. *countless* dp unārīmedum 10(a)/10
unāsecgendliċ adj. *unspeakable* ap unāsecgendlice 7/58
unbefohten adj. *unopposed, without a fight* npm unbefohtene 12/57
unbindan III *unbind, loosen* p ptc unbunden 11(h)/15
unc see **wit**
unclǣne adj. *unclean* npm 3/79; apm unclǣnan 3/80
uncūð adj. *unknown, strange* ns 5/78, 8/27; gsn uncūðes 18(a)/876 [MnE uncouth]
undēadliċ adj. *immortal* nsf 1/33 [archaic MnE undeadly]
under prep. w.d.a. *under* 1/5, 2/35, 4/12, etc.
underbæc adv. *behind, back* 2/66
underbeġinnan III *undertake* infl inf (tō) underbeginnenne 4/8
undercyning m. *underking* ns 4/166
underdelfan III *dig under* pret 3s underdealf 4/277 [MnE delve under]
underetan V *eat under, undermine* p ptc npf undereotone 13/6
underfēngon see **underfōn**
underfōn VII *accept* pret 3p underfēngon 7/61
understandan VI *understand* inf 4/15, 4/40, 4/75; infl inf (tō) understandenne 4/45; pres 3p understandað 4/25
underþēodan I *subject, devote* pret 3s underþēodde 8/16; p ptc underþēoded 9/84
unearh adj. *undaunted, not cowardly* npm unearge 12/206
unēaþe adv. *with difficulty, hardly* 3/139
unfæġer adj. *horrible* nsn 18(a)/727
unforcūð adj. *noble, of unblemished reputation* nsm 12/51
unforht adj. *unafraid* nsm 4/189, 14/110; npm unforhte 12/79
unformolsnod adj. *undecayed* nsm 4/264
unġehīrsum adj. *disobedient* nsm 4/120
unġelǣred adj. *unlearned, ignorant* npm ungelǣredan 4/25; dpm ungelǣredum 4/46
unġesǣlig adj. *unfortunate, wretched* npm ungesǣlige 4/274; dpm ungesǣlīgum 4/294
unġesǣlþ f. *misfortune* np ungesǣlða 7/73
unġesibb adj. *unrelated* dsm ungesibbum 11(k)/8
unhēanlīċe adv. *not ignobly, valiantly* 6/14
unlifġende adj. *not living, dead* gsm unlyfigendes 18(a)/744; asm unlyfigendne 18(b)/1308; dsm unlifgendum 18(b)/1389
unlūcan II *unlock, open* inf 4/278
unlȳtel adj. *great, not little* nsm 18(a)/885; asn 18(a)/833
unmyltsiendliċ adj. *unforgivable* ns 4/66
unnan pret. pres. w.d. of person and g. of thing *grant, allow* pret subj 3p ūþon 6/29
ġeunnan pret. pres. w.g. *grant* pres subj 2s geunne 12/176
unnyt adj. *useless* nsn 18(d)/3168
unorne adj. *simple, humble* nsm 12/256
unrǣd m. *ill advice, foolish policy* gs unrǣdes 11(f)/12; ap unrǣdas 7/73
unrihtwīs adj. *unjust, wicked* dsm unrihtwīsan 10(a)/18 [MnE unrighteous]
unrīm n. *countless number* ns 10(b)/44
unrōt adj. *sad, despondent* nsm 10(a)/30
unryht adj. *unjust, wrongful* dpf unryhtum 6/2 [MnE unright]
unstille adv. *not still, restlessly* 11(l)/5
unstilnes f. *disturbance* as unstilnesse 6/18 [MnE unstillness]
untrum adj. *infirm, sick* gp untrumra 9/91; compar. ap untrumran 9/91
untrymnes f. *infirmity* ds untrymnesse 9/88
unþinged adj. *unprepared for, unexpected* nsm 17/106
unwāclīċe adv. *not weakly, bravely* 12/308
unwærlīċe adv. *unawares* 3/44 [MnE unwar(i)ly]
unwearnum adv. *irresistibly* 17/63, 18(a)/741 (*eagerly, greedily*)
unweaxen adj. *not fully grown* nsm 12/152
unwillum adv. *unwillingly* 10(b)/24
unwittig adj. *stupid, ignorant* nsm 4/299; apn unwittigan 4/157 (*innocent*)
unwrītere m. *inaccurate scribe* ns 4/125
ūp see **ūpp**
ūpāstīġnes f. *ascension* ds ūpāstīġnesse 9/76
ūpcyme m. *up-springing, ascendancy* as 11(o)/9
ūpganga m. *landing, passage to land* as ūpgangan 12/87
ūphēah adj. *lofty* npf ūphēa 15/30
ūplang adj. *upright* nsm 18(a)/759
ūpp adv. *up* 7/10, ūp 10(a)/2, 11(n)/5, 12/130, 14/71, 15/3, etc.
uppan prep. w.d. *upon, on* 2/46
uppe adv. *up, above* 14/9
ūprodor m. *the heavens above* as 17/105
ūre poss. adj. *our* nsm 3/184, 4/162, 12/232, etc.; asm ūrne 4/87, 12/58; nsn 12/313; asn ūre 7/77; asf 4/87; dsf 4/68; dpm ūrum 12/56; npm ūre 5/34; npn 8/19; gpn ūra 8/16; dpn ūrum 3/210; dpf 4/71
ūrigfeþra adj. *dewy-feathered* nsm 17/25
urnon see **irnan**
ūs see **wē**
ūsic see **wē**
ūt adv. *out* 1/28, 3/76, 3/77, 3/80, 4/288, 5/8 (*outward*), etc.
ūtādrīfan I *drive out, expel* pres 2p ūtādrīfaþ 3/170, 3/176

ūtan adv. *from without, on the outside* 6/11, 18(a)/774, ūtene 7/31
ūtanbordes adv. *from abroad* 5/12
ūte adv. *outside, abroad* 3/145, 5/13, etc.
ūtene see **ūtan**
ūtgān anom. (§128) *go out* inf 3/8
ūtgong m. *exodus, emigration* ds utgonge 9/72
uton, wuton (1st pers. pl. subj. of witan used w. inf) *let us* 3/206, 3/208, 4/68, 4/69, 17/117, 18(b)/1390, wuton 9/115
ūtweard adj. *turning outward, striving to escape* nsm 18(a)/761
ūþon see **unnan**
uuiþ see **wiþ**

Visionis see note to 2/45

wā m. *woe, affliction* ns waa 10(b)/25; as interj. 15/52; cf. **wēa**
wāc adj. *slender* asm wācne 12/43; *weak* nsm 16/67; compar. npm wācran (as noun) 17/87
wācian 2 *weaken, turn coward* inf 12/10
wacian 2 *watch, keep awake* pres ptc waciende 3/31 [MnE wake]
wadan VI *go, advance, trudge* inf 12/140, 16/5 (*travel*); pret 1s wōd 16/24; 3s 12/130, 12/253, 18(a)/714; pret 3p wōdon 12/96, 12/295 [MnE wade]
ġewadan VI *pass, penetrate* pret 3s gewōd 12/157
wado see **wæd**
wāg m. *wall of a building* ns 13/9, ds wāge 11(j)/12
waldend see **wealdend**
waldendwyrhta m. *master builder, the king's builder* ap waldendwyrhtan 13/7
walo see **wæl**
wand see **windan**
wandian 2 *flinch, draw back* inf 12/258; pret 3s wandode 12/268
wanhygdig adj. *foolhardy, reckless* nsm 16/67
wanian 2 *diminish, lessen* pret 3s wanode 18(b)/1337 [MnE wane]
wāniġean 2 *bewail* inf 18(a)/787
wann adj. *dark, black* nsm won 16/103; nsn 18(b)/1374; nsf wann 14/55; dsf wanre 18(a)/702 [MnE wan]
warian 2 *attend, hold* pres 3s warað 16/32; 3p warigeað 18(b)/1358 (*guard, occupy, inhabit*)
warnian 2 *warn* inf 7/32
wāt see **witan**
ġewāt see **ġewītan**
waðum m. *wave* gp waðema 16/24, 16/57
wæċċan 2 *keep awake, watch* pres ptc wæccende 18(a)/708. See **wacian**
wæd n. *water, sea* ap wado 11(d)/2
wǣd f. *clothing, covering* dp wēdum 11(k)/4, wǣdum 14/15, 14/22 [MnE (widow's) weeds]
wǣdbrēċ f. pl. *breeches* ap 2/16
wǣdian 2 *equip* p ptc gewǣdod 7/37
wǣdla m. *poor person, beggar* dp wǣdlum 4/143
wǣfersȳn f. *spectacle* ds wǣfersȳne 14/31
wǣfre adj. *wandering* nsm 18(b)/1331
wǣg m. *wave* as 17/19; ap wēgas 16/46
wǣge n. *cup, flagon* as 18(c)/2253
wǣglīðend m. *seafarer* dp wǣglīðendum 18(d)/3158
wǣgun see **wegan**
wæl n. *slaughter, carnage* ns 7/15, 12/126, 12/303; as 7/37; ds wæle 12/279, 12/300 (*field of slaughter, battlefield*); np walo 13/25 (*slaughtered men, the slain*)
wælgǣst m. *murderous spirit* ns 18(b)/1331
wælgīfre adj. *greedy for slaughter* npn wælgīfru 16/100
wælhrēow adj. *fierce, bloodthirsty* nsm wælhrēowa 10(a)/24; asm wælhrēowan 4/198; npm 4/261; apm 4/205
wælhrēowliċe adv. *horribly* 4/302
wælhrēownys f. *bloodthirstiness, cruelty* ds wælhrēownysse 4/153
wælrǣs m. *murderous conflict* ds wælrǣse 18(a)/824
wælræst f. *bed of death, death in battle* as wælræste 12/113
Wæls pers. n. *Wæls* gs Wælses 18(a)/897
Wælsing pers. n. *son of Wæls, i.e. Sigemund* gs Wælsinges 18(a)/877
wælsleaht m. *battle, slaughter* gp wælsleahta 16/7, 16/91
wælspere n. *deadly spear* as 12/322
wælstōw f. *place of slaughter, battlefield* gs wælstōwe 12/95, ds 12/293
wælwulf m. *wolf of slaughter* (*Viking*) np wælwulfas 12/96
wǣpen n. *weapon* ns 11(j)/1, 12/252; as 8/60, 8/63, 11(n)/12, 12/130, 12/235; gs wǣpnes 12/168; ds wǣpne 12/228; np wǣpen 16/100; ap wǣpnu 4/203; gp wǣpna 12/83, 12/272, 12/308; dp wǣpnum 4/204, 12/10 (tō wǣpnum fēng *took up arms*), 12/126
wǣpnedcynn n. *the male sex* gs wǣpnedcynnes 11(g)/1
wǣpnian 2 *arm* p ptc gewǣpnod 7/37
wǣre see **bēon**
wǣron see **bēon**
wǣrun (= **wǣron**) see **bēon**
wæs see **bēon**
wæstm m. *fruit, result* ds wæstme 2/4, 2/5; dp wæstmum 8/48, 18(b)/1352 (*growth, stature, form*)
wǣta m. *moisture, blood* ds wǣtan 14/22

wæter n. *water* as 1/2, 4/64, 12/91, 12/98, 18(b)/1364; ds wætere 12/64, 12/96, wætre 15/49; ap wæteru 4/61

wæterian 2 *water, give water to* inf 3/19; p ptc apm gewæterode 3/32

wē pron. *we* np 1/29, 2/5, 2/6, 4/45, etc.; ap ūsic *us* 17/123; dp ūs 1/32, 2/6, 3/140, 3/173, 3/197, etc.

wēa m. *woe, misery* gp wēana 18(b)/1396

weal m. *wall* ns 13/39, 16/98; ds wealle 16/80, 18(a)/785, 18(a)/891, 18(d)/3161; np weallas 16/76

wēalāf f. *survivors, woeful remnant* ns 10(b)/22

Wēalas m. pl. *Cornwall, Cornishmen* dp Wēalum 7/9 [MnE Welsh]

*ġe***wealc** n. *rolling, tossing* as 17/6, 17/46 [MnE walk]

*ġe***weald** n. *control, dominion, power* as 4/123, 4/163, 10(b)/38, 11(f)/14, 12/178, 14/107, 18(a)/764, 18(a)/808

wealdan VII w.g. *wield, control* inf 12/83, 12/95, 12/168, 12/272; (w.d.) pret 3p wīoldon 10(b)/48 [MnE wield]

*ġe***wealdan** VII *rule, control* pres 3s gewielt 2/35

wealdend m. *ruler, the Lord* ns 14/111, 14/155, waldend 11(h)/6, Waldend 12/173; as 14/67; gs wealdendes 14/17, 14/53; ds wealdende 14/121; np waldend 16/78

wealhstod m. *translator* ap wealhstodas 5/52

weallan VII *well, surge, boil* pres ptc weallende 18(a)/847; pret 3s wēol 18(a)/849

weallwala m. *wall-brace* ap weallwalan 13/20

wealstān m. *masonry* ns 13/1

wealsteal m. *foundation* as 16/88

weard m. *guardian* ns 9/42, 14/91, 17/54, 18(b)/1390; as 9/36 [MnE ward]

weardiġan 2 *occupy* pres 3p weardiað 15/34

wearg m. *criminal, felon* np weargas 4/283; ap wergas 14/31

wearoð m. *shore* as 10(b)/14

wearp see **weorpan**

wearþ see **weorðan**

wēaspel n. *tidings of woe* ds wēaspelle 18(b)/1315

wēaþearf f. *grievous need* ds wēaþearfe 15/10

weaxan VII *grow* pret 3s wēox 10(b)/5 [MnE wax]

Weċedport m. *Watchet* (*Somerset*) ns 7/14

wēdan 1 *be insane, rave* pret 3s wēdde 8/67

weder n. *wind, storm,* (*bad*) *weather* is wedre 11(o)/2

Wederas m. pl. *the Geats* gp Wedra 18(d)/3156

wēdum see **wǣd**

weġ m. *way, path, road* as 14/88, 17/74, 18(a)/763, 18(a)/844, 18(b)/1382; ds wege 4/197; ap wegas 11(l)/6

wēgas see **wǣg**

wegan V *carry* inf 8/63; pres 3s wigeð 11(m)/3; 3p wegað 11(j)/14; subj 3s wege 18(c)/2252; pret 3p wǣgun 11(f)/3, wēgon 12/98 [MnE weigh]

weġnest n. *viaticum, provisions for a journey* isn wegneste 9/111

wel adv. *well* 3/32, 3/69, 4/42, 4/315, 9/63 (*readily*), well 14/129, etc.

wela m. *prosperity, riches* ns 16/74; as welan 5/35 [MnE weal]

weler m. *lip* ap weleras 4/111

welhold adj. *very kind* nsf 11(k)/4

welhwǣr adv. *well-nigh everywhere* 5/79

welhwylc adj. *every* (*one*) gpm welhwylcra 18(b)/1344; pron. asn welhwylc *everything* 18(a)/874

weliġ adj. *rich, well-to-do* dsf welegan 10(b)/37; dp weligum 3/133

wellan see **wille**

welm m. *fervour* ds welme 9/85

welwillendnys f. *benevolence* ds welwillendnysse 4/144

wēn f. *expectation* ns 18(a)/734

wēnan 1 w.g. *think, expect* inf 4/10; pres 1s wēne 5/17, 14/135 (ic wēne mē *I look forward to*), 18(b)/1396; pret 3s wēnde 10(b)/78, 10(b)/82, 12/239; 3p wēndon 5/44, 7/51, 8/66, 18(a)/778 [archaic MnE ween]

wendan 1 *wend one's way, go, turn, translate* inf 5/43, 5/67, 12/316, 14/22; pres 3s went (*goes*) 1/10; subj 1s wende 12/252; pret 3p wendon 5/49, 12/193, 12/205

*ġe***wendan** 1 *return, turn* pres subj 2s gewende 2/41, pret 3s 4/135, 4/152, etc.

wēndon see **wēnan**

wenian 1 *accustom* inf 16/29 (*entertain*); pret 3s wenede 16/36

went see **wendan**

wēofod n. *altar* as 2/57; ds wēofode 4/270

wēop see **wēpan**

weorc n. *work, task, deed* ns 4/7; as 2/61, 9/38, 14/79; ds weorce 2/38, 4/284; dp weorcum 4/43

*ġe***weorc** n. *labour, workmanship, handiwork* ns 13/2; ds geweorce 3/196, 4/84; np geweorc 16/87

weorode see **werod**

weorpan III *throw, cast* pres 1s weorpe 3/76, 3/77, 3/80, 11(f)/7; pret 3s wearp 13/38 [MnE warp]

weorþ n. *worth, price* ds weorþe 3/144, 3/147

weorð, -e adj. *worthy, dear, valuable, in possession of* nsm wyrðe 4/24, 4/190, weorð 11(f)/1; gsn wyrðes 9/47, 10(b)/67; nsf wyrðe 4/314, weorðe 8/37; np wyrðe 10(a)/8, 10(b)/37; compar. nsm wyrðra 18(a)/861

weorðan III *become, happen* inf 5/45, 11(m)/

10, 16/64, wurðan 18(a)/807; pres 2s wierþst (*wilt return*) 2/42; 3s weorþeð 16/110, 17/69; pret 3s wearþ 4/156, 6/18, 11(k)/8, 12/113, 12/186 (wearð ... on fleame *took to flight*), 12/295; 3p wurdon 4/129, 4/254, 13/27; w. p ptc forming passive (§202) inf 18(d)/3177; 3s wearð 4/234, 12/106, 12/114, 12/116, 12/135, 12/138, etc.; 3p wurdon 2/15, 4/243; subj 3s wurde 2/59, 4/225, 12/1; p ptc geworden 9/118, 14/87

*ġe***weorðan** III *please* pres 3s gewyrð (impersonal: *it pleases*) 4/114

weorðful adj. *honourable, venerable* nsm wurðful 4/137; dsm wurðfullan 4/314

weorþian 2 *respect, honour* inf 3/208, 14/129; pres 3p weorðiað 14/81; subj 3s wurþige 4/315; pret 3s wurðode 4/138, 4/271

*ġe***weorþian** 2 *honour, exalt* pret 3s geweorðode 14/90, 14/94, geweorþade 17/123; p ptc geweorðad 9/2, asm geweorðod 14/15

weorþlīċe adv. *splendidly, in splendid fashion* 14/17, wurðlīce 4/253, 12/279; superl. weorðlīcost 18(d)/3161 [MnE worthily]

weorðmynd n. or f. *honour, dignity* ds wurðmynde 4/255, wurðmynte 4/273; gp weorðmynda 10(b)/51

weoruld see **woruld**

weoruldhāde see **woruldhād**

wēpan VII *weep* inf 10(a)/31, 15/38; pret 3s wēop 14/55

wer m. *man, husband* ns 4/280, 11(a)/1, 16/64; as 18(d)/3172; gs weres 2/35, 18(b)/1352; ds were 2/14; np weras 11(b)/1, 11(j)/3, 11(j)/12, 11(o)/6; ap 4/157; gp wera 3/166, 11(c)/3, 13/26, 17/21; dp werum 11(f)/1 [MnE were(wolf)]

wēr f. *covenant, pledge* dp wērum 17/110

werede see **werian**

werg see **wearg**

werian 1 *defend, protect* pret 3s werede 6/14; 1p weredon 18(b)/1327; 3p 12/82, 12/283

wēriġ adj. *weary, exhausted* nsm 17/29, nsn 16/15; asm wērigne 16/57; npm wērige 12/303

wēriġmōd adj. *disconsolate* nsm 15/49, 18(a)/844

werod n. *troop, company* ns 12/64, 12/97; as 12/102; ds werode 4/164, 12/51, weorode 14/152; is werode 6/10, 14/69, werede 14/124; gp weruda 14/51

werþēod f. *people* gp werþēoda 13/9

weruda see **werod**

wesan anom. *be* inf 14/110, 14/117, 15/42, 18(b)/1328. See **bēon**

west adv. *west* 12/97

wēste adj. *deserted* nsm 16/74

wēsten n. *desert, wasteland* ds wēstene 4/82

wēstenstaþol m. *deserted place* ap wēstenstaþolas 13/27

Westseaxe m. pl. (§46) *West Saxons* gp Westsexena 4/155, Westseaxna 6/1, 7/63

wīc n. *abode* ns 15/32; ap 11(d)/2, 15/52, 18(a)/821

wiċċecræft m. *witchcraft* as 1/14

wicg n. *horse* ns wycg 11(j)/5, ds wicge 11(j)/14, 12/240

wīcian 2 *dwell* infl inf (tō) wīcianne 3/198

wīcing m. *Viking* as 12/139; ap wīcingas 12/322; gp wīcinga 7/11, 12/26, 12/73, 12/97; dp wīcingum 12/116

wīd adj. *broad* apm wīdan 13/39; apm wīde 18(a)/877; compar. wīdre asn 18(a)/763

wīddor see **wīde**

wīde adv. *far, far and wide* 4/148, 4/322, 4/329, 11(d)/5, 11(f)/1, 13/25, 14/81, 15/46, etc.; swā wīde swā *as far as* 7/57; compar. wīddor 11(k)/10; superl. wīdost *farthest, most widely* 17/57 [MnE wide]

widewe f. *widow* ns 4/267; dp widewum 4/143

*ġe***wīdost** adv. superl. *as far apart as possible* 15/13

*ġe***widre** n. *weather, storm* ap gewidru 18(b)/1375

wīdwegas m. pl. *distant regions* ap 18(a)/840

*ge***wielt** see *ge***wealdan**

wierþst see **weorðan**

wīf n. *woman, wife* ns 2/4, 2/11, 2/18, 2/24, 11(m)/5; as 3/149; gs wīfes 1/31, 2/36, 6/17; ds wīfe 2/2, 2/8, 2/31, 4/19, 17/45; np wīf 11(o)/6; ap 4/16, 4/32, 4/157; gp wīfa 4/20, 14/94; dp wīfum 4/183, 11(a)/1

wīfcȳþþu f. *company or intimacy with a woman* ds wīfcȳþþe 6/10

Wīferþ pers. n. *Wiferth* ns 6/25

wīfian 2 *take a wife, marry* inf 4/21

wīġ n. *war, battle* ns 16/80; gs wīges 12/73, 12/130, 18(a)/886; ds wīge 5/9, 12/10, 12/128, 12/193, 12/235, 12/252, 18(b)/1337; is 10(b)/22

wiġa m. *warrior* ns 11(j)/1, 11(l)/6, 11(m)/1, 12/210, 16/67; as wigan 12/75, 12/235; np 12/79, 12/126, 12/302; gp wigena 12/135

wīġbed n. *altar* ap wīgbedo 8/47, wīgbed 8/54, 8/75

Wīgelin pers. n. *Wigelin* gs Wīgelines 12/300

wīġend m. *warrior* np 12/302

wigeð see **wegan**

wīġfruma m. *war-chief* ds wīgfruman 18(c)/2261

wīġhaga m. *battle-wall, wall of shields* as wīhagan 12/102

wīġheard adj. *hard in war, fierce* asm wīgheardne 12/75

wīġhyrst f. *war trappings* dp wīghyrstum 13/34

wīġplega m. *battle-play, fighting* ds wīgplegan 12/268, 12/316

wīġsteal n. *place of war, place of idols* (?) np 13/27

wīhagan see **wīġhaga**

wiht f. and n. *creature, being* ns 11(b)/1, 11(g)/6, 11(h)/2; as 11(g)/1; ap wuhte 11(l)/1 [archaic MnE wight]

wihte adv. *at all* 11(c)/6, wiht 18(a)/862 [MnE whit]

wiites see **wīte**

wilddēor n. *wild beast* np 3/63; ap 3/49, 3/50; gp wilddēora 3/43; dp wilddēorum 2/29

wile see **willan**

wilġehlēþ m. *familiar companion, comrade* ap wilgehlēþan 11(j)/5

willa m. *will, desire, pleasure, delight* ns 14/129, 18(a)/824; as willan 4/116; gp wilna 18(b)/1344

willan anom. *wish, desire, will* pres 1s wile 3/146, wille 12/247, wylle 12/216, etc.; 2s wilt 3/95, 3/119, 3/144, wylt 4/166; 3s wile 12/52, wyle 4/22, etc.; 1p willað 12/35, 12/40; 3p 12/46; subj 1s wille 12/221; 2s 5/21, 12/37; 3s 4/10, 5/62, 16/14, 16/72, 17/43, 17/97, 17/99, 17/113; pret 2s woldest 2/65; 3s wolde 1/14, 2/43, 2/58, 2/61, etc.; 3p woldon 4/107, 4/255, 4/275, 4/305, 7/50, 9/85, 12/207, 14/68; subj 3s wolde 16/28; 3p woldan 8/5. With negative: nyllan *be unwilling, will not* pres 1s nyle 3/125, 3/129, nelle 4/118, 4/186, 11(h)/15, 12/246; 3s nyle 3/215, nille 17/99, nele 4/125; 3p nyllaþ 3/166, nellað 4/32, 4/310; pret 2s noldest 2/72; 3s nolde 4/140, 6/20, 7/74, 12/6, etc.; 1p noldon 5/38; 3p 12/81, 12/185, 12/201

wille f. *fountain* ds willan 8/5; ap wellan 11(g)/3 [MnE well]

wilnian 2 (w.g.) *desire, petition for* pret 3p wilnedon 10(b)/35

*ġe***wilnian** 2 (w.g.) *desire, wish* pres 1s gewilnige 4/181

wilnung f. *desire* ds wilnunga 5/45

wilsumnes f. *devotion* ds wilsumnesse 9/119

wilt see **willan**

Wiltūnscīr f. *Wiltshire* ds Wiltūnscīre 7/72

wīn n. *wine* as 3/141; ds wīne 11(a)/1, 11(j)/17

*ġe***win** see *ġe***winn**

wind m. *wind* ns 18(b)/1374; ds winde 11(j)/14, 11(o)/1, 16/76

windan III *fly, wave, circle in the air* inf 12/322; pret 3s 12/43; pret 3p wundon 12/106

*ġe***windan** III *go, turn* inf wīdre gewindan *reach a more remote place by flight* 18(a)/763

windiġ adj. *windy* apm windige 18(b)/1358

wine m. *friend, lord* ns 12/250, 15/49, 15/50; as 17/115; ap winas 12/228

winedryhten m. *beloved lord* as 12/248, 12/263, 18(d)/3175, winedrihten 18(a)/862; gs winedryhtnes 16/37

winelēas adj. *friendless* ns 15/10, 16/45

winemæg m. *beloved kinsman* ap winemagas 12/306; gp winemæga 16/7; dp winemagum 17/16

wīngāl adj. *flushed with wine* nsm 13/34, 17/29

*ġe***winn** n. *war, strife* as gewinn 12/214, gewin 10(a)/1, 11(h)/2, 18(a)/798, 18(a)/877; ds gewinne 12/248, 12/302, 14/65 (*agony*)

winnan III *suffer, struggle, fight* infl inf (tō) winnenne 4/205; pres ptc nsm winnende 11(l)/6; pret 1s wonn 15/5; 3p wunnon 18(a)/777 [MnE win]

*ġe***winnan** III *conquer, win* inf 12/125; p ptc gewunnen 10(b)/17, 10(b)/28, dsm gewunnenum 4/153

winnende see **winnan**

wīnreced n. *wine hall* as 18(a)/714

wīnsæl n. *hall* np wīnsalo 16/78

wīnsele m. *hall* ns 18(a)/771

Wintanċeaster f. *Winchester* as Wintanceastre 6/41

winter m. *winter, year* ns 3/10; as 3/154, 8/34, 17/15; gs wintres 8/32, 16/103; ds wintra 3/121, 8/33; gp wintra 6/7, 6/41, 10(b)/29, 16/65; ip wintrum 12/210

wintercearig adj. *desolate as winter* nsm 16/24

wintersetl n. *winter quarters* as 4/164; ap wintersetle 7/62

wintertīd f. *wintertime* ds wintertīde 8/28 [MnE wintertide]

wioldon see **wealdan**

wiotan see **wita**

wiotonne see **witan**

wīr m. *wire, metal rod* dp wīrum 13/20

wīrboga m. *twisted ornamental wire* ip wīrbogum 11(j)/3

wirċean see **wyrċan**

wīs adj. *wise* nsm wisa 3/186, 10(b)/51, 12/219, 16/64; asm wīsne 3/183, wīsan 18(b)/1318; dsm wīsan 4/58; apm wīse 5/52

*ġe***wis** adj. *aware* nsm 9/125; *trustworthy, unfailing* asn 17/110

wīscan 1 *wish, desire* pret 3p wīscton 4/326

*ġe***wīscan** 1 (w.g.) *wish, desire* pres 1s gewīsce 4/181

wīsdōm m. *wisdom* ns 4/58; as 5/12, 5/23, etc.; ds wīsdōme 5/9

wīse f. *way, manner, wise* as wīsan 2/57, 2/60, 4/102, 4/105 (*idiom*), 9/58 (*task, assignment*), 9/85; ap 3/109; dp wīsum 17/110

wīse adv. *wisely, prudently* 16/88

wīsian 2 *guide* pret 3s wīsode 12/141

wīsliċ adj. *wise* nsn 8/21

*ġe***wislīcost** see *ġe***wisslīċe**

wisse see **witan**

wissian 2 *guide, instruct* inf 4/42; p ptc gewissod 3/184

*ġe***wissian** 2 *guide, direct* pret 3s gewissode 4/144

*ġe***wisslīċe** adv. *certainly* 3/184; superl. gewislīcost 18(b)/1350

wissung f. *guidance* ds wissunge 4/235

wist f. *feasting* ds wiste 16/36

Wīstān pers. n. *Wistan* ns 12/297

wiste see **witan**

wistfyllo f. *fill of feasting* gs wistfylle 18(a)/734

wit dual pron. *we two* n 11(e)/7, 15/13, 15/21; a unc 11(e)/2, 11(e)/7, 14/48, 15/12, 15/22; d unc (refl.) 2/51; g uncer 15/25

wita m. *wise man, counsellor*, pl. *the witan* ns 8/24, 16/65; np witan 7/27, 7/59, 18(a)/778, wiotan 5/3, 6/2; ap 10(b)/66; gp wiotena 5/41; dp wytum 8/4, witum 8/8, 10(a)/15

witan pret. pres. *know* inf 4/33; infl inf (tō) witanne 4/106, (tō) wiotonne 5/55; pres ptc np witende 2/11; pres 1s wāt 8/19, 16/11, 18(b)/1331; 3s 2/9, 4/185, 4/310, 12/94, 16/29, 16/37, etc.; subj. wite 18(b)/1367; pret 1s wiste 4/13; 3s 8/67, 12/24, 18(a)/764, 18(a)/821, wisse 18(a)/715, 18(b)/1309; 3p wiston 5/32, 9/106 (see note), etc.; subj. 3s wisse 16/27 (see note). With negative: pret 3s nyste (*did not know*) 4/17

*ġe***witan** pret. pres. *know, ascertain* inf 18(b)/1350

*ġe***wītan** I *depart* inf 17/52; pres 3s gewīteð 18(b)/1360; subj. 3s gewīte 8/31; pret 1s gewāt 9/30, 15/9; 3s 12/72, 12/150, 14/71, 15/6, 16/95; 3p gewitan 13/9, gewiton 14/133, 18(a)/853; p ptc npm gewitene 17/80, 17/86

wīte n. *punishment, torment* as 11(h)/6, 15/5; ds wīte 14/61; gs wiites 9/78; np wītu 5/24; gp wīta 14/87

wītega m. *prophet* ds wītegan 4/286

*ġe***witenes** f. *departure, death* gs gewitenesse 9/87

witod adj. *appointed, decreed, ordained* nsm 11(e)/7

witodlīċe adv. *certainly, verily* 4/189

wiþ prep. w.a.d. *against, in return for, from, with* 3/144, 3/146, 4/78, uuiþ 6/7, 7/53, 7/74, etc.; w.g. *to, toward* 12/8, 12/131; wið þon (þām) þe *provided that* 4/175, 7/60, 7/65

wiðerlēan n. *requital* ns 12/116

wiðfōn VII *lay hold on* pret 3s wiðfēng 18(a)/760

wiðhabban 3 w.d. *withstand, hold out against* pret 3s wiðhæfde 18(a)/772

wiðmetenes f. *comparison* ds tō wiðmetenesse w.g. *in comparison with* 8/27

wiðsacan VI w.d. or a. *renounce, forsake* inf 4/215, 8/51; pret subj 3p wiðsōcen 4/325

wiðstondan VI w.d. *withstand* inf 16/15, wiðstandan 4/167

wlanc adj. *proud, splendid* nsm wlonc 11(j)/1, 13/34, 17/29, wlanc 18(b)/1332; asm wlancne 12/139, wloncne 11(m)/10; dsn wlancan 12/240; nsf wlonc 16/80; npm wlance 12/205, wlonce 11(o)/6; apm wlonce 11(j)/17

wlætta m. *nauseating substance* ds wlættan 3/165

wlenco f. *prosperity, riches* gp wlencea 10(b)/76

wlītan I *look* pret 3s wlāt 12/172

wlitiġ adj. *beautiful* nsm 11(j)/12; nsn 2/12

wlitiġian 2 *brighten, make beautiful* pres 3p wlitigiað 17/49

wlonc see **wlanc**

wōd see **wadan**

wōdlīċe adv. *furiously* 4/211

wōdon see **wadan**

wōg n. *error* ds wōge 4/123; ap wōh 4/125

wōh see **wōg**

wōh adj. *curved, bent, twisted* ipm wōum 11(j)/3

wolcen m. or n. *cloud, sky* gp wolcna 11(d)/5; dp wolcnum 10(b)/76, 14/53, 14/55, 18(a)/714, 18(b)/1374 [archaic MnE welkin]

wōldæg m. *day of pestilence* np wōldagas 13/25

wolde see **willan**

wom m. *sin, iniquity* dp wommum 14/14

wōma m. *tumult* ns 16/103

womb f. *womb, belly* as wombe 11(b)/5

won see **wann**

wong m. *ground* as 13/31; ap wongas 17/49 (*fields, meadows*)

wonn see **winnan**

wōp m. *weeping, lamentation* as 18(a)/785

word n. *word* as 12/168, 14/35; ds worde 14/111; ap word 4/287, 8/1, 8/41, 9/35, 9/46, 9/56, 11(c)/1, etc.; gp worda 10(b)/81; dp wordum 4/75, 4/188, 5/1, 8/24, etc., wordon 12/306

wordġyd n. *lay, elegy* as 18(d)/3172

*ġe***worhte** see *ġe***wyrċan**

worhton see **wyrċan**

wōrian 2 *decay, moulder* pres 3s wōrað 13/12, 3p wōriað 16/78

worn m. *large number* as 16/91, 18(a)/870

woruld f. *world* ns 17/49; as 16/58, weoruld 16/107, 17/87; gs worulde 4/18, 9/8, 15/46, 16/74, worolde 18(b)/1387; ds worulde 4/113, 4/298, 5/25, 9/94, 12/174, 14/133, etc., weorulde 10(b)/51

woruldcræft m. *secular occupation* ns 3/191

woruldcund adj. *secular* gpm woruldcundra 5/4

woruldcyning m. *earthly king* gp wyruldcyninga 18(d)/3180
woruldġesæliġ adj. *prosperous, happy* nsm 12/219
woruldhād m. *secular life* as 9/62; ds weoruldhāde 9/18
woruldrīċe n. *kingdom of the world, the whole world* ds 15/13, 16/65
woruldsǣlþa f. pl. *worldly prosperity* dp woruldsǣlþum 10(a)/28
woruldþēaw m. *worldly custom* dp woruldþēawum 10(a)/13
woruldþing n. *worldly affair* gp woruldðinga 5/22
wōum see **wōh**
wrāh see **wrēon**
wrāð adj. *hostile, cruel, angry* dsm wrāþum 18(a)/708; gp wrāðra 14/51, 16/7; dpm wrāþum 11(j)/17 [MnE wroth]
wrāðe adv. *cruelly, fiercely* 10(a)/9, 15/32
wræc see **wrecan**
wræcca m. *wanderer, exile* ns 15/10; gs wræccan 17/15
wræclāst m. *path of exile* ns 16/32; ap wræclāstas 16/5, 17/57, 18(b)/1352
wræcsīð m. *misery* ap wræcsīðas 15/38; gp wræcsīða 15/5
wrǣtliċ adj. *wondrous, strange, splendid* nsm 11(h)/2, 13/1; asm wrǣtlicne 18(a)/891; asn wrǣtlic 11(n)/3; nsf wrǣtlicu 11(c)/2; asf wrǣtlice 11(l)/1
wrecan V* *utter* inf 17/1, 18(a)/873, 18(d)/3172; pres 1s wrece 15/1
wrecan V *avenge* inf 12/248, 12/258, 18(b)/1339; pres subj. 3s wrece 18(b)/1385; pret 3s wræc 6/5, 18(b)/1333, wrec 12/279; subj. 3s wrǣce 12/257 [MnE wreak]
*ġe***wrecan** V *avenge* inf 12/208, 12/263
wrēgan 1 *accuse* pres 3p wrēgað 4/74
wrēon I *cover, wrap* pres 3s wrīð 11(m)/5; pret 3s wrāh 11(k)/5
wreotan see **wrītan**
*ġe***writ** n. *writing, writ* as 5/61, 5/65; gs gewrites 9/74; ds gewrite 4/310
wrītan I *write* 1p wrītað 4/45; pret 3p wreoton 9/70
wrītere m. *writer* ds 4/100
wrīð see **wrēon**
wrixendlīċe adv. *in turn* 9/107
wrixlan 1 w.d. *change, exchange, vary* inf 18(a)/874
*ġe***wrohtan** see *ġe***wyrċan**
wudu m. *wood, forest, tree* ns 2/55, 11(n)/16, 14/27, 18(b)/1364; as 2/52, 2/58, 12/193; ds wuda 3/122, 4/232, 4/237, 4/247; dp wudum 3/64; gp wuda 15/27
wudutrēow n. *forest tree* as 11(n)/3
wuhte see **wiht**
wuldor n. *glory* ns 4/330; gs wuldres 4/264, 14/14, 14/90, 14/97, 14/133, 17/123; ds wuldre 11(o)/2, 14/135, 14/143, 14/155
Wuldorfæder m. *Father of Glory, God* gs 9/38
wulf m. *wolf* ns 4/156, 4/234, 4/241, 16/82; gs wulfes 4/244; np wulfas 3/25
Wulfgār pers. n. *Wulfgar* ns 7/19
wulfheafedtrēo n. *gallows, cross* as 11(n)/12
wulfhliþ n. *wolf-slope, retreat of wolves* ap wulfhleoþu 18(b)/1358
Wulfmǣr pers. n. *Wulfmær* ns 12/113, 12/155; as Wulmǣr 12/183
Wulfstān pers. n. *Wulfstan* ns 12/75; gs Wulfstānes 12/155; ds Wulfstāne 12/79
*ġe***wuna** m. *custom* ns 4/149
wund f. *wound* as wunde 12/139, 12/271; np wunda 4/260; dp wundum 12/293, 12/303
wund adj. *wounded* nsm 12/113, 12/144
wunden adj. *twisted* nsn 16/32; asn 11(n)/3; dsn wundnum 18(b)/1382 [MnE wound]
*ġe***wundian** 2 *wound* pret 3s gewundode 6/15; p ptc gewundad 6/22, 6/40, gewundod 12/135
wundon see **windan**
wundor n. *wonder, miracle* ns 4/234, 4/257, 18(a)/771; as 11(c)/2, 18(a)/840; np wundru 4/254, 4/327; ap 4/325, 4/329; gp wundra 4/245, 4/309, 4/322, 9/38; dp wundrum as adv. *astonishingly, wonderfully* 11(m)/1, 13/20, 16/98
wundorliċ adj. *remarkable, wonderful* nsf 1/19; dsm wunderlicum 4/81
wundorlīċe adv. *wondrously* 4/280
wundrian 2 *wonder, marvel at* pret 1s wundrade 5/40; 3s wundrode 9/95; 3p wundrodon 4/282
wundru see **wundor**
wundrum see **wundor**
*ġe***wuneliċ** adj. *customary* nsn 4/184, 4/237
wunian 2 *dwell, subsist, occupy* inf 3/154, 14/121, 14/143, 15/27; pres 1s wunige 11(e)/6; 3p wuniaþ 3/64, 14/135, 17/87; pret 1s wunade 17/15; 3s wunode 6/3, wunade 6/4; 3p wunedon 14/3, 14/155 [MnE won(t)]
*ġe***wunian** 2 *remain, be accustomed to* inf gewunigen 10(b)/37; pret 3s gewunade (*was accustomed to*) 9/2; p ptc gewunod 10(a)/28
wuniġe see **wunian**
*ġe***wunnenum** see *ġe***winnan**
wuolde (= **wolde**) see **willan**
wurde see **weorðan**
wurdon see **weorðan**
wurðan see **weorðan**
wurðful see **weorðful**
wurþige see **weorðian**
wurðlīċe see **weorðlīċe**
wurðmynde see **weorðmynd**

wurðode see **weorðian**
wuton see **uton**
wycg see **wicg**
wyle see **willan**
wylm m. *surge* ds wylme 13/39
wylt see **willan**
wyn see **wynn**
wynlēas adj. *joyless* apn 18(a)/821
wynliċ adj. *delightful* compar. apn wynlicran 15/52
wynn f. *benefit, joy* ns wyn 15/46, 16/36, 17/45, 18(c)/2262; as wyn 17/27; gp wynna 12/174, 15/32; dp wynnum 14/15 (as adv. *beautifully*), 16/29
wynsum adj. *delightful* npm wynsumu 9/69 [MnE winsome]
wyrċan I *make, form, produce* inf 9/3, 9/11, etc., wircean 4/69; pres ptc wircende 7/58; pres 1s wyrce 3/152, 3/203; 2s wyrcst 3/150; 3s wyrcð 4/329; 3p wyrcað 4/322; subj. 3s wyrce 18(b)/1387; pret 3s worhte 4/56; 3p worhton 2/16, 4/253, worhtan 7/23, wrohton 7/54; subj 1s worhte (w.g.) 4/184 [MnE work, wrought]
*ġe***wyrċan** I *make, form, perform* inf 12/81, 12/264; pres subj. 3s gewyrce 17/74 (*accomplish*); pret 3s geworhte 1/37, 2/2, 4/53, 9/80; 3p geworhton 14/31, 18(d)/3156, gewrohtan 7/41; p ptc asn geworht 9/7, asm geworhtne 17/115 (his geworhtne wine *the friend he has made*), npn geworhte 4/327
wyrd f. *fate, event* ns 10(b)/29, 11(c)/2, 13/24, 14/74, 16/5, 16/100, 17/115, 18(a)/734; ds wyrde 16/15; np wyrde 13/1; gp wyrda 14/51, 16/107 [MnE weird]
wyrdan I *injure, destroy* pret 3s wyrde 18(b)/1337
wyrhta m. *workman* np wyrhtan 3/206; dp wyrhtum 3/210 [MnE wright]
wyruldcyninga see **woruldcyning**
wyrm m. *worm, serpent, dragon* ns 11(c)/3, 18(a)/897; as 18(a)/886, 18(a)/891
wyrman I *warm* p ptc gewyrmed 8/29
wyrmliċ n. *serpent shape, serpentine pattern* dp wyrmlicum 16/98
wyrnan I w.g. *withhold* pret 3s wyrnde 12/118
wyrp f. *change* (*for the better*) as wyrpe 18(b)/1315
wyrs adv. (compar. of yfele) *worse* þȳ wyrs (*by so much*) *the worse* 10(b)/76
wyrt f. *herb, plant, vegetable* ap wyrta 2/40, 3/170; gp 3/162; dp wyrtum 18(b)/1364 [MnE wort]
wyrtġemang n. *mixture of herbs and spices, unguent* as 3/141
*ġe***wyrð** see *ġe***weorðan**
wyrðe see **weorð, -e**
wytum see **wita**

ȳcan I *increase, cause to grow* inf 11(o)/9 [MnE eke (out)]
yfel adj. *evil* dsm yfelum 4/303; asf yfelan 1/37; npm yfele 4/306
yfel n. *evil, harm* ns 10(b)/55; as 2/11, 4/125, 7/41, etc.; gs yfeles 12/133; ap 7/58, 10(a)/14; dp yflum 10(a)/10
yfele adv. *ill, badly* 10(a)/9
ylcan see **ilca**
yldan I *delay* inf 18(a)/739
yldrena see **ieldran**
yldu f. *age, old age* ns yldo 17/70, 17/91; gs ylde 9/19; ds ældo 13/6
yldum see **ælde**
ylfetu f. (*wild*) *swan* gs ylfete 17/19
ymb prep. w.a. *about, concerning, with regard to, after* 3/65, 5/10, 6/7, 6/36, embe 4/259, 4/290, 12/249, 12/271, etc.
ymbclyppan I *embrace* pret 3s ymbclypte 14/42
ymbsettan I *surround* p ptc npm ymbsette 8/55
yrhðo f. *cowardice* as 12/6
Yrmenlāf pers. n. *Yrmenlaf* gs Yrmenlāfes 18(b)/1324
yrmþu f. *hardship* gp yrmþa 15/3
yrnan see **irnan**
yrre n. *anger* as 18(a)/711
yrre adj. *angry* nsm 12/44, 12/253; npm 4/211, 18(a)/769
yrremōd adj. *angry* nsm 18(a)/726
ys (= **is**) see **bēon**
ȳtmæst adj. *last* ap ȳtmæstan 9/122 [MnE utmost]
ȳþ f. *wave* as ȳþe 11(l)/5, 11(p)/4; gp ȳþa 15/7, 17/6, 17/46, 18(a)/848
ȳþan I *lay waste, destroy* pret 3s ȳþde 16/85
ȳþġeblond n. *commingling of the waves, surge* ns 18(b)/1373
ȳwe see **īewan**

Indexes to Part One

INDEX OF SUBJECTS

The references are to the numbered sections. The abbreviations n. and fn. stand for 'Note' and 'Footnote' respectively.

You may find it useful to remember that §§252–268 comprise the Bibliography, and to note the entries 'sound-changes', 'spelling variations', and 'technical terms explained'.

This Index does not give references to what are merely passing mentions of persons, poems or prose texts, places, or things.

INDEX OF WORDS

The references are to the numbered sections.
The letters LV mean that the word in question will be found in 'Learning the Vocabulary' in the section 'How to Use this Guide'.
The abbreviations n. and fn. stand for 'Note' and 'Footnote' respectively.

æ follows *a*, *þ* follows *t*.
ċ is to be found under *c*, *ġ* under *g*, and *ð* under *þ*.
ġe- is ignored, so that *ġemunan* appears under *m*.

Nouns, adjectives, and pronouns, will be found under the nominative singular, and verbs under the infinitive. Verbs discussed in Appendices A and B only are excluded.

You may find it useful to remember that lists of conjunctions used in adverb clauses are given in §168 (non-prepositional) and §171 (prepositional).

NOTTINGHAM
UNIVERSITY LIBRARY